A PRACTICAL GUIDE TO EARLY CHILDHOOD CURRICULUM

Ninth Edition

Claudia Eliason
Weber State University, Ogden, Utah

Loa Jenkins
Bonneville Early Intervention Center, Idaho Falls, Idaho

PEARSON

Boston   Columbus   Indianapolis   New York   San Francisco   Upper Saddle River
Amsterdam   Cape Town   Dubai   London   Madrid   Milan   Munich   Paris   Montreal   Toronto
Delhi   Mexico City   São Paulo   Sydney   Hong Kong   Seoul   Singapore   Taipei   Tokyo

Vice President and Editorial Director: Jeffery W. Johnston
Senior Acquisitions Editor: Julie Peters
Editorial Assistant: Andrea D. Hall
Vice President, Director of Marketing: Margaret Waples
Senior Marketing Manager: Christopher D. Barry
Senior Managing Editor: Pamela D. Bennett
Project Manager: Linda Bayma
Production Manager: Susan Hannahs
Senior Art Director: Jayne Conte
Cover Designer: Suzanne Duda
Cover Image: iStockphoto
Full-Service Project Management: Niraj Bhatt/Aptara®, Inc.
Composition: Aptara®, Inc.
Text Printer/Binder: Edwards Brothers Malloy
Cover Printer: Edwards Brothers Malloy
Text Font: Garamond Light

Every effort has been made to provide accurate and current Internet information in this book. However, the Internet and information posted on it are constantly changing, so it is inevitable that some of the Internet addresses listed in this textbook will change.

Credits and acknowledgments for materials borrowed from other sources and reproduced, with permission, in this textbook appear on the appropriate page within the text.

Photo Credits: All photos by Paul L. Jenkins

Library of Congress Cataloging-in-Publication Data
Eliason, Claudia
  A practical guide to early childhood curriculum/Claudia Eliason, Loa Jenkins.–9th ed.
    p. cm.
  ISBN-13: 978-0-13-259513-1
  ISBN-13: 0-13-259513-3
  1. Early childhood education—Curricula.   I. Jenkins, Loa   II. Title.
LB1139.4.E54 2012
372.19–dc22

2011010236

10 9 8

PEARSON
www.pearsonhighered.com

ISBN-10:   0-13-259513-3
ISBN-13: 978-0-13-259513-1

PREFACE

Many are the times
we will teach.
Many are the times
we will be taught.
. . . But only once, a child.

PHILOSOPHY AND PURPOSE

While preparing to teach, preservice teachers become imbued with educational theories, but then often find themselves in the classroom as student teachers or professional teachers without practical knowledge of what and how to teach. They understand the theories of learning, but they often are unable to blend these theories with practical applications appropriate for young children.

In this textbook, we not only emphasize *how* to teach, but also we provide a solid foundation for the theoretical basis of the concepts being applied. We want students to understand *what* can be taught to young children, *why* it is important, and *how* it can be accomplished. We also emphasize the importance of a child-centered curriculum that encompasses the whole child—physical, social, emotional, creative, and cognitive. We take a developmental approach to teaching young children; that is, experiences are planned in accordance with the developmental needs of the children in the classroom or center. This book focuses on cognitive areas of the curriculum and effective methods of curriculum implementation. Its purpose is to explore how children learn; what children can learn; and the specific concepts, ideas, and strategies that are developmentally appropriate for young children.

NEW TO THIS EDITION

When writing new editions, it is both exciting and challenging to research and address current topics and ideas, while still maintaining our own basic philosophy and approach to early childhood education. In this revised edition, our goal has been to add available resources that will provide additional suggestions and supports to students and new and seasoned teachers of young children. Theories and historical perspectives are important and readily available in many textbooks, so we have condensed some information in this text in order to expand the practical approach.

- Assessment material has been updated and consolidated into one stand-alone chapter. The new chapter is easier to read and understand as a chapter than spread through several chapters.
- Developmentally appropriate practice, previously a stand-alone chapter, is now included in Chapter 1, where it helps determine the approach maintained throughout the text.
- Two chapters, separately addressing "Myself and My Family" and "Myself and My Body," have been combined into a single chapter, "Myself and Others."
- More national standards have been included throughout the book. Students will find numerous ideas for incorporating these standards into the daily curriculum.
- Specific "Ideas" that support particular topics have been added.
- New photographs visually support areas of study, with captions reminding readers of important concepts.

A Practical Guide to Early Childhood Curriculum evolved from the constant inquiry and search for meaningful teaching ideas by preservice and professional teachers. It also evolved from our teaching experiences in the primary grades, in Head Start, and in college and university classrooms and laboratories. The concepts selected for inclusion are those that most often meet the needs, interests, and developmental levels of children ages 3 through 8 years. However, they should not limit your thinking, planning and imagination, but rather should serve as a springboard for selecting projects and themes to explore, both in course work and in classrooms with young children.

CHAPTER PEDAGOGY

The unified pedagogy follows a specific format for most chapters: introductory comments, including content information; approach to teaching; chapter summary; student learning activities; and suggested resources.

The Introduction provides an overview of the chapter as well as specific background and guidelines on the concept or concepts; the Summary reviews the notions presented. The approach to teaching provides very specific content information, precise concepts, ideas that are developmentally appropriate for young children, and many explicit ideas for classroom activities and experiences. In addition, as appropriate, unit plans or webs are shared or illustrated within the approach-to-teaching section.

Lesson Plans

Occasionally within the chapters a lesson plan is included to show students how one teacher might apply the concepts in the chapter. However, most lesson plan illustrations appear in Appendix A, and recipes are presented in Appendix B. The format for the lesson plans is very simple and may be modified or adapted. There are many instructional design formats, and the ideas presented in this text can be adapted to various designs. In Chapter 4, we suggest a comprehensive design format called Teacher Work Sample (TWS). We believe TWS is the most appropriate design format available today because it adopts all of the very best practices relating to curriculum planning. It begins with the teaching context and ends with reflection on the unit or lesson. The components of the TWS model are sound, and we encourage students to develop expertise in this format.

Other Applied Features

To make the text more readable, we have included some boxed content in every chapter. In addition, in the chapters that include "Concepts and Ideas for Teaching" sections, we have consistently boxed this section. The Student Learning Activities at the end of each chapter offer discussion questions and many suggestions for applying chapter concepts within the university or college classroom.

Also included in this edition are standards from various professional associations. Chapter 1 provides an overview of the present impact of standards on early childhood classrooms and curriculum planning. Content area chapters include standards from national organizations.

CONTENT COVERAGE AND ORGANIZATION

In this current edition, a number of major changes have been made, including some reorganization of the chapters. The text is divided into four parts, each presenting a solid theoretical discussion and rationale.

Part One includes four chapters and provides an introduction and framework for the text. **Chapter 1** is an overview of early childhood education and addresses its past, present, and future. The importance of early

childhood education is also considered in depth. Developmental appropriateness of early academics, assessment, curriculum, and the physical setting has been incorporated into Chapter 1, along with theories of learning and children's excitement for learning. **Chapter 2** provides direction for developing partnerships among families, schools, and communities. **Chapter 3** addresses purposes and administration of various assessments appropriate for young children, and **Chapter 4** presents a detailed discussion on curriculum planning.

Part Two presents skills and concepts related to understanding and dealing with the self and others. Helping children learn about people and appreciating their diversities, focusing more on similarities than differences, is presented in **Chapter 5.** Although multicultural and anti-bias education is integrated throughout the text, it is also considered in greater depth in this chapter. Helping children learn more about families and themselves, social and emotional health, character education, resiliency, physical and nutritional fitness, and general health issues are all included in **Chapter 6.** Some instructors might choose to include parts of this particular Chapter along with **Chapter 11,** "Life Science Experiences." We feel it fits more appropriately with the Personal and Social Development section of the text.

Part Three includes six chapters that directly relate to cognitive development in the early childhood years. All curriculum development rests on the child's literacy ability, and **Chapter 7** focuses on language development, including speaking and listening activities. **Chapter 8** reflects our beliefs regarding the importance of comprehensive literacy development, including reading and writing. Many new sections and much new information have been added to this chapter. Young children should not only be taught to learn, memorize and take in facts, but they must also learn to think deeply—to classify, explain, investigate, question, observe, sort, wonder, synthesize, communicate, analyze, compare, hypothesize, and predict. Science concepts and ideas for incorporation into the curriculum are discussed in **Chapter 9, Chapter 10, and Chapter 11**, and **Chapter 12** relates to math concepts and emphasizes problem-solving skills. Children should learn to solve problems initially by working with concrete ideas; then, equipped with some process skills, they become able to generalize and handle more abstract problems.

Finally, Part Four includes a chapter on music and movement **(Chapter 13)** and creativity, art, and dramatic activities **(Chapter 14).** These vital experiences should be incorporated frequently throughout the curriculum, and not planned as only occasional endeavors.

Occasionally, we suggest the use of foods as art media; but we consider it imperative that children learn early the value of using and preserving, rather than wasting, food. Sometimes a food item, such as macaroni, may be more economical than purchasing beads for stringing necklaces. Also, discarded items such as oranges and potatoes from the grocery store or from family kitchens often expand the possibilities for creative art activities.

Previously, we read a statement that delightfully supports our own feelings regarding working with children, and we include it here: "Young children keep us from stalling in neutral gear. They make us drive in the heart of the center lane of life" (Chenfeld, 1995, p. 71). We find that working with young children is refreshing and helps to keep us focused on the importance of the early childhood years. Our desire is that this text, which supports the child-centered and constructivist points of view, will assist you in planning and implementing a fully integrated, developmentally appropriate early childhood curriculum.

NEW! CourseSmart eTEXTBOOK AVAILABLE

CourseSmart is an exciting new choice for students looking to save money. As an alternative to purchasing the printed textbook, students can purchase an electronic version of the same content. With a CourseSmart eTextbook, students can search the text, make notes online, print out reading assignments that incorporate lecture notes, and bookmark important passages for later review. For more information, or to purchase access to the CourseSmart eTextbook, visit www.coursesmart.com.

INSTRUCTOR'S RESOURCE MANUAL AND TEST BANK

Many suggested resources for each chapter are provided in the Instructor's Resource Manual. Literally hundreds of new books and audiovisual and technology works are published each month in early childhood alone. Based on the kind of computer you have and your budget, we suggest that you periodically evaluate new software choices for your school, classroom, or center. The software you select should be developmentally appropriate, utilize a variety of approaches, emphasize a variety of concepts, and encourage problem solving.

Assessment items for this edition appear in various formats: a Test Bank in Word, the same items in a cus-tomizable MyTest, and also for Blackboard and WebCT. Both supplements are available online. To download and print the supplements, go to www.pearsonhighered.com and then click on "Educators."

ACKNOWLEDGMENTS

We express appreciation to the many people who have assisted, supported, and encouraged us in this project. We are indebted to Paul Jenkins for the photographs throughout the book. We appreciate his sensitivity, skill, time, and effort. We also thank the many children and adults who cooperated in the photography, including the Bonneville Early Intervention Center and various elementary schools in Bonneville Joint School District Number 93, Idaho Falls, Idaho.

A special thanks to Jana Jones for her assistance in providing information on teaching children with special needs. We also express our appreciation to the publisher's reviewers for their valued contributions to the completion of this book: Nancy E. Bacot, Arkansas State University, Jonesboro; Sue Boyd, Central Carolina Community College; Madhu Lodha, Cabrillo Community College; Graham P. Matthews, Tennessee State University; and Maureen Provost, Mount Wachusett Community College.

Lisa Warner, of Eastern Kentucky University, shared materials with us, and Patrice Liljenquist Boerens contributed her graphics and artistic talents.

For editorial assistance, we thank our editor, Julie Peters; her wise direction, patient prodding, and demand for excellence were valued. Penny Burleson and Linda Bayma provided comprehensive guidance as we prepared our manuscript for production, and Carol Sykes was especially helpful with photo coordination.

We are grateful for our interaction with the children, parents, and students we have taught. Their inspiration, incentive, behavior, and thoughts have influenced whatever understandings we have.

We are indebted to our friends and families, especially to our husbands, Glen and Paul, whose patient support, interest, and encouragement were vital to the completion of this new edition. We express our thanks to our children-Megan, Eric, Erin, Kyle, Kristen, Catherine, Jason, Cathrine, Anne, and Matthew—whose examples have enlightened our understanding of the truths of childhood.

BRIEF CONTENTS

CONTENTS

part 1
Introduction to Early Childhood Education

The chapters in Part I provide an introduction to and overview of this textbook. The focus of this book is on children ages 3 to 8 years or prekindergarten through third grade, and the curriculum emphasis is on play. During early childhood, more concepts and structure should be added to the curriculum very gradually. We emphasize that even though there have been major sociological and technological changes in our society over the past years, developmental rates have remained constant. Children need environments and learning experiences that are geared to their needs, not highly academic curricula planned around what adults think children ought to be learning and doing. Young children need child-centered environments that offer many opportunities for choices and encourage learning through play, exploration, and discovery.

chapter 1

Early Childhood Education and Developmentally Appropriate Practice

The beliefs of many philosophers, psychologists, and educators dating back to the 17th century have influenced early childhood education as it is practiced in the 21st century.

> To know where early childhood education is going, it is important to know where it has come from.

The needs and values of early childhood education are multifaceted, and caring, qualified early childhood teachers are paramount to the learning of the developing child. To implement developmentally appropriate teaching practices in the child's early years, it is vital for teachers and caregivers to be aware of the developmental characteristics of the children with whom they are working. This will allow teachers to successfully support the children's progress toward becoming well-adjusted, confident, and thoughtful learners. It is also important to understand the components of children's learning.

A HISTORICAL LOOK AT EARLY CHILDHOOD EDUCATION

The field of childhood development and education began centuries ago and has recently experienced a resurgence of attention. It has been shaped by a range of influences from philosophers to individual teachers (whose perspectives have the most significant influence on the actual educational experiences of children). Federal laws and programs have also focused on the value of early childhood education for young children, and the importance of standards for programs and curriculum is currently receiving widespread attention.

A Brief Historical Overview of Contributors to Early Childhood Education

John Locke (1632–1704), English Philosopher

- Recognized individual differences.
- Stressed the importance of play and early years.

Jean-Jacques Rousseau (1712–1778), French Philosopher

- Believed that children should be treated with sympathy and compassion.
- Recognized the value of early childhood education.
- Explained that children progress through developmental stages.
- Asserted that children learn through direct instruction.
- Wrote the classic, *Émile*.
- Stressed the importance of play.

Johann Pestalozzi (1746–1827), Swiss Educator

- Proposed that the purpose of education is to develop physical, moral, and intellectual skills and powers.
- Stressed the importance of positive teacher–child relationships.
- Asserted that all persons have the right to an education.
- Founded one of first European schools to focus on children's developmental characteristics.

Friedrich Froebel (1782–1852), German Educator

- Originated the first kindergarten, based on play and materials.
- Recognized that children have innate gifts to be developed.
- Created first curriculum designed to meet the specific needs of young children.
- Stressed importance of teacher–child relationships.

Elizabeth Peabody (1804–1894), American Educator

- Established the first U.S. kindergarten in Boston in 1860.

John Dewey (1859–1952), American Educator

- Emphasized experimentation and discovery learning.
- Stressed the importance of exploration in active, free-play environment geared to own interests.
- Promoted problem solving based on real-life experiences.

Margaret McMillan (1860–1931), English Educator

- Established the first nursery school in London in 1911.

Patty Smith Hill (1868–1946), American Educator

- Was an early pioneer in kindergarten education in the United States.

Maria Montessori (1870–1952), Italian Educator

- Developed the Montessori method, which focuses on development of the intellect through the exploration of materials.
- Opened Casa dei Bambini (Children's Home) in Italy in 1907.
- Believed senses were the source of all intellectual development.
- Developed set of materials (autotelic, or self-correcting in nature) for teachers to use in prescribed manner.
- Emphasized importance of school and family working together.

Arnold Gesell (1880–1961), American Psychologist and Pediatrician

- Developed norms of children's growth.
- Developed concept of individual differences.

Jean Piaget (1896–1980), French Psychologist

- Proposed a theory of children's cognitive development.
- Believed that children learn through experimentation.
- Described periods of cognitive development.
- Explained that time and experience are needed for maturation.

Lev Vygotsky (1896–1934), Russian Psychologist

- Proposed a theory of development describing social process of learning and impact of development of language.
- Developed a concept of scaffolding.
- Developed ZPD (zone of proximal development).

Erik Erikson (1902–1994), Danish-German-American Developmental Psychologist

- Emphasized social and emotional aspects of growth.
- Developed a theory of personality development.

Other Contributions to Early Childhood Education

- Project Head Start, 1960s. A composite of federally funded preschool programs for children from impoverished backgrounds.
- Public Law 94-142, the Education for All Handicapped Children Act of 1975 (renamed the Individuals with Disabilities Education Act [IDEA] in 1990). Required that all children be given the opportunity to reach their fullest potential and that children with special needs be included in regular public school programs when possible. As a result, much more emphasis was placed on understanding children with special needs or disabilities.
- The Ypsilanti, Michigan, Early Training Project, 1980s. An ongoing research study supporting early intervention programs.
- Public Law 99-457, Education of the Handicapped Act Amendments of 1986. Far-reaching federal policy supporting early childhood intervention for children 3 to 5 years of age.
- A Nation at Risk: The Imperative for Educational Reform, a report from the National Commission on Excellence in Education, 1983. Report resulted in educational program reforms throughout the country.
- Developmentally appropriate practice (DAP), 1997. A policy statement issued by the National Association for the Education of Young Children, defining its position with regard to appropriate

practices in early childhood education. This approach considers the whole child, while taking into account the individual child's needs.

- No Child Left Behind Act of 2001 (NCLB). (Reauthorization of the Elementary and Secondary Education Act [ESEA] of 1965). Bipartisan education reform effort that was signed into law on January 8, 2002. It addresses four main principles: stronger accountability, greater local and state flexibility and control, more choices for parents, and emphasis on using methods based on scientific research. Because of this law, states developed plans to improve schools and raise student achievement.
- Reauthorization of IDEA that became effective on July 1, 2005. Designed to improve results for infants, toddlers, children, and youth with disabilities. It aligns closely with the NCLB Act to ensure equity, accountability, and excellence in education for all children with disabilities. It emphasizes both access to education and improved results, based on data and public accountability, for students with disabilities.

The historical perception of childhood has evolved from considering it of little value, to seeing it as a "mini-adulthood," to the present day when childhood is valued as a foundation for learning and development. Various aspects of educational focus over the years have included religious development, character and moral development, self-esteem, physical development, social development, emotional well-being, and cognitive and academic achievement. Most recently, professionals have emphasized total development, or the whole child. Focusing on the child's development guides curriculum, instruction, and assessment. Early childhood professionals have benefited from Rousseau, Froebel, Montessori, Gesell, and Erikson, but it is from Piaget that the current philosophy of developmentally appropriate practice (DAP) has emerged. From Piaget, early educators have learned the importance of development and the limits it sets on learning. They have learned that from rich, developmentally appropriate experiences, children can construct their own knowledge and understanding. The aim is to provide the kind of environment and stimuli that will stir children to be curious, active, and thoughtful learners.

DEVELOPMENT OF THE WHOLE CHILD

Historically, preschool and child care have been two separate traditions in the United States. Research literature suggests that care and education of young children must no longer be thought of as separate entities: "Adequate care involves providing quality cognitive stimulation, rich language environments, and the facilitation of social, emotional, and motor development. Likewise, adequate education for young children can occur only in the context of good physical care and of warm affective relationships" (Bowman, Donovan, & Burns, 2002, p. 2).

Political, social, and economic changes in our society have made families increasingly dependent on outside social institutions to aid not only in educating young children, but also in providing for all their needs. Three major trends that have focused public attention on the care and education of young children include the demand for child care as more mothers enter the labor force; agreement among parents and professionals that young children should have educational opportunities; and research evidence that young children are capable learners and that early educational experiences have a positive effect on later school learning (Bowman et al., 2002).

There is a renewal of interest in strengthening the American family, particularly to help families to develop a moral orientation and to build stronger values within the family unit. To this end, parents must have a genuine desire to learn and make changes, must be committed to their families, and must take charge of themselves and their children. They need to focus on high standards, values, and integrity.

Businesses are recognizing the importance of contributing to schools and early childhood programs to ensure a strong and capable workforce for the future and thus the importance of providing child care options for employees. These efforts should be expanded. Many agencies and businesses are involved in school partnerships, providing financial help, administrative assistance, or employees' volunteer time as tutors or mentors.

Public schools have expanded the number of safe, affordable child care options for parents by administering Head Start, child care, or other school-based programs. For example, schools are often used for after-school programs for those who would otherwise be home alone. However, child care programs in public schools should not emphasize formal, structured, academic instruction for young children. Young children learn best through firsthand experience and concrete encounters, through active exploration and guided discovery. The public must join forces with parents to demand excellence in the education of administrators and teachers; excellence in early childhood education has been equated with effective and high-quality teaching.

Features of Quality Early Childhood Programs

- Support cognitive and social–emotional development.
- Provide responsive interpersonal relationships with teachers.

- Have small class size and low adult–child ratios.
- Integrate curriculum goals across domains.
- Require ongoing professional development of teachers.
- Employ teachers who are actively engaged and provide high-quality supervision.

Source: Based on *Eager to Learn: Educating Our Preschoolers,* by B. Bowman, M. S. Donovan, and M. S. Burns (Eds.), 2002, Washington, DC: National Academy. Press.

Quality in early childhood programs is often difficult to assess because program goals are by necessity less specific. Standardized achievement tests are not developmentally appropriate for children, so it is difficult to define effective ways to evaluate quality early childhood programs. According to the National Association of Elementary School Principals (NAESP) (1990), quality programs enhance the child's self-image, strengthen social, and emotional development; expand communication skills; and stimulate an interest in the world's surroundings. In addition, they expand concepts and notions, encourage independent thinking, and develop problem-solving skills. Quality programs advance motor skills, identify special needs, reinforce respect for others and for the rights of others, promote creativity and aesthetic appreciation and expression, and increase the child's capacity for self-control and self-discipline. Providing quality early childhood education is not an easy task; it requires a well-trained, committed staff; a rich curriculum; and adequate resources.

"Children are not innately *ready* or *not ready* for school" (Maxwell & Clifford, 2004, p. 42). Their development and skills are greatly influenced by their families, interactions with other people, and environments

In a quality early childhood program, teachers are actively engaged with children.

during the younger years (Maxwell & Clifford, 2004). Early education experiences that promote readiness for kindergarten include a child-centered, age-appropriate, and engaging environment; a curriculum and assessment approach that supports individual differences; and responsive, knowledgeable teachers who facilitate learning (Cassidy, Mims, Rucker, & Boone, 2003). As much as possible, children who are ready for school should have "physical well-being and muscle control and coordination; healthy social and emotional development; positive approaches to learning, such as curiosity and motivation; adequate language development; and a foundation in cognition and general knowledge" (Biggar & Pizzolongo, 2004, p. 64). Experts generally agree that school readiness involves three important elements: "children's readiness for schools, schools' readiness for children, and the capacity of families and communities to provide developmental opportunities for their young children" (National Governors Association, 2002, p. 1).

GOALS FOR EARLY CHILDHOOD EDUCATION

Educators and other concerned people need to determine how to best provide for the needs of young children and enable *all* children to reach their full potential.

Goals for Early Childhood Professionals

1. Understand the nature of development and learning as well as the individual nature and characteristics of each child.
2. Know what to teach, how to teach, and how to assess what children have learned, as well as how to adapt the curriculum to the needs and interests of individual children.
3. Create a caring and responsive learning environment that is inclusive of the diverse cultural and linguistic backgrounds of all children.
4. Establish positive, mutual relationships of trust and respect with families, recognizing that shared goals benefit children and their education.
5. Pursue perpetual professional training and knowledge.
6. Treat every child with respect, dignity, and positive regard; recognize that every child has great potential.

Educators need to be competent and have a sound set of beliefs, goals, and actions. Early childhood professionals need to be focused on and accountable for accomplishing their goals. Another priority is to continue involving the family in early childhood programs. The more the teachers collaborate with the family, the greater the child's strides. This involves embracing family diversity, sharing responsibility, and striving for an understanding of each family's values.

Still another priority is to improve our professional image by educating the public about the importance of high-quality early childhood programs and seeking to protect and strengthen licensing in states and local communities. Ideally, program standards, regulations, and expectations should be uniform among states, and need to be followed.

When a child has rich, high-quality early childhood experiences with stimulating activities enhancing his or her development, the effect will likely be lasting. This benefit should be sought for all children.

Strong families strengthen the fabric of our society. The threads are strong individuals who have hope, enthusiasm, and a desire to become educated. Our children must be strong threads—responsible, unselfish, self-disciplined, and positive.

IMPORTANCE OF EARLY CHILDHOOD EDUCATION

Factors Influencing the Need for Early Childhood Education

All children deserve high-quality early childhood education; this is especially true for children from disadvantaged backgrounds. Effective preschool experiences help children to overcome the influences of poverty (Children's Defense Fund, 2005). We can and must provide high-quality child care and enriching preschool experiences for poor children.

Children from homes where both parents work or from single-parent homes need child care. There is a need not only for more child care programs, but also for upgrading the quality of the care given. Because many young children are still cared for by untrained caregivers, our efforts should be not just providing quality training to those caregivers, but also reaching the large number of other people who are caring for our nation's young children in community agencies, churches, clubs, and other groups, who also need training.

Children with special needs also benefit from early childhood education. Early education can be viewed as the time to mitigate problems by providing special programs: programs focusing on children who are economically disadvantaged and on the problems often associated with poverty; programs treating learning disabilities at an early age; programs in special education; or programs reaching children with emotional difficulties at a time when negative behaviors have had little time to become ingrained. All children need the opportunity to learn at their highest potential in an inclusive environment.

Developmental Need for Early Childhood Education

Several aspects of young children's growth point to the need for early childhood education. To foster a balanced human being, it is important to pay attention to social, emotional, physical, moral, and academic development. *Socialization* takes place in the early years, with the family being the first and most important group to which the child belongs. The early childhood group, in which children relate to other children of their own age, is an ideal situation for furthering social skills and development. Through their play, children learn to develop friendships that enable them to refine their social behavior. Sharing, listening to others, developing leadership skills, learning to follow others, gaining confidence in dealing with others, and learning to conform to the rules of the group are all examples of by-products of early childhood socialization.

The *emotional development* of the child has long been of paramount concern; children need schools that foster warm, supportive relationships (Baker & Manfredi/Petitt, 2004.) This relates closely to the development of either a positive or a negative self-image. Children must like themselves. The feelings of being "okay" and important and of having strengths and direction make up the positive self-image. Although these feelings are generated from within, they are influenced from outside the child. Teachers and parents can encourage these positive feelings in children. Positive feelings provide motivation and encourage growth, whereas negative feelings stimulate failure and engender bitterness and resentment.

The significant people in children's early environment reflect back to the children how they are viewed, and the children, in turn, decide how to see themselves. These views will form their self-concepts, which will determine their behaviors, attitudes, values, feelings, experiences, and success. The early childhood years are the most effective time to nurture a loving and caring approach to life (Swick & Freeman, 2004). "A child loved by us at two will reflect that love at seven. A child encouraged by us at age three will show confidence at age seven. A child affirmed by us at four will demonstrate self-esteem at seven" (Bakley, 1997, p. 21).

Generally, children who feel good about themselves also feel good about their world; their emotions are characterized by spontaneity, enthusiasm, joy, interest, and happiness. Children who do not feel good about themselves view the world with disappointment, anger, resentment, prejudice, and fear. Children cannot be protected from negative emotions and situations, but to be emotionally healthy, they should be equipped to cope with these feelings. Early childhood programs offer experiences that help to develop this coping ability, which is necessary for emotional health. Much depends on the classroom atmosphere. A supportive classroom increases students' ability to learn how to solve problems in stressful situations, as well as to learn academics (Pohan, 2003).

A basic ingredient in the development of a healthy self-concept and emotional foundation is love. The power of love in the very early years of life is strong enough to make sick children well; the lack of it can make well children sick. Love has such a positive force that it can decrease the child's inevitable moments of pain, frustration, and anger. Love can change, modify, and channel negative feelings into constructive actions and lead toward success later in life. Children's earliest memories are usually associated with people and the relationships the children had with them: "It is important that children are connected to their role models through loving relations, because these early positive emotional patterns of behavior provide them with schema on how to live throughout their lives" (Swick & Freeman, 2004, p. 3).

Because of liability concerns amid allegations of child abuse in child care settings, some programs have instituted policies that do not allow physical displays of affection toward young children. These policies fail to recognize the importance of touch to the healthy development of children, especially to infants and toddlers. Young children need positive nurturing touch to feel secure and loved. As teachers, we must understand that "withholding touch can be just as physically and emotionally harmful to a child as sexual abuse or physical abuse such as hitting, grabbing, spanking, and shaking" (Carlson, 2006, p. 3). If children are denied touch, or experience touch only through punishment or aggression, they do not learn to tell the difference between appropriate and loving touch from inappropriate or dangerous touch (Carlson, 2006): "When positive, nurturing touch and learning about it are lacking, young children miss out on things that might very well have made them safer from potential abusers" (Carlson, 2006, p. 61). Warm responses such as pats on the back, hugs, face touches, or ruffling a child's hair show care, concern, and love. However, these responses should always be developmentally appropriate, acceptable to the child, and consistent with each individual child's needs and cultural expectations.

Children have a right to "to learn and develop, work diligently in school and career, achieve, and pursue a happy and fulfilling life" (Washington & Andrews, 2010, p. 2). It is particularly important that teachers assist young children to become contributing members of society by supporting their moral development, providing opportunities for their success, and helping them become involved in their communities (Robinson & Curry, 2005/2006). The relationships we have with children today are helping to form them into the adults of tomorrow (Baker & Manfredi/Petitt, 2005).

Early childhood experiences also aid in the *development of physical and motor functions.* Materials and apparatus should be provided that enable the child to use and exercise both large and small muscles. Large-muscle equipment and activities include climbing equipment, tricycles, wagons, rocking boats, tumble tubs, and locomotor and rhythmic activities. There are also many appropriate physical–motor games for children in the early childhood years. They should be simple to play and noncompetitive. Small-muscle activities include puzzles, lacing games and toys, scissors, and crayons, as well as fingerplays and any other activities and materials that encourage use of hands and fingers.

The term *early childhood education* implies teaching the child. Thus *intellectual* or *cognitive* aspects become an ingredient in the growth and development of the young child. It is well documented that the early years are of crucial importance to the child's intellectual growth. Early childhood education opens up the world to young children through experiences with people, events, animals, places, and other things. A child cannot have an understanding of what a strawberry is, for example, without some experience with it—either a real experience or a vicarious experience through a picture or an explanation, in specific detail. The richest and most meaningful experiences for children are first-hand, concrete, or sensory. These experiences may be in school or on field trips.

Although young children need opportunities for learning, mastering skills, and thinking, the process must be slow and organized. Young children must be given time to experience who they are on their road to becoming responsible adults. Pressures for early achievement and academic learning have intensified, but the way that young children grow and learn has not changed.

Some cognitively oriented programs focus simply on accelerating development of the child's IQ. However, the individual child should be the focus, and the curriculum should be planned to help each child to reach his or her fullest potential. Basic concepts presented in an exciting way are stimulating, fun, interesting, and involving, and they provide the foundations for both learning and initial attitudes toward learning. Teachers of young children thus have the challenge of providing a curriculum that meets their needs and is relevant for them.

Early childhood educators seek to educate children not only to think, but also to feel and act. When planning lessons and writing objectives, teachers should ask, "What is it that I want these students to know, do, and feel as a result of this lesson?" Teachers should not separate the cognitive from the affective; rather, they should see these domains as integrated parts of the whole and try to gear their instruction to build on this interdependence.

Early childhood education can thus be one of the primary means for meeting and satisfying some of the basic needs of young children: social, emotional, physical, intellectual, and linguistic. The early years are times for the development of language, creativity, thinking, and self-concept. Therefore, the importance of high-quality education during this period cannot be overemphasized.

COMPONENTS IN HOW YOUNG CHILDREN LEARN

Children need active, engaged, relevant, experiential learning that provides them with both **structured learning** and **incidental** or **spontaneous learning**. Much of the learning taking place in today's classrooms and early childhood centers results from planned curriculum experiences and activities based on children's needs. However, opportunities for learning abound in the child's environment beyond that which is teacher prepared. Incidental or spontaneous learning is refreshing to observe a young child in the process of discovery during a spontaneous learning experience, as in the following illustration.

> Jalana painted with horizontal strokes of alternating black and white paint that had been placed at the easel. As the two colors ran together, her eyes expressed discovery, and she exclaimed, "I made gray!"

Hands-on or real experiences are important for children in the stage of early childhood. These children need a strong base of experiences that will provide a foundation for later learning. They need a variety of experiences around a single notion, remembering that a single experience is not usually enough to build a reliable intellectual concept. Children need experiences that encourage them to manipulate, explore, use their senses, build, create, discover, construct, take apart, question, and ultimately understand the world in which they are living. They use their experiences to provide the basis for interpreting, conceptualizing, and categorizing into meaningful ideas.

Young children construct their knowledge through many different experiences of the world in which they live. As bits of knowledge collected through these experiences are combined, meaning results. These become the pieces that make up children's schema, "maps," or understanding of their world and dictate to them their thinking and how to behave. The larger the stock of experiences, the more meaning they develop, the more elaborate is their schema and, ultimately, the clearer their thinking.

Real experiences provide concrete knowledge from which clear understanding evolves.

> Ms. Harris, in her Head Start center, told the children a story about a donkey. When she asked what a donkey looked like, she realized that the children had never actually seen one. The next day when school began, Ms. Harris confidently walked into the classroom, leading behind her a reluctant donkey—one that the children could experience firsthand.

Learning and information must be congruous with what has already been understood. When the child understands a notion, it is stored in the mind with the related schema of other concepts. In further experiences, the child calls on the prior knowledge already compiled to understand the new ideas. Teachers need to make the information that they teach compatible with what each child knows from previous experiences, the prior understanding. Teachers do this through preassessments prior to units of study.

Children make generalizations as they build relationships among concepts by relying on information previously accumulated. Without a broad base of direct encounters from which to generalize, children cannot move toward abstract reasoning. Before certain conceptual strategies can be learned, specific levels of cognitive development must be achieved. Children can understand only those things that past knowledge has prepared them to grasp.

Curiosity, questioning, and **inquiry** motivate children to learn about and explore their world. Curiosity impels a child to reach out to the environment to learn, explore, and understand (Cartwright, 2004). An adult can help foster children's curiosity by encouraging them to explore, and creating surroundings that allow them to satisfy their inquisitiveness. To touch, observe, listen, think about, and evaluate the things around them; to take apart and put together, explore and look for alternatives; to try and fail and try again and again until they succeed—these are all ways that a child learns through curiosity. To ask "why" and "how" questions is a means for coming to know and learn. Early childhood educators should be especially interested in the questions that young children generate, because they are tenacious questioners even before they enter formal schooling. However, something happens when they begin their formal schooling that inhibits their natural questioning, and they learn to answer the teacher's questions, but not to ask. Perhaps they are conditioned early in their education to *know* information, rather than to *question* ideas. If we desire child-centered early childhood classrooms, we need to discipline our teaching behavior to expect and support inquiry from children and to use their questions as a springboard for planning projects, activities, and learning episodes.

Questioning is significant to learning, and it should be encouraged as a part of communication. The child asks a question, and the teacher listens to determine whether the information has been correctly interpreted. Then the teacher either reinforces and praises the child for the right information or corrects the misconception. A child's questions may lead the discussion in a direction unplanned by the teacher and provide feedback for concepts not understood. Following a story and discussion about watermelons, the children observed a real watermelon that was quite small. Joanna asked, "Why don't you water that thing?" and then pointed out that the teacher should "dump it in water." The teacher wisely sustained the inquiry and through feedback from the children learned that many of them thought that if they put the watermelon in water it would grow bigger. After a lengthy, unplanned discussion, the children learned the valuable notion that because the watermelon had already been picked from the vine, it could not grow any more.

Through communication from the child, many **misconceptions are identified, which must be clarified and corrected.** Only then is a child able to obtain further knowledge of concepts in the continuing search for meaningful relationships in the environment. Thus, student questions become a means of early childhood assessment. An example of a child's misconception follows.

> The children had spent a week exploring the theme of the dairy cow. A number of concepts and a variety of activities were included. On the last day of the theme study, the children visited a dairy farm, observed some cows being machine-milked, and watched the milk flowing through clear plastic tubing. A child asked the teacher, "How can they tell when the cow is full?"

This child's questions provided the necessary communication feedback to the teacher about that child's understanding. Additional experiences may need to be planned and concepts retaught, perhaps in different ways, to correct misconceptions or to extend meaning.

Modeling is another component of learning that is important in early childhood education. The teacher models both concepts that are to be understood and correct language usage. In addition, teachers model attitudes; enthusiasm for learning is caught, not taught. Prosocial behaviors are often best learned when they are modeled or when children can observe them in others. Other behaviors and attitudes that influence learning are also modeled for the young child. Teachers who are caring, questioning, and thoughtful learners, for example, are more likely to have students with these same academic qualities. Skills and behaviors, in particular, are learned through imitation or modeling. To tie a bow based on a word description of that skill would be very difficult, but when the skill is modeled for a child who is developmentally ready, with practice it can be learned. If a child is praised for work, efforts, or a particular behavior, the praise serves as reinforcement for that child. In addition, other children will desire to receive the praise, so they too will try to accomplish the work or skill. This is observational learning: Children observe others and then model or imitate that person's efforts, skills, or work.

Scaffolding is adult assistance or support to young children as they build a firm understanding. Scaffolding consists of giving clues, reminders, encouragement, support; breaking problems or challenges into steps; or anything else that allows the child to grow in independence as a learner. It is always built on the child's previous knowledge.

Another component in how children learn is the **sociocultural base or heritage**—the context—of their experiences and lives. Their knowledge is not just individually constructed, but is also influenced by their particular families and the culture from which they come. Cultural habits and traditions in homes and communities serve as contexts for children's development. Learning takes place through children's active participation in the traditions, routines, and rituals of their culture, lives, and contexts. As a child interacts with the significant people in his or her environment, the shared understandings between child and others will eventually become internalized knowledge, skills, and dispositions. The broad range of various experiences and perspectives that diverse students bring to school is a powerful way for all children to learn more.

STANDARDS IN EARLY CHILDHOOD EDUCATION

Teacher education and early childhood preparation programs at universities across the country use standards as a guide. For example, if a university is accredited by National Council for Accreditation of Teacher Education (NCATE) or Teacher Education Accreditation Council (TEAC), it will need to show evidence of desired educational outcomes based on standards such as those of the Interstate New Teacher Assessment and Support Consortium (INTASC). These are standards for licensure adopted by states across the country. The 10 INTASC standards define knowledge, performance measures or skills, and dispositions that new teachers should possess. Teacher candidates are expected to have opportunities to develop professional knowledge,

INTASC STANDARDS

Standard #1: Knowledge of Subject Matter

The teacher understands the central concepts, tools of inquiry, and structures of the discipline(s) he or she teaches and can create learning experiences that make these aspects of subject matter meaningful for students.

Standard #2: Knowledge of Human Development and Learning

The teacher understands how children learn and develop and can provide learning opportunities that support their intellectual, social, and personal development.

Standard #3: Adapting Instruction for Individual Needs

The teacher understands how students differ in their approaches to learning and creates instructional opportunities that are adapted to diverse learners.

Standard #4: Multiple Instructional Strategies

The teacher understands and uses a variety of instructional strategies to encourage the students' development of critical thinking, problem solving, and performances.

Standard #5: Classroom Motivation and Management Skills

The teacher uses an understanding of individual and group motivation and behavior to create a learning environment that encourages positive social interaction, active engagement in learning, and self-motivation.

Standard #6: Communication Skills

The teacher candidate uses knowledge of effective verbal, nonverbal, and media communication techniques to foster active inquiry, collaboration, and supportive interaction in the classroom.

Standard #7: Instructional Planning Skills

The teacher plans instruction based on knowledge of subject matter, students, the community, and curriculum goals.

Standard #8: Assessment and Student Learning

The teacher understands and uses formal and informal assessment strategies to ensure the continuous intellectual, social, and physical development of learners.

Standard #9: Professional Commitment and Responsibility

The teacher is a reflective practitioner who continually evaluates the effect of his or her choices and actions on others (students, parents, and other professionals in the learning community), and who actively seeks out opportunities to grow professionally.

Standard #10: Partnerships

The teacher fosters relationships with school colleagues, parents, and agencies in the community at large to support students' learning and well-being.

Source: The Interstate New Teacher Assessment and Support Consortium (INTASC) standards were developed by the Council of Chief State School Officers and member states. Copies may be downloaded from the Council's website at www.ccsso.org. Council of Chief State School Officers. (1992). Model standards for beginning teacher licensing, assessment, and development: A resource for state dialogue. Washington, DC: Author.

skills, and dispositions in the above 10 standards and then be able to show evidence of these standards in practice and in their INTASC portfolio.

Currently, American schools and early childhood programs focus on standards-based education. The passage of the No Child Left Behind (NCLB) Act, along with additional state and federal legislation, has led to greater accountability and a need for teachers to become familiar with standards set for students at each level and grade and to refer to them when planning lessons. For example, standards in literacy have been developed by organizations such as the International Reading Association (IRA) and the National Council of Teachers of English (NCTE). Standards in math have been developed by the National Council of Teachers of Mathematics (NCTM), and standards for social studies have been developed by the National Council for the Social Studies (NCSS).

The standards in a variety of the content areas for early childhood as well as the standards for professional teachers and programs in early childhood education (ECE) have been established by the National Association for the Education of Young Children (NAEYC), which has often collaborated on position statements and standards with the National Association of Early Childhood Specialists in State Departments of Education (NAECS/SDE). Most states have developed their own standards, which most often emerge or have been developed from the standards of the variety of professional associations such as those previously listed. Most recently (June 2010), the Council of Chief State School Officers (CCSSO) and the National Governors Association (NGA) have developed a Common Core State Standards to help ensure that all students are college- and career-ready by the end of high school. Teachers use the various standards as

NAEYC EARLY CHILDHOOD PROGRAM STANDARDS

Program Standard 1: Relationships

The program promotes positive relationships among all children and adults to encourage each child's sense of individual worth and belonging as part of a community and to foster each child's ability to contribute as a responsible community member.

Program Standard 2: Curriculum

The program implements a curriculum that is consistent with its goals for children and promotes learning and development in each of the following areas: social, emotional, physical, language, and cognitive.

Program Standard 3: Teaching

The program uses developmentally, culturally, and linguistically appropriate and effective teaching approaches that enhance each child's learning and development in the context of the program's curriculum goals.

Program Standard 4: Assessment of Child Progress

The program is informed by ongoing systematic, formal, and informal assessment approaches to provide information on children's learning and development. These assessments occur within the context of reciprocal communications with families and with sensitivity to the cultural contexts in which children develop. Assessment results are used to benefit children by informing sound decisions about children, teaching, and program improvement.

Program Standard 5: Health

The program promotes the nutrition and health of children and protects children and staff from illness and injury.

Program Standard 6: Teachers

The program employs and supports a teaching staff that has the educational qualifications, knowledge, and professional commitment necessary to promote children's learning and development and to support families' diverse needs and interests.

Program Standard 7: Families

The program establishes and maintains collaborative relationships with each child's family to foster children's development in all settings. These relationships are sensitive to family composition, language, and culture.

Program Standard 8: Community Relationships

The program establishes relationships with and uses the resources of the children's communities to support the achievement of program goals.

Program Standard 9: Physical Environment

The program has a safe and healthful environment that provides appropriate and well-maintained indoor and outdoor physical environments. The environment includes facilities, equipment, and materials to facilitate child and staff learning and development.

Program Standard 10: Leadership and Management

The program effectively implements policies, procedures, and systems that support stable staff and strong personnel, fiscal, and program management so all children, families, and staff have high-quality experiences.

Source: Excerpt reprinted with permission from National Association for the Education of Young Children (NAEYC), *NAEYC Early Childhood Program Standards and Accreditation Criteria: The Mark of Quality in Early Childhood Education,* (rev. ed., 2008) (Washington, DC: NAEYC, 2008). NAEYC Early Childhood Program Standards and Accreditation Criteria are available online at www.naeyc.org.

---

resources from which to frame their objectives and desired outcomes for programs as well as units and lessons. NAEYC has standards for various purposes; they have 10 Early Childhood Program Standards and Accreditation Criteria (2008) for the purpose of providing program standards with specific performance criteria for each standard that must be met for NAEYC accreditation. Performance criteria support teachers in planning program goals.

The focus of the NAEYC Early Childhood Program Standards and Accreditation Criteria is to ensure the quality of experiences in the early childhood programs and to encourage positive outcomes for the children (NAEYC, 2008). It is important to emphasize that incorporating subject-matter content standards will improve early childhood education and result in long-term benefits for children's development and learning.

NAEYC has another set of standards for the purpose of preparing preservice teachers in early childhood education. This set of standards includes six standards for preparation programs in guiding early childhood teacher candidates. These standards, NAEYC Standards for Early Childhood Professional Preparation Programs (NAEYC, 2009b), will be the focus of this text. Each of the six standards has key elements that guide teacher candidates as they prepare to be professional teachers.

EARLY CHILDHOOD EDUCATION TEACHERS

Because so many demands and expectations are placed on the early childhood classroom—standardized assessments, curriculum standards, NCLB—it sometimes seems impossible to achieve DAP (Geist & Baum, 2005). As teachers, we understand that there must be expectations and standards for our early childhood programs. But we must carefully plan how academics can be effectively and appropriately incorporated in order to maintain quality and successful programs (Gronlund, 2001). Wheatley (2003) provides the following recommendations to assist teacher educators in emphasizing subject-matter standards: "Learn about the content standards, reexamine beliefs about subject matter, emphasize content standards in coursework, develop resources that clearly reflect the content standards, [and] participate in the revision and improvement of state and national standards" (p. 97).

Piaget (1970b) believed that a teacher of young children should be highly intelligent and highly trained. Teachers who have quality training and education are more likely to make a significant impact on children's development and learning. Programs can be play-based, but "play with purpose and intent" (Gronlund, 2001, p. 42). After following the children's interests, the teacher defines this purpose and intent by setting up the environment and organizing the materials to help children explore, solve problems, practice skills, and learn concepts through hands-on experiences (Gronlund,

Teachers' attitudes should reflect interest, patience, enthusiasm, empathy, hope, understanding, and care.

Demonstrated Qualities of Effective Early Childhood Teachers

caring	competent	qualified	educated
credentialed	enthusiastic	flexible	creative
empathic	tolerant	understanding	good communicator
learner	nurturing	sensitive	aware
cultivate thinking	patient	high energy	high expectations
teaching strengths	planning strengths	positive attitude	curriculum aware

2001). The teacher is also the decision maker and most often determines whether a day is successful or unsuccessful. Teachers make numerous decisions each day in the classroom, and in doing so should remember the following questions: "Are we helping children to become contributing members of society?" "Are we teaching children the skills that are necessary for success in life" (Shidler, 2009, p. 91)? Because the attitudes of the teacher and the teaching staff influence every aspect of the program, their attitudes should reflect interest, enthusiasm, creativity, empathy, hope, tolerance, understanding, and care: ". . . children's behaviors are influenced by their teachers' behaviors and use of language" (Shidler, 2009, p. 88). Research on teaching effectiveness indicates that some of these qualities, in addition to flexibility, communication skills, a secure self-image, and the ability to involve children actively in learning activities, are the most desirable assets in early childhood education teachers. We must "make choices and take actions that allow children to become more competent and more confident than when we met them" (Shidler, 2009, p. 91).

> Early childhood educators must strive to be *learners* who are willing to continually study, grow, and change, and to think and solve problems.

Thinking teachers are people who reflect and think deeply while helping and inviting others to think well. The term *thoughtful teaching* is prevalent in the literature today, and it has a double meaning. Thoughtful teachers are those who are caring and sensitive to the needs of young children, and who also demand deep thinking, problem solving, study, and decision making of themselves and those that they teach. Such teachers do everything in their power to cultivate thoughtful teaching; they raise their own standards and expectations to the highest level.

Teachers who are successful in working with young children are likely to have warm and nurturing personalities. Children do not tune in or develop a rapport with cold, uncaring teachers. Children flourish in a classroom where they sense that the teacher deeply *cares* about them as people, about what they are learning, and about the skills that they are developing (Bosworth, 1995).

Another vital quality for effective early childhood teachers is patience, because children make mistakes as they learn. Energy and enthusiasm are also important characteristics. The excellent early childhood teacher must be on the move frequently, and often very quickly, for most of the day. Enthusiasm must highlight the teacher's personality and illuminate every activity, for enthusiasm is caught, not taught. The more excited and enthusiastic the teacher is, the more eager, enthusiastic, and positive the children will be.

> Teaching in early childhood is a complex task and requires teachers with positive teaching strengths and qualities, as well as excellent teacher preparation and practice.

To encourage high-quality teaching and competent teachers, the following criteria are important (Darling-Hammond, 1997; DeVault, 2003):

- The curriculum needs to be flexible.
- Teachers should have a voice in making curriculum changes.
- Teachers must understand how children learn and manage, and they must monitor student learning.
- Teachers must have early childhood subject-matter or content knowledge.
- Administrators and policy makers should trust teachers.
- Beginning teachers need a mentoring program.
- Teachers should understand and incorporate national, state, and district standards.
- Teachers should be regularly evaluated on their teaching strengths, areas for improvement, and skills.
- Teachers should be recognized for their knowledge, skills, and quality teaching.
- Schools should be organized for both student and teacher learning.
- Professional development needs to be a part of a teacher's daily work.
- Teachers need a realistic workload.

In the right kind of environment, one that is planned to include materials and firsthand experiences, coupled with an atmosphere of teacher competency, warmth, and concern, children are likely to flourish and have the groundwork laid for positive educational attitudes. Their needs will be met in such a way that they can proceed successfully to the next level of development.

DEVELOPMENTALLY APPROPRIATE PRACTICE IN EARLY CHILDHOOD

Developmentally appropriate practice requires both meeting children where they are . . . and enabling them to reach goals that are both challenging and achievable. All teaching practices should be appropriate to children's age and developmental status, attuned to them as unique individuals, and responsive to the social and cultural contexts in which they live. (Copple & Bredekamp, 2009, p. xii)

According to NAEYC (2009a, pp. 11–15), the following principles of child development and learning are research-based and theory-based and should be considered by early childhood educators when making decisions:

1. All domains of development and learning—physical, social and emotional, and cognitive—are important, and they are closely interrelated. Children's development and learning in one domain influence and are influenced by what takes place in other domains.
2. Many aspects of children's learning and development follow well-documented sequences, with later abilities, skills, and knowledge building on those already acquired.
3. Development and learning proceed at varying rates from child to child, as well as at uneven rates across different areas of a child's individual functioning.
4. Development and learning result from a dynamic and continuous interaction of biological maturation and experience.
5. Early experiences have profound effects, both cumulative and delayed, on a child's development and learning; and optimal periods exist for certain types of development and learning to occur.
6. Development proceeds toward greater complexity, self-regulation, and symbolic or representational capacities.
7. Children develop best when they have secure, consistent relationships with responsive adults and opportunities for positive relationships with peers.
8. Development and learning occur in and are influenced by multiple social and cultural contexts.
9. Always mentally active in seeking to understand the world around them, children learn in a variety of ways; a wide range of teaching strategies and interactions are effective in supporting all these kinds of learning.
10. Play is an important vehicle for developing self-regulation as well as for promoting language, cognition, and social competence.
11. Development and learning advance when children are challenged to achieve at a level just beyond their current mastery, and also when they have many opportunities to practice newly acquired skills.
12. Children's experiences shape their motivation and approaches to learning, such as persistence, initiative, and flexibility; in turn these dispositions and behaviors affect their learning and development.

Source: Excerpt reprinted with permission from the National Association for the Education of Young Children (NAEYC). NAEYC Position statement: *Developmentally Appropriate Practice in Early Childhood Programs Serving Children from Birth through Age 8.* (2009). Washington DC: Author. All current NAEYC position statements are available online at www.naeyc.org/positionstatements.

> *Developmentally appropriate teaching* means that we approach children from where they are and not from where we think they ought to be.

The NAEYC Standards for Early Childhood Professional Preparation Programs includes Standard 4, which is Using Developmentally Effective Approaches to Connect with Children and Families. Central to DAP is the knowledge teachers have in three areas: child development and learning, what is known relating to each individual child, and what is known with regard to the individual social and cultural contexts of children (NAEYC, 2009a). Thus, teachers begin by considering age and developmental norms, then considering each individual child "within the context of family, community, culture, linguistic norms, social group, past experience (including learning and behavior), and current circumstances. Only then can the teacher see children as *they are* to make decisions that are developmentally appropriate for each of them" (NAEYC, 2009a, p. 10). Everything teachers plan and do should focus on the individual child. They tailor, adjust, and adapt the curriculum to fit each child in the program, rather than expecting children to fit the program (Elkind, 1987). In a DAP classroom, children are allowed to progress at their own rate, and both the curriculum and teaching

strategies are relevant for all the children in the classroom. Thus, a great deal of flexibility is required, but this does not mean a total lack of structure and academics; rather, it means that the structure and academics of the program are based on individual and group needs and current understanding of child development (Raines, 1997).

NAEYC (2009a, pp. 16–23) proposes five guidelines for early childhood professionals to use in making decisions in practice to support DAP. These guidelines are addressed in several chapters of this text and should serve as the foundation of all decisions in early childhood practice. These dimensions incorporated into classroom teaching cultivate successful, high-quality, developmentally appropriate classrooms and programs. The guidelines are:

1. Creating a caring community of learners
2. Teaching to enhance development and learning
3. Planning curriculum to achieve important goals
4. Assessing children's development and learning
5. Establishing reciprocal relationships with families*

---

*Excerpt is reprinted with permission from the National Association for the Education of Young Children (NAEYC). NAEYC Position Statement. *Developmentally Appropriate Practice in Early Childhood Programs Serving Children from Birth Through Age 8.* (Washington, DC: NAEYC, 2009). All current NAEYC position statements are available online at www.naeyc.org/positionstatements.

DAP suggests recognizing the importance of positive, supportive, and caring relationships (Gallagher, 2005). It is creating an inclusive and caring community that extends from the classroom to the community, and fostering respectful and collaborative relationships among peers. Teachers must understand the developmental needs and characteristics of each age group as well as of each individual child. DAP focuses on the child while taking into account gender, culture, disabilities, and other factors. DAP includes some intentional or explicit teaching according to the needs of the children, but it also suggests that children, are playful: "We want them [children] to interact with teachers and peers as they sing, listen to stories, and engage in creative art and play. As they do so they will learn vocabulary, acquire information, and learn" (Morrow, 2004). In DAP there is a balance between play and direct, thematic, and spontaneous instruction (Morrow, 2004).

The curriculum is adjusted to meet the child's needs in DAP; this includes cognitive, linguistic, physical, and social-emotional development and needs. Learning activities and objectives match children's development, and adequate time is provided for exploring during the various stages of learning. Teaching is not simply a matter of collecting materials and toys and selecting projects and activities for children; rather, it requires a sensitivity and understanding of the children, their parents, and DAP. As teachers plan appropriate activities, they should ask three questions: Is this activity right for a child of this age? Is this activity right for this child? Does this activity match the social and cultural contexts in which the children in this class live? (Copple & Bredekamp, 2009).

Children should be encouraged to engage fully in each stage of development. Their learning should be a pleasant and fascinating journey, with their motivation for learning emerging from their "natural curiosity and desire to make sense of their world" (Hart, Burts, & Charlesworth, 1997, p. 5). Teachers, viewed as facilitators, play an active role in helping children to construct their knowledge and understanding (Raines, 1997). Recognizing the diversity in rates of intellectual attainment and mental abilities requires constant accommodation and flexibility on the part of the teacher (Elkind, 1996). Teachers thus need to view the early childhood age range as a continuum rather than as separate grade levels.

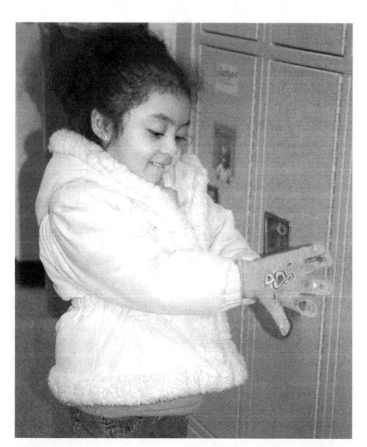

Encourage children to be independent, confident, and competent.

Characteristics of Developmentally Appropriate Practice

- Activities are age-based and developmentally appropriate.
- Plans and materials are individually appropriate.
- Students are provided with culturally and linguistically appropriate materials.
- Authentic instruction and assessment are used consistently.
- Children construct knowledge based on what they already know as well as what they want to know.
- Hands-on learning experiences are provided as a primary means of learning.
- Students have choices, although there are teacher-directed experiences.
- Students are encouraged to develop autonomy as learners and also socially.
- Play is a central ingredient in the curriculum.
- Adequate time is provided for exploring, questioning, and problem solving.
- The curriculum and school experiences are adjusted to meet the needs of the children in the classroom.
- Children progress at their own rate.
- The curriculum is dynamic and ever-changing.
- Families are important.
- A caring community is relevant to learning and development.

Even though many educators understand and support DAP, research tells us that as little as one-third to one-fifth of the early childhood programs studied actually exemplified the philosophy (Elkind, 2005; Neuman & Roskos, 2005).

Some common misconceptions relating to DAP include the following:

- The teacher is not in charge.
- There is no structure in the curriculum or the classroom.
- Few skills and concepts are taught.
- DAP is a set curriculum (Raines, 1997).

Although the teacher is in charge in a DAP classroom, children do have choices and many hands-on learning activities. There are teacher-directed experiences, but the many opportunities for choice build independence and responsibility in the young learners. There is structure in the classroom in terms of the curriculum, the space, the time, and the schedule, but this organization is sometimes hard to detect to an observer who sees children playing and choosing various activities. Children learn skills in authentic play experiences and activities, rather than with drills and worksheets. Children can and should develop as knowledgeable, skillful, and active problem solvers—not passive, inactive, fill-the-vessel learners.

DAP is reflected not in one particular curriculum, but in the way the curriculum is carried out (Raines, 1997). Teachers are influenced by the constructivist approach in encouraging students' points of view and supporting learners working in an authentic environment, making choices, and solving problems (Torp & Sage, 1998).

BALANCING DIRECT TEACHING AND CHILD-GUIDED PLAY

Generally, *how* we teach influences success or failure more than *what* we teach. Curriculum content, strategies, or teaching methods that put too much emphasis on intellectual achievement can misuse these early years (Elkind, 1987). There is pervasive acceptance of the proposition that young children are not smaller versions of older children (NAESP, 1990). However, there is a dangerous trend toward teaching skills earlier and earlier in educational settings, increasing the stresses and failures felt by our youth. The college curriculum is being taught in senior high school, the senior high school curriculum in junior high, the junior high in later elementary grades, the later elementary in early elementary classes, the early elementary in kindergarten, and the kindergarten in preschool.

The idea that education is a race, and the earlier you start, the earlier and better you finish, has become a well-established assumption in our society. . . . This notion, together with parental angst and early childhood amnesia, helps account for the current efforts to focus on academics and testing in early childhood education. (Elkind, 2005, p. 39)

Ten Boom (1971) writes that her father would not allow her to learn too much, too soon, too fast. She had asked him a question, the answer to which he felt she was not yet able to fully understand. He responded by asking her to carry his luggage from the train, which she was unable to do, and she said, "It's too heavy." He answered that it is the same way with knowledge. "Some knowledge is too heavy for children. When you are older and stronger you can hear it. For now you must trust me to carry it for you" (pp. 26–27). In our sometimes faulty evaluations of where children are at a specific stage of development and what they seem capable of handling, we often believe that they can "carry it." We need to consider seriously: Can they? And if they can carry it right now, how long will they be able to carry it? Is it necessary for them to carry it at this point in time?

Elkind (1996, 2005, 2007a) believes that the national trend toward pushing young children to achieve has led to using inappropriate teaching methods and developing unreasonable expectations, particularly for kindergarten and prekindergarten children. The end result has been that many of these children are pressured with too much, too soon, too fast, and they face stress and burnout early in their lives. "Parents or care givers who push children too fast or too hard can do as much damage as those who do not challenge children at all" (Newberger, 1997, p. 4).

The kindergarten scene of years gone by—children building with blocks, painting at the easel, and dressing up—has been replaced with one of formal education practices, including workbooks, worksheets, paper and pencil work, and basal-based instruction. Children who are pushed too fast, too far, too soon lose interest in learning, experience failure, are unable to think for themselves, cannot deal with stress, and often find it difficult to relate to peers. Some critics of national mandates such as the 2001 NCLB Act believe there have been negative consequences for young children "including narrowing the curriculum and testing too much and in the wrong ways" (NAEYC, 2009a, p. 3). In early childhood programs where children participate in developmentally appropriate academic experiences, the difference is in *how* number, literacy, and other content concepts are taught. When teachers use activities, centers, a variety of literacy modes, music, choral reading, work with puppets, reader's theater, manipulatives, and other appropriate materials, the learning environment is much different from one that focuses on scripted programs along with workbooks and worksheets. Children in this kind of learning environment do learn to read and do develop beginning number concepts.

The philosophy in this book is that children from 3 to 8 years of age benefit from a direct, explicit, or intentional teaching approach, but that such an approach should be individually appropriate, used for short periods of time, and integrated with self-initiated play (Copple & Bredekamp, 2009). Teachers need to be wise as they plan and develop appropriate curriculum experiences for these children and consider the value of play and child-guided activity.

Child-Guided Play

In a developmentally appropriate program, both the curriculum and the environment should reflect the teacher's knowledge and acceptance of the value and importance of child-guided play in early childhood. "Play is an active form of learning that unites the mind, body, and spirit" (NAEYC, 1998b). It is the most important activity in the day for young children (Auxter, Pyfer, & Huettig, 2009). Play shapes and guides the child's world and is an organizing force in the child's life (Hillman, 1995); it is, in fact, the way children explore their world. To help direct our thinking toward the importance of the playful environment, Rivkin (1995) suggests that we remember the places where we liked to play when we were young. Did they allow privacy, independence, or materials to arrange? Could we revisit those places now? Are they still accessible to children, or do they no longer exist? What can we do about providing "memory" places for children today? Play should be the very heart of the early childhood curriculum (Bodrova & Leong, 2003; Copple & Bredekamp, 2009; Elkind, 2003, 2005a; Fromberg, 1999, 2001; Isenberg & Jalongo, 2009; NAESP, 1990; NAEYC, 1998b, 2009a). Play provides a way for young children to reinforce worthwhile, meaningful learning and cooperation with others, rather than just acquiring facts and information alone (Fromberg, 1999, 2001). Meaningful play provides the support and components for academic learning, including using imagination, tapping curiosity, sustaining attention, finding application for newfound understanding, and solving problems. "Play is not a luxury, but rather a crucial dynamic of healthy physical, intellectual, and social-emotional development at all levels" (Elkind, 2007b, p. 4).

Theoretically, there is widespread acceptance of the idea that play is important—that it is serious business for the young child. Elkind (2003) has reviewed a variety of theories that support the role of children's play, including Montessori, Freud, Piaget, and Vygotsky, and points out that theorists, and many adults in general, support the healthy functions and value of play,

but the real value is in the personal experience and joy that play brings to children. Honig (2007, p. 78) suggests, "Play deepens a child's sense of serenity and joy." However, this is a time when the push for academics in early childhood is pressing, and at the practical level, play is too often being replaced with highly structured learning experiences.

> Children constantly remind us, through their behavior and interest, how compelling and essential play is to them.

Good play experiences unite and blend all aspects of development, reaping social, emotional, physical, intellectual, moral, creative, and cultural benefits for young children (Tsao, 2002; Van Hoorn, Nourot, Scales, & Alward, 2007). Good play strengthens skills and deepens understanding of concepts. It gives children opportunities to explore, experiment, create, and imagine (NAEYC & NAECS/SDE, 2002). As educators, we must recognize our responsibility to educate parents in the values and purposes of play for young children. This can be done through workshops, orientation meetings, newsletter articles, and by providing resource materials that teach the values of play.

Features of Early Childhood Play

Integrative

Meaningful

Worthwhile

Solitary or cooperative

Satisfying and personally motivating

Active

Imaginative

Symbolic (it represents reality)

Rule governed

Episodic (emerging and shifting goals)

Source: Based on "A Review of Research on Play," by D. P. Fromberg, in *The Early Childhood Curriculum: Current Findings in Theory and Practice,* 3rd ed. (p. 28), edited by C. Seefeldt, 1999, New York: Teachers College Press.

Purposes and Benefits of Play

Much has been written about the purposes and benefits of play. Here we discuss various purposes for play to help you to recognize its inherent values. This information will aid you in responding clearly and wisely to such queries as "Is that all my child does? Just play?" Some parents may believe that play is an important part of the home environment but question its value in school. They often feel that the school curriculum should be more involved in academics (Brewer & Kieff, 1996/1997). We need to be sensitive to these parental concerns and help parents to understand the benefits of play in a curriculum that fosters learning and development of children.

Play promotes significant mental or cognitive skills (Bodrova & Leong, 2003; Cooper & Dever, 2001; Stegelin, 2005). Research on brain growth and development supports the need for active and stimulating play for *all* children (Stegelin, 2005). Play gives the child opportunities to express thoughts and ideas. It provides occasions to organize, plan, solve problems, reason, try out solutions and skills, create and explore (Hatcher & Petty, 2004; Jones & Cooper, 2006). According to the work of Piaget (1952), play allows children to construct knowledge through assimilation, acquiring information through experiences, as well as through accommodation or modification of an existing point of view because information cannot be integrated into a particular scheme of understanding. Play contributes to the child's development of imaginative thinking (Fromberg, 1999, 2001). Play enables children to formulate ideas and then to test them, to problem solve (Miles, 2009). Much skill development occurs through play, and there is integration of cognitive skills such as literacy and math (Miles, 2009). During play, children have the opportunity to develop their senses of touch, taste, smell, sound, and sight—to assimilate new stimuli (Isenberg & Jalongo, 2009). In addition, their attention spans are expanded as they stay on task and remain attentive to activities in which they are involved.

Play facilitates both divergent thinking and convergent thinking. Convergent tasks have a single answer, whereas divergent tasks have multiple solutions or approaches. Both kinds of thinking are important, and play provides the opportunity to practice both. Even though it is a vigorous intellectual exercise, play does not create the pressure or tension that is often associated with more structured learning approaches.

Play assists communication, language, and literacy development. Many researchers think that communication skills are developed in part through peer play and the need for children to communicate with each other in their play (Chenfeld, 1991; Morrow, 2008). Play stretches the vocabulary and expands language development by providing opportunities to use new words, converse with playmates, listen to another's language and point of view, learn new semantics (meanings of words), and hear and subsequently use new syntax (parts of speech). Play synthesizes previous experiences and thoughts, allowing children to piece them together. Because children plan, communicate, listen, read, and write in their play, it offers the right conditions for learning language and literacy skills (Cooper & Dever, 2001; Stegelin, 2005). Play also fosters creativity and aesthetic appreciation, which can influence the way children think and solve problems.

Play promotes physical–motor development. Play is active; children are never passive recipients (Jones, Evans, & Rencken, 2001). Children use their bodies and increase large-muscle dexterity as they run, climb, skip, hop, jump, throw, and catch. Play, therefore, provides the exercise and physical activity needed to strengthen and coordinate children's muscles and bodies. Children need play for health reasons. According to the American Heart Association (2010), the U.S. obesity epidemic is currently affecting even young children, with more than 12% of 2- to 5-year-olds being overweight. The physical activity of play facilitates release of stress and helps children manage feelings in a positive way (Stegelin, 2005). Through physical play, children can learn appropriate ways to display aggression and other assertive behaviors without hurting themselves or others. When a group of kindergarten children was quizzed about their favorite part of school, a large majority stated that they liked recess best of all. During recess, the spontaneous, self-directed activities involve mostly physical–motor play.

Play encourages positive emotional development. Play affects the child's motivation (Bodrova & Leong, 2003). It is the means for fostering a healthy personality, and it provides the opportunity for each child to discover the self. Play lets children express thoughts and ideas and try out ways of behaving and feeling. Play experiences provide safe avenues for expressing both positive and negative emotions. As they express thoughts and ideas, children can learn and be directed to the most positive ways of handling their emotions through support and reinforcement by both peers and teachers.

Play is pleasurable and enjoyable (Elkind, 2003, 2007). Children use play to make up for unkindness, defects, and disappointments, as well as to play out frustrations, sufferings, fears, anxieties, and anger. In addition, play allows children to be powerful, in control, and assertive, depending on the decisions made in particular play situations. Play enables children to translate feelings, thoughts, fantasies, and inclinations into action, to literally be in control and in charge of their world and feelings. Perhaps the greatest asset of self-directed, self-discovery, or spontaneous play is the satisfaction it gives children of making choices based on their own interests, of attaining some control over their own learning.

Freedom to experiment with materials, feelings, words, and ideas gives impetus to the development of creativity. Through carefree, unpressured play, children's imaginations invent new solutions, different approaches, and unique ideas. Even though ideas are "pretend," it is important that the ideas are created; one day, children will realize that their ideas must be compatible with reality.

Play allows children to develop into social human beings.

Play allows children to develop into social human beings. Piaget (1970a) considered the theoretical relationship between play and socialization. He believed that children are naturally motivated to interact with other children and, as they do so, they become less egocentric and more aware of others. Solitary play is valuable; however, in early childhood, play usually means people. In play experiences, children learn to be both leaders (telling others what to do) and followers (being told what to do). They learn to try different roles and think of other possibilities (Chenfeld, 1991). They learn to give and take, to put themselves in another's position, to negotiate, to sense another's feelings, to hear another's point of view. They learn to share, cope with disappointment, play by the rules, and resolve differences (Brewer & Kieff, 1996/1997; Stegelin, 2005). Play provides practice in the social skills that society demands for success. It also provides practice in being less bossy, less selfish, less meek, or less shy. Play encourages a child to be a friend and a contributor, to cooperate, and to be flexible.

As teachers plan the time that children spend in their classrooms, they must remember the inherent value of play for its own sake and for the behaviors it directly affects. They must not structure and arrange so much of the school time that inadequate time is left for spontaneous, self-directed free-play periods. In terms of benefits, these periods may well be the most important times of the day, and children should not be robbed of

them. Every day should have one or more blocks of time for spontaneous play.

The lesson plans suggested in this book are activity oriented, and many of the activities listed are to be included in the free-play or self-directed spontaneous play period, in addition to the centers that are a regular part of the room environment.

Play Facilitates:

> Learning
> Development
> Motivation
> Thinking and problem solving
> Social development and social awareness
> Flexibility
> Skill development
> Sensory awareness
> Attention span and listening
> Language acquisition and communication
> Physical and motor development
> Healthy emotional development
> Autonomy
> Imagination
> Metacognition (thinking about one's own thinking)

The Teacher's Role in Fostering Positive and Meaningful Play Experiences

Contact with others, both adults and children, is more important in fostering positive play experiences than materials and toys. Children develop empathy, understanding, and sensitivity to each other by relating to each other. Human relationship skills come from firsthand experiences of learning to give and take, to sense another's feelings and needs, to share kindnesses in words and deeds (Glasser, 1997).

> Teachers have an important role during children's play as they provide models of human qualities and encourage their development during play situations.

The teacher's positive attitude, interest in individual children and groups, and enthusiasm for play experiences will influence children's attitudes toward play and the meaning that they draw from their play experiences. The teacher's role is to value, provide for, encourage, guide, and supervise the play of young children. However, the teacher does not become the object of the play or the center of attraction or dictate what the child can or should do in the play activity. Teachers should be available to support, assist, observe, scaffold, interact when appropriate to do so, and indirectly channel misbehavior, as well as to direct and encourage positive behaviors. Teachers encourage play by modeling, planning with children, and playing with language (Fromberg, 1999, 2001). For play to be sustained or extended, children often need adult suggestion, intervention, or stimulation, but once limits have been established and children are comfortable with their environment, adults should intervene as little as possible.

Teachers can make suggestions for play activity and, through play, expand the children's language development, increase conceptual understanding, answer questions, and encourage new social interactions and friendships. Perhaps the most important contribution that they can make to foster children's play is to provide ample time for play and create adequate protected space for playing (Balke, 1997).

During their play, children need opportunity for making choices; this is **student-centered** or **self-regulated learning.** Self-regulation is predictive of later functioning in areas such as problem solving, attention, and metacognition (NAEYC, 2009a). One of the best means for creating student engagement in learning is to allow children the opportunity to make decisions (Kohn, 1993). As they make choices, they feel in control, which results in their being able to accept responsibility (Kelman, 1990). However, children's interest will dwindle, and they may even stop playing, if teachers interfere too much or try to structure their play for them. Play is more valuable when children plan, define, shape, and carry out their own play activities (Kohn, 1993). Yet, the teacher's role must not be diminished. Play should not be used as a reward for children who finish their work. Rather, it has to be planned for by the teacher, expected of all children, and encouraged and understood by parents. Well-planned play during early childhood is more important than adult instruction or formal, structured learning activities.

Although the teacher is important, other children provide the greatest source of complex play. Toys and materials do not sustain play as well as other children. Peers are thus an important part of the play environment. No matter how elaborate the physical facilities are with regard to play, the quality of the environment is determined by teachers and caregivers. They are the ones who evaluate the function of materials, space, time, and people and determine how to appropriately meet children's needs.

PROVIDING DEVELOPMENTALLY APPROPRIATE MATERIALS

Children need carefully selected, developmentally appropriate materials that meet the age range of children in the classroom (NAEYC, 2009). The materials,

toys, and manipulatives are just objects until children use them to support ideas and understanding. To do this, they will need the guidance of thoughtful adults and caregivers to channel and support meaning making.

A particular piece of equipment can be enjoyed by children ages 3 to 8, but the older the child, the more advanced and complex it must be. The structure, as well as the style, of children's play and play materials become more diverse as children mature. For example, children in a broad age range enjoy puzzles and matching materials; however, younger children need fewer pieces to prevent frustration and foster success. Age is not the determining factor here, but rather the developmental abilities of the child. For younger children, simple concepts such as shape and color should be presented, rather than concepts such as time, money, and more complex shapes. Children gain most from materials matched to their stage of development.

Selecting and Using High-Quality Commercial Toys and Equipment

The market is saturated with toys and early childhood equipment. It is imperative that in a developmentally appropriate classroom, educators make wise and careful selections.

General Criteria for Selecting Commercial Equipment, Toys, and Other Materials

1. The equipment should be appropriate for the children's ages, levels of development, abilities, needs, and interests.
2. A good piece of equipment encourages participation and involvement, not just observation and entertainment. It should stimulate independent activity.
3. The equipment should be versatile or open-ended, allowing for additional creative and inventive potential.
4. The equipment should be simple and as free of detail as possible. This encourages versatility, imagination, variety, and appeal.
5. The equipment should be durable, safe, and sanitary and be repaired immediately when broken. When purchasing equipment, find out whether extra pieces or parts are available to replace those that may be lost or broken.

Teacher-Made Learning Materials

In many instances, limited budgets determine the quantity and quality of the equipment and materials

Play equipment should be appropriate for the children's ages, levels of development, abilities, needs, and interests.

that can be purchased. In addition, many commercial toys are restricted in terms of their learning potential. Equipment, materials, and games can easily be made from accessible and inexpensive supplies. This section focuses on materials that contribute to conceptual, perceptual, and language development, in addition to supporting the concepts presented throughout this book.

Equipment and materials are tools for the teacher to use in teaching and reinforcing learning, as well as for the child to enjoy through play. They provide the child with the opportunity to develop concepts such as color, shape, and number, as well as visual perception and eye–hand coordination. Children also use skills that provide the foundation for developing abilities and understanding in reading, writing, and mathematical operations.

Wisely selected equipment and materials can be used in a variety of ways, including child-initiated and teacher-initiated activities. Frequently, when children initiate the play, it may simply (but importantly) involve exploration. Teachers can suggest, model, or prod, but ultimately the children should determine how they want to use equipment and materials (Kohn, 1993).

To sustain and extend play, a teacher could suggest additional ways of working with a material or even establish rules for games, such as dominoes. The teacher could ask, for example, "Have you ever thought about how the beads would look on the string if they were strung in a pattern such as two reds and then one blue, two reds and then one yellow, and so on?" Both kinds of play, child initiated and teacher initiated, are valuable. The selection depends on the individual situation and children.

Although many materials themselves stimulate children's imaginations for use, guided help and teacher assistance are needed to focus on the concept being emphasized. A set of shape dominoes may be used as blocks, for example, or for building corrals and fences. This is important and of great value. However, as play progresses, the children should be shown how to play shape dominoes with the blocks. Teachers do not always need to play with and be near children, but there are both intellectual and emotional advantages in doing so. Positive teacher–child relationships can be strengthened when teachers enjoy focusing on the use of materials and discussing basic concepts with the children. This provides a valuable opportunity for learning about each child's conceptual development. It is also an excellent time for visiting personally with children and becoming better acquainted with their needs, emotions, desires, and interests.

In deciding which materials, equipment, and games to make for enhancing classroom learning, remember that teacher-made materials should be prepared using basically the same criteria for selecting commercial materials and equipment. Be flexible in considering the various ways that each material can be used. Many materials adapt to play by one child, many children, child and teacher, or children and teacher. Figure 1.1 shows some examples of teacher-made materials. Teacher-made materials are used in the same ways that commercial learning materials are used in classrooms. They provide hands-on learning, particularly during independent or small-group learning time.

Properly chosen toys and materials facilitate the children's play as well as foster a developmentally appropriate program. Wisely selected teacher-made learning materials contribute to conceptual, perceptual, and language development. The effectiveness of the equipment depends on its arrangement, display, and organization; periodic rotation; and care and maintenance. Consider the goals of the materials and games you choose and remember that children can learn cooperation and other prosocial behaviors or the games can foster "rejection, competition, failure, and humiliation" (Staley & Portman, 2000, p. 67). Play is valuable, whether it is child initiated or teacher initiated, when the materials have been selected wisely, with care and understanding of young children's developmental needs.

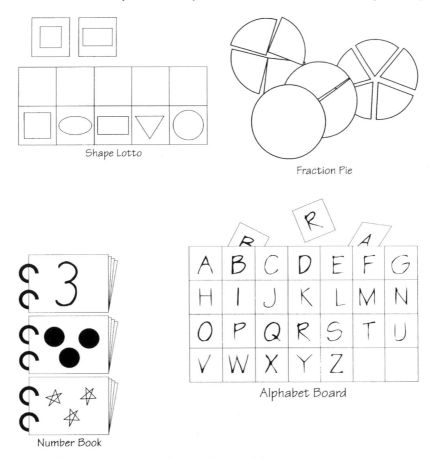

FIGURE 1.1   Examples of Teacher-Made Materials

PREPARING A DEVELOPMENTALLY APPROPRIATE AND CURRICULUM-SUPPORTIVE ENVIRONMENT

A key elements of Standard 1, Promoting Child Development and Learning, is "using developmental knowledge to create healthy, respectful, supportive, and challenging learning environment" (NAEYC, 2009b, p. 11). When teachers recognize and understand the developmental needs of young children, they are able to plan and organize appropriate play experiences and a suitable curriculum. This knowledge also positively influences the environment, which includes both the outdoor play area and the indoor classroom. The outdoor play yard offers children the sense of power, initiative, and opportunity for different kinds of activity and noise (Perry, 2003), but it does not happen by chance (Sutterby & Thornton, 2005). The outdoor environment is often neglected, so thoughtful preparation of it is as important as careful planning of the indoor environment (DeBord, Hestenes, Moore, Cosco, & McGinnis, 2002). Outdoor play benefits children in many ways, including health, fitness, and physical performance (Sutterby & Thornton, 2005). The neurological benefits of outdoor play affect children's healthy brain development (Sutterby & Thornton, 2005). With regard to providing developmentally appropriate play environments, Rivkin (1995, pp. 9–10) proposes a couple of thought-provoking questions: Is it possible that hyperactivity, in part, could be a "cultural disease" and "that if children were not as confined as they are, their activity level would not be so disruptive? Would active play, if in an outdoor setting rather than indoors, be more tolerated?"

The physical setting or environment has a great impact on the child in both an affective and a cognitive way. Feelings engendered in the child by the environment should include a sense of order, enthusiasm, interest, curiosity, cleanliness, and safety. The environment contributes to setting the tone of the school day for both the children and the teacher. An organized, attractive, clean, and cheerful or "warm" setting results in more positive behaviors and attitudes. When things in the environment are beautifully presented, young children have more respect for them and interact with them in a very different way (Wien, Coates, Keating, & Bigelow, 2005). In addition, the environment should offer opportunities for learning and increasing skill in all developmental areas: physical, social, emotional, cognitive, and language. Children need and deserve an environment conducive to learning, growing, positive behavior, and good play.

Guidelines for Arranging the Early Childhood Classroom

The materials and equipment should be appropriate for the developmental level of the children in the class (NAESP, 1990). Indoor and outdoor environments should be arranged to avoid situations that naturally frustrate or anger children. For example, a mixture of toys or materials should not be stored in the same box. If a child desires to play with a soldier that happens to be in the bottom of the box and dumps out the whole box of toys to obtain the soldier, the child may become angry or frustrated when told to pick up all the other toys. The child may honestly say, "But I didn't play with all the toys, only the soldier." Toys and equipment should be complete and in good repair. It is frustrating to put a puzzle together only to find that a piece is missing. Some incomplete or unrepaired materials are unsafe. For example, worn, rough wooden blocks can have splinters; vehicles missing wheels or broken parts can be dangerously sharp.

Guidelines for a Developmentally Appropriate Environment

1. Equipment and materials must be the correct size and height for children. This means that pictures and bulletin boards should be placed at the child's eye level, not the teacher's. Coat hooks, cupboards, shelves, and other materials or items should be where the children can reach them. For comfort and availability, chairs and other furniture pieces should be the appropriate size.

2. The room should be organized and uncluttered. A disorderly environment frequently ignites similar behavior in children. Classrooms are more orderly and interesting when teachers avoid putting everything out at once. For example, if your classroom has six puzzles, put only one or two out at a time. However, there must be enough toys for all children to have something to play with. Material for specific areas or learning centers in the room should be kept separate. As part of cleanup, encourage children to put away toys and materials where they belong.

3. Reflect the local culture in the classroom. Make certain the room is free of stereotypes. Pictures, toys, materials, dress-up clothes, and other objects should reflect the diversity of people and genders.

4. Consider the traffic flow when planning the room arrangement. Eliminate long corridors or "running spaces" that encourage children to run. Break up long spaces, for example, with a trough filled with sensory media. Arrange art areas near a sink for easy access to cleanup. By wisely planning the environment, teachers can indirectly manage behavior; this is referred to as *behavior prevention*.

5. Provide large-motor equipment both indoors and outdoors. Inside, large-motor equipment presents opportunity for active play (Curtis & Carter, 2005). Where possible, keep noisy areas close together and apart from quiet areas (Curtis & Carter, 2005). For example, it would not be wise to put a music area with a rhythm band right next to the story area. There should also be a place where children can get away and be alone; this is especially essential in full-day programs (Curtis & Carter, 2005).

6. The classroom and outdoor areas must be clean, neat, and cheerful. The physical environment must be clean for health and sanitary reasons alone. The classroom walls should be considered as part of the educational environment and not just something to be decorated (Tarr, 2004). Cheerful, bright touches, combined with carefully selected bulletin board pictures, can support the unit theme being studied. Photographs of the children at work on projects and activities should be placed at a level for them to enjoy. Their pictures and work should also be displayed in the room, and a comment or question a child makes during an

Play should be the very heart of the early childhood curriculum.

activity can be placed alongside the child's work (Katz, 1990; Tarr, 2004). But be careful not to add too many displays; simplicity is a guideline for the entire environment.

7. The organization and setup of the room should encourage children to keep the room orderly while developing classifying, categorizing, or matching skills. In the block area, for example, trace a pattern for each size and shape of the small unit blocks on solid-colored, adhesive-backed paper. Then organize and sequence these patterns on the block shelf so that the children can match the blocks to the pattern and, at the same time, organize the block area. Another possibility is to put hooks in the housekeeping area and then place a picture of a hat, dress, or slacks above specific hooks. This encourages children to sense that objects have a place to be put and facilitates matching and classifying. Pictures of fruits, vegetables, and dairy products can be glued in specific locations of the refrigerator. A similar method can be used in the stove and cupboard by gluing pictures that will help children to classify and match items to be placed in these areas. Tools can be hung on a pegboard and matched to their shape.

8. Teachers should be able to see and supervise all areas of the room. Place tall cabinets and shelves against the wall and use shorter cabinets and shelves as area dividers. In addition, create play places at different angles and levels to create interest (Curtis & Carter, 2005).

9. Consider the care and storage of equipment and materials. For example, to facilitate the cleanup of paint or glue brushes, have some cans or containers of water to put brushes into immediately after use so that the paint or glue will not harden. Ideally, there will be clean, orderly, organized storage areas outside the classroom, or higher than the children's reach, where some materials can be stored. Other materials and supplies such as paints, paper, pencils, and paint shirts should be accessible to children so that they can take responsibility for getting them and putting them away (Casey & Lippman, 1991).

10. Rotate areas and materials to create interest. You may ask, "Will children feel secure in an environment that is frequently changed?" The answer is yes. The teacher provides the security, while the changing environment encourages interest, learning, fun, and interaction among children. Children need variety and become bored with toys that are not rotated.

11. Each area, piece of equipment, and material should have purpose and meaning. In evaluat-

ing areas and equipment, ask such questions as "Why am I using this?" and "What am I trying to accomplish?" Remember that the physical setting should serve the needs and interests of the children in the classroom.

12. Choose versatile materials and equipment that lend themselves to a variety of uses and activities. Materials should be open-ended (Curtis & Carter, 2005).

Arranging the Environment with Areas to Meet Developmental Needs

Classrooms should be divided into areas, with each area providing opportunities to satisfy children's developmental needs. If a child avoids a particular area over a period of time, encourage the child to use this area. Avoidance may be an indication of insecurity or uncertainty with the area.

Kindergarten and first- and second-grade children may find a contract helpful to promote on-task behavior. A contract is an individualized activity plan that incorporates both teacher guidance and student interests. Contracts can also effectively guide children to learning areas. Figures 1.2 and 1.3 include examples of sample contracts for use with young children. As a child participates in each activity or area, he or she colors in the square or makes a check mark or an "X" in the box. Study of individual contracts for several days alerts teachers to areas or activities that the children are not participating in as well as those in which they are interested. Contracts also serve as a means of assessment and as a springboard for parent–teacher discussions and conferences. Figure 1.2 would be used for children 3, 4, and 5 years of age, and Figure 1.3 would be used for 6-, 7-, and 8-year-olds.

Allow children to choose areas or centers by placing pictures or names of the centers on a board and hooks under each that determine how many children can be in this center. When children want to go to a particular center, they put their name or picture on the hook under the name or picture of the center. Even preschool children can be effective planners, and approaches such as this help them to focus on their choices (Casey & Lippman, 1991).

Because these areas of the room satisfy various needs, they should be organized, orderly, inviting, and on the child's level. Areas can be changed or modified occasionally to maintain motivation and interest. For example, weekly rotation of toys in the manipulative area will stimulate new exploration. Sensory and creative areas can be changed more frequently, depending on the space, the theme or project, and the balance of planned activities.

FIGURE 1.2 Sample Contract for Preschoolers

The environment should support the curriculum, with the room setup and outdoor playground supporting the unit theme being presented, whenever possible. For example, if the current theme is "fish," the block area could be converted into a large fishing pond, with the large hollow blocks set up as the banks of the pond. Fish cutouts with attached paper clips could be caught in the pond, using fishing pole magnets. An aquarium or trough containing live fish could be used as a learning area. Bulletin boards could feature fish and fishing. Another example of adapting a room area to a theme,

in this case "mail and the mail carrier," is to convert the jungle gym into a mail truck by using colored butcher paper and a little imagination.

The following areas are suggested for early childhood classrooms. The size of the room may limit the use of all areas at one time, and the more areas in a classroom, the more complex the environment.

Outside play area. These will be determined by the facility and what is available, but there is evidence from current research that increasing the

FIGURE 1.3 Sample Contract for Primary-Grade Children

quality of the playground environment encourages children's overall health (Frost, Wortham, & Reifel, 2007). The play yard should be mapped out and carefully planned to meet outcomes and objectives, remembering that complex learning happens outdoors (Perry, 2003). The play yard for primary-grade children is used for structured play experiences as well as recess. Recess is unstructured playtime when children have choices as well as the opportunity to release energy and stress (Council for Physical Education for Children,

2006). Recess is developmentally appropriate and contributes to the physical, social, emotional, and cognitive development of the child (National Association of Early Childhood Specialists in State Departments of Education, 2002).

The playground should have appropriate permanent pieces of equipment such as domes, slides, various climbing apparatus, nesting climbers with boards and bridges, and an adjustable basketball standard and backboard. Items such as barrels, inner tubes, and other salvage pieces can often be purchased inexpensively. Versatile modular gym systems can be set up in a variety of ways for use both indoors and outdoors. Specific and purposeful playground equipment can help children develop skill in climbing, swinging, and balancing (Sutterby & Thornton, 2005).

Large-muscle area. Include equipment for large-muscle development. Dome climbers or jungle gyms are ideal for large rooms because they can be moved to different areas. Some types of smaller jungle gyms fold flat for easy storage and are more appropriate in smaller areas. Other large-muscle development equipment includes balance beams, slides, indoor jumping trampolines, and nesting climbers set up in a variety of ways. It is important to plan *how* the equipment will be set up each day and to plan in a way that facilitates the physical and motor needs of both the group and individual children (Poest, Williams, Witt, & Atwood, 1990).

Dramatic play area. These areas provide opportunities for role playing, trying out, pretending, and acting out familiar and imaginary experiences. "Preparing for and engaging in sociodramatic play provides a nonthreatening, child-centered environment where children teach, learn, and experience real-life roles" (Cooper & Dever, 2001, p. 62). Playing house seems to be the most preferred theme for young children; grocery stores and doctor's offices also spark interest. Teachers or other adults can function in a variety of roles, including onlooker, stage manager, supporter, or play leader (Cooper & Dever, 2001). Additional possibilities are suggested later in the chapter.

Drama center. In this center, include activities such as puppet plays, readers' theater, or choral reading activities.

Sensory play area. May include a trough, tubs, or other methods of setting up media for sensory exploration. Such media might include water, sand, clay, wheat, Styrofoam packing pieces, sawdust, or other available material. Such tools as funnels, bottles, shovels, scoops, cups, beaters, or other items also add occasional interest.

Creative arts area. Provide media such as paints, collage materials, chalk, charcoal, crayons, felt-tipped markers, colored pencils, and other sources to be used with paper on easels, tables, floors, or walls.

Block area. These are often near or part of the large-muscle area. Many classrooms are large enough to accommodate both large and small unit blocks. The block area (especially when it includes large, hollow blocks), the large-muscle area, and sometimes the outdoor play area give children opportunities to develop strength, coordi-

nation, and balance. Manipulative and creative toys such as small cars, farm animals, zoo animals, or human figures used together with blocks can stimulate block play and provide variety. If you use human figures, make sure that they reflect diverse people.

Science area or interest centers. These are often part of the early childhood classroom, especially for supporting science unit themes. For example, during a theme on "color," provide different activities such as color mixing. The science area could be a table with items, displays, or simple experiments that focus on helping children to explore their environment. Magnifying glasses or microscopes encourage additional exploration and study. Also include items involving math and measuring.

A "book nook" or library area. This area provides a place to explore the world through books. Select books to meet the children's developmental needs and to support the theme or concepts being taught. The entire book supply should not be displayed at one time; occasional book rotation stimulates renewed interest. There should always be a rug, chair, or table nearby for reading or being read to. Some of the children's favorite books will be those that they author; these may be individual or class projects and may or may not relate to the theme or project being explored. Also include magazines, newspapers, puppets, flannel board stories, paper, and writing implements.

Music area. These are places where children listen to music, sing, play musical instruments, or perform creative dances. Additional equipment should include appropriate tapes or CDs and/or rhythm band instruments.

Manipulative play area. This area includes small blocks, pegboards, puzzles, number games, bead-stringing activities, magnetic games, and other like equipment. Puzzles and other toys should show diversity and should not have any stereotypic images (Derman-Sparks & A.B.C. Task Force, 1989). Display shelves, tables, and chairs help to extend interest spans.

Computer or technology area. This area includes computers with developmentally appropriate software. Carefully selected hardware and software require teachers with technology training. Young children are becoming very savvy and confident users of technology. They have watched the many facets of computer use in their homes and in the world around them. Teachers need to take advantage of their interest and skill in using computers.

Lockers or cubbies. These may be inside or outside the classroom. Each child should each have a place labeled with his or her name for storing belongings and hanging outerwear. If these spaces are inside the classroom, they could also serve as places for children to sit for quiet meditation or solitude. These areas need to be carefully and appropriately selected according to the developmental needs of the children and the concepts being taught and reinforced.

Learning centers. These are designed to promote concepts and competencies to be explored independently and are planned according to the developmental needs and abilities of the children in the group. Some early childhood teachers use learning centers to structure direct teaching of particular concepts. For example, assign small groups of children to different learning centers. With the assistance of parents, teaching aides, and others, the groups work at a different center each day, so by the end of the week they have participated in all five centers. Other examples of learning centers include Making Words Center where children participate in a variety of developmentally appropriate activities to work with and construct words (McLaughlin, 2010).

Interest centers. These are based on the interests of the children in the classroom. For example, if a child brings in a rock, this may be the stimulus for an interest center on rocks that could include rock collections, books, and other rocks brought by the children.

Although we have not attempted to list the room areas in the daily plans and lesson plans, we assume that they will be well thought out. Remember to vary using these areas and change them often to ensure continued interest and variety. In the plans suggested in this book, we have included individual activities that could be used on specific days and for theme reinforcement.

LOOKING AHEAD

We all recognize that the formative years are birth through eight years of age. As teachers of young children, we can shape the world that the children and their parents will live in (Hernandez, 2010). Currently, many of the public efforts and budgets address fixing problems in young children after they occur. We need to change that focus to providing healthy environments for young children so we can decrease the development of those problems in the first place. This will involve parents and professionals who recognize, understand, and support such ideas as the learning potential of young children; the value of play and outdoor activities; the importance of family culture and racial identity; and the value of social-emotional development. Are we, as educators, spending too much time debating play *or* academics, child-initiated *or* teacher directed, cognitive *or* social? It should be *both* play *and* academics, *both* child-initiated *and* teacher-directed, *both* cognitive *and* socio-emotional (Bredekamp, 2010). Goldilocks searched for the best solutions that were neither too hard nor too soft, but were "just right." As early childhood teachers, we must also find the middle ground as we encourage and support children's development and learning (Bredekamp, 2010). We need to make sure that the focus on early academics and early learning does not prevent our children from experiencing the joys of childhood (Hernandez, 2010).

> The "Hope for the children of 2020: That all children live in a world free of violence, where they know they are loved and respected, and supported to reach their full human potential— physically, spiritually, emotionally, and intellectually" (Washington & Andrews, 2010, p. 18). "The research is clear: we create tomorrow by what we do today" (Washington & Andrews, 2010, p. 1).

Summary

We have looked at early childhood education historically and have found that its roots go back for centuries. We have examined early childhood education today and recognize that great strides have been made, and that we need to continue making progress. All children should be provided with high-quality child care, regardless of their gender, race, religion, or economic situation. There needs to be increased support for the strengthening of family traditions, experiences, and expectations. Early childhood teachers should be highly trained, thoughtful, enthusiastic, creative, empathetic, hopeful, tolerant, understanding, warm, and nurturing.

In addition, our concern is for the quality of kindergarten and primary-grade education, which too often have an academic focus. We have cautioned against inappropriate, pressurized early learning. We propose that children want to learn, and successful DAP begins with, and builds on, concepts that are relevant during the early years. Early childhood education should be different from other kinds of education. We need to provide experiences that contribute to the development of the whole child, and these experiences should be available for *all* children to help them reach their full potential.

Developmentally appropriate early childhood education means providing a curriculum and environment that are right for the developmental needs of children. The developmental needs and characteristics of age groups and individual children need to be understood, and learning activities and goals should be based on the knowledge that children in early childhood are ready for learning through their senses, utilizing experiences, materials, and concrete activities.

Play is an integral part of the early childhood environment and curriculum. Play does not stifle or prevent learning; rather, it enables children to learn (Bodrova & Leong, 2003). It is imperative that teachers recognize the inherent values in play, organize an environment that reflects these values, and plan a curriculum based on play. Play is developmentally right for children 3 to 8 years of age; it is what they need, based on our understanding of their developmental characteristics.

The physical environment is an important ingredient in determining the feeling or tone of the classroom or center and should focus on DAP. Early childhood educators must recognize their responsibility in creating a physical environment that has positive influences on the learning and growth of the children who use the environment. Toys and materials must be properly selected, used, stored, and cared for. Time spent creating an appropriate and inviting environment offering many opportunities for play will benefit learning.

Student Learning Activities

1. Make a time line depicting the history of early childhood education. What people and/or events do you personally feel have made the most significant contributions to early childhood education?

2. From your reading and observation, make a summary chart of the characteristics of children ages 3 to 8 years. Why is it important that early childhood teachers be aware of these characteristics in the children that they teach? What precautions should be taken in applying developmental characteristics?

3. Visit an early childhood classroom or center and write a brief report of your visit. Answer as many of the following questions as possible: In what activities were the children involved? What is the nature of the facilities, both indoors and outdoors? What kinds of resources did you observe? What kind of program is offered? How many children and teachers were there? Based on your visit, what are your feelings about early childhood education? In terms of your visit, evaluate the program with regard to its advantages and/or disadvantages for the young children it serves.

4. Describe characteristics of DAP. Visit at least three different early childhood classrooms or centers and evaluate them on the basis of DAP. What did you learn?

5. Why do you think child-guided play is important? Visit an early childhood classroom and evaluate the kinds of and opportunities for play.

6. Using the criteria for room arrangement suggested in this chapter, draw a sample room arrangement. Describe the intended age group. Explain why you included the specific areas. Does the arrangement support a particular curriculum theme?

7. After reading the chapter, observing in early childhood classrooms, and reflecting on and creating your own philosophy of how young children learn, write a one-page paper on your thoughts on DAP.

Suggested Resources

Colker, L. J. (2008). Twelve characteristics of effective early childhood teachers. *Young Children 63*(2), 68–73.

Epstein, A. (2007). *The intentional teacher: Choosing the best strategies for young children's learning.* Washington, DC: NAEYC.

Espinosa, L. M. (2002). High-quality preschool: Why we need it and what it looks like. *Preschool Policy Matters 1.* Retrieved December 21, 2006, from http://nieer.org/resources/policy-briefs/1.pdf

Hyson, M. (2000). Growing teachers for a growing profession: NAEYC revises its guidelines for early childhood professional preparation. *Young Children 55*(3), 60–61.

Hyson, M. (2003). Preparing tomorrow's teachers: NAEYC announces new standards. *Young Children 57*(2), 78–79.

Hyson, M. (2003). Putting early academics in their place. *Educational Leadership 60*(7), 20–23.

Jalongo, M. R., & Isenberg, J. P. (2012). *Exploring your role in early childhood education* (4th ed.). Upper Saddle River, NJ: Pearson.

McDaniel, G. L., Isaac, M. Y., Brooks, H. M., & Hatch, A. (2005). Confronting K–3 teaching challenges in an era of accountability. *Young Children 60*(2), 20–26.

Noddings, N. (2001). The caring teacher. In V. Richardson (Ed.), *Handbook of research on teaching* (4th ed.). Washington, DC: American Educational Research Association.

Wien, C. A. (2004). *Negotiating standards in the primary classroom: The teacher's dilemma.* New York: Teachers College Press.

Online Resources

www.census.gov/population/www/socdemo/children/html   A variety of census data relating to many aspects of childhood are available on this site.

www.childrensdefense.org   This site promotes advocacy for American children, particularly poor and minority children. See the interesting piece titled "Moments in the Lives of American Children."

www.naeyc.org   The National Association for the Education of Young Children is a professional association. They have an information-rich site including standards, position statements, articles, and information on program guidelines for young children.

www.aap.org   The American Academy of Pediatrics has a variety of resources on selecting safe, appropriate toys; search for *toys.*

www.cpsc.gov   The Consumer Product Safety Commission advises about toy selection and provides safety alerts about products on the market.

www.lekotek.org   The National Lekotek Center makes play accessible to children with disabilities. Play and learning centers for children and families are located throughout the country.

www.lionlamb.org   The Lion and Lamb Project works to stop the marketing of violence to children through guides, training, and advocacy. The dangers of marketing media violence (television, video games, movies, music, toys, etc.) to children's health and well-being are addressed.

www.ipausa.org   The International Association for the Child's Right to Play (IPA) publishes a quarterly newsletter and offers its *Declaration of Child's Right to Play.*

www.nncc.org   Information on many facets of developmentally appropriate practice is provided.

chapter 2

Family, School, and Community Partnerships

The term *partnerships*, by very definition, denotes a relationship of equality among the partners (*The American Heritage Dictionary of the English Language*, 2010). It also assumes that each partner has unique and valuable knowledge and contributions to make to this relationship. The importance of partnerships is easy to recognize, but actually practicing as equal partners requires willingness, acceptance, determination, understanding, and communication. We know that early childhood programs benefit from partnerships with families. How much more benefit is realized when we include the community in the relationship (Starbuck & Olthof, 2008). "Children do not grow and develop in isolation—they are members of families and communities" (Dockett & Perry, 2008, p. 274). Research continually shows long-lasting benefits for children when families are involved in education programs. Increasing attention has recently been given to the importance of parent involvement in young children's learning (Baker & Manfredi/Petitt, 2004; Copple & Bredekamp, 2009; NAEYC, 2004; Daniel, 2009; Epstein, 2009). All families want to help their children to be successful—academically, socially, and in their careers (Ball, 2006; Koralek, 2007). As teachers of young children, we must understand that parents are essential partners in their children's education. Families, not just children, are in our programs (Keyser, 2006)! When families feel we care about them, they will be responsive. When they are responsive, we are able to work with them and provide support. When they feel supported, we can work together for the success of their children (Arndt & McGuire-Schwartz, 2008). "The partnership centers on the child and relies on mutual respect, information sharing, inclusiveness, and a sense of community" (Raikes & Edwards, 2009, p. 55). To meet the challenges facing families in today's rapidly changing society and to avoid the potential ill effects, parents should provide learning opportunities for children in the home, become more involved in their children's schooling, form partnerships with their children's teachers, and participate in parent education.

Most of us, as teachers, have chosen the early childhood education profession because of our love for children and a desire to work with them, " . . . but almost all of us have discovered that working with children's families is as much a part of (our) jobs as working with children" (Keyser, 2006, p. xi). Although teachers and administrators recognize the need for developing partnerships with families in the early childhood programs, there is still a significant lack of actual family involvement in the schools. "Most parents want to be involved; they just need a little support to make it happen. So, how do we get there?" (Narvaez, Feldman, & Theriot, 2006, p. 52). This chapter will explore many of the barriers that prevent effective partnerships and discuss how we can turn these barriers into avenues of success.

Even though the importance of school–family partnerships is generally accepted, there is often little or no training for helping teachers to implement this valuable relationship. "Too often the center approach to adult relationships (between family and caregivers, as well as among center staff) resembles the dynamics of a dysfunctional family" (Baker & Manfredi/Pettit, 2004, p. ix). Partnerships and collaboration are frequently mentioned when discussing the importance of teacher–family relationships, but putting them into actual practice is more difficult. Often the parental involvement is limited to back-to-school events at the beginning of the year, occasional help with scheduled parties and field trips, or periodic parent–teacher conferences, usually formal in nature and with a set time limit. Parents and

Parents feel more comfortable in the classroom as they get involved in activities.

teachers may not feel secure working with each other; attitudes, ideas, values, previous experiences, cultures, and other influences all may make communication with one another difficult. Not only are *we* not always confident in knowing how to work with parents, but *they* are often uncertain about how they can become involved in their children's education. Parents may not even be aware that they can, and should, be an important part of their children's lives during early school years. Still, teachers are expected to involve parents, and parents are expected to become involved, and so the partnership needs to begin by building a trusting relationship. Teachers and parents must search for common ground for children to achieve optimum academic, emotional, speech–language, social, moral, and physical development. We need to recognize and accept that both teachers and parents have the experience, knowledge, expertise, and resources that are needed for the best care, support, and education of their child (Gonzalez-Mena & Eyer, 2004). "Family involvement is critical to children's developmental and educational progress . . ." (Souto-Manning, 2010, p. 88).

Families and schools share a mutual responsibility in helping children to learn (Myers & Myers, 2005; J. Thompson, 2004). This resulting relationship should be "reciprocal," or based on mutual respect, appreciation, and exchange of ideas (NAEYC, 2008). Every effort must therefore be made to strengthen this important link. These desired relationships must reflect a basic concept of equality and shared responsibility. "Teaching young children is a shared task" (Myers & Myers, 2005, p. 1) that neither teachers nor parents can effectively accomplish by themselves. Powell (1998) refers to an imagined woven fabric typically made when the threads of the children and staff of an early childhood program are woven together, and the threads of the parents are woven into a separate parent involvement section. He suggests that a much better design results when the parents' threads are interwoven with those of the children and staff throughout the fabric pattern.

The National Association for the Education of Young Children's (NAEYC) Code of Ethical Conduct helps teachers to clarify their professional responsibilities. Mutual trust, respect for the family's values, and involvement of the family when important decisions are being made are essential components. It is imperative that teachers be familiar with and base their program practices on current knowledge in the fields relating to child development, recognize and respect the uniqueness and potential of each child, and recognize the special vulnerability of children (NAEYC, 1998a). Failing to incorporate these personal ethical responsibilities often results in breakdowns to the partnerships between families and schools.

"The two most influential environments in which young children develop are their homes and their early childhood programs" (Halgunseth, 2009, p. 56). The family is the young child's earliest educator, and parents have a lasting influence on their child's attitudes, values, learning, concepts, emotions, and ideas. Even though many parents are not aware of how important they are in their child's education, there is extensive and convincing evidence regarding the benefit of parent involvement (Keyser, 2006; Koralek, 2007; Myers & Myers, 2005; NAEYC, 2004; Souto-Manning, 2010). When families are involved, children tend to have higher achievement levels, more positive school behaviors, improved parent-child relationships, improved attendance, better homework habits, more positive attitudes toward school, and greater gains in reading.

Parents make the difference between a mediocre school and a great school. Everyone benefits when parents are involved in their child's education, and all parents have competencies that will help their child to succeed in school. The school and the home must be partners, because they are both vital parts of the child's life and education. Family involvement in school rewards children in terms of attitudes and achievement; and the earlier the family becomes involved, the greater the benefits! A two-way flow of support and information between home and school strengthens the child's experiences in both.

Because of differences in their experiences and backgrounds, families and teachers can move beyond their "present knowledge and explore understandings" as each contributes to the relationship (Myers & Myers, 2005, p. 1). Families know the values and goals they desire for their children, and the kind of person they want their child to grow up to be. Families can become better acquainted with the school's programs, and teachers can become more aware of children's home situations. As they learn each other's values and goals, they are able to be more supportive of each other. Parents who are involved in their children's school are more knowledgeable about child development, have increased self-confidence in parenting, and are aware of the importance of the home for student learning environment. Teachers also reap benefits from parental involvement in the classroom. They generally report a greater understanding of families' cultures, have increased appreciation for parents' interest and desire to help their children, and develop more respect for parents' abilities and time.

Some teachers believe that planning for families' involvement takes too much time. However, despite the difficulties, research has accumulated on the positive effects of family participation in educational programs. Although many parents want to become involved in the classroom, some prefer not to become involved; we must make both kinds of parents feel comfortable in their preferences. Often those who do not want to be in the classroom will change their perspective as they become more familiar with the curriculum and environment. Teachers can begin by developing positive attitudes toward family involvement, helping parents and staff to understand the benefits that will come. There is a clear relationship between the teacher's attitude toward parent involvement and the actual level of involvement; the more positive a teacher feels about involving parents, the higher the level of parent involvement.

Many strategies and techniques will assist schools and homes in developing partnerships that benefit everyone involved and help parents to realize that their participation makes a difference. Developing a positive attitude toward working with families is a major step in developing good relationships with parents.

For clarity, we use the term *parents* in this chapter to include parents, single parents, grandparents,

guardians, and foster parents. Keep this in mind as you adapt the activities and suggestions to the needs of your students' families.

Because of early childhood education's focus on parents and families, we assume that fathers are automatically included. However, early childhood educators tend to become more involved with mothers than with fathers. "Even without research, it is clear that involving fathers in the everyday care of their children benefits everyone" (Parlakian & Rovaris, 2009, p. 64). Some professionals still consider the father in the family as the disciplinarian and the mother as the nurturer. But the child and family both benefit when parenting is a partnership. This, in turn, enhances the partnership that develops between schools and families. Most fathers want to be, and should be, involved in the decisions affecting their children. Fathers and mothers should both be included and valued as volunteers in the classroom. Research suggests that fathers want to participate in their children's programs and that this involvement results in more positive outcomes for the children and the rest of the family (Gadsden & Ray, 2002; Nelson, 2002; Nelson, Carlson, & West, Sr., 2006; Parlakian & Rovaris, 2009; Rump, 2002). Sanders (2002) suggests ways to support the involvement of male family members in the early childhood education classroom:

- Invite men to take part in school activities involving families.
- Address communications to fathers/grandfathers.
- Find out what activities fathers would be interested in at the school.
- Involve males in parenting education classes.
- Schedule meetings/volunteer times considering available hours for fathers.

"Parents are critical components of the family microsystem that nurtures children. Within this microsystem, fathers especially warrant and need attention" (Gadsden & Ray, 2002, p. 34). Effective parenting programs plan activities and experiences in which both parents can become involved (Gadsden & Ray, 2002). When children see both men and women as caring, nurturing, skilled, and involved adults in the classroom, they learn that women and men do not have to be limited or confined by gender (Sanders, 2002). More books and articles about men who teach have been written in the last 15 years than ever before. Also, more movies are focusing on men as being involved in teaching children. More schools, universities, organizations, and programs are welcoming more men as teachers (Nelson, Carlson, & West, Sr., 2006). The ability of men "to care *for* and care *about* . . . children is just as fierce and powerful as that of women . . ." "Men do care; let's give them a chance to do it" (Sanders, 2002, p. 48).

When Fathers are Involved in School

Children are more likely to:

- Enjoy school (U.S. Department of Education, 1997)
- Achieve higher grades (U.S. Department of Education, 1997)
- Participate in extracurricular activities (U.S. Department of Education, 1997)

Children are less likely to:

- Repeat a grade (U.S. Department of Education, 1997)
- Be suspended or expelled from school (U.S. Department of Education, 1997)
- Behave violently in school (Smith, 1995)
- Be involved in acts of juvenile delinquency (Elias, 1996)

Source: Information from "Father's Involvement in Programs for Young Children," by V. P. Turbiville, G. T. Umbarger, and A. C. Guthrie, 2000, Young Children, 55(4), pp. 74–79.

IMPORTANCE OF ACTIVE FAMILY INVOLVEMENT

Children's achievement improves, they are more successful learners, and they make friends more easily when their parents become involved in school (National Coalition for Parent Involvement in Education [NCPIE], 2006). Programs vary in the kind and amount of family involvement, but we do know that schools cannot work in isolation. If programs in early childhood education are to succeed, parental support and participation are significant factors, and children need to continue to receive stimulation from parents. The early, formative partnerships between families and teachers affect the connections between families and schools later in the child's schooling. When parents are supported in their initial attempts to offer suggestions and participate in decision making, they will likely continue their efforts in their child's later school years (Dabkowski, 2004). Remember that all parents care about their children and most understand the value of partnerships. Also, all parents have strengths and knowledge to contribute. Be careful, and do not assume that parents' absence implies lack of caring!

#3 Even though as educators we are aware of these principles, we are not always sure how to achieve positive and effective relationships. We can involve parents when schools are developing standards and implementing new teaching methods and strategies. We can appeal to parents' interest, strengths, experience, and knowledge; parents need to know that they are needed.

Traditionally, teachers have met with parents twice yearly for parent–teacher conferences and report sessions. Today, however, teachers realize that more interactions between parents and teachers are necessary, with much more communication between the two. Parents should feel welcome not only at school and program activities, but also in the classroom. They must realize that they have a direct influence on their child's education. Children should be made to feel safe and secure as they move back and forth each day between their two worlds of home and school.

Parent involvement takes many forms, and it ought to encompass a broad range of activities. Involving parents as volunteers is one of the most successful avenues for developing high-quality family involvement in the classroom. This is achieved by recruiting volunteers, making them feel welcome, planning ways to involve them, and supervising them. They can be involved in such areas as art, woodworking, blocks, dramatic play, manipulative play, music, library, writing, science, and outdoor play. If parents are unable to be in the classroom, there are many other ways to involve them—they can create a webpage or newsletter for the classroom, make homemade learning toys and games, read and record stories or music, sew clothes for dramatic play, and so on (DiNatale, 2002). Following are suggestions for involving parents in classroom activities:

Activities for Involving Parents

- Help on field trips
- Assist with art and craft projects in the classroom
- Do work at home: sewing, mending, cutting out materials, and so on
- Share their careers or hobbies with the students
- Bring in a pet or other animal
- Become a special friend to a particular child
- Read to the students
- Share a food, game, or book from particular cultures
- Assist with music and recreational activities
- Help to plan curriculum activities
- Help in planning and evaluating involvement activities
- Be a room parent
- Serve as members of committees and governing boards
- Contribute to newsletters
- Help with support groups
- Mentor in the classroom
- Assist in learning and computer centers
- Help to reach and involve other parents

Parents can provide resources for the classroom and *be* resources for particular units of study. Parents can be assistant teachers or teacher's aides working in the classroom with the children. One teacher found that a successful way to involve parents is to invite them into the classroom to talk one-on-one about the books that the children are reading.

In addition, parent involvement helps parents to become effective teachers of their own children. Parents' involvement may be as simple as letting their child know that they value education, reading to their child at home, encouraging their child with homework, and supporting at-home projects. Remember that teachers instruct to both the children and their parents. The concepts being taught at school will be supported at home when parents also understand the concepts. Provide frequent avenues for parents to learn about the information being experienced by their children. Not only does it increase their own understanding, but it also provides numerous opportunities for them to reinforce concepts learned at school.

Often when parents ask their children what they did in school, the response is, "Nothing." Teachers know that the child's response may be because the child is tired or not really interested in talking about the day. Parents could be left wondering what actually did take place during the school day. They need occasional reassurance and confirmation that the program is actually great (Gennarelli, 2004). It is helpful if teachers take advantage of using individual child portfolios, photographs, videotapes, handmade classroom books, calendars, newsletters, bulletin boards, and other activities to keep parents informed and aware of the many activities that children are involved in during the school day.

Provide frequent "tips" to parents to help them become more involved in their child's play and learning. For example, here are some ways to make reading a part of every day (Ulmen, 2005, pp. 96–97):

- Read and reread your child's favorite books.
- Read comics to your children.
- Let your child read to you.
- Let your child be the storyteller.
- Subscribe to a child's magazine.
- Save and recycle junk mail.
- Leave closed captioning on while watching television.
- Play different versions of tic-tac-toe.
- Find some giant sunglasses and play "I spy."
- Talk to your child.

Because children learn through playing, the home environment should include games, toys, and activities that support playing. It is also valuable for parents to become actively involved with children in play. Playing with children provides opportunities for parents to bond socially, physically, intellectually, and emotionally with them. Such involvement includes talking about the toy/game, physically interacting with the child while playing with a toy/game, and singing/saying nursery rhymes and songs. Traditional games such as The Farmer in the Dell; London Bridge; Duck, Duck, Goose; I Have a Little Doggie and He Won't Bite You; Peek-a-Boo; Pat-a-Cake; Jump Rope; Ring Around the Rosie; Drop the Handkerchief and other familiar activities provide opportunities for enjoyable interaction with children. These types of activities are also valuable in helping children learn crucial social skills as they explore peer relationships (R. B. Jones, 2004).

Another current trend is to extend the curriculum into the home through the support of parents. School hours pass quickly, and children have an added advantage if their parents can support what is being taught at school by teaching, reinforcing, and extending these same ideas and concepts at home. They can help children with homework, talk with them about their school days and activities, and listen to them read. Remember: Not only is it important that parents support children's learning to read, but children also never get too old to be read to! What parents *do* certainly does make a difference in the child's life.

In addition, schools and teachers are one of the best support systems for the family. Recognizing that parenting is a difficult task and one in which many persons have had limited training, schools frequently offer parenting classes. These classes allow parents to participate in discussions, lectures, and demonstrations that focus on parenting skills, guidance and discipline, child-rearing practices, home-based learning activities, and family relationships. Teachers can also suggest sources of assistance to parents who are coping with crises. Sometimes, teachers can be of great help by listening and demonstrating concern. It is also imperative that teachers remember the diversified nature of the family today and find ways of encompassing and communicating with parents from diverse cultures, working parents, grandparents, single parents, guardians, and foster parents. Just as each child is unique, so is each child's family situation.

Recognizing the diversity of parents, teachers should realize that their own patterns of child rearing and attitudes regarding education might differ from those of the parents with whom they work. This is especially apparent when children of various cultural backgrounds are in the classrooms. "Intercultural communication" lets teachers become familiar with each child's values and traditions. Children need to know that their parents are valued and respected by the teacher, which leads to acceptance and unity in the partnership. When parents feel that they are part of an equal partnership, they are more likely to become involved in their child's school life (Lundgren & Morrison, 2003). "To develop and sustain a feeling of camaraderie, belonging, and satisfaction, we must provide ongoing parent training, treat parents with respect, and provide activities throughout the year that demonstrate appreciation for their work" (DiNatale, 2002, p. 94). Offer encouragement rather than praise. "Telling your students and parents that they are doing a great job is 'hollow

Positive relationships are developed as children begin to feel comfortable with, and trust, the parents in the classroom.

praise'" (J. Thompson, 2004, p. 8). Give specific examples of when and how a parent or child has participated in a positive experience in the classroom. Parent involvement in the classroom allows them to feel a sense of ownership in their child's educational experience.

With ongoing and interactive communication, *all* parents can contribute to the classroom. When we develop good relationships with the families of our students, parents become our greatest ally. We all—children, parents, and teachers—miss out when we fail to build bridges between home and school (Keyser, 2006).

Benefits of Parent Involvement for Children

- Make greater gains in reading
- Have a more positive attitude about school
- Have higher attendance
- Have better homework habits
- Make better home–school connections
- See parents as important part of education

Source: Information from School and Family Partnerships: Preparing Educators and Improving Schools, *by J. L. Epstein, 2000, Boulder, Co: Westview.*

Benefits of Parent Involvement for Parents

- More willing to help students at home with their homework
- Have more positive attitudes toward involvement at school
- Tend to rate teachers higher
- Support teachers' efforts more consistently
- Are more familiar with what children are being taught
- Understand better the functioning of the school and its programs
- Have more confidence in their parenting skills
- Have more understanding of child growth and development

Source: Information from "Parent Involvement: It's Worth the Effort," by D. Eldridge, 2001, Young Children *56(4), pp. 65–69.*

Benefits of Parent Involvement for Teachers

- Have more time to spend with individual children
- Appreciate parents' involvement
- Respect parents' time and abilities
- Are more respected and appreciated by parents
- Feel more comfortable having parents involved in school

Source: Information from "Parent Involvement: It's Worth the Effort," by D. Eldridge, 2001, Young Children *56(4), pp. 65–69.*

GUIDELINES FOR WORKING EFFECTIVELY WITH FAMILY MEMBERS

The first step in working effectively with parents is to establish a warm and supportive relationship. Frequently, there are barriers to overcome. In any job involving human relationships, forming positive and constructive associations is often the most challenging aspect. Because some parents' contacts with schools and teachers have not been positive, teachers often have to work diligently to combat negative attitudes. Some teachers view parents as threats, and some parents develop the same view of teachers. Keep in mind the challenge to serve families and not just children. Remember that children come from families and spend much time within those families.

Be careful not to appear too strong or too authoritarian. You are a professional, and you do have much skill and expertise. However, some teachers give parents the feeling that they "know it all" and that they consider their ways and values to be the best. This attitude almost immediately breaks down relationships with parents.

Social, linguistic, cultural barriers, or separations may interfere with effective communication and work with parents. These barriers may involve differences in values, approved child-rearing methods, behavior standards, accepted foods, and many other areas. Complete agreement on everything is unrealistic, but through communication and daily contact, effective parent–teacher partnerships can be formed. Recognize that although a child may have two parents, both parents might not be living in the home together all the time. Separations can be the result of employment where a parent is gone for periods of time, divorce, death, illness, or military deployments. Children respond to separations in individual ways, but anxiety, depression, withdrawal, hypervigilance, regression to prior developmental levels (thumb sucking, toileting accidents, dependency and clinging behaviors), aggression, and anger may be exhibited (Kim & Yeary, 2008).

In working to overcome some of the barriers to effective relationships with families, show interest and respect for cultural differences and variations in family values. Cultural differences include ethnic, racial, and linguistic diversity; region or geographic location; religion; and socioeconomic status (Bradley & Kibera, 2006). The various practices and beliefs of these cultural differences can affect how we interact with families. Be aware of these variations when considering the following issues: eye contact, touch, silence, smiling, personal space, time concepts, gender roles, adult authority, and autonomy (Epstein, 2009). Spend time listening to parents and learning about their feelings, values, and culture. Becoming effective at cross-cultural communication will minimize misinterpretations and biases.

Common Barriers to Effective Partnerships with Families

- Type of household (two parent, single parent, foster parent, grandparent, divorced parent, legal guardian, same-sex parent, other relative, teen or much older parent, blended or split family, extended family)
- Lifestyle and culture of family (language, dress, traditions and holidays, norms, rules, foods, employment, education level, economic level, siblings, religion, attitudes toward child rearing and discipline, expectations *for* teachers and school, expectations *of* teachers and school, housing, nutrition, health, amount of support for academic practices in home)

- Time and work schedules (of teachers and families)
- Transportation (access to car or bus, ability to drive)
- School (distance, ease of finding location, adequate parking, parents' level of comfort in situation)
- Communication (ability to understand and/or read information from teacher, ability to respond verbally or in writing; need for interpreter)
- Siblings (need for child care, any with disabilities)
- Misunderstandings and unclear expectations between parent and school
- Attitudes and feelings of parents and teachers (discomfort, awkwardness, insecurity, lack of mutual trust)
- Parents not involved in mutual decision making
- Strengths and abilities of parents not recognized or utilized
- Previous negative school experiences of parents

All families have something to contribute to the classroom, and they need to be encouraged to share these valuable contributions. Request the help of parents in singing songs, leading dances, supervising ethnic food preparations, or making costumes or decorations. Invite them to play music, recite poetry, or help to portray celebrations or cultural events. Barriers usually disappear when parents sense teachers' honesty, sincerity, and professionalism. In addition, parents need to feel appreciated and be recognized for their contributions and efforts.

The importance of listening as a means of building effective teacher–parent relationships cannot be stressed enough. Because parents are especially knowledgeable about a child's past development, current attributes, and abilities, it is imperative that teachers listen to and learn from them. As teachers, we see only one side of children, and it is important to find out from parents what kind of person their child is at home and other places. We need to know children individually if we are to make developmentally appropriate decisions for them. This is accomplished through becoming more acquainted with the child and family (Copple & Bredekamp, 2009). When teachers ask families about their children, it lets the parents know that their insights and knowledge are valued. This two-way partnership encourages communication and respect from both partners (Copple & Bredekamp, 2009).

Frequently, parents will have insights into their child's behavior that the teacher could not possibly know from associating with the child only in the school setting. The parents may have developed methods for handling the child's behavior challenges at home that would work equally well for the teacher in the classroom. Perhaps the parents have deep concerns, complaints, or irritations that can be resolved through listening and effective communication. Sometimes simply airing concerns to sensitive and understanding teachers helps parents to feel more comfortable in the relationship. Provide parents with a constant opportunity to share these feelings—there are many ways to do this. An open communication line regarding very young children can be established through daily contact as parents pick up their children from preschool. Remind parents that their feelings and suggestions are welcomed by making such comments as, "How are you feeling about (child's name's) school experience? Is there any way I can be more supportive?" At the initial meeting or conference, indicate the time of day when you can be contacted. Encourage parents with concerns to call you. Parents will sense the sincerity and honesty of the suggestion. Begin developing this trusting relationship from the very start before a need actually arises for problem solving. "If we first connect with parents in positive ways, then strong trusting relationships will already have been established when problems come along" (Kersey & Masterson, 2009, p. 35). Trusting relationships are developed over a period of time through shared understandings, communication, and empathy (Bennett, 2007). Empathizing with parents—imaging what they might be feeling or thinking—helps parents feel valued, understood, and cared for (Gillespie, 2006). When a parent makes a comment, demand, or request that seems unusual or inappropriate, we should try to think why the comment might have been made (Keyser, 2007). This will help us understand more about the family and its beliefs or practices. Unless we have developed a positive relationship with families, they will not be receptive to our suggestions addressing parenting, education, or interventions (Hyson, 2008). To summarize, here are some specific suggestions for working effectively with parents:

1. Listen. Set up a specific open time when parents know that you will be available for listening and communicating. Sense their needs to share and discuss, and find some time—lunchtime, after school, a home visit, an evening telephone conversation—for meeting these needs by being an effective listener. If parents know that as teachers we are available and approachable, parent–teacher relationships are more cooperative and productive (Kersey & Masterson, 2009). "As we focus on families, we must remember to listen and appreciate them as they are, not how we think they are or should be" (Arndt & McGuire-Schwartz, 2008, p. 281). Daniel (2009, p. 10) suggests that we utilize a "two-way conversation (listening carefully as well as speaking)."

2. Treat all children and their families with respect and caring concern. Take advantage of the little opportunities that occur daily for showing concern and interest in children and their families. For example, send home a short note apprising the parents of a particular skill that the child mastered that day or telling them something the child said or did that you enjoyed. A quick phone call on the day a child is absent lets the parents and the child know that they are important and cared for. Treat the parents with the kind of respect that conveys the belief, "I see you as an equal partner, having more and superior understanding of the child in some areas than I, the child's teacher."

3. Be sure to know the child well enough to relate specific information about him or her to the parents. Record keeping is important, and a list or chart of the items that you wish to discuss will be helpful for both you and the parents. Anecdotes or other kinds of dated observation notes can also be supportive. In addition, it is helpful for the parents to see samples of the child's work; over a period of time, they can observe progress in specific areas. For the preschool child, even progress in art stages is easily apparent from selected samples of the child's artwork.

4. Convey to the parents positive, warm feelings regarding their child. Make sure that they know how much you like the child and how interested you are in the child's growth and development.

5. Be objective and realistic about goals for working with the child. Involve parents in determining appropriate goals for their child. Where necessary, make appropriate referrals for assistance from such professionals as speech therapists, psychologists, and medical doctors.

6. Be a source of help in many parenting areas and help to extend what you are teaching into the home. Parents may need suggestions for age-appropriate good books, meaningful learning activities that can be done at home, toy selection, and where to find helpful materials on guidance. Remember, too, that the school and family alone may not be able to handle the range of children's needs. Schools should seek to help families to access community services that they need; teachers should draw on the full range of community resources to strengthen the child. What does your local library offer for parents who indicate a particular need? If there is a nearby college or university, what particular services could be recommended to parents? You may want to keep a current file of resources appropriate for the parents of the children that you teach.

7. Remember that it will take numerous encounters and meetings to build positive and supportive relationships with parents.

To work effectively with parents, apply the same attitudes used in working with children: Be positive, supportive, interested, caring, objective, friendly, and warm. Work hard, using a variety of techniques to motivate, teach, build, and strengthen. Following is a list of practical suggestions for involving families.

Checklist for Effective Family Involvement

1. Provide opportunities for parent association and training: practical skills workshops, support groups and social events, school policies and procedures, how to help with homework, developing language and communication skills, basic child development and learning, discipline and guidance, career planning.
2. Conduct conferences and meetings in family-friendly settings.
3. Make initial contacts friendly and inviting.
4. Involve parents in ongoing assessment and evaluation of involvement opportunities.
5. Train administration, teachers, and other staff in the development of skills for relating to parents and families.
6. Recognize that early childhood programs serve families, not just children.
7. Clearly define expectations and objectives (teacher's and school's). Parents need to know what they should do, why it should be done, and how they should do it.
8. Involve families in choices and decision making.
9. Work toward achieving positive relationships of mutual trust, confidence, understanding, acceptance, and cooperation.
10. Determine and build on strengths, skills, expertise, and abilities of the child and family.
11. Maintain frequent, open, two-way communication with parents (use an interpreter, if needed).
12. Establish an open and accepting classroom environment.
13. Invite meaningful and appropriate parental involvement.
14. Demonstrate empathy, patience, respect, and acceptance of families, their ideas, uniqueness, diversity, decisions, values, priorities, characteristics, and circumstances.
15. Consider the needs of the family (transportation, concerns, priorities, important issues, work schedules, child care).
16. Be knowledgeable about community supports and services for families, and collaborate with them when necessary.

STRATEGIES FOR ACHIEVING FAMILY-FRIENDLY SCHOOLS AND SCHOOL-FRIENDLY HOMES

Now that we have some guidelines for working with families, we need to focus on strategies for developing the desired partnerships between schools and homes. Family involvement works best when parents are invited to play a variety of roles; their involvement will take different forms depending on their needs and interests. How much more effectively children will learn if parents and teachers are partners in the teaching process! Because learning occurs through repetition and many experiences, children will learn more successfully if what is being taught in the classroom is extended into the home. The following sections discuss ways for the teacher to support the development of partnerships between home and school.

Written Communication

Written communication transmits as much information as any other form of communication (Keyser, 2006), and it allows people time to read and understand information. Also, some people (teachers and families) feel more comfortable with written communication than with telephone calls or talking in person. It is a two-way process for sharing information, knowledge, and expertise. Information should be relevant, inviting, friendly, interesting, understandable, and manageable, not too lengthy or overwhelming or filled with professional jargon and phrases.

Written communications can take many forms and are a vital link between home and school. It may take repeated invitations to motivate parents to become involved. Upcoming events and activities, as well as snack assignments or main-course lunch menu items, can be included on a monthly or weekly newsletter–calendar. A few specific guidance or management hints might be shared. Child quotes or anecdotes from recent activities might also be included.

Teachers can list simple activities that parents can do in their homes to be actively involved in their child's learning. For example, activities listed in any chapter in this text could be shared with parents. Or, for each general curriculum area (that is, math, science, language and literacy, music, art), choose several activities that could easily be done at home and share them with parents. For example, for math, children can:

- Sort laundry and match socks. When finished, they can count pairs of socks for each family member and then add them together.
- Make a number lotto game and play it with parents.
- Circle numerals in the newspaper beginning with 1 and going to 10, or as far as the child can recognize.

- Estimate the weight of several household objects such as a ball, a gallon of milk, and so on. Once the items are weighed, the child can order them from lightest to heaviest.
- Do matching, sorting, and categorizing activities using beans, buttons, groceries, cards, and newspaper pictures or photographs.
- Use calendars for matching or for counting days until a specific event, days in the week, days in the month, weeks in the month, months in the year, and so on.

Find time each week to send a note or newsletter home with the children to tell parents what concepts or ideas are being focused on that week, as well as to provide an overview of planned activities. In addition, write down any individual notes that may be helpful or enjoyed by the parents regarding their child. Parents will be interested in knowing when field trips are being taken. Include words to new fingerplays they can teach their child. Children will also enjoy having their parents tell them of the activities planned for the next week or the next day in school; it creates interest, enthusiasm, and eagerness. For example, if parents are aware of the upcoming unit on color, they can add support by reinforcing color concepts at home, even during spontaneous experiences such as eating dinner or going to the grocery store. Parents frequently ask children what they did at school, and it is often difficult for young children to remember or to single out the concept being studied. It is helpful to the child for the parent to ask something like "What did you learn about color today?" or "What did the police officer tell you when he visited your classroom today?" An excellent practice to encourage inquiry is for parents to ask children what questions the children asked at school that day.

Notes from the teacher are also appropriate when the children have enjoyed a particular food, music, or science experience: "Today the children were amazed with the 'growth' of the chemical gardens we made in class yesterday. You may wish to make them at home. The recipe is . . ." or "Today the children enjoyed the playdough we used. The recipe is . . ." Parents appreciate these ideas, and knowing that their children enjoy the activities, they will often do them at home.

Send notes of appreciation to parents. When parents participate in a field trip, they have donated several hours of valuable home or work time and should know that their efforts are appreciated. These short notes help to build warm parent–teacher relationships. Also, send a note if a parent sends a snack or assists in the classroom in any way. It is helpful to keep thank-you notes and cards readily available so that they can be sent soon after the parent has participated.

Parents are valuable resources for providing opportunities that enrich and support the curriculum.

A bulletin board is a source of information for parents that might include general school information, lesson or activity schedules, parenting classes, upcoming events, meeting new people, and messages for children and teachers. Another effective avenue for two-way dialogue is to write journal entries. Teachers and/or children write in journals that are then taken home to the parents. Parents can also be encouraged to send return notes or messages with their children to the teacher. For preschool and kindergarten children, their journal "writing" may actually be pictures or picture stories, and they might also dictate to a teacher or assistant words for their entries.

It is important to remember that a child might have two parents who are not living together in the home. It is important that, when possible, both parents should be involved and kept informed of the progress of their children (Kim & Yeary, 2008). Suggestions include telephone, postal service, e-mail, webcams; child could make two projects instead of one; teachers could make two copies of information, reports, notes, and photographs. The more parents are informed, the more successful are the partnerships among families, school, and community.

Parent Conferences or Conversations

Conferences with parents are traditionally called *parent conferences*. As we address developing strong partnerships with families, it would also be very appropriate to refer to these meetings as *family conferences* (Carter, 2008). Both terms will be used interchangeably throughout this chapter. When a family realizes that each member is an accepted and valued participant, bridges are more easily spanned, and bonds are more readily formed. "Conferencing with families is one of a teacher's most important responsibilities" in helping to establish, strengthen, and maintain supportive relationships with families (Seplocha, 2004, p. 96). Family conferences allow opportunities for building trust and partnership by meeting face-to-face. They provide a more private time to share information back and forth without interruption. Information about the child, the program, and community resources can be discussed, and mutual goals can be developed for the child (Keyser, 2006). Parent–teacher conferences require trust and goodwill, even though the backgrounds and personalities of the teachers and parents are not always compatible.

Face-to-face encounters with parents contribute to student success and should be planned frequently. Generally, the more contact there is between home and school, the more the child benefits (McWayne, Hampton, Fantuzzo, Cohen, & Sekino, 2004). For some parents, the most convenient direct encounter is at the parent's home or place of work. It is unrealistic to predetermine the exact number of times per year that these conferences should be held, because some parents may need them every 6 to 8 weeks, whereas once every 3 or 4 months may be sufficient for others. The important thing to remember is to meet with parents as often as is necessary to maintain close contact and to be an advocate for the child and his or her best interests. Conferences, to be successful, should be well prepared, relate to the parents' needs, and facilitate the cooperation between home and school. When parent–teacher conferences are well planned and conducted, parents feel more comfortable in becoming involved.

The teacher should begin (and end) the parent conference by saying something positive about the child or sharing some of the child's strengths (Kersey & Masterson, 2009). Then the parent should be encouraged to talk—ask their perspective or seek their help. As a teacher, you gain much knowledge and understanding from parents by listening to them. This encourages information sharing and discourages confrontation between parent and teacher. Questions are very useful in eliciting two-way conversation—start conversations with a question, use open-ended questions, answer questions with questions (Keyser, 2006).

Consider the following points with regard to communicating with parents:

1. Many parents do not share their concerns unless asked.
2. Parents derive their concerns by comparing their child to others.
3. Regardless of educational level or parenting experience, parents can share concerns that are often accurate indicators of children's development.
4. Parents' concerns can be useful in developmental or behavioral screening when necessary.
5. By carefully interpreting parents' concerns, professionals can make evidence-based decisions about any services families may need.

One way of gaining information from parents is to have them complete a preconference worksheet designed to get feedback from them about concerns that they would like to discuss and also what primary successes they believe their child is experiencing. Parents should feel supported, relaxed, comfortable, and wanted. They should be made aware of the child's strengths and needs and of specific ways that they can help their child at home. A postconference worksheet can be filled out in collaboration by the teacher and parent. Desired actions and steps to reach goals can be specifically delineated.

Teachers should be sensitive to the strong emotional investment parents have in their child, which may manifest itself as defensiveness, anger, denial, or anxiety. Tension during conferences and interfacing with parents can be reduced as teachers use "I" messages, seek parents' suggestions, and stress positive aspects. What is best for the child should always be paramount. Be cautious with criticism, and instead of giving advice, give suggestions or guidelines. Never betray a confidence; this applies to children as well as to parents.

A suggestion regarding the physical setting for the conference: Sometimes chairs set side by side or at right angles to each other are more conducive to successful parent conferences than chairs set facing each other. This is especially true when a particular problem is being discussed and the teacher is able to show the parent related paperwork. Focusing on something physical frequently diminishes defensiveness or discomfort by diverting direct eye-to-eye contact.

The initial conference of the year may consist primarily of questions. Many schools distribute questionnaires with which the parents can become familiar before the first conference: How does your child feel about himself or herself? What expectations do you have for your child during the coming school experience? What kinds of learning experiences or activities does your child enjoy most? Is the child developing a particular talent or interest? How does your child relate to and get along with siblings and/or neighborhood friends? These questions allow parents to become familiar with some areas of discussion that are often difficult to think about without prior preparation. They generally provide the teacher with much more feedback and also open the lines of communication, because the parents have had time beforehand to think about something that they want to discuss.

Once the child is in school and conferences are scheduled, the teacher should be well prepared with ideas and materials to share with the parents. Portfolios with a sampling of the child's work can show progress being made in specific curriculum areas. The teacher should be able to discuss the child's progress in a number of areas: socially, emotionally, physically (both large- and small-motor areas), and intellectually. Parents are anxious to know of their child's progress in each of these areas and need to see materials that validate the teacher's appraisals. Anecdotal records can strengthen the teacher's evaluations and help parents to appreciate individual attention. Parents are usually anxious to hear about any ideas and activities that they can implement at home to help their child to improve. Especially when a child is having difficulties in one or more areas, the teacher can give the parents concrete suggestions for helping the child to progress.

- Keep language simple and direct—without educational and professional jargon.
- Listen and respond with empathy, sensitivity, and diplomacy.
- Allow parents to express concerns, problems, ideas, and information.
- Observe nonverbal communication.
- Encourage and validate questions and concerns without judging.
- Appreciate parent's input, personally and publicly.

Summarize and document conference.

The essential ingredients for effective school–family relationships are frequent, informal contact and warm, respectful, candid conversation. Omitting relevant information is not being honest with parents. Again, it is important for the teacher to listen to the parents—to their suggestions for working with the child or about strategies and activities that work in the home. The skills found to be important in family–teacher relationships are valuing, accepting, listening, perceiving, guiding, understanding, helping, responding, and empowering.

In addition to formal scheduled conferences, teachers should take advantage of informal daily or weekly opportunities for brief but friendly conversations. These may occur when the parent picks the child up from school or when the teacher and parent meet casually in the grocery store. Regardless of how the situation develops, the teacher should make good use of any opportunity for free discussions and for answering any questions that the parent may have. These informal conversations are often the building blocks to effective home–school relationships. School administrators could also schedule lunch meetings with parents to address concerns and suggestions.

Seplocha (2004) provides some tips for parents regarding successful parent–teacher conferences.

Following are some guidelines for planning parent conferences:

1. Contact parents before scheduling to determine convenient time.
2. Send a notice of meeting including date, time, length, location, purpose, agenda, and what program staff will be attending. Invite them to bring family members and any support persons if they desire. Let them know they will be participating as a partner, not just as a listener!
3. Create inviting environment

   - privacy (no interruptions)
   - seating (comfortable chairs, arranged to create feeling of equality)
   - atmosphere (soft instrumental music, children's art work, comfortable temperature, plants or flowers)
   - refreshments (help break ice)

4. Allow sufficient time

Following are some guidelines specifically for the teacher during parent conferences:

- Maintain two-way conversation.
- Use names of family members during conference.

Tips for Parents Relating to Parent–Teacher Conferences

1. Get to know your child's teacher when school begins.
2. Talk to your child about the upcoming conference and write down any questions.
3. Be familiar with the child's schoolbooks and homework.
4. Try to have both parents at the conference.
5. Remember the appointment and be on time.

6. Find out what the teacher expects and ask questions about various aspects of the curriculum.
7. Find out if there are any scheduled tests; and if there are, what can you do to help your child?
8. Ask about your child's relationship with both adults and peers.
9. Share any information about your child and family that might help the teacher.
10. Find out ways you can help your child at home to be successful in school.
11. Stay focused on your child.
12. Be aware that children can hear and remember what is said.

Numerous benefits result from effective parent conferences and conversations: School programs and climate improve; parents' knowledge and leadership skills increase; family support is maintained; family, school, and community connections are built; and there is more family support of teachers. However, the most important benefit is the impact that the partnerships have on students.

Parent Meetings or Parent Education Programs

Parenting classes and workshops have been found to ease parents' tensions and anxieties, improve skills, and teach child development concepts. Parent education programs that actively involve parents and require several sessions have been found to be more effective than single sessions. These meetings, workshops, or programs are planned by the teachers, by the parents, or by the two in collaboration. Because the focus is on parent education, take a poll of the parents' interests and then strive to meet these needs as meetings are planned. The number of meetings per year will depend on parental support and interest. Topics for these meetings could include guidance, facilitating antibias development, and making home learning materials, and curriculum topics such as art activities, science at home, or nutritious food activities. Parent meetings could include such activities as an icebreaker for opening, demonstrations and discussions, interactive projects, networking opportunities, family culture activities, and interactive presentations (Keyser, 2006). Successful parent meetings also provide opportunities for parents to share knowledge, expertise, and experience with others.

A variation in parental meetings could involve children in both the planning and presentation. An open house could be planned, with the children acting as hosts and hostesses. A display of some of their work and activities would be shown, with the children acting as chefs for the refreshments. Parent evenings or afternoons could focus on a single topic, such as "Foods We

Like to Make and Eat," or a science fair. The children enjoy the preparation and planning involved in these events, but they especially look forward to sharing their school and activities with their parents.

Parent meetings, workshops, and programs can be very beneficial in enhancing parents' skills, knowledge, attitudes toward their children, and ways to increase their parenting skills. Parent education opportunities are of paramount importance in helping to develop effective partnerships between families and school.

Many authors support the idea of parenting/caring education for children. "Teaching students parenting skills has a great deal of support because it addresses children's immediate social and emotional needs while also laying the groundwork for a more socially and emotionally fit next generation" (McDermott, 2003/2004, p. 71). Preparation for parenting and life skills development can begin with very young children in the preschool years. "Teachers believe that the same caring process taught in parenting classes could be used to improve how teachers, parents, and students relate to each other" (McDermott, 2003/2004, p. 73).

Technology and Telephone Calls

Computer and telephone technology affords opportunities for quick and open communication. Parents should feel free to contact teachers and teachers to contact parents. Telephoning need not be only a means of conveying emergencies or reporting negative behavior and problem situations. It also provides a valuable opportunity to let parents know the positive things that occur in the classroom. Using e-mail and answering machines enables parents to leave messages for teachers, and lets teachers transmit general class or curriculum information and homework assignments to parents.

If a child has had particular success with a concept or curriculum activity, convey this information to the parents by telephone. For example, a telephone message from the teacher might be: "Today we mixed the three primary colors together to make the secondary colors. We used water colored with food coloring, a white Styrofoam egg carton, and an eyedropper. You should have seen how much Christopher enjoyed this activity! For 30 minutes, he continued to experiment with mixing the colors. I am sure he would enjoy doing this activity in your home."

Or, if a child is having particular difficulty with a concept presented at school, do not wait until the formal conference to alert the parents. A phone call can suggest, in a warm and positive way, what the difficulty is and how the parents can help. For example, in a first-grade classroom, the children have had their first activity involving concepts related to money. Rachel has difficulty understanding the values of coins and becomes very frustrated with the activity. In a call that day to the home, the teacher might say: "Today we began work with the values of money and coins. Rachel seemed unusually concerned, and I plan to give her individual help at school, but you may wish to work with her at home, too. You may want to role-play store situations in giving change or develop simple games to match equal values. For example, if you lay down 10 cents, from the change Rachel has at hand, she needs to come up with another combination representing 10 cents. You may also want to encourage her in making actual purchases at stores, such as allowing her to purchase an item, giving the grocer a dollar bill, and receiving the change." The parents usually eagerly welcome these kinds of suggestions. It is not as helpful simply to state the learning difficulty, offering no suggestions for action. Technology can serve as a bridge between home and school, and it can strengthen the partnership between them.

Home Visits

A visit to the family's home provides opportunity for the teacher to see the family in their most comfortable surroundings (Keyser, 2006), and for the child to meet the teacher in the safety of the family's home environment. "Home visitors provide an intense service in the most personal of all spaces—the family's home" (Bouhebent, 2008, p. 83). This also sends the message to the family that they and their culture are valued. In this more familiar, comfortable setting, two-way conversations are more likely to include additional information that will help in determining goals for the child (Keyser, 2006).

Through child-centered home visits, a teacher can gain insights about the child that can be obtained in no other way. These visits provide the opportunity to relate to families in their own familiar surroundings and to gain valuable information about the child's needs and his or her interaction in the home environment. Home visits can be especially beneficial for families who might otherwise be economically, socially, and/or geographically isolated (Bouhebent, 2008). These visits build closer ties between parents and teacher, strengthen the child's self-esteem, and communicate to the family that the child is important to the teacher. To be successful at home visits, the teacher must be able to accept different homes, the diversity of families, and the variations in values, beliefs, and attitudes. Some particularly enlightening information relating to curriculum planning can occur naturally and spontaneously in a home visit. For those who visit the child and family at home, confidentiality, flexibility, and being able to respond to critical situations must be maintained (Bouhebent, 2008).

A Head Start teacher visited a home where the mother was just preparing dinner. She was preparing peas and happened to mention that she never made Rebecca eat them; as a family, they had learned that the texture of peas made Rebecca sick. The Head Start teacher recalled one lunchtime when peas were being served, and Rebecca had been rather persistently made to taste some of them. Reserved Rebecca had sat at the lunch table longer than the other children, and the teacher thought Rebecca was just testing to see if she really must taste at least some of the peas!

A kindergarten teacher was making a home visit and discovered that Stephen, with the help of his geologist father, had assembled a collection of rocks and knew many interesting facts and concepts relating to them. This suggested a unit on rocks. Stephen proudly brought his specimens and shared his information with the other children.

When arranging for home visits, teachers need to request a visit to the home. Parents should be informed that the teacher is visiting to learn more about the child, to have an opportunity to spend some time with the child, to meet the family, and to allow the family to become better acquainted with the teacher. Pressure should not be put on the parents to have the teacher in their home. There may be special problems in the home at that time, and the parents may view a teacher's visit as one more problem or pressure to be handled. Teachers usually can sense whether the time is appropriate for a home visit and if they are welcome. If home visits for a particular child do not seem to be appropriate, the teacher may consider visiting a parent at work.

When making a home visit, the teacher must be relaxed, friendly, and alert to the needs and responses of the family. The length of the visit should be determined by the needs of both the family and the teacher. Generally, home visits should not be lengthy unless the teacher has been invited for a special occasion, such as a family meal or a birthday party.

Home visits also provide an opportunity for the teacher to introduce into the home a game, activity, or book that the child has enjoyed in the classroom, to be shared with the child and perhaps other family members. Depending on the receptiveness of the parents, the visit may be a good time for giving suggestions about learning activities, materials, or equipment appropriate for home use by the child. At the end of the visit, some teachers leave the parents a newsletter or handout relating to learning ideas for home use.

Family Involvement and Observation in the Classroom

There are many ways of involving families in the classroom and a great advantage in doing so. Other activities involving parents could include family social events (opportunities for parents and children to play together) and family workdays (parents, program staff, and community work together to take care of maintaining or building facilities) (Keyser, 2006). Gains made by children

Social interactive skills with peers are encouraged and supported through parental involvement.

in early childhood education programs are maintained to a greater extent when families are involved in the program. When parents take the time to be involved in the classroom, this acts as a teaching experience for them, giving new ideas for home activities and guidance principles and helping them to observe and learn about the child in the school situation. It is also valuable for the child to know that he or she is important enough for the parent to spend time in the classroom. Parent–teacher rapport is strengthened as the "team" works together in the classroom. Parents become more understanding of the teacher's role as they view the teaching situation from the inside. This results in more positive attitudes toward the school and the staff.

Many teachers prepare a parent-involvement calendar at the beginning of the year, quarter, or month based on parents' needs and schedules and inviting all parents who are able into the classroom as volunteers. This is preceded by a parent meeting scheduled at the beginning of the year to help parents to understand their responsibilities and opportunities in the classroom. Teachers should convey to the parents the value of their participation, helping parents to understand that they have expertise and skills that will contribute greatly to the classroom. Most working parents, if they have adequate advance notice, are able to arrange time to be in the classroom. When parents are aware of the projects and activities at school, they can more often contribute with shared expertise or experiences.

Expectations and responsibilities need to be very clear when parents are assisting in the classroom; duties assigned to them should be important and relevant. Parents should view themselves as participators, and not just as cleanup persons. They can become involved with the children in the various activities and experiences. For example, parents could sit at the manipulative table and visit with the children while helping them with the play materials. Parents might also read to children, sing with them, participate in their games, eat with them, build with them, and otherwise interact with them. Where cleanup is necessary or when assistance in dressing or undressing is needed, they will do it. In primary-grade classes, teachers should give parents the opportunity of working with their own children, hearing them read, helping them to write a story, completing an assignment, or working on a project. Parent volunteers in the primary grades are especially valuable when working with children who have emotional, social, physical, or academic problems.

To interact with parents more, one teacher did a unit titled "What Do Grown-ups Do All Day? The World of Work." The unit lasted all year and integrated many curriculum areas. The unit included parent questionnaires; field trips to some parents' workplaces; and activities such as mapping where parents ate lunch, having parent visitors who described what they did, and having children draw their parents at work.

Parent visits to the classroom may also be for the purpose of observation. Make sure the parents feel welcomed to visit the classroom anytime they want—appointments should not be necessary (Raikes & Edwards, 2009). Many early childhood programs in colleges and universities have observation booths with one-way viewing mirrors for student and parent observation. In other classrooms, the teachers encourage the parents to visit and observe their child in action.

Another occasion for parent involvement in the classroom is when extra help is needed. For example, food activities and field trips may require additional help or supervision. Perhaps a parent has a particular skill that lends itself to a unit of study. During a unit on fish, a father who was an avid fisherman visited the class and brought his fishing gear to demonstrate. He showed the children how to prepare the fishing pole, how to use the many different kinds of flies and other gear in his tackle box, and then how to cast. He brought slides of a fishing trip that he and his son had taken and of his young son catching a fish. The children watched as he demonstrated how to fillet a fish. Then he cooked the fish in a skillet and served it to the children. Teachers should find out parents' hobbies and professions to learn of special skills or talents that can be shared with the children.

Sensitive teachers and staff should recognize that the needs, schedules, backgrounds, time, skills, and values of parents are all unique, so the participation of parents should also be geared to their individual capabilities.

Policy Planning, Decision Making, and Evaluation

Positive effects will be felt when parents are included as members of policy-planning committees or boards involved in decision making and/or evaluations related to the children and the school. However, parents must have information to participate in a meaningful and rational way in policy-making decisions. When parents are invited to be involved, their thinking and suggestions must have merit and be a meaningful part of the decisions made.

Family Resource Centers

Facilities should be set up to allow parents to visit the classroom and benefit from school resources offering parenting help and methods for extending what is being taught into the home. A parent room or parents' area can be organized to include books on child development; materials, books, and toys that can be checked out for home use; videos; and other resources such as free pamphlets and brochures. Let parents know what is available so they can make use of the program. In one community, the school puts together age-appropriate materials into packets that are given out by the hospital when a child is born and then sent to the family on each child's birthday until the child enters school. This project ties the family to the school before the child even enters school.

Many school districts are now providing parent resource centers, which supply these same kinds of services. Even a small private preschool or a single kindergarten can make available materials and equipment to support parents in teaching their children at home. Parent bulletin boards or displays can be set up where parents can check for information.

Summary

All families, regardless of backgrounds, characteristics, and circumstances, are generally interested and active in their children's lives, and positive family–teacher partnerships are vital in high-quality early childhood environments. Teachers can begin by developing positive attitudes toward parent involvement and helping parents to understand the benefits that will come from their participation and involvement.

Effective work and communication with parents are necessary in any good early childhood program, and we must look to parents as friends and helpers. It is vital to establish a positive partnership between the home and the school and to make sure parents and teachers see each other as playing an important role in the children's education. We should validate families without judging, assist families in finding needed resources and services in the school and community, utilize a variety of communication strategies, and model patience and empathy. Parents should get the message that their values, ideas, and decisions are respected.

The purpose of any parent–teacher or parent–school activity is to develop school–home relationships, to promote school–community activities, and most of all, to strengthen the child. We must understand family priorities, needs, and resources if we are to effectively develop school–home partnerships. Parent involvement can be the catalyst for lasting beneficial effects.

Although planning for parent partnerships takes time and can be challenging, the positive effects and outcomes are well worth it. Parents and teachers need to nurture and build one another in partnerships that draw on one another's strengths. Without parent involvement, programs or schools cannot achieve the ultimate objective of excellence for which both are striving. Partnerships with parents must be built on positive approaches, with patience and confidence that the efforts will result in strong and supportive relationships among children, parents, and teachers.

Student Learning Activities

1. Arrange to observe during a professional teacher's home visit to encourage the development of a partnership with the family.
2. Interview an early childhood teacher and find out what methods are being incorporated for developing a partnership with the family and extending the curriculum into the home. Ask which methods the teacher feels are most valuable for helping parents to carry out learning activities in the home.
3. Visit the home of a child between the ages of 3 and 8 years. It may be a child in your neighborhood, or your instructor may provide a list of parents who would enjoy having you in their home to teach a home-learning activity. Plan a learning activity that would be appropriate for the child's age; there are many

suggestions throughout this book. Call the home and arrange for the visit, and then evaluate the visit and the experience. What went well? Were the parents and the child interested in the learning activity that you presented? Did the child become involved? What would you do differently on your next visit?
4. Visit your local library and make a list of some of the services it offers parents. Summarize the good parenting material available and also some of the materials that you would suggest to parents for providing meaningful learning activities in the home.
5. Attend a parent–school meeting in a school district or center and evaluate it in terms of the ideas that you read about in this chapter.

Suggested Resources

Allen, J. (2007). *Creating welcoming schools: A practical guide to home-school partnerships with diverse families.* New York: Teachers College Press.

Christenson, S. L., & Reschly, A. L. (Eds.). (2009). *Schools and families: Creating essential connections for learning.* New York: Routledge.

Crawford, P. A., & Zygouris-Coe, V. (2006). All in the family: Connecting home and school with family literacy. *Early Childhood Education Journal 33*(4), 261–267.

Dodge, D. T., & Phinney, J. (2007). *A parent's guide to preschool.* Washington, DC: Teaching Strategies.

Epstein, J. L. (2007). Families, schools, and community partnerships. In D. Koralek (Ed.), *Spotlight on young children and families.* Washington, DC: NAEYC.

Gestwicki, C. (2007). *Home, school, and community relations.* Clifton Park, NY: Thomson Delmar Learning.

Glasgow, N. A., & Whitney, P. J. (2008). *What successful schools do to involve families: 55 partnership strategies.* Thousand Oaks, CA: Corwin.

Grant, K. B., & Ray, J. A. (2009). *Home, school, and community collaboration: Culturally responsive family involvement.* Thousand Oaks, CA: Sage.

Keyser, J. (2006). *From parents to partners: Building a family-centered early childhood program.* St. Paul, MN: Redleaf Press.

National Education Association (NEA). (1996). *Building parent partnerships.* Washington, DC: Author.

Souto-Manning, M., & Swick, K. J. (2006). Teachers' beliefs about parent and family involvement: Rethinking our family involvement paradigm. *Early Childhood Education Journal 34*(2), 187–193.

Vazquez-Nuttall, E., Li, C., & Kaplan, J. (2006). Home-school partnerships with culturally diverse families: Challenges and solutions for school personnel. Special issue, *Journal of Applied School Psychology 22*(2), 82–102.

Xu, Y., & Filler, J. (2008). Facilitating family involvement and support for inclusive education. *The School Community Journal 18*(2), 53–71.

Online Resources

www.k-state.edu/wwparent/aboutdads/Blog/Blog.html A website for parents with programs, courses, story time, opinions, and humor.

www.fatherhood.org National Fatherhood Initiative provides support networks, research, resources, and multimedia products to help fathers.

www.pta.org/documents/National_Standards.pdf This page features National Standards for Family–School Partnerships, by the National Parent Teacher Association.

www.hfrp.org/publications-resources/browse-our-publications/family-involvement-in-early-childhood-education This website provides information about the Harvard Family Research Project on family involvement.

www.parentsasteachers.org This association provides parents with child development knowledge and parenting support.

www.ncpie.org This site provides information for developing meaningful partnerships that meet the needs of family, school, and community. Also, on the home page, search for the article titled "What's happening. A new wave of evidence: The impact

of school, family, and community connections on student achievement."

www.edpartnerships.org/Content/NavigationMenuResource_Centeer/Parent_Family_Engagement/Resources.htm This page provides explanations of, and resources on, parent/family engagement in children's education.

www.teachersandfamilies.com Resources to help parents work with schools and with their children are available here.

http://parenting.org This site offers resources for helping parents deal with day-to-day teaching, guidance, and development of children.

http://positiveparenting.com Resources and information to help make parenting more rewarding, effective, and fun can be found on this site.

www.tnpc.com National Parent Center provides tips, information, and links to other excellent parenting sources.

http://users.stargate.net/~cokids/dap.html Information is available on developmentally appropriate practice in early childhood education as well as links to other sites.

chapter 3
Assessment

Assessment is an important part of early childhood teaching, instruction, and learning (Copple & Bredekamp, 2009; Johnston & Rogers, 2002; NAEYC & NAECS/SDE, 2003). Assessment should be based on the goals of the program, used to benefit children, and be child centered (NAEYC, 2009; NAEYC & NAECS/SDE, 2003). Assessment allows teachers to track children's progress toward goals and monitor and report on individual student achievement. The purposes of an assessment will determine what kind of assessment is used. Assessment is one of the standards in both the Program Standards (NAEYC, 2008) and the NAEYC standards for preservice teachers (NAEYC, 2009b).

DEVELOPMENTALLY APPROPRIATE ASSESSMENT

Educational reform and concerns about accountability have fueled a testing mania in our country that is affecting early childhood. There is increased use of standardized testing at all levels of education, as well as mandated state-level achievement tests. High-stakes testing is not appropriate in early childhood because the results often lead to penalties, disapproval, rewards, or endorsements for teachers, programs, districts, or other educational systems. With tests driving teaching and the curriculum, many educators are concerned that this drive to measure everything may result in a more academic approach to early childhood curriculum (Wortham, 1997). Young children in any class do not begin the year at the same place, they certainly do not learn in the same way, and they do not learn at the same pace. In addition, assessment should reflect the diversity of children and be free of biases (NAEYC & NAECS/SDE, 2003).

Purposes of Early Childhood Assessment

Assessment functions to improve instruction and to communicate progress. It is the process of observing, measuring, or recording what learning has occurred or documenting the work of the child for the purposes of benefitting children and making wise educational decisions, not just to note disability and deficit (Johnston & Rogers, 2002). The purpose of all assessment is to provide teachers with the information to best inform their teaching and work with individual children (Teale, 1990). Classroom teachers work with resource teachers, psychologists, administrators, and in professional learning communities in selecting and administering appropriate assessments that will inform instruction and enhance students' learning and achievement (Stiggins & DuFour, 2009; Stiggins & Duke, 2008). These should involve hands-on activities, rather than pencil-and-paper tests (NAEYC & NAECS/SDE, 2003).

Assessments inform teaching and instruction and document children's learning and achievement.

Purposes of Assessment in Early Childhood

Benefit students
- Inform teaching and instruction
- Diagnose individual special needs
- Communicate accurate information about children to their families
- Document children's learning and achievement
- Monitor development of the whole child: physical, cognitive, socioemotional
- Identify and serve special needs
- Identify those who need early intervention
- Evaluate the program, school, or center with regard to evidence of the child's growth, learning, and progress in meeting program goals
- Use for accountability to school district, to parents, and to the community

Assessment provides information and documentation of all children's achievement and growth in specific areas of development in order for teachers to talk specifically with parents and others, such as special education teachers, about progress and goals for each child. Classroom assessments are linked to accountability through standards that provide direction in expectations for programs as well as individual student achievement. Standards are set up as benchmarks, the knowledge and skills that are typically mastered by children at particular ages or grade levels. Professional organizations such as NAEYC and state departments set up standards; teachers are then accountable for planning instruction and outcomes to meet these standards. Teachers must understand the goals, benefits, and uses of a variety of assessments (NAEYC, 2009b, p. 13).

Developmentally appropriate assessment means using knowledge of age-appropriate, individually appropriate, and culturally appropriate expectations as a context for individual children's growth and learning (Copple & Bredekamp, 2009). Planning assessments that meet the various personal and distinct needs of each child in the class is challenging, but can be done. It is differentiating the curriculum for individual needs, and also differentiating assessments to the needs and interests of each child.

Inappropriate Uses of Assessments in Early Childhood Education

- Use of entrance tests to determine readiness and admittance to kindergarten
- Judging the success of a program on the basis of children's performance on standardized tests
- Use of tests to determine retention of children
- Use of tests to compare teachers, schools, and school districts
- Use of test material to determine what should be taught
- Use of tests to accelerate learning

Guidelines for Early Childhood Assessment

USE ETHICAL CONSIDERATIONS.   Teachers must be ethical in all assessment decisions in early childhood. Tests should be ethical, appropriate, valid, and reliable (NAEYC & NAECS/SDE, 2003). Early childhood teachers need support from principals and professional learning communities, teams of teachers who teach the same grade level, in designing and implementing assessments that are ethical and appropriate and that lead to student achievement (Popham, 2009; Stiggins & DuFour, 2009; Stiggins & Duke, 2008). Both new and seasoned teachers need professional development training to learn the critical elements of effective classroom assessment (Popham, 2009).

RECOGNIZE ASSESSMENT BENEFITS FOR CHILDREN
Assessment is used *for* learning to support the achievement

of all students in meeting standards (Stiggins, 2005). Another key to suitable assessment is that it be used to benefit children and not to retain, track, or segregate them (Bredekamp & Shepard, 1989; NAEYC & NAECS/SDE, 2003). Educators should recognize the strengths and weaknesses of various assessment options and advocate for sound assessment practices for young children. In addition, assessments need to be carefully aligned with objectives, both program and instructional, and should cause no harm to young children (J. Jones, 2004).

and possible referral or intervention. Diagnosis is never on the basis of a single assessment.

Source: Reprinted with permission from the National Association for the Education of Young children. Excerpts adapted from Position Statement: NAEYC and National Association of Early Childhood Specialists in State Departments of Education Joint Position Statement. Early Childhood Curriculum, Assessment, and Program Evaluation: Building an Effective, Accountable System in Programs for Children Birth through Age. (Washington, DC: NAEYC, 2003; NAEYC, 2009). Full-text versions of all NAEYC position statements are available online at www.naeyc.org.

The following suggestions for appropriate assessment of young children are included in guidelines from the National Association for the Education of Young Children (NAEYC) and the National Association of Early Childhood Specialists in State Departments of Education (NAECS/SDE), two groups consisting of individuals knowledgeable about young children's development (NAEYC & NAECS/SDE, 2003; NAEYC, 2009):

- Assessment of the children's growth and achievement is purposeful, ongoing, and systematic; it is formative and therefore an ongoing process in the classroom.
- Children should enter school on the basis of their chronological age and actual legal right to enter school, rather than on what they know.
- Assessment relates to the goals of the program and should be integrated through the program; in addition, assessment should focus on individual children's progress toward developmentally appropriate goals and achievement.
- Assessment is used to benefit children, to improve learning.
- All domains of learning and development, including physical, social, emotional, and cognitive, are routinely and informally assessed.
- Assessment recognizes and welcomes individual differences in learning styles, experiences, and rates of learning.
- Assessment focuses on what children can do, on their strengths and progress in learning and development.
- Assessment relies on multiple sources of evidence over time, such as observations, interviews, portfolios, anecdotal records, and teachers' summaries of children's development and progress.
- If assessment is used to place children in learning groups, the grouping should be flexible.
- Families and children should be viewed as important sources of assessment information.
- Assessment methods should be appropriate for the age and developmental level of individual children.
- When an assessment or screening identifies children with special needs, there is always follow-up

Forms of Assessment

Different forms of assessments are used for different reasons. We can think broadly about forms of assessment as two different types: formal assessments, which include screening assessment and standardized assessment, and informal assessment, which is a term that encompasses classroom assessments such as observation anecdotal records, checklists, interviews, work samples, and portfolios.

Assessments may be tests or test-like procedures such as teacher tests or quizzes or textbook tests. Assessments may be very informal, such as group meetings, student–teacher conferences, or student questions or comments during class. Not only are teachers more able to understand how children learn, but they can also help others to recognize this learning as they collect, interpret, analyze, and display various evidences of learning (Helm, Beneke, & Steinheimer, 1997).

FORMAL ASSESSMENT. The primary purpose of formal assessments is to help teachers make informed and responsible decisions about materials, grouping students, and what students need to practice. Those involved in any aspect of assessing children must have the training required to participate in the selection, administration, and evaluation of the particular assessment.

Standardized, formal, or accountability testing is limited in early childhood education to situations such as identifying potential disabilities to determine how to serve individual children's needs. When standardized tests are used, they need to be valid, reliable, and used only for the purpose for which they were designed (Bredekamp & Shepard, 1989).

Screening Assessments. A number of authors have cautioned against the use of entrance tests to determine readiness and admittance to kindergarten and suggest that these tests are often a form of bias and might be abusive (Shepard, 1994). A score on a developmental readiness test may be the result of inadequate social and physical experiences in the home environment, and the kindergarten environment may be the only place where the child could obtain these kinds of experiences (Shepard, 1994). Our focus should be on making schools more ready for children, rather than making children ready for schools or classes. Too often screening or readiness tests deny children the opportunity of having the kinds of developmental experiences they need, which is considered developmentally inappropriate practice.

Assessment should not be a diagnosis for success or failure, advancement or retention, but a means of determining the needs and goals of individual children (Shepard, 1994, 2001). Data from school readiness assessments should not be a factor in determining whether the child is eligible for kindergarten, and research suggests that delaying school entry does not, in most cases, benefit children (H. Marshall, 2003). Developmental screening can be used to apprise how teachers, parents, and others associated with helping the child can best support progress and achievement.

Screening and assessment results need to be utilized carefully. The child's rights must be protected, and teachers and other staff must realize that all assessment results are confidential. Results must be interpreted accurately and carefully, and these interpretations must be shared with others who work with the child, including the parents, in such a way as to not be misunderstood or misinterpreted.

> We must make it very clear that group-administered standardized achievement tests are not recommended before the third grade (Kamii, 1990). "Individually constructed meanings cannot be measured within the constraints of standardized tests" (Heuwinkel, 1996, p. 30).

Standardized Assessments. Standardized tests are tests that are administered, scored, and interpreted in a standardized way. Even though volumes of literature have been written suggesting the inappropriate use of standardized achievement tests for measuring student learning in the early childhood years, the practice still continues. Too often standardized testing is required for schools to be eligible for some federally funded programs. Standardized tests may be useful to gain services for children with special needs, to estimate level of risk, or to provide evidence about needs for the program (Lidz, 2003; Shepard, 1994). However, when making "high-stakes" decisions, educators need to remember that multiple sources should inform those decisions (Lidz, 2003).

Far too often, when children do not measure up to preconceived readiness standards on a standardized assessment in early years, they are held back for remedial work or intervention. Individual growth rates are pronounced during these early years. The different rates at which children acquire various abilities are independent of their IQ and should not be used as a judgment for retention (Scherer, 1996). When we

understand these important principles and accommodate children's vast diversity in competencies, we focus on creating a liberating, active, and engaging program, rather than on assessing children to determine which should be held back (Scherer, 1996). In a longitudinal study of retention, the authors concluded that both retention and transitional classrooms do not benefit children (Allington & McGill-Franzen, 1995).

Some believe that the effort to use testing in tandem with raising standards has actually lowered the standards (Shepard, 2001). Many caution that standardized achievement group tests are especially inappropriate for assessing learning in children younger than third grade (Meisels, 1993). In more traditional forms of assessment such as standardized tests, teachers learn what children know; in more authentic classroom assessments, teachers learn what children can do and apply.

> In appropriate early childhood assessment, children do not compete for grades or scores; letter or numerical grades are not used in reporting progress to parents. Rather, in regular, intermittent sessions, progress is reported with detailed information using documented sources such as observation and anecdotal records, portfolios, and the focus is on what the child can do (NAEYC & NAECS/SDE, 2003).

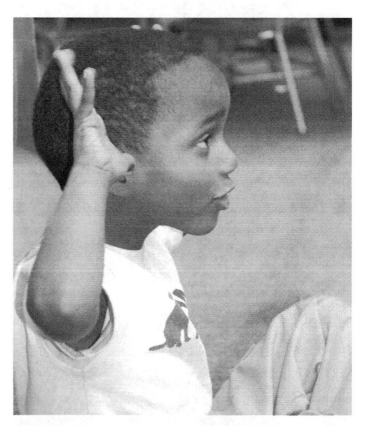

Assessments may be very informal, such as a student's commenting in class.

INFORMAL CLASSROOM ASSESSMENTS. Informal or classroom assessments, sometimes referred to as ongoing or formative assessments, include observations, anecdotal comments, brief conference summaries, checklists, rating scales, performance samples, portfolio entries, journals, learning team reports, and other measures of the child's achievement and progress.

Johnston and Rogers (2002, p. 386) suggest that "assessment in early childhood is essentially formative in nature." Elaboration of some of the specific kinds of informal classroom assessments will follow.

Observation-Based Assessment.   Observation is one of the most effective means of assessment in early childhood (McAfee, Leong, & Bodrova, 2004). Standard 3 for preservice teachers emphasizes the importance of knowing how to use observation documentation for the purpose of assessing young children (NAEYC, 2009).

The traditional street-crossing safety reminder, "Stop, look, and listen," can help us to identify developmentally appropriate practices in assessing the development of young children. We should often stop what we are doing, look around to see where we and the children are, and listen for feedback, or what is being said. Then, with cau-

tion, we can go ahead. The education of young children is influenced by the quality of the assessments used.

> The essence of developmentally appropriate practice is knowing where children are on a continuum of learning and then offering them challenging yet achievable experiences to gently nudge them along the way (Dodge, Heroman, Charles, & Maiorca, 2004, p. 24).

Observation is one of the best measures of children's needs, success, and development. Observations by teachers and professionals, who are trained observers, inform instruction and determine future goals for individual children. Observations consider the whole child, not just the child's academic abilities. Children's physical, social, emotional, and cognitive development is routinely assessed while observing what they do and listening to what they say (NAEYC & NAECS/SDE, 2003). Early childhood educators and staff always have a notebook or checklist nearby to record anecdotal observations in all of the developmental areas. Figure 3.1 is an activity

FIGURE 3.1
Activity Participation Checklist

(For specific activities, teachers can mark a + for participation or a – for nonparticipation. Teachers can also give anecdotal information indicating the level of participation, skill development, or interest the child appeared to have in the activity.)

Specific Activity: Today (April 3) we did a class book titled "Our Favorite Animals" with each child invited to contribute a page to the book if he/she chose to do so.

Name	Participated (+) Did not participate (−)	Describe the child's level of participation, skill development, or interest in the activity.
Rebecca H.	+	Rebecca loved drawing a rabbit and told about her experiences with "wild" rabbits in their backyard. The rabbits ate the lettuce her family grew in their garden.
Stacy M.	−	Stacy did not want to participate in this activity. She said she did not have a favorite animal and today she did not want to draw.

participation checklist on which the teacher or observer notes the specific activity, for example, a class book titled "Our Favorite Animals." title of the activity, for example. Then, after each child's name, the teacher enters a+ for participation or a– for nonparticipation. There is also space to describe the level of activity and skill development for the individual child.

In observation-based assessment, data about learning are collected during normal instructional activities throughout the day (Maxwell & Clifford, 2004; Shepard, 2001). Teachers can learn the most about what children know, do, and feel by carefully observing them and noting behaviors and comments. The work they do tells a great story of their development and understanding, and assessment should focus on their strengths and abilities (Charlton, 2005). "The key is to observe purposefully and document examples that provide rich data" that lead to informed curriculum decisions and give insight to the individual child's progress (Dodge et al., 2004, p. 20).

Documentation. Helm, Beneke, and Steinheimer (1997, p. 200) suggest that "documenting children's learning may be one of the most valuable skills a teacher can learn." Documenting or providing **evidence and artifacts,** expands informal assessment from the traditional observation techniques by including technologies such as video- and audiotaping. Interviews with children also depict what they understand and can do. Thus, documentation may include photographs, drawings, audiotape transcriptions, and videotapes. Documenting individual growth, development, learning, and achievement requires observing in all areas of development over a significant time span, and then creating a documentation piece that tells the story of that child (Seitz, 2008). Additional forms of observing and documenting the child's growth and progress include work samples; anecdotal observations of events, experiences, and development; transcribed conversations, parent or teacher comments and feedback on events, experiences, and development. It is suggested to report a complete, in-depth story of an event or experience, rather than trying to tell everything, and focus on positive progress and learning (Seitz, 2008).

Emphasis on standards, accountability, and research-based practice is increasing and intensifying. For teachers to succeed in this atmosphere, they must provide evidence of student achievement. It is suggested that "comprehensive, careful, systematic documentation of the learning that occurs when children are involved in meaningful learning experiences can meet the demands for both effective teaching and accountability" (Helm et al., 2007, p. 9). Documentation enables the teacher to verify that learning outcomes are met; that children master knowledge, skills, and dispositions expected; and that the individual child is meeting the program goals or standards (Helm, 2008). Teachers use documentation artifacts and evidence to bridge curriculum planning and standards; the documentation is the evidence that standards are met. As an important part of assessment, documentation provides depth in understanding individual children's needs and supports curriculum planning that meets the needs and interests of all children.

How to Observe Young Children

- Know the purpose of your observation (you might be observing physical and motor development, social development, emotional development, language development, or specific cognitive characteristics such as mathematical or literacy characteristics).
- Write down specific facts that you observe and not opinions.
- Observe each individual child over time and note changes.
- Describe specifically what you see and hear.

Recording Observations

- Observation recording tools might be direct, written notes for the purpose of understanding the child's behavior, responses, learning, and growth.
- Anecdotal records may serve as a way to record behavior growth, and learning over time. They are a series of notes that are taken anywhere that show patterns relating to areas of growth such as physical, social, cognitive, language, and emotional development.
- Developmental checklists (such as the one included later in this chapter) may be used to record observations on individual children. Teachers can create their own checklists based on standards or their specific goals, or they can use commercially prepared developmental checklists.

An effective piece of documentation tells the story and the purpose of an event, experience, or development (Seitz, 2008, p. 88).

Documentation: Types of Evidence and Artifacts

- Videotapes, audiotapes, and transcriptions showing the child at work and play or discussing opinions or understanding
- Photographs

- Work samples including artwork and drawings, writing samples and other work
- Anecdotal observations of events and experiences that are factual and nonjudgmental
- Check lists of standards met through an event, experience, or project
- Parent/family members, teacher, or child comments, responses, and observations
- Inventories and checklists of traits, behaviors, and personal characteristics and preferences
- Portfolio collections with a specific purpose
- Projects and presentations
- Journal entries
- Narratives
- Self-assessment

Anecdotal Records. Anecdotal notes or records describe events that occur in the classroom with specific children. They may be comments, responses, expressions or body language, dispositions, or social sketches that describe specifically the child's behaviors or reactions. They can be noted or taken anytime or anywhere, should record facts, and be unbiased. When gathered over time, patterns emerge that show the child's development and needs and support instructional decision making.

Authentic Assessment or Performance Assessment. This type of assessment appraises what children can *do* or *apply* rather than what they *know* (Pierson & Beck, 1993). These kinds of assessments provide various ways to demonstrate knowledge, and each child's progress is compared to his or her own prior work. Authentic or performance assessment is the process of gathering information by organized observation to make decisions about a student, and it is conducted in the meaningful context of the child's work and play environment. The documentation focuses on children's experiences, thinking, ideas, and memories (Katz & Chard, 1997). It may be in the form of performance tasks such as the completion of a project or writing a story; a portfolio that would include such things as writing, art, or other work samples (Collinson, 1995; Katz & Chard, 1997; NAEYC & NAECS/SDE, 2003). Additional examples include interviews, games, self-assessments, or narratives. When authentic assessments are combined with written summary reports or documentation and an organized record-keeping system, a clear picture of each child's progress and learning can be obtained, shared with parents, and used for informing teaching.

Portfolios, projects, or self-evaluations used as alternatives to tests are considered to be more authentic and appropriate.

Portfolios. These are an effective assessment tool for charting progress, recognizing achievement, and showing work in various areas (Shepard, 2001). Using portfolios for assessment can prompt teachers and students to become more systematic in analyzing student growth and learning (Shepard, 2001). Portfolios allow students the opportunity of seeing their progress and telling the stories associated with their learning; the assessment, therefore, should focus on *potential* and not just *performance* (Herbert & Schultz, 1996). Portfolios provide a means of organizing various types of resources and materials into a collection that can then be used to evaluate the child's progress. They can be organized by integrated units or projects, developmental domains, content areas, or a combination of topics or themes. Reflection is the key component in portfolio assessment (A.F. Smith, 2000) and portfolios "foster continuous reflection and richer, deeper communication among all the members of the learning community" (Harris, 2009, p. 84). With modeling, training, and prompting, even young children can be encouraged to look back on their work and make decisions about which work should be included in the portfolio. In reviewing and studying portfolio assessment, A. F. Smith (2000, p. 208) drew these conclusions:

- Preschool children who are given time and who practice reflection will provide meaningful, reflective responses.
- Preschoolers who share their portfolios will teach and help one another expand their reflective abilities.
- Decision making in the classroom encourages and enhances reflective thought.
- Reflective portfolios provide a "meeting place" for parent, teacher, and child to be informed about the preschooler's learning.

Journals. These are children's own record keeping and insights relating to growth and achievement. Journals help the teacher learn what most interests the children. Journals or diaries also give information on how children feel about themselves and their work. Young children's early journal entries can be in the form of pictures.

Self-assessments, self-evaluations, and self-monitoring. These are assessments by students evaluating their own work and performance. Teachers support children in accepting responsibility for their own goals and achievements. One form of self-assessment is a teacher-planned or class-planned rubric with specific criteria for a learning task or project (Andrade, 2008). Teachers support students in self-assessment by modeling how they can be accountable for their own progress using rubric or other means. Brown (2008) developed a graphic tool named "Quick Check" to support children in evaluating and owning their goals and achievements. With training, it encourages students to note specific criteria and develop an awareness of progress toward improvement. The following is an example of "Quick Check."

Early Quick Check

1. ___ I tried this, I can't do it by myself. I need help.
2. ___ I can do some of this. I need some help.
3. ___ I can do this by myself. I am good at it.
4. ___ I am an expert at this. I can help someone else.

Later Quick Check

1. ___ I don't know what to do. I need help.
2. ___ I can do some of this. I need some help.
3. ___ Good Quality. My work meets all of the criteria. I could improve it. I feel OK about it.
4. ___ Excellent Quality. My work meets all the criteria. It is the best that I can do. I feel great!

Source: Brown, W. (2008). Research to Practice. Young children assess their learning: The power of the quick check strategy. Young Children, 63(6), 14–20. Reprinted with permission from the National Association for the Education of Young Children (NAEYC). www.naeyc.org

---

Checklists. These are used to identify and document children's needs and interests. Following is an example of one that can be used in whole or part, based on observations of the child and the child's work, or on interviews with the child. It is suggested that the assessment *not* be given in the framework of a test. Remember to take chronological and developmental age into consideration. This is a general inventory and should not be scored; either should it be used for judgment or placement of the child. The results are used to help the teacher plan classroom instruction and learn more about each child's interests, abilities in limited areas, and developmental characteristics. While observing and questioning the children, the teacher can take notes with specific actions and comments described directly on the assessment sheet. For example, with the item "Knows and recognizes colors," a teacher could write down the colors that the child knows and recognizes. For the item "Cries easily," if the child does cry easily, the teacher could note what frequently causes the child to cry. In other words, the degree to which the child accomplishes the task, or the *hows* and *whys* of the behaviors and skills, can be noted. Based on careful observation, this assessment becomes more meaningful to those who work with the child. Indicating words such as *frequently, occasionally,* or *rarely* could be noted on many of the items.

It is important to use this assessment carefully. It should be used to plan how to effectively meet the needs of individual children and to help determine appropriate learning activities. The observations and notes taken should be regarded as confidential information. In NAEYC program standards (NAEYC, 2008) one of the accreditation criteria is that all children receive developmental screening.

Developmental Checklist

- Knows first and last names _____
- Recognizes first and last names in print _____
- Writes first name _____
- Writes last name _____
- Knows address _____
- Knows phone number _____
- Knows how many brothers and sisters he or she has _____
- Has a favorite color _____
- Has a favorite toy _____
- Has favorite kinds of activities _____
- Draws recognizable pictures _____
- Names right hand and left hand _____

Checklists are used to identify and document children's needs and interests.

- Names some physical characteristics, such as eye color, hair color _____
- Draws a self-portrait that includes a human figure with arms, legs, and features _____

Physical and Motor Checklist

- Walks across a balance beam _____
- Hops 5 times or more on one foot _____
- Balances on either foot _____
- Balances on either foot with eyes blindfolded _____
- Skips _____
- Walks up and down stairs with one foot per step _____
- Jumps using both feet _____
- Throws a ball or beanbag overhand _____
- Kicks a ball _____
- Climbs confidently up and down climbing equipment such as a jungle gym or dome _____
- Catches a ball or beanbag _____
- Dribbles a ball at least 3 times _____
- Rides wheeled toys confidently _____ What kind? Big wheel _____ Tricycle _____ Bicycle _____
- Easily uses fingers and hands in fingerplays and games _____
- Writes with a pencil and holds it correctly _____
- Writes with a crayon or marking pen _____
- Snaps fingers _____
- Uses most cooking utensils, such as knives and peelers _____
- Uses scissors and cuts on simples lines around shapes _____
- Has good finger dexterity using manipulative materials and toys, such as nuts and bolts, pegs and pegboards, small plastic fit-together units, puzzles, snap beads, etc. _____
- Copies a pattern, such as a geometric shape or letters _____
- Traces around shapes, such as geometric or animal shapes _____
- Draws various geometric shapes and designs based on chronological age _____
- Ties shoelaces _____
- Snaps, zips, and buttons clothing _____
- Builds a tower with cubes _____ How many cubes? _____
- Weaves strips of paper together _____

Social and Emotional Checklist

- Has one best friend _____
- Is accepted by at least 5 children _____
- Engages in cooperative play _____
- Initiates play activities with other children _____
- Is primarily friendly with other children _____

- Is primarily assertive with other children _____
- Is primarily shy with other children _____
- Is afraid of _____
- Is overly serious _____
- Cries easily _____
- Is bossy with other children _____
- Manipulates other children _____
- Is sensitive to the needs of other children _____
- Has empathy for other children and their problems _____
- Is learning to share _____
- Has self-confidence _____
- Is able to assume some responsibility _____
- Asks for help when needed _____
- Is trustworthy _____
- Usually has good self-control _____

Language and Literacy Checklist

- Is bilingual _____
- Enjoys conversation with others _____
- Initiates conversation with others _____
- Articulates most sounds correctly _____
- Sounds the child does not articulate (list) _____
- Speaks and responds in sentences _____
- Average length of sentences _____
- Repeats a five- to six-word sentence with correct word order _____
   (Show 10 picture flash cards, such as of a watch, for the child to label and tell what they are used for.)
- Number labeled correctly _____ Can describe the use or function of how many? _____
- Understands questions and communications from others _____
- Answers questions _____
- Follows simple directions _____
- Participates verbally in songs, fingerplays, stories, and games _____
- Uses all parts of speech (i.e., nouns, pronouns, verbs, adverbs, adjectives) _____
- Listening skills are appropriate for age _____
- Can tell a story or rhyme in sequential order _____
- Likes to use new words _____
- Understands puns or plays on words _____

Cognitive Checklist

- Attempts most tasks or projects _____
- Has adequate attention span to stay on task and complete activities _____
- Is curious _____
- Asks thoughtful questions _____

- Enjoys sensory materials and explorations _____
- Understands and follows given directions _____
- Grasps ideas and concepts quickly _____
- Follows spatial directions such as "Draw a circle above the box" _____
- Recognizes and matches colors _____
- Names colors _____
- Counts by rote up to _____
- Counts by 2s to _____ by 5s to _____
- Recognizes numbers up to _____
- Does addition up to _____
- Does subtraction up to _____
- Understands basic money concepts _____
- Can tell time _____
- Matches basic geometric shapes _____
- Names basic geometric shapes _____
- Recognizes likenesses and differences, and groups things that belong together _____
- Recognizes alphabet letters (upper- and lower-case) _____
- Names alphabet letters (upper- and lowercase) _____
- Knows consonant sounds and can circle pictures representing beginning consonant sounds (e.g., for the *b* sound, can circle pictures such as ball, bear, or button) _____
- Knows vowel sounds and selects correct vowels in words _____
- Makes comparisons _____
- Classifies things according to similarities _____
- Is willing to make predictions _____
- Analyzes a problem or situation _____
- Is able to hypothesize a problem to approach a solution _____

Other informal assessment tools include cards or matrixes for noting and recording children's development and learning.

> **IDEA:** A card or sheet could be used for each child, and sections for each developmental area might include large- and small-muscle motor and physical development, cognitive development, language and literacy development, and social–emotional development. In each section there would be space for recording anecdotal notations, observation records, evidence of participation, preference activities, descriptions of specific competencies or knowledge in each area, and other key pieces of information. This information can be used in planning appropriate learning for each child and during parent–teacher conferences and planning sessions.

Rubrics. Rubrics, even for very young children, help the teacher and parents determine a child's inter-

ests and feelings about many different aspects of the school environment.

> **IDEA:** Make a list of activities or draw simple pictures of activities, such as looking at books, drawing pictures, playing with toys, singing songs, listening to a story, playing outside, and having individual play inside. Next to each, draw three faces: one smiling, one with a straight mouth or neutral expression, and one frowning. Read each activity on the list and have the children color the face that represents how they feel about that activity.

Rubrics can also be used for authentic assessments such as presentations, projects, or portfolio entries. The teacher can design these by asking questions such as: "What are the qualities or characteristics of an excellent presentation?" or "What should a response report on a book include?" As the questions are answered, criteria are suggested and can be described in levels, gradations or degrees, or with indicators. Rubrics provide clear standards or expectations for projects or assignments.

Assessment tools need to "take into account variations in children's skills and knowledge based on cultural and linguistic differences" (Santos, 2004, p. 48). Assessment information should be readily available for reference and for adding to what has previously been documented. Parents and families are resources for information, so teachers should communicate with families and involve them in the assessment process (NAEYC & NAECS/SDE, 2003).

CURRICULUM ASSESSMENT

Why are we doing what we are doing? How does what we do benefit the learners in our classroom? What worked in this lesson and why, or what did not work and why? These are reflective questions that should always be in the forefront of the teacher's mind. A curriculum is planned to meet the needs of the individual children in the group or classroom, using standards that result in meaningful objectives or outcomes. The integrated teaching units or projects provide avenues for the communication of this curriculum. But the desired achievement of the program for young children depends on continual and effective assessment. Effective teachers use assessment data to evaluate and improve their teaching and instruction (Shepard, 2001).

Evaluation and **assessment** are the processes of determining the degree to which children's needs are met and desired objectives are achieved (NAEYC & NAECS/SDE, 2003). This includes assessing the general curriculum, including units or projects as well as activities; evaluating the performance of the children and teacher; and determining if the objectives were achieved. One measure of successful teaching is student achievement of desired outcomes; that is, did the child actually learn what he or she was supposed to learn? Lessons and units are planned to align objectives, assessments, and learning activities. After teaching lessons and units, teachers must analyze the data from the assessments, including assessments that measure what students know before instruction (pre-assessment) compared to what they know at the end of the lesson or unit (post-assessment), and then be accountable for individual students' achievement of the objectives.

Teachers must know the purpose of assessment ("What will this assessment tell me about the child?" "Why am I doing this particular type of assessment? What will I learn from it?") in order to select the most appropriate approach ("Now, which type of assessment should I choose to find out what I need to learn about this child?" "What is the best way [assessment approach or type] to learn what I need to learn about the child?") In addition, classroom assessments must align to or be congruent with the objectives and the learning activities for the lesson or unit (Shepard, 2001). After evaluating the results of the assessments, professionals and classroom teachers work together to determine goals for individual children.

Assessments given "along the way" are often termed formative and are informal assessments that give feedback to teachers and staff in terms of progress and achievement of the daily lesson objectives. In contrast, the assessments at the end of the unit of study are often termed summative or "at the gate," and are used to determine individual student achievement and learning; they are assessment FOR learning (Stiggins, 2005). They may be documented or provide evidence in the variety of ways already discussed in this chapter such as portfolio entries, drawings, observations, and so forth. Summative assessments may indicate a need for some children to have intervention, correctives, or reinforcement of concepts for content mastery.

As the curriculum is organized and carried out, knowledge of what the child needs and is able to do assists the teacher in captivating and motivating the child. In addition, it allows the teacher to promote self-direction and intrinsic rewards in learning. In "learning-centered classrooms, the teacher moves away from dispensing information and toward guiding students' efforts to make sense of their work" (Heuwinkel, 1996, p. 30).

Questions that educators can ask to assist in the development of curriculum assessment are:

- What do I want the children to know and be able to do as they complete a unit of instruction, when they leave my classroom (program), or at other appropriate times?
- What will be assessed in each developmental domain and content area?
- What methods will I use to assess and document the progress of each child?

- How will assessment data be used to inform instruction and benefit each child?

These reflective questions can encourage teachers to think about the assessment of young children and recognize that assessment needs to be thought of in the planning stage and not at the end of a lesson or unit. To determine each child's achievement in a unit of study, teachers can consider developmentally appropriate assessment as a pre- and post-assessment. Children and parents delight in seeing evidence of learning from integrated units of study in content areas.

The curriculum in early childhood needs to be assessed on an ongoing basis to ensure that it is doing what it is supposed to be doing and remains in harmony with children's abilities and needs. In-progress assessment allows any necessary adjustments to be made in the unit or project to make it more beneficial for the children. Because children are constantly developing, the curriculum must be constantly adjusted to supplement their development. The evaluation or assessment can be made using the following questions as guides:

- **Goals:** Did the project or unit meet the overall goals of the program? What evidence is there to validate this?
- **Objectives:** Did the objectives of the unit, project, or activities match children's needs, abilities, interests, and knowledge?
- **Preparations and procedures:** Were the necessary preparations for the unit, project, or activities considered and completed? Were activities prepared in advance? How else might the procedures have been carried out? Were staff members made aware of their assignments and responsibilities? Thoughtfully consider if alternative methods, strategies, or procedures would have been more efficient or appropriate.
- **Activities:** Did the activities support the objectives of the unit? Were the children interested in the activities? Was there motivation to learn? Was interest captured? Did the activities promote learning, competence, enjoyment, engagement, thinking, and success? Were the activities substantive and relevant? Were the children able to make choices and decisions? Were they involved in suggesting and planning the activities? Were the children interested and challenged by the activities? For children who needed them, were there appropriate extensions? For children who did not understand, were correctives, reteaching, or feedback provided? For children who needed to be challenged, were extensions provided? Were the activities sensitive to the diversity of the children in the classroom? Was there adequate variation in the scheduling of the activities and routines? Was each activity successful or not successful? (Include reasons and analysis of why or

why not.) Were there appropriate transitions between activities?

- ***Culminating activity(ies) to bring closure and provide feedback:*** Did the summary or closing action bring closure to the unit or activity and help children synthesize the planned objectives? (Evidence?) Do you, the teacher, have a way of knowing if you accomplished what was to be learned? What kinds of changes in the activities and unit would bring about overall improvement?

In evaluating early childhood curriculum, achievement in performance-based objectives can be observed. Examples may be the children's work, comments, or behaviors. This can be combined with the assessment approach in which the teacher evaluates the project, unit, or activities on the basis of questions such as those given in the preceding list.

All staff should be involved in ongoing evaluation and should assess each unit or project as it is completed using questions such as those suggested. They should discuss the effectiveness of the unit or lesson and individual student achievement. Attention should be given to accommodations or adaptations for the children with special needs or English Language Learners (ELLs). Staff should have data on individual student achievement of the objective or outcome of the unit with written narrative relating

All staff should be involved in ongoing evaluation and assessment.

to reteaching, practice, or reinforcement to meet individual progress. Finally, teachers and staff should thoughtfully reflect on their experiences and carefully evaluate what they have learned from teaching the unit. Evaluations should also direct the work with individual children in fostering their positive growth. Feedback from the assessments also provides useful information for parents when they have questions about their children and the influence of the curriculum on their learning and growth.

When evaluating, observations should be validated and specific comments and insights shared, not just general statements such as "The activity was very successful." Why? On what basis do you know that? Was the objective of the activity met and was it relevant? Statements such as "The majority of children were engaged and stayed with the activity for a long time" and "Each child was absorbed in the activity and anxious to participate" are more specific.

To be effective, evaluation must include both negative and positive aspects, or failures and successes, of the activities, units, or projects. For example, if an activity turns out different than planned, an objective evaluation may conclude either that the activity failed or turned out much better than originally planned. Successful and positive evaluations build confidence and ability in the teacher. Failures and negative evaluations show where planning may have been inadequate or follow-through insufficient. These discoveries, in turn, provide the groundwork for successes in similar situations.

Assessing Children's Learning and Involvement

The performances or learning outcomes of the children are, as discussed in this chapter, an integral part of assessment. Each child's learning and achievement needs to be assessed and written down. In staff oral evaluations, the group's participation throughout the unit should be assessed. Did the children accomplish the desired objectives? Were there measurable behavior changes when desired? Were the children interested and motivated to participate? Were they actively involved in the experiences, or were activities too difficult or too simple? Because the teacher keeps abreast of the child's development, objectives can be designed to increase the child's progress. Is the child interested in the program? Is the material too advanced for the child's abilities? Does it provide an adequate challenge? What is the child's relationship with the other children? Is the child socially, physically, and mentally healthy? Does the child have any particular problems that need concentrated guidance and effort? What are the child's strengths?

Assessing the Child's Development

Assessment of children's development is imperative. Knowing how the children that you teach are growing and developing is of primary importance in planning what will be taught and how it will be accomplished; it is basing curriculum plans on the context in which you are teaching. Effective assessment must take into consideration generalizations of growth and development, which include the following:

- Each child is an individual and grows in his or her own way.
- A child's self-concept affects how he or she learns.
- The child's total development, not just cognitive functioning, must be the focus of the learning environment.
- Children in the early years learn best through concrete, real experiences by experimenting and discovering.
- The learning experience must take into account the cultural background, needs, interests, and developmental levels of each child in the classroom.

Assessment yields important information for the teacher, child, and parents. Through evaluation, the teacher can plan learning experiences to match the needs of the child and to challenge the child's abilities. Assessment information is a must at parent conferences to validate the child's achievements and to give the parents some proof of the child's developmental level, as well as learning and progress. Checklists of developmental skills can be sent home for the parents to work on with the child, and to give them firsthand information on the child's progress. These checklists can be general and include cognitive skills, motor skills, social developments, and emotional characteristics, or they can focus on specific areas, such as math or reading.

Figure 3.2 is an example of an activity participation graph that can be used to evaluate each child's

FIGURE 3.2
Activity Participation Graph and Anecdotal Records

Name	Date	Art Center	Dramatic Play Area	Sensory Center	Block Area	Science Center	Reading or Literacy Center	Music Center	Manipulative Area	Technology Center
Jaden	4/3	✓ Participated at the easel.	✓		✓		✓ Particularly enjoyed reading Mother Goose Rhymes		✓ Did a sound sort with beginning sounds /m/ and /p/	

participation in various activities such as general curriculum areas like art. The graph is used over a period of time to illustrate the individual child's involvement in various kinds of activities. It graphically illustrates each child's participation or nonparticipation in classroom activities in particular curriculum areas.

Evaluating the Teacher

Being a reflective teacher means taking time to reflect on practice as a teacher. Effective teachers continually seek to highlight the positive, but be committed to making improvements. By means of a continuing assessment of the curriculum, units, and children, the role of the teacher automatically receives evaluation. Where changes are needed in the program or activities, the teacher makes the alterations. The teacher continually works to build on the strengths that already exist in the curriculum and children. The teacher should ask the following questions: What is my relationship with the children individually? Collectively? Am I planning the curriculum to meet the abilities and needs of the children? Are my desired objectives being achieved? Am I providing adequate challenge, guidance, and direction to the children? Am I enjoying what I am doing? What changes do I need to make? What are my strengths? What are my weaknesses? Do I have dispositions that need to be improved?

Summary

Assessment of individual children, instructional units, program goals, and teachers is an integral part of early childhood. The trend in early childhood assessment is away from formal assessment (group or individual standardized tests) and toward more informal methods of assessment that are more authentic or meaningful (NAEYC, 2009). Such assessment practices and tools as observations, individual conferences, projects, performances, and written and verbal explanations of students' work are much more realistic and accurate than paper and pencil tests for measuring children's progress. Anecdotal records should be kept for each child, with notations of growth, achievements, regressions, and concerns. These can be stored on the computer or they can be a card file, calendar recordings, charts, or in notebooks. An especially effective assessment tool is a portfolio of the child's work. Progress in art, writing, math, language, science, and other areas are assessed through viewing the child's work over time.

Teachers should assess young children to guide and plan for their learning and to communicate in a knowledgeable way with parents. Using documentation in our assessment benefits the children, school, and parents (Dodge et al., 2004; Helm et al., 1997). However, any assessment should be used for the benefit of children and should never be used to keep students out of a program or retain them in a particular grade. In early childhood, authentic assessments such as observations, interviews, projects, presentations or performances, and portfolios are used to determine needs, evaluate growth and learning, guide the curriculum, and evaluate the program.

Student Learning Activities

1. Visit with several early childhood teachers and discuss the forms of documentation that they use. How do they use them? Are the examples developmentally appropriate? What suggestions would you have for these teachers?
2. Interview three early childhood teachers and ask them what assessment tools or means they use. How often do they use them? How do they evaluate their program, curriculum, children, and themselves? As they meet in parent–teacher conferences, what do they share with parents as criteria for evaluation? Make comparisons of your findings and draw some conclusions of your own, from your reading and from the interview, as to what you think are the most effective means of assessment and evaluation for early childhood education.
3. Suppose the objective of a third-grade lesson is: Students will describe what a community is, as well as the type of community they live in (rural, urban, or suburban). Describe an appropriate assessment for this objective.
4. Create an assessment for a K–3 classroom (choose one grade) that might be used for assessing children's language growth. Describe your teacher-created assessment in detail.

Suggested Resources

VIDEOS AND DVDs

Assessing the Whole Child. Insight Media. This DVD examines new assessment techniques and shows how they relate to the whole child.

Classroom Moments. NAEYC. This DVD features interviews with experienced teachers who discuss the purpose, benefits, challenges and common misunderstandings of child assessment.

Focused Observation. Insight Media. The DVD provides realistic observation techniques for early childhood teachers to apply in their classrooms.

How to Grade for Learning, K–12. NAEYC. This DVD includes information on assessments that accurately reflect student strengths and weaknesses and measure achievement separate from behavior.

How to Informally Assess Student Learning. Association for Supervision and Curriculum Development (ASCD). This DVD explores informal assessment techniques for various grade levels.

Observation of Young Children: The Eyes Have It! NAEYC. This DVD illustrates how to use observation methods and explains how to use assessments to individualize instruction.

Voices: Child Assessment. NAEYC. This DVD features interviews with experienced teachers who discuss the purpose, benefits, challenges, and common misunderstandings of child assessment.

Online Resources

There are thousands of websites that provide guidelines for early childhood assessment. We suggest you explore them and bookmark the ones that will be most helpful to you. Following are a few suggestions:

www.naeyc.org National Association for the Education of Young Children (NAEYC) & National Association of Early Childhood Specialists in State Departments of Education (NAECS/SDE). (2003). Early childhood curriculum, assessment, and program evaluation: Building an effective, accountable system in programs for children birth through age 8. (Position statement.)

www.naeyc.org National Association for the Education of Young Children. (1995). *Responding to linguistic and cultural diversity: Recommendations for effective early childhood education.* Washington, DC: Author. Brochure.

www.nap.edu/catalog/12446.html National Research Council. (2008). *Early Childhood Assessment: Why, What, and How?* Committee on Developmental Outcomes and Assessments for Young Children, Catherine E. Snow and Susan B. Van Hemel, editors. Board on Children, Youth and Families, Board on Testing and Assessment, Division of Behavioral and Social Sciences and Education. Washington, DC: The National Academies Press.

www.uen.org/k-2educator/assessment.shtml Most state departments of education have documents on early childhood assessment. This document is from the Utah State Office of Education.

chapter 4
Planning the Curriculum

The early childhood curriculum should be planned around the developmental needs of the children in the classroom. Young children need teacher planned or teacher-guided experiences as well as child-guided experiences (Copple & Bredekamp, 2009). In other words "Children benefit *both* from engaging in self-initiated, spontaneous play *and* from teacher-planned and -structured activities, projects, and experiences" (Copple & Bredekamp, 2009, p. 49). The curriculum planning suggested in this book is adaptable and sometimes requires curriculum and planning that is explicit and direct and other times can be prompted by the child's own ideas and planning.

A position statement by the National Association for the Education of Young Children (NAEYC) and the National Association of Early Childhood Specialists in State Departments of Education (NAECS/SDE) urged early childhood educators to "implement curriculum that is thoughtfully planned, challenging, engaging, developmentally appropriate, culturally and linguistically responsive, comprehensive, and likely to promote positive outcomes for all young children" (NAEYC & NAECS/SDE, 2003, p. 1). A culturally sensitive curriculum helps children to make sense of their world, creates harmony between the home and school, and helps to make the concept of diversity and acceptance a natural part of children's understanding. Rigid, uniform, and structured interpretations of developmental appropriateness, however, can lead to insensitivity to multicultural issues (Lubeck, 1994; New & Mallory, 1994).

Curriculum development should draw from many sources, including knowledge of early childhood, children's individual characteristics, the knowledge base of various disciplines, the values of our culture, parents' desires, and the knowledge children need to function proficiently in society (NAEYC & NAECS/SDE, 2003). Shepard (2001, p. 1074) suggests the following principles of curriculum:

- All students can learn.
- Challenging subject matter is aimed at higher order thinking and problem solving.
- Diverse learners are given equal opportunities.
- The relationship between learning in and out of school is authentic.
- Students foster important dispositions and habits of mind.
- Students enact democratic practices in a caring community.

Experiences should be developed to help young children improve their skills in problem solving, thinking, reasoning, and creating, not just their skill in rote memorizing. Facts may eventually become outdated, but the skills of thinking, making meaning, developing understanding, and problem solving never will. An old proverb says, "Give me a fish, and I will be fed today. Teach me how to fish, and I will be fed forever." Simply, learning how to solve a problem is more important than the solution.

The joint position statement on curriculum and assessment from NAEYC and NAECS/SDE (2003, p. 2) proposes the following indicators of effective curriculum:

- Children are active and engaged.
- Goals are clear and shared by all.
- Curriculum is evidence-based.
- Valued content is learned through investigation, play, and focused, intentional teaching.
- Curriculum builds on prior learning and experiences.
- Curriculum is comprehensive.
- Professional standards validate the curriculum's subject-matter content.
- Curriculum is likely to benefit children.

Source: Reprinted with permission from the National Association for the Education of Young Children. All current NAEYC position statements are available online at www.naeyc.org/positionstatements.

The curriculum should provide opportunities for healthy social, emotional, and physical development.

Research on brain development indicates that the more active children are, the better they learn (Jensen, 2000). Howard Gardner advocates: "The brain learns best and retains most when the organism is actively involved in exploring physical sites and materials and asking questions to which it actually craves answers. Merely passive experiences tend to attenuate and have little lasting impact" (Gardner, 1999b, p. 82). Therefore, learning should be a process of active involvement with rich, meaningful content, using developmentally appropriate practices and approaches, not just focusing on an end result. Learning should include many hands-on experiences. The many kinds of active learning experiences include role-playing, creative dramatics, simulations, pantomime, games, art activities, and storytelling (Kline, 1995).

Curriculum has deeper meaning for children when it connects them to real-world experiences, including their culture, and gives them opportunity to share and plan based on their own sociocultural experiences (Patton & Kokoski, 1996). The more input we have from the children in curriculum planning, the closer we come to achieving that direction. One approach is to begin units or lessons with the K-W-L chart (Ogle, 1986). The chart is divided into three columns: K: what do we know; W: what do we want to know or wonder about; and L: what we learned. Williams (1997, pp. 78–80) suggests four similar questions to ask children when we involve them in curriculum planning:

- What do you wonder or want to know about?
- What can we do to find out?
- What materials do we need?
- What will you bring? What would you like me to bring?

The curriculum should provide opportunities for development in areas besides intellectual or cognitive growth. It should also provide encouragement of, and opportunities for, healthy social, emotional, and physical development. Most early childhood educators and parents think preschool education should strengthen children's social competence and language skills. It should allow adequate time and opportunity for children to express themselves freely through various media: creative materials, large- and small-muscle materials, dramatic or role-playing materials, manipulative toys and materials, books and other literature, sensory media, and resource people.

There is no such thing as a universal curriculum that is appropriate for all. The outcomes or objectives of the planned curriculum need to link with developmental tasks for the ages of the children and be comprehensive in scope. The objectives of the curriculum should be based on standards. To create a meaningful curriculum with respect to how children learn and what children know, VanScoy (1995) has suggested that we trade the three Rs (reading, 'riting, and 'rithmetic) for the four Es: experience, extension, expression, and evaluation. In other words, 3- to 8-year-old children need rich experiences with opportunities to study and go into depth in understanding the meaning of these experiences. They need to question and talk about the experiences. Parents need specific evaluative feedback on the child's progress and needs.

Recent changes in early childhood curriculum perspective have created more emphasis on academic content, even in preschool programs (Copple & Bredekamp, 2009). Many early childhood programs have particularly strong foci on literacy and math. With this point made, it is still important to remember the value of additional disciplines such as art, music, science, social studies, and plenty of opportunities to learn through play.

PLANNING BASED ON OBSERVATION

Curriculum planning should focus on promoting learning and development in all areas of development (NAEYC Program Standards, 2006). Units and lessons are based on themes that will be both interesting and developmentally beneficial for all children. On the other hand, "projects" are based on the interests or passions of the children in the classroom or are responsive to student inquiries (Ferguson, 2001; Mindes, 2005).

What we know about children should be at the center of our work (Goldberg, 1997). We know from research that all children pass through stages of growth in the various developmental areas; however, children do not pass through these stages at the same rate (Elkind, 1996; NAEYC & NAECS/SDE, 2003). In a classroom of children within a 1-year age range, there may actually be a developmental range of several years in cognitive, social, emotional, and physical areas. Teachers must expect a wide range of individual differences (NAEYC & NAECS/SDE, 2003). The challenge comes in determining where each child is developmentally and then matching appropriate learning activities and curriculum to that developmental stage. This requires observation, listening, planning, organization, assessment, and often help from other professionals.

If all children are asked to do the same things, in the same way, and all at the same time, we are not honoring their distinct, individual learning styles, abilities, and interests. When programs or classrooms are geared to individual children, the teacher cannot *control* all the children all the time; on the contrary, children become self-disciplined as they take responsibility for their own learning. Then they learn from their own initiative and action. From the constructivist perspective, autonomy should be the aim of education; to foster autonomy in the classroom, children need encouragement to make their own decisions and also to enforce their own rules (Kamii, Clark, & Dominick, 1994).

Frequently, teachers plan the curriculum for an entire school year before they have even met the children that they will be teaching. Too often the teaching focus considers only the scope and sequence guides and standards established by national, state, and local organizations and pays little attention to the developmental needs of individual children in the classroom. It is more effective to begin the year with a needs assessment and observation that determine the strengths, developmental levels, and needs of the children; these also identify the best place to begin and the competencies that should be stressed. Throughout the year, additional observations and performance assessments or alternative assessments determine the children's progress and help the teacher and students to select appropriate curricula.

In addition, nearly every classroom has children who have learning difficulties. More and more, schools are utilizing programs for early recognition of children who may be displaying signs of impending special needs. Screening and assessment can alert the school to the existence of developmental deviations that may be due to physical, psychological, or neurological circumstances. Early diagnosis decreases the possibility of the conditions becoming more severe and increases the opportunity for successful corrective treatment.

As a teacher answers the questions "Which standards will I use and how will I attend to those standards?", "What are my objectives?", "What will I do?", "Why will I do it?", "How will I do it?", and "How will I assess it?", the curriculum is designed. Answers to the above questions also depend on the teacher's training, the materials available, and the purposes or long-range program goals, based on the needs of the children. Besides carefully observing children and determining their needs, support in planning and writing objectives for units and lessons also comes from national content standards, such as those in mathematics and social studies, and from state core standards and objectives. Meaningful lessons and units are planned when integrating standards and goals into active, engaged learning that meets students' interests (Helm, 2008). Additionally, there are new Common Core State Standards in English Language Arts, Math, History, and Social Studies. How these will be implemented remains to be determined; they are broader than most state standards. Standards articulate what all students are expected to know or be able to do, but teachers and districts should determine how to best reach the objectives and what additional topics and activities meet the needs of individual students in the program or class. As part of curriculum planning, teachers review the standards to which their program or school are expected to comply. These standards are found on various websites, and teachers are expected to align their teaching to these standards. Teachers are accountable to teach with attention to standards, but there is room for teachers to decide how to teach to meet the standards. Gronlund (2006) suggests three steps as children progress toward accomplishing a standard: (1) First steps, (2) Making progress, and (3) Accomplishing the standard. Teachers are expected to document each child's progress toward achievement of the standard.

To review, the curriculum is established first by the needs of the individual children that are determined through careful observation. Consideration is then given to standards from which to write specific outcomes or objectives of a lesson or unit. Knowing the outcomes desired, an appropriate assessment is planned to determine if the outcomes of the lesson or unit are met. Then learning activities are aligned to the objectives and assessments that are developmentally appropriate for the age and needs of the children in the class.

Goals are absolutely essential to each program. They give something to move toward, a larger framework from which to plan. Every center, program, or classroom teacher should make a list of purposes or long-range goals: What is the mission of this program or classroom? What should a parent expect a child to achieve by attending this school, program, or class for a given length of time? What is the approach, and where is the emphasis? Goals should be posted so that parents, teachers, and administrators can read them. Some programs or schools offer the goals in the form of a mission statement, which provides an overall direction for the program or school and allows stakeholders a clear vision of its intent. When there is alignment or integration of curriculum objectives with assessment information for the purpose of meeting individual needs, programs and classrooms are strengthened and children benefit.

Goals and Objectives Answer Why

Goals and objectives constitute the *why* of the curriculum. They provide the reasoning behind the program—the purposes or outcomes of the teaching. Why should we have this particular activity? Why should we have this activity at the time it is planned? Why is it of value to the children? Why will it benefit the child? If there are no purposeful goals or objectives, reevaluation and redirection are needed.

It is necessary to make a distinction between the terms *objectives* and *goals*. Long-term goals should be based on the NAEYC Early Childhood Program Standards (NAEYC, 2006) or similar standards as defined by the state or district. From the long-term goals, the teacher can make short-term objectives that will guide the curriculum. Remember, these objectives are derived from standards previously discussed in Chapter 1. When we refer to the long-term desires of a program, we are alluding to **goals;** when we refer short-term outcomes, we are alluding to **objectives.** Specific daily objectives add up to the long-term goals that the teacher is trying to reach. Objectives should be specific; clearly state the purpose of the unit, lesson, or activity; and suggest the desired outcome of the lesson.

> Objectives should be planned and written from the perspective of "What do I want my students to *know, do,* and/or *feel* as a result of this unit or lesson?"

Objectives are student centered and guide learning activities and assessments. Curriculum alignment occurs when objectives, learning activities, and assessments match or are aligned with one another. For most teachers, Bloom's taxonomy (Bloom, 1956) is helpful in designing objectives that move children into higher-level thinking activities and projects by the nature of the verb selected. In early childhood, teachers rarely go beyond application and analysis, but by third grade many students are able to synthesize and evaluate and should be encouraged to do so by the objectives and outcomes expected.

Bloom's Taxonomy

Competence	Skills Demonstrated	Verbs
Knowledge	Observe and recall information	list, define, describe, identify, show, examine, name
Comprehension	Understand information or ideas, grasp meaning	describe, summarize, interpret, contrast, predict, discuss, illustrate
Application	Use information or use methods in new situations	apply, demonstrate, complete, illustrate, change, experiment, discover
Analysis	See patterns and relationships	analyze, compare, contrast, separate, order, classify, infer, explain
Synthesis	Combine ideas to form a new whole	create, invent, develop, design, plan
Evaluation	Compare and discriminate between ideas	judge, critique, decide, assess, conclude

Source: Based on *Taxonomy of Educational Objectives: The Classification of Educational Goals, Handbook I: Cognitive Domain,* by B. Bloom, M. Englehart, E. Furst, and D. Krathwohl, 1956, New York: Longman Green.

Anderson and Krathwohl (2002) revised the original Bloom's Taxonomy into two dimensions, the Knowledge dimension and the Cognitive Process dimension. By developing these two dimensions into a table, the objectives, standards, or assessments can be classified into what the authors refer to as a Taxonomy Table. Teachers can use the table to improve instruction and carefully examine curriculum. Following is a comparison of the original Bloom's Taxonomy and the revised version (Buehl, 2009):

Original Version	**Revised Version**
Knowledge	Remembering
Comprehension	Understanding
Application	Applying
Analysis	Analyzing
Synthesis	Evaluating
Evaluation	Creating

Teachers can study Bloom's original taxonomy and the revision of the taxonomy and decide which of the verbs best meet their needs to develop instructional objectives. Some teachers find the original version more appropriate and other use the revised version as a personal preference. What is most important is that teachers carefully select the verb that will demonstrate what they want children to know or be able to do as they describe the desired outcome.

Well-Planned Integrated Units and Activities Answer What

What activities and materials are needed to carry out the desired goals and objectives? In effect, what will be done? The curriculum is planned with the themes, projects, and activities that are developmentally appropriate. The activities need to be aligned to or match the learning objectives or desired outcomes of the unit or lesson.

In addition to making a list of the broad program goals or purposes of the program, based on children's needs, some teachers plan themes for the entire year to provide direction and meaningful sequencing of themes and concepts; however, if we are to direct our curriculum to the needs of children, this practice either should be approached with flexibility or should be avoided. Others, taking a more child-centered approach, seek to learn what experiences the children bring to class and use these experiences along with children's questions and interests to guide the curriculum (Chard, 1998). Through careful selection of themes, projects, units, and daily activities (some supporting the theme), days will be balanced with varied experiences, and the question "What will we do?" will be answered.

Defining Instructional Contexts Answers How

How will the selected activities (*what*) be presented and carried out for the desired goals and objectives (*why*) to be achieved? Will whole groups, small groups, or individual activities be planned? Answering this question includes preparing and planning materials and procedures, as well as gathering needed supplies and determining the approach for following through. It encourages the teacher not only to plan the activity, but also to organize work. In the approach to lesson planning suggested in this book, the procedures sections answer this *how* question. With this question answered, the teacher knows the procedures or sequence for the activity, from beginning to completion.

> Too often in early childhood curriculum we have resorted to narrow approaches to teaching that deprive children of higher order thinking, questioning, discovering and that leads them to development of ideas, concepts and knowledge. Neuman and Roskos (2005, p. 26) argue we do a disfavor to, in particular, the economically disadvantaged children who lack the rich language and literacy heritage of more advantaged children when we use a "limiting, marginalizing, and reduced curriculum that is devoid of any real thinking." They continue that "these children need just the opposite: content-rich instruction that blends meaningful learning with foundational skills (Neuman & Roskos, 2005, p. 26).

As a teacher carefully thinks through these three questions, the curriculum becomes stronger. Teachers need to know *why* they are doing *what* they are doing, and *how*, specifically, they will accomplish their plans.

RIGID PLANNING VERSUS FLEXIBLE CURRICULUM PLANNING

Curriculum planning in the early childhood years does not mean planning a rigid time schedule. "Allowing children to move freely about the classroom, initiating learning experiences in a variety of ways, requires a movement away from rigid scheduling of discrete, subject-driven activities to an integrated, holistic view of curriculum, development, and learning" (Patton & Kokoski, 1996, pp. 39, 40). Too often, programs for early learning are geared to the clock or to a lesson plan, rather than to children. Perhaps the reason young children often become bored, restless, and uninterested in school is not that they are actually tired of school per se, but that they are tired of the daily routines and time schedule. Many routines in early childhood classes waste untold hours, with no real

Be flexible! Rain does not need to cancel an outside picnic, just move it inside!

learning taking place. Routines such as greeting, roll taking, and sharing can be changed to foster learning, problem solving, and creativity. The child comes to school knowing that certain things will take place: There will be snacks, centers, free play, singing, reading, math, and a warm, responsive teacher. Knowing that there are daily occurrences provides security, but not knowing exactly how the goals and plans will be carried out or what approaches or strategies will be used in the learning activities creates interest, curiosity, and enthusiasm. This does not mean, however, that the *teacher* does not know how the day will proceed. The order and planning of activities must be formulated.

The teacher needs to have a general idea of the time and sequence of activities, but then it is necessary to observe, feel, and determine the needs of the children, allowing for flexibility. For example, free play may be planned for about 30 minutes; but because of the children's involvement and interest, the period may be extended to 45 minutes. This, in turn, may make it essential to have another activity shortened or even eliminated during that particular day. Far too often children are rushed from one activity to the next, or an activity is prolonged just because the lesson plan indicates that music is scheduled at 2:00 P.M. Young children need well-planned, integrated units of study that are carried out through activities with objectives, but the amount of time taken by specific activities must be determined by children's interest and involvement (Katz, 1990).

There is great value in a well-structured curriculum of sequential learning plans, but considerable flexibility and skill must be used in following these

through. An integrated curriculum does not segment into specific content areas such as math, reading, science, or social studies. Rather, it allows children to learn through relevant and meaningful real-world experiences (S. J. Stone, 1995/1996). In an **integrated curriculum,** content areas such as art, music, technology might be combined in a social studies integrated unit of study; in most all units, language arts/literacy are integrated. Integrated curriculum interconnects content domains within one activity or a unit (Schickedanz, 2008). The suggested planning in this text integrates curriculum; the unit ideas are just that, integrated curriculum. Children enjoy both the process and content of learning through exploring, discovering, problem solving, inventing, experimenting, imitating, and dramatizing. The teacher who has planned activities, but has built them on a flexible base, is not disturbed when opportunities for taking advantage of teachable moments arise. For example, one day an Angora sheep wandered close to the play yard. The children were fascinated with it and had numerous questions. The wise teacher encouraged the sheep to enter the play yard and allowed the children to smell, romp with, touch, and feed tree blossoms to it. This necessitated eliminating a planned activity, but the advantages were of far greater value than those that would have been obtained through an inflexible time schedule.

As curriculum is planned consideration is also given to the learning or instructional contexts in the early childhood classroom. Some of these instructional contexts are more flexible and some more structured. Consideration needs to be given to the developmental and individual needs of the children, to the intended objectives of the lesson or unit, and to other contextual factors of the students and classroom.

EARLY CHILDHOOD INSTRUCTIONAL CONTEXTS

There are various instructional contexts for teachers to contemplate generally as they plan curriculum. Some of these instructional contexts are incorporation of free play, whole- and small-group activities, learning centers, and cooperative learning strategies and structures.

Free Play Including Individual Activities

Becoming a master player is a goal worth achieving for young children. Every day there should be some time for free play, a time when children individually choose areas of involvement. Weather permitting, the children should have daily opportunities for play both inside and outside. Outside, the core of the play will be large-muscle activities: climbing, running, sliding, balancing, jumping, and so on.

Free play should not be a time for teachers to relax and take a break. For children to receive maximum benefit from their play, guidance from teachers is necessary; they should be nearby to give assistance and encouragement. Teachers can acknowledge creative and constructive efforts, invite questions, ask thought-provoking questions that extend and expand children's play, and redirect play that needs changing (Crosser, 1992). The teacher helps to create meaning and purpose, then moves to another child or group of children. Much learning, teaching, and interacting should go on between children, between individual children and the teacher, and between small groups of children and the teacher. Free play is a great time for the teacher to assess each child's development and needs through careful observation.

Young children should have opportunities for computing, exploring, measuring, investigating, constructing, and experimenting. They not only need *many opportunities*, but they also need *adequate time* to do it. *Enough time* refers particularly to large blocks of time, rather than to numerous short periods of inadequate length (Copple & Bredekamp, 2009; NCTM, 1989; Patton & Kokoski, 1996). Free play should be long enough for children to carry out their play ideas. The length of the play period directly affects the quality and level of play. To promote both group dramatic and constructive play, it is necessary to provide longer play periods. It has been suggested that it may be wise to occasionally reduce the number of activities available during free play so that there will be less distraction and greater opportunity for involvement in particular play activities.

Whole- and Small-Group Activities

In addition to free play (or individual) activities, which may also include centers or project work, the children will participate in small-group and whole-group activities. If all the children are participating at the same time in the same situation and general location, they are engaged in a **whole-group activity.** A traditional whole-group activity is *community* or *circle time*, when the children sit in a circle and discussions relating to the theme, experiences, music activities, stories, or other activities are presented to the entire group. When teachers give explicit or direct teaching relating to a specific topic, it is often in a whole-group setting. For **small-group activities,** the children are divided into groups of three to five. Sometimes they are grouped by their ability level, and sometimes they are grouped in cooperative learning groups; it will depend on the nature and desired outcomes of the activity which type of grouping will be used.

Many activities are best suited for one of the three approaches: individual, small-group, or whole-group activities. For example, the use of sensory media in the trough is generally best suited to individual play. Other activities, such as finger painting, can be carried out as either individual, small-group, or whole-group activities, depending on the desired objectives, available space, and other planned activities for the day.

Effective transitions to move children from one activity to another must be carefully planned. Children can be "enticed" to move to the next activity (Crosser, 1992, p. 26). A designated piano chord, a bell, or a word can signal that it is time to clean up or change activities (Crosser, 1992). Give fair time warnings before expecting children to move to the next activity.

Learning Centers

Learning centers are another instructional context that allow children opportunity to explore, extend learning, and often have hand-on experiences with materials that have been introduced in a whole-group or small-group setting. Children do need to be taught explicitly what they are expected to do in a learning center if an adult is not present to support their learning. Learning centers give children a chance to try out, talk about, or work with materials or ideas that have been previously introduced (Schickedanz, 2008).

When working in centers children may be assigned with 3 to 6 children per center or they may choose in which center to work. If there is choice of the activity or center, it is usually referred to as free play. Many specific early childhood centers are suggested in Chapter 1. If there is more structure, the teacher needs to provide direct and explicit instruction to the children.

Cooperative Learning

Cooperative learning is a versatile approach that can be used in small groups, during free play, or in whole groups. The cooperative learning strategy is not meant to be used exclusively, but rather should be integrated and used as the teacher feels appropriate. When children are in whole groups, they are divided into pairs or teams to solve a problem, discuss a question, or brainstorm an idea. In cooperative learning activities, children work together with a common goal in mind (Gillies, 2007; Jacobs, Power, & Loh, 2002). Research has shown that there are impressive academic and social gains for children who consistently participate in cooperative learning activities (Jolliffe, 2007; Kagan & Kagan, 2009). Many "research studies demonstrate that cooperative learning has a positive impact on classroom climate, student self-esteem, empathy, internal locus of control, role-taking abilities, time on task, attendance, acceptance of mainstreamed students, and liking school and learning" (Kagan & Kagan, 2009, p. 32). All children, regardless of their backgrounds or abilities, can benefit from being in single, inclusive classrooms that incorporate techniques of cooperative learning (Jolliffe, 2007; Putnam & Slavin, 1993).

Cooperative learning emphasizes social skills—learning to work together and helping one another. Children learn that no one in the group succeeds until they all succeed; this is positive interdependence (Johnson & Johnson, 1999). Even though the focus appears to be on group behavior, the real purpose is to create stronger individuals. Cooperative learning also encourages children to develop friendships with children who are different from themselves (Kagan & Kagan, 2009). Additional social skills developed in cooperative learning experiences include taking turns, self-direction, positive self-esteem, and the ability to take different roles (Kagan & Kagan, 2009). Cooperative learning encourages peer tutoring, staying on task, and individual accountability, and it promotes interdependence. There is more motivation, enthusiasm, and participation on the part of all children when cooperative learning is incorporated into the curriculum.

Cooperative learning experiences prepare young children today for the democratic world that they will live in tomorrow (Kagan & Kagan, 2009). Our democratic ideal promotes equal participation by all members; if children have had no experience participating as viable members of a group, they will have difficulty participating as contributing members of society in the future.

GOALS OF COOPERATIVE LEARNING. The following are goals for cooperative learning:

- Build positive interpersonal social skills and habits among students by giving more opportunity for group interaction.
- Give children the opportunity to teach and learn from one another. This builds leadership skills, strengthens self-esteem, and enhances learning.
- Provide experiences that encourage flexibility, cooperation, and problem solving.
- Provide the kind of learning structure that fosters communication skills. In cooperative learning groups, more children have the opportunity to share ideas, exchange information, and talk.

GUIDELINES FOR USING COOPERATIVE LEARNING. The following are guidelines for cooperative learning activities:

- Children need to be shown how to use the cooperative learning strategy, and it must be discussed thoroughly before the children go into their groups.
- The content and objectives of the lesson plan, as well as the developmental level of the children, determine which particular cooperative learning strategies are used.
- To be an effective member of any group, children need to learn that they will be expected to share ideas (talk), as well as listen to what other group members have to say.
- Cooperative learning can be used during free play as children work together on activities, play with manipulatives, paint at the easel, work on a science project, or participate in any variety of cooperative group activities. The group size may be two, three, four, or more members.
- Cooperative groups can be used to solve a single problem such as a math problem, for more complicated activities, or for a group discussion. Cooperative learning can be used in art, science, language explorations, or virtually any curriculum area. This approach is especially valuable in the language area, because all children can then share, discuss, evaluate, write, act out, plan, play a part, have a turn at the game, listen to another, or otherwise participate in whatever the lesson or activity involves.
- Cooperative learning is different from regular small groups in that the focus is on interactive group behavior. All children must participate and support the group effort.
- After the groups have worked together, it is wise to "debrief" the children. This means that group members decide what went well and what did not go so well. It is a form of evaluation and feedback, as well as an opportunity to bring the activity to an end.

DIVIDING CHILDREN INTO GROUPS. There are many ways to divide children into groups, whether they are small groups or cooperative learning groups. They might be divided by ability or a mix of abilities. They might be randomly grouped; the following are some suggestions:

- Divide the children into two circles, one inside the other, and have the circles move in opposite directions. When a signal is given, the circles stop and the children facing each other are partners.
- Put numbers, colors, animals, shapes, book titles, or songs in four corners or areas of the room (if you want more than four groups, use more than four areas). Have the children go to the corner or area that designates their favorite number, shape, or whatever category has been chosen.
- Put badges or stickers of different colors, animals, numbers, or even different children or class members. The children go with the group that has the same badge as theirs.
- Cut a picture into three, four, or five parts and give a part of the picture puzzle to each child. Children are to find the other parts of their picture to form their group (Kagan & Kagan, 2009).
- Split lines by lining children up, then "folding" the line in half to create a partner for each child. Fold each line again to form groups of four (Curran, 1991).
- Mount a picture of each child on an index card or small piece of cardstock paper. Shuffle the stack of pictures and then draw out three to five per group with the first one being called assuming the role of group leader.

COOPERATIVE LEARNING STRATEGIES.   Following are a few suggestions for structures and strategies used in the context of cooperative learning:

- *Numbered Heads Together.* Each of the students in a group has a number. For example, four children in a group would be numbered 1 through 4. The teacher asks a question or gives a problem to solve. The children work on it and agree on their team's answer. The teacher calls a number, and the children with that number share their group's answer (Curran, 1991).
- *Think–Pair–Share.* An idea is given for the children to think about. Each child finds or is assigned a partner, and the two discuss the problem together. Then they report back or share what they have learned.
- *Interviews.* Children are assigned to groups of four. Child 1 interviews child 2, and child 3 interviews child 4. Then they reverse so that child 2 interviews child 1 and child 4 interviews child 3. They share what they have learned. This can be used for a review, for end-of-unit feedback, or for focusing on a particular concept.

For additional suggestions regarding strategies used in cooperative learning, we refer you to Curran (1991), Gillies (2007), Jacobs, et al. (2002), Jolliffe (2007), and Kagan and Kagan (2009).

APPROACHES TO CURRICULUM PLANNING

There are a variety of specific approaches to use when planning early childhood curriculum. Some curriculum approaches include comprehensive units of instruction such as the Teacher Work Sample (TWS) model. Other methods such as the thematic approach to instruction, project-based instruction, or emergent curriculum might be used or incorporated into the TWS. Whatever the approach to instructional design, teachers must carefully align objectives, learning activities and assessments or documentations. Collaboration is also an important part of curriculum planning as teaching teams meet together to plan (Dodge, Heroman, Charles, & Maiorca, 2004).

No matter what approach or model is used in early childhood education, teaching young children requires much preparation. Vital components of planning include the following:

- Appraising and evaluating carefully the contextual factors of the classroom, school, and community.
- Choosing a theme or project and the objectives of the entire unit or project.
- Selecting the assessment or documentation of the unit or lesson that aligns to the objective. This informs you if the objective or desired outcome of the unit or lesson was achieved.
- Brainstorming activities to teach or support the theme or project (unit plan or web). If you are doing a project, the children will do the brainstorming.
- Determining daily activities, ensuring a balance among various kinds of activities (daily activity plan).
- Deciding on a daily schedule of activities (what will be done first, second, etc., and about how long each activity will last).
- Organizing the unit or lesson plan.
- Preparing materials and resources and planning for each activity.
- Arranging the room's environment. Major room changes may be made each week or less often, and minor room changes can be made daily to accommodate the activities planned.
- Planning for and preparing accommodations and adaptations for students' diverse needs. This is differentiating the curriculum.

Teacher Work Sample Approach to Planning

The Renaissance Partnership for Improving Teacher Quality (n.d.) developed a comprehensive approach to planning units that is used in many teacher preparation programs in the country. The model is called Teacher

Classroom arrangement should include a quiet reading area with comfortable seating and an appropriate selection of books.

Work Sample (TWS) (see Table 4.1). TWSs are exhibits of teaching performance that provide evidence of a candidate's ability to design and implement standards-based instruction, assess student learning, and reflect on the teaching and learning process. TWSs are teaching exhibits that can provide credible evidence of a candidate's ability to facilitate learning for all students. They are one source of evidence, along with classroom observations and other measures, to assess candidate's performance relative to national and state teaching standards. The TWS is a more broad and inclusive approach to instructional design than past approaches to unit planning; it is a comprehensive unit of instruction from beginning to end. More than designing the instruction, it includes a thoughtful analysis of *contextual factors,* including the community, school, and the students. The TWS includes writing clear *objectives* (based on the national, state, and local standards), designing an *assessment plan* for the unit as well as the individual lessons, and *designing the instruction* using sound lesson plan formats. Adaptations and accommodations for exceptional students including English language learners (ELLs) are part of the instruction design; thus, after teaching the lesson, the candidate writes about the *instructional decision making* that occurred in the unit. What accommodations and adjustments were used for special, gifted, or ELL students? How did these adaptations meet their needs? What adjustments were made to the curriculum to adapt to the needs of the lesson/unit? The TWS also includes an *analysis of student learning,* which means the candidate uses assessment information and data for the benefit of the students' progress and achievement. A clear interpretation of the assessment data is shared to give evidence of the unit out-

comes on student learning and achievement. The last section of the TWS model is the *reflection and self-evaluation* completed at the end of the unit as the candidate reflects on personal learning and growth. Many "I learned . . ." statements should be included in the reflection and self-evaluation.

TWS methodology is a process requiring thoughtful observation, planning, and reflection, taking the needs of children into account. It provides a way for teacher candidates to be accountable for student progress and achievement. It is student-centered instructional design. The first four pieces are all preplanning, and the last three parts of the TWS follow the teaching of the unit.

We have found great success using this model. One of its advantages is that it is adaptable to whatever lesson model the candidate/teacher wishes to use. The fourth section, Design for Instruction, can include a variety of design formats, including formats suggested in this text. Table 4.1 shows the template of the model.

Thematic Planning

It is important for us to remember as we plan an integrated early childhood curriculum that "less is more" (Patton & Kokoski, 1996, p. 40). This means that we strive to teach fewer themes or concepts, but to teach them in greater depth. The challenge then comes in going deep rather than wide with regard to curriculum planning. It also means that we plan an in-depth study of a theme, with an open-ended time frame, rather than the traditional theme-of-the-week approach. The curriculum can focus on a topic or theme and at the same time allow for integration of more traditional subject-matter disciplines such as literacy and math. Using

TABLE 4.1 • Teaching Processes, TWS Standards, and Indicators

Contextual Factors

The teacher uses information about the learning-teaching context and student individual differences to set learning objectives and plan instruction and assessment.

- Knowledge of community, school, and classroom factors
- Knowledge of characteristics of students
- Knowledge of students' varied approaches to learning
- Knowledge of students' skills and prior knowledge
- Implications for instructional planning and assessment

Objectives/Intended Learning Outcomes

The teacher sets significant, challenging, varied, and appropriate objectives.

- Alignment with national or state standards
- Significant, challenging, and variety
- Clarity
- Appropriateness for students

Assessment Plan

The teacher uses multiple assessment modes and approaches aligned with objectives to assess student learning before, during, and after instruction.

- Alignment with objectives and instruction
- Clarity of criteria for performance
- Multiple modes and approaches
- Technical soundness
- Adaptations based on the individual needs of students

Design for Instruction

The teacher designs instruction for specific learning objectives, student characteristics and needs, and learning contexts.

- Alignment with objectives
- Accurate representation of content
- Sound lesson structure (i.e., Emergent curriculum, project-based lessons, Madeline Hunter, 4MAT (Bernice McCarthy), Inquiry, Multiple Intelligence, etc.)
- Use of a variety of strategies, activities, assignments, and resources
- Use of contextual information and data to select appropriate and relevant activities, assignments, and resources.
- Integration of appropriate technology

Instructional Decision Making

The teacher uses ongoing analysis of student learning to make instructional decisions.

- Utilization of sound professional practice
- Adjustments based on analysis of student learning and incorporation of accommodations and adaptations for special needs including gifted and talented students
- Congruence between modifications and objectives

Analysis of Student Learning

The teacher uses assessment data to profile student learning and communicate information about student progress and achievement.

- Clarity and accuracy of presentation
- Alignment with learning goals
- Interpretation of data
- Evidence of impact on student learning

TABLE 4.1 • *(continued)*

Reflection and Self-Evaluation
The teacher reflects on his or her instruction and student learning in order to improve teaching practice.

- Interpretation of student learning
- Analysis of student motivation
- Insights on effective instruction and assessment
- Alignment among objectives, instruction, and assessment
- Implications for future teaching
- Implications for professional development

Source: Adapted from and reproduced with permission from Renaissance Partnership for Improving Teacher Quality (http://www.uni.edu/itq). Director: Dr. Roger Pankratz.
Note: Your instructor may share a first-grade TWS on seeds that was planned and taught.

a unit theme or concept provides an opportunity for rich and meaningful conceptual development. The unit theme must be selected before further planning can take place. The possibilities for unit themes are infinite and often are selected on the basis of student interest or suggestion, with the use of textbooks, or by studying the standards and objectives suggested in the state core curriculum. Children at differing stages of development approach a concept from different levels. They first develop an awareness, then explore it, then use inquiry, and finally use the concept or learning. Thus, any child can benefit and gain something from almost any theme.

A large portion of this text will deal with specific themes and integrated approaches to teaching them. However, a beginning list of possible themes or projects appropriate for children in the early childhood years follows:

Air
Animals: specific categories (farm animals, insects), kinds (bees, dogs), animal homes, animal babies, hibernation
Color
Family
Fire
Flowers
Houses
Magnets
Numbers
Nuts
Paper
People: emotions, self-concept, senses, body parts, family, friends, cultures, professions
Pollution
Rocks
Seeds

Shape
Shoes
Texture
Trains (or other forms of transportation)
Trees
Water (or other resources)
Wheat
Wheels

Many of these suggestions could be narrowed down to even more specific concepts, projects, or themes. Teachers, parents, and children can brainstorm themes and topics appropriate for their classroom. Themes should support the standards on which the program is based.

Project-Based Learning

Project learning is advocated by Chard (1998), Katz and Chard (2000), and Wolk (1994) as a constructivist approach to learning that puts the responsibility for decision making, planning, and learning with the child, therefore encouraging more autonomous learning. Distinctive characteristics of Chard's approach include group discussion, fieldwork, some type of representation, investigation, and display or sharing of understanding (Chard, 1998). A **project** is defined as an in-depth study of a topic, theme, or concept and may be done individually, in small groups, or as a whole group (Chard, 1998). Each project goes through three basic phases: (a) reviewing and building on the children's present knowledge and interests; (b) giving children new experiences and also opportunities for research; and (c) evaluating, reflecting on, and sharing the project work (Chard, 1998).

Project-based learning (PBL) is a child-centered approach that integrates curriculum. Children find a variety of ways to demonstrate their learning and share what they have learned; they may draw, talk about, or write about the topic they have studied. One of the values of project-based learning is that it invites **process skills** including observation, problem solving, analyzing, comparing and contrasting, and forming hypothesis and conclusions (Helm & Beneke, 2003). In one first-grade class the children did a project on hurricanes. Their research and reporting was quite different from the research and reporting on the same topic done by older children. However, using invented spelling and more simple approaches to their research, the first-graders were still able to garner new facts and information as they read, researched, and documented their study of this topic (Diffily, 2003). Because of developmental differences, there were different approaches in the research process, but all children who participated in this project benefited in a variety of ways as they gained meaning of and insight into hurricanes.

> The following are characteristics of project-based learning (adapted from Diffily, 2003, p. 76):
>
> • Children select topics for study.
> • The undertaking is initiated and directed by children but supported and guided by the teacher.
> • Learning is research-based.
> • The program concludes with an end product and with a celebration and sharing of their learning.
> • The plan is carried out over time, sometimes days, and for older children, possibly weeks.

Children should also be a part of curricular planning (Chard, 1998; Kohn, 1993). They can make suggestions for themes or topics to investigate; or once a theme is selected, they can help to select specific aspects or activities to study. In the project approach, children work individually or in groups with the teacher guiding the child's work (Chard, 1998; Katz & Chard, 2000). Project work is defined as "children's in-depth investigations of topics that interest them" (Hartman & Eckerty, 1995, p. 141). Either children or teachers may initiate projects, but the children provide the main impetus for direction and depth. The subjects are generally related to events and ideas with which the children are familiar. Children tend to stay motivated and focused on projects for longer periods of time when they have a personal interest in them (Diffily & Sassman, 2002). Pressing children to think beyond what they already know inspires understanding. As children realize that their ideas result in action,

their self-esteem and initiative are enhanced (Perkins & Blythe, 1994).

When children are allowed the luxury of defining curriculum content, when they are able to move in academic directions that interest them, and when they actually *do* something, they become engaged in their learning (Perrone, 1994). Ultimately, the teacher is accountable for determining what is best for the individual child, as well as the whole class, and then doing it; however, what is usually best for the child is to allow the child some agency and responsibility for his or her own learning.

Emergent Curriculum

The foundation of emergent curriculum as an approach to curriculum planning is the Reggio Emilia. The Reggio Emilia is not a model nor is it a program; rather it is an early childhood education approach that works for the Reggio Emilia region in Italy but has been used to inspire educators in this country to adapt it to fit North American education culture (Wien, 2008). Philosophically, this approach views children and their teachers as capable, resourceful, creative, and collaborative. Emergent curriculum views the learner as sharing and responsive, especially to the living things in the environment. This responsiveness is not predetermined.

In emergent curriculum, teachers may have standards or outcomes dictated by the state or the particular program, but consideration is given to children's thinking, interests, and choices, and too many different means to reach the desired end or outcome. In this approach there is not a single, linear plan for a unit of study, but rather multiple routes and possibilities teacher and children can choose to reach the learning (Wien, 2008). Other key factors in emergent curriculum are open ideas for processing, collaborative work, recognizing that learning occurs through a variety of modes of expression, scaffolding ideas to expand and go deeper in thinking and responding, and documenting carefully and thoughtfully children's work and thinking. Children tackle real problems and have many hands-on experiences with the environment. Drawing is a significant strategy to learning more. Classrooms that engage children in emergent curriculum are characterized by a positive energy that contributes to the culture of the community. Motivation of children and teachers is natural, intrinsic, inspiring, and makes learning effortless.

Unit Ideas

In this text, **unit ideas** include numerous possible integrated activities for carrying out the theme or topic of study. It could be completed as a web. It results from selecting a topic and creating outcomes or objectives for the unit, and then brainstorming ideas for experiences in various areas of the curriculum (e.g., nutrition or food experiences, science experiences, art activities, field trips, visitors, music experiences, and literary experiences), resulting in an integrated curriculum approach. The unit brainstorm includes far more activities than could be realistically incorporated into the actual plan. Nevertheless, it provides a variety of possibilities and encourages the teacher to plan coordinated activities that support the desired outcomes and meet the needs of the children in the classroom. Following observation or documenting contextual factors, writing specific objectives, one could begin a TWS, project-based unit, or emergent curriculum planning with integrated unit ideas.

Appropriate subjects for unit themes are those that strengthen and broaden the young child's understanding of the world. State or common core standards for grades K–3 provide many ideas for developmentally appropriate unit topics. For instance, a unit on seeds geared to 5-year-old children could include some of the suggested activities in the unit ideas on seeds.

UNIT IDEAS ON SEEDS

Lesson plans or projects on seeds can be effectively planned in the fall, when so many plants, particularly weeds and trees, are shedding seeds; or they can be planned in the spring, which is the planting season for flowers, grains, and vegetables. Select activities based on the desired objectives, the concepts to be taught, the season of the year, and the needs and interests of the children. Integrate several of the content areas in order to add variety to the curriculum.

ART

- Seed collages
- Seed shakers (used in rhythm activities)
- Finger painting with seeds added to mixture
- Screen painting with seeds and pods
- Painting with wheat stems, especially bearded wheat
- Paperweight made with potter's clay with seeds pressed in

FIELD TRIPS

- Nature walk, to look for seeds
- Home garden or farm, to plant seeds or to watch gardener or farmer planting seeds
- Seed distributor, to see kinds and varieties of seeds and how they are sold
- Grocery store, to look for foods that are seeds (sesame seeds, sunflower seeds, peas, beans, corn)
- Granary, to observe storage of seeds (grains)
- Farm, to observe harvesting of grains or use of seeds (corn, barley, wheat) in feeding some animals

FOOD

- Chili
- Lima bean soup
- Green bean salad, casserole
- Corn casserole or chowder
- Corn on the cob
- Whole-wheat cereal
- Pea salad or casserole
- Bread sticks sprinkled with sesame seeds
- Seed sprouts (may be used in salad)
- Popcorn
- Food experiences using the seeds of fruits and vegetables that we eat (tomatoes, bananas, beans, peas, corn)
- Seeds that must be cooked before they are eaten
- Seeds that can be eaten without being cooked

SCIENCE

- Seeds that need the shell removed before eating
- Need for water, warmth, food, and air for seeds to sprout
- Differences among seeds in size, shape, color, and texture
- Avocado seed supported with toothpicks in a jar of water (observation of growth)
- Seeds sprouted and tasted (alfalfa, wheat, and beans work especially well)
- Planting seeds
- Study and tasting of seeds that we eat; comparison with inedible seeds
- Study of where the seeds are obtained
- Study of how and why seeds travel
- Comparison of the numbers of seeds produced by various plants
- Study and observation of seed pods

- Observation of the growing stages of seeds: Seeds (such as lima beans) are placed between glass slabs or between a plastic or glass jar and a (constantly) wet paper towel lining the jar; start new seeds every day for 3 to 5 days so that the day-by-day changes can be observed.

MUSIC

- Musical chairs. Place a seed package on the front of each chair (everyone has a chair). When the music stops, give directions, such as "All the carrot seeds stand up and jump around the circle" or "All the petunia seeds change places."
- Songs about seeds
- Decorated seed shakers used as rhythm-band instruments
- Seedpods such as dried honey-locust pods used as shakers; used to accompany a drumbeat or musical selection
- Creative movements relating to seeds, such as milkweed moving and floating through the air, or the growth and sprouting of seeds
- Creative dramatics involving the care of seeds

VISITORS

- Gardener
- Farmer
- Seed distributor
- Grocery store clerk
- Seed nursery worker
- Member of child's family to demonstrate seed planting and care
- Forest ranger

LANGUAGE AND LITERACY DEVELOPMENT

- Stories about seeds
- Informational or expository texts relating to seeds
- Poetry and choral readings on seeds
- Distributing seed or package of seeds to each child, who describes it, tells whether it is edible or inedible, says what it will grow into, how it is cared for, and so on
- Writing, telling, or dictating stories such as "If I were a seed, I would . . ." or "Seeds I like to eat are . . ."

Webbing or Clustering

The process of **webbing**, or **clustering**, is similar to doing an integrated unit brainstorm and, although the

end product looks different, it has the same result. The approach is to pick a theme, project, or concept and then brainstorm activities and ideas for teaching the concept. In developing engaging and productive themes through curriculum webbing, the following four steps are helpful (Barclay, Benelli, & Curtis, 1995, p. 206):

1. Identify a theme and related subtopics.
2. Brainstorm.
3. Identify desired learning outcomes.
4. Prepare for teaching.

Figure 4.1 is an example of a web on seeds. Throughout the text you will see examples of other webs. Teachers should not find it necessary to do both a unit idea brainstorm and a web, since they serve basically the same purpose.

Using the project approach to planning a study on seeds, the teacher may help the child brainstorm using his or her own experiences, knowledge, and ideas and then organize these into a topic or concept web. Figure 4.2 is an example of a child's project web on seeds. Note that the focus of these two webs (4.1 and 4.2) is the same, but they are approached in a different way. One is teacher brainstorming and the other is the child's ideas to consider for a project. Figure 4.3 illustrates a child's question web. The child's questions and inquiries guide the study.

A teacher's own preferences, teaching style, and background determine whether the unit ideas plan, theme web, or project web is used. In addition, the teacher's philosophy will drive actions. If the teacher desires to be in control of the curriculum, more direct, intentional methods will be chosen and may begin with unit ideas or theme webs to generate possibilities. On the other hand, the teacher may begin with ideas, but then seek input from the children based on their interests, ideas, backgrounds, and needs. In the case of the project approach, the teacher can begin the project or generate some interest in it, but then, with the teacher's guidance and following the web brainstorm, the children work individually or collaboratively on a level that they choose and with experiences that they select (Chard, 1998; Katz & Chard, 2000). In addition to science topics, social studies topics in early childhood work well as projects (Mindes, 2005). Maple (2005) described a 9-week project on the post office in a kindergarten/first-grade classroom. This project involved the whole class and included a field trip, journal writing, a mail carrier visit, and some role play with mail preparation and delivery.

Activity Plan

Using a more teacher-directed approach, once the unit brainstorm plan or web has been developed, the

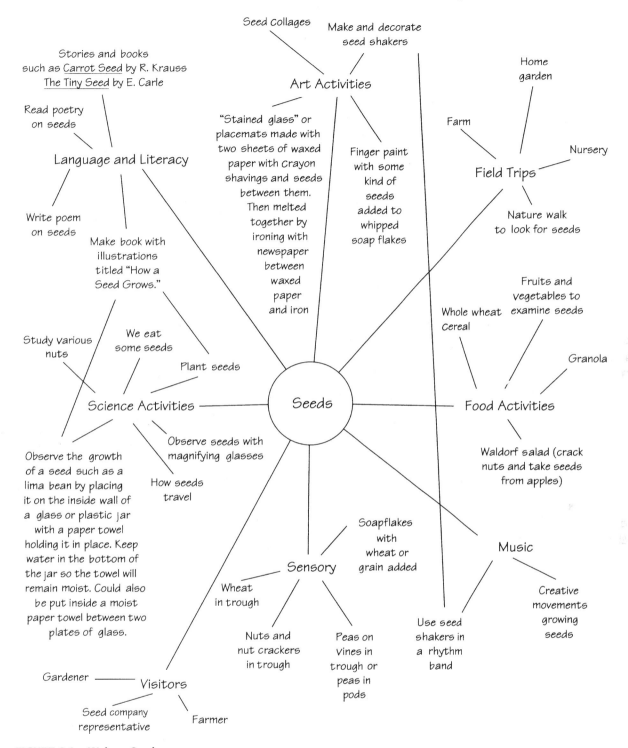

FIGURE 4.1   Web on Seeds

teacher selects from it the specific experiences to include in teaching. These selections should be made with respect to the goals that the teacher desires to accomplish. Most important, the needs and interests of the children need to be considered. Next the teacher formulates an **activity plan,** which is a sketch of the activities planned for each day throughout the duration of the unit. It provides an overview of the unit so it can be viewed in perspective. As a teacher moves from a unit brainstorm plan to an activity plan, there should be a balance of kinds of activities (art, music, language and literacy, etc.), as well as types of groups.

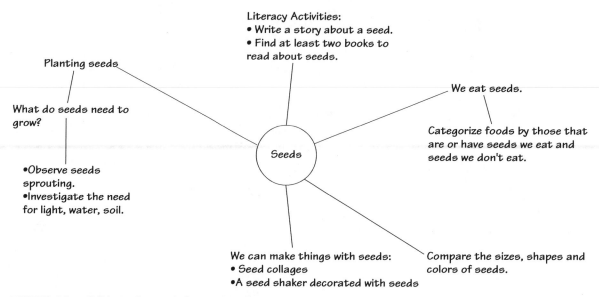

FIGURE 4.2   Child's Project Web for Seed Study

In the construction of the activity plan, include activities that correlate, reinforce, and support the theme and desired objectives. However, not all activities during the school day need to be, or should be, related to the theme. Too much constant exposure to one particular theme results in boredom, lack of interest, and frustration.

Following is an example of a 5-day activity plan on seeds. These experiences have been selected from the array of possibilities listed in the unit brainstorm plan or from the seed web. The activities are designated as individual, small group, and whole group so that a balance of these three kinds of participation can be achieved.

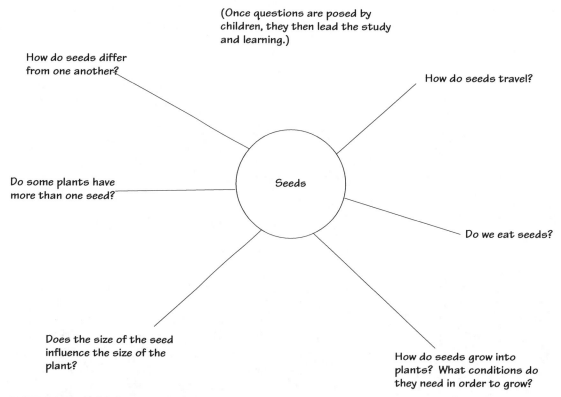

FIGURE 4.3   Child's Question Web for Seed Study

Sorting various kinds of seeds or beans increases skills in matching, identification, discrimination, and classification.

ACTIVITY PLAN ON SEEDS

DAY 1

Whole-Group Activity

SCIENCE

- How seeds grow
- Planting a lima bean seed

Small-Group Activity

FIELD TRIP

- Seed walk

Individual Activities

- Bubble blowing
- Seeds in sensory area

DAY 2

Whole-Group Activities

MUSIC

- Rhythm experience using seed pods

SCIENCE

- Seeds that travel

Small-Group Activity

ART

- Seed shakers

Individual Activities

- Easel with seed-shaped paper and green paint

SCIENCE

- Observing growth of lima bean planted yesterday and planting another bean today

DAY 3

Whole-Group Activity

VISITOR

- Musician and playing seed shakers

Small-Group Activity

ART

- Seed collages

Individual Activities

- Paperweight made from potter's clay with seeds pressed in

SCIENCE

- Observing and exploring foods with seeds
- Observing growth of bean plant and planting another bean today

DAY 4

Whole-Group Activity

SCIENCE

- Seeds we eat

Small-Group Activity

FOOD

- Chili

Individual Activities

- Peanuts and other nuts in the sensory area
- Shape tracing and cutting

SCIENCE

- Observing growth of bean plants and planting another bean

DAY 5

Whole-Group Activity

- Photographs on bulletin board to teach positional words and enhance self-esteem

Small-Group Activity

ART

- Finger painting with seeds added

Individual Activities

- Sorting and classifying seeds

SCIENCE

- Observing the growth of bean plants and planting another bean

Daily Schedule of Activities

The daily schedule of activities is an elaboration of the activity plan and a simplification of the lesson or unit plan. For experienced teachers or students who are at an advanced level, the daily schedule of activities may replace both the activity plan and the lesson plan, even though the objectives must be carefully thought through. The daily schedule of activities specifies the order of activities, approximate length of time, person responsible (if you are working with several teachers), specific responsibilities of individuals, and materials needed. This plan adapts easily to chart form with different columns added, depending on the needs of the program. Such assignments as setting up outdoor equipment, cleaning, and greeting may be included. Routines of the program, such as snacks, may also be added to the chart, showing the teacher assigned to the preparation and the time it is to be presented. When doing a daily schedule of activities plan for a full-day program, include such additional routines as lunch, rest time, and reading and writing workshops. (Your instructor may show you an example of a Daily Schedule of Activities plan for seeds.) The plans can be adapted to either half-day or full-day programs. The number of activities remains basically the same, because longer programs have additional routines of meals, individual play, and quiet periods.

Transitions are another issue to be taken into account when planning the daily schedule. Without strategies to eliminate challenging behaviors, transitioning from one activity to another is often an invitation for chaos in the classroom. Songs, clapping particular rhythms, piano chords, turning off the lights and other signals are nonverbal ways of telling the children to prepare for a change in activity or setting. "Designing a schedule that minimizes transitions and maximizes the time children spend engaged in developmentally appro-

priate activities is the first step in decreasing challenging behavior" (Hammeter, Ostrosky, Artman, & Kinder, 2008).

Lesson Plan

In the direct, teacher-centered approach, after the unit is seen in broad perspective through the activity plan and the specifics are defined in the daily schedule of activities, lesson planning takes place. Or, if you are preparing a TWS, after you have completed the Contextual Factors, Objectives, and Assessment sections, you are then ready to do the Instruction Design work, which is the lesson plans for the unit of instruction. It may be helpful for you to do a unit ideas brainstorm and even an Activity Plan before planning the lessons for your unit. The **lesson plans** include specific procedures for the learning activities. The teacher has selected a theme and has determined its benefit and value to the developing child. Through listed objectives, the teacher harmonizes the lesson plan's activities, using a variety of instructional contexts, with the children's abilities and needs. Specific accommodations and adaptations for meeting special needs can be included. Objectives are directed to the children's cognitive, language, social/emotional, and physical development. Objectives are also specifically written outcomes of the content for children to know as a result of the lesson or unit. Assessments are aligned to the desired outcomes or objectives.

If a more child-centered approach is desired, at this stage, before the specific activities are planned, seek input from the children. Their interests determine which activities to select. Students are more engaged and interested when they make decisions about their own learning. The webs and plans shared as examples in this book cannot reflect this child-centered focus. All are examples, and it will be up to the individual teacher to develop a philosophical, child-centered approach that will result in children making choices and decisions about their own learning activities.

When viewing the lesson planning in perspective, the teacher should keep in mind some general, overall objectives to be accomplished during the unit. For example, if the unit plan or TWS is on seeds, what will be the general objectives and/or concepts to be stressed and taught? What are the various interests of the children, and what variety of background knowledge do they have? The value of the TWS model is that these questions are answered in the Contextual Factors portion of the lesson or unit. In addition to theme-related objectives, child-related objectives help to meet the specific needs of the children. For example, a child-oriented objective may be that "the children will put away their own equipment and materials" or that "the children will become more independent in solving their own problems." These objectives are valuable in meeting nonacademic objectives or outcomes. The goals for a program are general, and the objectives for the unit are overarching, but lesson objectives are specific. They are clear and concise, describing what the children should know, do, or feel as a result of the lesson. The verbs in the objectives deal with concrete outcomes or tasks that can be observed and checked for achievement or completion. (Use the verbs suggested in Bloom's taxonomy on page 67.) In addition, the objectives should be based on content standards for various disciplines or outlined in the standards for each state.

Keep in mind that as teachers gain experience and insight, the amount of writing in lesson plans will diminish. Also, remember that the more children can make choices and use their own questions regarding what is to be learned and the activities involved, the more powerful and motivated they feel and the more engaged and meaningful their learning is.

Multiple Intelligences

Howard Gardner has proposed a theory of multiple intelligences, and teachers in every grade level, including early childhood teachers, are finding appropriate classroom applications of the theory. Howard Gardner's theory of multiple intelligences challenges the traditional notions of IQ as well as the SAT (Scholastic Aptitude Test). He suggested that intelligence refers to the ability of humans to solve problems or to make something valued in a particular culture (Checkley, 1997). In his book *Frames of Mind* (2011), Gardner proposed that our culture has too narrowly defined intelligence and that actually there are at least 8 basic intelligences. His theory has become ubiquitous and is known as the multiple intelligences theory (MI theory). Gardner also suggested that intelligence has more to do with the capacity for solving problems and fashioning products than with the isolated tasks on standard IQ tests.

Armstrong (2009, pp. 15, 16) suggests four key points in MI theory:

1. Each person possesses all eight intelligences. Some people have high levels of functioning in most intelligences; others are highly developed in one or two intelligences and more modestly or underdeveloped in the other intelligences.
2. Most people can develop each intelligence to an adequate level of competency.
3. Intelligences usually work together in complex ways. Intelligences interact and support one another.
4. There are many ways to be intelligent within each category. There is no standard set of qualities, characteristics, or attributes that a person must have to be intelligent in a particular area.

Gardner does not advocate a single way to teach and does not believe that there is a blueprint for teaching (Checkley, 1997). However, he does believe that MI the-

ory, when understood, encourages teachers to take individual differences into account and help all children to use their minds well (Checkley, 1997). In applying the MI model in the classroom, teachers move away from traditional forms of teaching, including lecturing and requiring students to do written work and assignments. Rather, an MI classroom looks much like a DAP (Developmentally Appropriate Practice) early childhood classroom. The MI classroom, like the DAP early childhood classroom, includes a variety of presentation methods and activities, including music, art, and creative activities and hands-on experiences in science, nature, drama, and other areas, and gives children opportunities to interact with others in both small and large groups. The MI classroom also gives time to work alone and reflect quietly or even write in one's personal journal. In terms of assessment, Gardner advocates that teachers allow students to demonstrate understanding in a variety of ways (Checkley, 1997).

When teachers apply the MI model to their teaching, it is suggested that they think of the intelligences and how they may be appropriately integrated into a particular unit or lesson, providing a balance of the eight intelligences in the activities. By doing this, all students can have their strongest intelligences incorporated at least some of the time. Armstrong (2009, p. 65) suggests that once the objective of a unit or lesson is in mind, teachers can ask the following questions to address the eight intelligences:

1. *Logical–Mathematical:* How can I bring in numbers, calculations, logic, classifications, or critical thinking?
2. *Linguistic:* How can I use the spoken or written word?
3. *Spatial:* How can I use visual aids, visualization, color, art, or metaphor?
4. *Musical:* How can I bring in music or environmental sounds, or set key points in a rhythmic or melodic framework?
5. *Bodily–Kinesthetic:* How can I involve the whole body or use hands-on experiences?
6. *Naturalist:* How can I incorporate living things, natural phenomena, or ecological awareness?
7. *Interpersonal:* How can I engage students in peer sharing, cooperative learning, or large-group simulation?
8. *Intrapersonal:* How can I evoke personal feelings or memories or give students choices?

ADDITIONAL CONSIDERATIONS FOR INSTRUCTIONAL PLANNING

Following are some additional considerations when designing instruction. In the chapters that follow, several of these are included in unit ideas and in unit and lesson plans. All four are areas than need to be integrated into early childhood curriculum planning. General guidelines are shared for planning field trips, visitors, service learning, and integration of technology.

Field Trips

Programs establish relationships with and use community resources to support the achievement of program goals (NAEYC Accreditation Standards and Criteria, Standard 8, 2008). Because field trips are an integral part of the early childhood curriculum and are not discussed elsewhere in this text, we have included them in this curriculum-planning chapter. Teachers need to follow important guidelines in both planning and implementing field trips.

GUIDELINES FOR FIELD TRIPS.   Field trips must have a purpose in order to have meaning for children. They are planned as an extension of the children's experiences and to clarify subjects about which the children may have misconceptions or misinformation, not just to have fun, provide variety, or take a trip someplace. Field trips should be tied closely to the curriculum; they are often the means by which children make sense and meaning out of what is being taught in the classroom. They need to be kept simple so that they are manageable and developmentally appropriate for young children.

Every school is located in a unique community to explore, and many successful field trips can be planned as walking trips. When planning field trips, consider the type of transportation available. Budgets may provide for buses for a monthly field trip or may prevent the frequent use of buses. Some programs have parent volunteers to provide cars for transportation.

VALUE AND BENEFITS OF FIELD TRIPS.   When field trips are planned carefully and with purpose, they provide numerous benefits.

- Children participate in real experiences with people, places, and things; what is seen, heard, smelled, and felt is most often what is remembered. Also, when experiences are firsthand, the opportunity for knowledge and understanding is enhanced.
- Field trips provide excellent opportunities to reinforce and extend concepts and notions.
- Field trips expand children's knowledge of the world about them, including the diversity of people and cultures.

PLANNING A FIELD TRIP.   When planning field trips, carefully consider a number of important points.

1. *The length of time that the trip will take.* For half-day programs, the actual bus or car ride to the site should take no more than 20 minutes. For full-

day programs, plan no more than 1 hour of riding time each way. Young children tire too easily to travel farther. If the zoo is a 90-minute ride one way, wait until the children are older, and it will be much more effective for them. Third- or fourth-grade children would still be able to enjoy the zoo even though they had a long ride to get there.

2. *The children's safety.* Every effort must be made to ensure the safety of the participants. Whether walking or riding, getting to and from the field trip site must be carefully considered. If the children are riding, drivers should be provided with maps so that they know exactly where to go and the route to be followed. If riding in cars, the children must be required to wear seat belts. Arrange for enough vehicles to comply with this rule. Drivers must be properly licensed, and their vehicles must have appropriate insurance. During the field trip, count the children often. *Never leave a field trip site, or a stop along the way, without making certain that every child is accounted for.*

3. *The ages, attention spans, special needs, and interest levels of the children.* Field trips must be carefully evaluated with respect to the children being taken, with particular consideration given to children with special needs. For example, if there are children in wheelchairs, the transportation, site access, and restroom facilities must accommodate their needs.

4. *Adult supervision.* Plan for adequate adult supervision based on the number of children going on the field trip. For children ages 2 to 3, there should be one adult for every 3 to 4 children; for ages 4 to 6, there should be one adult for every 4 to 5 children; for ages 7 to 8, there should be one adult for every 5 to 6 children. Encourage the supervising adults to ask and answer questions, explain, and extend desired concepts.

5. *Permission.* Permission must be obtained from parents or guardians. Some schools or programs allow for a single written and signed permission to be obtained from parents at the beginning of the year that covers all field trips during the year. The permission should give legal permission for the child to go on field trips, and it should also release the school from liability in case of accident. Parents must be notified of all field trips that the children take and know when and where they are going.

6. *Visit site before the actual field trip.* The teacher should visit the site of the field trip before the children visit. This provides information regarding the required travel time and route and an estimate of the approximate length of the visit. If applicable, the teacher should inform the person on site who will be responsible for the discussion regarding the purpose of the visit, concepts to be

taught, the age level of the children, and the amount of time available. The availability and locations of restrooms should be noted.

7. ***Need for snacks or lunches.*** Preparations for snacks or lunches should be made if warranted by the length of the field trip experience.

8. ***Preparation of the children.*** Children need to be adequately prepared for and introduced to the field trip. They should be told why they are taking the trip, what to expect and look for, what safety precautions they should follow, and any limits that must be observed. Small groups of children should be assigned to individual adults who will supervise them and with whom they should stay at all times. For safety reasons, children should *not* wear nametags.

Suggestions for Field Trips

The following are suggested field trip ideas. Add other possibilities to this list, especially those unique to your own community.

- Community nature center
- Zoo
- Farm
- Neighborhood business, park, or home
- Pet store or a home with pets
- Bus ride
- Grocery store
- Park
- Cemetery
- Department store
- A parent's place of work
- Fire station
- Post office
- Police department
- Library
- Nursing home
- Shut-in neighbor
- Children's museum
- Field, park, or open space to fly kites
- High school, college, or university music department
- Music store
- Touch, sound, or smell walk
- Train station
- Butcher shop or fish market
- Treasure hunt
- Historical site or monument
- Warehouse
- Weather bureau
- Fish hatchery
- Art gallery
- Observatory
- Bakery
- Aquarium
- Newspaper printing facility

FIELD TRIP FOLLOW-UP. Field trips are the most successful when the learning is extended with both pre- and post-activities (Patton & Kokoski, 1996). Pre-activities could include reading about the topic of interest, looking through magazine pictures, or watching a video. A variety of classroom learning activities could focus on the concept or theme of the field trip. Post-activities might involve writing notes of appreciation, journal entries, art projects with materials gathered while on the field trip, group or individual story writing, and so on.

Following the field trip, teachers should get feedback to determine comprehension. Use pictures, books and stories, filmstrips and videos, dramatic play, visitors, music, art, and discussions to clarify and enrich the experience, as well as to provide outlets for expressions of feeling. As the children recall their experiences, the alert, observant teacher can evaluate the benefit of the field trip and catch any misconceptions that need to be clarified or concepts that need reinforcement. Language experience charts can be used to record the children's memories, and over time these can be used to recall trips taken. Depending on the age of the children, letters can be written or pictures drawn as a "thank you" to adults who provided transportation and supervision or to those who guided the children at the field trip site.

Visitors

Sometimes people are willing to visit the center or school. For example, instead of having the children go to the fire station, firefighters may prefer to bring equipment to the school. Therefore, determine whether it is best to plan for a field trip or a visitor. Inviting visitors into the classroom is less disruptive to the school day and requires less paperwork and concern than field trips. To determine whether a visitor or field trip would be best, think about the objectives for the experience. A general guideline is that students should be taken on field trips only for the experiences that cannot be duplicated in the classroom.

When visitors come into the classroom, they give the children the opportunity to interact with and glean information from someone from the community. The teacher can guide the children in using the information from the visitor to strengthen and add to the concepts

Visitors and field trips allow learning to extend beyond the immediate classroom.

and notions that they are working on with their project or unit of study.

When inviting visitors into the classroom, follow some of the same guidelines outlined for field trips: The visits should have meaning and be tied to the curriculum. The visitors should know precisely the purpose of their visit and what is expected of them. They should be encouraged to talk on a level that the children can understand. They should be given a specific time limit. Some people should not be invited because they cannot speak on a level that the children understand or lack an understanding of young children and their needs.

Just as the children need to be prepared ahead of time for a field trip, they also need to be prepared beforehand for a visit from someone in the community. Knowing in advance the purpose of the person's visit, they can be encouraged to think of questions to ask the visitor and be reminded of courtesies that should be extended to any classroom guest. The following are suggestions for classroom visitors; for almost any topic, there are several community resource people. One of the best resources for visitors is family members of students. They have jobs that are interesting and hobbies and talents to be shared with the children.

This list is just a beginning; a teacher's own thinking and imagination will provide numerous other possibilities.

Suggested Classroom Visitors

Person to demonstrate a hobby or skill such as coin collection, bread making, tortilla making, flower arranging, origami, or gardening

Community helpers

Musician

Person to share language, traditions, artifacts, foods, or customs from his or her culture or from one that he or she has visited

Parent to bring an infant

Pet store owner or parent, grandparent, or neighbor with a pet

Angler

Magician

Dancer

Elected official

Baker

Librarian

Medical personnel

Dentist

Banker

Service Learning

The phenomenon of service learning is sweeping our classrooms and schools. There is growing research and evidence that points to school-based service learning as an effective means of influencing children and the needs of the community. Some programs are obtaining grants to infuse service learning into the curriculum. However, many classrooms and programs are able to integrate service learning into the curriculum without additional funding. In some communities, service learning is part of districtwide or schoolwide projects, but many individual classrooms or programs plan and implement service learning projects that involve substantial hours of service to agencies or programs in the community (Melchior,

2000). Service learning strengthens the bond and often creates a partnership between school and community. Research concludes that the work and effort of students is appreciated and viewed as valuable by community members and agencies (Melchior, 2000).

Technology and Computers

Although we were once asking whether we should include the use of computers in our classrooms, we are now asking how we can incorporate the technology into our ever-expanding curriculum! Young children can and should have access to a variety of media, and technology should be used to extend and enrich the curriculum. Early childhood teachers should know basic operations of the computer, guidelines for choosing appropriate software, how to use the computer for instructional purposes, and how to use the computer for instructional support such as keeping records and communicating with parents via e-mail (Bewick & Kostelnik, 2004). Technology can give families opportunity for consistent communication with their children's teachers (Ray & Shelton, 2004).

There is evidence that almost 94% of public schools in the United States have access to computers and the Internet (U.S. Department of Education, 2006), but many teachers do not use the technology available to them (Bewick & Kostelnik, 2004). National organizations have given early childhood teachers standards and guidelines for integrating technology into their classrooms. ISTE (International Society for Technology in Education) has created technology standards for all grades including PreK–2 (ISTE, 2007). NAEYC has prepared a position statement on the use of technology in early childhood (NAEYC, 1996c).

We must critically examine the effect of computers in children's lives and determine how they can be used for the children's benefit. A variety of media and technologies can be incorporated in the early childhood classroom, but whatever is added must be connected thoughtfully and appropriately to get positive results (Rafferty, 1999). Children are attracted to technology and intrinsically motivated to use computers (Guthrie & Richardson, 1995). The purpose of computer technology in the classroom is to supplement, not replace, classroom activities such as art, music, blocks, dramatic play, books, writing, and outside play (NAEYC, 1996c). Computers become valuable as they enhance, not substitute for, discovery and exploration through sensory experiences. They offer unlimited opportunities for learning through manipulation, creative problem solving, and self-directed exploration (Clements & Swaminathan, 1995).

The ISTE (2007) developed the following National Educational Technology Standards for Students that identify competence, skills, and knowledge all students need to succeed in technology:

1. Demonstrate creativity and innovation
2. Communicate and collaborate
3. Conduct research and use information
4. Think critically, solve problems, and make decisions
5. Practice digital citizenship
6. Use technology effectively and productively

In addition, ISTE developed Profiles or indicators of achievement for particular stages. Teachers should use the following as they plan technology experiences in early childhood. They are the PreK–2 (ages 4–8) Profiles for technology literate students:

NATIONAL EDUCATIONAL TECHNOLOGY STANDARDS FOR STUDENTS PreK–2 (2007), P. 12

Technology and digital learning activities for PreK–2: (The numbers in parentheses following each activity identify the standards, 1–6, linked to the activity described.)

- Illustrate and communicate original ideas and stories using digital tools and media-rich resources. (1, 2)
- Identify, research, and collect data on an environmental issue using digital resources and propose a developmentally appropriate solution. (1, 3, 4)
- Engage in learning activities with learners from multiple cultures through e-mail and other electronic means. (2, 6)
- In a collaborative work group, use a variety of technologies to produce a digital presentation or product in a curriculum area. (1, 2, 6)
- Find and evaluate information related to a current or historical person or event using digital resources. (3)

- Use simulations and graphical organizers to explore and depict patterns of growth such as the life cycles of plants and animals. (1, 3, 4)
- Demonstrate the safe and cooperative use of technology. (5)
- Independently apply digital tools and resources to address a variety of tasks and problems. (4, 6)
- Communicate about technology using developmentally appropriate and accurate terminology. (6)
- Demonstrate the ability to navigate in virtual environments such as electronic books, simulation software, and Web sites. (6)

Problem-solving skills must be developed through real-life experiences. "The real test of a pupil's competence is not the mere possession of a skill, but rather performance in a real situation" (Tener, 1995/1996, p. 100). The most important strategy for children using computers in solving problems is for them to create their own solutions. When accomplishing a task on their own, they feel empowered, have increased self-confidence, and develop a keener sense of identity (Bauer, Sheerer, & Dettore, 1997). Children receive the most benefit when computer experiences are supported by concrete activities. Two ways for teachers to ensure that this occurs are: (a) design specific supplemental activities, or (b) integrate the computer experiences into the general curriculum (Haugland, 1995). Technology should be integrated into the curriculum in such a way that it supports instruction, intellectual thinking, and curiosity (Guthrie & Richardson, 1995); in addition, it should prepare students for tools that they will be expected to have mastered as they live and work in the world of tomorrow.

Computer effectiveness in the early years of learning can be achieved only when teachers develop competence in computer literacy by understanding how a computer functions and the basic principles of programming. Computer literacy programs should teach teachers to assess the appropriate use of computers in the classroom, locate suitable computer hardware and computer-related materials, and evaluate software for young children.

Before we discuss the selection of software, a caution: Because some of the children's families will not have computers in their homes, it is important to take that into consideration as we plan our curriculum. It is also helpful if we determine where parents and children can have access to computers (public libraries; college, high school, or elementary school computer labs; community centers; and so on).

Selecting the computer is not as important as selecting the software. A proliferation of software programs have been developed at a much more rapid pace than we can keep up with. Many make excellent contributions to early childhood education, but even more do not! Frequent in-service training should be helpful in preparing teachers to make wise selections of the software that is available for the classroom. Computer software should not be used to fill empty time or because it happens to be convenient and readily available. We should ask two pertinent questions when evaluating the software programs for our schools: Why is a particular program in the classroom? What does the program teach young children?

Computers should not just entertain; they must support and extend children's learning. For children to benefit from technology in the classroom, software must be reinforced with concrete activities, be open ended and exploratory, teach about cause-and-effect relationships, emphasize the discovery process (Haugland, 1995), and be developmentally appropriate (Copple & Bredekamp, 2009).

When selecting software for children to use on the computer, consider the four criteria suggested by computer experts Susan Haugland and Dan Shade, in Diffily and Morrison (1996, p. 104):

- Is it age appropriate for the child?
- Is it designed to give the child control?
- Is it easy for the child to understand?
- Is it relatively easy for the child to use alone?

These four questions will aid us in our choice of children's software.

Because of the challenging bombardment of continually changing and advancing technologies and programs, it is difficult for us, as educators, to feel competent in directing the uses of computers in our schools (Gatewood & Conrad, 1997). In fact, most teachers do not receive adequate training for using technology in the classrooms. Technology training needs to be ongoing and tailored to the needs of individual teachers (Hurst, 1994). As inadequate as we may feel regarding the computer in our curriculum, remember: Good teachers are not those who know the most facts or information, "but rather those who continually incorporate new information in creative ways" (Riel, 1994, p. 465).

Let us consider computer technology as simply another avenue through which all children learn. Use of the computer, like the use of other media, must be carefully planned to meet the level of understanding of the children in the classroom. Care must also be taken to teach the children how to use the computer. How exciting it is to see the effects of computer exploration on young children when it is carefully integrated into a well-planned early childhood curriculum. Computers offer children opportunities to develop greater control, expand their ways of learning, connect with classrooms all over the world, and access vast amounts of information.

The thrill of being on the cutting edge of technology can permeate your entire building or center, giving confidence, vision, and life skills to faculty as well as students. It will foster a positive image of your school and engender dynamic, mutually beneficial partnerships with parents, businesses, and other community organizations (L. J. Wilson, 1997).

Summary

Brandt (2000), thinking futuristically, envisions a structure for curriculum in the future with the following characteristics:

- Has greater depth and less superficial coverage
- Focuses on problem solving that requires using learning strategies

- Emphasizes both skills and knowledge of the subjects
- Provides for students' individual differences
- Offers a common core to all students
- Coordinates closely
- Integrates selectively
- Emphasizes the learned curriculum
- Pays greater attention to personal relevance, while drawing on other streams as well

These characteristics are those that early childhood educators must consider seriously. They might well be a guide for teachers in planning and designing curriculum changes based on the content in this chapter.

The curriculum is everything that takes place in the classroom to meet the needs of the children. This includes attention to the context, the determination of goals and objectives, the needs assessment, and the scheduling of the curriculum, including planning the unit, project, or lesson. Following the unit or lesson attention should be given to *if* and *how* diverse needs were met and to analysis of student achievement of desired outcomes. Teachers must be accountable for student achievement. Teachers must also be reflective practitioners, and continual evaluation should take place regarding the curriculum; the children's learning, involvement, and development; and the teacher.

Because the teacher in most cases does the planning, scheduling, and evaluating, the teacher is the key to their combined success. The cooperative learning strategy is a versatile and valuable approach that encourages children to learn from their peers in a cooperative environment. Field trips, visitors, and service learning activities are valuable elements of the curriculum and

Computer software should be developmentally appropriate and supplement, not replace, traditional classroom activities.

often teach and share things with young children that the teacher alone could not do. Early childhood teachers need to become experts at using and incorporating technology into the curriculum. They need to be discerning and wise as they critically select the software for their computer, making sure it is developmentally appropriate and can be used while children work alone at the computer. With commitment, responsibility, and dedication, an exciting and meaningful program can be planned and implemented. When this happens, children not only benefit, they reap great rewards.

Student Learning Activities

1. Visit an early childhood classroom and talk with the teacher about the method or methods of instructional planning used. Compare the approach to those presented in this chapter. Even though the approach will most likely differ from the one in this book, are the basic ingredients and questions (Why? What? How?) part of the planning? You may wish to visit with several early childhood teachers to discuss and evaluate various approaches to instructional design.

2. From visits or observations you have previously made in early childhood classrooms or from currently planned visits, evaluate the scheduling. How did the scheduling in the class-

room compare to that suggested in this chapter? Were you able to observe some free play during each visit? How do you feel about free play in early childhood classrooms, and what can it accomplish?

3. Select one of the themes suggested in the chapter or one of your own choosing and complete a TWS, integrated unit brainstorm plan, web, or project according to the format suggested in this chapter. Do not select a theme for which a unit plan or web has already been completed in this book. Follow with preparation of a daily activity plan, daily schedule of activities, TWS or unit plan, lesson plan, project outline, or whatever your instructor suggests.

Suggested Resources

VIDEOS AND DVDs

A Children's Journey: Investigating the Fire Truck. (video on the project approach). Teachers College Press.

Instructional strategies for the differentiated classroom: Tiered assignments. Insight Media.

Lesson planning. Insight Media.

Portfolio assessment. School Improvement Network.

Using the power of technology to improve student achievement. Insight Media.

A visit to a differentiated classroom. Insight Media.

Online Resources

There are thousands of websites that have great ideas for lesson planning and other aspects of instructional design for the early childhood classroom. We suggest you explore them and bookmark the ones that will be most helpful to you.

www.homepage.mac.com/dara_feldman/Techcon.html   This website is the creation of Dara Feldman, a kindergarten teacher in Montgomery County, Maryland, who compiled technology resources to assist teachers in using computers effectively in their classrooms.

www.teach-nology.com/teachers/early_education/curriculum   Articles, teaching tips, lesson plans, and other tools for early childhood teachers are available on this site.

www.education-world.com/a_earlychildhood   This site offers lesson plans, professional development, newsletters, and other support for early childhood education instructional planning.

part 2
Personal and Social Development

All children need to learn people skills. We do not live alone, and people everywhere need to learn to relate initially to themselves and then to others around them. The ability to relate to others depends on one's attitude toward oneself and toward other people. Positive relationships among children, teachers, and parents are the foundation of everything we do in early childhood education. The ability to live effectively within the family and later to function capably within the community—neighborhood, classroom, and peer group—hinges on social skills that we begin to learn in early childhood.

Children are all unique, with strengths and characteristics singular to themselves. They recognize differences in people, and begin to develop attitudes and ideas about these differences. As children also learn about these diversities, we can also help them realize that there are more similarities than differences among people. All children—indeed, all people!—should be accepted and valued for these differences, yet accepted and valued as separate individuals who share common concerns, feelings, desires, hopes, and dreams. Attitudes of respect, trust, and care should permeate the entire environment of our early childhood classrooms!

Developing social skills is not an easy task. It takes knowledge of correct relationship skills, in addition to time, experience, and practice. We must be patient as we provide assistance and guidance to children who struggle to develop positive social and emotional skills. These skills can be taught and learned, but most importantly "caught" from the teacher, who provides the model. A teacher's own attitude toward the self, children, and adults is one of the most powerful forces in this process. If the teacher likes and enjoys others, particularly children, the child receives the message that people are to be liked, respected, and esteemed.

The world is the only limit in creating socioemotional skills studies for children! During the early childhood years, teachers can select units from areas such as sociology, economics, geography, history, and anthropology. Remember: Gear the units and concepts to the level of the children, and provide social studies activities with concrete learning experiences, such as classroom visitors and field trips. Many of these concepts, elementary as they may seem, remain abstract unless they are made concrete through carefully planned learning. Through exploring rich thematic units relating to social studies, children develop a sense of who they are, the culture they live in, and their civic responsibility. Planning for social studies units and experiences needs to be based on "both content (organized around important child questions) and process (action-oriented strategies)" (Mindes, 2005, p. 17).

Along with all the cognitive notions about the self and others, we hope that children are taught, by example as well as concept, that people are important and have feelings, and that all of us need to be sensitive, respectful, and caring about the feelings of others. Children learn good citizenship and what a democracy is through firsthand experiences in pulling together as a group (Cartwright, 2004).

chapter 5
Appreciating Differences

In the twenty-first century, young children must operate in a society that values respect for diversity and appreciation of conventions and rules in a broad spectrum. (Mindes, 2005, p. 15)

Our country is more culturally diversified now than it has ever been in its history (Washington & Andrews, 2010). Although children are alike in many ways, each is uniquely different from any other: gender, age, physical and mental ability, ethnicity, family structure, linguistics, geographical location, socioeconomic status, religion, beliefs, attitudes, values, customs, and culture. How children feel about and treat others is influenced by their own regard for themselves, as well as the social skills that they have learned from home, school, and other cultural and community groups. "Culture influences our thoughts and behaviors and is shared by a group, passed on to members of the group, and changes over time" (Bradley & Kibera, 2006, p. 35). From the earliest years, children need help and guidance in developing positive social values and skills in learning to relate to others effectively. Once again, warm, responsive, and attentive teachers are models for treating, speaking to, and behaving toward others. Early childhood teachers need patience as they work with children who are often very inexperienced in social behaviors. Teachers should display positive attitudes that serve as models for having friends, learning how to treat others, and understanding the social environment.

A multicultural, antibias approach to learning is a way of looking at the world that challenges our often narrow and distorting views of culture and seeks more thoughtful and inclusive teaching. It involves respecting others and their differences. Spring (2004) suggests four goals of multicultural education:

1. Work to build tolerance of other cultures.
2. Abolish racism.
3. Teach substance from various cultures.
4. Teach and help students to view the world from different cultural perspectives.

When young students develop a spirit and attitude of acceptance, an understanding of various cultures, and an ability to understand a different frame of reference, this increases their sensitivity and knowledge and promotes actively working for social justice as they mature (Spring, 2004). Multicultural education "is a movement designed to empower all students to become knowledgeable, caring, and active citizens in a deeply troubled and ethnically polarized nation and world" (Banks, 1993, p. 22).

As concepts about people are taught on a daily basis and in specific units, the focus must be primarily on similarities, as well as promoting an appreciation for differences. Learning to identify similarities and respect and accept the nature of differences among peers helps children to realize how much we all actually have in common. Differences are to be celebrated recognized as sources of strength. "The goal of diversity is unity. Only when we can come together freely, as we are, feeling good about who we are, can we create a healthy unity among all people . . ." (Gonzalez-Mena, 2008, p. 14). Valuing diversity means that we see differences in group or personal attributes as positive and normal (Epstein, 2009). "Respecting diversity means treating people as individuals, not as stereotypes, and recognizing that individuals simultaneously share common characteristics and differ in others" (Epstein, 2009, p. 91).

In stressing similarities rather than differences, it becomes evident that all children live in some type of family unit, participate in family activities, play games and enjoy toys, learn songs and stories, celebrate holidays, express similar feelings and emotions, and communicate with one another. By discussing differences, children can see that their specific behaviors are simply one way of doing things, not the only or the best way. Children will then be able to understand and appreciate how people are different. Our world will be richer as we "celebrate and respect different perspectives and ways of approaching learning and life . . ." (Washington & Andrews, 2010, p. 66).

Accepting and understanding similarities and differences is also very important with respect to children who have special needs, those whose learning and behavioral characteristics differ substantially from others and who require special methods of instruction. A basic understanding of particular categories of exceptionality (their characteristics, possible teaching strategies, and available community specialists) helps teachers in caring for children and planning programs.

Children's orientation to the social world and their initial development of social skills begin in the family unit and with the formation of early friendships. The most critical time for shaping positive cultural understanding is during the early childhood years. This is the time to start preventing children from developing biases and prejudices as their attitudes, values, and beliefs begin to form.

Focusing on how lives are similar, yet sometimes different, helps children to expand their awareness of others, increases their capacity to accept and cooperate with others, and enhances their own positive self-concepts and esteem. "Respecting diversity means being able to honor ways of being and doing things that are different from one's own, even practices that may feel wrong when we first come into contact with them" (Keyser, 2006, p. 9).

> We must be very careful that we do not teach children that others who are different are inferior. Often teachers ignore these differences as if they do not exist, assuming that children will naturally grow up to approach the differences in positive ways.

Derman-Sparks and Edwards (2010) emphasize the need for teachers to confront, rather than ignore, the issues of diversity in their classrooms. When we do not openly discuss concerns, prejudices, racism, and feelings, children resort to physical confrontations and find unacceptable ways to get rid of their anger, intolerance, and frustrations. By opening the lines of communication and discussing diversity issues, we give children ways of dealing with their feelings and, at the same time, overcome negative emotions and reactions.

TEACHING AND VALUING DIVERSITY

Developing the Perspective of Diversity

The United States, with a broad range of ethnic and cultural groups, is one of the most diverse countries in the world. Recognizing the value and importance of each individual, while respecting and accepting one another's differences, is essential to maximum growth and development. "Culture is the fundamental building block of identity . . . . Through cultural learning, children gain a feeling of belonging, a sense of personal history, and security in knowing who they are and where they come from" (Lally, 1995, p. 66). Even though culture is often referred to when addressing diversity of minorities or specific groups of people, we must remember that we are all members of cultures and are greatly influenced by them (Copple & Bredekamp, 2009). Our individual cultures are shaped by such things as family structures, customs, and rules; educational backgrounds; interpersonal relationships; travel experiences; and religious beliefs. Culture also includes all the subtle aspects of both verbal and nonverbal communication that people use all the time. We all have language and culture, which are the very essence of who and what we are. Through activities and discussion, we should respect and develop children's ideas and encourage input from their various cultures. Such aspects as gender, race, class, personality, and ethnicity influence the development of a child's sense of identity, and it is sometimes challenging to develop programs in early childhood education that support the identity of all young children.

As young children begin maturing and acquiring a positive self-concept, they also begin relating to and accepting others. These early years are the time to start influencing children's basic cultural attitudes, values, and beliefs. Development and implementation of a diversity perspective is, therefore, imperative. Parents, peers, teachers, and extended families all play a major role in helping children to accept and have pride in their cultural identities.

Culturally diverse classrooms foster genuine respect, acceptance, and openness for all children and their families regardless of race, gender, ethnic orientation, or physical ableness. Sensitive educators challenge some of the common myths relating to diverse cultures. For example, some teachers believe that some families do not value education and do not support their children in learning. This is disputed by some studies, which found that in fact families from marginalized communities do indeed value education and find effective ways to support their children in their learning, maybe not the same ways classroom teachers might, but nonetheless, supportive (Volk & Long, 2005).

Volk and Long (2005, p. 18) offer the following suggestions to teachers for incorporating children's home cultures into literacy activities in the classroom:

- Validate children's home language.
- Use familiar, culturally relevant literature.
- Let the children shape activities.
- Use environmental print.
- Help children share personal stories.
- Create activities around songs from home.

Young children usually begin to notice racial and gender differences during the first two years of life; during the third year children begin to learn the names of different colors and start to apply this knowledge to variations in skin color. Soon they begin to identify with members of a particular race and may wonder why they are a different color than other children or adults.

> Bradie, who attended a culturally rich preschool, had been helping her family work in the garden one sunny weekend. When she returned to class, she showed her suntanned arms to her teacher and announced, "Look, teacher! My skin is just about Spanish!"

Children notice observable characteristics such as skin color, language, and dress. How they respond to these differences is, to a great extent, determined by the direct and indirect messages and feelings of those around them. Children who are biased consider others to be inferior because of their differences. Teachers should work to overcome ethnocentrism, the attitude that one's own culture is correct, right, or natural. Accepting and respecting diversity should be a way of life, a value that is lived, felt, and woven into all areas of the classroom and curriculum. This means helping children to value others and to express positive feelings and behaviors toward them. It is an active approach to countering attitudes and behaviors that sustain prejudice, ethnocentrism, racism, stereotyping, sexism, discrimination, and oppression.

As teachers, we can learn about other cultures through personal interactions with parents and children, reading books on various cultures, discussions with other teachers and adults, visiting community cultural events, and utilizing media sources.

School may be the first place where children and families encounter cultural differences from their own (Kirmani, 2007). School practices often contribute to misinformation regarding various cultures: omission of materials from the curriculum, inaccurate information,

stereotyping, and cultural insensitivity (Moomaw & Jones, 2005/2006). During the early childhood years, children develop stereotypic attitudes about gender roles, racial and cultural biases, and negative attitudes about having different abilities. Not only are attitudes negatively affected, but experiences become narrow and limited as a result of the stereotyping associated with race, sex, and disabilities. Teachers should, therefore, foster positive attitudes of acceptance and tolerance. Children need to learn to value one another's differences while recognizing that they have many similarities. The similarities, rather than the differences, ought to be the focus.

Children can learn very early that, while individuals may view things differently, they still have many common needs, feelings, hopes, and desires; it is this common ground on which we should build.

Teaching diversity means modifying the early childhood environment, including the curriculum and the people involved, so that it is more reflective of the diversity within society. Curriculum activities that emphasize and show respect for various aspects of multiple cultures have a significant, positive influence on all children. Teaching diversity involves helping children understand empathy, to take the perspective of others, to look and see through their hearts, eyes, and minds. Students should recognize that all class members are equally important and deserve equal educational opportunities.

We live in a complex, global, diverse society today, and this should be reflected in our schools and neighborhoods. All schools, no matter the diversity of their population, should acquaint students with the broad range of our nation's racial, ethnic, cultural, and religious diversity. Teachers who teach all-white or predominately white groups still have a responsibility to engage these children in multicultural activities and experiences (Derman-Sparks & Ramsey, 2005). For example, create opportunities with materials or experiences that encourage conversations and discussions about diversity, prompt children to appreciate their own differences, invite stories of their lives and experiences, value community and cooperation over individual achievement, and challenge the dynamics of privilege (Derman-Sparks & Ramsey, 2005). If we expect children to function cooperatively in this diverse society, we must teach them attitudes, concepts, and skills that will enable them to do so.

A variety of terms have emerged as the basis for programs and practices relating to the pluralism of our world: *diversity, multicultural education, multiethnic education, ethnic studies, antibias curriculum,* and *global education.* Each has a somewhat different perspective. We have selected the term *diversity* as our approach, both in this text and as we teach young children, for several reasons. First, young children understand the concept of *different* and can expand this understanding to include the word *diversity.* Also, the term *diversity* is positive, and our goal as we teach diversity is to help children develop positive feelings and attitudes toward others. Diversity among people encompasses differences in gender, social class, religion, race, ethnic group, and physical or mental abilities. Compatible with our approach and focus, we prefer this broad implication of the term *diversity* as it relates to people, and we feel it is the most appropriate term to use with young children.

Teaching diversity enriches the classroom by providing various ways to solve problems and to view people, events, and situations (Copple, 2003). When children are able to view the world from the perspective of its diversity, their views of reality are broadened.

> Teaching diversity and adopting an antibias approach is not just an idea, fad, or educational movement that will pass with time. It is here to stay—an active process that focuses on the idea that *all* children have a right to learn and to reach their individual potentials.

The following are questions that teachers can consider in evaluating responsiveness to diversity in their classrooms:

- Am I respectful and accepting of each child's gender, race, sex, capabilities, culture, and linguistically diverse background?
- Do the literature, resources, and materials in my classroom reflect the diversities, cultures, and languages of all the children?
- Does the curriculum that I offer celebrate diversity?
- Do I encourage families to maintain their cultures and first languages?
- Do I integrate the various traditions, values, history, interests, games, music, art, languages, and families into my curriculum and program whenever appropriate?
- Do I encourage and provide many opportunities for cooperative learning and interaction with others?
- Do I show respect for the differences in family cultures and incorporate their customs and beliefs into the curriculum?

The Family

"In your efforts to partner with families in their child's learning and development, you are the experts in child

development and education, but they are the experts in their child and the child's ability" (Ray, Pewitt-Kinder, & George, 2009, p. 22). Families are important cultural resources that can be utilized in the classroom to support play and learning (Cohen, 2009). Bradley and Kibera (2006) suggest the following recommendations when working with families: learn from them, practice a nonjudgmental attitude, include cultural backgrounds in all aspects of your program, look for commonalities among children and families, and network with cultural/ethnic community groups. Families also reap many benefits from accessing the resources of their cultural communities and realizing the strengths of their own cultures (Bradley & Kibera, 2006).

Halgunseth (2009) provides the following recommendations for engaging diverse families in our early childhood programs:

- Provide a welcoming environment.
- Integrate culture and community.
- Make a commitment to outreach.
- Provide family resources and referrals.
- Set and reinforce program standards.
- Strive for program-family partnerships.

The Teacher

Teaching diversity is a professional and moral responsibility. How we think influences our teaching and expectations, and affects achievement and performance of our students. We must recognize our own cultural beliefs and attitudes about differences before we can appreciate these differences in children (Diversity and Equity Interest Forum, Derman-Sparks, Amihault, Baba, Seer, & Thompson, 2009). Teachers set the stage, and they must begin by evaluating their own culture and eliminating personal biases. It is sometimes difficult for us to set aside our own cultural beliefs, values, and habits as we work with diverse family situations. "Culturally relevant teaching requires teachers to learn about children's home cultures, and use that knowledge to make schooling relevant to the children's lives" (Hyland, 2010, p. 84). We need to acquire knowledge of other races, ethnicities, and cultures so that we do not unknowingly pass on our misunderstandings as stereotypes to our students. To be able to meet the needs of the children and families, "we need to understand the children we serve, their unique strengths, the conditions of their early learning environments, and how to effectively respond to their specific educational needs" (Espinosa, 2010, p. 10).

Teachers may need to change their attitudes and expectations, realizing that differences in lifestyle and language do not mean ignorance. They may need to be more positive toward children from minority groups and those who are different in any way. A genuine desire to know more about other people is absolutely necessary. The following are questions for a teacher to consider when identifying any possible personal, unrecognized biases (Association for Childhood Education International [ACEI], 1996b, p. 160-L). Analyzing personal prejudice allows us to make any necessary changes in our own attitude, which, in turn, affects the diversity climate in the classroom.

- Which 5 students do I like most and feel most comfortable with?
- Which 5 students do I like least and feel least comfortable with?
- When I need an assistant, do I tend to ask the same few students?
- Do I spend more instructional time with one group of students than others?
- Am I quicker to give prompts, cues, and/or answers to low achievers?

There is no way that we can be familiar with all the values, norms, and expectations of all the cultural groups represented in our classrooms. However, a genuine respect and appreciation for the students' cultural backgrounds helps us to interpret their needs, feelings, and behaviors appropriately and respectfully. "For the optimal development and learning of all children, educators must *accept* the legitimacy of children's home language, *respect* (hold in high regard) and *value* (esteem, appreciate) the home culture, and *promote* and *encourage* the active involvement and support of all families, including extended and nontraditional family units" (NAEYC, 1996b, p. 5).

Teachers need to affirm diversities of their students, and demonstrate that they value and appreciate the differences. Early childhood teachers need to develop awareness for the feelings of all people and become cognizant of the things that they say and do—some very subtle—that demean, oppress, dehumanize, or exclude others. For example, what we say ("Let's sit 'Indian style'"), what we do (make Indian headbands and decorate them with feathers, or sing "Ten Little Indians"), or what we don't do (we seldom sing Jewish songs or include symbols of that culture) all affect children and their feelings about who they are and the cultures with which they identify. Teachers must set examples of positive actions and attitudes and use teaching approaches and materials that are sensitive to the backgrounds and experiences of all students. We must nurture and celebrate the diversities of children and their families.

Teachers should be trained in the importance of, and approaches to, teaching diversity education. They must learn about different ethnic and cultural groups' lifestyles, patterns, values, and interests. They must be taught *how* to behave toward and communicate with minority children and their parents.

Goals of a Classroom Focused on Diversity

". . . a multicultural, multi-ethnic, and multi-ability student population demands a unique and nontraditional approach, characterized by individualism and sensitivity . . ." (Filler & Xu, 2006/2007, p. 92).

The following are the goals we see as important for teaching diversity in the classroom.

All children must be given opportunities to reach their potential regardless of their gender, social class, religion, race, ethnic group, or physical or mental abilities. Each child is different and has unique behaviors, thoughts, and needs. When we teach children from where they are, according to their needs, and help them to reach their distinctive potential, we are using developmentally appropriate education and beginning our approach to teaching diversity. In addition, when diversity is taught and practiced within a school, academic achievement improves.

Children's diverse cultural, social, family, and ethnic backgrounds create differences in the ways they think, feel, and behave. It behooves teachers to understand these differences to enable them to identify the individual needs of each child. "Participating with families in their worlds and learning from them is key in understanding the wealth of knowledge in homes and communities" (Volk & Long, 2005, p. 18).

All children should feel included and valued as worthy members of the class and of society. Our classrooms and centers must become inclusive, with children developing a sense of dignity and a tolerance for all people. "Inclusion is much more than simply opening up our doors; we must open up our hearts" (Elswood, 1999, p. 66). We must adapt our curriculum, physical space, and interactions if we are to be truly inclusive of all children.

Children should be helped to clarify and feel positive toward their own identity, including their sex, ethnic background, race, and physical abilities. Children need to understand who they are and why they behave, feel, and value things the way that they do. "How prominently race figures in children's perceptions of themselves and others depends, in part, on their majority or minority status in their local community and on the extent and quality of contacts that they have with other racial groups" (Ramsey, 1995, p. 20). Culturally integrated cooperative learning groups help children develop friendships and decreases stereotypes and prejudices.

Even though early childhood educators recognize differences in biracial children (children from interracial unions) and their families, the curriculum usually does not adequately address these differences. We must acknowledge this reality and help the children to accept and mesh together this dual parentage. Until they accept their own differences, they will surely have difficulty accepting the differences in other people.

Teachers should help all children to gain greater self-esteem and self-understanding as they view themselves from the perspective of differences and similarities. Early childhood teachers should respect the various backgrounds of the children and make them aware of other cultures in the community. Children can learn to appreciate what they have in common with others, while recognizing characteristics that distinguish them from other children (NAEYC, 1996b). Children need information on their culture and need to develop pride in their heritage. Their family, local community, economic or political level, and particular cultural or ethnic group determine children's expectations and experiences.

Some children wear glasses, and some don't.

Some children wear braces, and some don't.

Some children write with their left hand, and some don't.

Some children have missing teeth, and some don't.

Children can learn to take the perspective of children who are different from themselves. In a classroom that appreciates differences and reinforces similarities, children develop empathy, get along with others who have differing views and traditions, and take pride in their own culture (Byrnes & Kiger, 2005). Children can develop empathy for many other children, not just those in their own class. They can do this only through positive exposure to and experiences with other children. They must see how they are alike and how they are different and be taught to value the differences. Diversity education that focuses on respect and love for our fellow human beings will be well worth the effort. We must create classroom climates where everyone is accepted and respected, and where equity, empathy, and advocacy are practiced (Williams & Cooney, 2006).

> "Ongoing, face-to-face contact is the best way to break down barriers, recognize similarities, and see differences as enriching rather than as uncomfortable or strange" (Derman-Sparks & Ramsey, 2005, p. 24).

The diversity perspective should be integrated into all aspects of the school or program. If, as teachers, we only do "other people" units of study or an occasional multicultural activity, we are not solving the problem. These activities do not allow adequate time for exploring or developing concepts, and they often misrepresent various aspects of a particular culture. Separate units of study also tend to perpetuate stereotypes and emphasize differences. Children become more amenable to others' diversities when multicultural activities are integrated daily into the curriculum.

When the curriculum includes a particular ethnic group only in a specific unit of study on that group, children do not learn to view the group as an inherent part of our total society. They view it as being separate, and they often assume this separateness means inferior. One author (Derman-Sparks & Edwards, 2010) refers to this curriculum approach as the "tourist" approach. By this she means that we "tour" a country and provide a sampling of that country—its foods, holidays, and traditions, for instance. We look at "things" from that country. When we do this, we teach on the surface but do not build or teach understanding of other people. All groups have specific attributes that influence their attitudes, values, and behaviors in complex and subtle ways. Sometimes the identifying factors of a culture are so subtle that we may not be aware that we are skimming the surface in our efforts to know more about that culture. Another danger of this approach is that we tend to select units on some groups of people and leave others out completely.

If we are really going to solve the problem, the concept of diversity must be infused into our materials, environment, and curriculum, and it must be reflected in staff attitudes and beliefs. Content from diverse groups of people must be integrated into all parts of the curriculum.

Diversity is not a separate subject that should be added to the curriculum, nor is it the study of isolated facts, cultures, or countries. It is not a specific curriculum or formula, but an everyday attitude of acceptance. It is not teaching isolated lessons such as cooking ethnic foods or discussing achievements of African Americans during Black History Month. Although these activities have purpose, by themselves they are inadequate. Rather, there should be both planned and spontaneous integrated learning activities that build positive and reliable concepts about all people.

Children need to understand the classroom rule that discriminatory or insulting actions, language, or attitudes toward others will not be tolerated. Biased, racist, or other unkind remarks are to be taken seriously and addressed directly by teachers who must validate the feelings of the children who are on the receiving end of these comments. When children know that adults expect particular behaviors, they will seek to live up to these expectations. Our classroom norms must reflect respect and tolerance for all differences in people.

These goals must be tailored to fit the context and specific needs of each classroom; however, it is important to recognize the need for some foundation goals that provide direction in teaching diversity. It is important to discuss these goals with children in the classroom at the beginning of the school year. If children can read, the goals should be posted and reviewed as needed.

Gender Bias

It is important that children learn to appreciate the contributions to society that are made by those who have diversities relating to religion, age, culture, race, abilities, and gender. Positive attitudes toward differences develop from the early years and affect behavior throughout children's lives (Ramsey, 2004). Between the ages of 3 and 8, children sort out their understanding of gender and what it means. They use external attributes for identifying gender: names, hairstyles, hobbies, clothing, and play materials. This is why it is important that teachers help children to realize that anatomy, not external attributes, determines gender. We can help them to move from gender role stereotypes to gender fairness (Ramsey, 2004).

Gender bias is often subtle and difficult to recognize. Overt stereotyping relating to gender bias is not as common as it used to be, but subtler bias persists, and it hurts both males and females, especially those from minority cultural backgrounds. The ways teachers treat students can reflect these biases. Gender bias is found in curriculum materials, in the learning environment, and in teacher expectations and interactions. Teachers must diligently strive to overcome intentional or unintentional gender bias in classrooms so that *all* their students will feel important, respected, and equal to their peers. Once again, teachers' attitudes either overcome or reinforce biases. Gender bias takes many forms. Several of these are described in the following paragraphs.

Stereotyping

When teachers assign traditional and rigid roles or attributes based on sex, the abilities and potentials of each gender are limited. Stereotyping is damaging and debilitating to young children and does not promote equity. Stereotyping denies students an understanding of the diversity and variation of genders. Young children need to understand that both boys and girls can do all the activities offered in the educational program. Children who see themselves portrayed only in stereotypic ways may internalize these stereotypes and fail to develop their own unique abilities and interests and their full potential.

One common gender stereotype assumes that boys are better in math and science and girls are better in language skills. We expect qualities of caring and sharing in girls and qualities of assertiveness, competitiveness, and critical thinking in boys. Girls are expected to be more courteous and kind than boys. Girls are rewarded for appreciative, dependable, considerate, and dependent behavior; boys are rewarded for active, curious, and questioning behavior. Interests are stereotyped by expecting boys to prefer carpentry, cars, sports, and science, for example, and expecting girls to be interested in such things as housekeeping, cooking, and quiet activities. Many children's books present stereotypical roles, attitudes, and behaviors. Teachers should make a very mindful effort to provide books and materials that are free of gender stereotypes (Roberts & Hill, 2003).

Children should know that discriminatory comments or actions will not be tolerated. Studies have shown that gender stereotyping can be altered as a result of good literature, especially where strong characters are viewed in a variety of roles and with a variety of characteristics.

Inequitable Attention

Often, boys are given more attention by the teacher in the classroom. Girls frequently form a quiet background to the active role of boys. Teachers interact more frequently with boys, reward them for their academic work more often, and talk to and question them more often than they do girls. Females are often omitted or included less frequently than males on bulletin boards and in discussions of famous people, books, and dis-

plays. Girls are not called on as often as boys, and they are not rewarded as frequently for their academic achievements. Too often females are left out of our culture, creating the impression that the male experience is the norm. When we make anyone feel "invisible," we are making them feel less valued or important.

Dividing Students by Gender

By separating boys and girls in classroom procedures such as lining up, forming groups, and organizing sports or recreational activities, teachers promote isolation and division of the sexes. Teachers ought to take measures to ensure mixed grouping. If children are given guidance and opportunities to break down gender barriers, they are able to do so. This can be accomplished by mixing genders in activities that frequently separate children by gender, such as when boys form one line, girls form another; girls get their coats on first, then the boys; boys go to the science table, girls go to the math table; boys against the girls in kickball; and so on.

Linguistic Bias

Curriculum materials, teacher conversation, and other forms of communication often reflect the discriminatory nature of our language. Masculine terms and pronouns such as *forefathers, mankind,* or even the generic *he* all exclude women. In addition, masculine labels such as *fireman, mailman,* or *chairman* deny the legitimacy of women working in various fields or in different capacities. Other forms of biased language include frequent reference to all doctors, construction workers, or lawyers as *he* or all secretaries or nurses as *she.* In conversation and in books, the pronoun *he* is often used when we refer to something or someone whose gender is unknown. Teachers must carefully monitor what they say and realize the impact of their words on young children. For instance, when reading books that refer to an animal as "he," sometimes substitute "she."

Behavior Expectations

Too often teachers expect certain kinds of behavior from one sex or the other. For example, boys are expected to behave in a courageous and chivalrous way; swearing is more likely tolerated from them; and more boisterous behavior is acceptable. Girls, on the other hand, are expected to be neat and clean; submissive, gentle, and kind; and not to take the lead in any activity. Even duties and chores within the classroom are too often assigned on the basis of sex. Acceptable behavior should be expected from all students, and unacceptable behavior not tolerated from any students. All activities in the early childhood classroom should be available to all children. As both girls and boys hammer nails, construct buildings, shovel dirt, pilot boats, drive road graders, tend babies, cook dinner, sweep floors, paint pictures, kick balls, repair tricycles, sing, dance, follow ants, carve pumpkins, extinguish fires, plant seeds, dress up, and play in the beauty shop, avenues of learning and exploration become limitless.

Teachers should be aware of unintended biases, assess their areas of responsibility, review materials for content and form, evaluate their learning environments, and become aware of their interaction and language patterns with others, particularly young children. The total learning environment must foster integrity, equality, and initiative in all children, both boys and girls, to prepare them for sound and vigorous futures. By establishing a nonsexist educational atmosphere, we allow young children to explore freely and identify gradually the roles that they find most comfortable and fulfilling. Gender-equitable classrooms provide a wide variety of gender-fair experiences that allow for participation and exploration by both boys and girls.

Suggestions for Eliminating Gender Bias

- Give *all* children in the classroom attention, and equal time to respond or comment.
- Give equal opportunities for *all* children in class responsibilities.
- Allow equal choices in toys, games and activities to all children.
- Praise *all* children for their efforts and abilities.
- Use nonbiased (not gender specific) language and labels.
- Provide bias-free role models.

Religious Bias

There is great diversity in religious preferences in our society today, and children's religious preferences have a considerable effect on how they behave; the traditions that they share from their homes; and their beliefs, values, and moral standards. Religious beliefs about human events such as birth and death and the very purpose of life all influence what children think, say, and do in the classroom. The degree of religious influence in the school varies from one community to another; however, if a school has a dominant religious group, the perspective of that group may be reflected in the school and its curriculum. A family's religious beliefs will influence what parents expect from the school, the teacher, and the child.

Children are aware of religious diversity early, and they can usually describe their own religious identity by the time they are kindergarten age. By the time they are in the fourth grade, they know whether someone is religious or nonreligious, and they can tell you what religion some people have by their actions and behaviors.

Teachers must be sensitive to the religious beliefs of all the children in the classroom. Again, the teacher's example of respect and tolerance for different beliefs helps children to build this same regard and consideration for another person's way of life and belief system. Teachers can better understand their students if they know the children's religious identifications. Sometimes religious identity is combined with ethnic identity, as it is for the Russian Jew, the Irish Catholic, and others. A child's membership in two microcultures can help a teacher to better understand the child's behavior and self-concept, and the teacher can then assist other children in gaining the same understanding. Religious perspective affects children's friendships, dress standards, social activities, customs, and dietary habits, and language. Teachers must not tolerate criticism from the children's peers with regard to these obvious differences. Rather, teachers can openly teach and model patience, tolerance, and respect for habits and behaviors that reflect a child's religious beliefs and teachings.

CHILDREN WITH SPECIAL NEEDS

Beyond gender, cultures, and ethnic groups, the concept of recognizing similarities and differences among peers includes children with special needs. "When we work to ensure that the children with special needs are truly included in all aspects of the program, not only these children benefit but all the children in the group gain understanding and acceptance of the differences in people" (Copple & Bredekamp, 2006, p. 27). Children who have severe disabilities as well as those who are gifted are considered as being exceptional or having special needs. Children with **special needs** are those who have learning or behavioral characteristics that differ substantially from others and require special methods of instruction. All children, with wide ranges of disabilities, should be accepted, appreciated, and celebrated in our early childhood education programs (Filler & Xu, 2006/2007). Although children with special needs have differences, they are actually more like other children than unlike them. They must be treated as individuals, not labeled as members of a particular group. "Every child needs to be understood both as a whole child with developmental needs similar to those of age mates and as an individual with unique needs" (French & Cain, 2006, p. 84).

Suggestions for communicating about individuals with disabilities:

1. Avoid focusing on a disability and instead focus on issues that impact quality of life for the individual.
2. Avoid portraying successful people with disabilities as superhuman.

> 3. Avoid sensationalizing a disability.
> 4. Avoid using generic labels.
> 5. Always put people first.
> 6. Emphasize abilities and not limitations.
> 7. Show people with disabilities to be active participants in society.
>
> *Source:* Developed by Research and Training Center on Independent Living, University of Kansas, Lawrence. Adapted by and cited in *Special Education in Contemporary Society: An Introduction to Exceptionality* (p. 8), by R. M. Gargiulo (2006), Belmont, CA: Thomson Wadsworth.

A **disability** is a reduced capacity or inability to perform a task in a particular way (Gargiulo, 2006). A disability becomes a handicap only when the condition limits or stops the person's ability to function normally. A child's disability is not as great a problem as how the special need affects the child's participation in activities. Effective early childhood programs ensure "that all children can interact with materials, activities, teachers, and peers to the fullest extent possible and with equal frequency and enjoyment" (Watson & McCathren, 2009, p. 21). We must have an attitude of openness and acceptance and realize that exceptional children are members of our society and can make valuable contributions. Of children who have disabilities, many have only mild impairments. Children with disabilities can be classified into any of 13 categories according to Wolery and Wilbers (1994, pp. 3, 4), and many of these children do require specialized attention.

- Deafness
- Dual-sensory impairments
- Hearing impairment
- Mental retardation
- Multiple disabilities
- Orthopedic impairments
- Serious emotional disturbance
- Specific learning disabilities
- Speech (language) impairments
- Visual impairments and blindness
- Traumatic brain injury
- Autism
- Other health impairments

With these individual needs in mind, Congress passed Public Law 94-142 (the Education for All Handicapped Children Act) in 1975. This law mandated that a free and appropriate education be provided for all children aged 5 through 18 years with disabilities in an environment closest to that of a "normal" child (the least restrictive environment, or LRE). Schools implemented an approach whereby children who need special services are identified and then assessed or evaluated to determine their degree of impairment.

Then intervention is planned to best meet their needs. The child's teacher, qualified school personnel, and, most importantly, the child's parents develop an **Individualized Education Program (IEP)** for the child. Public Law 94-142 is considered to be the legislative heart of special education and is often viewed as a "Bill of Rights" for children with exceptionalities (Gargiulo, 2006).

An amendment to PL 94-142 has significantly influenced and enhanced early intervention with young children who have special needs. PL 99-457, the Education of the Handicapped Amendments of 1986, did not mandate universal service for children younger than 5 years of age, but it strengthened incentives for states to serve 3- to 6-year-old children and established a new discretionary program for services to children from birth to 3 years of age. In 1990, the Individuals with Disabilities Education Act (PL 101-476, IDEA, 1990) was passed as an amendment to PL 94-142. This legislation replaced the word "handicapped" with "disabled" and expanded services for the disabled. In 1997, amendments to IDEA were passed, which resulted in early childhood educators assuming more responsibility for the education of children with special needs. IEPs are required for all children who receive special education services, and they outline the adjustments that must be made so that children with disabilities can participate in the appropriate activities provided to children without disabilities (IDEA, 1997). These IEPs, which are reviewed at least annually, identify measurable goals and benchmarks necessary to achieve the following IEP goals (IDEA, 1997):

- Specify the behavior or behaviors that the child is to perform.
- Describe the conditions under which the desired behavior is to be performed.
- State the degree to which the behavior is expected to be performed.

Teachers often find it challenging to work with the requirements of the IEPs, because it is sometimes difficult to write these goals, plan instructional experiences to meet these goals, and document the child's progress toward accomplishment.

Effective July 1, 2005, in the Individual with Disabilities Education Improvement Act of 2004 (IDEA), the U.S. Department of Education issued proposed regulations that created additional changes in special education. The purpose of the national law is to work to improve results for infants, toddlers, children, and youth with disabilities and to more closely align IDEA to the No Child Left Behind Act (NCLB). Detailed information on IDEA 2004 can be found at www.ed.gov/policy/speced/guid/idea/idea2004.html.

The amended changes in IDEA 2004 that critically affect children with disabilities and their families focus on the IEP process, due process, and discipline provisions. A section of the act also suggests that states minimize the number of rules, regulations, and policies relating to special education to which school districts are subject.

Teachers at every grade level need to be aware of and sensitive to the needs of children with disabilities as they transition into a new grade. Felon (2005) suggests some best practices focused on transitioning children with disabilities into kindergarten. Every grade is a transition for these special needs children, so we have adapted Felon's suggestions to early childhood:

- Use a collaborative team approach that includes families, sending and receiving teachers, special education staff, and administrators.
- Set goals and outline anticipated outcomes.
- Encourage family involvement in the process of the transition and enhanced communication between all staff involved.
- Focus on the strengths and needs of individual children.

One additional legislative issue is Section 504 of the Rehabilitation Act of 1973 (PL 93-112). This is a civil rights law that protects children against discrimination due to a disability. Creating inclusive environments in developmentally appropriate classrooms for young children suggests a framework of six curriculum areas that are important for all children to achieve (Edmiaston, Dolezal, Doolittle, Erickson, & Merritt, 2000):

1. Functioning independently
2. Fulfilling the responsibilities of membership in the classroom community
3. Engaging in classroom learning experiences
4. Establishing satisfying interpersonal relationships
5. Communicating effectively
6. Meeting academic expectations

Using this framework in defining goals and benchmarks makes it easier to embed them within the practices of a developmentally appropriate classroom and curriculum.

Physical education is such an important part of the curriculum for children who have special needs that IDEA (1997) mandates that all children with disabilities receive physical education services. It is important that we, as educators and advocates of children, make certain that all children participate in physical education as part of a free and appropriate education

Working with Children with Special Needs

It is important for teachers to understand the conditions that children in their classrooms may have. Based on the interests, needs, and abilities of *all* children in the classroom, accommodations are made to the curriculum

and are reflected in differentiation. In differentiated classrooms, teachers find out where children are and what their individual needs are and accommodate the curriculum to those various needs. Thoughtful assessment practices allow teachers to determine if each child makes continuous progress. Following are nine general categories of special needs, giving characteristics, possible teaching strategies, and specialists in the community whom teachers may consult. Keep in mind that these are generalizations; not every child with special needs exhibits the same set of characteristics, but some of the most persistent features are included. All children have diverse abilities and needs, regardless of their particular labels or previous experiences.

Speech and Language Impairments

CHARACTERISTICS. Many problems can occur in a young child with a speech and/or language deficiency. Knowing the normal development of language and speech sounds helps a teacher to determine whether there is a problem. Some signs include omissions, substitutions, distortions, or additions of speech sounds. Such articulation disorders are common during the early years, but most often disappear after second or third grade. Stuttering is less common, but also more distressing, and may result from anxiety or difficulty with particular sounds. Use of single words and/or gestures, along with difficulty in following directions, is an indication of a developmental problem. An early childhood teacher may also have children in the classroom who are bilingual (learning two languages).

Reaching a child by using his or her first language is also very important. This language is the familiar vehicle of oral communication, and the student needs acceptance and understanding in the use of the language in any program. If a child in an early childhood setting is bilingual, that is, learning and using two languages, someone should be available to communicate with the child in both languages.

TEACHING STRATEGIES. A teacher can do many things to assist a child in speech and language development. When working with a child who has communication disabilities, be a good listener; use parallel or play-by-play broadcasting during activities; use alternative communications; model good language; and encourage specific reasons for language expression (Russell-Fox, 1997). Give simple directions, using phrases or short sentences. When addressing the child, do not talk down or use baby talk. Provide daily oral experiences, such as singing, language activities, or answering questions. Always listen and respond to the child; concentrate on what is said, not on the trouble that the student has in saying it. Avoid finishing a student's sentences or correcting articulation problems in front of peers. Provide good models for the child to listen to. Cooperative and small-group activities give opportunities for children to use language skills in less threatening situations. If problems persist or do not appear to be developmental, refer the child for testing. If the child is bilingual, have an interpreter, seek to understand the culture, and keep the vocabulary as basic as possible. Provide ELL (English Language Learners) students with opportunities to teach about their culture and language, and encourage class members to learn words from an ELL student's first language. Unless the school community understands the culture of the ELL student, the student will have trouble making steps toward any type of successful integration.

SPECIALISTS. Communication disorder specialists are among the community specialists in the area of speech and language development who can assist or consult with the early childhood teacher.

Mental Impairments

CHARACTERISTICS. For many years, levels of mental impairments were measured by intelligence testing. Other factors to consider and evaluate when assessing a child's potential in the classroom include the child's developmental gains in motor, language, social, and self-help skills for his or her age; physical difficulties or illnesses; and the length of the child's attention span. Teachers should observe the rate of learning and comprehension of abstract concepts.

TEACHING STRATEGIES. If a child is delayed in two or more of the previously mentioned areas, the teacher should refer the child for developmental testing. Adjustments can be made in the classroom that will assist the teacher and child. Low child–staff ratios are necessary to provide the individualized attention that the child will need. Specific learning objectives should be based on an analysis of the child's learning strengths and weaknesses. Tasks should be broken into small, logical components, and these should be repeated often and reinforced. The presentation should be consistent and the directions brief and simple. Materials should not insult the student. Skills and concepts should be practical, based on the demands of living. Students with mental impairments must overlearn, repeat, and practice more than children of average intelligence. Children need to experience success; teachers should chart the children's growth.

SPECIALISTS. The following specialists can help in evaluating and programming for children who have mental impairments: psychologist, special education teacher, developmental specialist, communication disorder specialist, occupational therapist, and physical therapist.

Hearing Impairments

CHARACTERISTICS. The following characteristics may indicate a hearing problem: limited communication skills, inability to understand or respond to the speech of others, misbehavior, inattentiveness, watching the speaker's face and lips, turning one ear toward the speaker, and complaints of earaches. If a hearing test has been given, a loss of 20 to 60 decibels (measurement of sound density) is considered hard of hearing, and a loss of 60 decibels or more is considered deaf.

TEACHING STRATEGIES. In the classroom, seat a child with a hearing impairment near the source of instruction and where there is good visibility. When working with a child who has hearing disabilities, develop a professional working relationship with the child's parents, speech–language therapist, audiologist, hearing specialist, and other involved care providers; keep the lines of communication open among all people; use visual and tactile aids; get the child's attention (call the child by name) before giving information or beginning an activity; speak normally; and allow adequate time for the child to speak (Russell-Fox, 1997). Articulate clearly, do not exaggerate, and face the child when speaking. If the child is using hearing aids, be familiar with them, check to see whether they are operating, know how to put them in the child's ear, and be prepared to charge the battery. Provide constant language stimulation. The teacher may need to learn some sign language and, if applicable, give the whole class some exposure to sign language.

SPECIALISTS. Specialists to be consulted in case of a hearing impairment are the audiologist, communication disorder specialist, and itinerant teacher for students who are hard of hearing. The parents should also be consulted.

Visual Impairments

CHARACTERISTICS. A child who has been diagnosed as having a severe vision problem falls into one of two categories: partially sighted or blind. Children who are partially sighted have a field of vision that is 20/200 (that is, they can see at 20 feet what a normally sighted person can see at 200 feet) or better in the corrected eye, but not greater than 20/70. Children who are blind have a field of vision of 20/200 or less in the corrected better eye. Characteristics of children with visual impairments are excessive blinking; rubbing, crossing, and squinting of the eyes; holding things close or far away; tilting the head when trying to focus; and dizziness or headaches.

TEACHING STRATEGIES. To adjust materials and activities to meet the needs of a child with a visual impairment, rely on the use of the other senses. When working with a child who has visual impairments, develop a professional working relationship with the child's parents, vision specialist, and other involved care providers; learn about the degree of impairment; orient the child to the layout of the classroom and materials, including any changes; provide tactile, auditory, and manipulative experiences; encourage independence, but be ready to provide physical prompts when helpful (Russell-Fox, 1997). Assign a buddy to help the child orient quickly and develop social interactions. Access and use materials and equipment to help the student who is visually impaired. For readers, make sure that the quality of the print that you expect the child to use is readable.

SPECIALISTS. The teacher may consult with the child's ophthalmologist or an itinerant teacher of children with visual impairments to find materials and adjust the program for the child.

Physical Impairments

CHARACTERISTICS. Indications of a physical problem include poor coordination or control of fine or gross motor skills, poor balance, and frustration and discouragement when attempting motor skills. Children with a physical disability may have normal intelligence. Common physical disabilities that can be identified in young children at birth or shortly afterward include cerebral palsy, epilepsy, and spina bifida. In addition to congenital impairments, there are impairments caused by diseases and accidents.

TEACHING STRATEGIES. When working with a child who has physical special needs, develop a professional working relationship with (and seek suggestions from) the physical and occupational therapists and the parents; arrange environments so that the child can access toys, materials, and equipment; learn the types, uses, and care of adaptive equipment; allow adequate transition time; support and encourage, yet foster independence (Russell-Fox, 1997). One of the major changes necessary when a child with a physical disability is in a regular classroom is acquiring appropriate structures and equipment (for example, ramps, walkers). Learn as much as possible about the physical problems and what limitations they may have on the child. Help the child develop motor, language, speech, and social skills to the fullest potential. Be sensitive to the child's feelings about the disability.

SPECIALISTS. To develop a program that is appropriate for a child with physical problems, the teacher should consult with an occupational therapist, a physical therapist, the child's physician, and the child's parents. In extreme cases, a neurologist should be consulted.

Emotional, Social, or Behavioral Problems

CHARACTERISTICS. Children with emotional, social, or behavioral problems may exhibit them to a marked degree in two different ways: passively or aggressively. A passive child may stare for long periods of time; seldom communicate; be withdrawn, afraid, sensitive, or shy; and have poor eye contact. An aggressive or hyperactive child may be overcompetitive, rebellious, easily distracted, disruptive, hostile, assaultive, overly active, impulsive, defiant of authority, inattentive, and restless. These children often have difficulty building positive relationships, staying on task, and being attentive, and they may experience depression. Children with autism also fit into this category.

TEACHING STRATEGIES. A child with behavioral problems may need a change in environment to receive the individualized attention needed to verbalize his or her feelings. Children with these problems need love, patience, and understanding. Communication appears to be a key ingredient. Most of all, they need consistency in expectations and positive reinforcement for appropriate behaviors. Teachers may need to draw information from specialists in the field to assist them in the class. Working with children who have **ADHD (attention deficit hyperactivity disorder)** requires a multimodal approach, including behavior management techniques. The most important technique is positive reinforcement, in which the child receives a rewarding response after demonstrating a desired behavior. Classroom success may require a range of interventions depending on how the disorder affects the child. The following classroom characteristics that promote success for children with **ADD (attention deficit disorder)** have been identified:

- Predictability, routine, structure
- Shorter work periods
- Reduced teacher–pupil ratio
- Individualized instruction, breaking tasks into smaller steps when necessary
- Positive reinforcement

The following are teacher characteristics that appear helpful in teaching children diagnosed with ADD:

- Positive academic expectations
- Frequent monitoring and checking of work
- Clarity in giving instructions
- Warmth, patience, and a sense of humor
- Consistency and firmness
- Knowledge of different behavioral interventions
- Willingness to work with a special education teacher
- Focus on potentials and strengths, rather than on the disabilities and limitations
- Ability to provide a highly stimulating learning environment

SPECIALISTS. Early childhood teachers may need to consult with a psychologist, physician, social worker, counselor, or special education teacher when working with children with emotional, social, or behavioral problems. A comprehensive evaluation and medical exam is necessary to establish a diagnosis

Chronic Illness

CHARACTERISTICS. Children who are chronically ill generally have a disorder that is always present and that may limit their physical activity. Some examples are asthma, cystic fibrosis, diabetes, tuberculosis, arthritis, muscular dystrophy, and hemophilia. Children who are chronically ill usually have normal intelligence.

TEACHING STRATEGIES. When working with a child who has a chronic illness, develop a professional working relationship with the child's parents, physician, school nurse, and other involved care providers; keep the lines of communication open among all people; learn about the child's health needs, diet, and medications; learn what to do in case of an emergency; develop a program plan that may include home visits, phone calls, care packages, activity packets, and so on (Russell-Fox, 1997).

If you are the teacher of siblings of a child with a serious illness, be aware that these siblings are often forgotten and lose the needed support from parents and other adults. There is also a disruption in the friendship between the child who is ill and the child's siblings. It is important for the teacher to provide support and understanding to these siblings.

SPECIALISTS. The child's parents, physicians, and the school nurse are the best consultants for teachers when dealing with children who are chronically ill.

Learning Disabilities

CHARACTERISTICS. The category known as **learning disabilities** has existed for 30 years. It refers to a disorder in one or more basic psychological processes associated with either understanding or using language, reasoning, or math. Some characteristics include motor disinhibition (being unable to refrain from responding), disassociation (responding to the elements of a stimulus rather than to the whole stimulus), figure–ground disturbance (confusing a figure with its background), perseveration (not changing from one task to another), absence of a well-developed self-concept and body image, poor gross and fine motor skills, and lack of established handedness.

TEACHING STRATEGIES. Children with learning disabilities often need one-on-one teaching with simple tasks and simple instructions. Proceed slowly and make, sure

that the child is paying attention. Be sure that the child has mastered skills at one level before proceeding to the next. Frequently, children with learning disabilities seem to have mastered the skills being taught, but they actually need to relearn or receive extra reinforcement and practice to retain the information. Increase the amount of time allowed for completing tasks. Provide opportunities for cooperative learning or small-group work, peer tutoring, and learning centers. Provide concrete examples. Use positive reinforcement when a child is learning each task. When working with a child who has learning disabilities, concentrate on the strengths, not the weaknesses of the child; patiently provide for overlearning and practice; use multisensory approaches to experiences; praise progress and successes, and encourage parents to do the same; provide clear, simple directions and transitions (Russell-Fox, 1997).

SPECIALISTS. Specialists in the area of learning disabilities include psychologists, special education teachers, developmental specialists, and social workers.

Gifted and Talented Children

CHARACTERISTICS. Gifted children are the most underserved group of exceptional children. There is no consensus about what constitutes a gifted child. Children have many individual gifts, and teachers should learn to think of *gifted behavior*, rather than *being gifted*, because giftedness is not an absolute and predetermined condition. It is a set of behaviors that emerges when certain traits interact with one another. Children who are gifted show above-average ability or potential in one or more of the following areas (Gargiulo, 2006, p. 360):

1. General intellectual ability
2. Specific academic and learning aptitude
3. Leadership ability
4. Creative or productive thinking
5. Visual and performing arts

Giftedness is exhibited in many forms. Children who are gifted may peak in some areas at particular times, but not necessarily in all cognitive areas. Karnes and Johnson (1989, p. 56) agree that "giftedness comes in many forms. Is the child an unusually creative thinker? Artistic? Musical? Mentally sharp? Good grades and giftedness are not the same thing." However, isolated incidents do not indicate giftedness. Also, gifted children may not necessarily score high on all parts of intelligence tests.

Professionals and those involved in evaluating should look at what children can do instead of what they cannot do. Parent reports and teacher observations should also be used in describing children's strengths, talents, and capabilities. Children who are gifted and talented are creative and observant, ask numerous

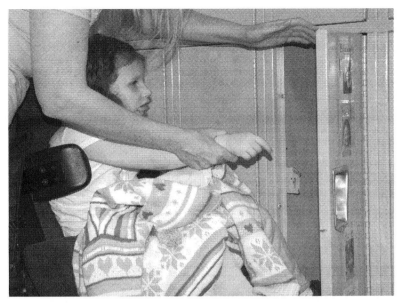

Every classroom should model accepting and appreciating differences among people.

questions, and learn quickly and easily. They possess a large store of information. They are attentive, have a capacity for seeing relationships and patterns, enjoy problem solving, exhibit an early interest in printed material, and have exceptional memory. They also have in-depth interests, a high energy level, and good reasoning and insight ability. They are sensitive and have high expectations. These children usually have large, accurate vocabularies and use expanded language. It is difficult for children from minority groups, young children, and underachievers to be identified and served by programs for gifted children.

TEACHING STRATEGIES.   Provide a differentiated curriculum (activities within units and lessons oriented toward students with different levels of achievement). Provide stimulating, challenging, and varied enrichment opportunities to develop knowledge, talents, and work habits. Provide relevant extra assignments or extensions. Build on language skills. Encourage the use of computers. Encourage independence and self-direction. Involve students in planning their own curriculum. Use delayed, intrinsic, and social reinforcement rather than immediate and concrete rewards. Focus on problem solving, divergent thinking, and other higher level thinking strategies. Older children (5 to 8 years) often need academic acceleration and enrichment (extending the regular curriculum), whereas younger children (3 to 5 years) benefit from individualization, discovery learning, and encouragement of talents. Flexible groups allow for continuous progress and can be used in a variety of types of classroom organizations.

SPECIALISTS.   Itinerant teachers of children who are gifted and talented, psychologists, or resource teachers

can assist the early childhood teacher in planning activities to enhance the child's program in the regular classroom setting.

Programs for Meeting Special Needs

Although children with special needs are similar in most respects to children without disabilities, they have additional needs, such as curriculum or environment adjustments, or individualized supports. The needs of children who have multiple disabilities (children with more than one of the disabling conditions described previously) must be met according to each child's disabilities and abilities.

Consultants from all areas can provide appropriate programs for the children to achieve their greatest potential. When it is necessary to consider referring a child with special needs to a specialist, it may be difficult to approach the subject with the parents. Instead of talking about *treatment* for the child, suggesting the need of an *evaluation* for services tends to help parents to be more receptive. "While traditional assessments serve the purposes of diagnosis and eligibility, they do not provide the type of information needed to make appropriate intervention decisions regarding functional and developmentally appropriate programming" for all children with special needs (Grisham-Brown, 2000, p. 3). Appropriate transdisciplinary activity-based assessments actively involve the family, allow teams to view the whole child, limit the number of people who interact with the child, and result in intervention strategies that are functional and developmentally appropriate (Grisham-Brown, 2000).

After the teacher comes to an understanding of a child's disabling condition, his or her acceptance of that child as a whole child, not just one who has a disability, is critical. The teacher becomes a model in showing acceptance for the child who has a disability for the other children in the classroom. Through the teacher, the other children will come to understand and accept this child. Research suggests that social integration of children, both with and without disabilities, does not occur automatically; it develops only when sensitive teachers structure experiences for social integration. Children with disabilities often need some direction with prosocial interactions. They need us to help them to learn how to make friends, to enter a playgroup, and to sustain interactive cooperative play. It may be challenging to include antibias philosophy in developmentally appropriate settings, but educators must foster social interactions among all children. Everyone benefits and learns from their relationships with exceptional children. It is the expert teacher who makes the presence of children with special needs an advantage rather than a disadvantage for everyone in the classroom.

A Comprehensive Program for Exceptional Children

1. A teacher knowledgeable in education and special education who accepts children at their level of development
2. A teacher who understands that children need consistency, a dependable schedule, and gentle but firm limits
3. A differentiated curriculum
4. A curriculum that has a multisensory approach
5. A curriculum that enhances growth in all areas of development and learning
6. A curriculum that provides various hands-on, relevant experiences
7. A classroom in which play is valued
8. Assessment accommodations including presentation, response, setting, and timing accommodations (S. Thompson, 2004)
9. Utilization of a multidisciplinary team of professionals
10. Application of universal design for learning, which means the design of materials, lessons, and activities that allow the objectives to be achievable by individuals with a wide range of abilities

A basic understanding of typical child development is necessary if a teacher is to work effectively among children with special needs. This understanding provides the teacher with a guideline to devise developmental instructional activities, a basis to modify the activities to meet the individual needs of the children in the classroom, and a guideline to form realistic expectations for all the children.

With knowledge of typical child development, early childhood teachers can adapt and individualize their programs to meet the needs of the children in their classroom. This individualization process involves breaking down tasks into small steps so that the child can progress successfully, providing appropriate models for the child to follow, maintaining accurate records of the child's progress, and altering the physical makeup of the building and equipment to meet the child's special needs. Consulting with specialists and following through with the programs outlined also assist the teacher in developing individual plans and directions.

Early intervention for young children with disabilities positively affects learning and development, and often decreases the possibility of more serious problems later. This translates to the need for early childhood special education teachers and staff to be prepared and qualified to implement effective and supportive programs.

We should not limit our expectations or predetermine possible outcomes, but explore all potentials, abilities, and interests. Include these children in regular education classes and activities. Remember: Success leads to more success, and failure leads to more failure!

Children with varying disabilities are frequently mainstreamed into regular classrooms. **Mainstreaming** means teaching children who are disabled in regular classes for part or all of their school day. To prepare for these children, teachers should learn as much as possible about typical child development, research the disabilities that they will be dealing with, seek help from specialists who work with the children, attend workshops or in-service training sessions, and talk with the children's parents. Teachers need extra skill, flexibility, and tolerance to work effectively with children who have special needs.

"By streamlining the instructional planning process, teachers implementing inclusion may experience less stress, greater confidence, and more success" (Winter, 1997, p. 216). Winter (1997) proposes a practical 5-point system (SMART) that helps teachers plan for inclusive education programs:

S   Select curriculum and approaches
M   Match instruction to the child
A   Adapt when necessary
R   Relevant skills targeted
T   Test to inform instruction (assessment)

Mainstreaming can be a positive experience for all children in the classroom. The benefits of mainstreaming for the typical child are learning to accept differences in people, learning to be a helpful and caring person, and learning how and when to help. Students who do not have disabilities experience an increase in self-esteem, tolerance, and growth in moral and ethical principles as a result of the inclusion of children with disabilities in the classroom. The benefits of mainstreaming for the child with special needs are the opportunity to choose friends with whom to play, to realize potential skills more fully, and to learn from peers without disabilities.

The potentials of special children inherent in heterogeneous groups, including mainstreaming, are greater for language and social development than for academic achievement. Educational services should be individually planned to best serve the needs of each child. Once a child has been placed, ongoing evaluation and observation should be undertaken to determine whether the program is providing optimal education for the child. To determine whether a program or service is effective, the student needs to demonstrate that he or she is progressing successfully.

The development of *all* children is enhanced when children with disabilities are included in regular classrooms as much as possible. For inclusion to be successful, both teachers and students with disabilities must receive support from parents, peers, extra personnel, special equipment and materials, and related in-service training. Although including children with special needs in learning environments with their typical peers presents many challenges, the rewards, benefits, and teamwork make it worthwhile. An effective inclusive classroom community empowers families, provides training and encouragement to teachers, and supports a 6-step process for inclusion:

1. Focusing attention on the value of inclusion
2. Involving key stakeholders in the planning
3. Finding and implementing easy successes
4. Identifying long-term service delivery partners in the community
5. Promoting ongoing systems support for inclusion
6. Evaluating the impact of change

Successfully incorporating these 6 steps results in an atmosphere that celebrates diversity, in which all children are able to grow, develop, and play together.

In addition, teachers or caregivers should respond to children's curiosity or questions with simple, accurate responses. Disabilities should be introduced to all children through books and materials that depict various disabilities, while still stressing the abilities and similarities among all human beings. All adults should model sensitivity to all people.

CREATING A DIVERSE CURRICULUM AND CLASSROOM

Copple and Bredekamp (2009) incorporate ideas for meeting the needs of young children who have disabilities, while supporting the importance of providing appropriate activities to support all children with different types of learning experiences. The most important goal for early childhood professionals is to provide *every* child with a responsive learning environment (NAEYC, 1996b). Creating a classroom, curriculum, and atmosphere that focus on diversity is challenging. In addition to broadly incorporating the goals stated earlier in the chapter, specific things can be done to create and teach diversity in the classroom.

Derman-Sparks and Edwards (2010, p. xiv) identified four goals for developing an antibias approach:

- Each child will demonstrate self-awareness, confidence, family pride, and positive social identities.
- Each child will express comfort and joy with human diversity; accurate language for human differences; and deep, caring human connections.
- Each child will increasingly recognize unfairness, have language to describe unfairness, and understand that unfairness hurts.
- Each child will demonstrate empowerment and the skills to act, with other or alone, against prejudice and/or discriminatory actions.

A curriculum program that promotes diversity not only fosters personal identity development in young children, but it also helps them to accept differences and diversities in others. Experiences should include exploring languages, customs, traditions, foods, and cultural activities through play, thematic units, field trips, visitors, stories and books, manipulatives and puzzles, dolls and dramatic play clothing, creative art, and music. Throughout all these activities, we must be sensitive to racism and prejudice, and provide support and encouragement as children develop their personal identities.

The following suggestions are not inclusive; add your own ideas to this list. In addition, each chapter of this text contains specific ideas for including and teaching diversity within the framework of various concepts.

Changing Attitudes and Practices of Teachers

Perhaps most important of all is that teachers do not just add the component of diversity to their curriculum; rather, the entire classroom and curriculum must be revised to reflect a change in attitude and practice that indicates genuine acceptance of all people. Teachers can do much by helping children to get rid of themselves the we–they attitude and replace it with the we–us attitude.

Selecting Books, Materials, and Resources

All children need to see images of themselves depicted in early childhood classrooms. Depictions of children with disabilities can be included in photographs, pictures, and posters; materials and equipment; and books and magazines. When children in the classroom see depictions of various diversities, they are more accepting and understanding of children who actually have these differences.

> When all children in classes are depicted in various ways, it sends a message that everyone belongs, that everyone is important, that everyone is accepted. This results in higher self-esteem and more positive personal identities for everyone.

Diversity materials need to be consistently available (Derman-Sparks & Edwards, 2010), and teachers must consciously evaluate the messages that are contained in these materials. Teachers should be cautious and careful in selecting materials such as books, pictures, games, and toys that are free of biases and stereotypes. Select materials that show diversity of culture, ethnicity, gender, and racial groups and that take the perspective of various minorities. Images of the elderly and people with disabilities should also appear.

One approach to assist young children in transitions and other activities in the classroom and, at the same time, to allow children to literally see themselves in books is to create "social stories—teacher-made books written for children on topics relevant to an individual" (Briody & McGarry, 2005, p. 38). These books include photographs of the child or children in transitions and activities within the classroom. As children read the books they share the experience and talk about it. The stories help them organize, remember, and interpret events during the day and they encourage prosocial behaviors. These kinds of stories encourage empathy by helping children understand different perspectives, cultures, and points of view (Briody & McGarry, 2005).

Children's picture books provide children with opportunities to read about and discuss differences they see. They provide a natural avenue for opening up communication and fostering environments of respect and understanding. Children's literature helps children appreciate diversity and develop prosocial attitudes and behaviors, and helps to build bridges and understandings between the known and the unknown (Feeney & Moravcik, 2005). Books and stories can generate attitudes of respect for diversity by discussing differences in people, talking through differences in people, and talking about topics that relate to diversity issues.

> How literature contributes to children's growing understanding of self and others (Feeney & Moravcik, 2005, pp. 22–24):
>
> 1. Increases positive self-concept
> 2. Increases respect for and appreciation of human diversity
> 3. Raises awareness that people live in many different ways
> 4. Aids the development of empathy
> 5. Aids the development of positive values
> 6. Models for ways to cope with problems and crises

We should work to provide all children with the experience of seeing themselves in their books and then learning to care for the others that they see. Children also need to be able to identify with heroes and heroines of their own culture. Avoid the practice of tokenism—selecting just one book, picture, or doll that includes an ethnic minority.

Throughout the year, pictures, toys, and books should reflect the diversity of people:

> Books that feature characters from diverse cultures help children become accustomed to the idea that there are many language, points of view, and ways of living. Books that focus on human universals help children recognize that all people need nurture, food, clothing, and shelter; tell stories, dance, and sing; and make things that are useful and beautiful—and do so in different and interesting ways. (Feeney & Moravcik, 2005, p. 23)

Classroom centers are also valuable resources for supporting diversity understandings. They make it easier to

- Meet the needs of a diverse group of children;
- Address particular goals and objectives of children with special needs;
- Develop varied and interesting activities;
- Promote efficient use of time and resources;
- Balance the number of structured and unstructured activities; and
- Coordinate schedules and responsibilities of teachers and staff.

> Successful centers in the early childhood classroom result when teachers understand the developmental goals, interests, and characteristics of the children; are aware of the environment; and know what materials and personnel resources are available.

Bulletin boards, films and videos, visitors, and field trips should constantly confirm the diversity of our world and present the minority perspective. During the year, invite several visitors from various cultures so that children may capture the variability that exists within and among cultures. Calendars should include dates of ethnic holidays and note outstanding citizens of diverse ethnic origins.

Dolls in the classroom should reflect different ethnic identities, physical abilities, and genders. "Persona" dolls can be used to introduce differences, particularly some of the differences not found among children in the classroom (Derman-Sparks & Edwards, 2010). These dolls have names, and the children personally identify with them through playing, interacting, associating, and listening to stories about their lives. For example, one doll might be named Jenny. Jenny might be blind and live with her mother and grandmother. Throughout the year, the teacher can build on Jenny's story and help the children to understand not only Jenny, but that her blindness is a way that she is different.

Games from other cultures are enjoyed by children and help broaden their perspectives. Music and art from other cultures can be included as a natural part of the early childhood environment.

Dramatic play offers ready opportunities to share clothing and items that reflect such diversities as the different physical abilities, genders, and ages of people.

If available materials are screened and found to be biased or presenting obvious stereotypes, the materials may need to be disregarded or altered. If this is the case, teachers should be honest with the children, pointing out biases and discussing them in ways that children can understand. Teachers can develop or make supplementary materials that help correct some of the misconceptions or biases found in materials.

Exposing Children to the Diversity of Cultures

There are more than 100 ethnic groups in the United States. Teachers cannot include curriculum content about each one, but they can focus on different groups that have a variety of customs, values, and traditions. Children should be acquainted with art, music, literature, and foods from various ethnic groups. Musical instruments, songs, dances, and stories can be presented and taught by people from various cultures. These should not be presented in ways that suggest tokenism, but rather so that children gain the perspective of and feel respect toward other people. As diversity is integrated into the curriculum, teachers should be mindful that the differences found among people are not to be interpreted as deficiencies or inferiorities. Cultures should not be described in terms of how they deviate from the mainstream culture. Diversity must be recognized as a strength and not considered as a weakness, so young children are able to understand the value of differences. People have different beliefs, eat many different foods, live in different ways, practice different religions, and have different names—and that is the way it should be.

Visitors with all kinds of talents, skills, and hobbies should be invited into the classroom. Field trips, a valuable resource for learning about differences and diversities, could be arranged for the same purpose of exposure. Focusing on similarities among all people throughout the classroom and the curriculum is a notion that might be referred to as the "common thread idea." We acknowledge the commonality of all people: We are all alike in that we are all people with feelings and hopes, and we are all more alike than different (Wardle, 1990). Yes, we are of different genders, social classes, religions; we come from a variety of ethnic backgrounds; and we have various physical abilities; but we share many similarities.

Accepting Language and Dialect Diversity

"Children enter preschool rich in their own language, and the important teaching builds on that strength rather than immersing children in a new language and ignoring the language and literacy development they have experienced so far" (Youngquist & Martinez-Griego, 2009, p. 94). The child's home language influences the child's overall development, and teachers should support its use at home and in the classroom (Kirmani, 2007).

Teachers must support language and dialect diversity, including sign language, and even teach words in other languages. If there are bilingual children in the classroom, they should often teach words or phrases relating to topics that are being discussed. Preferably in bilingual classes, children should use their native languages about half of the time, and the teacher should be fluent in the language of the majority of the students from minority groups. If there are no bilingual children in the classroom, the teacher could teach words or phrases from another language. For example, numbers, shapes, colors, units of money or time, the alphabet, songs, and fingerplays can all be taught in many languages.

Marcrina, Hoover, and Becker (2009) suggest that we consider the following strategies when no adult in the classroom speaks a child's home language:

- Model good English.
- Provide reading materials in the child's language.
- Encourage parents to use their home language with the child.
- Learn to correctly speak a few key words or phrases in the language, and teach them to everyone in the classroom.
- Make a picture chart showing the daily routines.
- Use pictures or props to help understand the meaning of new words.

All people speak different dialects, which includes both vocabulary and word pronunciation. Children have the right to their own language, and no dialect should be considered unacceptable. When we provide environments that support children's cultures and languages, they feel accepted and safe (Nemeth, 2009).

Using the Daily News as a Springboard for Cultural Awareness and Understanding

When discussing news and current events, locate other countries or states on maps. Brief dialogues about people in these areas can be included.

Teaching Differences in Occupations and Lifestyles

Children should become familiar not only with the obvious differences among people, but also with the varieties of people's occupations and lifestyles. These varieties can be found in pictures, books, visitors, and field trips. Teachers must connect the classroom with the diversities in the community and neighborhood. Parents and extended family members are great resources; they can share their interests, leisure pursuits, and professions. To overcome sexism, be sure to include women and men doing nontraditional jobs and having hobbies or interests that are nontraditional for a particular gender. This can help children to overcome the biases and stereotypes regarding sex roles and occupations.

Children learn that people have all kinds of jobs. Your challenge as a teacher of young children is to expose them to a variety of jobs. Be careful not to stereotype jobs so that the children develop misconceptions, such as only boys can be firefighters or police officers. A caution: If you begin discussing the jobs of some of the children's parents, in some way address the jobs of all the parents so that no child is left out.

Visits to or from elderly people and people with different physical abilities help children to overcome stereotypes. Books and stories also help to develop accurate concepts relating to older people or those who have physical limitations.

Diversity in family lifestyles needs to be taught, valued, and accepted. Some families have a single mom or dad; some have a mom who works and a dad at home; some have a dad who works and a mom who is at home; some have both parents who work; some have two moms and two dads (stepparents); some families are headed by grandparents or foster parents; some have interracial parents; some families have members with special needs.

Modifying Curriculum Approaches to Promote and Facilitate Achievement Among Children from Diverse Groups

Teachers can practice a number of strategies to ensure that all students have opportunities for success. Examples include using the language and traditions that children bring to school from their own culture to bridge the gap between what they know and what they need to learn. Learn the child's native language well enough to teach some academic content, and help other children learn basic words so they can communicate with each other. Cooperative learning should be used as a strategy. This approach to teaching and learning can promote integration of children from minority groups. As children come to know one another through working together, they naturally develop the respect, tolerance, and sensitivity that we are trying to achieve.

INCORPORATING THE NCSS STANDARDS

There is a developmental sequence for social studies content. Social studies is an opportunity for problem-solving life skills as well as development of coping skills. The National Council for the Social Studies (NCSS) suggests the main purpose of social studies "is to help young people develop the ability to make informed and reasoned decisions for the public good as citizens of a culturally diverse, democratic society in an interdependent world" (NCSS, 1993, p. 3). Teaching social studies seeks to engender a commitment to American democratic principles and ideals. NCSS has organized social studies content around 10 big ideas or themes from which or around which social studies is planned. A few general suggestions for applications are offered in the right column of the accompanying table.

These standards serve as both a framework and a guide by providing expectations regarding the knowledge, skills, and dispositions essential in social studies. Mindes (2005, p. 17) suggests some guidelines to consider when planning social studies curriculum:

• Build on what children already know.
• Develop concepts and processes.
• Provide hands-on activities and experiences.
• Select relevant social studies concepts.
• Take advantage of children's interests.

SPECIFIC CURRICULUM ACTIVITIES

Once we have adopted the diversity perspective, many ways of integrating it with our educational goals and implementing it in the classroom become obvious. All aspects of the curriculum should avoid stereotypes and include the diversity approach through experiences and materials that accurately reflect all cultural groups. Activities should be concrete, comprehensible, and linked to experiences in which the children can become involved. These activities will enrich and expand their overall experiences. As teachers, it is important that we make comparisons of similarities and differences among cultures whenever possible, focusing on the ways they are alike.

Theme	Early Childhood Applications or Performance Indicators
Culture Understanding various cultures, including the beliefs and traditions of the cultures, enables children to understand themselves and others.	• Compare and contrast cultures. • Recognize people have different perspectives. • Recognize characteristics of cultures including art, literature, foods, language, traditions, music, etc. • Describe the value of cultural unity and diversity within and across groups.
Time, Continuity, and Change Developing a historical perspective and locating self in time answers questions about self.	• Place stories, situations, and events into a historical perspective. • Analyze and explain changes over time. • Identify historical periods of time. • Compare and contrast families today and long ago.
People, Places, and Environment Increasing geographic perspectives bridges understanding between self and the environment.	• Use a variety of maps and globes to determine location and direction. • Recognize physical changes in the environment due to seasons, weather, and climate.
Individual Development and Identity Personal identity is molded by a variety of influences and affects human behavior.	• Recognize how factors such as family, religion, gender, and other cultural influences develop individual identity. • Recognize components of healthy self-identity including beliefs, attitudes, and perceptions. • Recognize influences on mental and emotional health. • Practice kindness, acts of service, and collaboration to and with others. • Identify personal changes over time, such as interests and physical development.
Individuals, Groups, and Institutions Institutions influence groups and cultures.	• Practice a variety of roles within group interactions. • Identify ways in which groups and institutions meet individual needs.
Power, Authority, and Governance Governments are essential for our democratic society.	• Identify rights and responsibilities of individuals. • Explain the purposes of government. • Identify features of the U.S. political system and of our country, such as our flag and national anthem.
Production, Distribution, and Consumption We live in a world with an interdependent economy.	• Recognize our economic system depends on the production of goods and services. • Relate how supply and demand determine what is produced and distributed.
Science, Technology, and Society Technology and supporting science influence the way we live today.	• Identify how science and technology have influenced our present society.
Global Connections Our diverse world requires making global connections among one another and societies.	• Learn about and develop respect for other cultures. • Describe our interdependence with other communities and nations. • Recognize forces for unity and cooperation among nations and people.
Civic Ideals and Practices Understanding the ideals of good citizenship is critical for positive participation in our communities.	• Identify what liberty and justice for all means. • Recognize and practice good citizenship.

Source: Themes from the National Council for the Social Studies, *Expectations of Excellence: Curriculum Standards for Social Studies* (Washington, D.C.: NCSS, 1994).

The following are some activities that can be incorporated into general areas of the basic curriculum. Additional activities are found in this chapter under the heading "Activities and Experiences." Also, each chapter in the text includes specific ways of integrating diversity into the teaching of specific concepts.

Communication Skills

Here are suggestions for increasing the acceptance and understanding of children's primary languages.

• View and listen to CDs and DVDs, and practice singing a variety of songs in different languages.

- Have the children learn many words and phrases in languages other than their native language, and especially in the languages of children in their class. Use names, foods, greetings, and other appropriate words and phrases.
- Translate children's names into other languages.
- Expose the children to sign language, the fourth most frequently used language in the United States.
- Talk to the children using words from different languages. Ask them whether they can understand the words. How does it make them feel when they are unable to understand the words?
- Have the children share and describe objects that are important to their culture.
- Interview parents and people in your community about their cultures, jobs, traditions, beliefs, or other things that will help the children capture a feeling of diversity.
- Share human-interest stories from news programs and photographs from the newspaper; locate on a map or globe where the stories take place.
- Have parents, staff members, or community members make tapes reading the children's favorite stories in different languages. These can be enjoyed as a group or with earphones, individually.

Literacy Skills

Stories and poetry have been used for many years to transmit values, traditions, skills, and practices important to various cultures. Here are some activities that can point out similarities in language and literacy experiences.

- Use open-ended and problem-solving situations about children from different backgrounds and of different abilities to help increase sensitivity to others. End with such questions as "How would you feel if . . . ?"
- Have the children observe and discuss pictures from ethnic magazines, calendars, cards, or professional journals so that they can learn about people who are different from themselves. Include a variety of cultures, children or adults doing nontraditional activities for their gender, and children of different physical abilities.
- Provide blank books for the children to dictate and illustrate stories about their families.
- Make a comparison of how alphabets are written in different cultures. Let the children experiment by writing their own.
- During the year, share books, stories, poetry, and folktales that represent the cultures of each child in your class.

Motor and Physical Skills

The following are some activities for increasing awareness that children everywhere develop and enjoy similar motor and physical activities.

- Acquire books, CDs, or DVDs that describe in detail traditional games played by children of different cultures.
- Identify and play such games as hopscotch and tag that may be found in all cultures. Describe specific culture variations.
- Teach the children how to play various card or board games using toys and manipulatives from different cultures.
- Teach authentic dances from other cultures, especially dances that offer cultural insights. Listen to music and sing songs from other cultures.

Creative Arts

Music and art offer many opportunities for providing cultural experiences for young children.

- Frequently listen to music from other countries, even as background music while the children are working or playing.
- Have pieces of art from different cultures displayed in the classroom.
- Invite artists and musicians from different cultures to visit and perform; discuss what feelings or messages they might be trying to portray.
- Have children share music that they listen to in their homes or art that their family appreciates.
- Provide paints or marking pens in such skin colors as brown, black, or peach (Derman-Sparks & Edwards, 2010).

Dramatic Play

The following dramatic play activities offer opportunities to explore various aspects of cultural diversity.

- Provide dress-up clothes and objects from different cultures in the housekeeping area, allowing both sexes to try out a variety of roles. Teachers may need to intervene if they hear stereotypic comments such as, "You can't wear the mail carrier's hat because you are a girl."
- Provide equipment that is used by people with disabilities. Allow the children to explore such things as crutches, wheelchairs, glasses, even a prosthesis.
- Cut from magazines, old sewing pattern books, and other sources pictures of children from various ethnic backgrounds and abilities. Laminate the pictures, mount them to sticks, and use them for telling stories, exploring language, or dramatizing.

Food Activities

Snacks and food activities from various cultures can often be added to the curriculum. Be careful of stereotyping by saying, for example, "This is Mexican food." Instead say, "This is a snack enjoyed by some Mexican Americans." Do not allow children to comment negatively about a food from another culture and do not force any child to eat a particular food (Derman-Sparks & Edwards, 2010). The following are a few examples of food activities:

- Share a particular culture's differences between daily foods and holiday foods.
- Visit ethnic restaurants to capture feelings, smells, and flavors.
- Make a recipe book of families' favorite recipes.

Math Skills

Children can learn about and compare counting systems used by various cultures by participating in some of the following activities:

- Teach the children to count in different languages.
- Study the development of calendar and time systems from different cultures.
- Compare money systems from different cultures. Compare coins and their sizes and values. Convert a dollar into rubles, lira, yen, and marks.
- Compare how numerals are written in various cultures.

Personal and Social Skills

Children's self-concepts grow when they feel that they are an important part of their environment. Some activities that may enhance children's self-concepts as well as build acceptance of diversity follow:

- Names are basic to a person's identity. Explore this concept by asking such questions as these: Where did your name come from? Does your surname (last name) or first name have an ethnic origin? Who named you? How do you pronounce your full name correctly? Can you say your name in other languages?
- Make a friendship tree by hanging objects from many cultures on the branches of a tree. Have the children identify each object, talk about it, tell whether it has a meaning, and match it with children from that heritage in the class.
- Have the children bring photos of themselves to compile into a book or make a bulletin board in the classroom. Let each child know that he or she is an important part of the class.
- Explore a variety of jobs, in the home and outside of the home, that are nontraditional for either sex.
- Create a bulletin board on the variety of families in the class.

Cultural Comparisons

The study of all cultures should be based on the premise that all people share the same basic needs for food, clothing, and families. Provide activities demonstrating that these and other needs are met in varied ways by different people.

- Use films, videos, DVDs, and resource people to acquaint children with diverse people.
- Use maps and a globe to show geographic locations.
- Provide dolls from both sexes and various cultures for the children to play with.
- Have children bring in real objects used by their families that may be historical or typical of the child's cultural group (for example, a rice steamer, fish trap, or krumkake iron).
- Collect ways the families and children recognize special days, seasons, rituals, and holidays. Make a scrapbook or display to share with the class.

PROSOCIAL SKILLS

There are many social skills in which young children learn and develop competence. Practicing the skills helps children accept and appreciate differences among classmates. The skills that we are eager to help children to develop are called **prosocial skills** or behaviors. Most prosocial skills come with experience and maturation. All children need guidance and correct modeling; many are aided by that spirit of self-confidence we call self-esteem. Many prosocial skills depend on the child's attitude; therefore, the teacher's goal in helping the child to develop prosocial behavior is to encourage the development of more positive attitudes. Much of their learning will come with practice. Once again, there are many great examples in literature that address positive social skills for young children.

The following are some of the prosocial skills encouraged by early childhood teachers (Vance & Weaver, 2002):

- Following classroom or center rules
- Learning to cope with social conflicts, such as name calling or teasing
- Treating others politely and courteously, and learning to use words such as "please" and "thank you"
- Being able to share the attention of others, including the teacher
- Developing eye-to-eye contact with peers and adults
- Learning to smile at others
- Being helpful and kind to others
- Showing empathy for another's feelings or situation and giving or expressing sympathy to others when they experience difficulties
- Being comfortable talking with others and being a good listener
- Following simple rules of games, taking turns, and cooperating
- Learning to gain attention from friends in positive and constructive ways
- Developing responsible behaviors, such as taking care of one's own possessions

Children learn prosocial skills, such as being helpful and kind to others, through modeling and guidance.

- Learning to compliment, rather than criticize, others
- Showing tolerance for others and their differences
- Sharing and cooperating with others in play situations
- Expressing sorrow when actions or words have hurt another
- Being able to accept the consequences of behavior and actions
- Learning to take the perspective of another person
- Cooperating with others in play and work, including in cooperative group activities
- Participating actively in class meetings, especially as a means to reason and solve conflict in a healthy manner

Children learn social skills when teachers give these skills the same attention and focus that they give to academic subjects. Although these skills will be taught and practiced daily, the teacher's modeling, feedback, reinforcement, and caring are critical to learning. For young children it is helpful for teachers to label and identify prosocial and antisocial behaviors and, in addition, to help children to become assertive concerning prosocial matters. Teachers should also model, acknowledge, and encourage understanding and expression of feelings.

Teachers can show pictured scenes of prosocial behaviors such as altruism and ask children to create verbal scenarios. It may be necessary to place a child who is experiencing social problems with another child who is more socially skilled to increase the antisocial child's positive peer interactions.

One relevant notion to explore is that people have feelings and that what we do and say can affect these feelings. Occasionally ask, "How would you feel if . . . ?" This question helps to sensitize children to the feelings of others. However, we need to emphasize that individuals are unique and have different feelings, so the same situation or event can result in different responses among various people.

Open-ended stories help to stimulate thinking about how other people feel in particular situations. Reading stories from children's literature also allows opportunities to discuss how children would respond in a similar situation and how they feel about a particular happening. Our responsibility is to select books with deep meaning that help children understand themselves and others, and touch heads and hearts. Stories can be powerful and can teach empathy and compassion. Trying to take the place of characters in the story will help children to become more sensitive to the feelings of others in real life.

In addition to sensitizing children to the feelings of others, teachers must also impart another important social skill to young children: conflict resolution. Children need specific tools or strategies for dealing with disagreements in positive ways. For example, teachers can teach children that when conflict occurs between individuals they can go through the following steps:

1. Both individuals stop and think.
2. Both take a turn to share what is wrong.
3. Each person listens to the other without interrupting.
4. Each thinks of possible solutions.
5. Both choose a solution that they both like.
6. The two people shake hands and smile at each other!

APPROACH TO TEACHING

Concepts and Ideas for Teaching

1. People are born (all people are babies at one time).
   a. Infants have particular characteristics and needs.
   b. There are differences and likenesses among babies, young children, and adults.
   c. The day of the year on which a person was born is called his or her *birthday*, and it is celebrated each year.
2. People die (all people will die at some time).
3. People do different things at different times; they have different experiences.
   a. People generally sleep during the night.
   b. Sometimes people sleep in the daytime.
   c. Children are in school part of the day and at home part of the day.

4. People have different capabilities.
   a. Most people can see, touch, hear, taste, and smell.
   b. Some people cannot do one or more of these things.
   c. Some people are athletic.
   d. Different people have different talents.
5. Different people have the same capabilities.
   a. A barber and a parent can both cut hair.
   b. A teacher and an orchestra member can both play the clarinet.
   c. A sibling and a friend can both play ball.
   d. A parent and a mechanic can both repair cars.
6. People are different sizes.
   a. Babies are smaller, adults bigger.
   b. Not all babies are the same size.
   c. Some people are tall, some short.
7. People are different shapes.

   Some people are thin, some fat.

8. People are of different races and nationalities. (Concepts include differences in homes, foods, clothes, and physical characteristics.)
9. People have different thoughts and ideas, and each person's ideas are important.
10. People have various religious beliefs and points of view.
11. People have various likes and dislikes.
    a. Some like spinach, some do not.
    b. Some like winter weather, some do not.
12. People have jobs. (Concepts include what these people do; how their jobs help; what equipment, machinery, and materials they use; and that they are important for more than the job they fill. Be sensitive to children who have a parent or parents who are unemployed.): doctor, mechanic, musician, carpenter, telephone operator, engineer, teacher, secretary, upholsterer, salesperson, gardener, accountant, janitor or custodian, photographer, author, electrician, server, pilot, police officer, jeweler, artist, dentist, clerk, farmer, or computer operator.
13. People change.
    a. Growth and age bring change. (New skills may be learned as a person grows older; sometimes older age curtails activity.)
    b. Makeup, cosmetics, clothes, costumes, jewelry, wigs, and hairstyles alter appearance.
    c. Voice changes from infancy through old age; the same voice can sing, talk, and cry.
    d. Exposure to sun may cause suntan or sunburn.
    e. Accidents or injuries result in physical or emotional changes.
    f. People increase in knowledge and learning (following directions; learning to read, walk, tie shoelaces, drive, delay gratification).

14. People eat food.
    a. Kinds of food
    b. Variations because of the time of day or season of the year
    c. Likes and dislikes in foods
    d. Cultural variations
15. People wear clothes.
    a. Names of particular clothing items; how they are worn
    b. When specific articles are worn (seasons, professions, occasions)
    c. Sequences of putting on clothing
    d. Fasteners on clothing
    e. Care of clothing
16. People live in homes. (Be sensitive to families who may be homeless.)
    a. Different kinds of homes
    b. Different building materials used: brick, lumber, rock, adobe, or canvas
    c. Inside and outside of homes
    d. Separate rooms, furnishings of rooms
    e. Different activities in different rooms
    f. Grounds surrounding homes
17. People travel.
    a. Places people travel: other homes, stores, churches, work or business, schools, recreation and sports locations, or on rides
    b. Ways people travel: automobile, airplane, train, taxi, van, bus, boat or ship, truck, motorcycle, bicycle or tricycle, tractor, ice skates/roller skates/roller blades, skateboard, skis, on foot, wheelchair, wagon or cart, horse, other animals (camel, elephant), snowmobile, or emergency vehicles (ambulance, fire truck, police car)
    c. Various methods of transportation have particular characteristics and related concepts (make selections appropriate to your specific curriculum plans).
       1. Speed and distance (miles per hour, time)
       2. Size and shape (dimensions, number of passengers, tires)
       3. Color (owner's choice, no choice, specifically designated)
       4. Sound (starting, running, stopping, horn or siren, wipers)
       5. Texture (inside, outside)
       6. Smell (fuel, engine, upholstery)
       7. Kind (models, company, use)
       8. Number (passengers, wheels, prices, speed, fuel, tickets)
       9. Shelters (garages, hangars, stations)
       10. Related jobs (mechanic, salesperson, attendant, driver, pilot)
       11. Parts (mechanical, physical)
       12. Purpose and use (recreation, business, education, shopping)

18. People have feelings and emotion: sadness, anger, fear, happiness, excitement, and loneliness.
19. People have names.
    a. Personal names
        1. Child's own name, first and last
        2. Names of others
        3. Others may have the same name
    b. Gender-related names
        1. Boy–girl
        2. Male–female
        3. Man–woman
        4. Father–mother
        5. Husband–wife
        6. Uncle–aunt
        7. Brother–sister
        8. Grandfather–grandmother
        9. Gentleman–lady
        10. Fellow–gal
    c. Other names (may also be roles, and people have more than one name or role): relative (cousin, etc.), family, people, person, child or children, boss, neighbor, friend, baby, adult, teenager or adolescent, names of professions, and employer or employee.
20. People have friends.
    a. Friends can be the same sex or the opposite sex.
    b. Friends can be the same age or different ages.
    c. Friendship takes effort and kindness.

Activities and Experiences

1. Make a neighborhood or community map, including schools, churches, homes, and businesses. Lay this map out flat, and provide small human figures and vehicles for the children to play with. Add cutouts of children's homes or apartments.
2. Make a set of flash cards or similar cards with pictures of community helpers. The children could be encouraged to bring pictures of their parents at their jobs or wearing clothing appropriate for those jobs. For another game, collect pictures of tools or items related to various jobs and have the children sort them. For example, for a hairdresser, use pictures of a comb, brush, scissors, and hair dryer.
3. Interviews with community helpers could be taped on a recorder or video if these persons cannot visit the classroom. Children will be especially proud to hear their parents tell about their jobs.
4. The children can interview their parents about their jobs, asking questions about what their jobs are and why, how, and where they are done. Charts or stories can be compiled; plan visits on site or invite parents into the classroom.

5. The children can tell and/or illustrate stories about their own roots or histories. They can tell about an ancestor, show a pedigree chart, or show family histories, journals, or scrapbooks; they can even invite a grandparent or great-grandparent to visit the class. Some children may have clothing or other antique items to share and discuss with the class.
6. Provide hammers, nails, blocks, lumber, canvas, and boxes for building different sizes, shapes, and kinds of houses, businesses, and transportation.
7. Obtain an old camera, or make pretend cameras. Give the children the opportunity of pretending to take each other's picture. They may wish to draw pictures to represent those that they "photograph." (Children could also use functioning camera.)
8. Make up riddles for different jobs or careers and have the children guess the answer to each riddle. For example: "I work with animals. I ride on a tractor. I grow wheat to make bread, and I grow other things that you eat. Who am I?"
9. Lotto or matching games can be made using pictures or words, depending on the skills of the children. The pictures or names of the community helpers can be matched with tools or items relating to their job. For example, a picture or the word *firefighter* is matched with such pictures or words as *hydrant, fire engine, fire hat,* or other related tools.
10. The children can draw or make a collage of their community and title it "Why (name of community) Is a Good Place to Live." Encourage children to contact community resources and agencies for information brochures that can also supply pictures for collages.
11. Use maps whenever you go on a field trip, helping children to understand that maps give directions and help us to know how to get to a particular destination.

 UNIT IDEAS ON PEOPLE

(This could most effectively be broken down into more specific units.)

FIELD TRIPS

- Hospital
- Doctor's office
- Grocery store
- Barbershop
- Beauty shop
- Service station
- Fire station

- Police station
- Dentist's office
- Clothing store
- Basketball court
- Landmark buildings or historical sites
- Skating rink
- Another school
- Livestock auction
- Eye doctor's office
- Airport
- Train depot
- Bus station
- Boat dock
- Farm
- Care center
- Court of law
- Museum

VISITORS

- Doctor
- Nurse
- Barber
- Hair stylist
- Grocery store clerk
- Grandparent
- Baby
- Mechanic
- Musician
- Train engineer
- Firefighter
- Dentist
- Clothing store clerk
- Pilot
- Farmer
- Auctioneer
- Garbage truck operator
- Janitor or custodian
- Athlete
- Soldier
- Clown

MUSIC

- Creative movements of various professions, children growing, traveling different ways, dressing up, and so on
- Music from many cultures

ART

- Decoration of handmade musical instrument
- Houses built from large cardboard boxes, poles, canvas, and so on, and decorated
- Boats, trains, cars, and wagons built from large cardboard boxes and decorated
- Collage of pictures of people and objects relating to people, cut from catalogs or magazines
- Litter bags

FOOD (ANY FOOD ACTIVITY)

- Common foods, unusual foods
- Foods specific to season
- Foods specific to holiday
- Foods for breakfast, lunch, dinner
- Foods from various cultures

SCIENCE

- Study how bricks, canvas, lumber, adobe, or other materials are prepared for use in building; bricks are made of straw and mud and then dried.
- Study germs under a microscope.
- Study effects of aging.
- Study effects of land, water, and air pollution.

LITERACY AND DIVERSITY ACTIVITIES

- Make a book titled "Our Families Are Different." All children will have a page to put drawings or photographs of their families and then write or dictate a few sentences about their families.
- Make a book titled "Families Do Different Things." All children will have a page to put drawings, photographs, and sentences that describe things that their families do. They may wish to include parents' or guardians' jobs and hobbies or things that the family does together.
- Make a book or bulletin board titled "How My Family Celebrates Holidays." The children can share through words, pictures, and photographs how they celebrate particular holidays. Be sure to point out the variations that exist even within a particular culture.
- Discuss and/or write about how families worship in a variety of ways. Point out that individuals and families have their own beliefs.
- Make a book on your community titled "Our Neighborhood." Visit, take pictures, and write a few sentences about a variety of neighbors. You may want to visit an elderly person, a person

with special needs, or businesses such as the grocery store, service station, restaurant, and bank. Put each neighbor or business on a separate sheet of paper, laminate the sheets, combine them into a book, and allow the children to read it during the year.

- Discuss stereotypes of certain holidays such as Thanksgiving. Share and critique pictures and books. Ask, "How would you feel if you were a Native American and you saw this picture?" (Derman-Sparks & ABC Task Force, 1989).

UNIT IDEAS ON AUTOMOBILES

VISITORS

- Auto mechanic
- Service station attendant
- New car dealer
- Person from auto body shop who paints cars
- Automobile seat upholsterer
- Parent showing how to care for car, wash car exterior, and change tire
- Police officer with police car
- Taxicab driver
- Chauffeur
- Racecar driver
- Older child with model car display

FIELD TRIPS

- Auto mechanic shop
- Used car lot
- Car dealership
- Auto seat upholstery shop
- Automatic car wash
- Manual car wash
- Service station
- Junkyard for useless cars
- Self-service gas pump
- Parking lot where numerous cars are parked (shopping center, school parking lot, golf course, etc.); notice colors, sizes, shapes, sounds
- Auto body and paint shop

SCIENCE

- Repair of a flat tire
- Discussion of value of keeping car's interior and exterior clean; vacuuming, washing, and drying inside and outside of car
- Demonstration of how wax finish repels water and other agents
- Discussion of parts of auto (depending on ages and understandings of children); children can experiment with no-longer-used engine parts (if not greasy)

FOOD

- Food items commonly eaten in cars: hamburgers, milkshakes, floats, sundaes, french fries, sandwiches, cookies, carrot and celery sticks, candy, ice cream cones

ART

- Tires, windows, doors, or other car-related items pasted on a car shape
- Shapes of cars used for easel painting
- Cardboard-box cars painted and decorated
- Decoration of shakers made from juice cans, then filled with screws, nuts, and bolts from cars

MUSIC

- Musical cars: played like musical chairs, but with decorated cardboard boxes
- Drums made from empty gallon tin cans (both ends cut from can) and rubber from inner tubes; rubber circles cut larger than can ends; rubber circles placed over ends and laced together
- Shakers made from cans and filled with screws, nuts, and bolts of various sizes used in cars
- Creative movements: pretending to be a car going fast or slow, having a flat tire, running out of gas, getting stuck in snow or mud

Webbing provides a visual picture for brainstorming and developing unit plans. See Figures 5.1 and 5.2 for examples of web drawings; refer back to Chapter 4 for a more in-depth description of webbing procedure.

Do any food activity as a cooperative learning experience.

Tell or read story of A Friend Is Someone Who Likes You.

Tell or read book Charlotte's Web and/or watch video. Discuss characters' friendship traits.

Food

Language and Literacy

Write or dictate letter to a friend.

Do fingerprints and compare similarities and differences among class members.

Each child completes page for booklet titled "How to Be a Friend."

Discuss and share how friends can have similarities and differences.

Science

In cooperative learning groups do an activity such as planting a seed.

In cooperative learning groups, make a collage of a picture titled "I Can Have Many Different Friends." Pictures can be cut from magazines and pattern books from fabric stores.

Art

Friends

Mail a letter to a friend.

Field Trips

Make a friendship bracelet or necklace to share with a friend.

Do a picture or simple craft for a friend.

Visit a dentist at a dental clinic.

Elderly person

Visitors

Learn a dance for which each child needs a partner.

Music

Make a "pretend" camera using a small jewelry box. "Take" pictures of friends. Put magazine pictures inside. Using a rubber band around the box, the children can "snap" pictures.

Librarian to tell about a book that focuses on friends. Example: Tell about friends in Indian in the Cupboard.

Police Officer

Teach songs such as "I Have a Friend" that focus on friendships.

Do a rhythm band and focus on sharing instruments.

Suggested Books
(Note: Complete references are provided in "Suggested Resources" at the end of the chapter.)

A Friend Is Someone Who Likes You (Anglund, 1983)   May I Bring a Friend? (DeRegniers, 1971)
Indian in the Cupboard (Banks, 1981)   Best Friends (Hopkins, 1986)
Do You Want to Be My Friend? (Carle, 1971)   Best Friends (Kellogg, 1990)
Will I Have a Friend? (Cohen, 1967)   Frog and Toad Are Friends (Lobel, 1970)
Best Friends (Cohen, 1971)   Charlotte's Web (White, 1952)

FIGURE 5.1   Project Web for Study of Friends

Summary

Children need to begin to develop social values and skills in their earliest years as they share different insights of people and culture. As children become aware of similarities and differences among people, emphasis should *always* be on the ways that people are more alike than different. However, they must recognize the rich diversity among cultures (Louie, 2006). This also helps to prevent the development of biases and prejudices.

As teachers strive to incorporate the perspective of diversity, they must successfully foster genuine respect for *all* children, regardless of gender, race, physical abilities, or ethnic orientation. Teachers must also promote

Study air or water purity or pollution.

Find out what happens to garbage.

Visit an elderly person at home or at a nursing home.

Science

Field Trips

Visit someone in the neighborhood who has an interesting hobby.

Explore how neighborhood is changing.

Visit someone in the neighborhood who has a flower or vegetable garden.

Business owner

Store owner

Read books and poetry about community helpers, stores and businesses, names, ways to travel.

Visitors

Public service employee to share what he or she does.

Each child completes page for book titled "What I Can Do to Be a Good Neighbor."

Literacy

Projects

Each child can make a map of his or her neighborhood.

Neighborhood

Do a three-dimensional map of the neighborhood immediately around the school.

Each child completes a page of booklet titled "What I Can Do to Make Our Neighborhood Great."

Art

Food Activities

Make a snack or treat to take to a lonely neighbor.

"Spreading Love in the Neighborhood." Each child designs a heart or love poster. Do a class letter that tells recipient that this is from someone in the neighborhood who loves him or her. The letter will also challenge the recipient to make a treat, make a letter and poster, and pass on the goodwill to another family. Let each child share the poster, and the treat made as a food activity, along with letter.

Make a treat to use and share in "Spreading Love in the Neighborhood" activity.

FIGURE 5.2 Project Web for Study of Neighborhoods

attitudes of tolerance and acceptance in order to prevent the acquisition of stereotypes relating to race, gender, or handicaps and other forms of discrimination. Children must be taught positive attitudes, concepts, and skills that enable them to function cooperatively in our diverse society.

It is the professional and moral responsibility of teachers to evaluate their own philosophies regarding diversity, and then demonstrate and model how differences are valued and appreciated.

All children must be given opportunities to reach their potential, encouraged to feel valued as members of society, and taught to understand differences among people. They must be taught that discriminatory actions and attitudes are not acceptable and be helped to feel positive identification with their own gender, race, physical and mental abilities, and ethnic backgrounds.

Teachers must be aware of biases and stereotyping with regard to race, gender, religion, and special needs. Public Laws 94-142 and 99-457 provide direction for identifying and providing educational programs for children who have disabilities. This chapter includes characteristics, teaching strategies, and specialists in such special needs areas as speech and language impairments; mental retardation; hearing, visual, and physical impairments; emotional, social, or behavioral problems; chronic illness; learning disabilities; and gifted and talented children.

In creating a diverse curriculum and classroom, teachers must change their attitudes and practices; carefully select books, materials, and resources; expose children to cultural diversities; focus on similarities among all peoples; accept language and dialect diversity; use the daily news for cultural awareness and understanding; teach differences in occupations and lifestyles; and use cooperative learning as a strategy.

Suggestions for incorporating unit plans and lesson plans into the diversified curriculum have been presented, along with the valuable tool of webbing for brainstorming and developing unit or project ideas.

Student Learning Activities

1. Describe yourself in terms of your own culture. Using professional journals or books, find at least two sources that help you to define and understand your own culture. Remember, your culture includes your ethnicity, religion, social class, physical abilities, and gender. Create a poster representing the cultures that help to define who you are.
2. Examine and describe some of your own biases. What do you specifically plan to do to overcome these biases?
3. Prepare a unit plan or TWS (Teacher Work Sample), web, or project on one or more of the following: a specific community helper, a type of transportation, homes, similarities among class members, differences among class members. Evaluate your work to see whether you included the diversity perspective.
4. Evaluate a lesson you have taught or will teach and see if you have made accommodations and adaptations for diverse learners including special needs children, ELLs (English Language Learners), gifted and talented, or other diverse characteristics.
5. Prepare a unit plan or TWS on a topic of your choice and find specific ways to integrate the diversity perspective into the plan.
6. Observe in a classroom of young children and describe how the diversity perspective was woven into the curriculum, environment, and discussions or conversations. What changes would you suggest?

Suggested Resources

National Association for the Education of Young Children. (1995). *Position statement. Responding to linguistic and cultural diversity: Recommendations for effective early childhood education.* Washington, DC: Author. Online: www.naeyc.org/about/positions/pdf/PSDIV98.PDF.

Ramsey, P. G. (2004). *Teaching and learning in a diverse world: Multicultural education for young children* (3rd ed.). New York: Teachers College Press.

Children's Books

Anglund, J. W. (1958). *A friend is someone who likes you.* New York: Harcourt, Brace & World.

Banks, L. R. (1981). *Indian in the cupboard.* New York: Doubleday.

Cohen, M. (1967). *Will I have a friend?* New York: Simon & Schuster.

DeRegniers, B. (1974). *May I bring a friend?* New York: Simon & Schuster.

Hopkins, L. B. (ed.) (1986). *Best friends.* New York: HarperCollins.

Kellogg, S. (1990). *Best friends.* New York: Dial.

Lobel, A. (1970). *Frog and toad are friends.* New York: HarperCollins.

White, E. B. (1952). *Charlotte's web.* New York: Harper & Bros.

Online Resources

www.ed.gov/policy/speced/guid/idea/idea2004.html This is the official site for IDEA 2004 news, information, and resources.

www.fcsn.org Links, information, and support for parents of special needs children provided from the Federation for Children with Special Needs. There is a link for Early Childhood.

http://specialchildren.about.com Information on this site is directed to parents, with links and information on a broad range of special needs and topics.

www.newhorizons.org/spneeds/front_spneeds.html This site offers information on a variety of special needs students.

www.chadd.org The site for the organization Children and Adults with Attention Deficit/Hyperactivity Disorder offers help and support materials for working with children with ADHD or ADD.

www.adhdsolutions.com Resources offered for parents and students seeking solutions for working effectively with ADHD children.

www.teachersagainstprejudice.org This site provides information and statistics from an organization created to combat prejudice.

www.tolerance.org The mission of this organization is to create a national community dedicated to human rights.

www.epals.com This website is dedicated to providing help in setting up a pen-pal program.

www.name.org The National Multicultural Education Association is an association providing information on celebrating diversity.

www.ncss.org/about/home/html The National Council for the Social Studies (NCSS) provides leadership, service, and support for K–16 teachers in a variety of content areas. The organization supports civic values necessary for fulfilling the duties of citizenship in a participatory democracy.

chapter 6

Myself and Others

An effective wellness program for young children should be developmentally and chronologically appropriate and contribute to the child's total development. Knowledge of health, safety, and nutrition is crucial in meeting life goals and providing for the total needs of each child. (Marotz, Cross, & Rush, 2005)

In educating the whole child, we must consider both the physical and psychological health of the children in our classrooms (Bales, Wallinga, & Coleman, 2006). The child's healthy development includes a variety of components, including physical and motor development; spiritual, emotional, social, and intellectual health; nutrition fitness and good eating habits; and attention to general health and safety issues. Establishing early patterns of healthy lifestyles is important in enhancing physical and psychological well-being for a lifetime (National Association for Sport and Physical Education [NASPE], 2001). ". . . mounting research strongly suggests that attention to children's health is critical to improving the school performance and academic outcomes for all children" (Winter, 2009, p. 287).

PHYSICAL HEALTH

Physical *inactivity* is a major public health problem in the United States. In addition, more than half of American children are overweight and regularly inactive (Huettig, Sanborn, DiMarco, Popejoy, & Rich, 2004). Childhood obesity increases the risks of several adult health issues, the early onset of type II diabetes, and depression and other psychological outcomes (Huettig et al., 2004).

There seems to be a close correlation between early positive social relationships and later adult adjustment.

Because children are less physically active than ever before, early childhood educators must recognize the importance of including regular physical activity in the curriculum. Classroom strategies to encourage greater activity include incorporating more dance and movement; providing opportunities to use large muscles both indoors and outdoors; inviting dramatic responses to literature and poetry; taking walks inside and outside the building; providing many large-motor materials such as balls (all sizes), hula-hoops, ropes, and parachutes (Huettig et al., 2004). The American Academy of Pediatrics (AAP) recommends that children in the early childhood years should be involved in some form of age- and developmentally appropriate physical activity (AAP, 2003). Movement activities are essential to learning, and physical fitness is important to brain development. Especially in early childhood, more activity meaningfully applied makes significant contributions to the learning process. Quality programs in physical education are developmentally appropriate and improve children's mental alertness, their academic performance, their readiness to learn, and their enthusiasm and interest in learning and coordination (Epstein, 2007). "Physical coordination is essential to accomplishing many, if not most, everyday tasks" (Epstein, 2007, p. 88).

Units, activities, and projects relating to the children's health should be planned so they learn about good health, gain competencies that will guide their choices and behavior, get exercise, and have fun. Activities relating to healthy development should be integrated throughout the curriculum. For example, as children participate in food activities, snacks, or meals, they can learn about good nutrition. Concepts relating to healthy eating can be taught using the U.S. Department of Agriculture's MyPyramid (USDA, 2005), and when preparing and eating snacks. Also, many locomotor and fitness activities can easily be combined with creative movement and music activities or with fingerplays.

Teachers often become passive and lack thought or planning when it comes to physical education. As more and more attention is being given to academic performance in our schools, less and less attention is being given to physical activities. Teachers may believe that adding an activity here or there or making sure the children get to play outside is enough. During the early years, children's brain development is expanding rapidly; but without proper environmental experiences and movement, the brain will not be able to develop properly. We cannot ignore the physical and emotional health of our students and expect them to be able to concentrate on learning.

Children's physical, social, emotional, and intellectual lives are a crucial part of the curriculum. Programs should be designed to represent a developmental sequence and can be integrated or stand as independent experiences, but they should provide a challenge for young children and allow them to progress in physical and motor development.

Appropriate instruction in physical education includes (NASPE, n.d.):

- Full inclusion of all students
- Maximum practice opportunities for class activities
- Well-designed lessons that facilitate student learning
- No physical activity for punishment
- Regular assessment to monitor and reinforce student learning

Physical Fitness

Physical movement and activity are essential for healthy growth and development and can provide many opportunities for both fine- and gross-motor skill development (NAECS/SDE, 2003). Physical activity has many short- and long-term benefits for physical, cognitive, and affective well-being. Regular, vigorous physical activity in a supportive environment helps build healthy habits that continue throughout life. All young children should have daily instruction in movement concepts and motor-skill themes (NASPE, 2004).

In addition to physical activity to support physical fitness in the classroom, teachers should encourage families to provide more physical activity for children at home. Teachers can suggest the following to families (Huettig et al., 2004):

1. Children should accumulate 30 to 60 minutes of physical activity every day.
2. All children should be encouraged to watch less TV every day.
3. Children should watch videos or shows that encourage physical activity.
4. Children should be encouraged to participate in exercise routines and basic physical movements.

Benefits of Being Physically Fit

- Weight control
- Decreased blood pressure
- Improved concentration, attention, and retention
- Decreased disruptive behavior
- Reduced risk of diabetes and heart disease
- Healthy bones, joints, and muscles
- Better overall health
- Decreased anxiety, depression, and stress
- Increased energy, endurance, and strength
- More positive self-esteem

The National Association for Sport and Physical Education (NASPE, 2004, p. 11) has outlined national standards for physical education, similar to other content areas. "Physical activity is critical to the development and maintenance of good health. The goal of physical education is to develop physically educated individuals who have the knowledge, skills, and confidence to enjoy a lifetime of healthful physical activity" (NASPE, 2004, p. 11). The following are the six national standards for a physically educated person:

Standard 1: Demonstrates competency in motor skills and movement patterns needed to perform a variety of physical activities.

Standard 2: Demonstrates understanding of movement concepts, principles, strategies, and tactics as they apply to the learning and performance of physical activities.

Standard 3: Participates regularly in physical activity.

Standard 4: Achieves and maintains a health-enhancing level of physical fitness.

Standard 5: Exhibits responsible personal and social behavior that respects self and others in physical activity settings.

Standard 6: Values physical activity for health, enjoyment, challenge, self-expression, and/or social interaction.

Source: Reprinted from *Moving into the Future: National Standards for Physical Education* (2004), with permission from the National Association for Sport and Physical Education (NASPE), 1900 Association Drive, Reston, VA 20191, www.naspeinfo.org.

Movement and motion are basic to the needs of young children, in developing their bodies and also in developing the whole child. To educate the whole child, we must first recognize that children are naturally often active and moving. Much of the physical fitness activity in early childhood is in the area of movement, because children are acquiring competence in fundamental locomotor movements such as walking, running, skipping, climbing, throwing, and kicking. During early childhood, the child's gross movement abilities begin to expand dramatically. Movement can be added to any classroom without any special equipment; all we need is our bodies, imaginations, and willingness to try. In most areas of the curriculum, teachers will be able to find opportunities for children to participate in movement experiences and, as they do, children can be creative and also use problem-solving adeptness. The development of movement skills (locomotion, gross- and fine-motor manipulation, and stability) requires multiple opportunities for practice, positive reinforcement and encouragement, and quality instruction. More than 14 years ago, Gallahue (1996) provided suggestions for creating a positive movement environment for early childhood, which are still appropriate today.

- Allow for individual choices and decisions.
- Create simple and appropriate fitness activities.
- Provide demonstrations and modeling.
- Keep directions and instructions simple.
- Provide variety.
- Allow adequate time for practice and participation.
- Encourage more active play.
- Focus on the process, not the product.
- Eliminate competition.
- Be patient.
- Allow and encourage creativity.

"For children to gain the basic physical skills they need, adults must plan movement experiences and structure physical activities that introduce a range of movement options" (Epstein, 2007, p. 87). NASPE (2000) defines the components of the movement environment: scheduled

Physical activity, both inside and outside, must be a major part of the early childhood curriculum.

activity, class size, equipment, play, facilities, repetition and success, participation for every child, and movement integration into other subjects.

Fitness, Motor, and Movement Guidelines

1. To develop their large muscles adequately, young children need teacher or adult guidance in physical activities, not just the opportunity to play on large-muscle equipment. This is facilitated by planning motor and physical activities and centers.

2. Physical and motor activities should be rewarding and positive experiences. Children should soon sense that moving and exercising make them feel more energetic and strong.

3. Teachers should emphasize fitness, not competition. Competition must be avoided by early childhood teachers. Competitive pressures result in decreased self-esteem and quality of learning and increased rivalry, anger, withdrawal, and sense of inadequacy. A child should be taught early to compete with himself or herself, to try to improve and do better.

4. Teachers should observe carefully so that children do not overdo. Gear your guidance and expectations to the needs and abilities of individual children.

5. Teachers should provide positive models for the children by participating in physical and motor games and activities whenever appropriate.

> **The optimum environment must be:**
>
> - Physically and emotionally safe
> - Free of teasing, humiliation, stress, intimidation, comparison, competition, failure, and rejection
> - Full of acceptance, encouragement, creativity, success, support, discovery, enjoyment, and fun

FUNDAMENTAL PHYSICAL MOVEMENTS

Locomotor Movements

Developing and exploring **locomotor movements** are important aspects of physical fitness. These movements adapt readily to music and rhythm activities. Some of the basic locomotor movements include walking, climbing, marching, running, hopping, jumping, skipping, galloping, rolling, crawling, leaping, sliding, and trotting. The most basic of these movements, and the one to begin with, is walking. Rhythmically, this movement has a basic, steady-beat pattern that can be slower or faster. Background stimulus for locomotor movements can be provided by a drumbeat or other instrument beat, a musical recording, a song, or an accompaniment on a tuned instrument such as a piano. As children

develop skill in each of the locomotor movements, they should be given the opportunity and encouragement to use the movements in a variety of ways and to find different ways of exploring the movements. For example, the following are some ways to explore walking; many of these same suggestions could be applied to other basic locomotor movements.

Fast	With eyes closed
Slow	On hands and feet
Heavily	Like . . . (a tin soldier, etc.)
Lightly	Happily, sadly, etc.
Low	In the wind
In the middle	In the cold
High	In the snow
With toes in	When it is hot
With toes out	Barefoot in the sand, on the grass, on pebbles, on hot pavement, in cold water
On heels	
On tiptoe	
On the outside of the foot	
Backward	
Sideways	In the dark
Diagonally	Following your hand as you walk
In big steps	
In short steps	Leading with your ear, eye, elbow, shoulder
Stamping	
Skating	
With knees out	
With knees high	
Lazily	
Long steps	When going someplace special
Tiny steps	
In slow motion	When going someplace you do not care to go
In the rain	

Further examples of exploring different locomotor movements might be variations of running. Children could run lightly or heavily, stop suddenly, or change directions. Bells and triangles could be used to evoke lighter running and drums and tambourines for more vigorous action. Marching is an often-used locomotor movement in early childhood classrooms. However, the goal there is usually to keep time to music, to keep in step, or to stay in the circle. We propose that the goal should not always be to keep time or to keep in step. Children should not always have to be in a line or circle; they can learn to march in different directions without interfering with others. Explore variations with marching.

Axial Movements

Other types of movements are often referred to as **nonlocomotor, axial movements.** They include the following (suggestions for stimulating these kinds of movements are given):

1. Swinging and swaying
   a. Swing arms like the pendulum of a clock, from side to side.
   b. Swing arms over and around, as though winding yourself up.
   c. Swing arms and body back and forth, as though getting ready to take off in flight or rocking in a chair.
   d. Swing and sway any part of your body like a monkey.
   e. Make some part of your body move like a railroad signal.
   f. Make some part of your body move like trees and leaves moving in the wind.
   g. Make some part of your body move like windshield wipers.
2. Bending and stretching
   a. How many different parts of your body can you bend? How many parts can you stretch? In how many different directions can you stretch?
   b. Bend yourself small and then stretch yourself tall.
   c. How many ways can you stretch your face?
   d. Can you stretch some part of you like a rubber band? If so, what happens when you pop?
   e. Pretend you are walking on stilts.
   f. Stretch, move, and bend your body through the stages of a sneeze.
   g. Move your body as though you were reaching for something on the highest shelf in your home.
   h. Pretend to be an inchworm.
3. Pushing and pulling
   a. Pretend that you are pushing a wagon.
   b. How many ways can you pretend to be pushing and pulling a piano?
   c. Pretend you are digging and hoeing weeds in the garden.
   d. Show me how you would move to work the oars of a boat.
   e. Pretend that you are swimming. How about pretending that you are rescuing someone who is drowning?
4. Rising and falling
   a. Pretend to be a jack-in-the-box.
   b. Show me how you would move if you were the sun rising and then setting.
   c. Pretend to be an airplane taking off in flight and then landing.
   d. Pretend to be a seed growing into a flower, and then a petal on that flower falling and blowing away.
   e. Pretend to be a ball bouncing up and down. Do you always bounce to the same height?
5. Twisting and turning
   a. How would you move if you were a top?
   b. Pretend that you are using a hula-hoop.
   c. Show me how you would move if you were an ice skater making a turn.
   d. Pretend that you are a lid being screwed onto a jar.
6. Shaking
   a. Shake like Santa Claus.
   b. Pretend to be some jelly.
   c. Show how you would move if you were being washed in a washing machine.
   d. Shake as though you were a milkshake being mixed.

Using Locomotor and Axial Movements

There are many ways to teach and use both locomotor and nonlocomotor movements. By getting children involved in these kinds of movements, you will enhance their coordination, give them experience with movement, provide opportunities for creative problem solving, and encourage physical activity and development. The following are further suggestions for accomplishing these goals:

- Many songs and musical arrangements offer opportunities for locomotor and nonlocomotor movements.
- Use a follow-the-leader approach.
- Suggest movements that resemble those of animals.
- Suggest ways to "cross the river" or go across the room.
- Use nursery rhymes to stimulate movements.
- Suggest ways to go around a dowel or other stick.
- Use records to stimulate ideas for movement.
- Lay out foot patterns on the floor for practicing fundamental locomotor movements.
- Draw shapes in the air using different parts of the body (include shapes, letters, and numbers, making them different sizes).
- Jump into the middle of a space and find various ways to move to get out.

Once children have explored locomotor and nonlocomotor movements, they are ready for what we often refer to as **creative movements.** Having had the basics of movement, they are ready to create on their own and use more freedom. Much of what we have suggested for both locomotor and nonlocomotor movements leads to creative movements, and the two categories become difficult to separate.

Physical activity is an important way to help children reduce stress. The rule should always be: "No helmet, no bicycle."

Fitness and Motor Activities

LARGE-MOTOR ACTIVITIES. Examples of these are walking, running, galloping, skipping, jogging, balancing, hopping, jumping, sliding, and climbing. Throwing and catching can include beanbag tosses, ball-throwing and ball-catching games and skills, or ring tosses. Other ball-handling skills include kicking, bouncing, dribbling, and rolling. Riding wheeled equipment is also a good large-motor activity. Balancing skills include walking a beam, stretching, bending, swinging, and twisting. Opportunities to run, walk, or jog should be provided daily to increase cardiovascular fitness.

SMALL-MOTOR ACTIVITIES. These include zipping, lacing, twisting, pouring, cutting, inserting pegs, pounding nails, tracing, and writing.

STUNTS OR SELF-TESTING ACTIVITIES. *Note:* These must be adapted to the developmental physical and motor abilities of the children in your group. Many are more appropriate for 6- to 8-year-old children. Many can be done to music.

- *Frog jump.* The children assume a squatting position with hands on the floor. They move forward with a springy jump, extending their legs and landing first on hands and then on feet.
- *No arms.* The children lie flat on their backs and fold their arms. The object is to get to a standing position without unfolding the arms.
- *Crab walk.* The children clutch their ankles with their hands and walk forward and sideways step by step.
- *Seesaw.* Two children sit on the floor facing each other with their feet together. They clasp hands and, as one leans forward, the other pulls back as far as she or he can. They seesaw back and forth.
- *Toe touch.* The children stand with their feet apart. They touch the right toe with the left hand and then alternate.
- *Back to back.* The children are in pairs, standing back to back. They try to sit down and then stand back up while keeping their backs together.
- *Partner pull-up.* The children are in pairs, sitting on the ground, facing each other, knees bent, feet flat on the ground, toes touching. With hands grasped, they try to pull each other up and then try to sit back down.
- *Jumping jacks.*
- *Forward roll.*
- *Backward roll.*

PHYSICAL GAMES

Active games in early childhood can promote a variety of life skills including social and cooperative skills, listening skills, and physical fitness. Games give opportunity for developing self-regulation or the ability to stay on task and to pay attention (Torbert, 2005). Games selected need to be developmentally appropriate and inclusive (Torbert, 2005). Young children play games much differently than school-age children. Consider the traditional games of Duck, Duck, Goose; Red Rover, Red Rover; Charlie, Charlie, Butcher Boy; The Farmer in the Dell; I Have a Little Doggie; Drop the Handkerchief, and so on. Just because they are traditional does not mean they are educational! They may be fun for some, but are they fun for all? Are we supporting physical activity, positive feelings, and developing skills, or are we actually doing activities that result in competition, rejection, and failure?

Guidelines for Effectively Playing Physical Games

1. Select games on the basis of the developmental characteristics of the children (Torbert, 2005).
2. Keep the games simple, with few rules. The older the children, the more rules that can be added.
3. Make sure that games are noncompetitive. Children cannot tolerate losing before 5 or 6 years of age. Focus on skill development, having fun, and encouraging a sense of fair play.
4. Make sure that the children experience accomplishment.
5. When selecting "It," be impartial. For example, draw from a set of class cards that includes each child's name.
6. When the game has reached its peak of interest, change activities.
7. Be aware of the physical abilities of all children. Plan how you will include children with physical disabilities.
8. Do not match boys against girls.
9. Make sure that all children are allowed to participate, but do not force children to take part.
10. Explain how to play the game and then demonstrate how to play.

Examples of Active Games

The following are some games that are appropriate for early childhood. Some are more suitable for younger children; most are more suitable for 5- to 8-year-olds. Some can be adapted to meet the needs of a particular age or group of children. Only a few suggestions are included here. Many other acceptable physical games can be found in game books available at your local library or in bookstores.

Hot Potato. Children sit or stand in a circle. The ball, rolled on the floor, is a "hot potato" and must be pushed or kicked away when it comes near.

Jump Ball. Players are in a circle, with "It" in the center of the circle. Players roll the ball, trying to touch "It," who jumps over the ball. If the ball touches "It," she or he changes places with the last child who rolled the ball.

Piglet. All players except Piglet form pairs in a circle. When Piglet says "face to face," the partners face each other. When Piglet says "back to back" or "side to side" or "toe to toe," the children follow the directions. If Piglet says "Piglet," everyone tries to find a new partner. The person left without a partner becomes Piglet.

Find the Leader. Players are in a circle. "It" is sent from the room, and a leader is designated. After returning to the room, "It" has a certain number of guesses to identify the leader. The leader changes the activity, and the players must copy the leader. If the leader is guessed, he or she becomes "It."

Cooperative Musical Chairs. Musical chairs can be played the traditional way, or you can supply a chair for everyone, or the children can share a chair with a partner. Leave no pair or partners out.

Freeze Tag. All children are "It" and can freeze other players by touching them and yelling "Freeze!" Players that are frozen must freeze in the positions that they are in when touched. When everyone but one person is frozen, that person says "Unfreeze" and the game begins again.

Balloon Keep-Up. Provide a variety of balloons about 7 to 8 inches in diameter. The children must keep the balloons in the air. They learn they have to work together to reach the goal of keeping the balloons off the ground (Torbert & Schneider [1992] 2005).

Railroad Cars. Players are in pairs, one behind the other. Each places his or her hands on the waist of the child in front. Put some train music on, and have the children try to add other cars onto their train.

Smile If You Love Me. Children are in a circle (if the group is large, make each circle about six to eight children). "It" goes to a player and says, "Smile if you love me." "It" can make faces, sounds, or movements as he or she tries to make the other child smile. If "It" makes the player smile, that child becomes "It." Make certain every child has an opportunity to be "It."

Run Home. The players stand in a single circle facing the center. "It" walks around the outside and then holds up a beanbag between two players. These two players run around the outside of the circle in opposite directions, each aiming to get back first and grab the beanbag. The one getting it may go and hold it up between two other players.

Who Has Gone? The children move about in the room. When a chord on the piano is played, or another signal is given, all children sit down and hide their eyes. The leader touches one, who quietly disappears. Then all look up and discover who is gone.

Other games of skill include those that require small-muscle coordination, such as passing a Lifesaver candy around a group of four to six children using a small wooden dowel or a straw. Other examples include beanbag or ball tosses, ring tosses, or coin drops (a coin is dropped into a soda bottle).

Outdoor Activities

Outdoor activities are an integral part of the early childhood curriculum (NASPE, 1995). Weather permitting, children should spend some time outdoors each day. The equipment on the playground should be inviting, challenging, durable, and safe. The playground must be fenced and provide built-in limits. Adults must always supervise children's play while they are outdoors. Some of the general areas for play include climbing equipment, sand, a playhouse, a paved area for riding toys, a shaded area for opportunity to get out of the sun, a developmentally appropriate basketball hoop, and additional equipment such as hula-hoops, balls, and riding toys. Many programs have garden plots that the children plant and care for during the spring and summer, and that they harvest in the fall. Outdoor explorations offer opportunities not available inside the classroom.

GENERAL HEALTH AND SAFETY ISSUES

> Programs should promote the nutrition and health of children and protect children and staff from illness and injury. (NAEYC Early Childhood Program Standards, Standard 5)

As a part of the total well-being of the child, attention needs to be given to general health issues. Teachers must be well aware of specific needs when teaching children with chronic health concerns such as diabetes, severe allergies, asthma, ADHD, and seizure disorder.

Child care health consultants or school nurses are excellent resources for keeping teachers abreast of emerging illnesses and treatments (Cianciolo, Trueblood-Noll, & Allingham, 2004).

Young children also need explicit instruction in health education issues. The most effective method for children to learn about health, nutrition, and safety is through direct experience. Health education should be included in the daily classroom activities and routines, with the support of adult modeling and direct teaching; it cannot be adequately addressed in occasional themes or units. Health education will include routine health practices, incidental learning (teaching moments), and planned activities. Teachers must also model the importance of health through personal example by frequently washing hands, brushing teeth, exercising, and so on. Many health concepts appear to be common sense, but many children have not learned these habits at home. Give gentle reminders, encouragement, and positive reinforcement when demonstrating appropriate behaviors.

Health Education Curriculum

An appropriate health education curriculum should give attention to the 2006 National Health Education Standards, PreK–12 (American Association for Health Education [AAHE], 2006). Following are the National Health Standards and ways to teach these in PreK through third grade.

NATIONAL HEALTH EDUCATION STANDARDS

Standard	Practical Application
1. Students will comprehend concepts related to health promotion and disease prevention to enhance health.	• Describe ways to prevent communicable diseases. • Describe various health care workers and why it is important to seek health care.
2. Students will demonstrate the ability to access valid health information and health-promoting products and services.	• Recognize health professionals who will promote and help determine health practices and behaviors. • Identify community health professionals.
3. Students will demonstrate the ability to practice health-enhancing behaviors and reduce health risks.	• Identify healthy behaviors. • Recognize behaviors that may result in compromising good health.
4. Students will analyze the influence of culture, media, technology, and other factors on health.	• Describe how the family and culture promote positive health practices. • Recognize the influence of media on health practices and behaviors.
5. Students will demonstrate the ability to use interpersonal communication skills to enhance health.	• Practice healthy ways to communicate needs, wants, and feelings to trusted adults in your environment. • Demonstrate ways to communicate in unsafe or dangerous situations.
6. Students will demonstrate the ability to use goal setting and decision-making skills to enhance health.	• Set and take action on short-term health goals. • Distinguish health care workers who can help you achieve your health goals.
7. Students will demonstrate the ability to advocate for personal, family, and community health.	• Advocate for healthy choices. • Know where to seek health information and demonstrate competence in locating or finding valid health information.

Source: This represents the work of the Joint Committee on National Health Education Standards. Copies of National Health Education Standards: Achieving Healthy Literacy can be obtained through the American School Health Association (ASHA), Association for the Advancement of Health Education (AAHE), or the American Cancer Society (ACS).

The following are some of the concepts to present, depending on specific needs, during early childhood:

- My hands need to be washed often with soap, because washing our hands is the most effective way to avoid illness. Following is a suggested list of times when hand washing is needed: anytime food is involved (before setting table, preparing or eating food); after using the bathroom, playing outside, touching money, playing with animals, handling garbage, or coughing or sneezing into hands or a tissue. (The best place to cough or sneeze is into your upper arm.)
- I must have immunizations to prevent diseases.
- If I am ill, I need to stay home so that I do not spread my illness to others. When I sneeze or cough, I need to cover my mouth and nose. After I use a tissue, I must throw it away in the garbage.
- I must brush my teeth every day, at least in the morning and before I go to bed.
- I must take a bath often and keep my clothing clean and my hair brushed.
- I must go to bed early every night and get a good night's rest.
- I must eat healthy foods.
- I must get adequate physical exercise.

Frequent hand washing is the best way to stay healthy.

Additional things that staff can do to promote good health and safety include the following:

- Take time to clean and disinfect toilet areas and surfaces.
- Open windows to let in fresh air.
- Make sure permanent health records and emergency cards are up to date for each child.
- Arrange for appropriate sick-child care for the child who comes to school ill or becomes ill during the school day.

The safety of the school, classroom, and playground also needs to be assessed continually. Close supervision is often the best measure for accident prevention. Other considerations include keeping the walking areas free of toys, cords, spills, or loose flooring. Toys should be evaluated constantly for safety, and any with sharp edges, toxic finishes, or small parts should be removed. All cleaning supplies, poisons, and other toxic materials should be out of the reach of children. The Centers for Disease Control and Prevention (CDC) also recommends that young children should not handle reptiles and amphibians at home or in a school setting (American Academy of Pediatrics, American Public Health Association, & National Resource Center for Health and Safety in Child Care [AAP, APHA, & NRCHSCC], 2002).

Safety in schools is also achieved through addressing cooperation and conflict resolution. Through conflict resolution, children participate in role-playing, mediation, and negotiating.

Fire safety particularly needs to be addressed with both children and staff. Make sure that your building meets all fire codes. Check fire extinguishers and smoke alarms regularly to make sure that they are in working order. Go over fire-safety procedures and a fire drill with the staff and children at least monthly. In early childhood education, follow these additional guidelines (Cole, Crandall, & Kourofsky, 2004):

- Discuss fire hazards such as the dangers of playing with fire or matches. Children should tell an adult if they see a match or lighter.
- Acquaint children with firefighters and what their roles are, and let them hear an actual fire alarm. Visit the fire station. Teach children exactly what they are to do in case of fire or when they hear the alarm sound.
- Role-play the "Stop, Drop, and Roll" drill often.
- Teach that the safest method for getting out of a room that is filling with smoke is to crawl low under the smoke.

More and more information is becoming available regarding the importance of providing sun protection for young children. This issue should be included as part of an effective physical health and education program in our schools. Young children can develop appropriate attitudes and behaviors toward protecting themselves from harmful exposure to the sun's rays (Fulmore, Geiger, Werner, Talbott, & Jones, 2009). Although not directly related to the school environment, water safety issues should also be addressed. The health and safety thread needs to be woven into the daily activities of the classroom in early childhood programs. It can be taught during specific units or lessons, but these are aspects of the program that need to be lived and attended to daily. Establishing safe and healthy patterns of behavior is much easier when they are learned and practiced in early childhood (Bales et al., 2006).

> **Basic Practices For Physical Health and Safety of Young Children**
>
> - Seatbelts
> - Car seats
> - Helmets
> - Immunizations
> - Frequent hand washing
> - Supervision
> - Sun protection
> - Physical activity
> - Good nutrition
> - Adequate sleep
> - Teeth brushing and flossing
> - Dental checkups
> - Physical checkups
> - Frequent bathing
> - Life jackets

NUTRITION AND FOOD EXPERIENCES

A significant aspect of personal and social development, especially the healthy development of self, is related to good nutrition. Children who have adequate rest, plenty of exercise, and nutritious, balanced diets are better prepared to learn and are able to handle the stresses in their lives (Huettig et al., 2004). During the early childhood years, teachers can have an important impact on fostering good nutrition and healthy eating habits.

> # Developing Good Nutritional Habits
>
> 1. Make eating a pleasant experience
> 2. When possible, allow children to assist in food preparation and serving
> 3. Model appropriate manners and behavior
> 4. Be positive; encourage, but do not force, children to try new foods; repeated presentations may be necessary before acceptance

To grow up healthy, with vitality and energy, children need adequate nutrition. Their early experiences of preparing, tasting, and eating nutritious foods can have an impact on their long-term eating preferences and habits. Many young children know little about foods with a high nutritional value.

For developmentally appropriate practices relating to the nutrition of young children, only healthy foods should be provided, and eating should be considered a happy and social time (Copple & Bredekamp, 2009). Children generally have a natural curiosity about and interest in food activities. From the time that they are born, food is vital to nurturing; it brings security, comfort, and love. To help children make proper food choices, a wide variety of wholesome foods should be available. In accomplishing these goals, food should neither be used for reward nor withheld as punishment (Copple & Bredekamp, 2009).

Being involved in food activities is an important way of teaching good nutrition to young children. "Cooking—like block building, reading, and the arts—should be an integral part of every preschool and kindergarten program" (Colker, 2005, p. ix). Cooking provides opportunities for young children to participate in activities that are most often reserved for adults. As children cook, their sense of competence and confidence develop as they follow a task through to completion. Cooking is a "domain that teachers can use to teach socioemotional, cognitive, physical, and literacy skills as well as to foster children's creativity and self-expression" (Colker, 2005, p. ix). In selecting a food experience or snack, one of the first questions that a teacher should ask is, "Will the food be nutritious?" Traditionally, early childhood classrooms offer prepared cookies, candies, ice cream, and other foods that provide little nutritional value or have a low nutrient density. To judge whether a food should be served as a snack, we must determine whether the food is nutritious. Acceptable snacks can be chosen from each food category. These are also excellent criteria for any other food prepared or served in the early childhood education classroom. Teachers must also be aware of food allergies and intolerances some children have and know how to manage these in the classroom with thoughtful planning and preparation (Holland, 2004). The foods that most commonly cause allergies for children are milk, eggs, peanuts, soybeans, tree nuts, wheat, fish, and shellfish (Duyff, 2002).

Nutrition Education

Research in countries with prevalent malnutrition indicates that there is an effect on cognitive and social development in children who suffer from undernourishment (Marcon, 2003). Many children are *mis*nourished because of poor nutrition choices, not because of what they don't eat (Marcon, 2003). Therefore, nutrition education is important for proper growth, and it is most successful in the early childhood years when health-promoting concepts and behaviors are more easily learned. When young children participate in nutrition-education programs, they are more inclined to eat desirable foods and have more positive attitudes about eating fruits and vegetables.

Nutrition can be integrated into many curriculum areas. Nutrition units, as well as food activities, should be planned carefully to teach nutrition concepts specifically and directly to children. Listed at the end of this chapter are many excellent curriculum guides on nutrition for preschool and primary-grade children. As a nation, we are becoming more concerned about this important aspect of health and well-being. Articles, books, programs, school units, extension programs, and White House conferences all have served to alert and educate us. Councils such as the national or state Dairy Councils® are an excellent resource for nutrition information and teaching materials. Nutrition activities should encourage children to explore the limitless potential for learning by providing open-ended experiences that allow them to extend their understanding beyond any specifically outlined objectives.

It is easier for children to learn to like new foods during the earlier childhood years than it is when they are older. Children are also very receptive during these early years to understanding the basics involved in nutrition and the importance it plays in our lives. Although we choose food and nutrition activities with objectives that we desire to achieve, other learning occurs as children are (and should be) allowed to explore in an attempt to answer the questions *How? Why? What if? How come?* and *I wonder . . . .*

Many early childhood programs, such as child care or Head Start, serve complete meals. The subject of nutrition provides many learning opportunities in these programs. It must not be viewed just as preparing, serving, and cleaning up food activities. The potential for nutrition education in the early childhood program is limitless.

It is more difficult today to remain aware of nutritional values because of prepackaging, vending machines, and fast-food restaurants. We subtly teach children that sweets are the best kinds of food when we make comments such as "Eat your salad and meatloaf, and then you can have your cake and ice cream."

It would be beneficial to plan parent meetings and workshops to educate families on good nutrition. Children are building bodies that are to last them a lifetime, and both children and parents must know that the food they eat has a direct relationship to the quality of their health. They must be informed of the interaction between early eating choices and habits and the development of diet-related diseases later in life. Nutritionally healthy eating habits are acquired early in life. The goal of nutrition education should be that children eat a well-balanced, nutritional diet that contains a variety of foods and that teaches children to make wise food choices. Eating habits that condition children to consume processed foods or foods high in sugar, salt, and fat are physically detrimental and instill in children a taste for foods that are unhealthy.

People in the United States each consume about 100 pounds of sugar annually. Sugar-laden foods provide empty calories and dull the appetite, leaving children uninterested in nutritious foods. In addition, overconsumption of sugar causes dental caries. Caregivers must try to reduce children's sugar consumption by avoiding high-sugar foods, selecting alternative natural sources of sweetness, and finding ways to celebrate special events other than with sugary foods. Sugar substitutes or artificial sweeteners should not be ingredients in the diets of young children unless specified by a physician. More than a decade ago, the surgeon general of the United States issued a report titled *Healthy People,* in which he urged Americans to eat a diet lower in cholesterol, saturated fat, sugar, and salt.

Value of Food Experiences

Families today are eating fewer meals together, and they are eating more fast foods and snack foods. All family members need to be taught to eat a well-balanced diet and to select nutritional foods. As teachers, we send many messages about food and nutrition to young children in the ways that we use specific foods for room decorations and teaching materials. Frequently, we display more desserts than fruits, vegetables, or grains.

The sensory experiences in food activities offer the greatest learning value. In addition, children enjoy working with and manipulating food—mixing, measuring, pouring, stirring, and eating. Food experiences provide natural means for exploring and developing basic concepts such as size, shape, number, color, measurement, weight, smell, taste, sound, touch, texture, flavor, preservation, and temperature change. Food activities provide opportunities for increasing language skills and labels. Teachers can teach what a particular food is, where it comes from, what it looks like, and how it compares to familiar and unfamiliar foods. Children can describe and label foods, equipment being used, and what is being done with the food (grating, mashing, kneading, stirring, beating, pouring, spreading, grinding, or peeling). Food experiences offer opportunities for teaching safety concepts and proper use of utensils, such as knives, forks, beaters, and peelers. If a stove, hot plate, or frying pan is being used for cooking, children can be taught safety concepts related to fire and heat. Cleanliness must also be stressed: Children should be encouraged to wash their hands before any food activity and to help clean up.

The value of snack time's contribution to the development of healthy social–emotional growth in young children is often overlooked. "It is an intimate, comforting break in which children gain physical and emotional nourishment" (Murray, 2000, p. 43). It also encourages the growth of cognitive learning as children practice valuable preschool concepts. So that children are not required to wait unnecessarily, food should be ready before they are called to meals or snacks (Copple & Bredekamp, 2009), unless they are involved in the preparation of the food. Especially for toddlers, bowls, spoons, and cups should be easy to handle. Children also benefit from working cooperatively as a team while interpreting directions in a recipe, following sequences, and keeping time. Social values include learning table manners, sharing, and developing appropriate eating habits. The children's self-images are enhanced as they set the table, prepare the food, eat their own product, and then clean up.

Many local health departments do not allow homemade food items to be brought into the classroom. If parents desire, they can bring recipes and ingredients into the classroom and make or bake the food with the children. Consider getting a small refrigerator, convection oven, microwave oven, electric frying pan, and an electric grill for use in the classroom.

Cooking provides an excellent way to integrate curriculum learning in the classroom. It can involve:

- Reading, writing, and drawing
- Math and problem solving
- Science
- Multicultural activities
- Creativity
- Social skills
- Independence
- Language and communication
- Following directions

Working with recipes provides young children with foundational understandings of measuring and fraction concepts. For example, they can best learn the concept of one-half by measuring

$\frac{1}{2}$ cup water

$\frac{1}{2}$ teaspoon vanilla

$\frac{1}{2}$ apple

and so on. Also, working with food recipes exposes children to concepts relating to various units of measure. Collecting and sampling recipes from diverse cultures helps children to develop an awareness of and respect for people of many cultures and backgrounds. This is also an excellent way to encourage family involvement.

Murray (2000) suggests using placemats that have been decorated with the child's name and photo during snack time and food activities. These placemats help to:

- Define "personal space"
- Provide visual cues to assist in organization
- Focus child's attention
- Facilitate matching, comparison, and contrast skills
- Contribute to feelings of belonging and sense of self
- Increase fine motor development skills
- Encourage understanding of one-to-one correspondence

Food and Nutrition Concepts

Many of the following food and nutrition concepts can be incorporated as objectives for food experiences, meals, and snacks. A teacher's understanding of these concepts makes classroom food activities more interesting and educational.

1. Nutrition is the process by which we assimilate or absorb food.
2. Food helps us live, grow, acquire energy, and stay healthy.
3. There are many varieties of foods.
4. Foods vary in shape, color, size, flavor, texture, smell, and sound.
5. The quality of food is influenced by how it is grown, processed, stored, and prepared.
6. Animals and plants are sources of foods.
7. Foods can be prepared for eating in various ways: raw, cooked (fried, boiled, steamed, baked), canned, frozen, or dried.
8. Food selection and eating are influenced by many factors: society, culture, economy, preparation, cleanliness, manners, appearance, season, traditions, availability, cost, individual and family habits, preferences, mass media, celebrations, atmosphere or environment, weather, taste, person's age, and health.
9. Foods may be classified into various categories: breads; cereal, seeds, grains; dried beans, peas, lentils; eggs; fruits; meat; milk, cheese; nuts; pastas; and vegetables.
10. A healthy diet includes foods selected from each of the categories in item 9.

Many children believe that foods originate in the supermarket, vending machine, or restaurant. Children need to know where foods come from and have opportunities to help in preparing wholesome foods. Children's diets often include large quantities of soda pop, potato chips, French fries, candy, and other sweets such as cookies, cakes, jams, and jellies. These may be termed junk foods; nutritionists label them *foods with low nutrient density*, which means that they have few nutrients in relation to their calories. These kinds of foods are not appropriate for preschool children because they lead to poor nutrition habits and obesity, and they take the place of more important foods.

As mentioned previously, childhood obesity is a critical health issue today (Huettig et al., 2004). In May 2010, The Task Force on Childhood Obesity delivered its report to the president of the United States. It reported that studies have found that "40% of obese children and 70% of obese adolescents will become obese adults" (TIME Custom Publishing department, 2010, pp. 51–52). The Centers for Disease Control and Prevention indicate that about 20% of children ages 2 to 5 are overweight and so are about 30% of children ages 6 to 11 (CDC, 2002). Early intervention is imperative because lifestyle patterns are established early (Huettig et al., 2004). Schools and teachers can help reverse the worldwide epidemic of childhood obesity by making health education and physical activity major components of the curriculum (Cook-Cottone, 2009; Winter, 2009). With the cooperation of family, school, and community, the obesity trends can be reversed, and chances for all children to be successful in school will improve (Winter, 2009). Teachers should be aware of opportunities to help children learn to select and enjoy nutrient-dense foods—those with a high ratio of nutrients to calories, such as fruits, vegetables, dairy products, and meats. The key to adequate nutrition is variety, which means that the body needs many different foods to develop and grow normally. General suggestions for helping children maintain a healthy weight include making it easier to access healthier foods (and harder to get unhealthy ones), increasing opportunities for physical activities, and providing education to help families make wise and healthy choices involving nutrition and physical activities for their children.

The primary focus in this text is on nutritious food activities for young children. In most recipes in this book, white flour is replaced by whole-grain or wheat flour; sugar content is reduced or completely eliminated; flavored gelatins are replaced by unflavored gelatin and fruit juices.

In 2005, the USDA released the MyPyramid food guidance system, replacing the food guide pyramid developed in 1992 (USDA, 2005). The new symbol and system provides options to help adults and children make healthy food choices and to be active every day. The new system acknowledges that one size does not fit all and so, based on the person's age, sex, and activity level, seeks to help the individual make appropriate food choices. The aim is to make smart choices from every food area, to find a balance between food and physical activity, and to get the most nutrition from food choices. Water should be available to children both indoors and outdoors (Huettig et al., 2004). Daily foods should include grains, with about half the grains being whole grains including breads, cereal, rice, and pasta; a variety of vegetables (lots of raw vegetables, especially for snacks) and fruits, with a main focus on fruits; calcium-rich milk products; lean meat, poultry, fish, beans, eggs, and nuts; and very small amounts of oils. Even young children can learn to plan for and follow the MyPyramid for Kids to eat right, exercise, and have fun (MyPyramid; see Figure 6.1). The five major groups that form the My Pyramid are described here.

Grains

- Half the grains selected should be "whole"; look for this word before the grain name.
- Include 3 ounces of whole grain bread, cereal, crackers, rice, or pasta every day.

Vegetables

- Include many dark green vegetables.
- Include many orange vegetables.
- Include dry beans and peas.

Fruits

- Eat a variety of fruits.
- Choose fresh, canned, frozen, or dried fruits.
- Go easy on juices.

Milk (including Yogurt and Cheese)

- Go low-fat or fat-free.
- Include milk in any form: whole, skim, low-fat, evaporated, buttermilk, and nonfat dry milk; also yogurt, ice cream, and ice milk; and cheese, including cottage cheese.

Meat and Beans

- Choose low-fat or lean meats and poultry.
- Bake it, broil it, or grill it.
- Vary choices with more fish, beans, peas, nuts, and seeds.

Most other foods fit into a sixth category of oils. This is not a food category. Foods in this group should be used sparingly.

Food Activities

Food experiences planned in the classroom must be well organized and explicitly planned, and adequate time must be allowed for completion. If the food activity takes place in small cooperative groups, take care to explain the procedures and methods to the teachers working with these groups, and make sure each group has its own copy of the recipe. If the activity takes place in a large group, the recipe could be written on the chalkboard or an experience chart. The teacher should discuss the recipe, ingredients, and procedures with the children before they begin.

Tasting experiences can easily be set up in a classroom as an interest center for use during free play, or

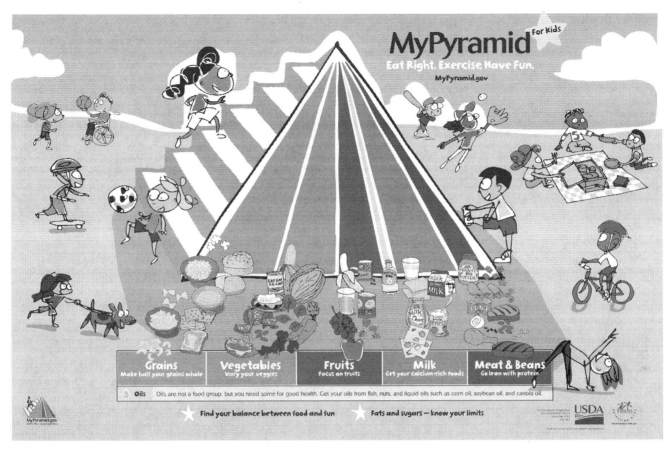

FIGURE 6.1 MyPyramid.gov
Go to www.mypyramid.gov to individualize the pyramid according to each child's age, gender, and physical activity level.
Source: U.S. Department of Agriculture, Food and Nutrition Service, "MyPyramid for Kids" (September 2005), www.mypyramid.gov.

they can be group activities. Children can taste several different foods, such as familiar foods, unfamiliar foods, different foods with similar flavors, or different forms of such foods as potatoes or tomatoes.

Children can also be introduced to new and interesting foods. It may be wise to begin with sensory experiences other than tasting. For example, the children may be encouraged to smell, feel, listen to, and look at a new food before tasting it. New foods can also be compared with familiar foods. For example, lima beans or kidney beans can be compared to familiar green beans, Brussels sprouts to cabbage, an avocado to a pear, a lime to a lemon, a kiwi to a strawberry. Also remember that, when first introducing children to a new food or unfamiliar recipe, give them very small servings. The family style of serving, in which the children serve themselves, is preferred.

Another food activity consists of acquainting children with the origins of foods. Many children assume that milk, for example, comes from the store or the milk delivery person, rather than from the cow. This activity provides an opportunity for teaching categorization games. Children can sort picture cards into categories, such as plant products or animal products. Even more specifically, cards could be sorted into underground plant products, tree products, vine products, cow products, and so on. Also, picture or flash cards can be used simply for naming the food item. Pictures can be found in magazines or discarded workbooks, or stickers can be purchased from variety stores.

Foods and food activities can be integrated into every aspect of the curriculum in early childhood. Cooking activities in the classroom lend themselves to a realm of marvelous learning opportunities for children including language arts–reading, math, science, fine-motor skills, art, health, music, and social studies. Most learning is through the senses, and since food appeals to all senses, it is a powerful learning tool. In physical development, there is opportunity for both small- and large-muscle coordination. In mathematics or number work, there are experiences for counting, classifying, and measuring. In science, possibilities abound for using the process skills in food activities—questioning, observing, interpreting, categorizing, and solving problems. There are opportunities for studying and discovering the nature and origin of foods, the changes that they make from seed to maturity, and their physical properties. In terms of social studies, children can study cultural aspects of foods and become acquainted with other people and the foods common to their culture, ethnic group, or region. For example, baking and studying about breads from many cultures and countries is an excellent activity for children of all ages (L. Bennett, 1995). Bread is an example of a common food staple among various peoples all over the world.

Opportunities for language and literacy development are limitless: Learning new words, reading directions and labels, following recipes, questioning, and naming and labeling foods are just some of the language activities inherent in food activities. There are also possibilities for art and creative expression. Many food projects, such as salads or sculptures, are creative processes in themselves. In music, children can do creative movements to interpret the growth of plants and changes made in preparing foods. Empty food containers are useful as shakers or music instruments. In addition, every food activity provides practice in socialization as children learn patience, sharing, respect for one another, and cooperation.

Some authors do not approve of allowing children to use food as a learning material such as in an art project, however. The rationale is that it teaches children that it is all right to play with food, that it wastes food products, and that it shows disrespect to the place of food in other cultures (Swim & Freeman, 2004). Whenever possible, use items other than food products for art projects. If using foods, include only those that would otherwise be discarded or thrown away because of age or condition.

Food Activity Guidelines

Foods, whether approached as a general area or as specific food items, make excellent choices for unit themes. The following ideas for activities have been grouped into basic food groups, although this approach to teaching is not the only possibility. For example, a unit may be presented on dairy products, the cow, milk, or the person who delivers milk. These suggestions for activities could fit into a variety of units. A food activity can be included in a unit as an unrelated activity; therefore, many of the suggestions given here could be used in any unit to support food activities.

APPROACH TO TEACHING

Fruits and Vegetables

Fruits and vegetables can be approached either in general units or in units featuring specific fruit or vegetable concepts. The children should first be made aware of the foods growing in the local surroundings, and units can easily take advantage of particular growing seasons.

Considerations for Integrating Food Activities into the Curriculum

1. Plan and organize all cooking activities. Generally, the younger the child, the more simple the project—perhaps one or two steps. Practice making the food activity yourself before doing it with the children.

2. Make sure that all foods, utensils, and other items necessary for cooking are ready and assembled.

3. Plan adequate time for the food activity, remembering that children take longer to prepare foods than adults. Allow enough time to question, taste, touch, smell, discover, and compare. Utilize each step in the food activity as a learning experience.

4. Show the children a copy of the recipe so that they know that specific directions must be followed. Write the recipe on a large chart or on individual cards for small groups. Draw pictures or use children's recipe books with directions in picture form. Review the recipe before starting the activity.

5. Adhere to rules of cleanliness: Wash hands before beginning, wipe up spills as you go, and involve the children in cleaning the area at the end of the activity.

6. Follow all safety rules appropriate for the particular food activity. Demonstrate proper use of utensils and supervise their use. Caution children about the dangers of hot items and electric appliances.

7. Provide for unlimited learning by allowing the children to explore the questions of *How? Why? What if? How come?* and *I wonder . . . .*

In general or specific units on fruits or vegetables, some of the following concepts could be incorporated:

- Where and how the food grows: on a tree, underground, on a vine, in a pod, on a bush; singly or in bunches
- Growing climate and season
- Number, size, and location of seeds
- How to tell when the food is ripe
- Various forms and preparations of the food: fresh or cooked; mashed, sliced, cubed, shredded, crushed, juiced, or chunked
- Varieties or kinds of the food (apples: Jonathan, Roman Beauty, Delicious; beans: kidney, green, lima, or pinto)
- Sizes

CHILD'S PROJECT PLAN ON BEANS

Beans can be planted.
•What do beans need
to grow?
•How do beans grow?
•What are the parts
of a bean plant?

We eat different kinds of beans—
dried beans, green beans, and
bean sprouts.
•Make a salad with sprouts.
•Make refried beans.
•Taste different kinds of beans.
•Make some chili.

Beans

Beans grow on vines or on
bushes. Sometimes they
grow on vines on poles.
•Pick some beans or find
pictures of how beans grow.

Beans come in different forms.
•Visit a grocery store to find out
the forms in which beans come.

I can make things using beans.
•Bean shaker using a milk carton.

FIGURE 6.2   Child's Project Plan on Beans

- Colors (ripe compared to unripe; variations in different kinds)
- Parts to be eaten (skin, seeds, leaves, and pulp)
- Methods of storage and preservation (freeze, can, or dehydrate)

See Figure 6.2 for a project plan on beans. There are actually foods from two different food groups in this project, green beans from the vegetable group and dried beans from the protein group. This can be explained during the project.

 UNIT IDEAS FOR FRUITS AND VEGETABLES (GENERAL OR SPECIFIC)

Note: Some of the listed activities may be related to specific fruits or vegetables. Make appropriate selections to suit your plans. Also see Figure 6.3 for a web on apples.

FIELD TRIPS

- Processing plant or cannery
- Orchard, garden, grove, farm; before, during, and after harvest
- Food stand
- Grocery store
- Sorting shed
- Ride on pickup wagon during harvest
- Fruit and vegetable picking
- Truck loading freight for store
- Bakery
- Ice cream store
- Nursery or greenhouse

VISITORS

- Orchard, garden, grove, or farm owner
- Person demonstrating food storage and preservation
- Grocer
- Fruit or vegetable picker
- Foods and salesperson
- Employee of cannery or processing plant
- Baker
- Ice cream maker, to demonstrate the use of fruits in ice cream
- Employee of nursery or greenhouse
- Home economist from county extension service

FOOD

- Making jam, jelly
- Making juice
- Blending fruits or vegetables into drinks or shakes
- Peeling, slicing, grating, or mashing foods
- Fruit or vegetable salad
- Fruit or vegetable pies, pastries, or turnovers
- Fruit or vegetable leather
- Sherbet or ice cream
- Gelatin salad
- Cobbler, strudel, or crisp
- Baked vegetables or fruits

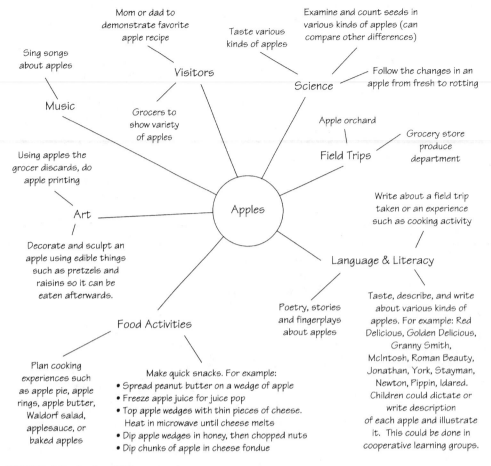

FIGURE 6.3   Project Web on Apples

- Fruit cocktail
- Stew
- Soup
- Casserole
- Fruit or vegetable cake, cookies
- Fruits and vegetables used with dips, cheese fondues, and white sauces
- Breads

SCIENCE

- Observation of food during the decaying process
- Tasting familiar and unfamiliar foods
- Observation of wormy food
- Where food grows: trees, vines, or shrubs; above, under, or on the ground; in gardens, orchards, or farms
- Edible parts: peelings, seeds, flesh, stems, roots, and flowers
- Number of seeds: many, few, one
- Size of seeds
- Number of sections

- Kinds of food that taste the same
- Kinds of food that taste different
- Sizes of food
- Textures of food
- Noise made during chewing: loud or soft
- Seed or plant in classroom, cared for by children
- Observation of various types of one specific food
- Smells of vegetables and fruits
- Climates and seasons of food
- Preservation of food
- Seeds sprouted for tasting or use with other foods
- Method of teaching how plants obtain water: cut a piece of celery in half lengthwise, but not all the way up; put halves in glasses of different-colored water; within a short time, the leaves at the top of the stalk will be the same color as the water, with the veins of the stalk also filled with colored water

ART

- Pieces of food traced on paper
- Food shapes cut from paper

- Pictures of food cut from magazines
- Seed collages
- Collages made from food pictures
- Shakers made from empty food containers
- Paintings or printings on food shapes
- Food sculpture: pieces of vegetables and/or fruits attached to a base with toothpicks (prepared for eating later)
- Food puppets: drawn or outlined; then decorated or given faces; then cut out and mounted on tongue depressors, dowels, or sticks

MUSIC

- Shakers made with seeds on inside and outside, shaken while singing and marching; shaken loudly, softly, quickly, slowly—like an elephant walks, like a kitten creeps
- Musical chairs: pieces of fruits or vegetables placed on chairs for children to identify when they sit down
- Creative movement: children pretending to be various fruits or vegetables being planted, picked, harvested, or falling to the ground
- Singing of expandable songs in which fruit or vegetable names can be included

LANGUAGE AND LITERACY

- Booklets made by class or individuals on "Fruits (or Vegetables) I (or We) Like"
- Fruits and vegetables cut from magazines and made into a booklet with children's descriptions of them

ADDITIONAL ACTIVITIES

- Unusual fruit or vegetable presented for tasting and for exploring with a magnifying glass
- Trough or tubs filled with soil, then foods planted; root vegetables or bush fruits placed in the soil just as they grow
- Trough filled with pea, potato, or bean vines (vegetables to be eaten)

See Figure 6.3 for a project web on apples.

Grain, Rice, and Pasta Products

Cereals, like the other food groups, can be approached in many ways as units. Units might be presented on wheat, breads, macaroni, rice, or oats. When any of these units are taught, some of the following ideas could be incorporated as teaching concepts or goals:

- Where and how the grain grows
- How it looks when it is ready to harvest

- How the seeds of some of the grains (for example, wheat) can be used: eaten raw, sprouted, or in food preparation.
- Number of forms in which the cereal or grain can be eaten.

Perhaps one of the most stimulating units features wheat, including experiences with raw wheat, cooked whole-wheat cereal, and wheat ground into whole-wheat flour to be used in many different food activities.

The following are unit ideas for bread; for unit ideas for wheat and flour, see Chapter 11.

 UNIT IDEAS FOR BREAD

ART

- Sculptured bread dough: worked and molded, then baked and eaten
- Sculpture made with different kinds of breads: small cubes or pieces of rye bread, sweet bread, sourdough, and so on, combined with chunked fruits and/or vegetables (prepare to be eaten later); Styrofoam base could be used

FOOD

- Open-faced sandwiches made in different shapes: cookie cutters used to cut shapes of bread; spreads or toppings added
- Toast or cinnamon toast (no sugar)
- French toast
- Rolls: any kind, in any shape
- Bread: pumpkin, zucchini, onion, honey, raisin, or garlic
- Dill bread, made with cottage cheese and onions
- Muffins
- Biscuits
- Blueberry muffins, rolls, or bread
- Scones, made from bread dough or sweet bread dough
- Eggs in a ring: cut hole in center of a slice of bread, butter both sides, put in frying pan, and break egg into center of bread; turn when white begins to look firm
- Canned refrigerator biscuit recipes (listed at the end of this chapter)

FIELD TRIPS

- Bakery
- Cafeteria or other restaurant where breads are prepared
- Child's home where a parent is baking bread

- Zoo or other place where animals are fed bread or bread crumbs
- Grocery store: kinds, shapes of bread; bread products

VISITORS

- Baker
- Parent: rolls made in interesting and unusual shapes
- Home economist or community nutritionist
- Bread deliverer: delivery truck brought, if possible; children encouraged to climb in and observe many kinds and forms of bread

MUSIC

- Songs relating to bread

SCIENCE

- Discussion of grains used to make breads (wheat emphasized)
- Kinds of bread and their different tastes; tasting activities
- Observation of process of grinding wheat into flour
- Comparison of taste, texture, and smell of raw versus cooked bread: dough form compared to baked form
- Comparison of size of bread before and after baking: combine

  $\frac{1}{4}$ cup sugar

  two packages dry yeast

  $\frac{1}{2}$ cup warm water

  Put mixture into pop bottle with balloon over neck of bottle; mixture causes air to expand in the bottle, just as it does in the bread; balloon inflates
- Animals that eat breads and/or bread crumbs (birds, insects); ant farm, with a focus on observing the ants as they carry bread crumbs

LANGUAGE AND LITERACY

- "Little Red Riding Hood": story adapted so that the children will not be frightened; used as object story by focusing on the different breads that filled her basket; sampling of such breads
- Making booklet of different kinds of breads

Dairy Products

Milk can be used in such foods as baked custard, yogurt, and soups such as cream of potato. Cream can be used in foods such as ice cream, or whipped cream can be used in desserts, in salads, and as a topping on gingerbread or other cakes.

Butter made by the children and then spread on bread or crackers can be made in several ways. Approximately one-half pint of whipping cream should be left out to warm to room temperature and then put into a container with a tight lid. As the children shake the container, the cream separates and becomes butter. Yellow food coloring and salt may then be added and the buttermilk drained off. To allow each child to make butter, a small amount of room-temperature cream can be put into a baby food jar and shaken until butter forms. How delighted the child will be to take the butter home and share it with the family (if it lasts that long)! From this activity, the children will learn that butter comes from cream, which is a product of the cow.

Sour cream and plain yogurt are used in making dips, fruit salads, and stroganoff and as a topping on baked potatoes. Cottage cheese is used plain, as well as in making salads, dill bread, chip dips, lasagna, and other dishes. Many recipes for casseroles, desserts, sandwiches, dips, tacos, and so on, use cheese. The children can learn that cheese comes in many different forms, such as spreads, cream cheese, bricks, curds, melted, or grated.

 UNIT IDEAS FOR DAIRY PRODUCTS

ART

- Cheese sculpturing: more economical if used in combination with additional foods, such as fruits and vegetables (then eaten)
- Collages made with magazine pictures of dairy products: additional media such as yarn and paper scraps can be added for variety
- Decoration of milk cartons to be used as litter containers, planters, or puppets
- Musical shakers made with milk cartons, cream cartons, cottage cheese containers; decorated with glue and collage items, or by dipping paper scraps, tissue paper, and other materials into liquid starch and then putting them on the carton

SCIENCE

- Milk separating
- Butter made from cream
- Milk curdling
- Discussion of the need for milk in the diets of both animal and human babies; actual experience of seeing babies drinking milk

MUSIC

- Creative dramatics: exploring such movements as milking a cow or dramatizing a cow chewing its cud, swatting flies with its tail
- Rhythm shakers: milk cartons (half-pint size easiest to handle) or cottage cheese cartons partially filled with rice, beans, wheat, or other grains

FIELD TRIPS

- Dairy farm
- Cheese factory
- Creamery
- Dairy
- Grocery store
- Milk depot

VISITORS

- Dairy farmer
- Grocer
- Ice cream shop proprietor: may discuss flavors, colors, and ingredients
- Person who delivers milk (and the milk truck, if possible)
- Person to make a food product in class using milk

FOOD

- Any of the activities presented and discussed previously
- Any food activity featuring dairy products
- Tasting different forms of milk (skim milk, buttermilk, evaporated milk, condensed milk, and cream)
- Tasting and using different kinds of cheeses
- Making butter
- Making ice cream

LANGUAGE AND LITERACY

- Experience charts relating to trips, visitors, movies, and other activities
- Poetry and story writing
- Movie, *The Cow:* opportunities for sensory experiences with young children; speaking or writing about experiences in the film
- Stories and poems about cows, dairies, and persons who deliver milk

Protein Products

Meat units most often tie in with animal units in which meat is the product of the animal. For example, a unit on beef cows could elaborate on different forms of beef: hamburger, steaks, roasts, wieners, liver, stew meat, and others. In a unit such as this, it is not necessary to have food experiences with each form of beef. The children synthesize the concept of beef and its different forms by observing pictures of these different meat cuts and by visiting a butcher shop or meat market to see various meat cuts.

Additional meat units could include pigs (bacon, sausage, wieners, pork chops, and pork roast), poultry (turkey, chicken, and eggs), and fish (tuna, salmon, halibut, trout, shrimp, cod, and turbot). A general area of meat could be approached as a unit, with subcategories such as those just listed (beef, pork, fish, poultry, etc.).

Whatever approach is chosen in developing units of study on meat, teaching should include both the origins and methods of preparation for the various meats. The taste of the meat changes as the method of preparation is varied: For example, the taste of chicken varies according to whether it is fried, put in a salad, baked, and so on.

The following unit ideas present each of the basic meat categories. Again, these categories can be combined and activities selected for teaching a general unit on meat. These suggested activities could also be applied to other meats, such as wild game or sheep.

Note: Foods such as cheese, bacon, eggs, and fried foods are high in cholesterol and should be used in moderation.

UNIT IDEAS FOR BEEF COWS AND BEEF PRODUCTS

ART

- Paper-sack cow puppets
- Pictures of cows painted or drawn
- Print with designs similar to cattle brands

MUSIC

- Creative movements or dramatics: dramatizing an auction or a roundup, lassoing a cow or calf, branding
- "Galloping" music: children pretending to lasso or herd cattle

FOOD

- Hamburger
  Foil dinners
  Spaghetti
  Pizza
  Casseroles
  Meatloaf

Patties: baked, fried, or broiled
Tacos
Lasagna
Unusual foreign foods

- Wieners
Pizza
Casseroles
Broiled, boiled, or fried
Sliced with cheese in the center and broiled or microwaved

- Stew

- Soups made from beef soup bone, hamburger, or stew meat

- Chili

- Beef pie or shepherd's pie made from leftover roast or stew meat

FIELD TRIPS

- Livestock auction
- Grocery store
- Farm to observe beef cattle
- Butcher shop to see beef carcass and meat cuts
- Child's home, where parent will show meat cuts in freezer and/or cook a beef cut such as a roast

VISITORS

- Leather tanner or tooler
- Parent to cook some beef cut
- Butcher
- Rancher
- Cowboy or cowgirl

SCIENCE

- Comparing size of meat before and after cooking (meat shrinkage)
- Preservation of beef: frozen, canned, or dried; discussion of what happens when not properly preserved
- Observing the processing of meats such as hamburger or wieners: grinding, seasoning, and others
- Observing a carcass
- Uses and preparation of leather
- Tasting different forms of beef: jerky, liver, steaks, roasts, and others
- Diet of beef cow: hay and silage in winter, grass in summer
- Calves: appearance after birth, diet, and growth changes

LANGUAGE AND LITERACY

- Stories and poems relating to cows
- Creative story and poetry writing
- Films, filmstrips relating to cows
- Class or individual booklet titled "I Like Beef"

UNIT IDEAS FOR POULTRY AND POULTRY PRODUCTS

ART

- Paper-sack chicken puppets
- Painting with chicken feathers
- Collages made with chicken feathers
- Eggshell collages: colored with egg coloring or food coloring mixed in alcohol or water; may be combined with media such as chicken feathers, cut straws, or paper scraps
- Chicken wings made to wear on the children's arms: attach with string and decorate with feathers, paper scraps, and other objects; beak made out of paper (could be used for creative movement)

MUSIC

- Creative movements or dramatics: dramatizing chickens and their movements; a chick pecking its way out of the shell, learning to stand and walk, drinking water, eating

FOOD

- Eggs
Eggnog (commercial or cooked)
Baked, fried, broiled, scrambled, or poached
French toast
Custard
Bakery products using eggs as ingredients
Desserts using eggs
Omelets
Chicken
Croquettes
Baked, fried, or broiled
Casserole
Salad
Sandwiches
Ground chicken used as chicken spread
Chicken and dumplings
Chicken pie
Chicken soup
Stir fry

FIELD TRIPS

- Poultry farm
- Grocery store: observation of chicken in meat section, eggs in dairy section, and canned chicken
- Hatchery
- Place where egg candling and sorting can be seen
- Child's home: parent to show poultry cuts in freezer, cook poultry cuts such as chicken, make chicken casserole or salad
- Restaurant selling or specializing in chicken

VISITORS

- Parent to prepare chicken product: possibly an unusual product such as an omelet, cooked eggnog, or chicken croquettes
- Poultry farmer
- Someone to demonstrate egg candling
- Butcher

SCIENCE

- Parts of eggs: shell, yolk, white
- Process of beating eggs or egg whites become foamy as air is beaten in
- Eggs used as thickening
- Various kinds of eggs: brown, white; chicken, turkey, swan, duck, or other bird
- Hatching of chicks in an incubator: watching as they peck out of the shell and then grow to be mature hens and roosters
- Candling of eggs
- Preservation of eggs: refrigerated, frozen, or dried
- Food eaten by chickens

LANGUAGE AND LITERACY

- Stories and poems relating to chickens
- Creative story writing: "Chicken Is Good"

Activities and Experiences

1. Prepare a "healthy" snack. Using MyPyramid, prepare a snack plate of small, bite-sized pieces of food. As the children use toothpicks to taste each snack, they should identify the corresponding food group. Make sure that at least one food from each food group is included. The following are examples:
   a. Fruits: fruit pieces such as apple, orange, or banana
   b. Vegetables: vegetable pieces such as carrots, celery, or cauliflower
   c. Grains: small crackers or pieces of bread (preferably whole grain)
   d. Milk
   e. Meat and beans: hard-cooked egg slices, small pieces of meats, such as cooked ham or beef
2. Sort the foods: Pictures of different foods are pasted on heavy paper or cardboard. The children then name the foods and sort them into the five basic food groups. Or, foods can be sorted into two groups: foods that are good for us, and foods that are not good for us. They could also be sorted according to their source or origin. These could also be made into a classroom book for the library.
3. Favorite food song: Sing to the tune of "Skip to My Lou":
   We have to eat so we might as well eat
   Some food we think is a special treat.
   _____'s my choice. It can't be beat,
   So serve it every Sunday.
   (Second time) So serve it every Monday.
   (and so on through the week)

   Assign cooperative groups each a day of the week. When the verse of that day is sung, the group names a favorite food to fill in the blank.
4. Discuss the relationship between food and exercise and the value of exercise. Food gives us energy to run, play, and exercise. We must eat right to have the energy that we need to play, run, and exercise.
   You can't feel fit
   If you just sit.
   Skip and jump and run!
   Play some ball,
   And stretch up tall.
   Exercise is fun.
5. Talk about the different parts of plants that are eaten as vegetables. Let the children taste a sample of each part, such as leaves (lettuce, spinach); roots (carrot, parsnip); flowers (cauliflower); stalks or stems (celery); and seeds (peas, corn).
6. Obtain a catalog from a nursery or seed distributor and cut out pictures of fruits. Have the children name each fruit and discuss individual characteristics, such as one large seed, skin that is peeled, skin that is eaten, or color. Have tasting samples of some of the unusual fruits, such as dates, fresh pineapple, cranberries, or other fruits of the season that the children may taste less frequently.
7. Food riddles: Make up riddles about foods. For example: "I am a fruit. I am yellow. I have a skin you peel off. I am long and thin and delicious to eat. What am I?" (banana). Break into cooperative learning groups and have each group make up a riddle.
8. Play "Which One Does Not Belong?" Have a group of 3 or 4 pictures. For younger children, three may

be foods and one not a food. They need to find the one that does not belong. For older children, have three in one food group and the fourth in another food group, or have three good foods and one food that is not nutritious.

9. Food sequence: Find or make pictures of the growing or processing stages of a particular food. For example, several pictures could be used in the sequence of wheat to bread. The children put the pictures in the proper sequence.

10. Compare raw and cooked vegetables. For example, compare raw to cooked broccoli or raw to cooked cauliflower.

11. Put different foods, one or a few at a time, into a "feely" box and have the children identify the food by feeling it. If possible, have them tell which food group it belongs to.

12. Divide the children into cooperative learning groups, using the strategy (see Chapter 4) Numbered Heads Together. Give each group an unfamiliar fruit such as a pomegranate, kiwi, mango, papaya, pineapple, raspberry, or whatever you can find in season and available. Each group will sample the fruit and then prepare a description using descriptive words. Call out a number, and that child in each group will be spokesperson to describe the fruit for the rest of the class.

SOCIAL-EMOTIONAL HEALTH

The socioemotional development of the person is a process involving feelings and thinking. To be able to relate to and work effectively with others, one must first be able to relate positively to oneself. Children come to the classroom with various backgrounds, values, and points of view regarding themselves and their family. They must be accepted as they are and encouraged to like themselves. Indeed, children need concrete experiences, moments, and ideas directed toward building positive feelings and attitudes about themselves.

> Positive relationships among children and adults are promoted in order to foster each child's sense of worth and feelings of belonging (NAEYC Early Childhood Program Standard, Standard 1).

Social competencies, interactions, and relationships are the foundation of social studies curriculum in early childhood. There is no aspect of the teacher's role in the early years more important than promoting social and emotional competence (Gullo, 2006). Epstein (2007) suggests that social-emotional competence is made up of four components: emotional self-regulation, social skills, social dispositions, and social knowledge. Gullo (2006)

identifies three basic skills to social and emotional competence: ability to form and sustain relationships, ability to regulate emotions and behaviors, and ability to cooperate with others and follow the rules of school and society. These two views express the same basic idea—the importance of developing social-emotional health during the early years. ". . . for many children, school becomes the first and only place where they can learn to regulate themselves. Thus, instruction in self-regulation in the early years deserves the same, if not more, attention as the instruction in academic subjects" (Bodrova & Leong, 2008, p. 58). Our daily classroom climates should be predictable, accepting, and responsive, (Jones, 2008), and should help children feel safe, confident, and successful. Much of social studies in early childhood is focused on self and family and then moves to culture, community, and the world around the child. Firsthand learning experience with daily family life activities helps build understanding of self and one's environment (Mindes, 2005). **Inquiry-based teaching** allows children to ponder a question, investigate, and gather information as an answer is found through *doing* and *thinking* critically (Mindes, 2005).

The basis of a high-quality program in early childhood is promoting feelings of self-esteem and dignity in each child. As caregivers, we are better able to help

A high-quality program promotes feelings of self-esteem and dignity.

children to develop positive feelings about themselves if we understand some basic generalizations and suggestions regarding building children's self-esteem. Katz (1995) presents six necessities that every child must have for healthy development:

1. *A sense of safety.* "The young child has to have a deep sense of safety . . . psychological safety, which we usually speak of in terms of feeling secure, that is, the subjective feeling of being strongly connected and deeply attached to one or more others. Experiencing oneself as attached, connected—or safe—comes not just from being loved, but from *feeling* loved, *feeling* wanted, *feeling* significant . . . . The emphasis is more on *feeling* loved and wanted than on *being* loved and wanted" (Katz, 1995, p. 4).

   Children need to feel loved because of who they are, not what they do. Qualities as kindness, helpfulness, and flexibility must be encouraged and appreciated more than children's accomplishments. Safety grows from being able to trust people to respond warmly, honestly, intensely, and sincerely.

2. *Optimum self-esteem.* Self-esteem is nurtured during the developing years by significant adults, siblings, and other children. We must be sensitive to the various criteria of self-esteem that children bring with them, formed from families, neighborhoods, ethnic groups, peer groups, and community, and not downgrade or undermine it.

3. *Feeling that life is worth living.* Whether children are at home, in child care centers, or in schools, they should be able to experience their lives as worth living, real, authentic, and satisfying.

4. *Help with making sense of experience.* We need to help children broaden their understandings of their worlds.

5. *Authoritative adults.* Young children need adults who accept their own authority, which has come from having greater experience, knowledge, and wisdom. These adults must set and maintain limits, while being warm, supportive, and encouraging. Children must also be treated with respect, even when adults may disagree with the opinions, feelings, ideas, and wishes of the children.

6. *Desirable role models.* Children need association with older children and adults who exemplify the personal qualities that we want children to acquire.

The Seven Irreducible Needs of Children

1. Ongoing nurturing relationships
2. Physical protection, safety, and regulation
3. Experiences tailored to individual differences
4. Developmentally appropriate experiences (DAP)
5. Limit setting, structure, and expectations
6. Stable, supportive communities, and cultural continuity
7. Protecting the future (Greenberg, 2001, p. 8).

It is also important that we recognize situations causing stress, how children react to stress, and how they can be helped to cope with stress. When we help children to develop resiliency, we fortify them for a lifetime.

Children's families are very much a part of how they feel about themselves; and even though family structures and makeup might vary, still the family's role in facilitating character education is paramount.

A Healthy Self-Esteem

One's attitude toward oneself is usually referred to as **self-esteem.** Children's self-esteem affects their actions, behavior, learning, and playing, and how they relate to others. Self-esteem is a feeling or attitude of personal worth, and it determines the extent to which each child believes himself or herself to be capable, attractive, worthy, responsible, important, and lovable. Self-esteem is enhanced when children feel competent and display the traits that are valued by their particular cultures.

A person with healthy self-esteem:

- Accepts the self and limitations, while trusting the self to cope with most situations that occur.
- Accepts and assumes responsibility.
- Is proud of successes and accomplishments, but does not have to use them in proving the self to others.
- Approaches new challenges, assignments, and experiences with enthusiasm.
- Has a broad range of emotions and feelings, but the general attitude and feelings focus on the positive.
- Is able to feel control of his or her personal life.
- Recognizes that an innate sense of self-esteem determines how he or she feels and acts.

A person with unhealthy self-esteem:

- Avoids situations or experiences in which he or she may not be successful.
- Feels incompetent, unsuccessful, untalented, unloved, and powerless.
- Blames others for anything that goes wrong.
- Tears down or views negatively any strengths or talents that he or she may have.
- Easily gives in to pressure from others.
- May have problems with drug and alcohol abuse, depression, hostility, or making friends.

Generalizations Regarding Self-Esteem

From significant research and study of self-esteem, we not only can describe what it looks like and doesn't look like in a person, but we can also understand the impact and implications of self-esteem on the individual.

- Our behavior matches our self-image. Much of children's behavior, both positive and negative, is influenced by the way that they view themselves, that is, their self-image.
- The significant people in children's lives have a great influence on how children see themselves. Children tend to view themselves as they think others see them.
- A child cannot grow in confidence and self-esteem without positive feelings or without being praised for appropriate behavior, accomplishments, and successes. Warm and loving approval from others is essential to the development of positive self-esteem.
- Children with healthy self-esteem are poised, confident, and pleasant to be with. Their social skills are generally good. They are less influenced by peers and tend to make better decisions.
- Whenever an act results in a feeling of satisfaction, this act is likely to be repeated. Children have an innate need for attention, preferably positive; but if no attention is given for positive behavior, children soon become conditioned to misbehaving to receive attention, even if it is negative attention.
- Self-esteem affects children's relationships, actions, interactions, and play. It influences stability, integrity, and creativity. Creative activities involve risk, and being able to take a risk requires self-confidence. Therefore, to be able to respond creatively, one must be able to trust that those one likes and loves will accept one through both failures and successes. Also, a child who is overly concerned with success, approval, and acceptance will not venture a risk, but will find security in assuming that it is better not to try at all than to try and fail.
- What we are and how we feel about the child has more effect than anything we do. Feelings are modeled and caught, not taught.
- Children with low self-esteem feel isolated, unloved, and defenseless. They often feel powerless to attain goals that they desire in life and are often withdrawn and passive about life and experiences.
- Children with low self-esteem are more influenced by the negative experiences in their lives and allow these experiences to control their feelings and perceptions of the environment.
- Because we cannot give away what we do not possess, because we cannot teach what we have neither learned nor understood, because we cannot build with materials we have not obtained, we cannot strengthen children with more positive self-esteem until we first find the courage, insight, wisdom, and determination to strengthen and build our own self-esteem. Thus, the stronger and richer the teacher's own self-esteem, the more successful she or he will be in creating like attitudes and concepts in the children being taught.
- Children and parents need to learn that "I can" is more important than IQ. Self-confidence can often compensate for deficits in other areas.

Positive self-images are developed as children learn more about themselves and have numerous successes resulting in increased confidence and a sense of self-worth. This, in turn, tends to give children the feeling that they are important to others and contributors to society. At the same time, children also develop feelings of the importance of and need for others. Children, in fact, cannot accept others until they accept themselves. Esteem for others begins with esteem for, and acceptance of, oneself. Teachers need to help children to find themselves.

Leslie and Megan were playing hide-and-go-seek and had hidden from Kyle and Curtis. When Kyle and Curtis became frightened because they could not find Leslie and Megan, the four children decided to play hide-and-go-seek all together at the same time. They covered their eyes and counted "One, two, . . . nine, ten." Then Megan instructed, "Come on, let's go find ourselves!"

Suggestions for Building Children's Self-Esteem

Knowing the significance of self-esteem, teachers need guidelines for fostering and facilitating children's self-esteem.

Here are some general suggestions for strengthening children's self-esteem:

- Be honest, sincere, and consistent in expressing feelings.
- Value the children's work and efforts, not necessarily the finished product or outcome. Praise them for specific accomplishments.
- Accept each child for himself or herself. This means not only accepting but searching for individual differences. Help children recognize their strengths, and work with their limitations.
- Do whatever is possible to help children overcome any physical problems, but also help them accept those things that cannot be changed.
- Encourage academic achievement. Knowledge and understanding are forerunners to feelings of worth.
- Encourage children to help, build, respect, and support others. This results in positive feelings of joy and internal satisfaction, in addition to

healthy social skill development. There appears to be a close relationship between early social adjustment in the peer group and later adult adjustment.

- Independence breeds self-esteem; allow children to do things for themselves. Children gain confidence in themselves as they accomplish new developmental tasks and acquire the ability to have some control. Giving children responsibilities and trusting them to complete these tasks helps build capabilities and self-confidence. Children learn to make competent decisions by being allowed to make decisions and accept responsibility for them.
- Smile and be cheerful, happy, and courteous and focus on the positive with children. These attitudes must be genuine and come from within; remember, your attitude is the key.
- Your actions must convey the worth and value of the children. Little acts of kindness, individual attention, and positive deeds become very important. For example, a short note or phone call expressing a positive feeling or congratulations for a new accomplishment can make a child feel valuable and accepted.
- Your words make a difference. Children perceive themselves as competent or the opposite by what teachers say and the tone in which they say it. Words or phrases such as "Congratulations," "I'm proud of you," "I'm sorry," "Excuse me," and "Thank you" should be included frequently in conversations with children. Phrases either build up or tear down, depending on how they are worded. For instance, put the "problem" on the item or action, rather than directing it toward the child. Say "That water fountain is too high," rather than "You are too short to reach the water fountain"; "That shoe is too hard to tie," rather than "You are too little to tie your shoe"; "That water is too deep," rather than "You're too young to go in the water."
- Listen to the child in order to understand the child. Pose questions to children that will help you to understand their self-concept, questions such as, "Tell me something about yourself" and "What do you like about yourself?"
- Invite the child to sit by or interact with you.
- Provide support groups in the classroom for resolving conflicts, for addressing personal problems and concerns in their lives, and so on.

Children's emotional well-being hinges on how well they accept themselves.

Regardless of the symptoms, most children with such problems suffer feelings of self-doubt, inadequacy, guilt, and helplessness. They may develop problems in behavior, motivation, and even physical health. Teachers need to do everything they can to inculcate in each child feelings of importance and self-respect—emotional well-being can be an indicator or predictor of academic success.

Teachers should help children to understand that this basic psychological need for self-respect is, to a degree, determined by their own attitudes toward themselves and their choice of values and goals. In other words, it is not totally up to parents and teachers to build this feeling; children need to find themselves. Healthy self-esteem comes from accomplishment and academic achievement; our challenge is to help students to become absorbed with learning, rather than focused on performance. Positive self-esteem is most powerful and has the greatest impact when it is competency based or comes from one's genuine, earned achievements, rather than from gold stars, blue ribbons, or stamped phrases. The key for development of self-esteem, then, is to develop strong inner self-esteem that comes from within. The following points are suggestions help teachers and parents

Children's emotional well-being largely hinges on how well they accept themselves. Psychotherapists have found that the most common denominator of mental health problems is a deficiency of self-esteem.

support children in developing strong inner or intrinsic self-esteem:

1. Believe in them, and let them know you do.
2. Help them recognize that their actions have logical consequences.
3. Help them understand that their efforts count.
4. Provide encouragement and support, not praise.
5. Eliminate negative comments and labels
6. Help children identify, and build on, their strengths and abilities

An integrated music program is an excellent way to enhance language development, creative expression, knowledge of musical concepts, a sense of collaboration, and self-esteem. It is important to select a variety of music that helps children feel successful, includes movement activities. Let children hear their names often included in songs. Our names are usually the first words we learn to write, and are an important part of our self-esteem.

Each Child Is Unique

Remember to stress children's similarities more than their differences. From the suggested teaching approaches presented in this chapter, children will gain insight into their feelings, names, roles, families, friends, abilities, foods, homes, clothes, travels, and many other characteristics. Children must sense that they are unique and special.

Stress in Children and Developing Resiliency

One precursor of self-esteem deficiency in young children is stress. Stress results when we cannot cope with either external or internal demands. Internal sources of concern or stressors may include hunger, pain, illness, fatigue, shyness, and emotions. External sources or stressors may include abuse, divorce, separation from family, illness, hospitalization, exposure to conflict, social conflicts, military conflicts with other countries, negative discipline, excessive high-achievement expectations, a death, violence, a blended family, accidents, or other traumatic happenings. Stress can be acute or chronic. Acute stress is sudden and intense and then gradually diminishes. Chronic stress, which has a more serious effect on children, is continual or ongoing. A child's reaction to stress depends on many things, particularly the child's coping skills, and the internal and external support systems available. Such stressors may include situations, events, or people and are not necessarily good or bad; they are just particular demands. Variables associated with different kinds of stress in children's lives include maturity, age, sex, intellectual abilities, neurological strength, living environment, socioeconomic status, family events or situations, and parenting practices. Even if we could avoid all stress, which we cannot, we would deprive children of valuable life-coping skills. The very

process of living produces stress. Many events in our lives over which we have little or no control create stress. One of the great stressors in the lives of young children is hurrying them: from one location to another, to get ready, to do well on work or assignments, to grow up. To counteract this, we can either decrease our demands or increase our supports.

Often the cause of the stress response in children is not the actual situation or person, but the child's attitude toward that particular situation or person. For example, stress in young children can be created by fears of unreal things such as monsters or witches. It is often a difficult task for very young children to make a distinction between reality and fantasy. Children misconstrue situations, events, or conversations to mean something that they do not mean. This results in worry, anxiety, concern, and stress. Children also experience personal fears and concerns that result in stress. Separation itself is not always stressful and harmful to children, but too much separation too soon is a major source of stress. When children become surrounded with fears, anxieties, quarreling, complaining, bickering, and other potentially anxious situations, they can experience emotional overload.

School often creates many stressors for children, and emotionally stressful classroom environments are counterproductive because they can reduce children's ability to learn. Many children miss school each year because they fear aggression there. Extremely demanding and developmentally inappropriate classroom practices and demands, such as too much emphasis on assessments, may also cause stress. There is competition for grades, high expectations, demand for excellence, and social concerns. At every educational level, there is a feeling that we must master certain concepts at this particular level; that is, we must get through this material by a specific time. On the other hand, school can stress some children if they find it dull, boring, and unchallenging. Children in this situation become fatigued, inattentive, uninterested, and stressed. Adults suffering job burnout, especially when their work is meaningless and repetitive, react with the same symptoms. Many adults have dreams relating to their previous school experiences, even though they may have been out of school for many years.

Violence and Conflict Resolution

Television and movies can create stress by giving children more information than they can understand and information that is too complex. This results in a discrepancy between the amount of information that children have and the amount that they are able to process. Of particular concern is the influence of violence in the lives of children. When children witness violence, their sense of security and predictability is threatened.

Violence results in children believing that there is no safe place and that there is no one to protect them. These feelings not only influence their emotional development, but also negatively affect all relationships. Witnessing violence or learning in detail about violent incidents can be very traumatic to children. When media repeatedly reports on the same incident, a young child thinks that it continues to keep happening over and over again. Exposure to media violence results in children viewing violence as a normal response to stress and as an appropriate way to resolve conflicts.

How children think affects how they interpret their experiences. They are not able to fully distinguish between fantasy and reality; they focus on the concrete, dramatic aspects of the situation; they are unable to make logical and appropriate cause-and-effect connections; and they concentrate on only one aspect of the situation at a time. Children who are exposed to violence often exhibit symptoms of posttraumatic stress disorder: nightmares or night walking, aggression or withdrawal, regression to prior developmental skill levels, irritability and emotional outbursts, increased concentration difficulties, or reliving the events. In addition, frequent exposure to media violence can result in children justifying their own use of violence, desiring to view increasing amounts of violence, selecting violent heroes as role models, mistrusting or fearing others, being desensitized toward violence and accepting it as normal behavior.

Young children can be taught skills that not only help them develop nonviolent behaviors, but also equip them to form nurturing and caring relationships throughout their lives. Loving, consistent, and reliable care are of utmost importance in helping children to feel the emotional and physical safety that is conducive to their growth, learning, and development. To assist children in acquiring these attitudes, teachers and families should provide a safe environment, build and foster supportive relationships, promote emotional and social competence, provide positive interactions with others, strengthen interactive skills, demonstrate positive role modeling, and foster problem solving (M. P. Anderson, 2001). In our daily interactions with young children, we must be aware of the words and language that we use, careful of our tone of voice, cautious of our own actions, positive in our approach to guidance, sensitive to the feelings and relationships of others, and mindful of the importance of creating a safe, harmonious learning environment in our classrooms.

Children need to use peaceful conflict resolutions to counteract the violent conflict approaches that they may learn from the media or from personal experiences in their lives. When children conflict with one another, it is important that we empower them with the skills to use problem solving as an opportunity for learning. Conflicts among young children are a natural part of

life, and valuable lessons can be learned through these conflicts. When we intervene too early in these conflicts, we prevent children from learning interpersonal skills and problem-solving techniques. Even though we may desire to resolve the conflicts ourselves, it is important for us to observe and allow time for children to find their own solutions, providing any needed guidance and support for their efforts and accomplishments. Children's literature is an excellent source for helping children to learn to resolve problems. Books show that, although conflicts may be a part of daily life, they can still be resolved in peaceful ways. Good books demonstrate finding common ground in conflict resolution as well as getting to know someone and valuing their uniqueness. Children can understand the basic elements for resolving conflicts peacefully. They should recognize that there are at least two sides to the problem and suggest possible solutions. Then they should select an agreeable solution and try it out to see if it works. If it does not work, then they should evaluate the situation and go back to choose another solution.

A "Fussbuster program" (Gillespie & Chick, 2001, p. 194) was developed to assist young children in a Head Start classroom to resolve conflicts. A "Peace Table" was designated, which was used only for the "Fussbuster program." Whenever a conflict occurred, the children involved and a mutual friend chosen by them immediately moved to the Peace Table. The teachers and children made up a list of rules and procedures that were to be followed. In the children's own words, they included:

1. No hitting; keep hands and feet to self.
2. Talk things over.
3. One person talks at a time.
4. Take a helper—a Fussbuster.
5. Stay until the problem is solved.
6. Shake hands at the end.
7. You get your spot back (where you were playing).

A sense of teamwork and ownership resulted as students developed the rules and procedures, chose Fussbusters, and were chosen as Fussbusters. The number of conflicts in the classroom dramatically decreased. The results supported the philosophy that young children, with proper training and modeling, can take control of their conflicts and find peaceful solutions to problems.

Children's Reactions to Stress

Considering individual differences among children, remember that what may cause stress in one child will not necessarily cause stress in another. Children respond to stress in various stages: A child is alarmed by event, tries to understand, searches for ways to cope, and then uses strategies for coping. Children have different coping abilities, as do adults, so what causes one child to fall apart may make another child stronger. Reactions also depend on individual stages of intellectual, emotional, and social development, which are usually determined by age (Mercurio & McNamee, 2006). Basically, validating their feelings and ensuring a safe, emotional, and physical environment are imperative (Wood, 2008). The child's reaction relates in part to the notion of accumulation: In one child, stress and anxiety build up faster than the natural adaptation process can handle; another child naturally adapts to the stress.

Signs That Suggest Children May Be Experiencing Undue Stress

Crying, fussing

Reverting to less mature behaviors

Nervous habits such as twisting or pulling hair; sighing deeply; nailbiting; thumbsucking; tapping feet, fingers, or pencils

Increased irritability, sometimes to the point of tantrums

Lethargy or withdrawal from activities

Distractibility

Daydreaming

Outbursts of anger

Sweating palms

Dry throat

Ulcers

Subtle reactions, such as a strained look about the eyes, tightened mouth, or furrowed brow

Excessive energy, restlessness, or aggression

Inability to stay on the task or concentrate

Nausea, eating disorders

Aches: head, stomach, neck, back, or muscle

Pounding heart

Susceptibility to colds and illness

Difficulty in breathing, asthma

Proneness to injury or accidents

Tiredness

Depression

Nervousness, tenseness

Forgetfulness

Difficulty sleeping and staying awake

Uncommon personality or behavior patterns

Picking at scabs or sores

Frequent physical, verbal, and/or emotional outbursts

Children's emotions are often expressed through gestures and facial expressions.

Helping Children to Cope with Stress

There is much literature on helping children cope with stress. Stress management helps children to develop coping skills, interpret events, and understand that they *can* cope. Sometimes it is helpful for children to learn about stress-producing events before they actually occur, which helps them to evaluate events when they do happen. Encouraging children to solve their own problems also increases their ability to cope with stress. It is imperative that they see the adults around them model appropriate and successful coping strategies. Our attitudes of confidence, love, acceptance, and understanding help children to get through stressful times.

When we allow children to determine the direction of learning and exploring, they become problem solvers and negotiators, planners, and thinkers. After a classroom pet rabbit died, the students, through the guidance and support of the teacher, initiated the resulting discussion and projects (Sandstrom, 1999, p. 15). The following unspoken messages were sent to each of the classroom children throughout the experience:

- I trust you.
- You are big.
- Your decisions are meaningful.
- You are valuable.

- Help is available.
- Questions are good.
- Death is another part of life.
- Grownups cry.
- People have different ideas, and that's OK.
- Feelings are important.
- Talking and discussion helps you understand.
- Writing is powerful.
- You can learn from everybody (not just teachers).

Respect conveys and fosters esteem. The atmosphere and feeling tone surrounding the child are vital. Listen to children and encourage them to communicate. Talking about the "worst thing that could happen" or asking them to "tell me what is worrying you" helps children to express such feelings openly. Care for the child. With loving guidance, the child can be emotionally equipped to face whatever life brings. Understand and accept (and sometimes encourage) crying, which seems to be a natural healer that helps us cope with stress.

Additional Suggestions for Helping Children to Cope with Stress

Reading

Lying down, resting, or taking a nap

Listening to music, playing music, singing, whistling, or humming

Daydreaming, mental imagery, or positive self-talk

Breathing deeper and slower

Laughter and humor

Slowing the pace down

Appropriate video games, computer activities, movies, or television

Physical contact: hugging, touching, or holding

Pets: playing, watching, or petting

Constructing or building

Eating; chewing gum or soft candy

Swinging (playground, lawn, or hammock)

Art activities and materials

Speaking quietly or softly to the child

Physical activity

Playing with a friend

Consistency, routines, schedules, or limits

Honesty and openness from others

Talking, drawing, or writing about concerns

Training in physical and mental relaxation or self-induced relaxation skills also tends to reduce stress and its effects on children (Bothmer, 2003). For example, one technique is meditation; the teacher's primary function is to provide a quiet, comfortable environment for relaxation and meditation (Bothmer, 2003). Another technique is progressive muscle relaxation, because one cannot be simultaneously relaxed and stressed, and because mental relaxation is a natural consequence of physical relaxation. By tensing and relaxing muscle groups, children can learn to relax muscles when necessary. Another technique, visual imagery, encourages children to imagine a peaceful and happy scene or experience. Or, they can imagine a warm ball of liquid gold that starts at the top of their head and slowly flows down their whole body. This visual imagery can be turned into creative brainstorming as children imagine similar kinds of things while both their minds and bodies relax.

Another way of teaching children to deal with stress is to encourage children to use positive, rather than negative, self-talk. Train them to think "I can" instead of "I can't." Have them brainstorm positive self-talk, that is, positive attitudes and ideas that they think about themselves. Help them to clarify their values by asking, "Is it worth worrying about right now?" or "Will my worrying about it solve it?"

Help children to develop a sense of humor and enjoy laughing. During the early childhood years, they enjoy telling riddles and "knock-knock" jokes; they learn that it is fun and relaxing to enjoy a good joke. A sense of humor helps children to cope with stress or conflict in their lives. Humor is a great moderator and stabilizer in our lives, and keeps us emotionally and physically healthy!

The curriculum and feeling tone in the classroom should model happy, peaceful living. This atmosphere will not only affect the children's feelings in a positive way, but it can also influence their attitudes toward and treatment of others in the classroom. In psychologically safe school environments, children are able to develop personal, meaningful social relationships. Children are able to form positive self-images as capable problem solvers, eager learners, supportive friends, and contributing family members. Faith that things will work out can be sustained in difficult times if children are supported by people who care for and scaffold them and offer a reason for commitment.

We remind teachers of the importance of fostering stress management for themselves, and suggest the following ways for teachers and other adults working with children to reduce their own stress:

- Take time for yourself.
- Form support groups with other teachers.
- Provide mentors or teaching buddies for new teachers.
- Let others know of your concerns or needs.

- Be realistic about your own expectations.
- Focus on the positive aspects of your teaching and students.

Fostering Resiliency in Children

Resiliency is the capability to cope effectively with life challenges. It is the ability to recover or "bounce back" and adapt to troubles, stress, and obstacles (Breslin, 2005) and to realize that problems can be worked on and resolved. This ability develops over time and is greatly influenced by the individual child's behavior and personality, family attributes, and social environment. It is not a fixed quality but a set of "protective mechanisms that modify a person's response to risk situations" (Breslin, 2005, p. 47). If early childhood professionals become familiar with the factors influencing resiliency, they will be able to positively affect the lives of the young children for whom they care.

Resiliency is directly related to a child's self-esteem and general attitude toward life. Children who are resilient usually have hope, a positive outlook, and good self-esteem. They are independent, confident, communicative, friendly, responsive, social, cheerful, and competent. They recognize their individual potential. Resilient children are accountable for themselves and act in a responsible way towards others; they have a sense of control over what happens in their lives and do not feel helpless (Kersey & Malley, 2005).

Teachers need to model respect and resiliency. We need to verbalize our respect and appreciation for children, for their talents, abilities, good qualities, and helpfulness. Such character traits as caring, helping, sharing, and being successful, competent, and sympathetic that we see children demonstrate should not go unnoticed! These same traits tend to be apparent in children who are more resilient. To prepare resilient youth for uncertainty, teachers should foster feelings of competence, belonging, usefulness, and optimism in the classroom. When children participate in classroom decision making, peer tutoring, problem solving, room arranging, or theme and project selection, they become more confident and resilient. Mistakes should be viewed as opportunities for growth (Kersey & Malley, 2005).

Developing resiliency in children requires care and support from significant adults, high expectations, and the opportunity for meaningful participation. Children need to be guided through self-directed understanding, and be able to recognize that they have emotional, mental, spiritual, and physical resources that can give them personal strength (Kersey & Malley, 2005).

A strong relationship with parents appears to be one of the most important contributions to resilience. Families have particular traits that help support and promote resilience in children—positive relationships with family members, appropriate supervision, involvement in school, fair and consistent discipline, and attitudes of acceptance toward others. As we model these strategies in our classrooms, it strengthens the families and helps children learn coping techniques through observation. Positive experiences in the school, neighborhood, and community provide additional resilient influences outside the home. Because of space, economics, work schedules, and time, many activities such as music, sports, and drama are not available in the home, but are readily accessible in the religious, educational, and community environments.

Because teachers can be mentors, models, examples, providers, and supporters, we can have a positive effect on children, reinforcing the belief that life is doable (Kersey & Malley, 2005). It is important that our attitudes convey: "I understand. I am here for you. I will help you. I care about you. You are important to me." As the children realize this, we help them to work with the stressors in their lives now and fortify them with confidence and abilities to handle the problems that they will encounter in the future. Bakley (1997, p. 21) confirms, "A child loved by us at 2 will reflect that love at 7. A child encouraged by us at age 3 will show confidence at age 7. A child affirmed by us at 4 will demonstrate self-esteem at 7." Caring breeds respect (Charney, 2002).

Character Education

Moral or character education is "the training of heart and mind toward good" (W. J. Bennett, 1993, p. 11). Schools are taking more specific approaches to character education, with much of the responsibility being delegated to teachers. "Teachers can be great role models for caring and altruistic behavior; they can demonstrate caring, empathy, and compassion toward others in their day-to-day interactions with students" (Robinson & Curry, 2005/2006, p. 70). **Character** involves possessing and demonstrating such qualities as self-control, honesty, courage, equality, compassion, integrity, self-discipline, industriousness, responsibility, empathy, patriotism, and loyalty. Most everyone recognizes that there is a core of values, often tied to our democratic beliefs, and that children do not innately possess these characteristics. In order to develop these

Factors Relating to Resiliency

- Heightened, positive sensory awareness
- High, positive feedback and expectations
- Developing a clear and accurate understanding of one's strengths
- A well-developed sense of humor (Breslin, 2005, pp. 48–50)

qualities, they need to be taught what is right and wrong, and to have positive examples and models. Children learn from what they see and hear! "If students practice behaviors associated with forgiveness, sympathy, and kindness, bullying behavior should decrease" (Bulach, 2002, p. 79). This does not merely refer to the traditional religious reference, but to the spark of fire in each person, the very essence of uniqueness (S. B. Turner, 2000). Children must develop clear values that help them to grow up being fair and considerate of others. Cooperation is an important part of building social relationships, and even young children can learn that success does not come at the expense of others (Heimes, 2009). These character values develop as children learn to express and understand not only their own feelings, but also the feelings of other people.

> Children need courage to face fear and heroism to truly care for others (C. A. Smith, 2005). Courage is persevering and overcoming fear. Its roots are:
>
> - To persevere or try again in spite of adversity
> - To remain thoughtful or mindful despite fear
>
> Heroism, "courage elevated by a noble purpose" (C. A. Smith, 2004), has its roots in:
>
> - Caring about self and others
> - Responding with compassion to another's suffering or trial
>
> "We must nurture courage, for we live in an age that requires noble deeds." (C. A. Smith, 2005, p. 87)

A variety of important character traits can be addressed in activities and units of study, or integrated across content areas. Exploring such traits as the following can help children examine and exemplify positive traits: responsibility, respect, courage, honesty, fairness, confidence, forgiveness, equality, kindness, loyalty, humor, restraint, and cooperation. Teachers should accumulate stories of real children in the community and school who exemplify these qualities, or seek resources with true stories profiling children demonstrating these traits (Lewis, 2005). Because the family is the first unit of society for the child, it has paramount responsibility for encouraging the character education of young children; however, more and more our schools have included character education as a significant aspect on the educational agenda. Research suggests that having secure relationships with at least one adult during the early years supports better intellectual development and social relationships in later years (Riley, SanJuan, Klinkner, & Ramminger, 2008; Bowman & Moore, 2006), and often that "one adult" is a teacher! Children tend to have fewer behavior problems when

they have warm, secure relationships with their teachers (Riley et al., 2008). In addition, "As their mastery of the social-emotional domain increases, young children's confidence in themselves, and positive interactions with others, become effective resources for learning in all other domains" (Epstein, 2009, p. 22).

Teachers and parents can assist young children in developing a lifelong prosocial attitude and a pattern of caring behavior by:

- Accepting individual uniqueness and needs of children
- Modeling and encouraging compassion, sympathy, and empathy
- Monitoring amount and types of activities involving television, computers, and handheld technological instruments
- Developing warm, trusting, and nurturing relationships with children
- Having children help solve problems and conflicts
- Expecting and appreciating age-appropriate responsible behavior

"Petting the classroom bunny and talking about how the bunny feels . . . are exactly the kinds of activities . . . we should be using to teach . . . perspective taking, empathy, and prosocial behavior" (Riley et al., 2008, pp. 2–3). The century-old child-guidance approach of helping infants, toddlers, and older young children to develop self-discipline and self-regulation is still applicable today!

Along with teaching democratic and civil values, our young people need to be taught to think for themselves and to make responsible decisions. As children develop positive character traits and internalize them as worthwhile values, their ability to function and behave as responsible, valuable citizens rapidly expands. **Values** represent standards or principles of worth. Human values are the core of our democracy, and many values are explicitly taught or implicitly caught within the family unit and the classroom. They are taught in a democratic classroom environment through cooperative learning activities, conflict resolution, practice, and modeling. Through example and specific curriculum activities, teachers and families teach responsible behavior and strive to help children to acquire a sound set of values with which to make decisions. We teach them what character traits are, and why they are desirable. "When young children do not know how to identify emotions, handle disappointment and anger, or develop relationships with others, a teacher's best response is to teach" (Fox & Lentini, 2006, p. 42). Nurturing and individualized teacher-child relationships provide important contexts for the promotion of children's emotional health (Bagdi & Vacca, 2005), as teachers build relationships, coach and model, and create healthy environments (Nissen & Hawkins, 2010). Children learn fair play, justice, and morality from how they are treated by their families, teachers, and peers. To interact cooperatively, get along well with others, and develop close social relationships, children must be able to understand the feelings and intentions of others, often referred to as the development of social understanding. When children behave prosocially, they do better in school, extracurricular activities, and other social situations (Petty, 2009). The benefits of early friendships are obvious—friends provide social stability for the children, they help children learn to get along with others, and they help children learn more positive problem-solving skills (Riley et al., 2008).

The foundation for strong values rests in empowering children with the following principles. The child must:

1. Develop self-esteem and courage to defend his or her convictions, values, and beliefs
2. Have the self-motivation to set and accomplish individual goals
3. Be tolerant of and show respect for *all* other people regardless of their gender, race, social class, or abilities
4. Have the ability to judge right from wrong as defined by laws and to make moral judgments
5. Be honest with self and others
6. Do his or her best and act responsibly

Because positive character traits are best fostered in a social environment of caring and respect, we must provide educational activities that allow students the opportunity of experiencing and internalizing desired values. As educators of young children, we have both the opportunity and responsibility to nurture their spirits during the years when their interests, values, and attitudes are taking root. Spiritual nurturing is not programmed into the curriculum routine at a particular time on a particular day. It must be present in our philosophies and approaches to teaching, classroom environments, and day-to-day interactions with each other (Wolf, 2000). "We cannot care for children without educating them, and we cannot educate children without caring for them" (Gallagher & Mayer, 2008, p. 86).

APPROACH TO TEACHING

Concepts and Ideas for Teaching

1. I am a person, and I have a name.
2. I have a body.
   a. Body parts
   b. How and why to care for various parts (hair, teeth, nails)

3. I have different physical characteristics: freckles; glasses, contacts; brown eyes; red hair; braces worn on teeth; braces worn on leg(s).
4. I am growing.
   a. I weigh more than I did a year ago.
   b. I am taller than I was a year ago.
   c. I was once a baby.
5. I am sometimes sick: colds, diseases, or headaches.
6. I have strengths, talents, and capabilities, but I also have some weaknesses.
   a. What are my talents?
   b. What are my strengths?
   c. What are my weaknesses?
7. I have some goals for myself. I would like to be . . .
8. I have a particular race and nationality.
9. I have feelings, and they are always acceptable, but I must learn to express them in acceptable ways.
10. I have unique thoughts and ideas that are important.
11. I live in a neighborhood.
12. I live in a city (on a farm, in a small town), in a state that is part of a nation that is part of the world.
13. I have favorite songs, colors, seasons, friends, things I like to do, television programs, movies or videos, holidays, foods, things to collect, and subjects in school.
14. When I grow up, I want to be . . .
15. I have a family.
    a. My family takes care of me.
    b. I learn many things from my family.
16. My family is unique.
    a. I may have one or two parents.
    b. I may have brothers and sisters.
    c. I may have a grandmother and grandfather.
    d. I may have cousins, uncles, and aunts.
    e. I may have a foster family.
    f. My family lives in a house, apartment, or shelter.
17. I have fun with my family.
    a. We play together.
    b. We go places together.
    c. We work together.
18. My family sometimes changes: divorce, death, parent remarriage, illness, disease, or moving to a different home or city.
19. I depend on many people and need the help of many people.
20. There are many elderly people in my community; I can serve and help them.

Activities and Experiences

1. Take photographs of individual children, especially in action shots. Photograph the entire child, not just the head. These photographs can be used to build the self-concept and can be displayed on the child's locker or desk.
2. Take or collect photographs of children with their families. These can be used to discuss family characteristics, diversity, similarities, and differences. Remember: Always stress how families and individual children are more alike than different.
3. Provide mirrors for the children to use on the tables for use during free play and on the walls in various locations. Every classroom should have a full-length mirror.
4. Draw body images of the children. The children lie on a sheet of butcher paper while a teacher (or another child, if older) draws around the body shape. After being decorated, the images are displayed around the room so that the size and shape variations of the children can be easily observed. As a variation, the children can cut body parts from magazines or newspapers for collaging onto the drawing.
5. Make hand- or footprints in plaster. They can be compared with those of other children in the classroom and also with the hands and feet of parents or other family members.
6. Do posters, sheets or booklets titled "All About Me" or "This Is Me." Include such topics as "My Favorite Things to Do," "My Family," "A Picture of Me," "Physical Characteristics," and so on.
7. Set up dress-up areas that include clothing and equipment/materials representing various roles and professions.
8. Provide charts, models, and pictures of the human body; include bones, muscles, and so on.
9. Make a neighborhood or community map, including the area and house where each child lives, if possible. Lay this map out flat, and provide small "people" and cars for the children to play with.
10. Have children complete open-ended sentences relating to their feelings. For example:
    a. I wish . . .
    b. The best thing I can do . . .
    c. I feel proud when . . .
    d. I feel angry when . . .
    e. I am happy when . . .
    f. When I get big, I'm going to . . .
    g. I get scared when ...
    h. I like it when my family . . .
    i. I wish my family would . . .
11. Have each child decorate an envelope with "Love Notes" written on the outside. The envelope can be left at school or taken home so that other children or family members can write or draw pictures of what they like about the child.
12. Make "I Can Do" cards with pictures or drawings of tasks and skills that the majority of the children in your class can do. As the cards are held up, the children do the skill or pretend to do it.
13. Make a puzzle of each child's name using first, or first and last names.
14. Make job or "To Do" charts. Assist children in individualizing these charts for their own responsibilities and activities. It is satisfying for children to see their accomplishments on paper as they mark off daily tasks. (See Figure 6.4.)
15. Use the following selection for role playing, creative dramatics, memorization, program presentations, ideas for visitors and field trips, development of literacy skills through reading and listening enjoyment, and so on:

When I Grow Up

I can't decide just what to do when I get big someday.
There are so many different things – it's really hard to say.
I know I can be more than one, more than two or three;
But what to be when I grow up? I'll have to wait and see!
Maybe I will drive a bus, a taxi, or tow truck;
And when the snow gets very deep, I'll help you get unstuck.
Maybe I will put out fires, or save a frightened cat.
I'll ride upon the fire truck and wear a fire hat.
I could become a dentist, too, and care for people's teeth.
I'd clean the ones in front, behind, above, and then beneath.
I could be a custodian and make the buildings shine.
They would ask, "Whose careful work?" I'd proudly answer, "Mine!"
Maybe I'll take care of hives, and learn about the bees.
When I serve honey sandwiches, they'll say, "Another, please!"
Maybe I will take a pen and write a reading book
'Bout how to plant, or how to fix, or how to jog or cook.
Maybe I'll a plumber be, and hear the people say:
"The pipes won't drain, the faucet drips. Please help me right away!"

	Sunday	Monday	Tuesday	Wednesday	Thursday	Friday	Saturday
 Get dressed							
 Set the table							
 Brush teeth							
 Pick up toys							
 Fold clothes							
 Take a bath							

FIGURE 6.4   Sample "To Do" Chart

Maybe I will sell new cars to folks who trade their old.

They'll say, "I think I'll take this one." And I will answer, "Sold!"

I could engineer a train, and speed along the track.

As people pass and wave at me, I will wave right back.

Maybe I will gather trash, and empty garbage, too.

I'll keep clean the city streets, the playground, and the zoo.

I could be a magician with a traveling magic show.

They'd ask me how it works, I'd say: "That's just for me to know."

Maybe I could sell new shoes – check fit at toe and heel.

I'd say, "Now walk around a bit, and see how those two feel."

Maybe I will fix up cars, and keep them good as new.

They'll ask me, "How long will it take?" "I'll call you when I'm through."

Maybe I'll help students learn – a teacher than to choose.

I'd work with 4's, or 8's, or 12's, 16's, or 22's.

Maybe I'll make people laugh, and be a circus clown.

I'll show them that a frown is just a smile turned upside-down.

I'll likely be a grandparent with tales about "Back when . . ."

After I am through, they'll say: "Please tell that one again."

I could become a baker, and make cookies every day.

They'd ask me which kind was the best. "Chocolate chip," I'd say.

You see, there are so many things that I could grow to be;

But what I'll be when I get big – I'll have to wait and see.

Source : Reprinted by permission from Loa T. Jenkins.

16. Help children to make character decisions about what is right and what is wrong. The following situations readily lend themselves to cooperative learning in smaller groups:

a. You are in a store and see something that you really want to have. But in your pocket is only enough money to buy milk for your family. What would you do?

b. You are supposed to take an object starting with the letter B to school, and you have forgotten to bring one from home. Your friend sitting next to you has a rubber ball in his coat pocket. What would you do?

c. You are shopping with a friend, and your friend takes a candy bar without paying for it. You are the only one who saw this happen. What would you do?

d. You are on the school playground, and a child is teasing and hurting another child. What would you do?

e. You are with a group of friends, and several begin saying negative and mean things about another friend who is not present. What should you do?

17. Seat the group in a circle. As each person's name is said, a positive adjective that begins with the same letter as the person's name is added: Friendly Frank, Happy Heidi, Jolly Justin. Or, do "Guess Who" riddles using children's positive characteristics.

UNIT IDEAS ON MYSELF

FIELD TRIPS

- Dance studio or ballroom where children can see themselves move in front of large mirrors
- Children's own homes, playgrounds, or yards
- Doctor's office
- Dentist's office
- Beauty shop
- Beauty college (children could have their hair done)
- Eye doctor's office
- Hospital nursery

VISITORS

- Dentist
- Doctor
- Nurse
- Barber
- Beautician
- Parent(s)
- Grandparent(s)
- Sibling(s)
- Person to perform and involve the children in mime

MUSIC

- Children making and decorating their own musical instruments and then accompanying familiar songs, as well as songs that they have created themselves.
- Body sounds to accompany the songs in rhythm (snapping fingers, clicking tongue, clapping hands, etc.)
- Music to skip, jump, hop, run, exercise, relax, and listen to
- Teaching sessions in which children learn to play musical instruments (depending on the ages of the children, these may be rhythm sticks, drums, autoharps, harmonicas, etc.)
- Songs (music and words) created from children's own ideas
- Songs and creative movement about feelings

ART

- Decoration of handmade musical instruments
- Body images: tracing around children's bodies while they are lying on paper; the children paint and decorate the images
- Shapes of eyes, noses, mouths, ears, and so on, cut out from paper by the teacher or the children and pasted onto a face-shaped base by the children
- Foot- or handprints set in plaster, dried, and then colored
- Self-portraits
- "Me Posters" (can be collaged or drawn)

FOOD

- Any food activity that allows and encourages children to develop skills and make something themselves
- Favorite snacks or foods

SCIENCE

- Health care activities that help children to understand and learn good health habits
- Looking at germs from their hands under a microscope
- Studies relating to growth: bones, hair, healing, and fingernails
- Magnifying glass for a closer look at eyes, teeth, freckles, fingers, pores, hair, nose, tongue, scars, and so on

LITERACY DEVELOPMENT

- Any stories that the children write themselves about their experiences, feelings, families, and selves (these can be dictated if the children do not have handwriting skills)
- Stories or thoughts that are the children's own ideas

Note: For a project web on families, see Figure 6.5.

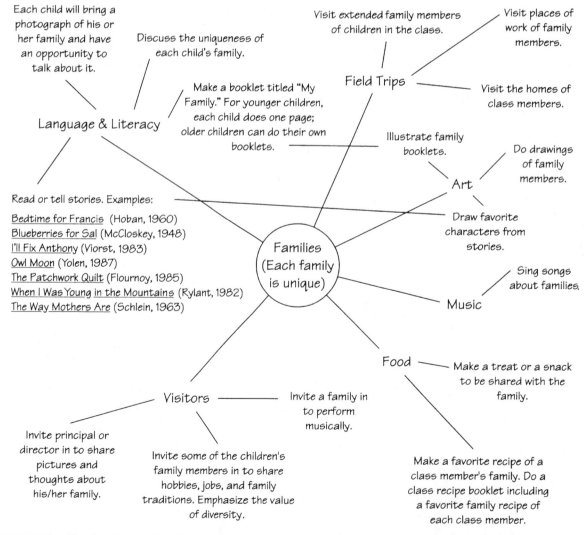

FIGURE 6.5 Project Web on Families

Summary

Physical education and motor experiences in early childhood must be developmentally appropriate and should be integrated into all curriculum areas. In all physical fitness activities and games, children should enjoy the opportunity of participating, being active, and having fun. Competition is not a necessary ingredient for success! Through physical fitness and play, children are able to develop understandings in socialization, values and ethics, sense of right and wrong, stress management and relaxation, creativity and curiosity, and occupations and vocations. Society as a whole is becoming more aware of the importance of nutrition during the early years in maintaining physical and psychological health. As young children participate in a variety of wellness activities, they develop habits that will help ensure their physical, spiritual, emotional, social, and intellectual health throughout their entire life.

Through the development of positive self-images, children are able to accept and value other people. The family provides the child's first social interactions, and it has a significant role in helping the child establish a positive self-image and healthy, realistic expectations. At the same time, teachers and caregivers need to accept children as they are and from this acceptance provide a caring, supportive, high-quality program designed to help the children to progress in their continuing quest for self-esteem. In our effort to understand the influences of stress in the lives of children, it is helpful to recognize situations causing stress, how children react to stress, how they can cope with stress, and how to help them become more resilient. We must understand the effects of violence on young children and empower them with the skills for solving conflicts peacefully. We also have a great responsibility to help children to learn and develop values and positive character traits. Children learn most from the examples of the significant adults in their lives. It is therefore important for teachers and caregivers to exemplify the character traits that they want children to acquire. A teacher's own self-acceptance and attitude are of utmost importance when seeking to assist young children in developing self-concepts that will destine them for success.

Student Learning Activities

1. Select two physical games for any early childhood age and prepare a game sheet with directions. Teach class members one of your games.
2. Select three unit topics and describe how you would integrate physical-motor activities into the unit.
3. Plan an appropriate food experience for children for each of the five food categories in MyPyramid.
4. Implement at least one of the food experiences that you have planned with children in item 3. Evaluate the experience. Was it appropriate? Was it organized in the most efficient way? Would you offer the same experience again? If so, would you make any changes?
5. Prepare a unit, TWS, or project plan on one of the following: "My Family," "My Friends," or some other concept relating to the self. For your web, unit, TWS, or project plan, include a section titled "Literacy" and include stories, poems, and other appropriate activities.
6. Using your plan prepared for item 5, prepare a 5-day activity plan. If you have chosen a project plan, invite the children to develop personal or group projects with their own ideas.
7. Observe in a classroom of young children and describe how the teacher enhances individual children's feelings of self-worth.
8. Study children's books relating to "myself and others." Select one to share with the class. How would you present this story to an early childhood class? Why do you like this book? Is it free of sexism and racism? What concepts relating to the self and/or family will this book support?

Suggested Resources

Carlson, F. M. (2006). *Essentials of touch: Meeting the needs of young children.* Washington, DC: NAEYC.

Connolly, P., Hayden, J., & Levin, D. (2007). *From conflict to peace building: The power of early child initiatives: Lessons from around the world.* Redmond, WA: World Forum Foundation.

Fulghum, R. (2003). *All I really need to know I learned in kindergarten.* 15th Anniversary ed. New York: Ballantine.

Greenman, J. (2001). *What happened to my world? Helping children cope in turbulent times.* No publisher listed.

Kieff, J. (2005/2006). Let's talk about friendship: An anti-bias unit on building classroom community. *Childhood Education 82*(2), 98-K–98-M.

Sutterby, J. A. (2009). What kids don't get to do any more and why. *Childhood Education 85*(5), 289–292.

Physical and Health Education Guides

American Academy of Pediatrics. (See website at www.aap.org.)

American Academy of Pediatrics. (2001). *Promoting optimal health for America's children.* Elk Grove Village, IL: Author.

Corbin, C. B., Pangrazi, R. P., Beighle, A., LeMasurier, G., & Morgan, C. (2004). *Physical activity for children: A statement of guidelines for children ages 5–12* (2nd ed.). Reston, VA: National Association for Sport & Physical Education.

Jensen, E. (2000). *Learning with the body in mind.* San Diego, CA: The Brain Store.

Kendrick, A. S., Kaufmann, R., & Messenger, K. P. (Eds.). (1995). *Healthy young children: A manual for programs.* Washington, DC: National Association for the Education of Young Children.

Lucarelli, P. (2002). Raising the bar for health and safety in child care. *Pediatric Nursing 22*(3): 239–241, 291.

National Association for Sport and Physical Education. (2000a). *Appropriate practices for elementary school physical education.* Reston, VA: Author.

National Association for Sport and Physical Education. (2000b). *Appropriate practices in movement programs for young children.* Reston, VA: Author.

National Association for Sport and Physical Education. (2004). *Moving into the future: National standards for physical education* (2nd ed.). Reston, VA: Author.

Pennsylvania Chapter of the American Academy of Pediatrics, Early Childhood Committee. (1993). *Preparing for illness: A joint responsibility for parents and caregivers.* Booklet. Washington, DC: NAEYC.

Silberg, J. (2000). *125 brain games for toddlers and twos: Simple games to promote early brain development.* San Diego, CA: The Brain Store.

Online Resources

www.aap.org/family/physicalactivity.htm The American Academy of Pediatrics site has numerous resources for early childhood educators. In addition to promoting physical activity, AAP sponsors the Healthy Child Care American Campaign at *www.healthychildcare.org.*

www.cpsc.gov/cpscpub/pubs/chldcare.htm The Child Care Safety Checklist for Parents and Childcare Providers provides information on child safety.

www.usda.gov The U.S. Department of Agriculture has a variety of information on nutrition education.

www.mypyramid.gov MyPyramid lists the five basic food groups and provides information on individualizing the pyramid according to each child's age, gender, and physical activity level.

www.aahperd.org/naspe The National Association for Sport and Physical Education (NASPE) aims to enhance knowledge and professional practice in sport and physical activity.

www.nfpa.catalog/home/index.asp The National Fire Protection Association seeks to reduce threat of fire by providing and advocating codes and standards. Fire safety tips are available on the site.

www.safekids.org The National Safe Kids Campaign includes safety tips and information on product recalls.

www.nccp.org/pub_cwr00h.html Article titled "Promoting Resilience: Helping Young Children and Parents Affected by Substance Abuse, Domestic Violence, and Depression in the Context of Welfare Reform" by Jane Knitzer. From *Children and Welfare Reform,* Issue Brief No 8. Published in 2000 by the National Center for Children in Poverty.

http://resilnet.uiuc.edu ResilienceNet provides comprehensive information about resilience. Includes a link to Internet resources.

www.kidshealth.org Kids Health.

www.ama-assn.org American Medical Association

www.cdc.gov Centers for Disease Control and Prevention

www.eatright.org American Dietetic Association

www.rwjf.org Robert Wood Johnson Foundation

part 3

Cognitive and Literacy Development

Development in cognition, language, and literacy allows young children to construct meaning and build understanding. Language and literacy encompass every aspect of the early childhood curriculum. Although art, music, social studies, science, and other content areas are not included in this part of the text, do not assume that these areas are not related to cognitive and language development—they are! All areas of the curriculum involve cognitive and language competence. However, in this part we focus primarily on language, literacy, and science mastery.

LANGUAGE AND LITERACY LEARNING

Language and literacy should be active ingredients in all curriculum activities and experiences, rather than separate elements assigned to be taught at specific times. Integrating reading, writing, speaking, and listening into all areas of the curriculum is important for teachers.

To enhance cognitive, language, and literacy development, teachers should value inquiry and thoughtfulness. The following unfinished phrases, spoken by teachers, will serve as springboards to deeper thinking for children and are especially appropriate for literacy and science explorations:

What if . . .?

I wonder why . . .?

Were you surprised that . . .?

Did you notice . . .?

Did you think about . . .?

Did it remind you of . . .?

What do you think happened . . .?

Can you think of another way to approach . . .?

Is there another alternative . . .?

How would you feel if . . .?

These kinds of inquiries encourage students to question, ponder, analyze, grapple, look for relationships, look below the surface, and think (IRA/NCTE, 1996, Standard 7). Children should also learn to explain, add to, and validate their responses and answers.

One approach for encouraging children to think is to have them become the teacher. When children explain an idea to someone else, they synthesize that idea into their own thinking more thoroughly (Vygotsky, 1962). They should be encouraged to observe, question, find out, and then share what they have learned with others.

Thinking—seeking for understanding and meaning—should be the center of all we do with young children. Critical thinking should not be a tacked-on lesson or exercise, but should be part of an integrated approach to the entire curriculum.

Literacy is more than reading and writing. It involves knowledge and skills in speaking, listening, writing, and reading. These skills develop concurrently and are interrelated. The knowledge and skills of literacy learning involve problem solving, gaining information, recalling and remembering, and communicating. The foundation of literacy is oral language development (Adams, 1990; Snow, Burns, & Griffin, 1998; Stahl, 2001). Because the development of oral language skills begins in infancy and relies heavily on experiences, and because families, environments, and experiences differ, children exhibit great differences in their language acquisition and growth. These differences are individual, normal, and acceptable.

chapter 7
Language Development

Oral language is the basis of the other language arts and the foundations for literacy development. A study by Hart and Risley (1995) found that the amount of talk and the richness of language (quantity and quality) young children are exposed to is correlated to the size of the vocabulary and their achievement in reading and math at age 10. It is that accumulation of rich language experiences by parents and teachers that impacts later intellectual development. Children need to hear language and be prompted and encouraged to use it.

Children's early experiences begin with language; they build spoken language by talking and listening. We stimulate young children's linguistic awareness with responsive verbal interactions, books, rhyming activities, storytelling, singing, and games, this early stimulation will influence the child's ability to read and write (Arnqvist, 2000). Children "learn what language *is* through what language *does*" (Novick, 1999/2000, p. 70). Through language, we are able to exchange and understand communicated thoughts and feelings.

Language functions in many ways for the child, and it may well be the most significant feature of the child's early learning. Language is the instrument of thought, personal expression, and social communication. Language empowers children to interact with a friend, to solve a conflict, to express a feeling (Novick, 1999/2000). Children's power to grasp, enter into, and reflect on their experiences depends largely on their facility in using verbal symbols. Thus, language is the device through which raw experiences are translated into meaningful symbols that can be dealt with coherently and used for both thinking and communicating. As experience broadens and deepens, language acquires meaning and further growth and learning becomes possible. Through language, we are able to express our own thoughts and emotions and share vicariously in those of others. Language competence is important in concept formation, school performance, and problem solving. To develop proficiency in organizing, classifying, categorizing, and understanding concepts, the child must have a wide range of appropriate vocabulary. A certain level of attainment in language acquisition is essential for the child to begin formal education successfully.

DEVELOPMENT OF EARLY LANGUAGE

Because the foundation of literacy is oral language development, early childhood teachers must be aware of the development of language, as well as the factors that influence its development. By the time most children reach 5 years of age, they have a large vocabulary, speak in sentences, and are often able to use proper syntax or grammar. Table 7.1 gives a brief overview of normal language development. However, it should be noted that experiences and maturation vary among children, so it is difficult to provide a definite age sequence or timeline for the development of language.

Children make the language of their family and neighborhood their own language as they imitate the accents, usage, structure, and colloquialisms of the people around them. Verbal imitation begins in the first year of life. Babies imitate rhythms and patterns of pitch and stress, and they begin to be aware of differences in word order and intonation. Children learn to pronounce words primarily through imitation. When children produce sounds, responding adults usually repeat actual words that closely

Children's early experiences begin with language. They build spoken language by talking and listening.

approximate these sounds, which provides auditory reinforcement. As children practice these sounds, correct or incorrect speech forms are reinforced through feedback. Careful observation of language progression determines that children's speech is actually a systematic reduction of adult speech, omitting function words that carry little information. For example, an adult might ask: "Do you want some more milk?" The toddler will often respond, "More milk." The fact that children learn the language of their environment reinforces the importance of imitation and modeling.

Vocalizations that normally occur in the first year of life are the forerunners of language. These vocalizations must be reinforced or rewarded by certain kinds of responses from others if they are to persist and develop into language. When adult reinforcement is minimal, language growth is negatively affected; the limited input limits the output of language. Children who grow up in poverty are often exposed to half as many words as their middle-class peers; this vocabulary gap remains five years later (Hart & Risley, 2003).

Motor and mental readiness are prerequisites for children to begin verbalizing or using oral language. Association of word meanings depends on memory and reasoning. Children begin using oral language by

blending real words in a stream of jargon, but the jargon quickly disappears and is replaced by one-word utterances. Initially, a sentence or phrase is combined and understood as one unit, for example, "awgone" instead of "all gone."

Language continues with the combination of words into utterances—two at a time, then three, and so forth. Whether the child is uttering a stream of jargon or a four-word sentence, others extend the child's language by filling in missing prepositions, conjunctions, verbs, and other parts of speech that reflect the way the language is used in the child's environment. Children flourish in their language growth when they are in a language-rich environment that includes exposure to the standard language spoken by their family, new words, and positive feelings toward language acquisition. A rich language environment includes descriptions, explanations, elaboration, and complex vocabulary and structure of language. Creating a "talk-rich environment is an accepting place where teachers encourage young children to talk" and refine their personal speech (Kalmar, 2008, p. 89).

Children progress in language just as they do in other developmental areas—at their own rates and in their own individual ways. Some are very talkative and engage in rather extensive language play or private speech, according to Vygotsky (1962). Others appear reticent in using oral language, and these differences are normal.

Before their second birthday, most children are forming sentences of two or more words. Although the grammar of these sentences is not identical to that of the adult model, we can usually translate the child's sentence by adding function words and inflectional affixes. There is no syntax in children's early utterances, but nouns, verbs, and interjections are the most common classes of words used. These reflect vocal stress, frequency in adult speech, or semantic importance.

Semantics

Children's development in **semantics,** or the meanings of words, is directly related to the experiences and interactions that they have. Children can program sentences that they have never heard before, but they cannot use a word they have not heard or read. Background knowledge (schema) and vocabulary are essential for successful comprehension. Building on the network or schema of the knowledge or meaning of a word is cumulative and the more words that a child knows, the easier it is to add additional words (Neuman & Dwyer, 2009). The more experiences children have, whether in the context of language, real experiences, or vicarious experiences such as books and other media, the more they expand their language meanings and vocabulary. A rich variety of well-planned experiences that involves labeling and drawing meaning helps children to expand their language and become more literate. However, an experience without

TABLE 7.1 • Normal Language Development

By the Age of	Development Activity
1 year	Imitates sounds
	Between 9 and 18 months, begins to use words intentionally to communicate
	Responds to many words that are a part of experience
	Understands simple instructions
2 years	Puts several words together in a phrase or short sentence (telegraphic language)
	Can recognize and name many familiar objects and pictures
	Has a vocabulary of about 30 words
3 years	Uses words to express needs
	Uses pronouns as well as nouns and verbs in speech
	Uses plurals and past tenses
	Identifies the action in a picture
	Displays a rapid increase in vocabulary—may average 50 new words a month (vocabulary ranges between 1,000 and 4,000 words)
	Creates three- to five-word sentences
	Answers questions that relate to realm of experiences
4 years	Follows simple commands
	Verbalizes experiences by putting many sentences together
	Recites songs and poems and retells stories
	Uses words to identify colors, numbers, letters, objects, places, and people
	With rich language exposure, can have 4,000–6,000 words in their vocabularies and their sentences grow longer (5–6 words) and are more complex
	Likes to make up new words and indulges in make-believe
	Likes rhyming
	Participates in discussions and asks and answers questions
5 years	Generally has few articulation problems
	Uses descriptive words—adjectives and adverbs
	Talks freely and often interrupts others
	Sentences are long and more complex, involving six or more words, and vocabularies can range from 5,000 to 8,000 words
	Describes artwork
	Most oral language is grammatically correct
	Knows common opposites
	Enjoys silly language
6 years	Asks the meanings of words and describes the meaning of words
	Takes more risks with language
	Senses language is socially useful
	Interested in new words and continues to add to growing vocabulary
	Makes few grammatical errors
	Talks much like an adult
	Able to tell a connected story
	May still be mastering some sounds or learning to articulate the following sounds: *s, z, r, th, wh*
7 years	Speaks and articulates well
	Follows fairly complex directions
	Relates complex and involved accounts of events
	Demonstrates that fluency is well established
	Has complexity of thought and speech
	Has an active vocabulary of more than 10,000 words and understands more

attached language does not develop understanding. The following example illustrates the importance of labeling children's experiences. Four-year-old Amy was given one-half of a grapefruit. When asked, "What is this?" Amy confidently replied, "It is vitamin C." Amy's association with grapefruit may have included the instruction "Here, eat your vitamin C." Therefore, the experience with grapefruit lacked real meaning because an incorrect label had been attached to it.

It is imperative that adults constantly share, converse, interact, extend, exchange language, and provide labels for words as children have experiences at the zoo, at the grocery store, at the park, at school, at home, in the car, in the classroom, or in any setting. A word with no meaning is an empty sound, not a word. The meanings of a word for a particular individual depend on previous associations with it, and the more limited the experience, the more limited the resulting language and meanings. Young children draw language meaning from the context in which it is used. In other words, children may not initially understand the meaning of a word, but they understand what the person using the word means.

A child's early utterances are often global or generalized, and a sound may represent several different objects or persons. As children continue hearing the verbal contexts of words and have a rich variety of labeled experiences, they increase their knowledge of meanings. For example, *dog* may refer to all animals. As vocabulary and experiences increase, the child is able to narrow the range and to organize, classify, and categorize words and their meanings. The child discovers not only that everything has a name, but also that "this is the name for that." As experiences are made meaningful through word attachments, these words are stored in the brain and used to understand later experiences and communications.

Syntax

Syntax is the set of rules for creating or understanding a sentence. It is the study of the patterns of formation of sentences from words applying grammatical rules. As children first begin to use words, they display no evidence of systematic grammar; yet, by about 4 years of age, most observers agree that the fundamentals have been learned. Since the sentence is the smallest complete unit of thought, sentence structure is a key to the logic of thinking. Symbols and sounds need to be put together correctly to make words that are understandable; then the words must be placed in a particular order to make a sentence that conveys meaning. Children's ability to form complete sentences is also an index of their growth in thinking and cognitive understanding.

Children learn syntax by first **imitating** sentences or phrases or by extracting their meaningful parts. For example, many children say "go" and "park," then advance to "Go park." **Expansion** is another process in the acquisi-

tion of grammar. Adults often expand what the child has said. If the child states, "Me drink water," the adult will often expand the phrase with a complete sentence such as "You want a drink of water." In effect, the adult is saying, "Is this what you mean?" as well as expanding the child's phrase to a complete sentence. However, these two processes, imitation and expansion, alone teach no more than the sum total of sentences that speakers have either modeled for a child to imitate or built up from a child's reductions. The child's linguistic competence extends beyond this. All children are able to understand and construct sentences that they have never heard but that are, nevertheless, well formed. Somehow, then, children process the speech to which they are exposed in order to derive from it underlying rule structures or innate abilities to think and form sentences on their own. Thus, children are intuitively able to master the rules of language and make inductive generalizations that go beyond what they hear. As children grow, they gain increased facility with syntactic structures, leading us to believe that maturation is a variable in syntax growth. The implication for teachers is that we need to speak to even very young children using correct grammar.

Language Acquisition Variables

There are many variables in acquiring language including each child's particular development but also the experiences in a language-rich environment or a language-deficient environment. Another significant variable in language acquisition is whether the child is a bilingual–bicultural learner. Many teachers recognize the need to support a child's native language and give enrichment in the second language, which is English. This philosophy is referred to as *additive* because it recognizes the need to *add* new language skills, but not to replace the child's existing language skills. A child's language reflects who that child is, for one's language is a reflection of one's culture.

Language Acquisition Variables

Maturation

Experiences

Amount and quality of verbal interaction provided

Relationship to and rapport with language model

Motivation for acquiring language

Television and other media habits

Language-rich environment

English Language Learner (ELL)

Teachers need to value and preserve children's native language and culture, build on students' existing language competencies, and also recognize that second-language acquisition follows the same stages as native-language development (NAEYC, 1996b). Instructional strategies in literacy for second-language learners or **English Language Learners (ELLs)** will likely need to be in their primary language (Snow et al., 1998). As teachers encourage oral communication among **English as a Second Language (ESL)** learners, it is recommended that children be taught the differences between their native language or dialect and the standard elements of conversational as well as formal speech such as academic English. Then they can be helped to identify the various contexts in which each style, formal or informal, is appropriate or inappropriate. However, English language learners are more likely to learn English when teachers show acceptance of them and sensitivity to their native language and their culture (Morrow, 2008). It has been suggested that learning activities for ESL students be context rich and that teachers work to build background knowledge and schema by using pictures, real objects, demonstrations, and graphic organizers to clarify (Williams, 2001). It is also recommended that teachers and parents work together to help children strengthen their native language and culture, while gaining the skills needed to participate in the shared language and culture of the school arena (NAEYC, 1996b).

Specific guidelines for oral language development with English Language Learners (ELLs):

1. Relate language to experiences in their lives and help ELLs to make connections.
2. Use clear and repetitive language; speak slowly and enunciate clearly.
3. Utilize gestures, pictures and props to make language meaning clear.
4. Anticipate words that might be challenging and provide explicit definitions (The Albert Shanker Institute, 2009).
5. Invite ELLs to "use new words in their own sentences" (Helman & Burns, 2008, p. 17).
6. Prompt, cue, build on, and question to elaborate and expand on what the ELL has said. For example, if the child says, "I have a cat," ask the child questions such as "How do you care for your cat?" Or "What does your cat eat?" etc.
7. Provide multiple methods to develop schema or background knowledge for concepts. For example, if children are learning about apples, provide a variety of experiences including pictures, a visit to an apple orchard or grocery store to focus on kinds of apples, food activities, stories, poems, songs, and tasting activities.

8. Give many opportunities for ELLs to interact and converse in natural situations such as small group activity and play. In play they initiate their own conversation.

General Guidelines for Oral Language Development

The following are general suggestions for encouraging language development:

1. **Model good listening and recognize that the teacher is the key to effective instruction in language development.** Modeling good listening behaviors such as repeating back what the child has said, using direct eye contact, and nodding your head at appropriate times sends the message that you are actively listening (Machado, 2010). Use the reading/writing workshop time as well as the free-play period to provide a prime time for teachers to interact with children on a one-to-one basis or in small groups to teach listening and literacy concepts and skills. One-on-one interactions support oral language development and provide foundation for later literacy learning (IRA & NAEYC, 1998). As children play with manipulative toys, work with blocks, enjoy books, play in the dramatic play area, use sensory materials, or use any of the areas provided during free play, teachers should encourage them to talk and listen to one another. Also, teachers should talk with, listen to, and read to children of all ages. One kindergarten teacher always puts paper and marking pens in the dramatic area, and children learn to label the things there. For example, during a unit on the farm, the dramatic area had a number of things, including a barn and rubber animals. Some of the child-made signs read: "One hors fur seele," "The tractr," and "R Farm." Early experiences with writing build confidence in children's belief that they can write. Often teachers use free-play time as a break period for themselves; they do not realize the valuable opportunity for individual and small-group speaking, listening, and reading so beautifully provided in free play. Discussions with children can address the project with which they are involved, or they can be unrelated and address their home, hobbies, or other interests.
2. **Provide many opportunities for talking, and listen actively.** Provide a model for listening. Do not talk too much—the voice that goes on and on is often tuned out. If you do not listen to children, how can you expect children to listen to others? Let the children know that you are listening to them by being attentive and focusing your eyes on them. Find time to listen to each child every day.

3. **Inquire of children often, and provide for stimulating inquiry. (Inquiry** refers here to the use of questions.) Two practices that stifle inquiry are emphasis on exact answers and emphasis on competition. Teachers should ask questions that require thoughtful responses; they should also encourage and respect the questions that children ask. "The ability to break patterns and pose new questions is as important as the ability to answer questions other people set for you" (Kohl, 2009, p. 273). Unusual questions and answers lead to deeper thinking; deeper thinking requires greater communicative ability; and greater communicative ability means language growth. Ask thought-provoking questions often.

4. **Acknowledge, accept, and celebrate individual language diversity in children** (NAEYC, 1996b). However, teachers must be diagnosticians. Thus, they must determine language deficiencies and then select the procedures that they will use in trying to overcome these deficiencies. They evaluate where the children are in their language development and how they can be stimulated and challenged to progress further. Teachers also determine individual needs for language instruction.

5. **Remember factors influencing the development of language, and therefore strive to be high-quality models—speaking distinctly, calmly, pleasantly, with well-chosen words, and using correct grammar.** Teachers should also give and encourage language feedback and provide new experiences. Assess and consider the complexities of learning language so you can provide developmentally appropriate activities and experiences involving language and literacy.

6. **Use the sentence as the basic unit of speech and teach children to speak likewise, in complete thoughts or sentences.** When we speak in sentences, we express complete and meaningful thoughts. This instruction is also excellent for emergent reading, because books are written in complete sentence form; point out the structure of text.

7. **Establish a comfortable, relaxed atmosphere that stimulates children to talk freely with others and focus on the expression of their ideas.** Engage children in conversations about their interests and experiences.

8. **Use strategies and provide experiences that develop phonemic awareness (that is, songs, fingerplays, games, poems, and stories with phonemic patterns such as rhyme and alliteration). Phonemic awareness** is the attentiveness in children that spoken language consists of a sequence of phonemes or the small units of speech that make a difference in our communica-

When children enjoy playing and visiting together, social language skills are reinforced.

tion and that exist independently of meaning (Cunningham, 2009; Wasik, 2001a; Yopp, 1995; Yopp & Yopp, 2000).

9. **Recognize that grammatical errors, particularly verb and pronoun problems, are typical in the early childhood years.** Rather than putting too much emphasis on exactness of speech, repeat the sentence to the child, using correct grammar so the child hears the proper form. Thus, the child will not feel a sense of failure, but will nevertheless be made aware of correct usage.

10. **Use specific words that will help to expand the children's vocabularies as well as teach the meanings of words.** Too often we speak in general terms such as "Put the book over there," as opposed to "Put the blue book on the middle bookshelf." Teach word meanings explicitly by giving examples of the word in a sentence and saying, "That word means. . . . "

11. **Verbalize what children are doing.** Paint word pictures for them about whatever activity they are involved in, for example, "I see Amy climbing very high on the jungle gym."

12. **Help children to draw meaning from listening, speaking, reading, and writing experiences with language.** For example, when someone speaks, it may be necessary to rephrase or ask, "Is this what you mean?" When a visitor comes or when the class goes on a field trip, it may be helpful to rephrase some of the conversation for the children to draw meaning from and understand what is communicated. Rephrasing may also be necessary as selections of children's literature are read and shared. Sometimes it is only necessary to define the meaning of one word for the context and ideas to be understood. Our goal in language and literacy development is to encourage children not only to speak, listen, read, and write, but also

to do so with meaning and with understanding of what has been spoken, heard, written, or read.

13. **Create a print-rich environment** (IRA & NAEYC, 1998). The classroom environment should include print in areas besides the book or story area. Research indicates that opportunities to engage with print during the early years may prevent reading difficulties (Snow et al., 1998). Even before children read, they should see words and print in their environment—word lists, word walls, phrases, charts, signs, labels, calendars, recipes, and so on. Label and read the items seen and used in the classroom. For example, during science or food activities, ingredient labels can be read to the children. When children are away from the classroom, labels on signs, doorways, billboards, and other areas can be read and pointed out. Take advantage of opportunities for using notes, charts, or written instructions, even when the children themselves cannot read. For example, the recipe should be available during a cooking experience so that the teacher can read the instructions and the children understand that the recipe communicates what to do. On a field trip, the children can follow a map of instructions that tells them how to get to their destination, as well as what to look for when they get there. As children begin reading, the written word should permeate the classroom, and written instructions for activities should be given to them to follow.

14. **Involve families with their children developing oral language.** Give them support, training, and encouragement in developing the skills and competencies to provide a literate environment for their children and to participate in many language-building activities and experiences with them.

Neuman and Roskos (2005, p. 26) suggest the features of effective content- and language-rich instruction include:

- Time, materials, and resources that actively build language and conceptual knowledge
- A supportive learning environment in which children have access to a wide variety of reading and writing resources
- Different group sizes (large, small, individual) and different levels of guidance to meet the needs of individual children
- Opportunities for sustained and in-depth learning, including play
- A masterful orchestration of activity that supports learning and social–emotional development

LISTENING AND SPEAKING

This chapter will focus on listening and speaking because these are two primary aspects of developing oral language. In Chapter 8, the focus will be on reading and writing. The four concepts are interrelated in the development of language and literacy, but for the purposes of this text we have chosen to separate them into two chapters.

Listening

"We hear with our ears, but we listen with our minds" (Garman, Garman, & Brown, 2009, p. 5) and "with our hearts" (Jalongo, 1995, p. 18). Listening is a skill that needs to be taught deliberately in the early childhood years. Modeling active listening by teachers promotes active listening in students. Listening is active, not passive (Jalongo, 1995). It is a serious mistake to ignore the need for instruction in listening (Roskos, Tabors, & Lenhart, 2009). Children do not necessarily need to do *more* listening; they need to learn to listen *better.*

Listening skills include **auditory perception,** the ability to perceive and understand what is heard; **auditory discrimination,** the ability to make fine discriminations among sounds; **auditory memory,** the ability to remember the sequence of sounds within words and sentences; **auditory association,** the ability to associate sounds or words with experiences, objects, ideas, or feelings; and **rhyming skills,** the ability to recognize and reproduce words that rhyme.

Simply because an experience has allowed a child to become familiar with an idea, we must not assume that the correct information has been assimilated. In the quest for meaning, a child often misunderstands; thus, an adult or peer needs to listen constantly to determine the functioning level of discernment. In the following examples, it is evident that communication from the child is also an important aspect in the learning process.

A child who had been encouraged to keep her shoes on commented to her teacher at the end of the day: "I wore my shoes all day today, but sometimes I wore my bare feet!"

During an excursion, various drums were shown to the children. It was explained that the kettledrum was so named because of its resemblance to a large pot or kettle that might be used on the stove for cooking. Later, as the concepts were being reviewed and reinforced, the children were shown a picture and asked the name of the kettledrum. Peter confidently replied, "Oh, that's a stove drum!"

Language, reinforcement, and review are constantly needed to correct, strengthen, and expand a child's understandings. As adults are receptive to the child's communications, they must be willing to listen (not just hear) and observe (not just see). Teaching entails much more than disseminating information. It involves listening and observing not only for the obvious, but also for the subtle ways in which the child makes perceptions and understandings known. Lastly, a teacher provides an exemplary role model for good listening by being a good listener.

Oral Language/Speaking

Children need oral language models that scaffold and support them; they need many opportunities to speak and be listened to or heard. Oral language encompasses the ability to listen, speak, and communicate effectively. Children learn to speak by being immersed in a verbal-rich environment, learning from people who love to communicate, talk, and use language. Oral language is the basis on which strong literacy is built (Palmer & Bayley, 2005). Later achievement in literacy is influenced by rich oral language experiences during early childhood (IRA, 2005; Strickland, 2004). Oral language builds background knowledge, and background knowledge greatly influences comprehension and vocabulary acquisition. Specifically, oral language ability of children impacts achievement in fluency and comprehension (Nation & Snowling, 2004). There is also a connection between oral language and reading and writing; as we support children in oral language development we are helping them learn to read and write (Roskos et al., 2003, Roskos et al., 2009). "Young children need writing to help them learn about reading, they need reading to help them learn about writing; and they need oral language to help them learn about both" (Roskos et al., 2003, p. 54).

Besides a language-rich environment, it is also suggested during the early childhood years that children have a high-quality oral language curricula, including:

1. Teachers should support children in oral language learning through integrated language learning. Knowledge-building units incorporating various disciplines strengthen language concepts (Neuman, Roskos, Wright, & Lenhart, 2007).

2. Explicit instruction, intentional teaching, or direct instruction in oral language is necessary in vocabulary, phonological awareness, and other areas of language development and should be included throughout the school day (The Albert Shanker Institute, 2009).

3. Self-guided play provides opportunities for small-group communication, teacher–child language exchange, discussions, and many opportunities to practice and use language. Activities that invite oral language include sensory play, blocks, dramatic play, cooking, and photo albums and scrapbooks (Kalmar, 2008).

4. Teaching strategies that support oral language development are also important. Mills (2009) proposed the following oral language (speaking and listening) strategies: making inferences, visualizing, generating and answering questions, and retelling and summarizing.

Activities for Listening and Speaking

The following are some suggested activities for listening and speaking, with a focus on helping children to acquire improved and continuing language growth. Remember, good listening skills influence reading abilities, and good speaking skills influence writing abilities.

1. Plan question periods in which questions are given and answers brainstormed and shared. The questions might be thought-provoking and realistic questions, or they might be thought-provoking nonsense questions. For example:

    What new machine might you invent?

    What would you do if you could only walk backward?

    What would you do to red to make it more beautiful?

    What would you do if you woke up one morning to a backyard full of elephants?

    What would be your one wish?

When a teacher and child read a book together, vocabulary and comprehension skills are enhanced.

What would you purchase if you could purchase anything in the whole world?

If you could make a contribution to the world, what would it be?

What would you like instead of school?

What would you give feathers to make them softer?

What is your greatest hope?

What changes would you like to make in yourself?

What if everyone had a long neck like a giraffe?

Once the children catch on to this type of questioning, they will enjoy making up questions. Perhaps this activity could be done in cooperative learning groups, using Think-Pair-Share as a strategy (see Chapter 5). Remember that all questions and answers are correct and acceptable.

2. Simple question-answer games can be played, in which the children sit in a circle while questions are asked. Then a ball or beanbag is thrown to a child, who answers the question in a complete sentence. This same child asks another question in complete-sentence form, and the beanbag or ball is tossed to another child for answering.

3. A sack of objects can be used for discussion and language development. The children can learn about and discuss the objects; then directions will be given, in complete sentences, about what will be done with the objects. The teacher or a child might say, "Put the green block on top of Jenny's head," or "Put the gerbil food underneath Stephanie's chair," or "Put the box on the floor and hop over it three times." This game not only teaches new words or labels, but also develops prepositional understandings.

4. Divide the children into smaller groups and give a picture to each group for discussion. The pictures could be snapshots that the children brought from home, which would encourage children to talk as their pictures are shown to the group.

5. Show-and-tell, or sharing time, is enjoyable if it is not presented too often. In one preschool class, the children are assigned a particular day during one week when they can bring something from home and tell about it. Each day during the set-aside time, five chairs are placed in front of the class, and five proud children bring their sacks holding the secret of the item that they are anxious to tell the class about. In another class, the teacher uses a large duffle bag and calls it the "mystery bag." Each day, one child brings something to show or tell about and places it in the mystery bag. The class can guess what is in the bag; if they have trouble guessing correctly, the child who brought the object can give clues. The child who guesses what is in the mystery bag is allowed to take the bag home that day if he or she has not had a turn for a while.

6. Rhyming couplets can be shared with children; the last word of the couplet, which rhymes with the word at the end of the first line, can be left off so that the children can guess what the word is. This activity can also be used with poems that rhyme, with the second word in a rhyming sequence left out for the children to guess. Younger children can listen to the couplet and tell the two words that rhyme. Children could work in cooperative learning groups on these activities.

7. Give three or four words in sequence, all but one of them beginning with the same consonant sound, and then ask the children to listen for the one that is not the same (for example, *tomato, trunk, egg, tumble*).

8. After a story with a definite sequence of events, have the children recall the events in the order in which they occurred. They could also prepare a reading flowchart by drawing pictures of the story in the order in which events occurred, and then the teacher could write a sentence or phrase for each picture.

9. Make use of sequence stories in workbooks or cartoons. The various parts of the story can be glued to wooden blocks, plywood, or poster paper to make sequence puzzles. The children must find the correct sequence and then tell the story. Older children might wish to write a sentence or phrase under each picture.

10. Make surprise boxes by wrapping them up and having the children guess what might be inside. Then unwrap them and have the children describe the object or objects and how they are used.

11. Have the children draw pictures representing specific experiences and then discuss the pictures. Instead of drawing the pictures, they can be asked to think of the experience and then relate it to the group. For example, they might be asked to share the most embarrassing experience, the saddest experience, the funniest experience, the most frightening experience, or the most exciting experience that they have ever had. An alternative would be to have children bring snapshots from home from experiences that they have had and describe them orally. Also, the experiences could be written down as the child tells them.

12. As stories, poems, or nursery rhymes are read or told, words or phrases can be left out, and the children can guess what the missing words might be.

13. A group of rhyming words can be shared (for younger children, three words are enough), including one word that does not rhyme. The children listen and then tell which word does not rhyme.

14. Give rhyming riddles for the children to guess. Examples: "I rhyme with *damp*. I sit on a table. What am I?" "I rhyme with *chose*, and I am on your face. What am I?"
15. Have each child pick an object out of a sack and describe the object.
16. Children form inside–outside cooperative learning circles and face their partners. The teacher gives a word and the outside-circle person thinks of a synonym for it for his or her partner; then the inside-circle person gives a word that rhymes with it. The activity can progress in this way with the teacher giving new words to explore. Other ideas: The children could give a word that begins or ends with the same sound and use the word in a sentence, or give a word that is an antonym. The teacher adapts the way that the word is approached to the developmental needs of the children.

Provide opportunities for students to recount experiences, present stories, recite selections, and give presentations. Encourage parents and students to share their cultural heritage and traditions with classes. Be alert throughout the day of the opportunities for developing speaking and listening. Also remember that children's attempts to express themselves and share their ideas are more important than perfect language usage. Do not drill on perfect grammar or articulation. Let children learn to enjoy listening and speaking.

Other Activities to Support Language Development

Several other areas of language/literacy development are vital to early childhood education and therefore need specific discussion. Stories, poetry, and finger-plays are delightful activities for scaffolding language growth in children. These activities all involve listening, speaking, reading, or writing. It is hoped that toward the end of the early childhood years, children will be given many opportunities and much stimulus for writing their own stories and poems.

STORIES/STORYTELLING.   Stories open minds to understanding, touch hearts, and capture imaginations. Stories help children to make sense and meaning of the things that they are taught. During early childhood, teachers should be aware that children will deepen their understanding as stories are repeated (Morrow, 2008; Schickedanz, 2008). When ideas and concepts are taught with stories, they are remembered. Events, facts, and bits of information in and of themselves are not meaningful and not remembered, but in the context of the story they become understood, intelligible, and retained. People express themselves through sharing the stories of their lives. Stories have a powerful effect

because they not only impart ideas, concepts, and information; they also engage emotions. Herbert Kohl (2009, p. 12) writes of "empowering stories" that encourage hope, creativity, imagination, and invite students to create their own stories. He states, "I've never had any problem trading formal learning for storytelling in my classes, and I believe the students have been richer for it. After all, seeding hope is at the center of the art and craft of teaching" (2009, p. 12).

Reading aloud satisfies emotional needs as the listeners enjoy physical closeness with the reader, and it facilitates development of social skills through pictures, content, and learning appropriate behavior during the reading experiences (Conlon, 1992, p. 15). Through stories we exchange experiences and feelings. Stories clarify what is being taught and enable children to make sense and meaning of what the teacher is trying to teach. Storytellers weave a story in their own words, create images, and stir emotions, but the listeners or readers bring their own experiences and imaginations into play to make meaning.

Values of Stories for Young Children

Stories assist children in the following ways:

1. Organizing their thoughts and expressing emotions (Booth & Barton, 2000).
2. Capturing the attention of children and adults and give enjoyment and relaxation.
3. Providing information, teaching new words and concepts, and encouraging an appreciation for literature (Birchmayer, Kennedy, & Stonehouse, 2008).
4. Teaching a concept or giving information that otherwise might be difficult to learn or remember.
5. Building social skills and values; children learn from the "friends" that they identify with in stories.
6. Offering opportunities for children to enjoy the world of pretend.
7. Encouraging appreciation of beauty.
8. Introducing young children to various cultures (Birchmayer, Kennedy, & Stonehouse, 2008).
9. Helping children learn to follow a sequence of events. Teachers should try telling a story and then retelling it using the "What happens next?" approach.
10. Providing and modeling appropriate patterns of speech and fostering language and literacy skills, including vocabulary and comprehension learning.

Children learn early to value stories, and they learn that the printed word is the key that opens the door to the world. Once children see storytelling modeled, they can become the storyteller; this fosters sharing their own culture and helps to build a sense of community and inclusion in the classroom. Often when children are restless or when the teacher is in need of an immediate activity, a well-told story is the best solution. For this reason, teachers of young children should know many stories and use a variety of storytelling techniques, such as felt boards, puppets, origami, photographs, music, chalk talks, and flip charts (Morrow, 2002). What a teacher needs most to tell a story effectively to children is a love of stories and enthusiasm for telling them.

Guidelines for Selecting Stories.   Remember the various ages and development of the children when selecting stories (Birchmayer, Kennedy, & Stonehouse, 2008). The following guidelines include additional criteria for selecting books and stories. Just because a story has been published does not meant that it is appropriate for the children.

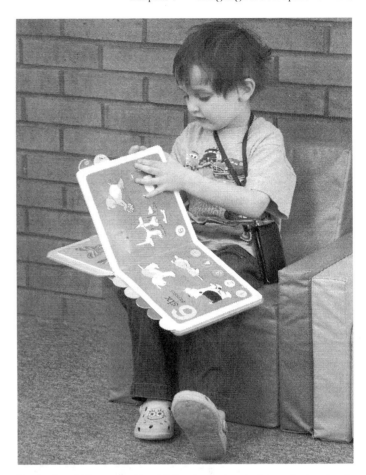

Books should be geared to children's age levels, interests, levels of understanding, and attention spans.

1. For *3- and 4-year-olds,* avoid stories with a strong fear element. For this reason, some of the fairy tales should be avoided until children can better separate fact from fantasy. The stories should be short; if a story is told from a book, there should be few printed words in relation to the number of pictures. Choose stories with a simple, linear plot, as well as stories with repetition; children enjoy chanting or saying the repetition after they have heard it several times. Stories should be realistic. Children prefer stories about animals, children, and other people.

   For *5- and 6-year-olds,* stories can be more complicated, and they can distinguish fact from fantasy. These children like adventure and nonsense stories and those with surprise endings.

   The *7- and 8-year-olds* like legends, folk literature, animal stories, fiction, science stories, stories that relate to their hobbies and other interests, and adventure stories. They enjoy longer stories and can be read to without having to see pictures; however, they still prefer hearing a story more than reading one themselves.

2. Select books and stories geared to the children's age levels, interests, levels of understanding, and attention span.

3. For younger children, a book or story that is being read should include illustrations that are colorful, attractive, clear, and appropriate. (Remember that you can tell a story with no visual aids or pictures and still be effective; however, for ELLs the pictures support the development of meaning.)

4. Select a comprehensive genre of books and stories to tell and have available for the children. Have samples of many categories, including those of various cultures, genders, and ethnic origins.

5. The books and stories that children especially enjoy will be repeated and retold often (Wolter, 1992). However, books that are selected for use in individual play should be rotated so that not too many are available at one time. Public libraries loan books to classrooms for this purpose.

6. The theme or main point of selected books should have value and importance. Books and stories used should have memory value; in other words, the children will remember good stories and books.

7. The characters in stories and books should be strong, having worthy character traits. Avoid stories that stereotype people and cultures.

8. Plots should be fresh and well paced.

9. Stories should be short and simple.

Guidelines for Preparing Stories.   Once the story is selected, it must be prepared and presented. Unfortunately, many teachers do not adequately prepare stories before reading or telling them. If stories are read, we suggest preparing ahead of time so that you are acquainted with the story and its message.

Preparing to Tell a Story

1. Careful preparation is needed to create a vivid experience for children (Wolter, 1992). Allow adequate time before presentation to learn the story thoroughly.
2. Outline in your mind the sequence of the story events; recall the characters, their names, and where they fit into the sequence of events.
3. Practice telling the story, but do not try to memorize the author's exact words.
4. If visual aids will accompany the story, practice using them.
5. Practice appropriate gestures.
6. Make a note of words or references that the children might not understand so that you can give explanations before the story begins; then the story can continue without interruptions.

Methods of Presenting Stories.   Remember, a story can be best told using your own body and facial expressions as the visual aids.

1. *Flip chart.* Illustrations or pictures representing the story are put on heavy paper and attached with large rings. Words for each page are printed on the back of the following page so that they are easily read, and then the page is flipped around. The children can view the illustrations while the teacher retains eye-to-eye contact during the presentation.
2. *Single object or picture.* A doll, animal figure, or puppet for single focus.
3. *Flannel-board story.* Use medium-weight Pellon® colored with marking pens or crayons. Often the figures can be traced from picture books or coloring books. A small piece of masking tape with a number on the back of each figure helps to order the sequence of each figure in the story.
4. *Record or record book*
5. *Tape-recorded story.* Presented with or without pictures.
6. *Demonstration*
7. *Dramatization.* During or following the presentation.
8. *Film, filmstrip, slides*
9. *Movie-box story.* Put story illustrations on a long piece of butcher paper, and then roll the paper on rollers or dowels. Show each illustration as it is unrolled and viewed in a box with a hole cut in it, resembling a television screen.
10. *Chalk-talk story.* Use simple chalkboard illustrations to accompany a story.

11. *Child involvement.* Give each child a picture or object to hold during a particular part of the story, or give each child a part in the story.
12. *Overhead transparencies*

Guidelines for Presenting Stories.   Stories can be read to children, but they are much more effective and meaningful when told. Oral storytelling is rich tradition for many cultures and families. It is an interactive experience involving the story itself, the storyteller, and the audience. Professional storytellers assure children they will create the story, but the children will produce their own pictures in their minds.

Suggested Guidelines for Presenting Stories

1. Make sure that all the children are comfortable and are able to see the storyteller; if visual aids are used, all children should be able to see them.
2. Generally, the smaller the group listening to the stories, the more effective the experience (Miller, 1990). Teachers can effectively group children by their developmental abilities, including their listening ability and their experience level (Wolter, 1992).
3. Use eye-to-eye contact in telling stories.
4. Keep a natural voice that is conversational and clear and that reaches all the children. Change the pitch and tempo of your voice to add interest.
5. Use gestures that are spontaneous and natural; use appropriate facial expressions. "Relax and allow your face to mirror your words and inner feelings" (Sherman, 1979, p. 26).
6. Relax and enjoy the story yourself. Keep it full of life, as well as simple and direct. Live the characters—feel their joys and sorrows, their laughter and struggles.
7. Draw on your own experience to add richness and meaning to the story.
8. Do not hesitate to ask an occasional question or give an explanation, but do not lose the flow and feeling of the story.
9. Younger children especially enjoy having their names in stories so that they become the characters in the story.

Guidelines for Evaluating Stories.   Once the story has been told, the teacher should evaluate whether the desired goals and objectives were reached.

1. Did I tell the story instead of reading it?
2. Did the story maintain high interest throughout?
3. Did I clearly make the point intended?
4. Was eye-to-eye contact maintained?
5. Were my facial expressions suitable to the actions of the story?

6. Was my voice natural, enthusiastic, and appropriate in tone and pitch?

7. Were my gestures natural and spontaneous?

8. Were visual aids appropriate and easy to use?

9. Did the children listen to and enjoy the story?

Teachers should constantly acquaint themselves with the best in children's literature, both old and new. It is also suggested that each early childhood teacher have an anthology of children's literature available. Good literature can be the means of integrating many activities and planning projects around a single book. As an example, see Figure 7.1 for a web constructed around the story *The Jolly Postman or Other People's Letters* (Ahlberg & Ahlberg, 1986).

Not only do teachers tell and share stories, but young children can also become storytellers. When children develop and present stories to others the "students' literacy is lived through their own performance" (Dillingham, 2005, p. 75). Some of the steps Dillingham suggests for the performance of stories include creating a visual portrait of the story as part of the preparation, followed by telling and retelling the stories in pairs or with partners. Students then draft their stories (younger children can dictate to an adult or on tape), and finally students rehearse and then perform their stories for classmates, other classes, parents, or community members.

POETRY. "Poetry paints verbal pictures for children, tells them stories, and expresses emotions that they are feeling" (Diffily & Morrison, 1996, p. 49). Poetry stirs imagination and creative thinking. Through poetry, children become more keenly aware of sensory impressions. They find enjoyment and satisfaction in these impressions as they are expressed through the imagery of poetry. Children also delight in the sound and rhythm of language as it is expressed. Poetry sings; it is rich, warm, and definite.

Poetry allows children to experience various emotions, feelings, and moods; become familiar with creative language; expand concept and language development; model desirable behaviors; and increase attention spans. Young children enjoy writing their own impressions in the form of poetry, especially when they learn that poetry does not require lines that rhyme.

FIGURE 7.1 **Project Web on a Storybook**

Many types of poems are appropriate for children in the early childhood years. Children throughout time have loved Mother Goose and other nursery rhymes, perhaps because of the variety of subject matter, the surprise quality, the rhyme, the musical movement, the repetition, and the short, easy-to-remember actions. Jump rope rhymes, also a form of poetry, are "part of an oral tradition that links communication and play ... and expose(s) children to the arresting qualities of rhyme, rhythm, and humor" (Buchoff, 1995, p. 149). As children get older, they generally tend to show less interest in poetry. However, their enjoyment increases with the inclusion of humor, rhythm, and rhyme (Cullinan, Galda, & Sipe, 2010). Once children's enthusiasm for poetry is rekindled through rhymes and chants, gradually add other types of poetry: ballads, free-form verse, haiku, limericks, and narrative poems (Buchoff, 1995). Since they are easily memorized, after just a few readings children will be saying them with you, and they should be encouraged to do so. Young children also enjoy nonsense verse or poetry, ballad and story poems, poems based on fact, and those that are make believe or fanciful. There are poems about nearly everything experienced in our world. If a poem cannot be found relating to a subject or concept, one can surely be written!

Poetry should not be read or presented in a singsong pattern, but with directness and sincerity. It should appeal to the emotions and flow with the right meter or rhythm. Most poems need not be explained, but read and enjoyed for the sake of the poem and its appeal to the individual child. Many of the suggestions presented in this chapter regarding stories are also appropriate for poetry. Poetry can be presented with pictures (or a single picture), puppets, objects, recordings, flannelboard illustrations, PowerPoint presentations or slides, overhead transparencies, or other visual aids.

In addition, many poems lend themselves to dramatization; even short nursery rhymes can be dramatized and put into action. For groups of children who are beginning to read, their favorite poems can be put on charts so that they can follow along as the poem is read. Children enjoy illustrating the poems that they hear.

Poems lend themselves to choral readings. The older the children, the more sophisticated the choral readings can be. Even young children can repeat their favorite poems and rhymes in choral speaking or reading. To begin choral speaking or reading, you will want to say the poem in unison first. Younger children can be divided into separate or solo parts from the group. For older children, there are other alternatives; for example, the children could be divided by voice pitch into groups of high, medium, and low voices or soft, medium, and heavy voices. When dividing a poem into choral speaking parts by voice pitch, have the high or soft voices take the delicate or lighter lines. Usually, these are the lines that ask questions. The low voices should take the lines that suggest mystery, gloom, or solemnity or that answer questions. The medium voices

carry the narrative, give explanations, or introduce characters. When teaching choral speaking, be careful not to drill, and remember that it should be enjoyable and therapeutic. Choral speaking also improves speaking ability by helping children to create a crisp, vigorous speech.

FINGERPLAYS. Fingerplays are short poems accompanied with finger motions; thus they are also a type of dramatization. They are useful attention getters and rest exercises. When children learn action songs and fingerplays, they learn about number, shape, color, size, order and sequence, and names of body parts; they also learn muscle control and manual dexterity, rhythm of music and speech, new words, to follow directions, to be attentive, listening skills, predictability, and auditory discrimination (Diffily & Morrison, 1996). Fingerplays and chants are especially suited for younger children, and very often they are repeated in unison as a type of choral speaking. Whenever you prefer, change dramatizations, finger motions, or words to fit the developmental level, desired objectives, and enjoyment of the children. To extend the opportunities for literacy development, have the children illustrate each part of the fingerplay and then put them together as a book to be read.

Fingerplay Examples

Five Little Monkeys

Five little monkeys jumping on the bed.
One fell off and broke his head!
Mama called the doctor, and the doctor said,
"No more monkeys jumping on the bed."

(Continue with four little monkeys, three little monkeys, etc., until:)

No little monkeys jumping on the bed.
They all fell off and broke their heads!

Frogs

Five little frogs standing in a row.
(Hold up five fingers.)
This little frog stubbed his toe;
(Point to each finger in turn.)
This little frog cried, "Oh, no!"
This little frog laughed and was glad;
This little frog cried and was sad;
This little frog did what he should—
He ran for the doctor as fast as he could.

My Senses

I have two eyes to see with,
I have two feet to run.
I have two hands to feel with,
And a nose, I have but one.
I have two ears to hear with,
And a tongue to say good-day,
And two red cheeks for you to kiss.
So I will run away!

Summary

Young children should sense that "language is a tool for exploring, discovering, discussing, and learning across the curriculum" (Reutzel, 1997). We advocate an environment rich in opportunities for speaking and listening to provide the foundation for future literacy development, specifically reading and writing. Adults need to model appropriate spoken expressions and also how to listen attentively to others.

The primary factors influencing the development of language appear to be (1) the child's innate ability to learn language, (2) the quality of the model or the early stimulation and variety provided by the model, and (3) the ability of caregivers to expand or extend the child's language. Oral language can be encouraged in early childhood by conversing, discussing, clarifying, reporting, explaining, reacting, dramatizing, storytelling, fingerplays, poems, and rhymes.

Student Learning Activities

1. As a teacher of young children, how can you be influential in helping young children to expand, refine, and enhance their language development? How can you support ELLs in developing language skills?
2. Plan, implement, and evaluate at least two activities to encourage listening skills in young children and two activities to encourage speaking skills in young children.
3. Based on the criteria given in this chapter for selecting appropriate stories, begin a story file with at least five excellent, culturally diverse stories for children 3 to 8 years of age. Make a card for each story. On the card, include the title of the story, author, illustrator, publisher, copyright date, age level for which the story is appropriate, and a brief summary of the story.
4. Prepare two stories using two different methods of presentation suggested in this chapter. For example, prepare a flannel-board story and a flip-chart story.
5. Begin a collection of appropriate culturally diverse pictures. The pictures can be used to prompt oral language with storytelling or discussion, or to accompany poems. Mount the pictures neatly and make them durable. If using with a poem, attach or write the poem on the back.
6. Memorize at least three fingerplays and teach them to children. Use cooperative learning strategies to teach at least one.

Suggested Resources

Cecil, N. L. (2004). *Activities for a comprehensive approach to literacy.* Scottsdale, AZ: Holcomb Hathaway.
A practical source for both language and literacy activities with an entire chapter on oral language activities.
Fry, E. B., & Kress, J. E. (2006). *The reading teacher's book of lists* (5th ed.). San Francisco, CA: Jossey-Bass.
A comprehensive resource for language and literacy development.
Morrow, L. M. (2008). *Literacy development in the early years: Helping children read and write* (6th ed.). Boston: Allyn & Bacon.
A textbook resource that includes theory and practice for developing language and literacy.
Children's Book Cited
Ahlberg, J., & Ahlberg, A. (1986). *The jolly postman or other people's letters.* Boston: Little, Brown.

Online Resources

www.ies.ed.gov/ncee/wwc What Works Clearinghouse: This site provides information on instructional techniques and curricula.

www.nieer.org/standards The National Institute for Early Education Research State Standards (NIEER) database lists language and literacy content standards by state.

www.naeyc.org The National Association for the Education of Young Children (NAEYC) website provides journal, magazine, and position statements related to early childhood education.

www.reading.org The International Reading Association (IRA) site provides journals, position statements, and links to related language and literacy materials.

www.highscope.org/EducationalPrograms/ReadingInstitute/readinginstitute.htm This website offers plentiful information on reading, listening, and speaking in addition to research reports from High/Scope.

www.teach-nology.com/teachers/early_education/subject_matter/language_arts This is a great site for many language arts activities and links to other sites.

www.nncc.org/Curriculum/fingerplay.html Resources for fingerplay and action verses for young children to promote language growth are available from this site.

chapter 8
Literacy Development

DEVELOPMENT OF LITERACY

Literacy, or learning to read, write, and think, is critical to the child's success both in school and in life. All children have a right to quality reading instruction (International Reading Association [IRA], 2000; International Reading Association [IRA] & National Association for the Education of Young Children [NAEYC], 1998). In literacy development, as in other areas, the teacher's challenge is to match best practices to the ways that children think, know, and understand.

> "Above all, reading means using your mind: asking questions, challenging the status quo, absorbing information with a critical eye." (Fountas & Pinnell, 2006, p. 3)

Literacy development means growth in communications skills, including initial speaking and listening and then writing and reading. Literacy is active; it is metacognitive problem solving or "in-the-head processes that enable the reader to pick up all kinds of information from the text and construct the author's intended meaning" (Fountas & Pinnell, 2006, p. 4). Early childhood teachers help children to develop competence in literacy, including knowledge about sounds, letters, words, and sentences. Development of these competencies begins early, even before the child enters school; they are shaped by instruction and do not emerge spontaneously (Bodrova, Leong, & Paynter, 1999). Literacy learning can be interwoven into the curriculum, with adults taking the role of modeling, optimizing children's play, and enriching the environment with literacy materials and experiences (Nel, 2000). Literacy activities are best provided in the context of meaningful, authentic activities (Novick, 1999/2000).

The International Reading Association (IRA) and the National Association for the Education of Young Children (NAEYC) agree that experiences during early childhood affect the development of literacy. Those who teach young children need to support the literacy development of children in their care. A joint statement from the two organizations is included in *Learning to Read and Write: Developmentally Appropriate Practices for Young Children* (1998). Following are summarized points from this joint statement:

1. Literacy learning begins in early infancy.
2. Parents have a responsibility to provide a literacy-rich environment at home to support children in acquiring literacy skills. Parents need to be actively involved in their children's literacy learning at school.
3. School staff must be aware that children come to school with prior knowledge and background experiences with reading and writing and that this knowledge varies from one child to another. Reading and writing should build on their existing knowledge.
4. Literacy education requires a supportive environment that builds positive feelings about literacy learning.

5. A rich literacy environment requires accessible materials and varied experiences.
6. All adults serve as models for literacy behavior by demonstrating strategies to be learned and interest in books and print.
7. During literacy experiences, children should have positive interactions within a social context, which motivates them to learn from one another.
8. Early reading and writing experiences should be meaningful and concrete and actively engage children in problem-solving experiences and explicit direct instruction of skills.
9. A literacy development program should focus instructional experiences that include oral language development and experiences with listening, reading, writing, and spelling.
10. Diversity in cultural and language backgrounds must be acknowledged and addressed in early literacy development.
11. Differences in literacy development will vary in children and individual needs must be met. Struggling readers, for example, should have opportunity for inclusion-based classrooms and early intervention programs.
12. Assessment of achievement should be frequent, match instructional strategies, and use multiple plans for evaluating student behavior.
13. Standards for early literacy grade-level benchmarks should be tied to instruction and assessment and used as a means for reaching goals for all children to read fluently by the fourth grade. The standards are only benchmarks and may not be achieved by all children at a particular time.
14. Programs should be designed with the concept of developmentally appropriate practice in mind.

Source: Excerpted and adapted from the joint International Reading Association and National Association for the Education of Young Children position statement *Learning to Read and Write: Developmentally Appropriate Practices for Young Children* (1998). All rights reserved. Full-text versions of all NAEYC position statements are available online at www.naeyc.org.

The IRA and NAEYC position statement gives teachers and parents an understanding of the goals of literacy instruction and enables them to assess children's progress toward these goals. Knowledge of the continuum of reading and writing development enables teachers to set goals for individual children and then adapt instructional strategies for children whose learning and development are either advanced or lag (IRA & NAEYC, 1998). The position statement also suggests the following in brief:*

Phase 1: *Awareness and Exploration* (goals for preschool). In this phase children explore their own environment and build foundations for preparing to read and write. They do this by listening to read-alouds, attempting to read and write, participating in literacy games, identifying some letters, and making letter–sound matches.

Phase 2: *Experimental Reading and Writing* (goals for kindergarten). During this phase young children develop basic concepts of print and begin to experiment with reading and writing. They do this by listening to read-alouds, using language in a variety of ways, recognizing letters and letter–sound matches,

becoming aware of rhyming and beginning sounds, writing letters, and matching spoken words with written ones.

Phase 3: *Early Reading and Writing* (goals for first grade). During the first-grade phase, young children begin to read and write. They read and retell stories, use a variety of strategies to aid comprehension, recognize many words by sight, and begin to use punctuation and capitalization.

Phase 4: *Transitional Reading and Writing* (goals for second grade). In this phase children read and write more fluently. They use a variety of strategies for comprehension and word identification. They increase their sight vocabulary. They write using a variety of topics.

Phase 5: *Independent and Productive Reading and Writing* (goals for third grade). This is a phase for extension and refining of reading and writing skills. Children in this phase can read fluently, utilizing a variety of strategies for comprehension and word identification. They can critically examine texts and structures. They can utilize all aspects of the writing process, including revising and editing.

Organizations such as IRA and NAEYC are committed to the goal of facilitating children in learning to read well enough by the end of their third-grade year "that they can read to learn in all curriculum areas" (IRA & NAEYC, 1998, p. 2). A number of authors have encouraged the use

*The suggestions given here are not meant to be exhaustive. In addition, students at any grade level will function at a variety of phases. Excerpted and adapted from the joint IRA and NAEYC position statement *Learning to Read and Write: Developmentally Appropriate Practices for Young Children* (1998). All rights reserved. Full-text versions of all NAEYC position statements are available online at www.naeyc.org.

of information or expository texts with emergent readers (Duke, 2000, 2003; Pentimonti, Zucker, Justice, & Kaderavek, 2010). Their proposition is that young children learn to read and read to learn at the same time. One way we can facilitate this is by focusing more attention on informational text and comprehension of text. Research indicates that informational texts are missing in many early childhood classrooms and incorporating them builds background knowledge, vocabulary, and motivation to read (Duke, 2000; Duke & Bennett-Armistead, 2003; Soalt, 2005; Yopp & Yopp, 2000, 2004, 2006). By using nonfiction texts children learn that literacy is a means of acquiring information, and that in the adult world nonfiction texts are a primary means of gaining information (Duke, 2003). In addition, some children prefer informational texts when given a choice (Duke, 2003). Expository texts are chosen for several reasons: "(1) knowledge gained, (2) choice, and (3) personal interests" (Edmunds & Bauserman, 2006, p. 416). It is suggested when planning units of study to pair text sets of fictional or narrative text *and* informational text (Soalt, 2005); when doing so, children make comparisons between the two texts.

Children seek to become literate for both survival and pleasure. "The central goal of literacy teaching . . . is to create a literate life for children in classrooms and enrich their home literacy as much as possible and appropriate" (Fountas & Pinnell, 2006, p. xxv). To teach in developmentally appropriate ways, teachers should understand the continuum of reading and writing development, as well as each child's individual and cultural variations (IRA & NAEYC, 1998). In addition, a developmentally appropriate environment for developing literacy in early childhood includes play, games, manipulative materials, dramatic play, and physical and motor play (Fields, Groth, & Spangler, 2007). Children need opportunities to use language in both the spoken and the written form. Children should frequently see a written copy of what they are hearing or what is spoken to them (Bear, Invernizzi, Templeton, & Johnston, 2008). Even when they are not yet able to read, seeing the written images helps them to make connections between what they hear and the written symbols. Bodrova, Leong, and Paynter (1999, p. 45) suggest a scaffolded writing approach for preschool and kindergarten children, in which the teacher "takes dictation" by drawing lines representing words that the child dictates for a message or story. The child will then fill in as many words or as much of each word as possible.

We can always find ways to create a print-rich environment regardless of what activities or materials we are using, and the print must make sense (Adams, 1990). Print-rich environments provide opportunities for students to see and use written language for a variety of purposes, and teachers can draw children's attention to the words and specific letters (Bennet-Armistead, Duke, & Moses, 2006; IRA & NAEYC, 1998; Strickland &

There is a strong correlation between listening, speaking, reading, and writing.

Schickedanz, 2009; Vukelich & Christie, 2009). Children frequently see printed words in their environment; they learn, whether they read or not, that things have spoken and written labels and meaning.

> Children who are successful readers in school have had written language as a dominant part of their daily activities.

COMPREHENSIVE LITERACY APPROACH

Literacy development includes ability in listening, speaking, reading, and writing. The interrelationships among these components should be obvious, because they all involve words. In listening, ideas are received through words; in speaking and writing, ideas are expressed through words; and in reading, ideas are communicated through printed words. Children learn to

Listen by listening

Speak by speaking

Read by reading

Write by writing

Listen by speaking, reading, and writing

Speak by listening, reading, and writing

Read by writing, listening, and speaking

Write by reading, listening, and speaking

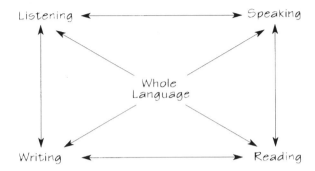

FIGURE 8.1 Language Interrelationships

Figure 8.1 shows the interactive relationships among listening, speaking, reading, and writing.

Comprehensive literacy instruction is grounded in scientifically researched practices (National Institute of Child Health and Human Development [NICHD], 2000). In a comprehensive literacy program, teachers provide developmentally appropriate literacy activities. There is structured, intentional, explicit, or direct instruction, but there are also more informal opportunities for extending practice in listening, speaking, reading, and writing. Instruction includes phonemic awareness, phonics, vocabulary, comprehension, and fluency. There are many opportunities for book reading, literature study, and writing instruction. There are whole-group and small-group instructions according to the needs of the learners. Teachers in a comprehensive literacy program must also provide explicit instruction that focuses on learning words and the strategies for decoding with instructions that build comprehension and thoughtfulness (McGee & Richgels, 2007).

Isolated skill-and-drill tasks and worksheets that fill so much time are ineffective and are not developmentally appropriate. More can and should be done in these early years to engage children in capturing the literacy vision. All children benefit from developmentally appropriate literacy activities. However, those children who come to programs and classrooms with limited literacy experience and proficiency particularly reap great value from activities such as reading stories aloud, sharing big books, working on a word wall, seeing the environment filled with meaningful print, and writing for the purpose of enhancing emergent reading abilities (Taylor & Heibert, 1994). In a comprehensive program, literacy should be integrated into every part of the early childhood curriculum. Music, science, art, food•activities, social studies, math, and any other kind of experience should provide opportunities for emerging literacy.

> Children learn about literacy through the practice of acquiring new knowledge, as they talk about and explore new ideas. "Any early literacy instruction that does not explicitly and systematically help children develop the conceptual knowledge base that underlies the meanings of words will never make much difference in overcoming the gap between children from low- and middle-income families" (Neuman & Roskos, 2005, p. 25).

In the past, heated debates have occurred about whether young children should receive whole language or phonics instruction. We propose, along with many other experts in the field, an approach that incorporates both methods, which theoretically means a subscription to both the bottom-up theory and the top-down approach. The bottom-up approach suggests that students derive meaning from the precise and sequential processing of words with the emphasis on the text instead of the reader's experience. The top-down approach is more holistic with the focus on the reader and the natural processing that occurs through immersion. Many refer to this as a **comprehensive or integrated approach to literacy.** With a comprehensive approach, teachers create a literate environment and then use the best tools available to teach the components of literacy.

The National Early Literacy Panel (Strickland & Shanahan, 2004) identified the key components of early literacy that affect later literacy achievement. These components are oral language development, phonemic awareness, alphabetic knowledge, print knowledge, and invented spelling.

Comprehensive literacy instruction includes a variety of reading and writing activities. For example, it may include the **language experience approach (LEA),** in which children dictate to the teacher their thoughts and ideas; the **sight- or whole-word approach,** in which children see the representation of the whole word and begin to read it; or **phonics,** in which children learn the letter sound in order to facilitate sounding out the words as they read. They learn word identification skills, develop vocabulary in a variety of ways, and always work on comprehension. Key skills are taught explicitly but are often embedded in and related to the reading, writing, and experiences of students. The USOE Cooperative Research Program in First-Grade Reading Instruction found that "the approaches that included both systematic phonics and considerable emphasis on connected reading and meaning surpassed the basal-alone approaches on virtually all outcome measures" (Adams, 1990, p. 9). This same study found that the single best predictor of students' achievement in reading at the end of the first-grade year was their ability at the *first* of the year to recognize and name upper- and lowercase letters (Adams, 1990). Understanding the **alphabetic principle,** the notion that spoken language is made up of sounds and that these sounds can be formed into written letters, makes both reading and writing achievement easier for young children (Adams, 1990).

Components of Comprehensive Literacy Instruction

- A literacy-rich environment, abundant with print, is evident. There is direct and explicit instruction in what the National Reading Panel (NICHD, 2000) refers to as the "big five": phonemic awareness, phonics, fluency, vocabulary, and comprehension.
- Comprehension instruction includes a focus on learning to activate prior knowledge, self-monitor, predict, clarify, question, and summarize.
- There is a focus on oral language.
- ESL (English as a Second Language) learners are provided with resources and visuals to support their learning and may be taught reading in their first language.
- Reading and writing are interwoven in shared reading and writings, in guided reading and writing, in the reading and writing workshop, and in read-alouds.
- Strong connections are made among the classroom, home, and community.
- Students access a variety of text types and genres.
- Assessments are aligned to the objectives and learning activities.

Additional Components in the Comprehensive Literacy Approach

HIGH-QUALITY CHILDREN'S LITERATURE. During the past decade there has been a dramatic increase in the emphasis on literature in classroom literacy instruction (Morrow & Gambrell, 2002). In early childhood classrooms, a substantive amount of literature is imperative and often is used to integrate the curriculum. Good literature is a model for accuracy and correctness in language usage and grammar. Meaningful literature can raise awareness of such values as empathy, generosity, and kindness and may be the impetus to move students to "compassionate action" (Miller, 2001, p. 381). Using literature as a basis for language in the early childhood classroom develops *readers* instead of just developing a set of *skills*; in addition, literature makes learning engaging and enjoyable (Morrow et al., 2009). Teachers

can enhance language and literacy opportunities for young children by increasing the volume and quality of children's experiences with high-quality books at an early age (Neuman & Celano, 2001). All children are entitled to great literature and books. "Children are universally entitled to meaningful experiences with memorable books" (Jalongo, 2004, p. 10). To be successful in using quality books, teachers need knowledge of excellent children's literature (Feeney & Moravcik, 2005; Morrow et al., 2009).

A variety of kinds of texts are included in a comprehensive literacy program to arouse children's interest and motivation. A **basal reading series,** which is a published reading series with stories and activities on increasingly difficult reading levels, may be selected by programs or school districts for early childhood classrooms. The **leveled texts,** like the basals, are arranged into levels of text difficulty. Some specific programs, such as Reading Recovery, use leveled texts and may have 12 to 16 levels of text difficulty for a particular grade. Some districts and programs have developed their own lists of leveled texts, and publishers often level texts according to their difficulty. In addition, comprehensive literacy programs should have a collection of authentic or quality literature, including fiction and nonfiction or informational texts. Providing children with opportunities to hear and read both narrative and informational text appears to improve reading motivation and also reading achievement (Duke & Bennett-Armistead, 2003; Kristo & Bamford, 2005). Providing this kind balance enables children to participate in reading for learning as they simultaneously learn to read. It is suggested that there be equal amounts of fiction and informational text in the daily read-alouds (Cunningham, 2005).

There is a plethora of choices of children's picture books, but not all are substantive and provide the meaningful literature that children need. Teachers need to be wise in their selection of books for their classrooms and use criteria and good judgment to ensure quality literature. Children enjoy rich stories about diverse cultural groups but care must be taken to check the authenticity of the story (Louie, 2006). The following are suggested as general characteristics of high-quality primary-grade picture books (Feeney & Moravcik, 2005; Hefflin & Barksdale-Ladd, 2001):

- Memorable, well-portrayed *characters*
- A clear, understandable, and engaging *plot* with an easy-to-follow sequence of events
- Well-crafted *language* that is concrete, vivid, and reflects the mood of the story
- A worthy and truthful *theme*
- Quality and authentic *illustrations* that enrich the story
- Messages about people, cultures, and race that convey *respect*.

The comprehensive or integrated literacy approach saturates the environment with wonderful books—about characters with which children can identify; about both familiar and unfamiliar animals, places, and events; and about experiences that encourage children to think, laugh, cry, or feel sad. "Humor helps children to grow cognitively as they act on what is seen and heard and resolve what is not understood in the spirit of fun. Literature that encourages or enables children to engage in such activity facilitates cognitive growth" (Zeece, 1995, p. 93). Suggested children's books involving humor include *Dog Breath: The Horrible Trouble with Hally Tosis* (Pilkey, 1994); *Frogs in Clogs* (Samton, 1995); *A Goodnight Opus* (Breathed, 1993); *Making Friends with Frankenstein* (McNaughton, 1994); *Prowlpuss* (Wilson, 1995); *Sheep Take a Hike* (Shaw, 1994); *Six Thick Thumbs: A Tongue-Twisting Tale* (Charney, 1994); *That Pesky Toaster* (Hillman, 1995); *The Three Little Wolves and the Big Bad Pig* (Trivizas, 1993); *Two Cool Cows* (Speek, 1995); and *Yo, Hungry Wolf!* (Vozar, 1993). (See Suggested Resources at the end of this chapter for complete references.)

Young children enjoy hearing the same stories or books over and over, about children their own age, animals, adventures with familiar things, humor, and the alphabet; they enjoy rhymes, the ridiculous, silly, fantastic, factual, and nonsensical. They enjoy their own creations, beginning reading books, poetry, and books with new words.

Good books, well selected, are not enough. The stories must be well delivered by either reading or telling the story with feeling, heart, and sensitivity. Good books well delivered introduce children "to the richness, diversity, sorrow, and joy that our human family has to offer" (Feeney & Moravcik, 2005, p. 27).

The literature selected must be developmentally appropriate (Morrow et al., 2009; Neuman & Celano, 2001; Neuman, Copple, & Bredekamp, 2000). For example, picture books should be provided for toddlers, with pictures that depict various ages, ethnic groups, and disabilities in positive ways. Song picture books promote language growth by "building on familiarity and enjoyment, providing repetition and predictability, expanding vocabulary and knowledge of story structures, promoting critical thinking and problem solving, and fostering creative expression and language play" (Jalongo & Ribblett, 1997, p. 16). They unite literacy development with music in an interesting way, provide a way for children to express their thoughts, stimulate the imagination, and teach literacy skills (Jalongo & Ribblett, 1997). Wordless books should include both the concept type, which works well for children at the labeling stage, and the story type, which can lead children to constructing their own stories (Raines & Isbell, 1988). Alphabet books use the sequence of the alphabet to present a story, teach the

letters, or organize information around a topic such as the circus. As children develop good reading skills, they should be guided toward making responsible choices and judgments in selecting reading materials. Certainly, not all children's literature is high quality. Providing children with reading lists appropriate to their reading level, including Caldecott and Newbery Award books, is helpful in guiding them to excellent choices.

Genres of Early Childhood Literature

Informational or nonfiction books: Provide realistic and authentic information about people, places, animals, plants, weather, and other real things in our world.

Traditional tales and stories: Handed down from one generation to the next and within cultures.

Multicultural books: Give the reader an accurate glimpse of another culture.

Fantasy: Amusing, pretend, or fantastic stories.

Folktales: A traditional tale with good prevailing over evil.

Fables: Tales about animals with an explicit moral.

Myths: Created to explain natural incidents.

Historical fiction: May include fictional characters, but the setting accurately reflects the time period in which the story is set.

Biographies and autobiographies: Accurate stories about the lives of real people.

Poetry: Usually anthologies or collections of poems; poetry appeals to the senses and includes imagery and rhythm, and may include rhyme.

Songbooks: Collections of songs.

Student-authored works: Collections of writings from individuals and groups of class members.

Good literature can also be used as a springboard for a study of a topic or an understanding of a concept, as well as a basis for integrating curriculum (Morrow et al., 2009). Books can evoke rich memories, raise awareness, and inculcate understanding. For example, as a springboard to a class service-learning project, a teacher might read *The Gift* (Brodmann, 1993), the story of a young girl deciding what to do with her Hanukkah money. The listeners or readers understand the true meaning of giving as they enjoy the girl's journey. The story provides a foundation for service learning, and children will come up with many ideas for service projects and sharing with others following this story of giving.

> **IDEA:** Another book that can serve as a means to integrate curriculum is *Sarah, Plain and Tall* (MacLachlan, 1985). This is a Newbery Medal–winning tale of life on the prairie frontier, so the story can help young children to better understand a part of history as well as a different culture. In the story, Sarah, homesick for her native Maine, tries to "bring some sea" to the prairie. She has brought some shells, stones, a snail, and a picture to remind her of her native home. An activity for young children that could emerge from this story is for each child or a group of children to create a sense box that would include souvenirs, pictures, or other items from a different place. Another activity is to compare Sarah's time with the present by making contrasts. A food activity might be preparing and eating something from the prairie days such as biscuits or scones.

Classrooms that support integrated and literature-based curriculum practices assure active and engaged learning.

LANGUAGE EXPERIENCE APPROACH AS PART OF A COMPREHENSIVE LITERACY APPROACH.   In the language experience approach (LEA), children write and read about their experiences. When they go on a field trip, for example, they return and write about it. Younger children dictate to the teacher; older children write their own stories, poems, ideas, or summaries. When stories or ideas are dictated to the teacher, the teacher writes the ideas in sentence format to model correct writing (Gately, 2004). Writing down the actual words that a child says when making storybooks helps them to recognize that "print is 'talk' written down" (Diffily & Morrison, 1996, p. 58).

> **IDEA:** Each child might draw a picture following the field trip and write or dictate to the teacher a description of the picture. These words could be compiled into a class book so that the experience can be enjoyed, as well as reinforced, in the future. When the story is completed the teacher reads and rereads the children's writing and points to each word as it is read, much as she or he does when sharing a big book with the whole class. When books and stories are reread, children become more able to eventually read the story independently. The stories children have written can be used for learning extensions. For example, specific words can be examined and compared for patterns, sound relationships, or word meanings (Gately, 2004).

In the language experience approach, children can draw, write, and read about their own experiences.

Another approach is to have the class participate together in writing an experience chart. The teacher begins with a statement such as "We had an exciting time at Mr. James's farm. Tell me about our trip, and I will write about our experience." The children are invited to participate as they dictate to the teacher where they went, what they did, what they liked, what they did not like, and any other individual perceptions and feelings. The language experience approach can also be used in writing a thank-you letter following a field trip or a meeting with a visitor. The children dictate to the teacher what to say, including their individual reactions.

Prior to the field trip, in addition to the discussion and other preparations (which include speaking and listening), the children could write a note home or take one written by the teacher that tells of the forthcoming field trip and activities. Directions for getting to the field trip destination could be written down and followed as the trip is made. Children then learn that we communicate with people by speaking, writing, listening, and reading. They also learn that their own thoughts can be both written and read, whether they do the writing and reading themselves or someone else does it for them.

Throughout the planning and carrying out of the field trip, the children listen for the purpose of gaining meaning and understanding. In addition, they are able to use oral language before, during, and after the field trip as they ask questions, participate in discussions, comment, make inferences, answer questions, and use other forms of oral language. Following the trip, they write about the experience by making an experience chart, individual or class book, or thank-you note. Afterward, they read, sometimes many times, what they have written.

The described environment and experiences focus on the values and meanings of literacy. In comprehensive or integrated literacy, all components of literacy are woven in a natural way throughout the curriculum.

READING AND WRITING ALOUD AS PART OF A COMPREHENSIVE LITERACY APPROACH. The comprehensive literacy approach encourages teachers to read aloud to children at least once a day from high-quality children's literature (Campbell, 2001; Hahn, 2002; McKean, 2000/2001). Effective interactive read-alouds include books matched to students' interests and developmental levels, preview and preparation by the teacher, establishing a clear purpose for the read-aloud, modeling fluency, stopping to question thoughtfully, and making connections to independent reading (Fisher, Flood, Lapp, & Frey, 2004). Additionally, read-alouds enrich vocabulary, build community, and address standards in the curriculum (Laminack & Wadsworth, 2006).

> "Read-alouds are the basis and foundation of literacy learning, as well as a springboard for activities such as role plays, reader's theater, shared readings, music, and art." (Campbell, 2001)

Children are never too old or too young to be read to. The most important exercise for building the knowledge and competence eventually needed for reading appears to be reading aloud to children (Adams, 1990).

Benefits of reading aloud with children:

- They learn to associate reading with pleasure and build background knowledge and vocabulary (Trelease, 2006).
- The reader provides a model for the sound, rhythm, expression, and fluency of reading.
- It fosters reading development, increases reading comprehension, develops listening comprehension skills, cultivates appreciation of literature, and expands oral language abilities.
- Children will have cherished memories of the stories that they hear (Trelease, 2001).
- Daily readings aloud will be one of the best parts of the day.

Guidelines for reading aloud with children:

- Teachers should read aloud daily and it will be one of the best parts of the day.
- Choose books suited to the experiences and needs of children in your classroom (Wolter, 1992).
- Provide sufficient time for questions, discussion, and response to the literature (McKean, 2000/2001).
- Incorporate discussion and make read-alouds interactive, engaging students, and supporting their comprehending of the text (Fountas & Pinnell, 2006; Morrow & Gambrell, 2002).

> "The more you read, the better you get at it; the better you get at it, the more you like it; and the more you like it, the more you do it. The more you read it, the more you know and the more you know, the smarter you grow." (Trelease, 2001, p. 3)

Big books (enlarged textbooks or children's oversized books) have become valuable tools for enhancing children's enjoyment and understanding of literature; they are great read aloud books. Big books can be obtained commercially or prepared by the teacher or individual children. In one kindergarten class, for example, after the children had listened to the song "What a Wonderful World," they each illustrated a phrase or word in the song and then put it together as a big book. In addition, interest centers for listening should be encouraged. Attach earphones to a tape recorder and let children listen to commercially prepared stories. Cassettes of teachers reading favorite stories can be enjoyed over and over again by the children, either individually or in a small group.

Beginning in about second-grade children still enjoy having teachers read aloud from picture books in small groups, but they also begin to enjoy books that are not completed in one sitting, but are carried over from day to day. These books are called chapter books and a few examples include *Charlotte's Web* (White, 1952); *The Indian in the Cupboard* (Banks, 1981) or its sequels, *The Return of the Indian* (1986) and *The Secret of the Indian* (1989); *The Cricket in Times Square* (Selden, 1960); *James and the Giant Peach* (Dahl, 1961); *The Hundred Dresses* (Estes, 1944); *Little House in the Big Woods* (Wilder, 1932) and others in the series; and *Sarah, Plain and Tall* (MacLachlan, 1985). (See Suggested Resources at the end of this chapter for complete references.) In addition to reading aloud to young children, it is also important to write aloud to model how to write. The teacher writes and comments out loud on the thought processes going on during the writing process.

GUIDED READING AND WRITING AS PART OF A COMPREHENSIVE LITERACY APPROACH. Using this strategy in the literacy program gives support to readers who need help. Texts are selected on just the right reading level for each group of children (Fountas & Pinnell, 2005). In **guided reading** the teacher or a peer guides students through the text, which they read silently and then discuss (Fountas & Pinnell, 2010). The teacher or peer leader might encourage students to make predictions, give background information to help students to construct meaning, ask questions, help students make connections, and give appropriate prompts.

During guided reading the teacher might stop and give a mini lesson on a phonics concept, word-identification skill, vocabulary concept, or any reading strategy that might benefit the children in the group. Guided reading provides opportunities to teach students strategies that they need to learn to read independently (Mere, 2005). In **guided writing** the teacher or peer guides the students through their own writing by prompting and asking questions to support them.

COOPERATIVE READING AND WRITING AS PART OF A COMPREHENSIVE LITERACY APPROACH. This approach is modeled after the principles of cooperative learning. Pairs of students take turns reading aloud text to each other, or they might read silently to a particular point and then stop and discuss their reading with each other. One approach to **cooperative reading** is called **discussion circles.** After students have finished reading a book or story, they get together in small cooperative groups to discuss the book. They may talk about what they liked or didn't like about the book, if they have experienced something similar to the characters in the story, or new and interesting words in the story. **Cooperative writing** allows partners to work together on a writing piece. This might be modeled after the LEA approach.

SHARED READING AND WRITING AS PART OF A COMPREHENSIVE LITERACY APPROACH. Text in this approach is shared by the teacher with students. The teacher reads aloud the book, story, poem, or song, and invites students to join in the reading when they feel comfortable. They respond to the text through art, writing, music, drama, and other activities. **Shared reading** gives young readers support in real reading. The big book concept models the shared reading concept. **Shared writing** is similar to the LEA approach in which a group works together on a writing piece and actually goes through the writing process.

LITERATURE CIRCLES. In small groups, children read and discuss books that they self-select or wish to read. Books that foster thinking and discussion require careful selection (Harvey & Goudvis, 2007). During discussion the children share personal responses, explore interpretations, reflect on their feelings about the story or characters in the story, and raise thoughtful questions of their peers (Daniels, 2002; Mere, 2005). In early childhood, children can learn to take roles as they participate in a **literature circle.** Making connections between home and school in literature response groups prompts dynamic discussion among group members (Bond, 2001; Miller, 2002).

INDEPENDENT READING AND WRITING AS PART OF A COMPREHENSIVE LITERACY APPROACH. As soon as children are able to read or write on their own, they should have time to do so by themselves. This type of reading and writing requires no support from others. Encouraging independent reading promotes motivation to read because children sense an ownership and enjoyment of their own literacy progress (Flippo, 2005). Independent reading allows children to focus on their interests, curiosities, and independent explorations (Miller, 2002). For example, journals provide a means by which students can respond in writing or, for children not ready to write, by drawing pictures. Encourage children to write their own books and stories, and place the books in the story or literacy area to be read and enjoyed again and again.

Book writing is more purposeful and meaningful than doing worksheets (Fields et al., 2007). Some kindergarten teachers have found that children learn their letters and sounds better by writing than by some of the other activities traditionally used in kindergarten for teaching letters and sounds (Moutray & Snell, 2003). Children's self-directed writings demonstrate how much they know and can do. If children are able to write, they can be encouraged to write and illustrate their own stories. If they do not write, they can illustrate their stories (pretend or real experiences) and dictate them to a teacher or caregiver.

> **IDEA:** Children in early childhood classes enjoy making calendar books. For each day of a particular month, cut a sheet of paper approximately 4 by 5 inches. Put the numeral representing the day at the top of the paper, and then put the papers on a bulletin board in the correct order for that month. After each day, have a child in the class draw a picture on the paper representing that day and perhaps something that happened at home, at school, or with the weather. Children who are able to write can write about what was drawn. Children who do not write should dictate something about the picture to the teacher. At the end of the month, take the numbered pictures down and put them in order. Add a cover sheet with the name of the month and then staple or bind the pages together. Add this "book" to the book center for the children to enjoy reading again and again. They will especially enjoy "reading" the pages that they have created.

Literature, books, and stories can often be a springboard for a class, group, or individual book. For example, the book *Fortunately* (Charlip, 1964) adapts easily to having the class do their own "fortunately–unfortunately" episodes. Or, after reading *All the Places to Love* (MacLachlan, 1994), the children can write about the places that they love. *The Jolly Postman or Other People's Letters* (Ahlberg & Ahlberg, 1986) is a great prompt for letter writing. (See the Suggested Resources for complete references.) Almost any story can serve to launch a writing activity. How proud children are when they realize that they can author stories or pages worthy of being bound as well as read and reread!

LITERACY LESSON AS PART OF A COMPREHENSIVE LITERACY APPROACH. A format for developing a literacy lesson in early childhood is fairly simple. Once the piece of literature has been selected, there are three parts to the literacy lesson:

1. *Introducing the literature.* Background knowledge and prior knowledge must be activated. This may also include discussion of key vocabulary words. In addition, children must be given a purpose for the reading.
2. *Reading and responding to the literature.* The literature can be read in a variety of ways including reading aloud, shared reading, and others. During this part of the lesson, students reflect on the meaning of the literature and summarize what is meant through discussion, questions, applications, and prompts.
3. *Extending the literature.* In this part of the literacy lesson, teacher and students are encouraged to go beyond, to invite a guest to the class, or to take a field trip to extend the piece of literature. The children do something with the literature: write about it, dramatize it, or sing songs about it. Or they may do an art or craft that extends or relates to the piece of literature.

EARLY CHILDHOOD LITERACY LESSON: THE VERY HUNGRY CATERPILLAR

OBJECTIVES

Students will

- Describe the life cycle of a butterfly;
- Discuss and chart the different types of food and categorize them into healthy or unhealthy snacks; and;
- Create a class book and write what they would eat if they were the caterpillars.

MATERIALS NEEDED

- Copy of the book *The Very Hungry Caterpillar* by Eric Carle (1969)
- Copy of the poem "Caterpillar" (author unknown)
- K–W–L (Know–Want–Learn) chart
- Flash cards of the physical changes that a caterpillar goes through

- Sock, with eyes and all colors of felt to make the different shapes of food
- Food cards of the foods that the hungry caterpillar eats
- Enough 8 1/2- by-11-inch pieces of cardstock for each class member to have one
- Hole punch, yarn, crayons, and pencils
- Copy of the "Caterpillar Song"

LESSON PLAN

Introducing the Literature

1. To introduce the book, first ask the children to think back to when they were on summer vacation and to imagine a summer day. Ask them, "Did you ever chase a butterfly?" Then ask, "Where do you think butterflies come from?" Pause and wait for the students to respond with a caterpillar as their answer.
2. Begin by reading the poem called "Caterpillar."

   A fuzzy, wuzzy caterpillar
   On a summer day
   Wriggled and wriggled and wriggled
   On his way.
   He lifted up his head
   To get a better view
   He wanted some nice green
   Leaves to chew.
   He wriggled and he wriggled
   From his toes to his head
   And he crawled about until
   He found a comfy bed.
   He curled up tight
   In a warm little wrap
   And settled himself
   For a nice long nap.
   He slept until
   One day he awoke
   And broke from his shell.
   He stretched and stretched
   And he found he had wings!
   He turned into a butterfly
   Such a pretty colored thing.
   On how happily
   He flew away
   And he flew and he flew
   In the sun all day!

3. Discuss what the children know about caterpillars by using a K–W–L chart. (What do you know about caterpillars? What do you want to know? What did you learn about them?) List on the chart the children's responses to the first two parts of the chart. Use prompts such as "What do caterpillars eat?" to guide their thinking if needed. Be

sure to write down what they want to know about caterpillars.

4. Following the K–W–L chart, use the flash cards to teach and discuss the physical changes that the caterpillar goes through during the life cycle.

5. To introduce the book *The Very Hungry Caterpillar,* do a walk-through of the book. Begin by pointing out the cover of the book, the back of the book, the title, and the author. Then quickly flip through each page, predicting what might happen in the story. Make sure that you open the discussion to the class so that children are able to voice their predictions. After the predictions, begin reading the story.

Reading and Responding to the Literature

1. While reading the story, use a green sock puppet and food made out of felt to dramatize the story.

2. While you read the story, stop at various places in the book to ask questions, point out special details, and talk about new words. For example:
   • What kind of egg do you think is on the leaf?
   • Why do you think the caterpillar is so hungry?
   • What do you think he will eat?
   • Do you know what kind of food an apple is? A pear? A plum? A strawberry? An orange? And so on.
   • Are these healthy snacks?
   • When you get to the salami, pause and ask, "What do you think might happen if he eats all of this food?"
   • Why did the caterpillar make a cocoon? What is a cocoon?

3. After reading the last page to the class, ask the children to share some ways that they have changed from the previous year to this year. Go back and discuss how much food the caterpillar ate by having the children count all the different food items throughout the story.

4. Next, the class will participate and join in while you reread the story. Before you begin, distribute the food cards and explain each card to the children so that they are aware of what picture they have. While rereading the story, have the children stand up when you read their particular picture in the story. This promotes listening and being involved during the story.

5. Using a sequence of picture cards that show the actual life cycle of the caterpillar to the butterfly, put the pictures in the proper sequence from the eggs, caterpillar (larva), chrysalis (pupa), to adult butterfly. Practice mixing these pictures up and having children order them in the proper sequence. (It is a great experience for children to observe the actual life cycle of the butterfly beginning with the caterpillar stage.)

Extending the Literature

1. Have the children return to their tables or desks and ask questions such as:
   • What part of the story did you like best?
   • What are your feelings about the story?
   • What kinds of food did the caterpillar eat? (Based on their prior knowledge, you might discuss categories of foods.)
   • What kinds of healthy foods do you like to eat?

2. Finish the K–W–L chart by discussing what they have learned about caterpillars.

3. Give the students an 8 1/2-by-11-inch sheet of cardstock with the sentence: "If I was the Very Hungry Caterpillar, I would eat _____." Have children finish the sentence and then illustrate a caterpillar and what food they chose for it to eat. Support those who need help with their writing. When the class is finished, punch holes down the left side of the cardstock sheets and tie them together with yarn. When it is completed, the children will have a class book to look at and read throughout the year.

4. Teach the song "Caterpillar." (The tune of the song is "I'm a Little Teapot.") Allow opportunity for the children to sing in groups in front of the class.

   I'm a hungry caterpillar walking slowly (slowly walk two fingers from right hand up your left arm)
   Looking for something (place hand above eyes searching for something)
   To fill my belly (rub belly)
   When I go to sleep (close eyes, tilt head, and rest on folded hands)
   I make a little cocoon (cup hands together)
   Pop! I'll be a butterfly soon (throw open hands, link thumbs, and make flapping movement)

5. Make a fruit salad using the same fruits that are mentioned in the book: apples, pears, plums, strawberries, and oranges.

Assessments

1. Individually, children will properly sort the picture cards of the life cycle of the butterfly.

2. Each child will write or tell one healthy and one unhealthy food.

READING

Reading and writing are the other two main ingredients of literacy in early childhood. The more children see us read, the more inclined they are to want to read; the more children see us write, the more inclined they are to want to write. The process of emergent literacy or learning to read and write is an ongoing process that begins when children become aware of the relationship of print and meaning. Before children learn about letter sounds and names, they must have numerous developmentally appropriate opportunities to observe the values and usefulness of reading and writing. Reading and writing are connected and integrated; one influences the other.

Often when parents are selecting a preschool for their children, one of the first questions they ask is "Do you teach reading?" The knowledgeable preschool teacher, aware of the importance and directions of the early years, should enthusiastically respond, "Yes, emergent reading." Many of the study areas presented in this book are specific emergent reading concepts (for example, shape, sound, and color). Before children have reading facility, they need to have had numerous experiences to sharpen their visual and aural perceptions. Before children can become readers, they learn about reading—why people read and what they read. They are aware that their environment is full of print. This is called **print awareness.** Reading involves the ability to differentiate similarities and differences in visual patterns, forms, and sounds. As children begin to read, they seek to make sense of the words. Others take this perspective when they point out that the reading process is no longer considered a word-by-word decoding process designed to unlock the meaning embedded in the print. Comprehensive literacy teachers view reading as a process of constructing meaning from interacting with the print, relating the information to what one already knows, and teaching specific skills. Neuman (2004, p. 90) found in a study of precocious early readers that "children's ability to read was related to skill development, not aptitude."

Children must also reach a certain cognitive maturity and readiness resulting in their desire to read. There are "two kinds of children: those who love to read and those who think they don't" (Fadiman, 1984, p. xviii). Fadiman (p. xix) refers to Fitzhugh's *Harriet the Spy* (1964), where "Harriet sits down to read. 'How I love to read,' she thought. 'The whole world gets bigger.' As for those who think they don't like to read, well, they're making a mistake, just as all of us do when we try to judge ourselves."

Like any other skill, learning to read takes time, patience, desire, and readiness. One of the most important ingredients in children's emergent reading is whether they have been read to. Basically, children learn to read by being read to. "Every time a child climbs on someone's lap to hear a story, literacy learning takes place" (Collins & Schaeffer, 1997, p. 68). Children who have enjoyed pictures, alphabet, nursery rhyme, and storybooks from early infancy will have a greater desire to read because they know that reading opens new doors, provides information, and is enjoyable. Some ask how old young children should be

when parents start reading to them. Our answer is: early infancy. From the earliest days, infants develop listening skills and learn how books look and feel, how to turn pages, how to be careful with books, and that words and pictures have meaning. Not only is it important that children have access to books, but they must have some books of their own. We advocate reading to very young children and suggest giving children as much as they are ready for and as early as they are ready for it. In addition to reading to children, speaking clearly, distinctly, and with a broad and ever-expanding vocabulary will also foster emergent reading.

Reading is a communicative art involving both recognizing and understanding words. Children cannot read with understanding and comprehension something that they do not have background knowledge about. As we speak to and communicate with children, we should endeavor to expand their vocabulary to include both word pronunciation and definition. A child who reads a word but attaches no meaning to it is not reading with comprehension. Learning the meaning of words evolves through experiences with them. The more experiences that children have and the more these experiences are labeled with words, the more effective their reading experiences become. During emergent reading stages, stories about the children's experiences should be written on chart paper and read aloud often. When children begin writing, they can write and read about their own experiences. Other related skills prerequisite to fluent reading include large- and small-muscle development, social and emotional maturity, and intellectual and language experiences.

Teachers can do much in the early childhood years to prepare children for reading. Ideally, effective early learning activities are combined with the teacher's understanding attitude, resulting in the development of

A child's name is a personal identity. It is exciting when it is recognized.

positive attitudes toward reading. The ability to read is important in academic success and life-long living. It is a slow, gradual process that emerges through regular engagement with print (Adams, 1990). Print awareness, letter familiarity, and phonemic awareness can all be developed through classroom instruction during early childhood.

Components of the Reading Process for the Emergent Reader

1. Growing vocabulary and concept development.
2. Recognize, name, and match the letters of the alphabet, both upper- and lowercase.
3. Associate sounds with letter(s).
4. Attend to, identify, and manipulate sound segments of speech (phonological awareness).
5. Recognize some basic sight words.
6. See a connection between speech and print.
7. See a relationship between letters and words.
8. See a relationship between words and sentences.
9. Hold a book correctly and recognize where to begin reading.
10. Know that we read from left to right, top to bottom.

Concepts of Print

Because of literacy artifacts such as wallpaper with alphabet letters and print, nursery pictures, picture books with print, stickers with print, cereal boxes, mail and letters, signs, newspapers, and many other things with print, children learn very early that print corresponds to oral language and represents ideas that can be read. Teachers can prepare a **logo chart** from newspaper ads, food labels, and other sources. These logo words (environmental print) that are common in advertising can be used in literacy skill lessons. For example, a logo chart could be used for teaching long or short vowel sounds, diagraphs, or such skills as plural possessives. Just spending a few minutes to read some of the logos is also a valuable strategy, because they make connections between school and the real world (Rule, 2001). Print on signs and recycling packaging can be used for alphabet instruction and reading practice activities such as word families, phonics, and compound words (Gerard, 2004; Xu & Rutledge, 2003). In addition, encouraging reading of environmental print helps children to recognize that reading helps us to survive and reading is everywhere. A word of caution, however, in overusing environmental print to encourage reading skills: "reading" logos does not necessarily transfer to learning words (Gately, 2004).

 IDEA: Children can help create their own "I can read" books. The teacher prints the phrase "I can read" on blank pieces of paper and following the phrase children cut out and paste logos from advertisement, magazines, food products, and other sources. Putting the pages together builds confidence in children as they "read" the book, page by page.

Reading is Everywhere that we Look and Helps us in Many Ways

Some of the places that we use reading include the following:

Mileage on roads

States on license plates, and cities and states on road signs

Signs about animals at zoos and in parks

Plaques on statues and at museums

Information on a ticket or pass

Washing instructions on clothing

Messages on doors or outside buildings

Directions on signs such as "Speed Limit," "Waiting Area," "One Way," and "No Smoking"

Dosage on drugs

Contents on labels and nutrition information

Menus at restaurants

Prices on items at stores

Children learn that the symbols called *words* convey meaning and tell something. Even though most preschool children cannot actually read, they have a great deal of competency and knowledge related to the functions and nature of print (Fields et al., 2007). Some early childhood **concepts of print** or **print awareness** include the following:

- Text is meaningful; we are able to read the words that are formed by the letters.
- Print exists and it is different from visuals or pictures.
- Print or reading goes from left to right and top to bottom.
- The cover of the book includes the name of the book, the author and sometimes an illustrator, and possibly a picture representing the story.
- Punctuation marks help to create meaning. Sentences begin with capital letters and end with periods, question marks, or exclamation marks.

- What people say can be written down and then read.
- Words are made from letters, sentences are made from words, and sentences combine into paragraphs and stories.
- A storybook or narrative has a beginning, a middle, and an ending.
- Informational or nonfiction text informs about people, places, or things.

Concepts of print and awareness of print may be developed intuitively, particularly for those children who have been read to at home prior to beginning school experiences. For children who come into early childhood classrooms without a feeling for and background in literacy, teachers need to provide a nurturing atmosphere of literacy—exposure to books (narrative and information), print, reading, and writing (Vukelich & Christie, 2009). One way to provide a positive literacy atmosphere is to organize literacy learning centers to motivate early readers and writers (Hill, 2000; Morrow, 2002). Instruction using appropriate techniques to present new concepts and skills that are slightly ahead of what a child can do independently provides developmentally appropriate early childhood literacy instruction (Bodrova et al., 1999). Being aware that many children need motivation to read helps focus on providing for a variety of needs in order to motivate. Edmunds and Bauserman (2006) recommend five components to motivate students to read: self-selection of text, attention to various characteristics of the text, matching books to personal interests, providing easy access to books, and providing opportunities for read-alouds and for peers to share what they are reading. Children who are motivated to read spend more time reading and ultimately demonstrate greater gains in reading achievement (Guthrie & Wigfield, 2000; Mazzoni, Gambrell, & Korkeamaki, 1999).

Phonological Awareness

Phonological awareness is an over-arching principle that includes detecting and manipulating speech sounds including words, phonemes, syllables, and onsets and rimes. Instruction in phonological awareness should be taught directly and intentionally (Yopp & Yopp, 2009). According to a number of researchers, phonological awareness plays a significant role in the teaching of reading, is a foundation for reading success, and is a predictor of early reading acquisition (Adams, 1990; IRA & NAEYC, 1998; Snow, Burns, & Griffin, 1998; Wasik, 2001a; Yopp, 1995; Yopp & Yopp, 2000, 2009).

Phonemic awareness is one aspect of phonological awareness; it is the awareness of the sound structure or sequence of our language. Activities that promote both the recognition and manipulation of

sounds in words foster phonemic awareness (Wasik, 2001a; Yopp & Yopp, 2000). Teachers need to intentionally teach segmenting and blending the phonemes or speech sounds of words. Phonemic awareness is an auditory skill in which children develop the ability to hear and differentiate the sounds in words. Developmentally appropriate activities for teaching phonemic awareness include songs, chants, nursery rhymes, fingerplays, and word–sound games that focus on rhyme, syllable units, onset and rime, and phonemes (Cooper, Kiger, & Au, 2009; Wasik, 2001a; Yopp & Yopp, 2009). Phonemic awareness is stimulated by providing a language-rich environment and through a variety of experiences throughout the day (Strickland & Schickedanz, 2009). It develops because of children's rich experiences with oral and written language in their surroundings (Cunningham, 2009).

 IDEA: Invite ESL family members into the classroom to share traditional books, poems and songs in their home language that focus on sounds.

Phonemic Awareness

The following categories are used to instruct and assess children in phonemic awareness:

- **Phonemic isolation or onset (word beginnings).** Example: What is the first sound you hear in *fish*?
- **Phonemic identity.** Example: What sound do these words have that are the same? (*bat, bee, boys*)
- **Phoneme categorization.** Example: Which word begins with a different sound? (*cat, come, map, cape*)
- **Phoneme blending** or the ability to put together an onset (beginning sound) and the rime (sound that follows the onset). Example: Put together these sounds and tell me the word you make. (/p/ig/) or (/tr/-/ee/)
- **Phoneme segmentation.** Example: How many sounds do you hear in *dog*?
- **Phoneme deletion.** Example: What is *spoon* without the *p*?
- **Phoneme manipulation** or the ability to manipulate beginning, middle, and ending phonemes. Example: Change the word *take* by changing the first sound or change the word *cap* by changing the middle *a* to a different vowel.
- **Rhyme.** Example: Think of a word that rhymes with *lamp* (*damp, stamp,* etc.).

Throughout the early years when children are developing emergent literacy skills and concepts, teachers should take advantage of spontaneous opportunities, teachable moments, to embed these concepts of print and reading into their teaching and interactions with children. For children who have rich home environments with much focus on literacy, these concepts of print will be understood; for many children they will require explicit teaching, reinforcement, and emphasis.

Alphabet

Alphabet understanding follows phonemic awareness or may overlap some. Before recognizing and naming letters of the alphabet, children must be familiar with letter shapes. The **alphabetic principle** is grasping the notion that sounds of the language (**phonemes**) are represented by letters; or, understanding that there is a relationship between letters and sounds. It is important for children to be familiar with letters and to recognize that these letters are related to reading (Strickland & Schickedanz, 2000; Wasik, 2001b). Snow et al. suggest: "Among the readiness skills that are traditionally evaluated, the one that appears to be the strongest predictor on its own is letter identification" (1998, p. 113).

It is difficult to teach letter shapes and functions without teaching the names of the letters. Usually, among the first letters that children are able to recognize and name are those in their own name. In teaching letter recognition, make children aware that 11 of the letters have basically the same shape in both upper- and lowercase (*Cc, Kk, Oo, Pp, Ss, Uu, Vv, Ww, Xx, Yy, Zz*). Seven of the letters are similar in upper- and lowercase (*Bb, Hh, Ii, Jj, Mm, Nn, Tt*). Differences between upper- and lowercase are greatest in the other eight letters (*Aa, Dd, Ee, Ff, Gg, Ll, Qq, Rr*). Adams (1990, p. 126) points out that letter recognition is extremely important in the development of word recognition: "For children with little letter knowledge on entry to school, current learning theory suggests it is unwise to try to teach both uppercase and lowercase forms of all 26 letters at once. For children who do not know letter names on school entry, special care should be taken to avoid confusion of names and sounds." It is also suggested that fluency in letter recognition is important (Duffelmeyer, 2002).

As children begin to recognize words, they discover that letters have sounds. Initially, children learn the characteristic sound of each letter. Eventually, they learn that some of the letters, such as the vowels, have more than one sound. Children learn alphabet recognition in context or as they interact with materials relating

Often the first word children recognize in print is their name. Many opportunities to practice are necessary before they are able to write it.

to their written language (e.g., books, chalk, chalkboards, paper, pens, markers).

Children can be encouraged to develop and strengthen reading skills. To become readers in the sense that they seek out and enjoy reading, children should develop skill in drawing meaning from the printed word, which gives purpose to reading.

Phonics

Phonics is a strategy using the sounds that letters represent and the resulting sounds made as they are combined with other letters to recognize words. Because English is an alphabetic code and oral language is put into a written form using letters, to represent the sounds, phonics becomes an important part of literacy instruction (Mesmer & Griffith, 2005/2006). Phonics instruction can be taught implicitly or explicitly and incidentally or systematically. The term *systematic* refers to the scope or content of phonics instruction and the sequence or order for teaching the letter–sound correspondences (Mesmer & Griffith, 2005/2006). The term *explicit* refers to the lesson delivery that in the case of explicit teaching is very direct (Mesmer & Griffith, 2005/2006). Good phonics instruction can also be more inductive or taught incidentally or spontaneously. The Reading First Initiative (Armbruster, Lehr, & Osborn, 2001) brought explicit, systematic phonics to the forefront and other writers support this approach (Adams, 1990; Beck, 2006; Cunningham, 2009; Savage, 2007). The focus should be on students' learning and achievement; therefore, good phonics instruction is always tied to formative assessment.

When children use phonics or letter/sound correspondence to decode words, this helps them master spelling patterns and also impacts their fluency (Mesmer & Griffith, 2005/2006). Further, there are many word families that once children recognize them, both in one-syllable and multisyllabic words, they will read more fluently (Rasinski, Rupley, & Nichols, 2008). When children are able to sound out words, they also begin to spell words. Spelling, in fact, is practice for phonics strategies. However, the same words that are difficult to sound out using phonics are also difficult to spell. For example, if you ask a young child to spell *wait*, a word unknown as a sight word, the child would probably apply some beginning phonics to the problem and spell it *w-a-t-e*. Some patterns in words have two different sounds. For example, the words *live* and *live* are spelled the same but have two different pronunciations and two different meanings.

Phonics work includes working with letters (upper- and lowercase), rhyming words, consonant letters and sounds, and vowel patterns and sounds. Vowels in the English language are the most unpredictable and challenging. There are so many patterns and combinations, it is a wonder that anyone learns to read and spell. According to Adams (1990) it is the patterns of our language and the words that enable children to learn to read and decode words. Manipulating, changing, and working with words as children begin to read gives them the kinds of daily experiences they need to build their repertoire of spelling and word patterns.

When reading, some words are not sounded out or decoded. Some words may be best tackled using the **sight-word** strategy; we refer to these words as **high-frequency words.** For example, if *hive* and *dive* rhyme, why doesn't *give* rhyme with them? *Give* cannot be decoded but must be a memorized sight word. Children are often faster and smoother readers when they build up a repertoire of sight words; otherwise, they tend to try to sound out each word, sound by sound. However, many words have regular patterns and can be decoded if children have never seen them before because they follow the rules of our language. Most of these words are either one- or two-syllable words.

> The National Reading Panel (NICHD, 2000) identified five phonics instructional approaches. They are:
>
> 1. *Analogy phonics*—Teaching children to decode unknown words by analogy or patterns of known words. For example, if they know the word *ran* they can decode the word *tan* because they make an analogy of the familiar rime segment of *an*.
> 2. *Analytic phonics*—Students analyze letter-sound relations in words they have previously learned in order to avoid articulating sounds disjointedly or in isolation.
> 3. *Embedded phonics*—Phonics skills are taught during text reading, so this is a form of incidental learning, or a more implicit approach.
> 4. *Phonics through spelling*—Students are taught to spell words phonemically, or to break words into sounds or phonemes and then to select letters that represent those phonemes.
> 5. *Synthetic phonics*—This is an explicit teaching approach in which students are taught to change letters into phonemes or sounds and then blend the sounds to form familiar words. In this approach children are taught to blend and synthesize all the rules of our language.

Phonics development is a vital part of literacy development. It is our hope that teachers sense their responsibility in helping children acquire both the ability and the desire to use phonics. Making word study fun, manipulative, and engaging is motivating to young readers (Lucht, 2006). We believe that too much emphasis in early childhood classrooms is put on worksheets and workbooks. "Many workbook tasks are not interesting, do not provide rich instructional possibilities, lack clear objectives, allow false-positive feedback, consume teachers' time in scoring them, and, most importantly, occupy time that can be otherwise spent teaching students what they do not already know" (Pincus, 2005, p. 79). We suggest that worksheets make reading a task and create a feeling of drudgery and boredom for many children. Also, in too many early childhood classrooms, the focus for literacy development is copying material off the board—board work. This task may have little or no regard for comprehension and meaning and often does not promote literacy.

There are a variety of excellent resources available for helping teachers to develop an understanding of phonics and how to teach it. Some of the resources we suggest are the following (see references for complete citations):

Phonics They Use: Words for Reading and Writing, 5th ed., by Patricia M. Cunningham

Sound It Out! Phonics in a Comprehensive Reading Program, 3rd ed., by John F. Savage

Phonics for the Teacher of Reading, 10th ed., by Barbara J. Fox and M. A. Hull

Self-Paced Phonics: A Text for Educators, 4th ed., by Roger S. Dow and G. Thomas Baer

Words Their Way: Words Study for Phonics, Vocabulary, and Spelling Instruction, 4th ed., by Donald R. Bear, Marcia Invernizzi, Shane Templeton, and Francine Johnston

These resources will also give the teacher many ideas for preparing teacher-made learning materials that focus on reading competency and word patterns giving children practice and experience without the drudgery of worksheet after worksheet.

> **IDEA:** One reading game involves making flowers. On a flower center (or circle), write a word ending, such as *er* or *est*. With a paper fastener, attach petals to the flower center. On each petal, write a word such as *fast, slow, bright,* or *light*. As the petals are rotated around the center, new words are formed. A variation could use *ing* or *ed* as center suffixes, with words such as *work, talk, jump,* and *walk* as petal words. This same concept can be used with two wheels made from card stock or tagboard attached in the center with a paper fastener. The inside wheel could have consonant sounds, blends, root words, or prefixes. The outside wheel could have suffixes or word endings.
>
> **IDEA:** Cut word cards out of heavy stock or use precut 3- by-5-inch index cards. Fold the right side of the card under about 1 inch from the edge. Write a word that uses the "silent *e* " rule on each of the cards. For example, use words such as *cape, tape,* or *care*. Write each word on the card in such a way that the *e* can be folded under. The children then read the word both without and with the silent *e* at the end.

Manipulative and word games can be made for working with consonants, vowels, and every other kind of spelling or word pattern. Lotto games could be adapted to a word game in which the children classify words as a person, place, or thing: A number of words (such as *girl, park, baby, ball, hammer, store, pen,* or *man*) can be written in boxes drawn on poster paper or card stock paper. A number of cover category cards would read *person, place,* or *thing*. The children match these cover cards on top of each word. This activity not only helps children to classify, but also facilitates drawing meaning from words.

Ideas for teacher-made phonics and reading games are limitless. There are also many great Internet sites with ideas and patterns for creating word study materials. When you recognize that a child needs help on a particular skill or strategy, make a game or activity for him or her to work with, rather than giving the child a worksheet to complete.

Vocabulary

Recognizing and understanding words is a significant component of being able to read. Cunningham (2009) emphasizes the importance of high-frequency words and suggests that about 100 words account for almost 50% of all words children read. Therefore, wide reading is one of the best ways to build reliable recognition and understanding of these high-utility words as well as to learn new and less familiar words (Cunningham, 2005). Direct and explicit instruction and using appropriate vocabulary strategies should also be a part of daily literacy instruction in early childhood classrooms. Remember that a single experience with a new word is not enough to build a reliable understanding; it will take repeated experiences with each new word. Encourage children to personalize their word learning; they do this by working independently with new vocabulary in such activities as concept wheels, semantic word maps, word banks, and other strategies.

In the report of the National Reading Panel (NICHD, 2000) from the review of many studies, the following implications for vocabulary teaching emerged:

1. Vocabulary should be taught both directly or explicitly and also indirectly, with repetition and everyday exposure to new words in rich contexts, including the use of computer technology.
2. Vocabulary tasks in direct instruction may need to be restructured or simplified and work best when students are actively involved.
3. For best results, teachers should use a variety of instructional methods and strategies.

The following are some suggested vocabulary teaching strategies that need to be carefully selected to accommodate the age and ability of the reader:

- Vocabulary study before reading a particular text. New words should be related to students' prior knowledge and background and be expanded and elaborated on with visuals, diagrams or graphic organizers, or concrete objects or actions.
- Computer-supported vocabulary learning. There are many programs that can assist children in the study of vocabulary.
- Substituting easier-to-understand words for more difficult words (especially helpful for ESL students and striving readers).
- Using a word wall and/or word bank (Cunningham, 2009). **Word walls** are walls or bulletin boards on

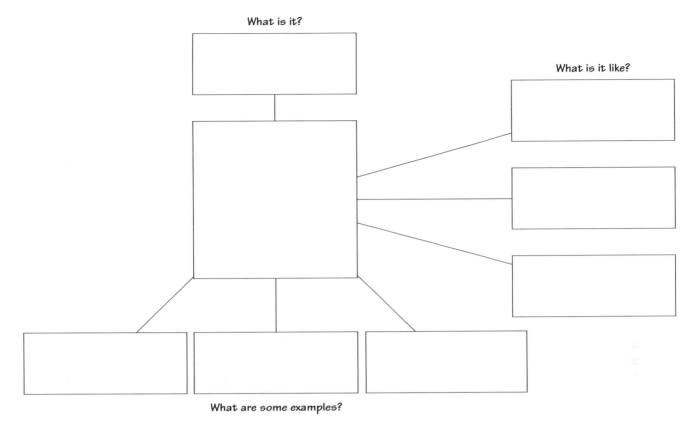

What is it?

What is it like?

What are some examples?

FIGURE 8.2 Word Map

which selected words are organized alphabetically or by themes or categories. Activities are planned to use the words as they are added. Words that children encounter often in their reading and writing are added to the word wall. **Word banks** are individual collections of words that children select and add to their file, notebook, or journal.

- Flash cards can be individually created with the word on one side and its definition or picture on the other side.
- **Word maps** or vocabulary graphic organizers assist children in analyzing and gaining the meaning of new words. Schwartz and Raphael (1985) suggested a word map that assists children in visually representing the components of a particular concept. An example of a word map is shown in Figure 8.2.
- **Word logs.** Children chart or log the word or words they independently learned on a particular day (see Figure 8.3).

Other activities include activities with making words, using the dictionary or thesaurus.

Fluency

Fluency is the ability to read smoothly and effortlessly with sufficient rate and accuracy. The findings from the

Date	New Words I Learned
March 3	Dew: moisture condensed from the air, especially at night, and found in the form of small drops. Sentence: The dew on the grass in the morning made the grass wet.

FIGURE 8.3 Word Log

National Reading Panel (NICHD, 2000, p. 11) state: "Fluent readers are able to read orally with speed, accuracy, and proper expression. Fluency is one of several critical factors necessary for reading comprehension. Despite its importance as a component of skilled reading, fluency is often neglected in the classroom." The association between fluency and comprehension has been shown in research. Strecker, Roser, and Martinez (1998, p. 306) refer to this as a "reciprocal relationship" with each promoting the other.

Steps to build reading fluency, according to Hudson, Lane, and Pullen (2005, p. 708), include:

1. Model fluent oral reading.
2. Provide direction instruction in teaching decoding of unfamiliar words and strategies that good readers use.
3. Provide oral support using such strategies as assisted reading, choral reading, paired reading, audiotapes, and computer programs.
4. Provide materials for independent reading on the student's appropriate reading level.
5. Give many opportunities for practice.
6. Encourage prosody by using punctuation and grammar to cue phrase boundaries.

Fluency refers to the efficient word-recognition skills that allow readers to gain meaning from text. It is manifested in oral reading, but for comprehension it must also be applied to silent reading. Accuracy in word recognition (word decoding) is related to phonics and fluency (Rasinski, 2008). Automatic word recognition is an important part of the development of reading, and automatic word recognition is a primary component of fluency. The rate of speed at which a child reads does matter, and teachers need to support slow readers in becoming more fluent (Rasinski, 2000). Prosody is another component of fluency. **Prosody** includes those rudiments of fluency that permit oral reading to sound like spoken language, including expression, intonation, pitch, and phrasing (Kuhn, 2004/2005).

Like other components or processes in developmental reading, fluency is likely improved by reading. Again, the more children read, the better they read; fluency takes practice. However, there is no convincing research demonstrating that increasing independent reading will increase fluency (Pikulski & Chard, 2005). Fluency is supported by a teacher or other model that uses intonation, expression, and fluency in reading aloud. Oral reading with feedback shared, repeated readings, shadow reading, choral reading, reader's theater, and buddy reading are other ways to develop fluency (Rasinski, 2010).

Comprehension

Understanding, comprehending, and creating meaning of that which has been read is the purpose of reading. It is seeking *meaning* that drives children's earliest experiences with literacy (Neuman et al., 2000). In short, reading *is* comprehending (Pinnell & Scharer, 2003). However, for comprehension to take place children must have phonemic awareness, print awareness, knowledge of phonics or other decoding strategies, as

well as a repertoire of sight words and some degree of fluency. The National Reading Panel (NICHD, 2000) found in their analysis of research that reading comprehension is complex and is influenced strongly by the role of vocabulary development. Comprehension is an active process that necessitates a deliberate and thoughtful interaction between reader and text. Children must learn to make sense of text, to "process and interpret the text" (Fountas & Pinnell, 2006, p. 9). Teachers can help children in the process of making sense of text; they "help readers simultaneously:

1. Process the text with understanding and accuracy.
2. Create reasonable interpretations of the ideas in the text.
3. Expand their processing powers in a way that transfers to other texts" (Fountas & Pinnell, 2006, p. 9).

The reader must relate the meaning of the text to prior knowledge or experiences. Strategies such as K-W-L (Ogle, 1986), in which children describe what they know about a topic or concept before they read about it, support activation of prior knowledge. The National Reading Panel (NICHD, 2000) noted the role of teachers in teaching students skill in applying a variety of reading comprehension strategies. Improving reading comprehension comes through expanding experiences. The more we experience and have language to label and organize those experiences into knowledge, the better we will read about similar experiences. For example, to read stories about the zoo and the animals in the zoo is most appropriate in the context of a field trip to the zoo. Building background and prior knowledge for children who do not have a rich background of experiences as a foundation is a prerequisite to a unit of study or a story. Building background knowledge provides children with **schemas,** organized sets of notions or ideas about a topic. In addition, to comprehend material it must be on the appropriate reading level. Teachers can use a variety of diagnostic assessments to determine each child's individual reading level to properly match reader with text.

The National Reading Panel (NICHD, 2000) identified seven categories of comprehension instruction that appear to be scientifically based. They are:

1. Comprehension monitoring *(metacognition),* where readers learn to self-monitor and think about their own understanding of the text. Readers continually activate and connect the new to the known.
2. *Cooperative learning,* where students learn and support one another in various strategies in learning communities.
3. *Graphic organizers* such as story maps, or semantic maps, where readers make graphic or

visual representations of the text to outline or support comprehension. Graphic organizers lead readers to extract the main ideas and other important notions from the text.

4. *Question answering,* where readers answer questions posed by the teacher.

5. *Question asking,* where readers pose questions about the text. Questions are used both to clarify unfamiliar ideas and discover new information. Questions raised may lead the reader to make inferences.

6. *Story structure,* where students unravel various parts or structures of the text to help them derive meaning.

7. *Summarization,* where readers synthesize and generalize from the information in the text to comprehend it.

In addition to narrative or story text, **informational, nonfiction,** or **expository text** should be integrated into the curriculum, and research suggests that strategies for using informational text need to be different from narrative simply because the two texts are very different in composition and format (Duke & Bennett-Armistead, 2003; Stead, 2005). Expository or nonfiction text is more complex than narrative text. One of the reasons some students find expository text challenging is that they lack awareness of expository text structure (Dymock, 2005). According to Dymock (2005), most text structures fall into one of two groups that can be taught. One is the descriptive pattern in which attributes of something are described in detail. The other group is sequential structures that present a series of events or changes over time. Both these structures can be taught with graphic organizers such as webs, lists, or sequence boxes.

With skillful reading instruction readers can develop reasoning competence to make inferences, analyze situations, compare and contrast characters and settings, make connections, ask questions, draw conclusions, form concepts, and apply a variety of strategies (Harvey & Goudvis, 2007). This necessitates that readers actively and purposely respond to text; they attend or give full attention and thought to their reading.

Strategies to Support Reading

ACTIVE READING. Explicitly teach and model for young children how to use the following active reading strategies:

- *Predict:* Take guesses based on what happened in the story and what you think will happen next.
- *Question:* Ask questions that arise in your mind as you read.

- *Clarify:* When something is not understood, clear up the confusion.
- *Summarize:* Review the main plot of the story or the main ideas in the text.
- *Evaluate:* Form some opinions, draw some conclusions, and share what you think about what you have read.
- *Connect:* Make some comparisons or connects between what you have read and something in your own experience. Make comparisons with something you have read in another text.

QUESTION ANSWER RELATIONSHIPS (QAR). The QAR approach is research-based and supports students in improving reading comprehension (Raphael, Highfield, & Au, 2006). Using the QAR strategy students ponder the differences between questions with answer sources in the book and those whose answer source is the students' own thinking or in their own head (Raphael & Au, 2001). They build further on this and make additional choices:

- In the book:
  Right There—The question and answer are "right there" in the text.
  Think and Search—The answer is in the text but requires thinking and searching or making connections within a paragraph or between paragraphs.
- In my head:
  On My Own—The answer is not in the text. Readers have to use their own ideas and prior knowledge to answer.
  Author and Me—The answer is not in the text. Readers need to fit together what the author says and what they already know.

Beck and McKeown (2006) suggest that by teaching students to question the author, to consider and converse with an author's perspective and ideas, students are better able to engage with the author and build comprehension.

STORY MAP. Use the **story map** for narrative text. Answer the following questions:

What is the title of the story?

What is the setting of the story?

Who are the characters in the story?

```
┌─────────────────────────────────────────────┐
│                                               │
│                                               │
│                                               │
└─────────────────────────────────────────────┘
```

What is the problem in the story?

```
┌─────────────────────────────────────────────┐
│                                               │
│                                               │
│                                               │
└─────────────────────────────────────────────┘
```

Describe some of the events in the story.

```
┌─────────────────────────────────────────────┐
│                                               │
│                                               │
│                                               │
└─────────────────────────────────────────────┘
```

What is the solution to the problem in the story?

```
┌─────────────────────────────────────────────┐
│                                               │
│                                               │
│                                               │
└─────────────────────────────────────────────┘
```

IDEA MAP.   Use the **idea map** for expository text. Answer the following questions:

What is the main idea of this book?

```
┌─────────────────────────────────────────────┐
│                                               │
│                                               │
│                                               │
└─────────────────────────────────────────────┘
```

What are the details that support the main idea in this book? (Add as many boxes as you would like.)

```
┌─────────────────────────────────────────────┐
│                                               │
│                                               │
└─────────────────────────────────────────────┘
```

```
┌─────────────────────────────────────────────┐
│                                               │
│                                               │
└─────────────────────────────────────────────┘
```

STORY SEQUENCE.   Answer the following questions:

What happened at the beginning of the story?

```
┌─────────────────────────────────────────────┐
│                                               │
│                                               │
└─────────────────────────────────────────────┘
```

What happened in the middle of the story?

```
┌─────────────────────────────────────────────┐
│                                               │
│                                               │
└─────────────────────────────────────────────┘
```

What happened at the end of the story?

```
┌─────────────────────────────────────────────┐
│                                               │
│                                               │
└─────────────────────────────────────────────┘
```

A story sequence could be visualized in a circle graphic or in a linear fashion from one box to the next, moving from left to right.

3-2-1 STRATEGY.   The **3-2-1 strategy** encourages children to summarize key points from their reading and provides an opportunity for them to ask questions about their reading (Zygouris-Coe, Wiggins, & Smith, 2004/2005). A chart to prompt the strategy might look like this:

Topic/book/text:

3 things you discovered:

2 interesting things:

1 question you still have:

RECIPROCAL TEACHING.   The **reciprocal teaching** technique fosters discussion and supports readers in comprehending text (Oczkus, 2003; Palinscar & Brown, 1984). It includes four specific strategies: predicting, questioning, clarifying, and summarizing. The technique or its specific strategies is especially useful in whole-class direct teaching, in guided reading groups, or in literature circles (Oczkus, 2003). The specific strategies of predicting, questioning, clarifying, and summarizing can all be used before reading, during reading, or after reading text. This is a research-based strategy.

WORD WALL AND WORD BANKS.   Word walls are bulletin boards or places on the wall for words that children are learning to decode and recognize; they serve as a visual scaffold to temporarily assist children in their independent reading and writing (Brabham & Villaume, 2001; Cunningham, 2009). They may be words from particular categories or themes, such as weather words or words that begin with the letter *b*. They may be words that cause children to stumble such as *because, brought, eight, neighbor, the,* or *have.* Word walls help learners to remember the words that they are learning and then make the words readily available for reading and spelling. For emergent readers, teachers could write the words on small cards and put them in a pocket chart so that they could be used at a child's desk or to match words to objects and pictures. A word bank is similar to the word wall except it is an individual file of words that the student is interested in learning. These may be in a book, card file, or individual chart. Word walls and other similar strategies must be interactive, and the children must *do* something with them; they are not classroom adornment (Cunningham, 2009; Pinnell & Fountas, 1998).

AUTHOR'S CHAIR.   A chair in the classroom is designated as the **author's chair.** When students have finished a writing project, they sit in the author's chair to share their work with class members. After a student has shared his or her writing aloud, other students are invited to make comments and ask questions about the writing.

READER'S THEATER. **Reader's theater** is a dramatic, interpretative production of a story using the dialogue of the characters in the story. It motivates children, develops fluency, and builds comprehension through the repeated reading of text (Larkin, 2001). Children can use scripts directly from books or they can create their own scripts. Students assume various roles and then read the character's lines in the script. No costumes or props are required, and a narrator may guide the audience through the story.

CHORAL READING. Poems, songs, or stories are read aloud by students. They may read the entire script together, or they can divide it and read sections in small groups, or assign sections or lines to individuals.

GRAPHIC ORGANIZERS. Graphic organizers are visual displays of information for structured overviews used for prereading, during-reading, and postreading tasks (Dunston, 1992; Merkley & Jefferies, 2000/2001). Graphic organizers such as webbing can be used to demonstrate learning (Bromley, 1996) or to prompt writing (Sidelnick & Svoboda, 2000). A variety of graphic organizers can be used in reading to help students focus on or organize information.

- The **K–W–L strategy,** developed by Ogle (1986) for the purpose of activating students' prior knowledge and then helping them to determine their purpose for reading informational text, can be put on a chart with three columns. The first column is what I know (K), the second what I want to learn (W), and the third what I learned and still need to learn (L).
- Another example of a graphic organizer is the **Venn diagram.** This graphic organizer encourages learners to compare and contrast similarities and differences. For example, the Venn diagram includes two overlapping circles. In the middle of the overlapped circles you may put the similarities or common properties of two characters or places. In the two portions of each circle left, put the ways that each of the two characters is different or their individual properties.
- **Semantic maps** help children to see relationships in a particular topic. For example, in teaching the concept of seeds, this would be represented by a circle in the middle and lines with arrows and words written on the lines that represent the various relationships. Several lines might give examples of seeds; others might say *are, are used for, have* (Cooper et al., 2009).

- Word maps (Schwartz & Raphael, 1985) are graphic organizers that increase students understanding of words. They include information for *What is it? What is it like?* and *What are some examples?*

SUPPORTING STRUGGLING READERS

Every early childhood classroom has students who are struggling readers and they need highly qualified teachers who know appropriate interventions for meeting individual needs (Dole, 2004; Woodward & Talbert-Johnson, 2009). Struggling or striving readers need teachers who differentiate instruction, reach out to parents, and use research-based instructional approaches to instruct these students. Struggling readers need early interventions. One approach is the three-tier model of instruction known as Response to Intervention (RTI). RTI is part of the 2004 reauthorization of the Individuals with Disabilities Education Act or IDEA (PL 108-446) and is directed to prevent unwarranted assignment to special education. RTI is a systematic, data-driven process that promotes student learning through prevention, early intervention, progress monitoring, and use of research-based interventions (Batsche et al., 2005). Figure 8.4 illustrates the three tiers. Tier 1 serves all students; they receive high-quality instruction in the regular classroom. Tier 2 is supplemental instruction or targeted group interventions with some students. This instruction is delivered by the classroom teacher and support staff such as reading specialist/literacy coach and other trained specialists and paraprofessionals. It is generally in a small group. Tier 3 is intensive, individual intervention delivered by a special educator or reading specialist/literacy coach.

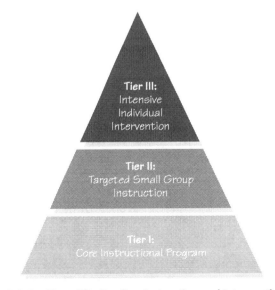

FIGURE 8.4 **Three-Tier Reading Instruction and Intervention**

Much research has been done on how to best meet struggling readers' needs. From their study of research-based practices, Ogle and Correa-Kovtun (2010, pp. 533–534) suggest the following: (1) provide reading materials at the student's level, (2) provide daily opportunities for oral language using academic or school vocabulary, (3) provide opportunities for students to ask and answer their own questions, (4) provide time for reflecting and clarifying understanding, and (5) provide guidance and support in using informational texts. From the perspective of a striving reader, the following suggestions were given to educators who work with readers who struggle: (1) teamwork among stakeholders, (2) build on the child's past successes, (3) connect that which the child reads to the world he or she lives in, (4) allow the child to self-select books and themes, and (5) provide the child with a variety of texts related to a single topic so that the topic is studied in depth (Jenkins, 2009).

When we recognize the processes good readers use in gaining meaning from text, we are better able to support struggling readers. Fountas and Pinnell (2009) suggest good readers are able to decode text efficiently, monitor understanding, and summarize material read. This is called "thinking within the text" (Fountas & Pinnell, 2009, p. 17). Good readers also make connections, infer, and synthesize new information and this is called "thinking beyond the text" (Fountas & Pinnell, 2009, p. 17). Lastly, according to Fountas and Pinnell (2009, p. 17), good readers are able to analyze and critique their reading and this is called "thinking about the text." Good readers use these skills and when a student is lacking some of these it can cause the child to struggle in reading. As early childhood teachers use assessments and monitor each child's progress in reading to determine what interventions are needed, support can be given to the struggling reader.

WRITING

Handwriting

Another ingredient in the language and literacy program is handwriting, which should be an integral part of the oral and written language program. There is a connection between listening, talking, reading, and writing. Diffily and Morrison (1996) suggest at least six different stages of writing: drawing, scribbling, invented letters, random letters, invented spelling, and common spelling. Matthew was drawing circle-type shapes on the fogged-up car window. "I'm writing in cursive," he proudly announced. "What does it say?" asked his father. "Oh, I don't know. I can only write in cursive, I can't read in cursive!" answered Matthew.

Before children can manage handwriting they need small-muscle coordination, eye–hand coordination, letter perception, or print awareness. Children need many experiences with tools such as paper, paints, pens, markers, chalk, brushes, pencils, and crayons to develop abilities not only in handling and using these tools, but also in making refined strokes. Adding envelopes and stamps encourages note "writing" to family, teachers, and friends. As children begin to understand symbols and expand their awareness that these symbols have meaning, alphabet letters begin to appear in their artwork (Dyson, 1990). Children should be able to copy simple shapes, differentiating likenesses and differences in both the shapes and sizes of objects and letters. Just as with reading, children must display a keen interest in learning to write and a desire to do so. For example, children who are ready for writing activities often try to write or copy letters, words, and even sentences.

Alphabet letters may be abstract to many children; allow them to explore and notice that words are made up of letters. Before children begin to write and use the alphabet letters in writing activities, they should have many experiences using alphabet and sight-word manipulative toys. For example, matching games with upper- and lowercase alphabet letters can be made by the teacher. Alphabet cards, either teacher made or purchased, can be used for various alphabet games and

Children must have many experiences involving the alphabet before they are able to read and write.

activities. Because many children develop writing skills at home, parents should be aware of when children might begin writing, aware of specific signs indicating readiness for writing instruction, and knowledgeable about how to teach correct skills.

Learning to form, remember, and read letters is a difficult, slow process, and each letter offers a unique challenge. Teachers must allow for mistakes, reversals, and incorrectly formed letters. It is challenging for children to maintain uniform size and stay within the lines. Writing takes much practice before it becomes natural, attractive, and neat. Teachers must be patient, allow plenty of time, praise positive efforts, and avoid pushing children who are not ready for the experience. Early experiences can be tracing activities; next experiences should be words, followed by short sentences and then short stories.

> Writing is thinking made manifest.

Writing or Composing

Readers use print or words to construct meaning, writers also use print or words to construct meaning. Preschool children may simply draw a picture to convey their story (Fields & DeGayner, 2000). Children learning to write need patient, supportive, accepting, and appreciative adults who realize that errors are a part of the learning process. Teachers should provide many opportunities for creative writing or composing, beginning with those experiences for which children dictate their ideas, stories, or poems to the teacher.

Reading and writing are interrelated (Schickedanz & Casbergue, 2009). Children learn to write as they are learning to read (Gentry, 2006). When children begin their first composition efforts, there should be no focus on the form of the writing, spelling, or punctuation. These mechanics can come later. Spelling, punctuation, neatness, and accuracy can be worked on once the child has had many experiences in writing for the sake of communicating an idea. Children's invented spellings for words help teachers to assess their level of understanding concepts and principles regarding the written word. Invented spellings are based on the sound of a word, rather than on sound–letter correspondence (Chapman, 1996; Schickedanz & Casbergue, 2009). As children invent their own spellings to represent the sounds of words, they are actually developing their abilities to use phonics (Diffily & Morrison, 1996). The initial focus in composing should be on the idea and the effort that the children make. Drill and practice writing are not appropriate for early childhood writing experiences.

The writing process (Calkins, 1994) involves the following components:

1. Prewriting (brainstorm the topic and generate ideas prior to writing)
2. Drafting (first attempt at writing the piece or story)
3. Conferencing (reflect and share writing with another for suggestions and changes)
4. Revising (making suggested changes)
5. Editing (attend to mechanics and refine the piece of writing)
6. Publishing (share the piece with others)

Emergent writers can use a modified writing process during the writer's workshop. The **writer's workshop** is a way of organizing some class time to do writing on a topic of the student's own choosing.

Teachers must be very flexible and cautious with emergent writers in using the writing process. It may be used only occasionally with those children ready for part or all of the process (Morrow, 2008). Many kindergarten children, for example, may not progress past the drafting stage because of their developmental phase. As children increase in their writing competency, additional steps of the writing process can be added. Some emergent writers, with excellent writing competency, will, over a period of time, reach the publishing stage with some of their work.

One of the most successfully used writing experiences in early childhood is journal writing. Children learn that here is an opportunity to express their thoughts and feelings and not have to worry about mechanics. They write to record things, and to share their thoughts and feelings. Journals are places where children write the stories of their experiences. Fields et al. (2007) advocate the teacher responding specifically to children's journal entries with comments that relate to the child's writing. At the end of the year, teachers and parents enjoy the sequence of activities and feelings expressed by the children, while seeing progress in the children's abilities to compose and write. The following guidelines for engaging children in journal writing:

- Set aside time daily to write or draw something in their journal.
- Each child should have a bound book for his or her writing.
- To start, tell children that writing or drawing is a way of recording or saving what you think or say, and tell them that they can begin by drawing and dictating or labeling their drawing.
- The teacher can suggest topics for children who have a difficult time getting started or thinking of something about which to write.

Generalizations for Effective Writing Experiences and Activities

1. Children should write every day.
2. Include a writing center in the classroom with writing and publishing materials.
3. Teachers should model effective writing behavior and share their own narrative stories with children.
4. Children's writing should grow out of real experiences.
5. Writing should be integrated throughout the curriculum.
6. Young writers should be given opportunities to share their work with others.
7. Expose emergent writers to aspects of punctuation as they are ready.
8. Invented spelling should be accepted (Schickedanz & Casbergue, 2009).
9. Give meaningful feedback through teacher–student conferencing and peer review of the child's writing to encourage progress (Bradley & Pottle, 2001).
10. Respect the children as writers, recognizing that there is a range of differences in every classroom (Bradley & Pottle, 2001).

In addition to journal writing, other writing activities are appropriate for the emergent writer. For example, children can draw pictures of a field trip or a family vacation and then write about each picture and put them into a book. They write a story for a roller movie by drawing the pictures and then writing about each picture. After completing the pictures and words, they can then put the long piece of paper on rollers and the rollers into a box. Another writing activity for young writers is to do their own flip-chart story and then read it from the author's chair. Very young children may need to dictate their story to an older child or adult. Almost any experience in the classroom or outside the classroom can be a prompt for a story. In early childhood, simple, self-authored books become texts for independent reading (Bradley & Pottle, 2001).

Writing can also be prompted in functional ways when children write birthday or other greeting cards to classmates, friends, or family members (Morrow, 2008). Notes to parents also offer opportunity for writing. Penpals and other letter writing experiences can be easily fostered, and using e-mail to correspond is another writing prompt.

When children are routinely involved in the writing process, their reading ability grows rapidly; readers become better writers and writers become better readers (Reutzel & Cooter, 2009). There is an interconnection between reading and writing. Children soon recognize that what they can think or say, what they can write (or someone can write for them), and what they can write, they can read.

Strategies to Support Writing

Some of the first reading experiences that teachers should provide for young children will be those that children have composed or "authored" themselves. Very early, children should learn that words they have spoken that has been written down could be read by someone. Therefore, as the children describe an experience, a picture that they have drawn, or their feeling about an idea, the teacher can write down their exact words, which can then be read back to the children. It is important to encourage *beginning* readers to write because children analyze their speech when they are writing and develop an ability to differentiate phonemes (Kamii & Manning, 2002).

IDEA: Class books can be made by giving the children an idea or they can create a book on a specific interest. The children will illustrate it and then dictate their description to an adult, which the adult writes on the illustration. Pages can be put together, with each child "authoring" a page. These books will become favorites to read again and again. Examples of class books are "Our Favorite Animals," "Zoo Animals We Like," "Favorite Dinosaurs," "Vacations We Have Taken," and ideas that tie into themes being explored.

Teachers should model and share their own personal writing. They should use picture books as models of good writing and the kinds of experiences and thoughts about which authors can write (McElveen & Dierking, 2000/2001). For example, books such as *Alexander and the Terrible, Horrible, No-good, Very Bad Day* (Viorst, 1972) or *When I Was Young in the Mountains* (Rylant, 1982) are the kinds of picture books that prompt students to discover their own personal experiences and thoughts to write about.

Many of the activities listed under "Activities for Listening and Speaking" in Chapter 7 can be adapted for reading and writing. Instead of listening, the children read; instead of speaking, they write. Simply adapt the activities to the developmental abilities of the children in your class.

There are a number of ways, beyond the early experiences just described, to help children who are ready for writing. To encourage children who are ready for more advanced writing experiences, you may wish to use one of the following approaches:

1. Show them how to build a web. For example, perhaps they will write about a summer vacation. The name of the vacation would be the center circle, and circles around that might be things that they did each day. One circle might be the beach, one an amusement park, one a visit to the zoo, and another a visit to Aunt Mary's. For each, ask children to describe what happened or what they remember about the experience, and then write these ideas around each circle, connecting them to the center circle. When they finish their web, each circle can represent a paragraph that they can write about.

2. A second approach is to give them steps to writing or the writing process. For example, you can teach them to think about their ideas and what they might write about and then brainstorm or organize these ideas and even number the order that the ideas should be in. Next, they should read what they wrote and make changes if they desire.

Students employ a wide range of strategies as they write and use different writing process elements appropriately to communicate with different audiences for a variety of purposes. (IRA/NCTE, 1996, Standard 5)

The following are some additional writing and reading activities that can be used in early childhood. Remember, just because children do not have handwriting skills does not mean that they cannot write. Instead, they can speak or dictate as an adult writes down word for word what they say.

- Early writing can begin with one-word labels of pictures or drawings of objects. Then children can write captions or phrases for pictures. Next they can write repetitive sentences such as "I like . . ." and put a different picture and word for each sentence. Soon children can write sentences for objects or pictures.
- Use open-ended proverbs. Give each child an open-ended proverb to finish by writing or dictating and then illustrating. The children fold their paper in half. On the left side, they write the part of the proverb assigned, and on the right side, they finish it. Or the first part of the proverb can

be written at the top of the paper and the children write or dictate the ending at the bottom of the page and then illustrate it in the middle of the paper. Examples of open-ended proverbs include the following:

Don't count your chickens . . .
He who is too greedy . . .
Think twice before . . .
Borrowed feathers . . .
Kindness works better . . .
You can't tell a book . . .
One good turn deserves . . .
The apple doesn't fall . . .
Half a loaf is . . .
Do unto others as . . .
Think before . . .
Biggest is . . .
Slow and steady . . .
A soft answer . . .
What goes up . . .
An ounce of prevention is worth . . .
Spare the rod and . . .
Silence is . . .

The following are some examples of how first-grade children completed some proverbs:

If you can't stand the heat . . . go in the snow.
A penny saved is . . . money in my bank.
The grass is always greener . . . on the ground.
Everything comes to him who . . . reads and makes money.
Money is the root of all . . . trees.
Early to bed and early to rise makes . . . me cry.
If at first you don't succeed . . . wait until you're stronger.
All that glitters . . . isn't the stars.
You can't teach an old dog . . . to read.

- Show the children a picture and have them dictate or write about it. Calendars, magazines, and photographs are sources for pictures.
- Have the children create an ABC of pretend monsters. Each child selects a letter of the alphabet, imagines a monster, and then writes or dictates a description of that monster. For example, A might be an "Atarox," a 17-foot-long garbage-eater that loves "rox" (rocks) for dessert. The children illustrate their monsters on their pages.
- Have the children bring a favorite possession from home in a paper bag. On the outside of the bag, they write at least five words that describe it without telling what it is. Class members guess what is in the bag.
- Give each cooperative learning group a different hat. Each group writes five words to describe the hat and then write who would use the hat.

- Give each cooperative learning group five words and have them write a synonym for each word. Examples include the following:

scream–yell	cent–penny
fast–speedy	little–small
glad–happy	leap–jump
pal–friend	share–divide
large–big	start–begin
hurry–rush	smell–sniff
town–city	smile–grin
skinny–thin	angry–mad
scared–afraid	save–keep
close–shut	stop–quit

This activity can be done with rhyming words, words that start with the same sound, antonyms, or other language activities.

- Have the children write recipes or directions for their favorite dishes.
- After reading a story, have the children orally describe or write about their favorite character.
- After reading a story or book, have the children describe a present that they would give to the main character or a character of their choosing.
- Pick an item that will change over time, and once every few days have the children write 5 to 10 words to describe it. Items might include a seed that will sprout, a flower, a glass of milk, a carved pumpkin, or a slice of bread in a moist wrapper.
- Assign each cooperative learning group a different topic or word and have them brainstorm and write as many ideas as they can for each spoke on the wheel shown in Figure 8.5. Topics might include insects, books, a yo-yo, homes, cages, umbrellas, spaceships, water, red, weekends, or spring, or topics might relate to a theme being studied.
- Set up a "mailbox" in the room and have the children write letters to a character such as Barnaby Bear or Lassie. When a child "mails" a letter, he or she should always receive a reply. Perhaps a volunteer parent could be assigned to answer each letter during the year.
- As a class, name a stuffed animal such as a bear. Each night one child will take the stuffed animal (the friend) home along with a binder with blank paper and stories about the friend written previously by classmates. The children are directed to take their friend with them to whatever activities they participate in and then at the end of the day make an entry in the binder about what they did with their friend. When the child comes to school the next morning, he or she sits in the author's chair along with the friend and reads his or her entry in the binder.
- Take advantage of the link between artwork and writing. When children draw or paint something and then describe their work, teachers can write on the children's papers what they dictate about their drawing or painting.
- Have writing materials in a specific area and use the computer as a writing center. Teach young children how to use the word processor on the computer for story writing (Fields et al., 2007). The writing center should have plenty of paper, pencils, and pens. It might also include envelopes, stamps, tape, staplers, paper clips, erasers, and anything else to encourage writing.
- Hold a consonant scavenger hunt. Throughout the classroom, put objects and pictures of objects

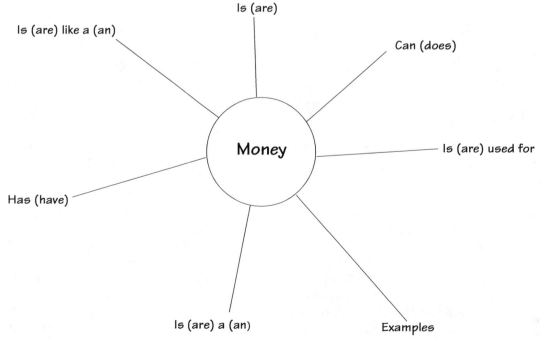

FIGURE 8.5 Topic Wheel to Stimulate Ideas

whose names begin with consonant sounds that the children have learned. Assign each child or pair of children a different consonant and have them search the room to find three items or pictures that begin with the sound of their consonant. After sharing their sound and the objects found to match it, they can return them, trade consonants, and do the scavenger hunt again (*Learning,* 1994).

- To make a game for working on compound words, use card stock paper or 5-by-8-inch index cards and write the first part of each compound word on the left side of the card and the second part on the right side. Laminate the cards and then cut them in half in a zigzag pattern so they become a puzzle. As children read them and match the correct pieces together, they will practice reading compound words.

- Have individuals or groups of children make reading flowcharts from a story, fingerplay, or poem that they have read. A flowchart shows pictures and words in the order of the events as they occurred in the story or phenomenon being described. They can also cut up newspaper cartoons, order them, and write new words for them. For younger children, cartoons can be cut up and used as an activity, ordering them from beginning to end.

- Following the reading of a favorite story, the children can make their own class big book of the story by having individual children illustrate each page and then author the words for their illustration (depending on their developmental level, they can either write the words or dictate them). When they are finished, they can put the pages together to be enjoyed in the reading center.

- The daily news can be used to benefit children's reading and writing. The children share events that are important in their lives. It can be written by the entire group or by small groups of students. This is motivating for children, because they enjoy reading about themselves, their friends, and the experiences of their classmates (Wiencek, 2001).

- Give the children open-ended similes to complete in the same way as completing the proverbs in a previous activity. Examples include the following:

As quiet as . . .	As busy as . . .
As sly as . . .	As slow as . . .
As slippery as . . .	As free as . . .
As wise as . . .	As red as . . .
As silly as . . .	As hungry as . . .

- Give the children story starters to complete. These can be done individually or in cooperative learning groups. Examples include the following:

  I make the most unusual sundae! First I take . . .

  I have an unexpected houseguest in the bottom drawer . . .

  While working in my lab late one night . . .

  I opened the door and . . .

  I know how to make a lizard laugh . . .

  My mom says, "Don't . . ."

- To encourage literacy learning with families, teachers can create family literacy bags. The bags might contain high-quality narrative or informational books relating to a particular theme, suggested activities, and a parent guide to explain the activities and how to read and discuss the books with children (Burningham & Dever, 2005). When working with ESL children, books can be sent in English and also in the native language.

Reading and writing should both be significant parts of the early childhood curriculum; they often are integrated together. Writing is thinking made manifest, and young children need to sense early that their thoughts can be put on paper and shared with others. Too often writing is left out of the curriculum, and then we wonder why older children lack writing skills.

In 1996 the International Reading Association (IRA) and the National Council of Teachers of English (NCTE) collaborated in publishing *Standards for the English Language Arts,* which suggests 12 standards for learning to ensure students are proficient language users. Table 8.1 includes the standards and some examples of our suggested applications.

Listening to, understanding, and following directions are all important aspects of literacy development.

TABLE 8.1 • Standards for the English Language Arts

Standards	What You Can Do
1. Students read a wide range of print and nonprint texts to build an understanding of texts, of themselves, and of the cultures of the United States and the world; to acquire new information; to respond to the needs and demands of society and the workplace; and for personal fulfillment. Among these texts are fiction and nonfiction, classic and contemporary works.	• Provide text in fiction and nonfiction as well as a variety of other kinds of works. Give children access to storybooks, alphabet books, and poetry books.
2. Students read a wide range of literature from many periods in many genres to build an understanding of the dimensions (e.g., philosophical, ethical, aesthetic) of human experience.	• Provide and read literature in genres such as folktales, fairytales, myths, biographies, fantasies, fables, legends, science fiction, historical fiction, or poetry.
3. Students apply a wide range of strategies to comprehend, interpret, evaluate, and appreciate texts. They draw on their prior experience, their interactions with other readers and writers, their knowledge of word meaning and of other texts, their word identification strategies, and their understanding of textual features (e.g., sound–letter correspondence, sentence structure, context, graphics).	• Teach specific literacy strategies (comprehension, vocabulary, decoding, interpreting, and evaluating) and teach the strategies to be used by children. Many examples are included in this chapter.
4. Students adjust their use of spoken, written, and visual language (e.g., conventions, style, vocabulary) to communicate effectively with a variety of audiences and for different purposes.	• Give opportunities to speak and write for different purposes. For example, children can write a letter to make a request, write a story to share an experience, participate in a reader's theater, share a book review, or a variety of other speaking and writing activities.
5. Students employ a wide range of strategies as they write and communicate with different audiences for a variety of purposes.	• Give opportunity to write every day: journal writing, roller stories, flip-chart stories, dictated stories, self-authored books, and other writing activities using various prompts and strategies.
6. Students apply knowledge of language structure, language conventions (e.g., spelling and punctuation), media techniques, figurative language, and genre to create, critique, and discuss print and nonprint texts.	• Teachers model and guide children in applying spelling and punctuation in their emergent writing. • Describe text structures such as expository text structures; for example, descriptive, sequence, comparison, cause and effect, or problem and solution text structures.
7. Students conduct research on issues and interests by generating ideas and questions, and by posing problems. They gather, evaluate, and synthesize data from a variety of sources (e.g., print and nonprint texts, artifacts, people) to communicate their discoveries in ways that suit their purpose and audience.	• Utilize the project approach in studying various topics and interests and orally share work with class members. • Conduct interviews on field trips or with classroom visitors to gather and chart information to be shared in class.
8. Students use a variety of technology and information resources (e.g., libraries, databases, computer networks, video) to gather and synthesize information and to create and communicate knowledge.	• Use technology for gathering and organizing information and data to share with class members. Internet searches on various topics can provide much information.
9. Students develop an understanding of and respect for diversity in language use, patterns, and dialects across cultures, ethnic groups, geographic regions, and social roles.	• Highlight the first language of class members and learn to speak some of the words in the various native languages. • Share stories and books that use the dialect of a unique culture; for example, *Flossie and the Fox* (McKissack, 1986).
10. Students whose first language is not English make use of their first language to develop competency in the English language arts and to develop understanding of content across the curriculum.	• Second language learners use their native language to communicate, learn, and bridge to the English language.

TABLE 8.1 • *(continued)*

Standards	What You Can Do
11. Students participate as knowledgeable, reflective, creative, and critical members of a variety of literacy communities.	• Organize book clubs in the classroom, school, or neighborhood for children to read, discuss, and share books together. • Literature circles provide opportunity for a small group of readers to interact with text.
12. Students use spoken, written, and visual; language to accomplish their own purposes (e.g., for learning, enjoyment, persuasion, and the exchange of information).	• Write notes, letters, cards, books; draw pictures and use other activities to communicate. • Use oral language to communicate in activities such as choral reading, singing, discussions, presentations, sharing books and personal experiences, author's chair.

Source: Standards for the English Language Arts, by the International Reading Association and the National Council of Teachers of English, Copyright 1996 by the International Reading Association and the National Council of Teachers of English. Reprinted with permission. Standards found at http://www.ncte.org/standards.

Summary

The early childhood years are a span of time when, for most children, there is an upsurge of growth in all areas of literacy. Children need a print-rich environment. They need to see adults reading and writing. They need access to a variety of genres and formats (e.g., fiction, nonfiction, poetry, alphabet books). They need to be given many and varied opportunities to make sense out of print and to express their thoughts in writing. They need teachers who understand that literacy is supported through rich, well-planned play-based experiences (Burke, 2010).

Teachers should make certain that practice in reading and writing is purposeful and that children see writing as a way to communicate meaningfully. Literacy should be integrated into every part of the curriculum, and young children should have many opportunities daily for writing and reading, even if that means reading and writing *to* or *with* the child rather than *by* the child on his or her journey toward independent work (Reutzel & Cooter, 2009). A variety of writing tools such as pencils, pens, markers, chalk, and crayons should be available.

Young children should have many opportunities to read for enjoyment from excellent literature, both narrative and informational. Children's experiences provide a frame of reference for them to draw on to make sense of and process what is read to them or what they read themselves. In addition, they need help if they are in reading trouble, ample materials for reading and writing, and much time to read and be read to.

The comprehensive literacy approach takes children from where they are, accepts what they do or do not bring with them, accommodates differences, and then builds on each child's language competencies and guides the child toward becoming literate and finding

joy, meaning, and pleasure in literacy. Children need to view others around them being literate; and then, as maturation, readiness, and experiences allow, children should be given many opportunities to talk, read, and write so that they view themselves as literate. Early childhood teachers can stimulate the child's interest in literacy and facilitate the child's efforts to become literate.

NAEYC EARLY CHILDHOOD PROGRAM STANDARDS

The National Association for the Education of Young Children (NAEYC) approved the Early Childhood Program Standards and Accreditation Performance Criteria (NAEYC, 2007). These standards guide programs in a variety of areas, including the curriculum. Standard 2 is Curriculum, and the Accreditation Criteria include some of the following under the heading Early Literacy Development*:

• **Children have varied opportunities to experience books individualized ways.**
What you can do: Read to individual children. Choose books according to their interests and abilities. Read to small groups of children and to the whole group. Read various types of books including narrative and informational books along with alphabet books, poetry books, and wordless

*Excerpted, adapted, and reprinted with permission, from National Association for the Education of Young Children, *NAEYC Early Childhood Program Standards and Accreditation Criteria: The Mark of Quality in Early Childhood Education* (Rev. ed.) (Washington, DC: NAEYC, 2008). Adapted from text of criteria associated with Standard 2, Curriculum (under Curriculum Content Area for Cognitive Development: Early Literacy). NAEYC Early Childhood Program Standards and Accreditation Criteria are available online at www.naeyc.org.

books. Listen to children read individually and in small groups as described in this chapter. Talk about the content of the books they are reading or that you are reading to them.

- **Foundations for early literacy are developed by building on children's enjoyment of books, songs, rhymes, and routine games and by planning daily opportunities for each child to hear and respond to various types of books including picture books, wordless books, and books with rhymes.**
  What you can do: Every day children should have opportunities to hear, respond to, and if possible read a variety of kinds of books. Use the strategies suggested in this chapter to help them respond to the books that you or they read.

- **Children participate in activities that allow them to become familiar with print.**
  What you can do: Help children capture the connection between print and spoken words. Guide children in making sense and meaning of environmental print in their classroom and home/community environment. Provide opportunities for children to use print.

- **Children have varied opportunities to learn to read familiar words, sentences, and simple books.**
  What you can do: Plan developmentally appropriate activities each day that give children opportunities to read. Use words they are working with in games and materials. Use words on word walls and other collections such as individual word banks. Encourage children to finger-point as they read books on their level.

- **Children have multiple and varied opportunities to write or dictate their ideas.**
  What you can do: Children can write in journals, on their artwork, in play and activity centers, or in writing books. Young children can dictate their journal entries or stories to an adult.

- **Children are regularly provided multiple and varied opportunities to develop phonological awareness.**
  What you can do: As children read or are read to, sing, do fingerplays, and hear poems, they are encouraged to play with sounds including phonemes, rhymes, and word families. They work with letters and letter sounds using manipulatives and a variety of activities and strategies. Daily experiences include systematic code instruction.

- **Children are given opportunities to recognize and write letters, words, and sentences as they are ready.**
  What you can do: Provide many materials for children to use in writing: letters for copying, paper, crayons, pencils, and other implements. Writing experiences initially use nonconventional forms such as invented spelling and over time more conventional forms. Children write different texts including stories, letters, poems, descriptions of art, reports, messages, and responses to literature they have read or listened to.

- **Children are encouraged to identify phonemes in words through varied activities, including writing and games.**
  What you can do: Use manipulatives and activities as outlined in this chapter in the section on phonemic awareness.

- **Books are displayed and writing is encouraged in one or more areas of the classroom.**
  What you can do: Set up centers that encourage writing and keep writing implements in a container at each child's individual desk or cubby. Have a mailbox available for children to write letters and assign volunteers to answer their letters. Children can take home a variety of writing activities to work on at home.

Student Learning Activities

1. Observe in an early childhood classroom with a focus on literacy development. What is the approach of this particular teacher to teaching literacy? What literacy components did you observe? Describe the activities that you observed, and identify the ways that each activity contributed to the development of literacy. For example, did the activity enhance listening or speaking skills? Did the activity teach new words? Were the activities appropriate, or can you think of ways to achieve the desired objectives and goals in a more appropriate way? Did the classroom integrate literacy development into all areas of the curriculum?

2. Plan, implement, and evaluate at least two activities to encourage emergent reading skills in young children.
3. Specifically plan, and if possible implement and evaluate, activities for teaching early childhood phonemic awareness, phonics, vocabulary, and comprehension.
4. Plan, implement, and evaluate at least two activities to encourage emergent writing skills in young children.
5. Select a meaningful picture book and then plan, implement, and evaluate a literacy lesson using the format described in this chapter.

Suggested Resources

The list of suggested resources for literacy development could be limitless, because there are so many excellent pictures, books, CDs, tapes, multimedia kits, films, videos, and computer software that could be used to stimulate speaking, listening, reading, and writing. Only a few of our favorites have been selected as examples here. Be selective in the kinds of resources that you choose to stimulate literary development in young children.

RESOURCES FOR CHILDREN'S LITERATURE

Cullinan, B., Galda, L., & Sipe, L. (2010). *Literature and the child* (7th ed.). Florence, KY: Cengage Learning/Wadsworth.

Gunning, T. G. (2000). *Best books for building literacy for elementary school children.* Boston, MA: Allyn & Bacon.

Hurst, C. O. (1997a). *Carol Otis Hurst's picture book guide: First and second grade.* DeSoto, TX: McGraw-Hill Learning Materials.

Hurst, C. O. (1997b). *Carol Otis Hurst's picture book guide: Prekindergarten and kindergarten.* DeSoto, TX: McGraw-Hill Learning Materials.

Justice, L. M., Pence, K. L., Beckman, A. R., Skibbe, L. E., & Wiggins, A. K. (2005). *Scaffolding with storybooks: A guide for enhancing young children's language and literacy achievement.* Newark, DE: International Reading Association.

Kasten, W. C., Kristo, J. V., McClure, A. A., & Garthwait, A. (2005). *Living literature: Using children's literature to support reading and language arts.* Upper Saddle River, NJ: Prentice Hall.

Lipson, E. R. (2000). *The New York Times parent's guide to the best books for children* (3rd ed.). New York: Times.

Lukens, R. J. (2006). *Critical handbook of children's literature* (8th ed.). Boston, MA: Allyn & Bacon.

Lynch-Brown, C., Tomlinson, C. M., & Short, K. G. (2005). *Essentials of children's literature* (7th ed.). Boston, MA: Allyn & Bacon.

Morrow, L. M., Freitag, E., & Gambrell, L. B. (2009). *Using children's literature in preschool to develop comprehension: Understanding and enjoying books* (2nd ed.). Newark, DE: International Reading Association.

Trelease, J. (2006). *The read-aloud handbook* (6th ed.). New York: Viking.

CHILDREN'S BOOKS CITED

Ahlberg, J., & Ahlberg, A. (1986). *The jolly postman or other people's letters.* Boston: Little, Brown.

Banks, L. R. (1981). *The Indian in the cupboard.* New York: Doubleday.

Banks, L. R. (1986). *The return of the Indian.* New York: Doubleday.

Banks, L. R. (1989). *The secret of the Indian.* New York: Doubleday.

Breathed, B. (1993). *A goodnight opus.* Boston: Little, Brown.

Brodmann, A. (1993). *The gift.* New York: Simon & Schuster.

Carle, E. (1969). The very hungry caterpillar. New York: Philomel.

Charlip, R. (1964). *Fortunately.* New York: Macmillan.

Charney, S. (1994). *Six thick thumbs: A tongue-twisting tale.* New York: Troll.

Dahl, R. (1961). *James and the giant peach.* New York: Knopf.

Estes, E. (1944). *The hundred dresses.* New York: Harcourt Brace Jovanovich.

Fitzhugh, L. (1992). *Harriet the spy.* New York: Harper & Row.

Hillman, B. (1995). *That pesky toaster.* New York: Hyperion Books for Children.

MacLachlan, P. (1985). *Sarah, plain and tall.* New York: Harper & Row.

MacLachlan, P. (1994). *All the places to love.* New York: HarperCollins.

McKissack, P. (1986). *Flossie and the fox.* New York: Dial.

McNaughton, C. (1994). *Making friends with Frankenstein.* Cambridge, MA: Candlewick.

Pilkey, D. (1994). *Dog breath: The horrible trouble with Hally Tosis.* New York: Blue Sky.

Rylant, C. (1982). *When I was young in the mountains.* New York: Dutton.

Samton, S. W. (1995). *Frogs in clogs.* New York: Crown.

Selden, G. (1960). *Cricket in Times Square.* New York: Farrar.

Shaw, N. (1994). *Sheep take a hike.* New York: Houghton Mifflin.

Speek, T. (1995). *Two cool cows.* New York: Putnam.

Trivizas, E. (1993). *The three little wolves and the big bad pig.* New York: Margaret K. McElderry.

Viorst, J. (1972). *Alexander and the terrible, horrible, no-good, very bad day.* New York: Atheneum.

Vozar, D. (1993). *Yo, hungry wolf!* New York: Bantam Doubleday Dell Books for Young Readers.

White, E. B. (1952). *Charlotte's web.* New York: Harper & Bros.

Wilder, L. I. (1932). *Little house in the big woods.* New York: Harper & Row.

Wilson, G. (1995). *Prowlpuss.* Cambridge, MA: Candlewick.

TAPES AND CDS

Many kinds of recordings can be used to stimulate language development. Using these can enhance listening skills. Children can listen to recordings to learn songs and sing along, they can be encouraged to listen for rhythms or beat patterns of rhythm records, and they will be anxious to listen to many story recordings. Using records, tapes, and CDs will stimulate oral language development of young children.

Online Resources

www.reading.org   This is the official site for the International Reading Association (IRA).

www.carolhurst.com   This is an excellent children's literature site.

www.acs.ucalgary.ca/~dkbrown/index.html   This site provides rich resources in children's literature for teachers, librarians, scholars, parents, and even children.

www.col-ed.org/   The Columbia Education Center's website is especially useful for student teachers and practicing teachers in grades K–12.

www.literacy.uconn.edu   This is a great literacy website.

www.nifl.gov   The National Institute for Literacy website provides great literacy information. The brochure *Put Reading First: Helping Your Child Learn to Read* is available at this website.

www.nationalreadingpanel.org   The National Reading Panel published the 2000 report, *Teaching Children to Read.* The report is available at this website.

www.ala.org/alsc   The American Library Association's children's division (ALSC) lists best books and award-winning books.

www.lii.org   The Librarians' Index to the Internet provides guides, children's book awards, and special pages of interest to kids.

www.ipl.org/ref/QUE/PF/kidmultilit.html   The Internet Public Library pathfinder on multicultural literature for children.

www.readingrockets.org   This is a great website with much reading and literacy information. It has a screening tool for parents and caregivers of preschool children to help in preparing children for kindergarten literacy. It gives information about teaching kids to read and helping those who struggle. The site includes current reading news, teacher's toolbox, curriculum ideas, tips for new teachers, and great articles.

www.billybear4kids.com   This is a fun and interactive site. It has materials you can copy and download, for example, the animal alphabet cards.

www2.nl.edu/reading_center/   This is the National Louis University site. Go to the Literacy link.

www.fcrr.org   Links for teachers and parents with materials and articles on all aspects of reading from the Florida Center for Reading Research.

http://readingserver.edb.utexas.edu/downloads/primary/booklets/word-study.pdf   The Word Study for Students with Learning Disabilities and English Language Learners site funded by the U.S. Department of Education offers myriad phonics activities.

www.janbrett.com   This is a fabulous website. Be sure to visit the activities pages and do some exploring.

www.starfall.com   This website is for children who are learning to read. It was created by Stephen Shultz, who struggled to learn to read when he was a boy.

www.randallklein.com   Lots of phonics materials are available for purchase at this site at reasonable prices.

www.fountasandpinnellleveledbooks.com   Learn about leveling books. You can subscribe to their leveled lists of books.

www.readwritethink.org   This is a joint project with IRA and the National Council of Teachers of English with MarcoPolo and MCI Foundation. The site offers standards-based, peer-reviewed lesson plans and other resources for teachers working with students aged 5 to 12.

www.bartleby.com   This is one of the largest and most comprehensive full-text free public reference libraries on the web.

www.kidsreads.com   This site provides information for children about their favorite books, series, authors, and characters, including the newest titles, in-depth author profiles, and more.

www.Funbrain.com   This site offers online games for children organized by grade level and a subject area maintained by Pearson Education.

www.rif.org   Reading Is Fundamental offers an educator's area where teachers will find lesson plans, book suggestions, and seasonal information to help in the classroom.

chapter 9

Physical Science Experiences

Young children have a natural curiosity about the world—they are full of eagerness, wonder, and enthusiasm for learning. They have an inherent desire to explore, investigate and to question (Bosse, Jacobs, & Anderson, 2009). This where science education begins! "Almost all young children in almost all environments 'do science' most of the time; they experience the world around them and develop theories about how that world works" (Conezio & French, 2002, p. 12). Young children are often referred to as "natural scientists," because they engage in many of the same behaviors that actual scientists do (Brenneman, 2009). This natural curiosity can lead them to exciting discovery and exploration (Conezio & French, 2002). These principles are captured in the goals recommended by the National Center for Improving Science Education (NCISE) (1990, p. 9). They are to:

- Develop each child's innate curiosity about the world.
- Broaden each child's procedural and thinking skills for investigating the world, solving problems, and making decisions.
- Increase each child's knowledge of the natural world.

In 1995, after nearly 5 years of development, the National Research Council (NRC) (1996) completed the National Science Education Standards. These standards suggest criteria for judging quality in:

- Scientific knowledge of students
- Excellence in teaching
- Professional development for teachers
- Assessment procedures
- Programs to support effective science teaching

These standards are of particular importance to teachers in early childhood education in two specific areas: science content and teaching science—or what should we teach and how should we teach it? These questions will be addressed throughout Chapters 9, 10, and 11. The standards suggest that the goal of science education should be science literacy, and promote wonder, inquiry, and understanding.

All children should develop abilities necessary to do scientific inquiry and an understanding about scientific inquiry.

Source: Reprinted with permission from "Content Standards K–4, Science as Inquiry, Content Standard A," *National Science Education Standards,* 1996 by the National Academy of Sciences, Courtesy of the National Academies Press, Washington, DC.

The National Science Education Standards, by emphasizing both excellence and equity, highlight the need to give all students the opportunity to learn science. Children need access to skilled teachers, a variety of learning materials, available workspaces, adequate classroom time, and community resources

This teacher is extending problem-solving skills by supporting children as they build a ramp.

(NRC, 1996). Science is action, and it must involve both "minds-on" and "hands-on" experiences (NRC, 1996). Science for young children is not just a list of facts and information that have been discovered by other people. It is a process of doing and thinking, a process that anyone can participate in and contribute to (Brenneman, 2009). "Science is what children do. More than just watch, they engage. They are exhilarated by small observations. They experiment and discover" (Shaffer, Hall, & Lynch, 2009, p. 19).

Children's natural curiosity provides the motivation for them to ask questions, then explore ways to answer their own questions (Cowan & Cipriani, 2009). Their questions reflect their interest in everything about them—nature, people, animals, plants, and so on. "Do snakes crawl backward?" "What does an earthworm eat?" "Do trees have birthdays?" "Why do magnets pick up pins?" Promoting inquiry-based learning in the classroom includes asking questions to learn prior knowledge, asking open-ended questions, encouraging children to think before answering questions, and repeating or rephrasing what children have said (Ogu & Schmidt, 2009). "What if . . . ?" questions are so valuable both for children and teachers to consider in science explorations. These endless questions often open avenues into the realm of science. As we answer questions through exploring, providing experiments and materials, and problem solving, we are encouraging the child's continued curiosity. This great emotion of curiosity and its importance in learning was discussed by Rachel Carson (1956, pp. 42–43) more than 55 years ago.

If I had influence with the good fairy who is supposed to preside over the christening of all children, I should ask that her gift to each child in the world be a sense of wonder so indestructible that it would last throughout life, as an unfailing antidote against the boredom and disenchantments of later years, the sterile preoccupation with things that are artificial, the alienation from the sources of our strength.

Although reasons for science instruction are usually stated in terms of cognitive objectives, Stone and Glascott (1997/1998) remind teachers of the importance of also including the affective (or emotional) side of science. This involves three important areas for consideration:

- Affective environment (risk-free, enjoyable, not bound by time limits, allows choices)
- Affective teacher (models excitement, enjoyment, and desire to know; values and supports children's explorations)
- Affective child (experiences autonomy, self-confidence, self-esteem, success, freedom to explore)

The benefits of science for young children also include the promotion of intellectual growth, greater potential for success in school, and opportunities for the development of positive self-image. "When science is in the air, infused into daily classroom life, we encourage wonder and help children develop a greater appreciation of the world and their place in it" (Bosse et al., 2009, p. 14).

THE TEACHER

"National and state standards stress that all children can learn science and that they have the right to become scientifically literate" (Colker, 2002, pp. 10–11). Early childhood educators agree that science should be included in the classroom.

The outcomes of too many science activities are controlled by the teacher, rather than by the children—by the product, rather than by the process. Our responsibility is to guide and facilitate, not dictate nor direct children's science explorations. One of the most fundamental goals of an early childhood science program is to develop children's inquiry skills. These inquiry skills include questioning, exploring, observing, describing, comparing, sorting, classifying, ordering, using tools, investigating, making predictions, gathering and interpreting data, recognizing patterns, drawing conclusions, recording, working with others, sharing, discussing, and listening (Worth & Grollman, 2003).

When children's natural inquiry and curiosity drive the outcomes of science experiences, understanding is expanded, motivation is maintained, and retention is increased.

Inquiry is a very active part of the physical science curriculum. Nonliving objects and materials can be acted on and manipulated in different ways. Simple investigations and experiments allow children to collect data, draw conclusions, question, predict, and theorize (Worth & Grollman, 2003). They are able to try things over and over again, with the same results, or exploring other possibilities. "Young children are highly capable of devoting long periods of attention to something that captures their interest and purpose" (Zan & Geiken, 2010, p. 14).

The teacher's interest and curiosity often kindles the child's interest in exploring and finding out. When the teacher's behavior demonstrates a sense of interest, wonder, and curiosity, the children model it. Answered questions add to children's reserves of knowledge and increase their interest in, awareness of, and understanding of the world in which they are living. However, it is best to allow them to discover the answers themselves through exploring, reading, listening, questioning, observing, and other process skills. Skilled early childhood education teachers "understand that direct exploration of materials and meaningful phenomena is the cornerstone of science for young children" (National Association for the Education of Young Children [NAEYC], 1996a, p. 83). Teachers must also recognize that there is a difference between a "science demonstration" and a "hands-on" science experience (Spangler, 2009, p. 62). Young children will learn much more about their physical world from the latter!

Moriarty (2002) reminds us that teachers must have a basic understanding of science, children should have access to materials that allow them to observe and explore scientific phenomena, and reflection is a valuable component of the science inquiry process. A rich science environment includes such materials as typewriters, printers, and supplies for making books; fraction and geometric materials; math manipulatives; balance scales, rulers, graded containers for liquid and solid materials; stethoscope, prism, magnifying glass; natural materials; animals and plants; and computer programs relating to language arts, numbers, colors, problem solving, and concept development (M. B. Bronson, 2004). The term *technology,* as it is used in Chapters 9, 10, and 11, refers to the tools and instruments involved in studying the sciences.

All children should develop abilities of technological design, understanding about science and technology, abilities to distinguish between natural objects and objects made by humans.

Source: Reprinted with permission from "Content Standards K–4, Science and Technology, Content Standard E," *National Science Education Standards,* 1996 by the National Academy of Sciences, Courtesy of the National Academies Press, Washington, DC.

"Because . . . children learn best by working with concrete materials, employing all their senses and discussing their ideas, early childhood teachers help children do science rather than only read about it" (NAEYC, 1996a, p. 84).

SCIENCE CURRICULUM

We need to revitalize our science curriculum through an integrated, interdisciplinary program that utilizes hands-on learning activities and experiences.

Science is, and should be, a natural part of a child's daily experiences. It is not a separate subject to be reserved for specific experiences in the curriculum; it is present everywhere in the world around the children, and they are anxious to explore it, discover answers, and build new understandings.

Keep science integrated into the entire curriculum, that is, where it naturally is, in math, history, health, literacy, and so on. Language and literacy development are strongly supported when science activities are included throughout the curriculum. Both receptive and expressive language skills are fostered as children expand vocabularies and increase their problem-solving abilities while participating in the daily routines of music, art, drama, cooking, book and story reading, field trips, visitors, outside play, sensory table, and manipulative toys. "Science learning provides a rich knowledge base that will become an essential foundation for later reading comprehension. It also provides the foundation for meaningful language and literacy development" (Conezio & French, 2002, 18). Do not treat science as a segregated topic to be explored every so often in designated themes or set time schedules. Science is much broader than doing science tables, science projects, science centers, having bug collections, and going on nature walks. Naturally occurring science explorations can best be included through meaningful, relevant, hands-on activities that are developmentally appropriate for children.

Take advantage of the unplanned experiences and select planned activities from the children's daily experiences. Many science activities are planned ahead of time. However, take time with the children to notice and enjoy the everyday wonders of science: fluffy clouds, lacy spider webs, soft breezes, the daytime moon, flower shoots, migrating insects, rain puddles, drifting snowflakes, darting fireflies, crisp leaves, snakeskins, singing birds, and so on. When materials for exploring the physical world are included in the daily learning environment, when we ask open-ended questions, and when children record their experiences, we are helping them to experience physical science.

It is important for children to be able to develop an awareness of physical materials and objects. Concepts of texture, color, shape, size, weight, softness/hardness, buoyancy, sound, light, temperature, position, and movement, can all be investigated both indoors and outdoors. Simple tools provide continued motivation and curiosity as they allow further exploration (Worth & Grollman, 2003). Creative thinking, problem solving, decision making, cooperative learning, social interactions, verbal skills, and self-confidence are all enhanced in an effective science curriculum.

> A high-quality early childhood science program should reflect the following six characteristics (Worth & Grollman, 2003, p. 14):
>
> - It builds on children's prior experiences, backgrounds, and early theories.
> - It draws on children's curiosity and encourages children to pursue their own questions and develop their own ideas.
> - It engages children in in-depth exploration of a topic over time in a carefully prepared environment.
> - It encourages children to reflect on, represent, and document their experiences and share and discuss their ideas with others.
> - It is embedded in children's daily work and play and is integrated with other domains.
> - It provides access to science experiences for all children.

VALUE OF SCIENCE ACTIVITIES

Science should not emphasize teaching children facts, but should involve them in the process of understanding their world through observing, manipulating, problem solving, and engaging with science activities and materials. "Doing science" can occur in any place at any time and should be integrated throughout the curriculum.

Process and inquiry skills provide the framework for science education in early childhood, and children should be encouraged to develop them as they participate in science experiences. Examples of skills include:

- Analyzing
- Classifying
- Communicating
- Comparing
- Computing
- Counting
- Creating
- Defining
- Describing
- Discussing
- Drawing conclusions
- Experimenting
- Explaining
- Exploring
- Gathering and interpreting data
- Hypothesizing
- Inferring
- Investigating
- Listening
- Measuring
- Observing
- Ordering
- Organizing
- Predicting
- Questioning
- Recognizing patterns
- Recording
- Sharing
- Sorting
- Using tools
- Verifying
- Working with others

These skills are important in the cognitive, reasoning, and thinking processes. Process skills are, in fact, thinking skills; these skills affect every area of learning and can be particularly encouraged and developed in science activities.

Teachers should pay careful attention to the skills just listed and should write direct objectives for science activities and other appropriate experiences that will assist in the development of these skills. Skillful, careful, and wise instructors teach children to observe, compare, create, communicate, analyze, and hypothesize. The kinds of comments, questions, and approaches to planned activities, as well as the activities themselves, aid in developing these process or thinking skills. Teachers should constantly be aware of children's individual development in science and try to stretch their abilities by expanding process skills and teaching higher-level process skills as children are ready for them.

To elaborate further on the process and inquiry skills that will be particularly utilized in early childhood: In **observing**, children are taught to use all their senses to learn about things and experiences. In **comparing**, children compare likenesses and differences among objects and ideas. In **classifying**, children are asked to group or sort by categories, to find something that does not belong, and to be able to name the group or say how the members of a group are alike.

Communicating is using words orally and, for children in the later early childhood years, writing to explain or describe an event or happening. In **measuring,** children are involved in using standard or nonstandard units of measure. In either case, the children give a quantitative description, which may involve time, distance, volume, temperature, weight, or numbers. When children **infer** something, they observe and add meaning to their observation. When they **predict,** they guess what they expect will happen. When they **record** information, they either dictate or write down what they observe.

In the science classroom, children's books and stories can help students develop the skills of observing, comparing, classifying, and predicting. Photographs are another valuable tool for helping support young children's science inquiry. They help children revisit and extend their investigations, reflect on building experiences and articulate their strategies, and analyze and synthesize data. Digital cameras have several advantages over the standard cameras, because they allow us to see the photos directly after they are taken; photos can be edited on the computer; print size can be manipulated; photos can be saved on the computer for later access; and individual children's learning can be readily documented. Early science learning can also be documented through records of children's conversations, anecdotal notes of their actions, and samples of drawings and constructions.

However, science is more than these processes alone. Science experiences in early childhood should help children to form scientific concepts. Science activities that build on children's natural curiosity help them to learn about physical properties and stimulate problem-solving skills.

Science, then, enables children to better understand their world. By understanding their environment, some of their fears are alleviated, they are more comfortable with nature, and they have an increasing awareness of the events, people, and materials surrounding them. Sciencing is of value because it creates high interest and is fun, exciting, and enjoyable. Through science studies, particularly open-ended or discovery activities, children develop methods of thinking that include problem solving, inquiry, reasoning, and rationalizing.

Science activities encourage children to observe, explore, inquire, and make generalizations, and they provide opportunities to use and develop sensory capacities—to see, hear, taste, smell, and touch. The children will gain scientific knowledge as they learn to use skills that scientists use: inferring, observing, interpreting, classifying, and drawing conclusions. Curiosity is what makes children want to wonder and explore, and it is curiosity that makes scientists want to do the same thing.

> All students should develop understanding of science as a human endeavor.
>
> *Source:* From "Content Standards K–4, Science as a Human Endeavor, Content Standard G," *National Science Education Standards,* 1996 by the National Academy of Sciences, Courtesy of the National Academies Press, Washington, DC.

> Children and scientific researchers have one thing in common—they are both scientists at play! (Ross, 2000)

TEACHING METHODS

"Teachers willing to invest in physical science activities will enable learning to be a challenging, yet joyful experience, and inspire a love for learning that lasts a lifetime" (Kato & Van Meeteren, 2008). Teachers must find the time to teach science, and they must have a strong motivation to do so (Buchanan & Rios, 2004). Two strategies that warrant consideration when addressing the ways that we approach children and science learning are the K–W–L (Ogle, 1986) and the learning spiral (Hobbs, Dever, & Tadlock, 1995). The **K–W–L** strategy encourages children to pursue their sense of wonder by sharing what they *know* (K) about a subject, determining what they *want* (W) to know about the subject, and then sharing what they have *learned* (L). The **learning spiral** suggests that we create developmentally appropriate practice in early childhood classrooms through engaging, investigating, sharing, and assessing. Both of these strategies support learning throughout all areas of the integrated curriculum. The primary objective is to create a learning environment that encourages children to use their developing skills to understand their physical and social surroundings (Dever & Hobbs, 1998).

Because concepts are built slowly from numerous activities and facts, teachers should plan many related science experiences to reinforce a single idea. Science activities become less meaningful to children if they are offered as isolated events. Random experiences are not sufficient to allow children to link important ideas together and fit them into other meaningful situations. Science notions and concepts should also be built on what the child already knows. Therefore, teachers need to inventory what the children know, understand, and are familiar with and then add concepts that are new and unfamiliar.

There are seven tasks teachers must do to effectively implement this high-quality early childhood program (Worth & Grollman, 2003, p. 14):

- They choose a focus for inquiry.
- They prepare themselves to teach the topic.

- They create a physical environment that supports inquiry.
- They plan a schedule that allows time for inquiry.
- They foster children's questioning.
- They encourage children's work and deepen their understanding.
- They observe and assess individual children and the group.

There is value in having some experiences that are structured; that is, the answers or conclusions are predetermined, and only one conclusion is correct. (For example, if a plant has neither water nor light, it will die.) However, many of the activities should have an open-ended or discovery approach; that is, there is no single correct answer, but rather many possibilities or hypotheses. (For example, while exploring with water, ask the children, "How many different ways can you think of that we use water?") Both types of activities encourage the kind of thinking that we are endeavoring to develop in young children.

Some science activities suggested in this book are of the more structured type in which a conclusion can be drawn as a result of the experience. Examples include the salt-chemical garden, as well as experiences involving changes in properties such as texture, size, and shape. However, even with these kinds of experiences, teachers should still take advantage of the discovery approach and not be too hasty in giving the answers or conclusions. Allow the children to discover them. *Caution*: Do not smother a child's interest and curiosity with too many facts and instructions.

There are also experiences that lead children to question and explore, but the conclusions must remain open ended. For example, one may ask, "How many hairs do I have on my head?" This problem may lead to a study of hair and the average number of hairs that a person may have, but it is doubtful that the child will be able to obtain a specific conclusion or answer, nor can the teacher supply that answer! Children should not be discouraged by unanswerable questions and problems. Remind them that thousands of scientists are working today to discover the answers to many questions.

One of the most exciting ways to teach science is by taking advantage of spontaneous learning experiences. Be aware of opportunities for daily science experiences, such as those with animals, plants, numbers, nutrition, creative art, music, social studies, and numerous others. The child may ask a question that could lead to an entire unit of study. A child may ask where a butterfly sleeps. This could result in a unit on butterflies, insects, or sleeping habits of animals. Children's inquiry and learning are encouraged when they become actively involved in projects.

Take advantage of the daily happenings and of the materials often brought into class. A child bringing in an icicle could stimulate a unit of study on the forms of water, especially focusing on ice and how it is formed and used. Illustrations from the authors' own experiences include the day a cement mixer poured a cement platform in the children's playground. A science experience emerged relating to the ingredients of cement and the mixing, pouring, and setting of cement. Another activity occurred when people entered the classroom to fix a broken radiator. The children were invited to gather around and watch as the radiator was repaired. The experience included a discussion of heat and its source. As steam escaped, it was discussed as a form of water, and the tools needed to repair it were named while the children observed them in use.

Another approach to teaching science is the use of a science center or science interest table. This area, like other areas of the room, can be used continually or occasionally. Materials can be put out for the children to explore, or science activities can take place on an individual basis in these areas. The materials used and activities selected need to be simple. For example, place some modeling clay and toothpicks beside a tub of water. Challenge the children to work with and model the clay to make cargo ships, with the toothpicks becoming cargo. In this subtle way, they can learn concepts of sinking, floating, and displacement. If a science theme has been selected as a unit of study, the science center or table can serve as reinforcement and review.

Science should be integrated throughout various aspects of the curriculum. As food activities are being carried out, there are many opportunities for exploring and including scientific concepts. What will happen to the butter when the electric pan is turned on? What will happen to the dry ingredients when the milk is added? What is happening to the cream as it is being whipped? Is something being added? Is it getting larger or smaller? Will it weigh the same before and after it is whipped?

Music activities also offer opportunities for exploration of science. Experiment with sound and the changes in sounds as the size of the strings of instruments changes. Explore the parts of instruments and how they work. Additional science opportunities can be found in the realm of art. What happens to media such as glue and papier-mâché as they dry? The secondary colors are often successfully taught through exploring and combining different colors of paints. Individual activities during free play, such as the sensory table or trough, blocks, easel painting, books, and manipulative materials, all offer opportunities for critical thinking and science exploration. Outdoor play offers limitless experiences in science concepts.

Field trips and visitors, by providing the firsthand experiences so valuable for scientific learning, offer nat-

Susan

How many days for the seed to sprout?

1	2	3	4	5
N	N	N	N	Y

N = No
Y = Yes

How many days before the chicks hatch?

N = No
Y = Yes

1	2	3	4	5	6	7	8	9	10	11
N	N	N	N	N	N	N	N	N	N	N
12	13	14	15	16	17	18	19	20	21	22
N	N	N	N	N	N	N	N	N	Y	

FIGURE 9.1 Sample Charts for Recording Observations

ural ways for teaching science. Field trips frequently require no resource persons other than the teacher; however, if field trip resource persons or classroom visitors are involved, they should be well informed about the concepts that you are teaching and should be given specific instructions regarding age-appropriate discussions or experiences.

When parents and families become involved with reinforcing children's science concept learning, they support and encourage the further scientific inquiry. Families can encourage children's self-initiated activities, and help them realize that science is everywhere (Crawford, Heaton, Heslop, & Kixmiller, 2009; NRC, 1996; National Science Teachers Association [NSTA], 2009). "If science consists of activities only in the classroom, children are less likely to see themselves as learners of science outside the classroom" (Chalufour & Worth, 2006, p. 102). If children are given a choice, they will usually prefer to become involved in outdoor activities before indoor activities, and do more hands-on projects than worksheets (Winters, Ring, & Burriss, 2010). We will be more successful in our teaching, and children will be more successful in their learning, if we extend our classroom to the outdoors.

Many activities in science lend themselves to record keeping, thereby enhancing measuring, observing, and recording skills. For example, when sprouting a bean seed in a glass jar between a wet towel and the jar, the children can record how many days it takes for

their seed to sprout (see Figure 9.1). On a daily basis, the children can record the weather with symbols on a calendar, and then at the end of the month they can compute how many days of sunshine, rain, clouds, or snow there were in that particular month. Still another example is observing the incubation period of eggs and recording how many days it takes for the eggs to hatch (see Figure 9.1).

The safety of the children should be of primary concern in planning science activities. As well as eliminating fears, science offers the opportunity to teach the use of caution. The teacher must model intelligent caution while encouraging exploration and investigation. The teacher should always know and understand what is going on and help children to understand where and why precautions are necessary. Never assign children a task or let them participate in an activity for which they are not developmentally ready. However, as they become ready for new tasks and adventures that involve safety factors, supervise them closely and carefully as they are learning. Give them rules that are necessary for their own health and safety, as well as those of their classmates.

Science activities can be planned on an individual, small-group, or whole-group basis. In small groups, cooperative learning works well as the children use experimentation and discovery to reach possible solutions. Often, when a science experience is explained and demonstrated to a whole group, it readily adapts to follow-up either individually or in small groups. This enables the children to try out the materials while the experience is clarified, explained, and reinforced.

As with other concepts, once a science concept has been taught, the teacher needs to receive feedback from the children to determine whether the ideas and information have been properly synthesized and understood.

Science is important. It is a way of life. It brings children into closer touch with themselves and the world that they live in. Children enjoy science; they love to discover, explore, and find out! "Young children's sense of wonder is a natural asset that can be refined in preparation for life-long inquiry skills" (Blake, 2009, p. 52).

Some Practical Suggestions

- *Do* have actual materials for children to explore. Make certain there are ample supplies of containers, magnifying glasses, paper and pencils, and crayons.
- *Do* use the sensory table or similar container for science materials and equipment. For example, fill the table with soil, often including some earthworms and/or insects. Put the balance scales in the table with boxes, blocks, or other toys, or even with sensory media such as sand or wheat. Put egg cartons, eyedroppers, and colored water in the trough for color-mixing experiences.
- *Do* frequently provide sciencing tools such as magnifying glasses, thermometers, magnets, and scales. Include them with the sensory media, at the science table or corner, or outdoors. When children are constructing, touching, etching, coloring, and exploring in the outdoors, they are better able to make connections with their natural world.
- *Do* develop an interested, curious, and enthusiastic attitude toward science yourself. The children have some inherent interest in and enthusiasm for science, but they will also catch much of the teacher's spirit.
- *Do* relate science activities and units to the children's environment and their daily experiences. For example, it may not be wise to do a whole unit on the walrus unless the children are familiar with it. However, such a unit would provide an excellent study in some locations. There are many possibilities for units and activities for children that relate to *their* world, *their* weather, the plants in *their* locality, and the animals in *their* environment.
- *Do* perform experiments and activities ahead of time to have confidence in what is being done. The success of many experiments depends on the specific ways that they are carried out. Previous tryouts provide knowledge and assurance in the performance of the experiment.

- *Do* remember to use open-ended questions such as: "What do you think . . .?" "What can you do with . . .?" "Can you . . .?" "What would happen if . . .?" "How else . . .?" "Do you think . . .?" "Why do you think . . .?" These questions have no wrong answers, and allow for unlimited and expandable possibilities.
- *Do* scale down ideas and concepts to the child's level of understanding. During activities, ask questions frequently to determine whether the information being taught is also being understood. Do not erroneously assume that the child already knows some of the basic concepts.
- *Avoid* making science activities magic; make them a part of the real world and help children to see the cause-and-effect relationship. Magnets are not magic; they are tools of science. Thunder and lightning are not magical or unidentified happenings; they are acts of nature that have a cause and an effect.
- *Be willing* to say "I don't know." Attempt to help children to find the answers to their questions. Seek answers through books, materials, computer software sources, and knowledgeable persons.
- *Prohibit* children from using dangerous equipment, materials, or substances. For example, when doing experiments involving fire, the teacher should perform the activity. However, teach children how these materials are used and the caution necessary in handling them.
- *Avoid* teaching only scientific facts; assist children in learning to think, discover, and solve problems.

Note: The remainder of this chapter addresses specific activities and experiences involving the physical sciences.

All children should develop an understanding of properties and materials; position and motion of objects; light, heat, electricity, and magnetism.

Source: Reprinted with permission from "Content Standards K–4, Physical Science, Content Standard B," *National Science Education Standards,* 1996 by the National Academy of Sciences, Courtesy of the National Academies Press, Washington, DC.

TEACHING ABOUT COLOR

Children delight in learning colors. Color is a concept that children live with daily. They see, feel, use, and respond to colors. Usually, when we teach young children about colors, we rely mostly on the visual aspects, even though we know that children learn best through multisensory discovery, experimentation, and investigation.

Excitement of discovery is experienced when children work with various media to mix colors.

Infants are quick to notice brightly colored objects and patterns in their surroundings. Using color names is one way that a child can describe his or her world. In addition, a child uses them for classification and seriation as he or she orders them from lightest to darkest.

Being aware of various properties of color enables us to understand better how color concepts can be approached in the early childhood curriculum. These properties include name (or hue), intensity or saturation (brightness or dullness), pure (primary) or mixed (secondary), and value (lightness or darkness).

Color Concepts and Labels

Color often is used as a clue in identifying and describing objects before other concepts, such as size, shape, and number, are used. When becoming interested in color, the child first recognizes what color is and describes items in terms of color. However, frequently the color label is wrong; it takes time to learn correct color labels. When beginning to learn colors, the child may be unable to label or name the colors, and yet is able to recognize that a particular item is the same color as another item. In effect, the child is able to *match* colors. Comments such as the following may be heard: "My shoes are licorice color" or "I want to wear the lemon shirt" or "I'll use the book that's fire-engine color."

One day as Creighton entered the classroom, the teacher asked him if he remembered the color of his eyes. When his expression indicated that he had forgotten, and because there was no mirror close by, the teacher gave him a clue by saying, "They're the same color as my eyes." As he looked at the teacher's eyes, he responded excitedly, saying, "Then there eyes are root beer!" The teacher recognized that, although he did not yet know the label *brown*, Creighton knew that his eyes and hers were the same color as root beer, surely the beginning of understanding the color brown.

Thus, do not assume the child is wrong if, in the process of naming colors of familiar items, he or she uses nontraditional names such as *chocolate brown, fire-engine red, lemon yellow,* and *lime green.* When a child uses such a label, the teacher might suggest that is one name for the color and then also say the traditional name.

Brady announced to his teacher, "Today I wore my coat with flag colors!" as he hung up his red, white, and blue jacket. A teacher asked a child to examine his plaid shirt and tell her any of the colors in the shirt. He responded with a quick "My shirt is rainbow-colored," and he was indeed correct.

Before young children are taught the labels of colors, they can be given many experiences in matching and sorting colors. A deck of cards can be sorted by color, or construction paper can be cut into squares, circles, or other shapes and then sorted into piles of similar colors.

Even before children label colors, they have the ability to point to a particular color when asked to find it. For example, on a particular page of a story being read, if there are several animals of different colors, the teacher might say, "Point to the animal that is yellow." Or, while eating, say, "Find something that is red." As long as this game is not overused, children enjoy playing it.

While learning a specific color (for example, yellow), the child may readily identify objects that are yellow, although not yet sure which ones are *not* yellow. The child who knows that apples, tomatoes, and stop signs are red may then ask whether a banana is also red. Or the child may know what green *is,* but not yet know what green *is not.*

Teaching Color Concepts

The world is saturated with colors, so there are numerous opportunities for encouraging children's awareness of the world of color. When experimenting with color, use all kinds of media: water, watercolors, oil paints, colored shaving cream, finger paints, tempera; hands, feet, brushes, eyedroppers, sponges, spray bottles, toy balls, squirt guns; leaves, sticks, canvas, sidewalks, paper, fabric, wood, and so on. There is no "right" way to teach or experience color. Color should be used often in everyday conversations with children. The teacher can comment on the color of the sky, trees, flowers, clothing the child is wearing, eyes, hair, or the book being carried. Questions such as "What else is this color?" or "This is the same color as what?" should be used often for problem solving relating to color.

To avoid confusion when teaching color, it is important to remember that color is an attribute, not an object. Grammatically, color names are both nouns and adjectives, but when they are taught as adjectives, children understand them more easily. In other words, use the name of both the color and the object being described. For example, of a seashell, say "That is an orange seashell" or "That seashell is orange in color," rather than "That is orange."

When preparing a lesson plan on color, be well aware of the needs and abilities of the particular group of children before deciding on an approach. Several alternatives are available, depending on the developmental level of the children in terms of their color understandings. For children who have little understanding of color, begin by focusing on what color is. Then spend perhaps one or two days or even a week on each of the primary and secondary colors. This approach will provide a sure understanding and knowledge of these six basic colors. Along with each color, the various shades could also be taught. For example, as blue is being studied, also teach dark blue, navy blue, light blue, turquoise blue, and so on. Another approach is to begin with the primary colors and then advance to the secondary colors. While learning secondary colors, the children discover that they are made by combining the primary colors. After the study of the primary and secondary colors, the children then go back to shades of colors. Since they have learned that the secondary colors are made by combining colors, it is exciting to learn how shades of a particular color are made by adding white paint to make it lighter, by adding black paint to make it darker, or by adding another color to change the shade. Color mixing provides other opportunities for young children to explore.

Concepts and Ideas for Teaching

1. Colors have names, and these names are used to describe objects.
2. Most objects have a color.
3. Some objects do not have a color.
   a. Water
   b. Clear plastic
   c. Clear glass
4. Many items are similar in color.
   a. Red: apple, cherry, tomato, berries, items of red clothing, or hair
   b. Green: plants, vegetables, books, or sweaters
   c. Yellow: lemon, sun, yellow butterfly, or corn on the cob
5. The same items may vary in color.
   a. Cars: red, black, green, and so on. The same model and kind comes in various colors.
   b. People: red, white, black, or brown
   c. Eyes: blue, black, green, brown, or hazel
   d. Apples: yellow, green, red, or brown

6. Single items may vary in shades of the same color.
   a. Trees: shades of green
   b. Fabric: shades of any color
   c. Paint: shades of any color
7. Single items may have various colors.
   a. Fabrics: plaids, stripes, or others
   b. Trees: In the fall, a tree may have leaves of many colors.
   c. Pictures or paintings
8. Color may be modified or changed.
   a. Combining: When two or more colors are combined, the color will be changed and a new one made, or the shade of the original color will be different. Working with colored water or paints offers many possibilities for exploring, making new colors by combining colors. The child should learn that the secondary colors (green, orange, and purple) are made by combining the primary colors (red, yellow, and blue): Red and yellow make orange, red and blue make purple, and yellow and blue make green. When combining these colors, start with the lighter of the two colors and then add the darker color. (It is easier to make colors darker than lighter.) The child who has learned these combinations can easily understand that every other color is made by combining the primary colors in various ways.
   b. Adding: In food, art, and science activities, colors can be changed by adding ingredients. For example, when making gingerbread, the original ingredients of sugar, eggs, and shortening change color when the molasses is added.
   c. Heat, cooking, or the sun: Exposure to the sun or the process of heating or cooking often changes the color of an item. Meats change, when cooked, from red to brown; bakery items such as gingerbread or chocolate cake often become lighter in color. Toast, waffles, or pancakes become darker, as does anything that burns. Roasted marshmallows or hot dogs become darker. Exposure to the sun often fades or lightens items, but people become tanned or sunburned.
   d. Freezing or cooling: Most items become lighter when frozen. When comparing the changes in color before and after freezing, make sure to have examples of the item both before and after the freezing process.
   e. Drying: The colors of fruits or other foods change as they are dried. The colors of some art media may change as drying occurs.
   f. Aging: Food in various stages shows changes in color. Physical characteristics of people

may change color during the aging process. The skin, hair, and eye colors of babies often change in a short period of time.

g. Natural changes: Weather changes, such as frost, freezing, rain, and sun, can result in changes in color. It is exciting to teach the changes of the autumn leaves resulting from cooler temperatures.

h. Camouflage: Some animals change color to camouflage, disguise, or hide themselves. Examples are the snowshoe rabbit and the chameleon.

9. Colors may be symbolic.
   a. Seasons: green for spring and summer; yellow, orange, and brown for fall
   b. Holidays: red and green for Christmas; orange and black for Halloween
   c. People: red, black, white, or yellow
   d. Clothing: Particular shades and colors are worn more typically during certain seasons; black clothing signifies mourning.
   e. Feelings: moods described in terms of color—blue for depressed, red for angry, or yellow for cheerful
   f. Safety: red meaning stop, green meaning go, yellow meaning caution
   g. Danger: red
   h. Sickness: yellow, red (flushed), white (pale), or green
   i. Injury: black-and-blue or red
   j. School colors
   k. Patriotism: red, white, and blue for the United States, or patriotic colors representing other native countries of students

10. Foods: There is a perceived alteration of taste when food is not the expected color (it is assumed that the taste *is* altered).

Activities and Experiences

1. Let the children observe and have opportunities for mixing colors, especially the primary colors into the secondary colors. Here is one example, using food coloring:

   Use either a quart jar or gallon jar filled with water and put enough drops of yellow in it to make it a deep yellow color; mix well. Then add a few drops of red and watch as the yellow water changes to orange; mix well. Repeat this experience with other colors. For a similar experience, use baby food jars, clear glasses, or plastic containers holding water colored with the primary colors. In additional containers, mix the secondary colors. (Always begin with the lighter of the two colors when mixing.) Using primary colors to make secondary colors can also be achieved when

finger painting, easel painting, and using cellophane sheets.

2. Take plastic six-pack can holders and cut them apart into separate rings. Thread a piece of yarn through the top of each, and then let the children glue pieces of colored cellophane on each one. They will enjoy hanging them as mobiles, hanging them at the window, or putting them on top of one another to form different colors.

3. From colored paper, cut patterns that have the same shape but are different colors. To make them more durable, laminate or cover them with clear adhesive paper. Spread them on the floor and tape them down. Cut smaller corresponding shapes and colors and give one to each child. Put on music and have the children march, slide, skip, and so on, to the music; when it stops, each child must find and stand on a shape the same color as the one being held. As an alternative, instead of giving each child a color, give verbal directions. For example, say "Donna, please stand on an orange circle."

4. Have the children sort colored items: buttons, paper shapes, marbles, colored macaroni, or pieces of fabric.

5. Have the children play color lotto. Use paint chips from a paint store or colored construction or poster paper. Cut two squares (or other shapes) the same size of each color. Children then match colors, or shades of the same color.

6. Make a color wheel of wood or heavy cardboard. The colors can be felt pieces or paper (colored with felt-tip pens) glued to the base. Now put corresponding colors on clip-type clothespins, using felt or colored pens, one color per clothespin. The children clip the clothespins to the corresponding colors of the color wheel. Older children may use shades of a single color, but younger children should use distinct colors.

7. Fill a glass or container partly full of water. Drop a single drop of food coloring into the water and stir. Add another drop and stir, continuing this procedure so that the children can see how the same color can change from light to dark. Let the children follow up with the same experiment. For a similar experience, instead of using the same container of water, use different or separate containers, such as clear medicine bottles. To each container successively, add one or two more drops of coloring than to the previous one. Then order the containers from lightest to darkest.

8. Sing songs that create awareness of the colors children are wearing and the colors in their environment.

9. Show outlines of objects such as fruits, vegetables, flowers, trees, and the sun. Do not show them

colored. Have the children name the color or colors of the object. You could also name a color and have the children respond with names of objects of that color.

10. Make up color riddles and have the children guess the color being described. For example, "I am the color of strawberries, cherries, and fire engines. What color am I?" Have older children make up the riddles and share them with one another. The riddles could be written and illustrated for a book. One page could have the riddle and the next page could have the answer, either written or drawn.

11. Have a color day when the majority of activities focus on one color. If the children are alerted to this event, they can be encouraged to wear clothing of that color.

12. Dye hard-boiled eggs. Use Easter egg dye or food coloring. You may wish to give the children the opportunity to mix colors or have them dip the egg into one color and then into another to discover the effect.

13. Make fishing poles of sticks or dowels (15 to 18 inches long). Attach screw eyes to one end of each for threading string. On the end of the string, attach a small magnet. Now let the children fish for fish of various colors that have been cut from colored paper and have paper clips attached. Encourage the children to name the color of each fish that they catch.

14. For older children who are ready to expand their color vocabulary, make word cards of the following color words and help the children to sort them into color piles. Find examples of each, if possible; paint chips are a good source.

   a. Red: scarlet, coral, terra cotta, crimson, vermilion, Castilian red, ruby, cherry, fire-engine red, calypso red, or poppy

   b. Green: shamrock, sea green, hunter green, olive green, chartreuse, avocado, army green, celery green, apple green, Kelly green, emerald, jade, verdant green, viridian green, grass green, cactus green, khaki green, or pea green

   c. Brown: chocolate, caramel brown, hazel, mahogany, maple brown, dirt brown, sepia, olive brown, or tan

   d. Yellow: mustard, lemon, saffron, chamois, blonde, canary yellow, sunshine yellow, citron yellow, buff, amber, sallow, primrose, tawny, or gold

   e. Purple: violet, lavender, orchid, amethyst, grape, lilac, burgundy, or damson

   f. Orange: carrot, peach, pumpkin, coral, mandarin orange, tangerine orange, copper, or rust

   g. Blue: indigo, royal, navy, cobalt, turquoise, sky blue, robin's-egg blue, baby blue, teal blue, azure, sapphire blue, midnight blue, or peacock blue

15. Make chromatograms (color patterns). Using water-based (not permanent) markers, make drawings or lines on paper towels. Put one edge of the paper towels into water, and watch what happens as the water rises up the paper to the dry marker patterns. The water loosens the pigments from the paper and carries them up the towel. Heavy pigments don't travel as far as the lightweight ones, so use more of the colors. Spray bottles can also be used.

UNIT IDEAS ON COLOR

FIELD TRIPS

- Color walk
- Art gallery
- Art department of college or other school
- Paint store
- Fabric store
- Flower shop
- Grocery store
- Nursery or greenhouse in the spring

ART

- Mosaic of dyed rice, macaroni, or other media
- Finger painting
- Painting with tempera paint or watercolors
- Collages with colored cellophane
- Mixing primary colors of clay or playdough to make secondary colors
- String painting
- Melted crayon pictures
- Blot painting
- Clay sculptures or modeling (use primary colors)
- Colored macaroni strung for necklaces or bracelets
- Collages using items that come in various colors: toothpicks, marshmallows, or cereal

MUSIC

- "Color Song" or "Color Parade" (Hap Palmer; see references at end of chapter)
- Songs that incorporate colors of the children's clothing, colors in their environment, or favorite colors
- Musical Chairs, with colors on the backs of each chair. After each child has a chair, give instructions for each color. For example, say, "All who have red on their chair stand up and hop in a circle." (Do not eliminate children in this game, as with any game for younger children.)

- In small groups, make shakers of different colors, or give groups of children baby food jars with objects of different colors or colored water in them. Say "All those with (name a color) shakers play on the next song (or on the chorus)."
- Creative movements with colors. Play some classical music; have the children decide what color the music represents and then move like that color or something representing that color.

FOOD

- Almost any food activity can be planned with a focus on color or color mixing.
- Make gelatin: Use flavored gelatin, or begin with one of the three primary colors, lemon, for example. After the hot water is added and the gelatin dissolved, use ice cubes that have been deeply colored another primary color. For example, if you add blue ice cubes to lemon gelatin, you will get green gelatin.
- Make a white cake and, before it is baked, marble it with drops of food coloring.
- Make cakes, cookies, or breads and add food coloring to change the color.
- Make fruit salad in small groups and have each group whip the cream and add food coloring, or use plain yogurt with color added to it, so that each group has salad of a different color.
- Make an apple salad using green, yellow, and red apples.
- Make any meat dish in which the children cook the meat first so that the change in color can be observed.
- Make colored popcorn.

VISITORS

- Paint dealer or distributor
- Artist to mix paints and paint picture
- Animals of various colors, perhaps with their babies to see whether they are the same colors (for example, a baby and adult mouse)
- A mother with her baby and a suitcase filled with clothing of different colors for the baby to wear
- A parent or other visitor to make snow cones, with children selecting the desired color and flavor
- A clown to put on different colors of face makeup

SCIENCE

- Chemical garden, made with food coloring of different colors on top (see directions later in this chapter)

- Coloring or dying carnations, Queen Anne's lace, or celery by putting them in glasses with food coloring or ink in water
- Any experience showing how particular animals use color camouflage
- Any experience in color mixing and color changing
- Color changes of autumn leaves
- Color changes resulting from aging, ripening, or molding

LITERACY

- Write or dictate stories on favorite colors. Story springboards might be "My Favorite Color Is . . ." or "I Like (color) Because . . ."
- Make a book for each color studied; the title of the book could be that color. Children could cut pictures from magazines or draw their own pictures of things that are that color.
- Encourage children to write or tell color similes and metaphors.

TEACHING ABOUT FIRE

Fire is an interesting part of the child's world, because it stimulates curiosity, but that natural curiosity needs to be tempered by a learned caution. Recent findings continue to support the fact that 1 in 4 fires is set by children who are 6 years of age and younger (Cole, 2004; Porth, 2002).

Children are not able to understand the risks involved with fires, and they do not have the cognitive abilities to understand that a small flame can grow into a disastrous fire. Another challenge in teaching young children about fire is complicated by the actions of many adults, who do not keep matches and lighters secured in locked containers. "A child who becomes interested in matches or lighters can find them" (Cole et al., 2004, p. 15). Not only must we educate adults about this concern, but we also must teach children what to do if they come across these materials. An effective fire safety program for young children must address two main issues: (a) preventing fire play, and (b) keeping children safe in a fire. Teach children that the firefighter is a friend; to crawl low under smoke; to stop, drop, and roll; and to go tell a grown-up (Cole et al., 2004). Young children's natural reaction to fear often is to hide, but they need to be taught that if they encounter a fire, instead of hiding they should to go to a place of safety. "Clearly, three- to five-year-olds are capable of understanding these lifesaving skills but will learn them only through a determined effort" (Cole et al., 2004, p. 18). Because of classroom and community fire safety programs, development of child-resistant lighters, and other factors, the number of fires started by children in the United States has been decreasing.

A unit on fire may be planned in conjunction with learning about firefighters. Often a unit of study focuses on the firefighter as a community helper, but never brings in concepts related to fire. We suggest teaching many concepts relating to fire to young children so that they know that fire has many uses, but that it is dangerous and is not to be played with.

On one occasion Smokey Bear visited the classroom of 3- to 5-year-olds. His role had been previously discussed—that he is a symbol of fire safety and is not actually a live bear. However, excitement ran high when Smokey walked in with the forest ranger; heartbeats stepped up, eyes widened, and one child exclaimed: "It's the real Smokey Bear. I thought I would never get to meet you." Even when Smokey Bear removed his head and an actual person's head emerged, the reality of Smokey Bear still remained in the minds of those 3- to 5-year-olds.

Concepts and Ideas for Teaching

1. Fire has many uses: heating, lighting, cooking, and burning of waste material.
2. Fire needs air (oxygen) and fuel (wood, paper, or other flammable material) to burn.
3. Fire can be ignited in many ways: striking rocks together, using matches or heat, focusing light on one spot for some time, combustion.
4. There are several ways to extinguish a fire: dousing with water or salt; smothering with dirt or a blanket; using a fire extinguisher.
5. People have different feelings toward fire. We may be frightened if our lives or homes are in danger because of a fire; we may experience pain if our bodies are burned with fire; we may feel warm and safe if we are gathered around the fireplace when it is cold and stormy outside; we may feel excitement and warmth as we are gathered around a campfire cooking our dinner and singing campfire songs; or we may feel relief and security when the power goes off and the candles are found and lighted.

Activities and Experiences

1. Demonstrate that fire needs air. ("Teaching About Air" in Chapter 10).
2. Demonstrate ways to put out a fire; role-play.
3. Demonstrate first aid in treating a burn: If it is not severe, put it under cold water and then treat it with ointment.
4. Demonstrate how to build a fire outdoors and then how to put it out.

UNIT IDEAS ON FIRE AND THE FIREFIGHTER

ART

- Collages of flammable and nonflammable materials
- Melted crayon pictures: Take care with the iron so that no fire will start and no one is burned

FOOD

- Hot dogs roasted over a fire
- Marshmallows roasted over a fire
- Any food cooked over a fire
- Foil dinners baked on coals
- Fondue

FIELD TRIPS

- Fire station
- Home or school on fire-safety inspection
- Picnic at a park, canyon, or picnic site; fire built in designated safe place; hot dogs cooked, marshmallows roasted; fire put out carefully

VISITORS

- Firefighter
- Smokey Bear
- Scout to show how to start a fire and how to put it out properly

SCIENCE

- Necessity of air in building a fire or keeping it going
- Ways to start or build a fire
- Ways to put out a fire

LITERACY

- Stories and poems about fires and firefighters
- Story of Smokey Bear
- Open-ended story: "I like fire because . . ."

MUSIC AND DRAMATIC PLAY

- Dramatization of putting out a fire
- Dramatization of sitting around a campfire cooking food and singing songs

---

TEACHING ABOUT LIGHT AND SHADOWS

The question posed to a group of preschoolers, "What would you do if you had no light?" resulted in some interesting comments and answers. One child said, "I would get a blind man's dog," and another said, "God

Exploring shadows helps develop concepts relating to sun, light, shadows; self-awareness; and physical body characteristics.

would help me." Another replied, "I would light a candle." "But a candle is one source of light," the teacher replied. "Then I would get a flashlight," the child responded quickly. "And that is another source of light," the teacher told him. "Then I guess I would just have to sit," concluded the child. It is difficult for children to imagine a world without light, and it is interesting for them to begin to understand the several sources of light. In every situation in which people are without natural light and there is a power failure preventing the use of electricity, there are still sources of light, such as flashlights and fire.

Shadows, an aspect of light, are so fascinating that even babies find them interesting. Very young children may find shadows frightening, but as preschool children learn the cause of shadows, their fears are alleviated, and they delight not only in watching them but in making them.

An activity children enjoy is to hang a sheet in front of a light. Have some of the children perform shadow dances, shadow dramatics, or shadow games behind the sheet (but in front of the light), so that the other children can watch the shadows on the sheet. After a story, one teacher decided to have the children dramatize it by means of shadow dramatics. There was awe, fascination, and excitement as the children in the audience watched the shadows of the performing children. Children also enjoy guessing who other children are by their shadows. One young boy said, "I know that is Stacy, because the shadow has pigtails!"

Concepts and Ideas for Teaching

1. Light is either natural (sunlight) or artificial (flashlights, lanterns).
2. Plants need light and grow toward the light.

3. Light has many uses.
   a. Used by people
      1. Lamps: used by people to see in the dark
      2. Lighthouses: used to warn ships and boats of nearness to land
      3. Freeway and street lights, lighted airport runways, traffic lights, headlights, lighted signs: used with forms of transportation to light the way and let people know where they are going
      4. Light or fire at a campsite: used for warmth and cooking, and to discourage wild animals
      5. Natural sunlight: used for warmth and also as a source of telling time
   b. Used by animals
      1. To see in the dark
      2. For warmth
      3. To determine the approximate time
   c. Used by plants: warmth and sunlight needed by most plants to grow
4. Shadows are produced when an object passes in front of light; shadows result from the interruption of light. If the object making the shadow is removed, the shadow also disappears.
   a. Relation of object's shape to its shadow
   b. Relation of the size and shape of a shadow to a change in the location of the object and the position of the light source

Activities and Experiences

1. Collect as many sources of light as possible: flashlights, lanterns, candles, matches, lighters, and so on.
2. Try growing a plant in a closet or room where there is no light.
3. Watch a plant "follow" the sun or light.
4. Show pictures or slides of the uses of light.
5. Show, discuss, and demonstrate the effect of sunlight on photographic paper, ice, cold water, colored construction paper, and fabric.
6. Explore shadows.
   a. On a sunny day, divide the children into pairs to trace each other's shadows.
   b. Play shadow tag, with the one who is "It" trying to step on another person's shadow.
   c. Make a sundial: tie string around the end of a dowel; put the other end of the dowel in some sand or soil next to cement; extend the string on the end of dowel across the cement and secure with tape. Throughout the day, draw a line on the cement with a piece of chalk where the shadow is being cast.
   d. Use an overhead projector for making shadows of objects, letters, numbers; encourage the children to make hand and finger shadows.

Note: See Lesson Plan on Light (Shadows) in Appendix A.

TEACHING ABOUT MAGNETS

"I've never seen a pin jump before," exclaimed one excited child as magnets were introduced. Another child said, "I didn't know pins were alive," as she observed the magnets attracting the pins. Magnets are fascinating for children to explore. Simply showing the children magnets and telling them what they can do takes away the excitement; children need opportunities to experiment and discover for themselves what magnets are and can do. Ideally, each child should have a magnet; however, magnets can be put on a science table for use in individual exploring.

The children need many objects to use for experimenting with the magnets so that they can determine what kinds of materials the magnets attract. A container of common objects such as a cork, scrap of material, pencil, eraser, paper clip, scissors, tack, coin, soap, washer, pin, needle, fastener, and tape provides continued motivation for exploration. The objects in the box could be sorted into two groups: those attracted by the magnet and those not attracted by the magnet. (A dog's two-sided food dish works very well for this sorting or classifying activity.) After adequate experimentation, the children will be able to see some similarities in the objects that the magnet attracts.

During a sorting activity, one child replied, "All the things that the magnet picked up are silver. Magnets must pick up silver things." True, many iron and steel objects are silver in color, but this concept was not accurate. Then the teacher said, "Let's test your idea to see whether it is correct." The teacher selected some silver paper, aluminum foil, a piece of aluminum, a nickel coin, a silver button, and silver fabric. After trying to pick up each of these objects with the magnet, the child concluded that magnets do not necessarily pick up items that are silver in color. The teacher took the opportunity to explain that the objects attracted by the magnet were made of iron and steel. Also, even though an object of iron or steel may be too large for the magnet to pick up, the pull or attraction can still be felt.

It is sometimes difficult to present an entire unit on magnets; therefore, they are presented here as a science concept, with several supporting ideas and activities. Perhaps an experience with magnets could be presented each day for a week or two or incorporated as a science activity within another unit of study.

Concepts and Ideas for Teaching

1. Magnets attract objects made of iron and/or nickel and/or steel. (Although it is not necessary to teach the components of magnets to young children, they are actually made from rock called *magnetite,* which does attract iron and steel. Magnetite is also called *lodestone.*)
2. Magnets come in many shapes, sizes, and strengths; some have stronger magnetism than others.
3. Stronger magnets attract through paper, glass, cardboard, wood, and water.
4. Magnetism can be transferred. It is possible to magnetize such objects as iron nails, paper clips, needles, and knitting needles by stroking them 30 to 50 times in one direction with a magnet. However, as the children will discover, these homemade magnets do not retain their magnetism for very long.
5. All magnets have a north pole and a south pole, and magnets are strongest at their poles.
6. Opposite or unlike poles attract (the north pole attracts the south pole), whereas like poles repel each other.
7. A compass needle is a magnet, always pulling to the north. When a magnetized needle is floated in water, it acts as a compass and points north.

Through experimenting, children discover which materials are/are not attracted to magnets.

Activities and Experiences

1. Collect magnets of different sizes, shapes, and strengths. Also collect objects that use magnets, such as clips for holding notes to bulletin boards or refrigerators, toys using magnets, and potholders with magnets attached.

2. Compare the strengths of magnets by counting or comparing the number of pins or paper clips that each magnet can pick up by "hooking" them one to another until the magnet can no longer hold another pin or paper clip. Order the magnets from strongest to weakest. In this experience, the children can discover that the strength of a magnet is not necessarily determined by its size.

3. Have the children put a piece of paper between their magnet and paper clip to see whether the magnet still attracts. During this activity, children will discover that magnetism works through glass, cardboard, wood, fabric, and other materials. Fill a glass bowl with water and drop the paper clip into it. The children will learn that the magnet attracts the paper clip through the glass and the water.

4. Suspend a bar magnet from a thread or string tied to its center; in a few minutes, the magnet will align itself with Earth's magnetic field and point north and south. It becomes a simple compass. Notice that as some types of metal are brought close to the magnet there will be an attraction and the compass will not work.

5. Put iron filings on glass, a paper plate, or cardboard. Put a magnet underneath and let the children discover what happens as the magnet is moved around. Sprinkle the iron filings over a glass slab and touch a magnet underneath the glass. Now put this slab on an overhead projector so that the iron filings designs can be enlarged on the wall or screen.

6. Make small fishing poles from 1/4- by 12-inch dowels and attach small magnets to them with fishing line. The children fish from a box containing assorted items: iron and steel, as well as objects that will not be attracted by the magnet. Cut fish from paper and attach paper clips to them so that they can be "caught." If desired, basic concepts such as color, number, and shape can be put on the fish to enable the children to tell about their catch. Larger poles can also be made from dowels or sticks, and a dramatic-play fishing area can be built in one area of the room. Use large-unit blocks for the rocks surrounding the fishing pond or lake; the children sit on these rocks and fish.

7. Place a horseshoe or bar magnet on a table and cover it with a white piece of paper. As iron filings are sprinkled onto the paper, they will align themselves with the magnetic field. If you put two bar magnets with like and then unlike poles next to each other, the iron filings will show the interaction of the magnetic fields.

Note: After a period of time, magnets may lose their force. They can be recharged in high school or university physics or electronics departments. Also, you can rejuvenate a weak magnet by pulling it lengthwise across the pole of a powerful magnet. To preserve magnetism when magnets are not in use, attach an iron keeper over the poles of a horseshoe or bar magnet, avoid storing the magnets with the north and south poles together, and do not store them in metal boxes. Remember, magnets can be damaging to electronic products.

TEACHING ABOUT WEIGHT AND BALANCE

Weight and balance are challenging but exciting concepts to explore with young children. Like other concepts previously discussed, these must be explored through concrete experiences. Children usually judge the weight of an object by its size. As a result, children often misjudge the weight of an object and how much strength they need to pick it up. An understanding of weight is necessary before children can comprehend the meaning of balance.

A group of children was learning about weight, and a scale was included in one of the centers. Melissa watched as some of the children stood on the scale and were weighed. Soon she said to the teacher, "Pound me next!"

A discussion of the relationship between gravity and weight depends on the age and understanding of the children. Weight is the result of gravity, and gravity is stronger closer to the center of Earth. Therefore, the farther away an object is from Earth's center, the lighter in weight it is. An object at sea level weighs slightly more than the same object on a high mountain.

Older children will be able to understand the effect that gravity has on an object. Younger children will understand weight in terms of heaviness.

Weight is the heaviness or lightness of an object as it is weighed on a scale by use of a standard of measure. The terms *heavy* and *light,* commonly used in defining weight, are relative, or comparative. We must have two objects to compare before being able to determine that one object is heavier or lighter than the other. It is impossible, technically, to state that a single object is heavy unless it has been determined that an amount greater than so many pounds is heavy. We must also consider to whom an object would seem heavy. What is heavy to a child is very different from what is heavy to a teenager or adult. What is heavy to a dockworker, a farmer, a furniture mover, or someone with great strength is very different from what is heavy to someone with little physical strength.

An object is **balanced** when stability has been achieved by an even distribution of weight on each side of a fulcrum, or point of support. A **fulcrum** provides the point of balance between two objects. It is not necessarily located at a central point between these objects, however. When objects are balanced, their weight or number is equalized on both sides. Thus, two objects of unequal weight can be balanced by either (a) moving the fulcrum or (b) moving the two objects in such a way that the lighter of the two is farther from the fulcrum on one side and the heavier is closer to the fulcrum on the other side. If objects are of equal weight, such as identical blocks or chips, two or more can be put on one side, closer to the fulcrum, and one on the other side, farther from the fulcrum, thus equalizing the weight on both sides. This discovery is exciting to children; it can be achieved in another way by having children of different weights balance on a seesaw.

Children acquire the concept of balance by balancing themselves. They may try to balance on one foot with their eyes open and then with their eyes closed. They may then change feet and try the same activity again. Soon they begin to recognize the state of stability of objects in balance.

Daily Experiences with Weight and Balance

Daily experiences are valuable in developing an awareness of weight and balance. Riddles are easily used in teaching weight and balance. For example, say "I weigh the same as a pound of hot dogs, and you use me on toast in the morning. What am I?" The answer is a pound of butter or margarine. Or one may say: "You use me in cakes and cookies and on your cereal, and I weigh the same as 5 pounds of flour. What am I?" The answer is 5 pounds of sugar. Guessing games are especially adaptable with weight and balance. Display objects of different weights and ask which ones weigh the same, which one weighs the most, and which one weighs the least. Which toy is heaviest? Which of these two books weighs more? Can you find at least three objects in our room that weigh more than 5 pounds each? Can you balance the balance board or the balance scales with sand on one side and blocks on the other side? A balance scale is an excellent piece of equipment to include in the water trough with small, dry media; it gives children an opportunity for practical exploration of both weight and balance. Similes and metaphors also can be used with weight. For example, the phrases "as heavy as _____" and "as light as _____" could be completed with the children's own ideas of heavy and light objects. Exploratory questions asking what makes an object heavier or lighter could also be used frequently.

As young children begin to have experiences with weight, they need many opportunities to compare weights by using their own muscles. They should have practice in determining **equivalents,** weights that are the same. Scales or balance scales can be used for these activities. Experiment with directive questions, such as "How many pennies are the same weight as 20 buttons?" or "How many little rocks weigh the same as two pencils?" Children also need activities requiring balance: using their bodies as the means of balance or using equipment such as a seesaw or the balance scales to achieve a balanced state.

Provide many opportunities for children to become familiar with weight vocabulary. As children have many exposures to words and their meanings, the words soon become possessions and active parts of the children's vocabularies. The following are examples of weight words:

> heavy, light
>
> heavier, lighter
>
> heaviest, lightest
>
> weighty

Children must also relate weight to the standard units of weight measurement. They must therefore understand that weight is measured in ounces, pounds, and tons. Eventually, they will need to know what these terms mean and how they relate to one another; for example, 16 ounces in a pound or 2,000 pounds in a ton. Children should also be exposed to the standard units of weight measurement in the metric system: grams, milligrams, kilograms, and so on. Simplify the prefixes; for the metric units as follows: $1,000 =$ kilo.; $100 =$ hecto.; $10 =$ deka.; $\frac{1}{10} =$ deci.; $\frac{1}{100} =$ centi.; and $\frac{1}{1,000} =$ milli. Ounces can be compared with grams and pounds with kilograms. In addition, inches can be compared with centimeters, feet with decimeters, yards with meters, miles with kilometers, and degrees Fahrenheit with degrees Celsius.

Children often relate weight to themselves and their own body weight. A child may know that she weighs 42 pounds, but not know exactly what that means. It would be interesting, then, for the children to find other things that weigh 42 pounds: How many large-unit blocks would it take to weigh 42 pounds? How many books could weigh 42 pounds? What could you pack in a suitcase to make it weigh 42 pounds? Probably anything the child can lift is "light," and anything that cannot be lifted is "heavy."

Concepts and Ideas for Teaching

1. Gravity determines weight and depends on an object's distance from the center of Earth. The farther from Earth's center, the less the

object's weight is. Weight is the force with which a body is attracted toward Earth by gravitation.
   a. A parent weighing 180 pounds on the seacoast would weigh less on a mountaintop and only 30 pounds on the moon.
   b. The higher in the sky that an airplane flies, the less it weighs.
2. Anything that takes up space has weight; even items having seemingly no weight still have weight that can be measured on a fine scale.
   a. Feather
   b. Scrap of paper
   c. Penny
   d. Small piece of candy
3. Weight is measured through the use of instruments called scales.
4. Weight can change.
   a. Additions
      1. People gaining weight by adding pounds
      2. Air added to an inner tube
      3. Water added to a dry sponge
      4. Balloon inflated
   b. Subtractions
      1. Release of air from a balloon
      2. Drying out a wet sponge
      3. Removal of a baby's clothes (making the total weight less)
   c. Physical growth and aging
      1. Children generally gaining weight as they grow
      2. Older people often losing weight as they become very old
      3. Stale, shriveled apples weighing less than fresh, firm apples
5. A change in weight may result in an alteration of appearance.
   a. Either adding or subtracting many pounds from a person
   b. An inflated balloon compared to a deflated balloon
6. Changing the form or rearranging the structure of an item will not change its weight.
   a. A pound of butter weighs the same when melted.
   b. A tower of 10 blocks weighs the same as these 10 blocks in a pile.
   c. An amount of water weighs the same when it is frozen into a solid as when it is a liquid.
7. Weight is not determined by size, shape, age, or equal amounts. Some items may look heavy but are light; and some items may look light but are heavy.
   a. A pound of nails is not equal in volume to a pound of feathers.
   b. A large Styrofoam container, such as that used to hold a tape recorder, weighs less

than a smaller cardboard container, such as a jewelry box.
   c. Older people do not necessarily weigh more than younger people.
   d. Gifts of various shapes do not vary in weight merely because of their variation in shape.
8. Different items may have the same weight.
   a. An 11-year-old child may weigh about the same as a bale of hay.
   b. A 10-pound bag of sugar may weigh the same as a child's dog.
   c. A pound of butter weighs the same as a pound of bacon.
9. Many items are sold and packaged in 1-pound units of measure: bacon, butter, rice, cereal, meat, candy, nuts, nails, plaster, and salt.
10. The same items may vary in weight: apples, people, boxes, rocks, marbles, and automobiles.
11. Air has weight.
12. Weight experiences may involve making comparisons between the weights of two or more objects, in addition to ordering items from lightest to heaviest.
13. Balance is not necessarily achieved by supporting an object or a group of objects in the middle, but by obtaining stability through an even distribution of weight on either side of a fulcrum, or vertical axis.
14. Materials do not have to be of the same kind, substance, or amount to be balanced.
   a. A roll of cellophane tape balanced on one side of the balance board, with a wooden block on the other side (heavier object moved closer to the fulcrum to achieve balance).
   b. Wheat on one side of the balance scale, rice on the other.
   c. Two wooden blocks balanced against one wooden block.

Activities and Experiences

Experiments with Weight Comparisons

1. Have the children place wrapped packages of different sizes and shapes in order, from lightest to heaviest.
2. Visit a pumpkin patch, or collect as many pumpkins as you can find. Weigh and measure them, and order them from lightest to heaviest. (Use other seasonal items such as potatoes or apples or other objects such as shoes, blocks, and so on.)
3. Have the children match duplicate weights of items—even when the items are not the same or the items are not the same size, shape, or equal in amount.
   a. Boxes of different sizes filled with various items and then wrapped (or use paper sacks)

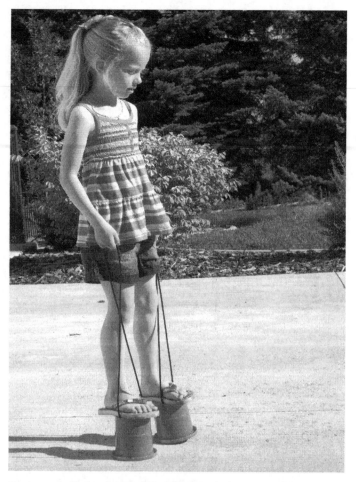

It takes practice and patience to learn to balance on stilts.

   b. Balance scales used to match items of same weight
     1. Scales or pans in the same position on either side of the fulcrum
     2. Children try to choose items of similar weight and verify the weights by using a scale
     3. If possible, a scale measuring both pounds and ounces showing actual weights
   c. Different amounts of various items: feathers, candies, nails, bolts, wheat, balloons, and dry cereal. Children weigh them to determine how much of an item is required to equal a pound.
4. Ask the children to examine groups or pairs of objects and decide by observation which are heavier. Have them follow up by lifting the objects or weighing them to determine whether their selections are correct.
5. Have the children keep a record of their own weight and record the changes. The children can then find things that weigh less than they do, things that weigh more, and things that weigh the same.
   a. Number of large-unit blocks equaling children's own weight
   b. Comparison of weights

- Children weighed on scales
- Children weighed holding an item such as a book, a pound of butter, or some blocks

6. Introduce the children to units of measure by introducing them to scales. Focus first on scales that weigh in pounds, and give them many experiences with pounds. Then introduce the concept of ounces (a unit for measuring less than a pound), and let the children measure items on an ounce scale (for example, a diet scale). After this exposure, introduce older children to a unit of measure that is less than an ounce, a gram, and try to locate a scale sensitive enough to weigh grams. In addition, older children may be exposed to the unit of measure representing 2,000 pounds, a ton. Many heavy items are weighed in tons. A weigh station or trucking corporation is a possible place to see items being weighed in tons.
7. Use the balance scales with sensory media such as wheat, rice, or buttons to enable the children to explore the concepts of balance and weight. Various kinds of items can be used with the balance scales for making weight comparisons, as well as for balancing items of equal weight and for distributing weight in order to make the scales balance.
8. Perform experiments to show that air has weight. (See Chapter 10 for additional experiments with air.) For example, select two balloons that are exactly the same (put them on the balance scales). Measure two lengths of string that are exactly the same kind and length (about 10 inches). Tie the strings to the deflated balloons. Suspend a yardstick with a string in the middle, or balance it on the spine of a book, using the book as a fulcrum. Tie a string with a balloon attached to each end of the yardstick in the same location. Whether the yardstick or a balance scale is used, the balloons should balance evenly. Now remove one of the balloons and blow air into it. Tie it back on in the same place on the yardstick. It will be obvious that the balloon containing air has more weight because the yardstick or balance scales will tip lower on the side with the inflated balloon.

Experiments with Sinking and Floating

1. Put a number of different objects (feathers, corks, small wooden sticks, hairpins, pebbles, coins) near a bowl, basin, or trough of water. Let the children predict which objects will sink and which will float. Have a box for the objects that sink and a box for those that float.
2. Give each child an equal amount of oil-based clay (a ball about 1 inch in diameter). Ask the children to see whether the clay will float in water.

Challenge them to see whether they can change its shape in such a way that it will float. If the children are not successful, show them how to press the clay flat and then mold the edges up to make a little boat. (This can also be done with pieces of aluminum foil.)

Experiments with Balance

1. From a school physics laboratory, obtain an analytical balance scale that is sensitive to weights of less than an ounce. Then have the children experiment with balancing such objects as feathers, scraps of paper, toothpicks, hairpins, needles, and thumbtacks. They can also determine which is the heaviest of the objects that they are using for the experiment. Working with this balance scale is the same as working with the larger balance scale, except that objects of lighter weight can be balanced.

2. Put two children of different weights on a see-saw and challenge them to find a way to make it balance. The heavier child will be closer to the fulcrum, and the lighter one will be farther away.

3. Provide a balance board made from plywood about $\frac{1}{2}$ by $2\frac{1}{2}$ by 24 inches. The fulcrum can be made with a block of wood measuring $\frac{1}{2}$ by $\frac{1}{2}$ by 3 inches. Starting at the middle and working toward the ends, mark off the board at 1-inch intervals,

and draw a line across the board at each mark. Label the center mark 0, and begin labeling the marks on either side 1, 2, 3, and so on. Now give the child six or eight 1-inch blocks (made by the teacher or commercially). Many experiments with balancing can be performed with these simple materials. One of the best ways to begin is to let the children experiment with balancing the materials without giving any directions. After the children have balanced the board on the fulcrum, some of the following activities will provide reinforcement (see Figure 9.2):

a. One block placed on each side of the fulcrum after balancing the board on the fulcrum; children determine whether each block must be placed at the same distance from the fulcrum to make the board balance

b. Two blocks placed on each side of the fulcrum; children discover ways to position the blocks and still have the board balance (continue this with three blocks, four blocks, and so on)

c. Two sets of unequal numbers of blocks used to balance the board on the fulcrum:
   - One block is placed on one side and two blocks on the other side of the fulcrum; one block is placed on one side, and three on the other; and so on.
   - The principle discovered here, that one or two blocks placed farther from the fulcrum

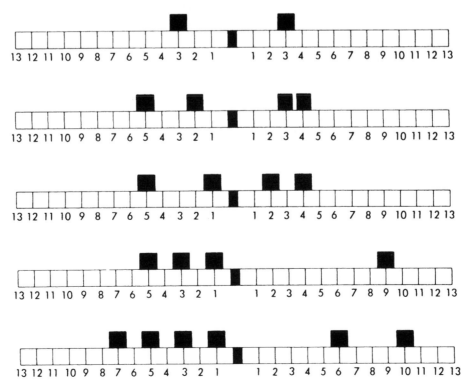

FIGURE 9.2 Balance Board Experiments

can balance several blocks closer to the fulcrum, can be taken a step further with older children; for example, show them that blocks placed on positions 1, 3, and 5 on one side balance one block placed on position 9 on the other side, since 1 + 3 + 5 = 9.

d. Fulcrum moved by the children so that it is not at the midpoint (perhaps under position 1 or 2 on either side). The children determine whether and how balance can be achieved.

UNIT IDEAS ON WEIGHT AND BALANCE

ART

- Wrapped packages of various weights decorated with paint or collage materials, then used for balancing or weighing
- Decorated music shakers: empty juice cans, milk cartons, or boxes filled with items of varying weight such as rice, rocks, and sand
- Papier-mâché molded around an inflated balloon; let dry, then pop the balloon, and paint or decorate ball as desired. Use to compare differences in weight.

FOOD

- Any food experience dealing with items sold in 1-pound quantities (bacon, rice, meat, butter, bread, etc.)
- Making a cake and weighing it in various stages: cake mix first, then weight change by adding water and eggs, and then again by putting it in baking pan
- Spaghetti or macaroni, which has changed weight from lighter when dry to heavier after being cooked in water

VISITORS

- Person from school physics department: various scales brought to the classroom
- Doctor or nurse: use of scales
- Grocery clerk with items in 1-pound packages
- Employee from state department of weights and measures
- Parent with bathroom scales

MUSIC

- Decorated music shakers to use with selected records

- Musical boxes (instead of musical chairs) of different sizes, shapes, and weights. (As music stops, children lift box that they are sitting on; then, when game is finished, see if they have been able to determine which box was lightest and which box was heaviest.)
- Creative movements: pretending to carry a heavy rock; pretending to toss a light rock into the air; pretending to be a balloon being filled with air and suddenly bursting

SCIENCE

- Deflated inner tube weighed, then inflated one weighed
- Deflated balloon weighed, then inflated one weighed
- Dry sponge weighed, soaked with water, weighed, allowed to dry, weighed again
- Seesaw set up for comparison of children's and teachers' weights; also for comparative weighing of various objects in the room
- Wrapped packages matched by weight
- Pound of butter weighed in cube form, then after melting
- Rice, wheat, or spaghetti weighed, soaked in water, then weighed again

FIELD TRIPS

- Physics department in a school: observation of scales and their uses
- Doctor's office: use of scales with people
- Medical supply store: observation of various scales and their uses
- Weigh station or trucking corporation: use of scales with vehicles
- Grain elevator: use of scales with crops and produce
- Grocery store: scales at checkout stand, meat scales, and scales in produce department
- Livestock auction yards: use of scales with animals
- Beach or sandy hills: different-sized containers for filling and weighing amounts of sand
- Post office: observation of weighing of packages

LITERACY

- Write and illustrate a story. "_____Is One Pound."
- Write and illustrate a story using the comparisons "_____Is Heavier Than _____" and "_____Is Lighter Than_____."

Children discover that wheels make it easier to move and transport objects.

PHYSICAL SCIENCE EXPERIMENTS UNRELATED TO SPECIFIC UNITS

Scientific explanations are presented simply in many of the experiences suggested in this chapter. Older children can understand and be introduced to scientific explanations in more detail. Younger children will find the demonstrations themselves adequate. Many experiments help children to understand about ecology and being sensitive to preserving Earth and its environment.

Vinegar and baking soda. To a small amount of vinegar (1/4 cup), add 1 teaspoon baking soda. Watch, hear, and feel what happens. (Carbon dioxide gas [bubbles] is formed when vinegar and baking soda are mixed together.)

Buoyancy of raisins, grapes, or alfalfa seeds in carbonated soda or in soda and vinegar solution. Add 3 tablespoons of vinegar and 2 teaspoons of baking soda to 1 cup of water. Add 1 teaspoon of alfalfa seeds or other tiny seeds; observe as the seeds rise to the surface of the water and then sink to the bottom of the container. Carbon dioxide bubbles pick the seeds up and carry them to the surface. When the bubbles pop, the seeds return to the bottom, where they are surrounded again by bubbles and are carried to the surface. Carbonated soda could also be used. (Concept: Gasses help objects float.)

Blowing up a balloon. Pour 1 inch of vinegar into a pop bottle. Put 1 or 2 teaspoons of baking soda inside a balloon and affix the balloon opening to the open top of the bottle. Then allow the soda and vinegar to mix together. The balloon will slowly inflate.

Crystals. Unique crystals can be grown with ordinary table salt or alum. Heat some water, and then dissolve as much salt as possible in the water. The solution will then be saturated. Pour the solution into an old open pie pan (the disposable aluminum kind works well, because the solution may be corrosive to some metals). Then place it in a corner of the room where it will not be disturbed. As the water starts to evaporate, small crystals will be observed forming. If these crystals are viewed through a microscope, they will show a crystal shape unique to that particular salt. Also note that the slower the water evaporates, the larger the crystals will grow.

Chemical garden. Combine the following ingredients: 2 tablespoons ammonia, $\frac{1}{4}$ cup bluing, $\frac{1}{4}$ cup salt, $\frac{1}{4}$ cup water. (Caution the children against smelling the ammonia, except at a safe distance.) Pour the mixture over coal, bricks, charcoal, or similar materials. Drops of food coloring may be added on top. In a few hours, salt-crystal formations will begin to appear. Use glass containers for this experiment, because the chemical may corrode aluminum. The chemical growth that occurs is made up of salt formations created when the liquid evaporates. The growth can be continued if more of the chemical ingredients are added or if 1 or 2 teaspoons of ammonia are added.

Floating an egg and pencil. Partly fill two containers, one with fresh water and one with salt water (4 tablespoons salt to 1 cup water). Let the children try floating the egg in each container. Try a hard-boiled egg. Now place a pencil in the water with the lead end up and the eraser end down. What happens to the pencil in the fresh water? What happens in the salt water? Do the items float in the salt water or the fresh water?

Rainbow. On a sunny day, stand a mirror in a bowl filled with water. Set the bowl near a wall.

Now turn the mirror to reflect (and refract) the sun's rays onto the wall. This exhibits the colors of the spectrum. What colors are seen?

Mirror images. Hinge together two mirrors with tape. Stand the hinged mirror on its edge. Place bits of colored paper in the mirror angle. Observe the different patterns in the double reflection. Try using a penny instead of the colored paper bits. How many pennies can you see? Open and close the mirror and observe as the number of pennies reflected in the mirror changes.

A–Z science fair. Hold an A–Z science fair during school, after school, or in the evening, with parents and other classroom students invited to attend. The teacher and children collaborate and think of a science experiment, activity, demonstration, or concept to represent each letter of the alphabet. Each child selects a letter of the alphabet or a science idea to be presented during the science fair. Flags or labels identify each letter, enabling participants to progress from activity A through activity Z, observing, trying out, manipulating, and inferring with each one. The following is a list of possible general concepts or ideas to represent each letter in the alphabet. These are only suggestions; there are numerous other possibilities.

- A   Air
- B   Bubbles
- C   Crystal garden
- D   Degrees (Celsius and Fahrenheit)
- E   Electric current
- F   Floating and sinking
- G   Gravity
- H   Hive
- I   Ice
- J   Jack (observe and try spinning a jack)
- K   Keys (which key fits the padlock)
- L   Light and shadows
- M   Magnets
- N   Nests
- O   Owl facts
- P   Plants
- Q   Quarts (measuring liquids)
- R   Rainbows
- S   Sounds
- T   Tasting
- U   Unhatched eggs
- V   Violin strings
- W   Water
- X   Xylophone sounds
- Y   Yards (measuring)
- Z   Zucchini (observe differences between zucchini and cucumber)

Following the science fair, write a book about the experience. Let each page represent a letter, with a picture drawn by the child and then a sentence or two in the child's words about that experiment or activity.

Summary

Because children are naturally curious about their environment, science is frequently a part of their exploration, play, questioning, and experimentation. Science can teach patience, inquiry, respect for evidence, self-reliance, and open-mindedness. Many science activities are preplanned into the curriculum, but often science-related experiences result from natural, spontaneous environmental stimulation. As children gain more knowledge in the areas of science, they become more able to understand their world. As they become more familiar with Earth, they also should learn that they can make a difference in protecting our environment, and that the quality of air, soil, and water is determined by human treatment and care. They become more aware of, and comfortable with, nature, people, events, and the materials surrounding them.

Valuable science activities for children include hearing, tasting, smelling, touching, inferring, observing, interpreting, classifying, drawing conclusions, solving problems, inquiring, reasoning, rationalizing, exploring, generalizing, comparing, creating, verifying, analyzing, predicting, and hypothesizing. Possibly no other single area of the curriculum involves as many process skills that are so important to the development of understanding and thinking in young children. Young children have a natural curiosity about their world and how it works; they constantly wonder, explore, examine, describe, manipulate, compare, and question things relating to the natural environment. They should be encouraged to observe carefully, note similarities and differences, make predictions, test their predictions, ask questions, and interact with one another and the teacher. They should be constantly encouraged to think and talk about what they are doing and seeing.

Student Learning Activities

1. From your reading and study of this chapter, develop criteria for science activities and units for children. For example, science activities and units should provide opportunities for firsthand or real experiences.

2. From your study of this chapter, write down at least five of the process skills that science helps to develop in young children. For each skill that you listed, suggest one science activity that would specifically give children practice in

developing this skill. For example, to develop the skill of inferring, a good activity would be to pass around a gift-wrapped box containing several objects, such as paper clips and pennies. Have the children guess or infer what might be inside the box.

3. Make a list of science equipment and materials that you would begin collecting for science kits. Examples might be rocks,

seed collections, thermometer, magnifying glass, tape measure, and others. Pick an area, such as magnets, and develop a science kit. Time will be provided in class to share your kits.

4. Plan and carry out with children at least three science activities.

5. Discuss why it is important to know, understand, and implement the National Science Education Content Standards in early childhood education curriculum planning.

Suggested Resources

See additional science resources listed at the end of Chapters 6, 10, and 11. There are so many books, songs, pictures, kits, films, videos, DVDs, CDs, and software relating to all aspects of science that teachers should check available resources for additional suggestions. Consult the Internet, multimedia computer encyclopedias, bookstores, and libraries.

National Audubon Society

National Science Teachers Association

National Geographic Society

National Wildlife Federation

Newbridge Education Publishing

Scholastic

Science and Children (journal of the National Science Teachers Association)

Science Channel

Society for Visual Education

Sunburst

Weston Woods

SCIENCE RESOURCES

Note: These resources will also provide many suggestions for Chapter 10, "Earth and Space Science Experiences," and Chapter 11, "Life Science Experiences."

American Association for the Advancement of Science. Available online at www.project2061.org.

Ashbrook, P. (2003). *Science is simple: Over 250 activities for preschoolers*. Beltsville, MD: Gryphon House.

Boston's Museum of Science. Available online at www.mos.org.

Desrochers, J. (2001). Exploring our world: Outdoor classes for parents and children. *Young Children 56*(5), 9–12.

Dr. Science. Available online at www.drscience.com.

Elchinger, J. *Activities linking science with mathematics, grades K-4*. Arlington, VA: National Science Teachers Association.

Evitt, M. F., with Dobbins, T., & Weesen-Baer, B. (2009). *Thinking BIG, learning BIG: Connecting science, math, literacy, and language in early childhood*. Beltsville, MD: Gryphon House.

Gelman, R. K., Brenneman, K., Macdonald, G., & Roman, M. (2009). *Preschool pathways to science (PrePS): Facilitating scientific ways of thinking, talking, doing, and understanding*. Baltimore, MD: Brookes.

Harlan, J. D., & Rivkin, M. S. (2012). *Science Experiences for the Early Childhood Years: An Integrated Approach* (10th ed.). Upper Saddle River, NJ: Pearson.

Manning, M., & Szecsi, T. (2004/2005). ESOL in every minute of the school day. *Childhood Education 81*(2), 104–106.

McNair, S. (2006). *Start young! Early childhood science activities*. Arlington, VA: National Science Teachers Association Press.

National Science Teachers Association. Available online at www.nsta.org.

Neises, M., Hogue, L., & Sarquis, M. (2009). *Marvelous moving things: Early childhood science in motion*. Big Science for Little Hands. Middletown, OH: Terrific Science Press.

Parentspage. Howard Hughes Medical Institute. Philadelphia's Franklin Institute Online. Available online at http://sln.fi.edu/educators.html/.

Public Broadcasting System. Available online at www.pub.org/teachersource/sci_tech.htm/.

Ritz, R. (2007) *A head start on science: Encouraging a sense of wonder*. Arlington, VA: National Science Teachers Association Press.

Sanders, S. W. (2002). Child-focused environments. In *Active for Life: Developmentally Appropriate Movement Programs for Young Children*, 17–29. Washington, DC: NAEYC.

Seefeldt, C., Galper, A., & Jones, I. (2012). *Active Experiences for Active Children: Science* (3rd ed.). Upper Saddle River, NJ: Pearson.

PERIODICALS

Chickadee: The Canadian Magazine for Children. Young Naturalist Foundation, 59 Front St. E, Toronto, ON., M5E 1B3.

Child Life. P.O. Box 10681, Des Moines, IA 50381.

Children's Playmate Magazine. Children's Better Health Institute, 1100 Waterway Blvd., Indianapolis, IN 46202.

Ladybug. www.ladybugmagkids.com

National Geographic Little Kids. http://kidsblogs.nationalgeographic.com/littlekids

National Geographic News. National Geographic Kids Magazine, National Geographic Society, 1145 17th St. NW Washington, DC 20036-41688.

Ranger Rick's Nature Magazine. National Wildlife Federation, 11100 Wildlife Center Drive, Reston, VA 20190-5362.

Scholastic Let's Find Out. Scholastic, Inc., P.O. Box 3710, Jefferson City, MO 65102-9957.

Scienceland, Inc. 501 5th Ave., Suite 2108, New York, NY 10017.

Science Weekly. CAM Publishing, P.O. Box 70638, Chevy Chase, MD 20813-0638.

Sesame Street. Children's Television Workshop, P.O. Box 2896, Boulder, CO 80322.

World. National Geographic Society, P.O. Box 98199, Washington, DC 20090-8199.

Your Big Back Yard. National Wildlife Federation, 11100 Wildlife Center Drive, Reston, VA 20190-5362.

Online Resources

http://members.tripod.com/%7Epatricia_F/mathscience.html This website includes a variety of activities for teaching color.

www.educationworld.com Search for specific topics such as color or magnets at this site.

chapter 10

Earth and Space Science Experiences

"In many ways earth and space science is the most complex of the sciences" (Worth & Grollman, 2003, p. 143), and often requires a basic understanding of concepts related to both the physical and life sciences. There are so many aspects of earth and space science that can be explore—air, water, rocks, soil, moon, sun, weather, and erosion. Studying earth and space science helps children to begin developing an understanding of more abstract concepts they will explore later on.

This chapter presents ideas, concepts, and activities relating to the environment, air, water, rocks, temperature, weather, and seasons. Again, science is best learned through hands-on exploration and experiences. It is virtually impossible to designate science only as a subject to be occasionally taught as a unit or theme. It should be child centered and activity oriented; it should provide children with a varied environment to explore at their own pace and according to their individual cognitive abilities. All children should be encouraged to participate in science activities and inquiry.

Kupetz and Twiest (2000) suggest that children today have less exposure to the world of nature than did children of the past. They propose the following reasons why children are not as interested in exploring their natural outdoor environments:

- Safety concerns (dangerous or unsafe materials or environments)
- Organized activities (team and individual sports, music lessons, and clubs)
- Travel (more traveling among family members, vacations, and more time spent in transportation)
- Technology (computers, television)

> Science is a part of everyday life, so it must be a part of the everyday curriculum!

TEACHING ABOUT ENVIRONMENTAL CONCEPTS

Environmental issues are complex, and "the way we educate young children about the environment will have a great impact on the future quality of life for generations to come" (Crim, Desjean-Perrota, & Moseley, 2008, p. 6). The study of the environment with young children should include not only information, concepts, and behavior, but also attitudes and values (Kemple & Johnson, 2002). Children's ability to appreciate and emotionally respond to nature's beauty is important in building environmental responsibility. "Environmental education for young children is about wonder, and curiosity, enjoyment of our world, and caring for one's natural surroundings" (Kupetz & Twiest, 2000, p. 61). When children interact with the world of nature, they develop positive feelings and attitudes about nature, and establish habits for principles of conservation. Louv (2008) believes that when children interact with nature, it fosters a sense of attachment and belonging, and gives meaning to both indoor and outdoor environments of children. Young children can develop an appreciation for the beauties in the natural environment and begin to respect and understand the value of appropriate ecological behaviors. They can

Earth and space science involves basic understandings related to both the physical and life sciences.

respect and care for plants, animals, and human beings; help pick up litter and trash; keep earth, water, and air free from pollution; and use only what they need to prevent unnecessary waste (Woyke, 2004).

Early childhood programs should be both developmentally and environmentally appropriate, with the latter reflecting care, concern, and responsibility for our natural environment. It should not just be an occasional holiday, celebration, unit, lesson, or activity, but should become a natural part of everyday life. Demonstration (modeling) and active involvement are both needed for children to understand the importance of protecting and preserving our natural environment. When children see adults demonstrating concern for the planet, they learn to care for the environment themselves. Teachers, share your own respect and appreciation for *all* living things, and children will learn the same. The aesthetic groundwork for environmental appreciation should begin during the early childhood years.

Children can begin early to learn the need to protect our environment and that they can make a difference. They can learn that there are many natural beauties and resources on our planet to be enjoyed, appreciated, and protected by all people. They can learn that the quality of the soil, air, and water is determined by human treatment and care. Kim and Lim (2007,

p. 42) suggest the value of "eco-early childhood education," which emphasizes the importance of harmony between nature and humans. It promotes sound ecological principles, and encourages attitudes of reusing, sharing, and preserving natural resources.

Some of Earth's problems are the following:

- ***Air pollution.*** This is caused by combustion and burning fuel. Factories, wood-burning stoves, and cars all emit harmful pollutants into our air.
- ***Water pollution.*** People allow waste into our water supplies or spill chemicals or oil into our oceans, rivers, and lakes.
- ***Soil erosion.*** We farm soil so much that it becomes nutrient poor, and we cut down trees and clear away land for cities and buildings, leading to erosion.
- ***Solid waste.*** We throw away tons of garbage each year, and Earth is running out of space to put this huge amount of garbage. Children can learn that preventing waste is much easier than trying to get rid of it.

   Tips (Association for Childhood Education International [ACEI], 1996c) for doing that include using:
   Both sides of writing and drawing paper
   Reusable loose-leaf binders, book covers, bookmarks, lunch bags, and food containers
   Refillable pencils and pens
   Scrap boxes for reusable paper
   Fewer handouts
   Discarded items for creative arts projects
   Food wastes for compost piles
   Washable plates, utensils, and cups
   Equipment that does not need batteries

Recycled items such as toilet paper and paper towel tubes, bread tags, peelings from food items used during snack times, juice lids, finger loops from pop cans, packaging peanuts, wrapping paper, milk jugs, and plastic rings from 6-pack cans can be used for sorting, matching, counting, and creative art activities.

The study of the environment for young children must provide for interactions with nature. As Hachey and Butler (2009) note, "contact with nature is as important to children as good nutrition and adequate sleep" (p. 42). Young children are busy people. Because they enjoy touching, poking, digging, patting, hearing, shaking, smelling, and pouring, children are ready candidates for exploring and investigating nature. There are endless sensory experiences in the natural environment that support the observation skills involving aesthetic awareness and scientific thinking (Torquati & Barber, 2005).

Experiences with trees, parks, flowers, and their community all help children to acquire an appreciation for and commitment to our world and its environment. The best approach to support environmental and nature themes and concepts is to provide hands-on activities. For example, children can adopt a tree by naming it, studying and learning everything they can about their kind of tree, watering it, having a picnic under it, enjoying its shade, observing it during different seasons, seeing how animals use it, and making sure it is free of insect or other problems that could be treated. Teachers have an important role in helping young children to cultivate an attitude and sense of caring, understanding, and appreciation for their natural environment. As teachers, we should examine our own feelings about the outdoors. Do our feelings enhance or discourage children's play and learning while outdoors? Our own negative feelings about the outdoors (e.g., dislike bugs and dirt, find it too cold or too hot, or consider outdoor play as a time for our own break) influence whether and how we support our children's outdoor play explorations.

Concepts and Ideas for Teaching

Remember: One child *can* make a difference! Teach the children what they and others can do to save Earth, protect our environment, and be environmentally responsible.

1. Encourage observation of the natural surroundings. Children learn the interdependency of living things and that the natural world is interesting and always changing. When children collect materials from the outdoors (wood, leaves, seeds, etc.), these should be returned to the natural environment, if possible, after study is complete.
2. Protect plants and animals. All living things should be treated with respect and care. Help children to be aware of this and not to disturb nests, trees and bushes, animals and insects, flowers, and so on. When animals or insects are kept for study, try to return them to their natural habitat whenever possible.
3. Reduce, reuse, and recycle. Children can learn and teach their families about excessive packaging; conserving water, energy, paper, food, and other resources; repairing and reusing containers, clothing, and other materials; and recycling paper, tin, plastic, aluminum, clothing, and glass.
4. Conserve water. Turn off the water while brushing teeth, and do not let the water run to waste outside in yards and on playgrounds. Keep cold water in the refrigerator for drinking so that it does not have to run from the faucet each time to get cold. Take a shower instead of a bath.
5. Encourage families to buy products that are biodegradable, that is, they rot or decompose when discarded. Learn to conserve such things as paper. For example, school lunches can be brought in lunch boxes instead of paper bags. Bags, sacks, and other consumables can be reused. As much as possible, avoid using disposable utensils, napkins, plates and cups.
6. Always put trash in a trashcan. Children can check the playground every day for any garbage or litter that can be gathered up and disposed of properly. *Note:* Any dangerous trash (broken glass, sharp metal) should be handled by an adult. Always put trash in a trashcan.
7. Pick only what they plant themselves, and leave other things in nature for all to enjoy. Involving children in growing some of their own food not only minimizes food packaging, but it teaches children about nutrition, food sources, and the environmental needs of plants.
8. Make a compost pile. Besides making one outside, individual compost piles can be made in individual cups. Allow a few days of decomposition and then plant a seed (bean) and care for it as it grows.
9. Care for toys and other possessions so that they do not need to be replaced and can be passed on to others.
10. Turn the lights off when leaving a room, turn appliances off when not in use, and turn the thermostat down in winter and up in the summer to conserve fuel.
11. Involve parents in helping to protect the environment.

As we are planning our science curriculum, be sure to consider the outdoor environment as an important part of the entire program. Most children would rather be outdoors than indoors, and many of the everyday activities we do inside the classroom can be moved outside (Jacobs & Crowley, 2010). Interest and involvement increase when routines such as snack, water or sand table, circle or gathering times, creative art projects, music and movement, and story reading are offered outside the building. This also fosters an appreciation for the natural environment and surroundings.

The outdoor environment should provide endless opportunities for observation of birds, insects, weather, other children, wildlife, ground, and sky. Items essential for facilitating observation include magnifying glasses, binoculars, empty unbreakable jars, and insect nets. These items should be readily available for expanding the study of the physical, life, earth, and space sciences. If we want to raise children's environmental awareness, we must allow plenty of time for exploration and conversation, then use the children's own reactions and questions to determine what to do next (Lewin-Behham, 2006). These studies "invite the children to question, to develop attitudes and dispositions such as curiosity, a sense of themselves as science learners, perseverance, and collaboration" (Chalufour & Worth, 2006, p. 101). Whenever we want children to learn about something, we should provide the materials, space, and time for them to actively use their hands, noses, ears, eyes, mouths, feet—even their entire bodies!

Activities and Experiences

1. Do a nature-based scavenger hunt. The collected items could be studied in class, and then returned to their natural environments.

2. Make a nature scrapbook with drawings, descriptions, magazine pictures, photos, stickers, and children's summaries (Patrick, Mantzicopoulos, & Samarapungavan, 2009).

3. As children gain basic science understandings of geography and its relationship to their environment, begin encouraging them to observe the physical features around them (playground, garden, zoo, sandbox, grass, stream, houses, parks, and hills). Then talk about how things came to look the way that they do. Use photos, drawings, and blocks to tell the story of the things that the children see.

4. Have a "class-repair" day when a fix-it person comes to the school and helps the children to find items that need fixing or do not work (broken toys, wobbly tables and chairs, dripping faucets, broken shelves or cabinets, torn books, burned-out light bulbs, loose door knobs, and so on). If the item cannot be repaired, determine if it can be recycled.

5. Make a trash collage or sculpture. Provide each child with a sack and go for a trash-collecting walk in a schoolyard, park, or other location. The trash that the children gather can be recycled into an art project. They could also bring some discarded items from home to use.

6. Set up a recycling center in the classroom, lunchroom, or school. Have three collection containers: paper, plastic, and aluminum.

7. When crayons are in pieces and no longer used for coloring, melt them for making candles, place mats, or other items.

TEACHING ABOUT AIR

Young children soon learn that air is all around us, is real, and takes up space. Air can also be touched and felt; we feel the blowing wind, the cold and hot temperatures of the seasons, our breath, or the air from a com-

pressor or pump. An exploratory science activity taking place in the preschool classroom is described in the following example: The teacher had given the children small boxes of various sizes wrapped as gifts. They were told to explore the boxes in any way that they wished (except opening them) and to try to discover what might be inside them. One young boy said, "I know for sure one thing that is inside." The teacher, wondering how he could "know for sure," asked, "What do you think might be inside?" He confidently answered, "I don't just think, I know for sure air is inside!"

Once children learn the concept that air is all around us, they can "know for sure" that air is in a wrapped package, even though they do not know what else is actually contained in the mystery box.

Air concepts could be taught as a separate unit or as individual activities supporting other themes. There are numerous supportive curriculum activities relating to air.

Concepts and Ideas for Teaching

1. Air is part of Earth and is all around us.
2. Air takes up space.
3. Animals, people, and plants need air for survival.
4. Fire needs air to burn.
5. Air has weight.
6. Air has force.
7. Air moves.
8. There is air in dirt.
9. There is air in water.
10. Bubbles are formed with air. If you are blowing bubbles, the air comes from inside your body.
11. Air expands when heated, and warm air rises.
12. Air helps many items to float on water.
13. Air has many uses.
14. Air can be hot or cold.
15. Air can make noise.
16. The quality of air is affected by humans.

Activities and Experiences

1. Have the children hold their hands close to their mouths and noses to feel the air as they exhale. Have them put their hands on their chests to feel their chests (lungs) expand and contract as they inhale and exhale air.

2. Obtain a flexible cardboard box no smaller than a gelatin box and no larger than a cereal box. Cut a hole in one end and wrap the box with paper, making sure to wrap around the hole but not cover it. Above the hole, glue tiny tissue-paper

You can feel air when you blow against your hand.

streamers so that they hang across the hole. Pass the box around so that all the children can shake it or feel it. Then squeeze the box so the expelled air moves the tissue paper. Help the children conclude that there is air in the box that makes the tissue paper move.

3. Place a tissue in the bottom of a glass. Invert the glass in a large glass bowl that has been filled with water. Explain that the glass is full of air and that air takes up space. When the tissue stays dry, it is because the glass is full of air and there is no room for water to enter. If the glass is tipped to the side, air bubbles will escape and water will take the place of the air, allowing the tissue to get wet.

4. Fill a glass or jar half full of dry soil or dirt. With the children gathered very close around the jar, pour water onto the soil. Ask the children what they see and hear. They should be able to both see and hear air bubbles come up out of the soil. Explain that there is air in dirt. Water that is poured onto the soil and seeps down into it takes the place of the air and forces the air to the surface.

5. Fill a clear glass container with water. Allow it to stand for a brief time. Soon air bubbles will begin to form against the edge of the container. The air from the water has formed the air bubbles.

6. Fill a trough, tub, or sink with water. Obtain a small plastic container with a lid, such as an empty detergent bottle. Put the lid on and place the container on the water. It will float because of the upward force (buoyancy) of the water and because the container is light, being full of air. Take the lid off and fill the plastic container with water. Will it still float? A similar activity can be carried out in a larger body or pool of water. Show the children a deflated inner tube. Will it float or sink? Now inflate it with air and see what happens. Air helps things to float.

7. To demonstrate that fire needs air, obtain three pie plates or saucers and put identical small candles on each (you may need to melt a little wax to hold the candle in place). Select three glass jars of varying sizes (pint, quart, and gallon jars work well). Light one of the candles, and then put a jar over the candle. Explain that fire needs air to burn or that air has oxygen in it, and once the oxygen in the jar is used up, the fire goes out; it cannot burn without the oxygen. This same experiment can be demonstrated at Halloween with two jack-o'-lanterns, one carved and one only hollowed out.

8. Discuss what would happen if people, animals, and plants did not have air. Put a glass jar over a plant and observe what happens in a few days. Make sure that the plant still has water and sunlight. The plant will die without adequate air. Do all plants need air? (Not all; mold will grow in an airtight jar.)

9. Give the children a container of water and a straw. While blowing, they will see and hear the bubbles created when the air inside them blows through the straw and makes the bubbles in the water. Once the children have mastered blowing (and not sucking), add a small amount of detergent to water in a bowl, cup, or other container. Give them a straw and let them blow bubbles. Keep sponges close by to absorb water.

10. Make kites and pinwheels. Explain that it is both the construction of the objects and the moving air that make them fly or move.

11. Blow soap bubbles outside and explain that air from inside the child fills the bubbles, whereas the air outside makes the bubbles move; the more wind (moving air) there is, the faster and farther the bubbles will move. A good solution for bubble blowing can be made from either 8 ounces liquid detergent and 1 ounce glycerin or from 8 ounces liquid detergent and 1/4 cup sugar. Wands can be made by bending and twisting wire coat hangers or other heavy wire such as pipe cleaners.

Note: For activities to teach that air has weight, see Chapter 9.

UNIT IDEAS ON AIR

ART

- Hummers decorated to be used as rhythm instruments
- Straw painting
- Inflated balloons decorated with paper scraps, felt scraps, rickrack, gummed stars, or other objects; perhaps they could be decorated as human heads
- Pinwheels
- Paper airplanes (to make and fly)
- Fans (to make)
- Miniature parachutes made from different materials
- Bubble-blowing liquid tempera paint onto paper at the easel

VISITORS

- Someone to play a wind instrument
- Someone to demonstrate household machines and how they utilize air
- Firefighter to show how a fire can be smothered (with the air taken away)
- Parent to help fly kites

FIELD TRIPS

- Dentist's office: use of air in the equipment (air hose)
- Service station
- High school, junior high, or college music department
- Pet store: observation of fish and how they breathe air through the gills
- Place where there are machines that use air: vacuum, hair dryer, clothes dryer, appliances, or fans

FOOD

- Food activity featuring whipped cream: air beaten into cream
- Food activity featuring meringue: air beaten into egg whites
- Homemade ice cream
- Homemade root beer

SCIENCE

- Pictures or slides of animals and plants: discussion of how they need air
- Pictures or slides of machines that use air
- Observation of what happens on a windy day when you open a milkweed pod
- Exploration of bubbles

LITERACY

- Using the language experience approach to write about the uses of air
- Writing or telling about things that fly
- Studying and writing about keeping the air clean

PHYSICAL–MOTOR

- Playing with a large parachute and developing simple games to use with it

MUSIC

- Creative movements interpreting bubbles or kite flying: faster music as wind increases
- Using hummers, with discussion of how the air vibrating on the waxed paper makes the sound (see Chapter 13 for directions on making hummers)

TEACHING ABOUT ROCKS

"Teacher, I have something really, really valuable for you in my sack. I was going to give it to my mom, but I have given her one before, so I decided to give it to you." As the first-grade teacher opened the brown paper bag, she found a rock with fool's gold on it. The child proceeded to tell her of the value of gold and, therefore, of this rock's value. Rocks are of interest to young children and are readily available. Early in life, children become aware that rocks come in different sizes, shapes, colors, textures, and weights. Children enjoy classifying rocks in many of these ways. Probably one of the first ways of classifying is by kind, even though specific names may not be known. The children learn that rocks are made up of minerals and are unique because of the variations and characteristics of these minerals.

Concepts and Ideas for Teaching

1. There are many kinds of rocks.
2. Most rocks are made up of minerals or smaller particles, and they are formed in different ways.
3. Rocks have different hardness values. Some rocks can be broken more easily than others. (Mineralogists and geologists use the Mohs scale of hardness to classify rocks according to relative hardness from 1 to 10; 10 is the hardest. The diamond has a hardness value of 10.)

4. Rocks have different uses, depending on their hardness (hard and long-lasting rocks may be used for buildings), beauty (many are used for jewelry), or other qualities.

5. Some rocks may be used for writing and drawing on other rocks.

6. The inside of a rock often differs from the outside.

7. Rock fossils are specific kinds of rock. During the rock's formation many years ago, a plant or animal became embedded in the rock and left its imprint.

8. A person who collects, cuts, and polishes rocks as a hobby or profession is called a *lapidary*.

9. Rocks cannot burn.

10. Small or fine rocks are called *gravel* and are used in making cement or concrete. *Sand* consists of extremely fine rocks.

11. Over time, water changes rocks, making most rocks smooth.

Activities and Experiences

1. Collect rocks to sort and classify by general groups such as igneous (formed from cooling lava; examples: pumice and obsidian); sedimentary (formed from rocks, sand, and stones that are compacted by pressure; examples: sandstone, limestone, and shale); and metamorphic rock (formed when igneous or sedimentary rocks are completely changed through pressure and heat; examples: limestone becomes marble, shale becomes slate, sandstone becomes quartzite).

2. Collect rocks to sort and classify by specific kind of physical characteristics, such as color, shape, or size; order by weight from lightest to heaviest.

3. Collect rocks from bodies of water, streams, creeks, and other locations, and note their smoothness.

4. Make "fossils" from clay, and then let the clay harden.

5. Visit a lapidary shop, a gravel pit to notice different sizes of gravel, a construction site to watch concrete being poured, or a geological museum.

6. Obtain the Mohs scale of hardness and classify rocks (minerals) by hardness. Determine whether they can be scratched with a fingernail, penny, or nail or by other means.

7. Crack rocks open to examine them on the inside. Make sure to take safety precautions to protect the eyes.

8. Invite a geologist, lapidary, or jeweler to visit your classroom.

9. Collect geodes for children to observe.

10. Investigate how weathering changes rocks.

11. Have each child bring a rock from home or the playground. The children will write or dictate descriptions of the rocks. They can weigh them, measure them, and describe their physical characteristics. They can draw illustrations of their rocks and then put the pages into a class booklet.

TEACHING ABOUT WATER

Both children and adults have a natural attraction to water. Not only does it provide such a ready source for problem-solving and critical-thinking skills, it also allows for emotional catharsis. It is relaxing, comforting, soothing, pleasing, rhythmic, calming, fascinating, and instructive. Even though it is one of the substances most familiar to children, they never tire of exploring it. We have found that even unusual media such as rock salt and Styrofoam packing material placed in a trough do not capture as much attention as water—ordinary water! Water play not only seems to interest all children, but it also holds and maintains their attention for longer periods of time than do many other media. When playing with water, children expand fine motor development, refine social skills, discover cause-and-effect relationships, increase science knowledge, and develop problem-solving capabilities.

Ordinary water is exciting, but adding new dimensions to water or changing its form adds further interest. New concepts can be learned as various changes are made in the water. In addition to using ordinary water as a sensory medium, the following ideas are suggested: adding food coloring, adding detergent to make bubbles (perhaps adding some straws to go with the bubbles), and adding ice to the water. On the other hand, you could begin with another medium, such as sand, and then let the children add water to it in the trough. These suggestions are only a few of the ways to utilize water in exploring and discovering.

You can teach many concepts relating to water. The children can, of course, learn that it is a liquid and therefore can be poured. It can be compared to other liquids, or you can point out that water is the base of many liquids, such as punch or reconstituted orange juice.

Water can be used as an independent experience or it can be developed and expanded into a unit. The following is a discussion of some of the possible units relating to water: characteristics of water, forms of water, uses of water by people, the water cycle, and general uses of water.

A natural extension of water study is the study of mud. Adding mud centers to our early learning environment allows children to express their creativity, enhance their fine motor skills, and practice math, science, and literacy skills. Mud, one of the most basic elements of the earth, is an art medium that can be molded, dried, and decorated. Many materials suitable for supporting and extending mud play are readily available.

Concepts and Ideas for Teaching

1. Characteristics of water
   a. Has weight
   b. Is a liquid
   c. Is colorless, but can be colored by adding substances (food coloring, gelatin, ink, bluing)
   d. Takes the shape of the container into which it is poured
   e. Natural taste is changed with the addition of chemicals used in purifying
   f. Temperature changed by heating and cooling
   g. Evaporates (goes into the air)
2. Different forms of water
   a. Liquid (as previously explained)
   b. Ice: water in frozen form
   c. Steam: water that has changed to a gas or vapor
3. Uses of water
   a. People: drinking for survival; washing and cleansing of self, clothes, home, food; watering crops, gardens, and other plants; cooking; ice for preserving and cooling foods; steam for cleaning; ironing; removing wallpaper, stamps, or other items glued to surfaces; in generators and in steam turbines
   b. Animals: survival; habitat
   c. Plants: survival; habitat
4. The water cycle: Water evaporates from the earth into the air and then condenses into clouds. It returns to the earth in various forms: rain, snow, and so on. It collects in lakes, ponds, and seas. From there, rivers and streams carry it to reservoirs and storage tanks. After purification, it is carried through underground pipes into homes, schools, buildings, and other places. Children may also be interested to learn that water collects underground, so a well can be dug to pump the water from the ground. Children could observe the water pipes in a home under construction or in a home where the water pipes are easily viewed.
5. Forms of recreation utilizing water: fishing, boating, swimming, water skiing, and surfing
6. Professions involving water: firefighting, for extinguishing fires; fishing; sailing; plumbing, repairing water pipes and water systems; water quality engineer; lifeguarding; freighting to other countries; research of oceans and seas and animals that live there
7. Objects that sink in water, and objects that float
8. Materials that dissolve in water, and those that do not
9. Items that absorb water, and those that do not
10. Human effects on the quality of water
11. Water on Earth: The surface of Earth is mostly water (400 billion billion gallons). Most of Earth's water is in the oceans (97%) and therefore is salt water. About half of our fresh water is in ice caps and glaciers, so we must conserve and protect the available fresh water.
12. Consumption of water: People use more and more water all the time. The average person uses 125 gallons of water each day. That is too much; we need to conserve.

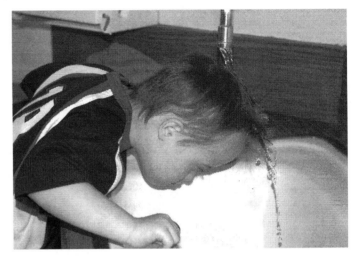

There are many ways to explore water.

Activities and Experiences

1. Observe the forms and cycles of water by first discussing ice cubes and how they are formed. Then put them in an electric frying pan with the temperature on low. Observe as the ice cubes change first to water and then to steam as the water boils. Hold an aluminum pie plate above the steam to collect some of the moisture, and then observe the drops of water on the pie plate.
2. Bring into the classroom animals that live in water: fish, tadpoles, and other aquatic life.
3. Allow the children to discover what kinds of objects float and what kinds of objects sink in water. Provide a container of water and a box of materials (paper clips, marbles, cork, sticks, beads, rocks, or sponges) for experimenting with sinking and floating. The children will discover that heavier items usually sink and lighter items usually float. (The concept of buoyancy and displacement can be addressed in simple terms for children to understand.)
4. Put an empty, capped detergent bottle in a bowl or tub of water. It should float. Put a small amount of water in it, and it should still float. As more water is added, it sinks lower and lower, because

an object will float if it is lighter in weight than the amount of water that would take up an equal amount of space. This same experiment can be performed with smaller plastic bottles. For younger children, a simple explanation might be that some objects are too heavy to float, or some objects are not porous enough (do not have enough air in them), or some objects need to be shaped like a boat in order to float.

5. Allow children to experiment with substances that dissolve in water and substances that do not. Compare sand, salt, marbles, an antacid tablet, flour, tapioca, soda, sugar, gelatin, and powdered drink mix.

6. Give children two ice cubes each. Have them sprinkle rock salt on one ice cube and then press the ice cubes together. The children should be able to see that the salt melts the ice. Try the same experiment with small rocks and note the difference.

7. Build a terrarium and observe the rain cycle. (See Chapter 11 for directions for making a terrarium.)

8. Fill a large glass or plastic container partly full of water and mark the water level. Put the container in the freezer, or outside if the temperature is below freezing. After the water freezes, determine whether the ice line is above or below the water line. The children should discover that when water freezes it expands. Allow the container of ice to melt back into a liquid. Compare ice and water lines again.

9. Fill two clear glass containers with water and mark the water levels. Leave the lid on one of the containers; leave the other container uncovered. Each day, observe and mark the water level in the uncovered bottle. Frequently compare the current water levels in both containers. Include the word *evaporation* often in the discussion.

10. Have the children take turns lifting different containers of water. They can lift a glass of water, but what about a pitcher or large bucket of water? Can they lift the pitcher or bucket without the water in it? Water has weight. Compare weight of wet vs. dry items like sponges or clothes.

11. Water play in a water table or basin can interest children for long periods of time. Many items are readily available to extend and support water play.

12. Place an ordinary drinking glass in a dish and fill it carefully with water. As it is filled, carefully pour more water into the glass; the water will bulge above the edge of the glass and form a convex shape. This is because of surface tension. To show the effect of detergents on water, a drop of liquid detergent placed in the water will cause it to flow over the edge of the glass.

UNIT IDEAS ON WATER

FIELD TRIPS

- Water laboratory
- Creeks, rivers, or streams
- Fire station
- Fire hydrant
- Ice pond
- Place selling bricks of ice and dry ice
- Car wash
- Frozen-food locker plant
- Gymnasium: water fountain, swimming pool, shower room, or steam room
- Pet store or place where children can observe an aquarium
- Fish hatchery

ART

- Painting with water (this works best outside on a fence or sidewalk)
- Watercolor painting
- Easel painting
- Paper-sack fish
- Mixing paint
- Papier-mâché
- Plaster of Paris molds
- Soapflake finger painting
- Salt–flour clay

MUSIC

- Moving like water: locations, stages, and sounds
- Sounds of water used for rhythms
- Rhythm sticks: tapping out rhythm of falling rain, thunder, and so on
- Containers with varying amounts of water; containers tapped with metal rod

VISITORS

- Someone who will bathe a baby in the classroom
- Animals that need water (fish)
- Person to cook with water
- Custodian: water vacuum
- Forest ranger

- Firefighter
- Parent to wash car

FOOD

- Boiled vegetables
- Cooked rice, macaroni: absorbing water
- Liquid for leavening
- Drinks
- Ice used for cooling
- Snow cones
- Homemade vegetable soup
- Gelatins
- Drink made from powdered mix
- Homemade ice cream

SCIENCE

- Floating objects
- Terrarium: rain cycle
- Stages and forms of water
- Items that absorb water and those that do not
- Items that dissolve in water and those that do not
- Uses of steam
- Uses of water in cleaning
- Animals that live and survive in water
- Overhead projector: colors mixed together in water
- Homemade ice cream: how salt changes the temperature of ice

LITERACY

- Writing or telling "I like water because . . ."
- Writing or telling "Water is . . ."
- Reading and reciting poems about water
- Reading stories relating to water

ADDITIONAL ACTIVITIES

- Water, ice, snow in trough
- Blowing bubbles
- Painting with water and brushes (outside)
- Role playing with firefighter's clothes, hats, fire trucks

Note: A lesson plan on water can be found in Appendix A.

TEACHING ABOUT TEMPERATURE, WEATHER, AND SEASONS

Weather easily integrates with science, math, literacy, and other parts of the curriculum.

> Because weather has such an influence on children, subject matter is readily available: rain, rainbows, prisms, clouds, precipitation, storms, temperatures, snow, hail, ice, sun, air, wind, barometers, thermometers, hygrometers, and so on. Weather and the changing seasons influence what we wear, what we do, what we eat, where we go, how we get there, and how we feel.

The concepts of temperature, weather, and seasons are related to one another because each influences the others. For example, the season often determines the weather for a particular locale. The temperature influences every aspect of weather and often determines the exact type of weather that is experienced. At the same time, the temperature is usually influenced by the time or season of the year. Thus, none of these concepts can be discussed without involving at least one of the others.

Both children and adults are greatly influenced by temperature, weather, and seasons. Activities, feelings, moods, and choices of games, recreation, foods, and clothes are often determined by the temperature, weather, or season. Everyone is interested in the weather report, because it often determines what we can and cannot do and where we can and cannot go. People listen to the weather report to decide whether windows should be washed, cars polished, or picnics planned. The weather report helps to determine whether it will be a good day for skiing, the fruit trees in blossom will be damaged by frost, or a planned trip can still be made.

Expanding children's awareness of weather and how it affects our lives enhances problem-solving skills, vocabulary building, observation abilities, and making predictions. Consider sounds, smells, and colors involved with weather and seasons. In teaching units relating to temperature, weather, and seasons, remember that young children should be exposed first to concepts regarding the seasons and kinds of weather that they actually experience. For example, it may not be practical to have units on snow and/or winter for children in Florida. Also, it is best to teach the kinds of weather and specific seasons at the time when the children are most apt to experience these particular conditions.

As with other concepts, the child may be able to group together pictures and objects relating to a season, but may not be able to label this season. Thus, a good approach to introducing and teaching a particular season or aspect of weather is to give the children the experience of classifying or grouping together objects and/or pictures of that season or aspect of weather. For example, the teacher may introduce winter by telling the children that they are going to talk about a time of year when the weather is very cold, when snowstorms are typical, and when the trees are usually bare. The label of the season, *winter*, is introduced. Then the teacher shows season pictures and objects, such as a snow shovel, a snowshoe, a swimming suit, a hoe, a rake, tire chains, a window scraper, and a flyswatter and asks the children to select those that are appropriate for the season being studied.

Another teaching approach involves helping the children to learn that the seasons always follow the same sequence. Thus, winter always follows fall, spring follows winter, summer follows spring, and fall follows summer, or whatever sequence is appropriate for your own region. In addition, children could draw pictures of scenes or objects, such as trees, in each season; then these pictures (or pictures provided by the teacher) could be arranged in sequence. It is interesting to teach the seasonal changes of animals: the snowshoe rabbit, monarch butterfly, and frog.

Because nature always foretells a coming season with signs, daily experiences outside offer the opportunity for spontaneous learning experiences. A sensitive teacher points to the buds on the tree and asks the children what season the buds signal. Or, as the children discover and explore the icicle hanging from the roof outside, the wise teacher relates it to temperature and season. The teacher may also ask such thought-provoking questions as, "What will happen to the icicle or to your snowman if the sun comes out and it gets very warm?"

Lesson plans relating to the concepts of temperature, weather, and season can be approached in a variety of ways. For example, it is possible to plan a unit on a particular season, with discussion of the most typical weather and temperatures accompanying this season. Thus emerge units on fall, wind, and cooler temperatures; spring, wind, rain, sunshine, and warmer temperatures; and summer, sun, and hot temperatures. On the other hand, each subject could be treated alone and approached as a separate unit. For example, during the fall season a unit could be done on fall, with perhaps a follow-up unit on wind. Temperature could be included in one or both of the units as it relates to the main subject. A separate unit on temperature could also be linked to the current season and a visit by the weather forecaster with weather instruments, such as the thermometer.

Weather, seasons, and temperature are part of the world in which children live; children are curious and interested and have a desire to learn more about them. Gear your units to the uniqueness of your own area and to the individual situations of the children in your classroom. Thus, depending on the seasons that the children in your locality experience, at least two and as many as eight or nine units could be developed from just these three concepts.

Concepts and Ideas for Teaching

1. Each day we experience a particular season, a particular kind (or kinds) of weather, and temperatures ranging from the high to the low for the day.
2. We live in a particular area where we experience certain seasons, certain kinds of weather, and a temperature variation.
3. The area where we live determines the characteristic temperature range that we experience, and this determines the climate in which we live. Thus, we live in a (warm, cool, cold, humid, dry, seasonal, constant, or changing) climate. (The children should describe the characteristics of their climate.)
4. Some animals are characteristic of our area because of the characteristic climate, temperature, weather conditions, or seasons of our area. (Describe animals of your own area.)
5. Some plants are characteristic of our area because of the characteristic climate, temperature, weather conditions, or seasons of our area. (Describe characteristic plants in your own area.)
6. A thermometer is an instrument used for measuring the temperature. The measured temperature goes up when the weather is warmer and down when it is cooler.
7. There are different kinds of thermometers.
   a. Thermometers for measuring the air inside and outside
   b. Thermometers for measuring body temperatures, especially during illness
   c. Thermometers for use in cooking, such as for meat and candy
8. When the temperature of some items changes, the items either expand (get larger) or contract (get smaller).
   a. Water expands during freezing.
   b. Metal expands during heating.
   c. Breads, cakes, cookies, and other foods that are baked expand in a hot oven because of the effect that high temperature has on their ingredients.
   d. Some types of meats get smaller when they are heated or cooked.
9. People, animals, and plants make changes in varying seasons, kinds of weather, and temperatures.
   a. Observation of a tree during each season
   b. Observation of what particular animals (bears, frogs, insects, birds, monarch butterflies) do during specific seasons or kinds of weather, or when the temperature changes
10. We are influenced in many ways by the weather, season, or temperature: how we feel;

what we do; what games and sports we participate in; how we dress; what foods we eat; how our bodies react to temperature changes, perspiring in excessive heat or getting goose bumps and shivering in cold weather.

11. The length of the day varies with the season; in the Northern Hemisphere, the days are shorter in winter and longer in summer.
12. There are many different kinds of clouds. We can often determine the approaching weather by the clouds.
13. Clouds have many different shapes and sizes, often resemble different objects, and may change shape rapidly.

Concepts and Ideas for Teaching Seasons

1. Each season has its own particular characteristics.
2. Each season has sensory characteristics: sounds, sights, smells, feels (or feelings), and tastes.
3. For each season, people make particular preparations involving their cars, homes, clothing, and outside grounds.
4. For each season, animals often make particular preparations or changes.
5. For each season, many plants make changes.
6. Each season has jobs, inside and outside the home, directly related to it.
7. Each season has characteristic kinds of recreation and activities.
8. Each season has characteristic foods.
9. Each season has holidays that always fall within its boundaries. (Note: Be sensitive to the fact that some families or religions do not celebrate particular holidays.)

In the following material, each season will be treated separately in terms of the preceding teaching ideas. The suggestions presented here are not meant to be inclusive; you may wish to contribute ideas more appropriate to your own locality. Encourage the children to brainstorm their own ideas as you study a season.

Winter

1. Winter has its own particular characteristics: cold, wet, quiet, white and gray, sleepy, and snowy. It is an indoor season for some and an outdoor season for others.
2. Winter has characteristic sensory qualities.
   a. Sounds: quiet, furnaces turning on, sleet hitting the windowpane, wind, cars stuck on icy roads, snowplows, children playing in the snow or sledding, snowmobiles, and road graders
   b. Sights: snow figures, snow, snowplows, warm and heavy clothing, boots, hats, frost on win-

dows, chains for tires, icicles, bare trees, and footprints in the snow
   c. Smells: crisp air, woolly clothing, wet clothing, soups, stews, Christmas smells, fire, homemade bread, furnace smells, and pine
   d. Feels: cold, toasty warm, tingly fingers and toes, wool, fur, blankets, fire, snow, ice, and wet clothing
   e. Tastes: soup, snow, icicles, hot bread, chili, turkey, hot chocolate; Hanukkah, Christmas, New Year's Day, and Valentine's Day tastes and foods
3. People prepare their cars, homes, clothing, and yards for winter.
   a. Cars: antifreeze, chains, snow tires, ice scrapers
   b. Clothing: purchased or taken out of storage; items such as boots, coats, hats, gloves, and scarves located and checked for fit and condition
   c. Homes: furnaces checked (if not previously done in the fall), windows sealed or shut tightly, air conditioners covered or stored away, and chimneys cleaned
   d. Yards and grounds: lawn furniture and gardening equipment stored, snow shovels purchased or taken out of storage, feed for animals obtained, shrubs tied up, and coarse salt purchased for icy walks
4. Animals prepare for winter in a variety of ways. Some animals hibernate; some grow thick, warm coats of fur; farm animals are usually provided with shelter; some animals, such as birds, migrate during the fall in preparation for winter; some animals store nuts, seeds, or other food; and some animals change color to blend with the environment.
5. Plants prepare for winter in a variety of ways. Some trees are bare and dormant during the winter; flowers often are nonexistent in the winter, unless they are grown in greenhouses; bulbs of such flowers as tulips and daffodils are dormant underneath the ground; and shrubs survive if the temperatures do not fall too low.
6. Jobs related to winter include shoveling the snow from the walks and driveways, feeding farm animals that in other seasons are on the range or graze in the pasture, operating snowplows or sanders, cleaning off snow-covered or icy car windows, and keeping the furnace in good working order. In addition, professional jobs include furnace repair, ski patrol, operation of ski resorts, and the sale of snowmobiles or other winter recreation equipment.
7. Recreational activities characteristic of winter include playing in the snow, building snow figures, snowball fights, hockey games, basketball games, skiing, snowshoeing, sledding, and ice skating.

8. Foods characteristic of winter include soups, chili, hot breads, Christmas foods, Hanukkah foods, Kwanzaa foods (vegetables, fruits, and nuts), Valentine cookies, traditional New Year's foods, oranges, and grapefruit.

9. Holidays of winter include Hanukkah, Christmas, New Year's Day, Kwanzaa, Martin Luther King, Jr., Day, Valentine's Day, Groundhog Day, President's Day, and St. Patrick's Day.

Spring

1. Spring has its own particular characteristics: warmer; sometimes wet and sometimes windy, and with more storms (tornadoes and thunderstorms), but mostly sunny and dry; active; alive; colorful; busy; home and grounds cleanup; gardening and planting; green; new growth; birds; snow melting; flowers blooming; and people wearing pastel colors.

2. There are many sensory characteristics of spring.
   a. Sounds: voices of children playing outside, roller skates, rollerblades, skateboards, songbirds, wind, rain, bees, lawnmowers, motorcycles, and cleanup crews using machinery to pick up and clean up trash
   b. Sights: kites, mud puddles, grass growing, newborn animals, new growth, flowers, people doing home and yard cleanup, children playing outdoors, and snow melting
   c. Smells: rain, earth and soil, newly cut grass, fresh paint, washed and cleaned homes (spring cleaning), flowers, fertilizer, and fresh-air smells
   d. Feels: chilly temperatures in morning and evening, warmer days; energetic; the feel of grass, earth, and soil (pulling weeds and cleaning flower gardens)
   e. Tastes: flavored ice pops, wiener roasts, ice cream, fresh vegetable salads, and fresh strawberry pie and shortcake

3. People prepare their cars, homes, clothing, and yards for spring in numerous ways.
   a. Cars: snow tires and chains removed, air conditioning checked
   b. Clothing: winter clothing put away, spring and summer clothing brought out of storage or purchased, and boots and raincoats kept close by
   c. Home: indoor spring cleaning, such as washing walls, cupboards, windows, floors, drawers, and closets, as well as sorting household items and discarding some of them; outside spring cleaning, such as cleaning out flower beds, planting flowers, trimming shrubs and trees, raking and fertilizing grass, painting or fixing up the outside of the home, storing snow shovels and equipment, and bringing gardening equipment and lawn and patio furniture out of storage.

4. What animals do in the spring: Many animals come out of hibernation, birds return, baby animals are born, animals may begin to lose fur coats, many livestock and farm animals are taken to the range for the late spring and summer months, sheep are shorn, and birds build nests.

5. What plants do in the spring: Plants that have been dormant during the winter come alive with buds, flowers, and leaves. Pussy willows are in season. Bulbs that have been dormant now poke up through the ground in the form of daffodils, tulips, and other early flowers. Some indoor plants are taken outdoors once the possibility of frost is over. Buds are seen on trees. Fruit trees blossom. Flowers, shrubs, and vegetable gardens are planted. Farmers plant vegetables, grains, and feed for their animals.

6. Jobs related to spring include those of city cleanup crews, gardeners, construction workers, farmers, professional carpet and rug cleaners, and nursery and seed people.

7. Recreational activities characteristic of spring include sandbox play, tricycle and bicycle riding, roller skating, in-line skating, skateboarding, baseball, golf, fishing, tennis, outdoor neighborhood games, and picnics.

8. Foods characteristic of spring include strawberries and fresh strawberry desserts, asparagus, avocados, fresh vegetable salads, Passover foods, Easter candy and hard-boiled Easter eggs, and picnic foods.

9. Holidays of spring include April Fool's Day, Passover, Good Friday, Easter, Arbor Day, Mother's Day, and sometimes Father's Day, Memorial Day, and May Day.

Summer

1. Summer has its own particular characteristics: hot, humid, lazy, sunny, dry, green, active, busy, vacations, flowers, gardens beginning to produce, lightweight and less clothing, sweating, visits from vacationing friends and relatives, usually no school.

2. Summer has many sensory characteristics.
   a. Sounds: lawnmowers, motorcycles, water splashing, hiking, parades, fire engines, birds, crickets, children playing outside, bees, water sprinklers, and sounds that often seem louder because windows are open.
   b. Sights: campers, boats, trailers; people wearing less clothing and people on vacation; fishing, camping, and hiking gear; gardens, flowers, and leaves on trees; parades, sunburned skin; green; people and animals sweating; sprinklers,

Water, mud, and sand are always great for exploring!

fans, and air conditioners; sunglasses; and swimming suits

  c. Smells: chlorine, beaches, flowers, sunburn ointment, earth, perspiration of people and animals, fresh fish, campfires, fresh fruit and vegetables, freshly cut hay, outdoor barbecues, hot asphalt, overheated cars, and bug spray

  d. Feels: going barefoot on grass, sand, or hot pavement; mosquito and other insect bites; bee stings; being sweaty, hot, and sticky; cool drinks and ice; and a refreshing swim

  e. Tastes: lemonade and other cold drinks, fresh fruits, melons, fresh vegetables, picnic foods, roasted hot dogs and marshmallows, potato salad, barbecued foods or charcoal-cooked meats, ice-cream cones, and fresh fish

3. People work in their yards and on their homes and wear cooler clothing in summer. They also take vacations.

  a. Clothing: swimsuits, shorts, and lightweight clothing for hot summer weather; sweaters or light jackets for cool evenings in the canyon or park; and shoes often not worn, especially by children

  b. Homes: yards and gardens watered often; flowers in bloom; harvest season in late summer; lawns cut often; bugs and weeds sprayed or treated; home repair; and screens put on windows

  c. Recreational activities and vacations: canyons, parks, beaches, and other places outdoors; a day spent away from home relaxing and having fun, or a vacation lasting for several days or weeks

4. Animals are seen in abundance in the summer, including those that are not seen in other seasons. Fish jump from lakes and ponds, insects buzz or move about everywhere (mosquitoes can be a nuisance), bats and fireflies may be seen at night, and crickets may be heard. Livestock are seen grazing in the fields and on the ranges, other farm animals are seen away from their winter shelters, and pets often rove freely about the neighborhood.

5. Plants are usually at the peak of their growth in the summer. Farmers are busy keeping their crops of vegetables and grains irrigated and weeded. Yards and gardens are beautiful with flowers, green trees, and green lawns. Fruit trees bear fruit, and vegetable gardens are productive. In late summer, the farmers harvest crops: grains, vegetables, and other plantings.

6. Jobs related to summer include city cleanup operations, gardening, construction work, farming, baseball umpiring, lifeguarding, ice cream sales, home-and-garden sales, and the harvesting of crops as a temporary job.

7. Recreational activities characteristic of summer include many outdoor activities. Vacations are often taken, and many activities are planned on vacations. The following summer activities are enjoyed by many: picnics, hiking, fishing, baseball, water skiing, sailing, swimming, tennis, golf, camping, boating, volleyball, tricycle and bicycle riding, roller skating, running through sprinklers, outdoor neighborhood games, and sandbox play.

8. Foods characteristic of summer include fresh fruits; melons, especially watermelon; hot dogs; hamburgers; lemonade and other cold drinks; ice cream; milkshakes and sodas; fresh vegetables; tomatoes; tossed green salads; picnic foods; barbecued foods such as steaks, hamburgers, and shish kebabs; and corn on the cob.

9. Holidays of summer include Father's Day (sometimes), Independence Day, and Labor Day.

Fall

1. Fall has its own particular characteristics: cooler days, quietness, colors (especially red, yellow, orange, rust, brown), harvest, school, new clothing, wind, the first frost, raking leaves, yard and garden cleanup in preparation for winter, warm days and cool nights, shorter days, dry leaves, first snowfall.

2. Fall has numerous sensory characteristics.
    a. Sounds: slower chirp of crickets, back to-school sounds of children, farm machinery sounds as harvesting is done, rain and wind sounds, blowing and crunching of dry leaves as children play in them, and football activities
    b. Sights: colorful leaves, harvest, wheat, raking and playing in leaves, falling leaves, apples, pumpkins, school buses, trees becoming bare, countertops and storage areas filled with freshly canned fruits and vegetables, and children in jackets and sweaters
    c. Smells: dry leaves, wet leaves, smoke, home canning, harvest smells, caramel apples, cinnamon, chili, brisk cool nights, and cut hay
    d. Feels: chilly nights, sometimes warm and sometimes cool days, and dry leaves as they are played in and raked up
    e. Tastes: cider, pumpkin pie, cranberries, squash, apples, turkey, chili, doughnuts, stew, hot soup, and caramel apples

3. People prepare their cars, homes, clothing, and yards for fall.
    a. Cars: snow tires, chains, and antifreeze
    b. Clothing: new purchases for school or last year's garments brought out of storage and checked for fit and good repair; warmer clothing substituted for summer's lightweight clothing; and sweaters, jackets, and other outerwear
    c. Home: screens taken off and windows shut tightly; air conditioners covered or put into storage; and furnaces checked and/or cleaned and new filters installed
    d. Yards and gardens: leaves raked; bulbs such as tulips planted; shrubs trimmed and tied; flower beds cleaned up; yard tools put into storage and hoses put away; outside water shut off so that pipes do not freeze; and fall harvesting of farm crops and foods

4. Some animals, such as bears and snakes, go into hibernation in late fall; other animals grow thick, warm coats of fur. Livestock are brought down from summer ranges; birds migrate; other animals store nuts and other foods; and some animals change color as a camouflage for winter. The caterpillar forms a pupa case (chrysalis) from which it emerges as a butterfly.

5. Leaves turn color and fall from the trees. Many trees, plants, and weeds bear seeds, and plants may dry or die. Some plants, like chrysanthemums, bloom in the fall. The first frost often kills many plants.

6. Jobs related to fall include raking leaves and yard and garden cleanup. Many jobs are associated with the harvest season. Farmers and farmhands are especially busy; in homes there is fruit and vegetable canning, and the busy season arrives for turkey farmers.

7. Recreational activities characteristic of fall include football, volleyball, soccer, playing in the leaves, and hunting.

8. Foods characteristic of fall include turkey, apples, caramel apples, apple cider, pumpkin pie, squash, Halloween candy, doughnuts, and cranberries.

9. Holidays of fall include Rosh Hashanah, Yom Kippur, Columbus Day, Halloween, Veterans Day, and Thanksgiving.

Concepts and Ideas for Teaching Weather

1. Discuss the particular kind of weather, how it is caused, and where it comes from.
2. Talk about what this type of weather does, what its uses are, and what its positive and negative aspects are.
3. Each kind of weather is manifested in different ways.
4. Each kind of weather has sensory characteristics: sounds, sights, smells, feels, tastes.
5. Each kind of weather makes us feel different inside, depending on our feelings toward that kind of weather.
6. Each kind of weather makes us dress differently.
7. Each kind of weather makes us do different things.
8. We participate in different games and activities in different places, depending on the kind of weather.
9. We go to different places in different kinds of weather.
10. The different kinds of weather are often related to other aspects or kinds of weather.

In the following material, each main aspect of weather (snow, rain, wind, and sun) is treated separately in terms of the foregoing ideas. The suggestions are not meant to be inclusive. You may have to contribute ideas that are more appropriate to your own locality. Encourage the children to brainstorm and to share the resulting ideas as you study and explore the various kinds of weather. Other types of weather can also be approached with these same questions.

Snow

1. Snow begins as frozen water vapor that forms around microscopic particles afloat in the air. When this water vapor freezes, transparent ice crystals are formed. As more water vapor condenses around these ice crystals, they become heavy enough to fall out of their clouds. Air currents then toss them about in the atmosphere, causing them to collide and to break into tiny chips of ice that form more ice crystals. The crystals clump together on their trip down to the earth, forming snowflakes. The crystals in a snowflake are always in the form of a 6-pointed star (hexagon). (*Note:* Select parts of this explanation that are suitable to your children's understandings.)

2. Snow falls in the colder climates and often blankets the earth during the winter months, especially in the mountains. Snow has many uses. Most of our water comes from snow, because when it melts it builds up the watersheds or melts into the lakes and reservoirs from which the streams and rivers flow to bring water to people. Snow is also used in many winter sports activities. Children play in snow and use it to build things such as snow figures. Snow also serves as insulation for plants and animals.

3. Snow comes in different forms. It comes as a blizzard, sleet, hail, large flakes, or small flakes. It can be wet or dry (powder).

4. Snow has many sensory characteristics.
   a. Sounds: quiet, light; snow falling against the windowpane, making a soft, tapping sound; and sleet and hail falling more loudly
   b. Sights: white, sparkling; each small, fragile snowflake quickly melting when touching a surface warmer than itself
   c. Smells: damp, wet; no other characteristic smell for snow
   d. Feels: cold, wet, icy; snow causing stinging or numbness, especially in the fingers and toes
   e. Tastes: wet, tasteless, like ice or ice water; clean, white snow inviting to taste because it looks good to eat

5. Snow creates different feelings in different people. The first snow of the season is welcomed by most people, especially children. However, usually the last snow of the season is not welcomed and creates negative feelings because most people are ready and eager for spring. Teachers must remember that feelings toward snow depend on whether snow is a favorite kind of weather or not. Children should be allowed to explore and share their feelings toward snow.

6. Snow makes us dress in warm clothing: wool, boots, mittens, heavy coats, hats, sweaters, and long socks.

7. Snow makes us do different things. When it snows, we play inside more often than we do in other seasons. We often do not travel very far or take vacations (some people vacation in warmer climates to get away from the snow and cold). We also build snow figures, play in the snow, go sledding, and participate in other winter sports.

8. We participate in different games and activities in different places when there is snow. We play many inside games, but we also play games and participate in snow activities: Fox and Geese, ice skating, sledding, skiing, building snow figures, having snowball fights, building snow structures, snowmobiling, and snowshoeing. Many of these activities take place in our neighborhoods and backyards, but others occur in winter resorts in the canyons or mountains.

9. We go to different places when it snows. Usually we stay home, but we may go to resorts or mountain areas to participate in winter sports or travel to warmer climates.

10. Other kinds of weather influence snow. Sun melts snow; wind creates blizzards and snowdrifts; rain melts the snow; if the temperature goes down after a snowmelt in the wintertime, it can create icy conditions.

Rain

1. Rain begins as moisture or water that has evaporated from the ground and from bodies of water. This water vapor collects (condenses) into rain clouds and then falls to the earth in the form of rain. Once again moisture from the ground and plants evaporates and forms vapor in the air, and the rain cycle continues. (*Note:* Use only those parts of the explanation that are appropriate for your children's understanding and levels of comprehension.)

2. Rain is useful in many ways. Heavy rainstorms, like snow, help build up the watersheds. Rain waters gardens and grass, helps farmers to irrigate crops if it comes at the right time, clears dust and smog from the air, and helps plants to grow. The water from rain is also used by people for washing, bathing, and drinking, as well as by plants and animals. Rainstorms may also bring rainbows, and their beauty is enjoyed by all, especially children. Rainstorms may cause damage and may occasionally have negative influences. They can be accompanied by thunder and lightning, and the

lightning can cause fires, especially forest fires, which are damaging and dangerous. Heavy rainstorms can also cause flooding.

3. Rain has different forms. It can come in a torrent, a drizzle, a mist, light rainfall, heavy rainfall, a thunderstorm, large drops, and small drops.

4. Rain has various sensory characteristics.
   a. Sounds: cars on highway, rain on roof or windowpane, thunder and lightning, windshield wipers
   b. Sights: rainbows, lightning, gray and dark, blurry, fresh and green after a rainstorm
   c. Smells: fresh, wet, musty, and moist
   d. Feels: wet, clean, fresh, humid, and cool
   e. Tastes: drops of water on the tongue have no taste

5. Rain creates different feelings in different people. On a rainy day, the following conversation between two children was overheard:

   DENNIS: I surely like rainy days—they are my favorite kind!

   SAM: They aren't your favorite kind—they are ugly, and they are the worst.

   DENNIS: They aren't ugly, and they are my favorite day. I love them because they are wet!

   For some, rain creates feelings of enthusiasm, exhilaration, and delight; for others, it stirs feelings of depression, sadness, and laziness. Our reactions and feelings toward rain may depend on the plans for the day or how long it has been since the last rainfall. For example, if a picnic is planned with family or friends, rain could bring disappointment or disgust. But after many long days of hot, dry weather, a rainfall is refreshing and welcome. Farmers also have different reactions to rainfall. It may be desperately needed and hoped for; but if farmers are just ready to plant or if the hay has just been cut or baled, rain is not a welcome sight. If rain has been falling for several days, it can often bring disgust or depression, especially to adults. As children discuss their feelings, give them actual situations to explore. For example, ask, "How would rain make you feel if it came on the day we were planning our field trip to the zoo?"

6. Rain makes us dress in special clothing. We wear boots and raincoats and carry umbrellas.

7. Rain makes us do different things. When it rains, we probably play inside more often. However, after a spring or summer rainstorm, we may especially enjoy playing in the sandbox or in puddles, or sailing boats down small streams caused by the rain.

8. We engage in different games and activities in different places when it rains. We play more inside games and activities and are often in a hurry to come out of a rainstorm. Immediately after a rainstorm, children like to play in the sandbox because the wet sand makes such good mud pies and molds so readily. They also like to sail boats and other objects in the streams created by rainstorms. Teachers often like to plan musical games and other inside activities for rainy days.

9. We go to different places when it rains. Usually, we stay home, and rainstorms often cause us to seek cover if we are enjoying outdoor recreational activities such as a picnic, hiking, or boating.

10. Other kinds of weather influence rain. Sunshine during or after a rainstorm creates a rainbow. A rainstorm on a hot day may create steam from the pavement or rooftops. Wind combined with rain often creates torrents or other miserable conditions. Wind can often blow away a potential rainstorm. Warm temperatures turn spring snowstorms into rain showers. Or cold temperatures can turn rain into sleet or freezing rain.

Wind

1. Wind is the result of moving air currents, caused when hot air rises and cold air takes its place.

2. Wind is good for flying kites, drying clothes or other items, moving storms or other kinds of air masses, making windmills work, and moving sailboats. It is not good for neat hairstyles; keeping dust in place; or freshly painted houses, garages, fences, or other outside structures. Most animals do not like wind. People who wear contact lenses do not like wind because it causes irritation to the eyes. Wind can also cause damage to the environment by contributing to soil erosion or causing other environmental problems. A farmer who has just planted a field does not like wind because of the soil erosion.

3. Wind has different forms, such as gusts, windstorms, hurricanes, dust storms, gentle winds or breezes, high winds, and tornadoes.

4. Wind has numerous sensory characteristics.
   a. Sounds: whistling, fluttering, gusting, rapping, whining, blowing, wailing; may be frightening or pleasant
   b. Sights: hair blowing, trees swaying, shrubs and flowers moving, branches blown down, people holding their hats on and moving in a hurry, women holding their skirts and dresses down, children flying kites
   c. Smells: dusty; may blow in unusual odors from nearby swamps, farms, industrial plants, lakes, or other areas; may bring the smell of a potential rainstorm
   d. Feels: gritty, dusty, cool, stifling, gentle, strong, cold, pleasant, irritating, welcome, unwelcome
   e. Tastes: sand that has blown into the mouth

5. Wind creates different feelings in different people, depending on what has been planned for the day. Children may enjoy spring winds because they can fly their kites. A cool breeze on a hot summer day or evening may be just the thing needed to cool off. Strong winds are most often unpleasant and unwelcome, at least to adults. During the winter, wind combined with already cold temperatures creates a chill factor that makes the temperature seem even lower and makes the weather more unpleasant. Gentle, light winds in summer are often welcome, but heavy, strong winds stir up too much dust in the air. On days when it is extremely windy, children often come into the classroom just like gusts of wind, and the emotional climate in the classroom on these days is often high.

6. Wind makes us dress in heavier clothing. In the spring or fall, we may need only a jacket or sweater. In the winter, if it is windy, we may need to put on extra-heavy clothing and coats.

7. Wind makes us do different things. We have to hold on to things we are carrying and hold down other things. If it is windy, we are often in a hurry to arrive at our destination or to go inside.

8. We engage in different games and activities in different places in the wind. We sail boats, enjoy windmills, and fly kites when it is windy. Children also seem to enjoy running outdoors when it is windy—almost as if they were chasing the wind or the wind were chasing them!

9. We go to different places when it is windy. Usually, we stay inside and enjoy inside activities. However, windy weather is also the time for flying kites and sailing boats, as well as enjoying windmills and pinwheels.

10. Other kinds of weather influence wind, and wind influences other kinds of weather. Wind may blow a storm in or blow one away. If wind occurs with a snowstorm or rainstorm, we have a blizzard or a gusting rainstorm. During dry weather or in dry places, wind creates dust storms.

Sun

1. The sun is a star in our galaxy. It is a source of light, heat, and energy. It does not turn off at the end of the day or on cloudy days. At the end of our day, it is making light and day for people on another part of Earth. On cloudy days the sun is still shining, but the clouds are in front of it so that we do not benefit as much from the rays of sunshine or from the sun's heat. Every day has a sunrise and sunset for most people; however, there are places on the earth (such as the North Pole and South Pole) where, during particular times of the year, because of the position of the sun, children do not see the sun for many days or the sun does not go down for many days, and there is no sunrise or sunset.

2. The position of the sun, or the position of Earth in relation to the sun, makes or changes the seasons. The sun produces light, heat, and energy, which are necessary for plant growth. The warmth of the sun creates good outdoor play conditions so that children and adults enjoy being outdoors. In the middle of summer, the sun can create so much heat and the temperature can get so high that it is uncomfortable to be in direct sunlight for long. In some places, it is necessary to have homes, schools, and other buildings air-conditioned because of the high temperatures. When the sun is very warm, it can melt such objects as crayons and objects made of wax. It can also fade colors, particularly in draperies, cars, or furniture, that are constantly exposed to the rays of the sun. It can make crops dry up, particularly on unirrigated farms, if rainfall is not adequate; it can wilt flowers and burn grass if they are not watered. It can cause painful and dangerous sunburns.

3. The sun has different effects, usually depending on the particular locality and the season of the year. It can feel slightly warm or extremely hot. In the winter when the sun shines, its rays are welcome and may create some warmth through a windowpane, but outside the temperature may be too cold for the sunshine to feel warm at all. Two of the beauties of nature are sunrise and sunset; they seem to have particular beauty and great variety of color in the summer.

4. The sun has various sensory characteristics.
   a. Sounds and tastes: no characteristic ones
   b. Sights: bright, yellow, orange, beautiful and colorful sunrises and sunsets, shadows, reflections of sunlight, glaring
   c. Smells: hot asphalt or tar, dry soil, melted wax or plastic, hot car seats, and hot rubber (created by the warmth of the sun's rays)
   d. Feels: warm, hot, sunburn, perspiration, lazy, dry, and sticky

5. The sun creates different feelings in different people. Most often the sun is a welcome aspect of weather. Children enjoy the sunshine because it means that they can play outside more often. During the winter, sunshine usually means that there will be no snow or rain; thus, even though temperatures may be cold, children can often play outside. In the springtime, everyone is anxious to see warm, sunny days because outside work and play are then possible. The sun also brings growth to trees, shrubs, flowers, and other kinds of plants. To farmers, the springtime sun means that the soil

There is only one way to get sand out of shoes and socks.

and land will begin to thaw and dry out enough for the ground to be worked and planted and for crops to grow. The summer sun means that many outdoor activities and games can be enjoyed. We plan many outdoor experiences in the summer, and the sun is welcome because it creates warmth and dryness. The fall sun casts more light on the bright colors of nature and makes them even more beautiful. For most people, the sunshine brings happy feelings. However, during the middle of summer, when the sun brings high temperatures, we may feel lazy, sweaty, and lacking in energy.

6. The warmer the sunshine, the lighter we dress. We wear less clothing and lighter-weight clothing when the sunshine is very warm. We wear sun suits, shorts, sleeveless shirts and blouses, and sundresses. We also wear sandals, and we do not need to wear sweaters and coats.

7. The sun allows us to do different things. We go on vacation. We play outside, run through sprinklers, and go swimming, wading, and on picnics. We play in the summer more than at any other time of the year. We enjoy projects such as lemonade stands, neighborhood plays, and hobbies of every kind. We go bicycle riding and play with outdoor equipment.

8. We participate in different games and activities in different places in the sunshine. We play outside, games and activities of every kind. We play in the sandbox, ride bicycles and tricycles, and play with other wheel toys outside. We play many neighborhood games, such as hopscotch. We ride skateboards and roller skates. We enjoy games and activities in the parks and other recreation areas and use equipment such as slides and swings.

9. We visit different places when the days are sunny, including recreation areas, parks, amusement parks, the zoo, the canyons, and mountains. Activities enjoyed at such places include picnics, barbeques, campouts, hikes, and boating. Visits to relatives and friends are more frequent, and families often plan outings and family reunions on sunny, warm days. Swimming is a favorite sport on sunny days.

10. Other kinds of weather influence the sun, and the sun influences other kinds of weather. Clouds may prevent the rays of the sun from reaching Earth, creating an overcast day. The wind may decrease the sun's warmth, lowering the temperature. The sun influences almost every other aspect of weather. It may melt the snow, shorten a rainstorm, and dry up puddles and mud.

Shadows are an interesting additional aspect of sunshine. They are created when objects pass in front of light. For example, clouds pass in front of the sun and cast shade on the Earth. In addition, the movement of the sun during the day creates different shadows. For example, a tree, building, home, fence, or other object casts shadows in different positions as the sun moves during the day. When the day is very hot, people move to the shade (places where shadows are cast) to escape the heat. When the day is cold, people like to move into the light of the sunshine to warm up. (See Chapter 9 for additional ideas on light and shadows.)

One additional concept is that day and night are caused by the movement of Earth around the sun. One child, in a discussion of day and night, said that it was the moon that made it dark. The teacher explained that it was not the moon, but the sun setting, that brought nighttime. It is also the sunrise that brings the beginning of day. Children can also understand that the length of daylight and nighttime will vary with the season.

Activities and Experiences

Very few specific activities and experiences are included here, because many of them are listed in unit ideas (particularly the science sections) and other places in this chapter.

1. Plant a garden indoors or outdoors.
2. Plant bulbs in the fall and observe their growth in the spring.

3. Discuss the thermometer and frequently check the temperature. Help the children to understand that the temperature goes up when it gets warmer and goes down when it gets colder. Chart the temperature on a graph at the same time each day for a month and observe any changes. The high and low temperatures each day could be graphed the same way.

4. Observe carefully the effects of temperature on a growing plant.

5. Visit a greenhouse and measure temperature variations in different areas of the greenhouse.

6. Visit a grocery store and measure and compare temperature variations in different food areas: shelves, frozen food case, refrigerated case, storage areas, and so on.

7. Fill a few containers with different temperatures of water and arrange them in order from hottest to coldest. Record the various temperatures in both Fahrenheit and Celsius (centigrade).

8. Make sets of sequence pictures to be ordered by season. One set might be of a tree pictured in fall, winter, spring, and summer. Another set might be of a child dressed for the four seasons.

9. Collect picture cards of things representative of various seasons: clothing, weather, trees in various seasons, tools, jobs, and others. Let the children categorize them by season. A similar set of sorting cards could be made to represent various kinds of weather.

10. Brainstorm with the children what they like best and least about each season. Graph the results or write their ideas down, and have them illustrated and put into a booklet.

11. Make a season scrapbook with a section for each season. Include pictures of jobs, recreation, weather, and many other aspects of the season. Write ideas for each page in a sentence or two.

From the foregoing material, many ideas for approaching lesson plans should emerge. However, we also include the following unit ideas for organizing activities for lesson plans. We have combined a season with the kinds of weather associated with that season. The units need not be combined, but they often fit together.

 UNIT IDEAS ON SUMMER OR SUN

- Beach or swimming pool for wading or swimming
- Picnic
- Backyard garden
- Canyon or park
- Zoo
- Outdoor walk to observe summer and sun characteristics
- Planetarium
- Aviary
- Farm
- Early morning sunrise breakfast or outing

ART

- Blot painting with white paint to portray clouds on gray or blue paper that represents the sky
- Flower pictures made with cupcake holders
- Flowers made out of nut cups, using pipe cleaners for stems; stems placed in clay base in paper cup
- Sponge painting of sunrise or sunset
- Folded paper fan decorating
- Collage of summer objects: sand, shells, rocks, pebbles, or grass
- Rock painting
- Paper-plate hats decorated for a summer parade
- Paint with water outside

SCIENCE

- Shadows
- Growing seeds and plants
- Life cycle of the frog
- Fire prevention
- Flowers
- Clouds
- Sunlight and its effect on growing plants

MUSIC

- Shadow dancing behind screen or sheet
- Creative movements relating to summer activities: fishing, swimming, throwing a Frisbee, and others
- Creative movements interpreting a sprinkler, fountain, or waterfall
- Creative movements representing the sun rising or setting
- Creative movements interpreting the growth of a seed into a plant, the wilting of a plant in the summer's heat or sunshine, and how it perks up when it is watered
- Creative movements interpreting animals seen in summer: birds, butterflies, insects, life cycle of a frog, fish, and others
- Marching parade with or without rhythm instruments

FOOD

- Homemade ice cream or frozen yogurt
- Marshmallows and hot dogs cooked over a grill on the playground or at a park
- Fresh fruits in salads and other forms
- "S'mores"—two graham crackers, piece of chocolate bar, marshmallow toasted by the child; "sandwich" put together while marshmallow is warm
- Sandwiches and other picnic snacks, even if the picnic is outside the classroom on the grass or at a nearby home or park
- Potato salad
- Making jams and jellies
- Fruits dried in the sunshine and eaten a day or two later
- Flavored ice pops, slush, or other frozen treats
- Gelatin squares

VISITORS

- Person from a nursery
- Lifeguard
- Farmer
- Gardener
- Florist or flower arranger
- Person who enjoys fishing
- Golfer
- Ornithologist
- Entomologist
- People to share vacation experiences
- Ice-cream vendor

LANGUAGE AND LITERACY

- Slides and/or pictures of summer scenes, with children discussing them, individually or in small groups
- Objects or pictures of food, recreational equipment, clothing, and so on, relating to all seasons; items are passed out to all the children, with each child who has something relating to summer telling about it
- Sharing of vacation experiences
- Sharing of favorite summer activities, foods, places to visit, and so on
- Stories, written or told, of most memorable summer vacation or experience
- Writing and illustrating booklets on "Why I Like Summer," "What I Like to Do in the Summer," "Summer Is . . .," or "What I Did This Past Summer"

UNIT IDEAS ON WIND

FIELD TRIPS

- Outdoor walk on windy day to observe characteristics of wind
- Kite flying or watching others fly kites
- Airport
- Dam on nearby lake to watch a sailboat
- Weather station or television station to watch the weather forecast
- University or high school band class where children can see and hear wind instruments
- Music store that sells wind instruments

ART

- Kites made by children
- Straw painting or blow painting
- Hummers made to use in musical activity
- Balloons decorated with papier-mâché or powdered paints

SCIENCE

- Study and observation of effects of wind: soil erosion, wearing away of rocks, sand dunes
- Observation of a weather vane to determine wind direction
- Study of the effects of strong windstorms such as hurricanes and tornadoes
- Study and discussion of positive and negative aspects of wind

MUSIC

- Hummer band (see discussion of hummers in Chapter 13)
- Creative movements interpreting leaves blowing in the wind, people moving in the wind, kites blowing in the wind, trees moving in the wind, feathers moving in the wind, clothes drying in a breeze
- Visitors with wind instruments: children allowed to try to play instruments; visitors asked to play their instruments while children play their hummers

FOOD

- Hot soup: children allowed to blow on it to cool it
- Hot chocolate
- Food activities related to air: egg whites or whipping cream beaten as a part of a food activity,

with emphasis on how air is beaten into it and the concept that wind is also moving air

VISITORS

- Musician to play wind instrument or harmonica
- Parent to fly kites on playground
- Meteorologist
- Pilot to tell about watching the wind direction and speed when flying
- Forest ranger to discuss the effects and influences of wind in the forest and mountains

LANGUAGE AND LITERACY

- Pictures or slides of different kinds of weather, with children identifying those that depict wind
- Stories about wind, written or told
- Poems about wind, written or told
- Variety of articles of clothing, with children determining which articles should be worn on windy days
- Booklet written and illustrated on wind, including why the children do and do not like it

 UNIT IDEAS ON RAIN

FIELD TRIPS

- Lake, pond, stream, or river
- Reservoir
- Fish hatchery
- Water laboratory
- Home where the family has a terrarium or rain garden
- Water tower

ART

- Painting or collage of rainy scenes
- Children mixing their own paint so that they see the water base; painting with watercolors
- Paintings of rainbows
- Screen spatter painting: screen mounted on a frame (or use an old window screen), which is placed several inches above and parallel to the tabletop; paintbrush dipped into paint and passed over the screen to give a spatter effect on the paper below; alternatively, shadow pictures made by placing an object or shape cutout (or cookie cutter) on the paper and spattering paint around it

SCIENCE

- Study and observation of the rain cycle: evaporation and condensation
- Building and observation of a rain garden or terrarium
- Study of rainbows
- Study and observation of what rain does to plants
- Study and observation of a prism

MUSIC

- Creative movements interpreting falling rain, plants, or flowers: how they wilt before a rainstorm, droop during the storm, and perk up after the storm
- Rain dance by children (perhaps after a visit from a Native American who performs a rain dance)
- Rhythm interpretations of rain: hitting a windowpane, falling slowly or very rapidly

FOOD

- Rainy-day foods such as soup or chili
- Hot chocolate
- Foods with a water base, such as root beer or lemonade
- Foods dissolved in water, such as gelatins or powdered drinks
- Foods cooked in water, such as vegetables, macaroni, or rice

VISITORS

- Weather forecaster
- A visitor to explain and build a rain garden or terrarium
- Farmer
- Forest ranger

LANGUAGE AND LITERACY

- Stories about rain, written or told
- Poems about rain, written or told
- Shared rainy-day experiences
- Pictures or slides of different kinds of weather, with the children identifying those that depict rain
- Variety of articles of clothing, with the children determining which articles of clothing should be worn on rainy days
- Writing and illustrating booklets titled "I Like Rain Because . . ." or "Rain"

Summary

This chapter has dealt with the widely varied subjects of the environment, air, water, rocks, temperature, weather, and seasons. As children become more familiar with Earth, they also should learn that they can make a difference in protecting our environment, that the quality of air, soil, and water is determined by human treatment and care. They become more aware of and comfortable with nature, people, events, and the materials surrounding them. Since the concepts of temperature, weather, and seasons are so closely related to each other, a discussion of one of them usually involves at least one of the others. All people are greatly influenced by temperature, weather, and seasons. These factors affect clothing, food, activities, games, recreation, feelings, and moods. Many people prefer one season over another because of the kinds of activities that are characteristic of that season. Weather, seasons, and temperature are natural parts of the world in which we live. The spontaneous curiosity and interest of children in their environment makes related learning both enjoyable and rewarding. Young children's natural curiosity about their environment makes the early years an excellent time to instill positive attitudes and practices regarding the world in which they live.

Student Learning Activities

1. Using one of the science unit plans or a science topic of a child's own choosing, discuss with a young child his or her ideas about plans for study with this theme. Invite the child to propose a project plan for this study. Evaluate results.
2. Write a paragraph or two on your attitudes about temperature, weather, and seasons. How might your own attitudes about the season, temperature, or weather influence the children in your classroom?
3. Begin a picture collection for weather, and seasons. Mount the pictures appropriately.
4. Begin a collection of children's poems relating to air, rocks, water, weather, seasons, and other aspects of the environment.
5. With a group of children, implement at least one of the activities and experiences related to a science concept suggested in this chapter. The group of children may be a classroom group, a gathering of relatives, or neighborhood children. Evaluate your experience.
6. Prepare an activity plan or web for one of the science concepts in this chapter.

Suggested Resources

SCIENCE RESOURCES

See additional science resources listed at the end of Chapter 11 and those relating to nutrition at the end of Chapter 6.

Claycomb, P. (1991). *Love the earth: Exploring environmental activities for young children*. Livonia, MI: Partner.

Council for Environmental Education (CEE). Provides programs and services to promote environmental education for young children and educators. www.councilforee.org

DeBord, K., Hestenes, L., Moore, R. C., Cosce, N., & McGinnis, J. R. (2002). Paying attention to the outdoor environment is as important as preparing the indoor environment. *Young Children 57*(3), 32–35.

Erickson, M. F. (2008). The Children & Nature Network: Ensuring that all children can spend quality time outdoors. Site provides information for studying and experiencing nature. www.naeyc.org/yc/pastissues/2008/january

Herman, M. L., Passineau, J. F., Schimpf, A. L., & Treurer, P. (1991). *Teaching kids to love the earth*. Duluth, MN: Pfeifer-Hamilton.

Kaser, S. (2001). Searching the heavens with children's literature: A design for teaching science. *Language Arts 78*(4), 348–356.

Keeler, R. (2008). *Natural playscapes*. Bellevue, WA: Exchange Press.

Kupetz, B. N., & Twiest, M. M. (2000). Nature, literature and young children. *Young Children 55*(1): 59–63.

Molland, J. (2009). *Get out! 150 easy ways for kids and grown-ups to get into nature and build a greener future*. Minneapolis, MN: Free Spirit.

Monhardt, R., & Monhardt, L. (2000). Children's literature and environmental issues. *Reading Horizons 40*(3), 175–184.

National Wildlife Federation. *Your Big Backyard*. A magazine published for young children. www.nwf.org

North American Association for Environmental Education. (1999). *Excellence in Environmental Education: Guidelines for Learning (K-12)*. Washington, DC: Author.

Sandall, S., & Ostrosky, M. (Eds.) (2000). *Natural environments and inclusion*. Longmont, CO: Sopris West; Denver, CO: Division for Early Childhood of the Council for Exceptional Children. Available from NAEYC.

Sherwood, E., Rockwell, R., & Williams, R. (2008). *Science adventures: Nature activities for young children*. Beltsville, MD: Gryphon House.

Ward, J. (2008). *I love dirt! 52 activities to help you and your kids discover the wonders of nature*. Boston: Trumpeter.

CHILDREN'S BOOK

Lionni, L. (1970). *Fish is fish*. New York: Pantheon.

Online Resources

http://members.tripod.com/%7EPatricia_F/mathscience.html This website contains classroom-tested ideas for earth science.

http://bubbles.org This is a great site to learn about bubbles.

http://kidsblogs.nationalgeographic.com/littlekids This site includes animal stories, science activities, puzzles, and games, as well as a special section for parents.

http://tryscience.org This site includes information on helping parents get involved in science activities.

www.councilforee.org This site provides programs and services to promote environmental education for young children and educators.

www.naeyc.org/yc/pastissues/2008/january Numerous articles relating to science and children appear on this site.

www.sciencemadesimple.com Includes a variety of science experiments and science projects.

www.tryscience.org An engaging site with a variety of experiments, virtual field trips, and adventures.

www.nwf.org National Wildlife Federation publishes a magazine for young children: *Your Big Backyard*.

www.weatherclassroom.com/WeatherEd/?gclid=CJXi5va7uogCFQSfYAodyni_2g The Weather Channel offers resources and lessons for teaching about the weather.

chapter 11
Life Science Experiences

The life science program in the early years focuses on living things and how they live in their natural environments. From these explorations, children learn to treat all things and their environments with respect and care (Worth & Grollman, 2003). A variety of activities, integrated throughout the curriculum, should include physical characteristics of living things, the basic needs of living things, simple behaviors, variation and diversity, habitats, stages of growth, and the relationship between living things and their environments (Chalufour & Worth, 2006; The National Research Council [NRC], 1996).

This chapter addresses teaching concepts included in the sensory-related, animal, and plant aspects of life science. Frequently, teachers rely too heavily on the sense of sight, or the visual process, rather than encouraging expansion and use of the other four senses. As children develop perception and the ability to distinguish differences in what they see, hear, taste, smell, and touch, they learn more quickly because all five senses are utilized instead of only one or two. Exploring nature effectively with young children must involve all the senses.

Children are naturally curious as they use their senses to explore the world. They try to touch, poke, pinch, taste, lick, chew, smell, watch, listen to, or examine objects, people, and situations in great detail. This is how they learn. We need to encourage children to maintain their sensory tools and use them to explore their world and answer their questions. Inquiry is probably the most important aspect of children's science learning. It is basically about questioning, wondering, exploring, studying, observing, and investigating (Chalufour & Worth, 2006; NRC, 1996). "Our world is a huge hands-on museum, a well-stocked laboratory, a fascinating never-ending field trip" (Ziemer, 1987, pp. 44–45).

> As children learn to use their senses with precision, they become more aware of their environment and use these senses to build and determine concepts.

In the outdoor playground, children can develop respect, appreciation, and understanding for the natural environment. This outdoor classroom also allows children to learn in ways that are not possible in the indoor classroom (Winters, Ring, & Burriss, 2010).

Animals and plants are living parts of the natural world and should be studied in their native locations and placements as much as possible. Many concepts can be gleaned from studies of animals and plants: size, shape, number, color, texture, weight, smell, sound, nutrition, appreciation and respect for life and environment, conservation, and so on. Environmental education is critical. Children discover that nature can be enjoyed and studied without interference or impact from observers.

Most children have limited experiences with animals and plants in their surroundings. More of the acquired knowledge they do have comes from schoolbooks and media than from direct experience, so we must increase direct-experience learning. Share your own respect and appreciation for all living things, and children will learn the same.

In the outside playground, children develop respect, appreciation, and understanding for the natural environment.

Animals have been considered an important part of human society since ancient times. Many fairy tales, nursery rhymes, stories, books, and movies have been (and are currently being), written about animals. Yet incidences of cruelty toward animals are increasing, and there is growing endangerment of the world's animals and the ecosystem. These conditions make it essential that young children become involved in learning animal welfare and advocacy activities. The early childhood curriculum should foster feelings of goodwill, justice, and humanity toward all life (Pattnaik, 2004/2005). "As future leaders, teachers, policymakers, and conscientious citizens, children can utilize their training and the spirit of animal advocacy to make this world a better place for all beings" (Pattnaik, 2004/2005, p. 100).

It is impossible to imagine going through a year of study at any level of early childhood without some units and experiences with animals. There are many advantages of having pets in the classroom: They help children develop caring and compassion, responsibility, social skills and interactions, personal worth, and self-confidence (Jegatheesan & Meaden, 2006). Young children have sensitivity to and seek an understanding of animals. Specific concepts relating to individual animals or to categories and classes of animals emerge as a result of animal studies. For example, children will become aware of the physical characteristics of the animals, where they live, what they eat, the uses of the animals, and how they reproduce and care for their young. Children will also enjoy making comparisons among animals as they become acquainted with the characteristics of the animal categories. In addition, children learn how to care for animals properly: how to hold them (if they can be held), how and what to feed them, and how to care for and clean their surroundings. Young children gain feelings of importance as they feed the classroom animals and provide for their care. Children can become aware of our tremendous reliance on animals as sources of food and clothing. They can also learn which animals are potentially dangerous and should not be approached.

Many children are afraid of animals, especially insects, but through experiences with them their fears can often be lessened or overcome. Generally, young children tend to describe insects as being gross or yucky (Korte, Fielden, & Agnew, 2005) or harmful to people (Shepardson, 2002). There is more to "bugs" than these definitions, and children are eager to learn about such insects and bugs as butterflies, worms, spiders, caterpillars, bees, flies, earwigs, mosquitoes, dragonflies, ladybugs, and grasshoppers. When children are provided with positive introductions to the life sciences, they will develop respect and appreciation for insects and other animals. "By encouraging and supporting classroom exploration of insects, with proper health and safety precautions, we can help young children study and appreciate insects rather than stomp and squash them" (Korte et al., 2005, p. 18). Teachers should provide hands-on experiences with a wide variety of insects, rather than narrowly limiting the curriculum to studying the life cycle of butterflies (Korte et al., 2005). As early childhood education teachers, we should be willing to start with nature, seize the moment, become a researcher alongside children, become a researcher alongside adults, and think of our classroom as a laboratory (Hawkins Centers of Learning, 2009).

By utilizing the senses while studying plants and animals, children become more aware of our reliance on plants and animals as sources for food, clothing, and shelter.

We have discussed in Chapter 10 the value of moving many of our typically inside routines to the outside environment in order to help children develop a relationship with nature. Now, we are also reminding you of the importance of moving the typically outside elements to the classroom inside. This also allows for many hands-on experiences with plants and animals (Jacobs & Crowley, 2010). Children learn about the life cycles, characteristics, survival needs, similarities and differences of plants and animals through such inside activities as pets, caterpillars to butterflies, seeds to plants, buds to flowers, and eggs to hatching. One classroom activity made caterpillars from old nylon stockings that were filled with soil and grass seed. Children predicted how long it would take the grass to sprout, then measured and recorded lengths as it grew, then trimmed the grass with scissors (Jacobs & Crowley, 2010, p. 44).

Hachey and Butler (2009) explain that everything early childhood education should be is included in nature play and gardening: "learning-centered, hands-on, inclusive, socially bonding, emotionally uplifting, physically stimulating, integrative, and aesthetically appealing" (p. 44). Children enjoy caring for and nurturing plants through their growing stages. There is particular excitement for young children the day that they discover that their little seed, carefully planted, watered, sunned, and cared for, is pushing its way through the soil and taking its first peek at the world. In addition to the satisfaction of planting seeds and caring for plants, there are many opportunities for learning about plant life through studies of seeds and plants. For example, children will become aware of the characteristics of plants, what plants need to grow, and the uses of plants. Children will also learn by making comparisons among plants: comparing sizes, colors, rates of growth, seasons of growth, and other factors. For example, as you observe a tall tree with young children, ask "I wonder . . ." open-ended questions. We do not need to know all the answers, because we are encouraging curiosity, rather than just teaching facts.

Children should have opportunities for exploring a variety of plants in the classroom environment. For example, building sculptures from wood scraps, knobs, shapes, and blocks allows children to increase their understandings of the natural world around them. They can learn about names of trees; what trees need to maintain life; proper care and treatment of trees; their uses and values; their types, colors, hardness, softness; their seeds, leaves, pinecones, acorns (Bisgaier, Samaras, with Russo, 2004).

With so many varieties of plants, teachers need to select those appropriate for the climate and season. Rubber plants and geraniums are especially hardy, and children enjoy watching geraniums bloom and observing the color of the blossoms. When there are plants in the classroom, allow the children to care for them: water them, put them in sunlight, give them plant food, and assume many other responsibilities. A number of plants are poisonous and should be avoided. Examples include English ivy, philodendron, laurel, and dieffenbachia. The specific varieties of plants that are in your environment, both inside and outside, should be named often. Ideally, children should have a garden space outdoors where they can plant and care for vegetables and/or flowers. Suggestions for plant gardens with young children should include plants that attract butterflies; plants that provide color, texture, scent, taste; and fruits and vegetables that are easily cultivated (Torquati & Barber, 2005). Before purchasing plants for your classroom or center, check with your local nursery to make sure that the plants are nontoxic.

When children are involved in growing some of their own food, they learn about nutrition, food sources, care of plants. ". . . children become increasingly adventurous in their tastes for vegetables the more they handle and understand plants . . ." (Matt, 2008, p. 98). When studying various aspects of plants, snacks could include the edible items from the six major plant parts: roots, stems, leaves, seeds, fruits, and stems (Matt, 2008). As children plan a garden, select and plant the seeds, and then tend and harvest the produce, they begin to understand the natural process of growth and are introduced to an area of science that can have lifelong influence. They realize the relationship of plant growth to other plants, animals, insects, humans, weather, temperature, sun, soil, and water, and seasons.

Through studies of plants, children become aware of our reliance on plants as sources of food, clothing, and shelter, as well as for aesthetic beauty in both indoor and outdoor surroundings. Children also learn that many plants, such as noxious weeds and poisonous plants, may be a nuisance or harmful to humans. We can encourage them to "predict and try out different conditions, enhancing their understanding of the influence of light, soil, and water on the growth and development of plant life" (Bosse, Jacobs, & Anderson, 2009, p. 13).

TEACHING SENSORY-RELATED CONCEPTS

Smell and Taste

Through the two important senses of smell and taste many new ideas are learned. These two concepts may be incorporated into a unit on the senses, taught together, or taught as separate unit themes.

Even though taste and smell are separate senses, they are closely related, and one greatly influences the other. Often a child may dislike a food because of its smell, not because of its actual taste. Chewing a food while holding one's nose diminishes the taste of the food. Likewise, nasal congestion from a cold results in a decrease in the sense of taste.

Understanding the location of the four taste-bud regions provides the foundation for learning about taste. The salt taste buds are located on the tip and sides of the tongue; sweet is on the tip of the tongue; and bitter and sour are on the sides of the tongue and on the palate.

Too often in learning activities, children are not encouraged to use their senses of smell and taste. They hear a teacher say "Look at it. What do you see?" But there are times when it is better to say, "Smell it (or taste it). Now what do you know about it?" Children should be given the opportunity to taste and smell different ingredients throughout the food preparation process and compare that to the taste and smell of the finished product. A child generally relies on previous experiences when learning through smell and taste.

When learning textures, the child can use other senses in addition to touch: taste, hearing, and sight. However, smells or tastes cannot be seen, felt, or heard unless the child has had previous experience with the items being smelled or tasted. For example, if a child who had never had experiences with a lemon was asked to describe its smell or taste, the child could not rely on touch or sound for clues; the child would have to taste or smell the lemon. Also, the way a child describes a taste or smell will depend on his or her experience with it. The child must have experience in hearing and using the word *sour,* for example, and must know the meaning of this word (the concept) before he or she can describe the smell or taste of a lemon.

Children understand that they learn about some things and identify them by smelling and/or tasting them. A good experience for assisting in this understanding is to fill opaque glasses or containers with root beer, orange juice, or other liquid. The children then taste this liquid, and the teacher asks them whether they would like to learn what they have tasted. The teacher can follow this experience with ways in which the children could learn what the bottle contains—by smelling or tasting the contents. In this case, it would probably be better to have each child smell the liquid to discover what it is. Approach this activity with one specific safety precaution: Teach children *never* to taste the contents of bottles or other containers unless they have been told and are certain that the contents are edible and something that they should taste. Make sure they understand that this practice can be very dangerous. Other health precautions to consider are sanitation and cleanliness when participating in all tasting activities.

Children should be encouraged to rely more often on their senses of smell and taste. Smells and tastes are frequently tuned out of daily experiences. One meaningful activity is to have children write down or discuss all the smells and/or tastes that they have experienced during a particular day. They might do a follow-up exercise in which they make it a point to be aware of smell and taste. In teaching smell and taste, exploratory questions can be asked. For example, you might ask "What else smells like _____?" or "What else tastes like_____?"

Smell

APPROACH TO TEACHING. A broad base for understanding smell can be built by increasing the child's vocabulary. Many opportunities for describing smells and using smell words should be provided, and new smell words should be introduced, along with their meanings. Whenever a smell word is learned, opportunities for smelling items described by the word should be provided. For example, learning the word *bitter* will have no meaning unless something bitter is smelled (or tasted), and it would be better if several bitter items were smelled. The following is an incomplete list of possible words describing smells; various objects representing these smells are easily accessible for meaning and reinforcement.

sour	lemony	strong
dusty	pleasant	burned
moldy	salty	smoky
rancid	rusty	fishy
sweet	bitter	fresh
dirty	offensive	clean
new	crisp	delicious
piney	sharp	

After experiences with these words, exciting brainstorming or creative writing sessions may evolve. Children can discuss or write about items, foods, or experiences related to the words. For example, they may think, talk, or write about an experience or memory related to anything that smells smoky. Simple poetry can evolve from smell words.

Smells can be divided into categories and unit themes can be developed on the sense of smell or on one or more of these "smell" categories. Each day the teacher can introduce a different category of smells, providing examples of smells relating to this category through experiences. For example, if the teacher chooses a unit on cleaning smells, a visit to a motel can be planned whereby the children meet the motel cleaning personnel, learn about the job, and smell some of the solvents and materials used for cleaning. Another experience during this unit might be a visit by the school custodian, in which cleaning materials are shared with the children. A salesperson who sells cleaning aids might also visit. The children could participate in a food experience, including the cleanup, with emphasis on smelling the cleaning aids. It is easy to see how exciting it would be to correlate a unit with the theme of cleaning smells.

The following is an incomplete list of some of the categories of smells:

inside	hospital	cleaning
outside	food	kitchen
animal	holiday	store
automobile	nature	school
seasonal	bakery	cosmetic

Concepts and Ideas for Teaching

1. Some smells give messages or direct behavior.
   a. Smoke leads people to discover what is burning and to take necessary action.
   b. Favorite foods may create hunger for a particular food, especially if a person is already hungry.
   c. Medicine indicates when someone is ill, has a cold, or is sucking a cough drop, which in turn points to sore throats, colds, coughs, and so on.
   d. Food smells are often strong and distinct enough to signal what is cooking.
   e. Fire or matches may tell us that children are playing with matches or warn us of danger.
   f. Unfamiliar smells may make a person curious about the source.
   g. Undesirable smells may remind a person of previous experiences and sometimes even cause nausea.
2. The same items do not always smell the same.
   a. People: perfume, soap, foods, culture, and other factors
   b. Automobiles: age, care, places parked, and so on
   c. Flowers: tulips, roses, violets, and others
   d. Perfumes: kind, type of container, age, and other factors
3. Items that look the same do not always smell the same.
   a. Potato flakes and soap flakes
   b. Strawberry gelatin and cherry gelatin
   c. Root beer extract and vanilla extract
4. Different items may have the same smell.
   a. Campfire smoke and cigarette smoke
   b. Vinegar taffy and liquid vinegar
   c. Various items with a lemon smell: lotion, cleaning solvents, and shampoo
5. Not all things have a smell: dish, wall, most water, some fabrics, and glass
6. Smell may be changed or modified.
   a. Cooking: foods in various stages of the cooking process, such as meat before and after cooking; bakery products before and after baking; any food product before and after burning; or bread before and after being toasted
   b. Aging: a tomato that is fresh and one that is spoiled; a freshly cracked nut and one that is becoming rancid because of age; new perfume and older perfume that is partially evaporated
   c. Temperature: frozen items, which lose their smell or develop distinct or stronger odors; melted butter; melted plastics
   d. Drying: fruits, paste, glue, and paints, which usually acquire a less distinct smell in the drying process.
   e. Additions: modification of smells in food experiences, science experiences, and art activities by adding or combining ingredients.

Activities and Experiences

1. The children can smell items and group them into categories, or the teacher can name a smell and the children tell which category or categories it fits into.
2. Colored bottles or containers with the outsides painted or taped can be used to identify the contents by smell. Take care to select mostly substances with which the children have had previous experience. If the substance is not edible, be sure to caution the children against tasting it.
3. To help the children differentiate by smell items that look alike, the teacher can select combinations of the following items within each category. Bottles or containers can be coded for older children; they can write down the number code of the bottle and its contents. Be sure to caution children that these items are to smell, *not* to taste.

1-A	Alcohol
1-B	Polish remover
1-C	Water
1-D	White vinegar
1-E	Clear carbonated drink
2-A	Perfume
2-B	Vanilla
2-C	Cider vinegar
2-D	Root beer extract
2-E	Steak sauce
2-F	Food flavorings (liquid smoke, maple, etc.)
3-A	White glue
3-B	School paste
3-C	Lotion
3-D	Cold cream
3-E	Thick dairy cream
4-A	Glycerin
4-B	Liquid detergent
4-C	Rubber cement
4-D	Honey
4-E	Baby oil
4-F	Some shampoos
5-A	Molasses
5-B	Maple syrup
5-C	Dark corn syrup
6-A	Soap flakes
6-B	Potato flakes
6-C	Onion flakes

6-D	Oatmeal
7-A	Salt
7-B	Sugar
7-C	Garlic salt
7-D	Onion salt
7-E	Celery salt
7-F	Sand
8-A	Powdered sugar
8-B	Cornstarch
8-C	Flour
8-D	Baby powder
8-E	Soda
8-F	Baking powder
9-A	Cinnamon
9-B	Chili powder
9-C	Cloves
10-A	Oregano
10-B	Parsley flakes

4. Once the children have identified an ingredient by its smell, they can then use descriptive words for it. Similes can also stimulate creativity: "It smells like a cinnamon roll," or "It smells like a cough drop."

5. For a "smell" walk or field trip, the children could walk around their own classroom, building, or neighborhood searching for smells.

6. Put sensory materials in a trough, large tub, or other similar container for exploring and smelling. Items could include mud, flour, lemonade, barley, and wheat.

7. Discuss with the children how their sense of smell can protect them from danger.

8. Brainstorm with the children their favorite or most pleasant smells and their least favorite or most offensive or unpleasant smells. These can be dictated or written into a booklet or chart.

9. Demonstrate the interrelationship of taste and smell. Have the children, while blindfolded, taste a piece of apple and at the same time hold a piece of cut onion near their nose. Some children may believe that they taste an onion.

 UNIT IDEAS ON SMELL

FIELD TRIPS

- Outside walk
- Bakery
- Meat market
- Paint store
- Cosmetic representative's home
- Drugstore or department store where a cosmetic counter could be visited
- Pet store
- Farm
- Hospital
- Flower shop
- Pharmacy

ART

- Collages with scented papers
- Collages made out of foodstuffs that have particular odors (this can be a good use of supermarket produce that would otherwise be discarded because of expired shelf life)
- Finger painting with soap flakes and/or whipped cream (no longer edible): comparison of smells of the two; alternatively, finger painting with creams that look like soap flakes but smell different
- Lemon halves dipped into tempera paint for lemon printing: the combination of lemon juice and paint releases an offensive odor (use lemons that are no longer edible)
- Coloring eggs or fabric using vinegar dye

MUSIC

- Various media are put into opaque bottles or other nontransparent containers to be used for rhythm shakers after an experience in smelling. The teacher says, "All those with cinnamon smell in their bottle, shake or play with me on the next song."
- Creative expressions and movements are dramatically portrayed as to how you would respond or move if you were smelling ammonia and other suggested smells.

FOOD

- Any food activity, planned with a focus on smell
- Pickles
- Root beer or milkshakes
- Vanilla ice cream, made and then flavored with peppermint or other flavoring
- Gelatin: different groups of children making different flavors and guessing individual flavors through their sense of smell
- Bread or other bakery products: smelled during the mixing process and then during the baking process

VISITORS

- Cosmetics representative
- Salesperson for cleaning supplies
- Paint dealer or distributor
- Father, to bring in shaving creams and lotions

- Mother, to bring in various cosmetics
- Custodian, to bring in cleaning solvents and other cleaning agents
- Animals
- Parent, to conduct a demonstration on smells of foods

SCIENCE

- Salt or crystal garden (see Chapter 9 for directions)
- Smelling of bread each day as it progresses toward the moldy stage
- Smelling of changes in any item as it is changed or modified
- Smelling and identifying substances in opaque bottles or other containers

LANGUAGE AND LITERACY

- The children write or dictate and illustrate booklets such as "Smells I Like" or "Smells I Don't Like."
- Write down a category of smells such as "Strong Smells" or "Summer Smells" and have the children write or brainstorm specific ideas.

Taste

APPROACH TO TEACHING. To build a broad base for understanding taste, begin with building a vocabulary of taste words. Provide many opportunities for describing tastes and using taste words; introduce new taste words and teach the meaning behind them. Whenever a taste word is introduced, the children should have an opportunity to taste an item that the word describes. For example, the word *sour* will have no meaning unless a child tastes something sour. It is best to provide several items that are sour tasting, such as a lemon, a grapefruit, or powdered drink mix. The following is an incomplete list of possible words describing tastes; various objects representing these tastes are easily accessible for meaning and reinforcement.

salty	tart	moldy	pleasant
soapy	sticky	bitter	spicy
sour	puckery	strong	burned
sweet	lemony	juicy	offensive
spicy	unpleasant	fishy	

After experiences with these words, exciting brainstorming or creative sessions can evolve. The children can discuss or write about items, foods, or experiences related to the words. For example, they might think about, write about, or discuss everything that they can remember that tastes fishy and the experiences that they have had in tasting items that are fishy.

Tastes can be divided into categories. Unit themes can be developed on taste or on one or more of these

Taste is one of our basic senses, and helps us identify foods and flavors. (This girl is tasting a cheese ball.)

categories. Each day a different category of tastes could be introduced, with examples of tastes fitting into this category provided through experiences. The following is an incomplete list of categories of tastes:

inside	fruit	bakery	holiday
outside	vegetable	sweet	seasonal
spicy	fish	bitter	bland

Activities and Experiences

1. Have a blindfolded child sample various items and then group them into taste categories, or name a taste and have the child fit it into a category or categories.
2. Have the children make a taste book. For example, at the top of a large piece of poster paper write the word *salty*. The children can then go through magazines and cut out pictures of salty foods or tastes for this page. The word descriptions should be included.
3. Have a child poke a toothpick into an opaque bottle or other container, withdraw the toothpick, and try to guess the contents (a food item) by tasting the flavor on the toothpick.
4. Have the children identify a food or ingredient by its taste and then think of descriptive words for the taste. Similes and metaphors can be used for

creative thinking and brainstorming. These can be written down and used later for a poem.

5. Tell a "taste" story, and at various intervals in the story have the children sample actual flavors.

6. Put sensory materials into a trough, large tub, or similar container, and encourage the children to taste them. Items used might include flour, wheat, gelatin, cornmeal, cooked or uncooked rice, and cooked or uncooked macaroni.

7. Encourage the children to list tastes they like and do not like. Develop an experience chart or graph that includes the children's likes and dislikes.

8. Brainstorm with the children the following: sweet tastes, sour tastes, bitter tastes, and salty tastes.

9. Let the children grow plants with characteristic flavorings, such as mint, onion, chives, sage, or parsley. Have the children taste these plants.

10. Prepare a food activity, but leave out the spice or seasoning. For example, make two custards, one with nutmeg and one without. Have the children taste the difference.

Concepts and Ideas for Teaching

1. Tastes may affect behavior or reactions.
   a. Lemons or chokecherries may make mouths pucker.
   b. Salty or sweet foods often create cravings or a desire for more, or create thirst.
   c. Bitter foods or other substances may make one want to spit out what is being tasted.
2. The same items do not always taste the same.
   a. Apples: Some apples might be sour, others sweet.
   b. Cakes come in many flavors.
   c. Gum comes in many different flavors.
3. Different items may have the same taste or flavor.
   a. Lemon-flavored items: ice cream, cakes, cookies, pie, pudding, gelatin
   b. Cherry-flavored items: lollipops, gelatin, cakes, soda pop
4. Items that look the same do not always taste the same.
   a. Salt and sugar
   b. Cinnamon, cloves, and nutmeg
   c. Olive juice, prune juice, and root beer
5. Tastes may be changed or modified.
   a. Cooking: foods in various stages of the cooking process, such as vegetables before and after cooking; bakery products before and after baking; overcooked foods, which may have been wet or juicy, but after overcooking have a dry or even burned taste
   b. Aging: change in the taste of foods, such as fresh bread to stale, moldy, or rancid; a fresh green-yellow banana to brown and overripe

c. Temperature: freezing or melting of foods, which often changes the taste as well as the texture
d. Drying: apricots, cherries, apples, or jerky
e. Additions: adding or combining ingredients, such as adding even a drop of flavoring to a bowl of frosting, causing the flavor or taste to change

---

UNIT IDEAS ON TASTE

FIELD TRIPS

- Restaurant
- Picnic
- Cookout
- Canyon or park: roasting marshmallows
- Grocery store
- Child's or teacher's home: tasting or cooking activity
- Factory where food is made or packaged

ART

- Finger painting with whipped cream: tasting it before and after it turns into butter
- Vegetable printing (use vegetables that are no longer edible)

MUSIC

- Creative movements: children pretend to milk a cow; to pull a carrot, peel it, grate it, and eat it; to eat something sweet, salty, bitter, or sour

FOOD

- Any food activity planned with a focus on taste: children are encouraged to taste the ingredients
- Gelatin: different groups making different flavors of red gelatin, for example, with children guessing the various flavors by taste alone
- Cooking of unusual foods
- Cooking of common foods in unusual ways

VISITORS

- Nutritionist
- Baker
- Butcher
- Parent: cooking or food demonstration featuring some aspect of taste, such as making something

using various spices, with the children tasting the spices beforehand
• Grocer

SCIENCE

• Pineapple juice colored red or green: will not change the flavor
• Children blindfolded and asked to guess various flavors by the taste or to describe the taste
• Various activities in which the children can learn that tastes can be modified by such processes as aging, adding, or melting

LANGUAGE AND LITERACY

• The children write or dictate and then illustrate booklets such as "Tastes I Like" or "Favorite Tastes."
• The children or teacher write down a category of tastes, such as "sweet" or "salty," and the children write or brainstorm specific examples. Illustrations can be made and pages collected into a booklet.

Texture (Touch)

APPROACH TO TEACHING.   Texture is an identifying quality. It is the way we describe substances or things in our environment when they are touched. Children are fascinated with different textures. It is important for children not only to identify things by the way they feel, but also to use descriptive words in explaining how things feel when touched.

Assisting children in learning about texture requires first increasing the teacher's own awareness of touch. Teachers need to acquaint or reacquaint themselves with touch sensations that they experience but do not notice.

After the teacher's own awareness of touch has been increased, the children are more likely to be made aware of the various common and uncommon textures in their environment. Becoming more cognizant of familiar textures automatically makes us more aware of unfamiliar or uncommon textures.

> Children need to know that the word *texture* refers to the surface feeling of an item. The words *feel* and *feeling* have various meanings that may need to be clarified so that the children can understand the relationship of feeling to texture. The children's first response to *feel* or *feeling* is likely to be in terms of happy, sad, tired, or other emotion-depicting words.

Texture words are usually adjectives, but often they are used in such a way that children may understand them as nouns. For example, when pointing to a brick, the teacher may say, "This is rough." It would be clearer to say, "The brick is rough" or "That is a rough brick." The child, having had no experience with bricks, may refer to the next brick seen as a "rough." It is important to clearly use texture words as adjectives.

The child can be encouraged to use many senses when exploring and building concepts related to texture. The sense of touch should be the main sense used in learning texture, even though many teachers point to an object and say, "Look, how does it feel?" Eyes are not always able to tell how objects feel; we must have had experiences in feeling or touching honey, pine needles, sheep's wool, or some kinds of plants to be familiar with their textures. Although textures can be described through seeing, perhaps even hearing, it is much more valuable to feel and then describe them. Even then, they are difficult to explain.

The way a child describes a particular texture will be based on previous experiences with this texture. The child who has never had experience with a wiry, stiff texture would have difficulty in describing the raw wool of sheep. Again, feeling a texture is one thing, but describing it is another. Knowing how grass feels is much easier, even for adults, than describing it in a way that can be understood by others; how much more difficult the task becomes for children, whose experiences are more limited.

To build a broad base for understanding textures, it is wise to begin by building the child's texture vocabulary. Provide many opportunities for describing textures and using texture words, and introduce and teach new texture words. Whenever a texture word is introduced, the child should have an opportunity to feel a texture that the word describes. For example, if the word *bumpy* is being learned, it will have no meaning unless the child feels what bumpy is; that is, unless the word takes on a meaning. The following is an incomplete list of words describing texture; various objects representing these feelings are easily accessible for meaning and reinforcement.

coarse	crunchy	prickly
rough	sticky	wiry
slimy	spongy	grainy
slick	gritty	sharp
smooth	sandy	wet
stringy	velvety	furry
hard	bumpy	dry
soft	fuzzy	slippery
crinkly	hairy	waxy

When teaching texture, begin with familiar textures and then progress to more difficult or unfamiliar ones. Children draw from previous learning experiences to build new concepts, and experiences with familiar textures will help them to understand and categorize the feelings of unfamiliar textures.

Textures can easily be narrowed down to specific categories, including words already mentioned as texture descriptions: animal textures, human textures, fabric textures, nature textures, food textures, and so on.

Concepts and Ideas for Teaching

1. Most things have a texture.
2. Single items may vary in texture.
   a. Trees: leaves, bark, limbs, buds, and others
   b. Cars: tires, seats, carpet, fenders, steering wheel, and other parts
   c. Interiors and exteriors of items: suitcase, sandpaper, fabric, corrugated cardboard, leaf, bark, banana, orange, and so on
3. Different items may have the same texture.
   a. Glass and ice
   b. Mirror and metal
   c. Brick and cement
4. Texture may be modified.
   a. Heat: items that become stiff or even "set up"; items that dissolve or become liquid; items that become hard, smooth, thick, or lumpy; foods, which offer many possibilities for changes in texture; items such as wood, plastic, and paper, which also change texture
   b. Cold or freezing: hardening of most items; making ice cubes and discussing changes in the texture of the water as it freezes and then melts
   c. Drying: change in the texture of wet clothes, fruits, paste, glue, and finger paint
   d. Sanding: change of a rough surface or edge to a smooth surface
   e. Additions: in food experiences, science experiences, and art activities, texture changed by adding additional ingredients
   f. Pressure: application of pressure to a rough surface, creating a smooth surface (such as wet cement), or creating a rougher one
   g. Aging: food in various stages showing changes in texture from hard to soft or from soft to hard; skin texture of an elderly person changed from childhood skin texture
   h. Chewing: food items changing texture in the chewing process
   i. Beating or whipping: whipping cream or egg whites showing changes in texture through the whipping and beating process
   j. Natural changes: weather changes such as frost, wind, freezing, and erosion creating changes in texture

Activities and Experiences

1. A texture book can be made by giving the children a standard-sized piece of poster paper and variable objects with different textures (Velcro, ribbon, sandpaper, etc.). The texture is pasted on the paper and then described in terms of how it feels or what else feels similar. The exact words, phrases, and sentences are recorded on the page, either by the child or the teacher, depending on the child's age level and ability. The pages can be put together with rings so that the children can enjoy their own book.

2. Place handprint shapes of various textures around the room at the children's level. When they match their hands on top of the shapes, encourage them to describe the textures that they feel.

3. Pass around materials of various textures (paper, wood, fabric), and when music or drumbeats stop, have the child describe the texture being held.

4. Pass around sacks or put them on a table or rug. Have each child put a hand inside a sack and then describe the texture and item without using visual clues.

5. Use texture collages to teach textures. Have a file folder with the sides taped shut and the top left open. After items of various textures have been put into the folder, a child puts a hand into the folder and then describes the texture of one item. The item may then be pasted on the front of the envelope. Many kinds of texture collages may be made by using items of various textures for background surfaces.

6. Put sensory materials into a trough, large tub, or similar container. Examples might be sand, soapy water, rock salt, and mud.

7. Invite a person who is blind to the classroom and have the person describe the importance of touch in the life of someone who is blind. If possible, have this person demonstrate reading Braille through using the sense of touch.

8. Let the children feel cornstarch and describe the texture. Now add some cold water and mix it to about the consistency of white glue. Give the children about $\frac{1}{2}$ teaspoon on the palm of their hand and let them experiment. Can they roll it into a ball? What does it feel like? Tell them to leave it on the palm of their hand without working it. What happens? How does it feel now?

9. Help the children to differentiate between how things can feel and how they can feel (emotionally) by making a list of each. The following are examples of each.

How Objects Can Feel

scratchy	hot	wet
bumpy	velvety	greasy
crinkly	slivery	silky

Touch the spines of a hedgehog very carefully!

ripply	waxy	oily
fuzzy	sticky	mushy
cold	rubbery	glassy
prickly	rough	gooey
slimy	grainy	gritty
slithery	oozy	pliable
slippery	sandy	hard

How I Can Feel (Inside)

empathetic	lucky	fearful
angry	rejected	sorry
in pain	sad	eager
depressed	hurt	pleased
delighted	joyous	happy
courageous	defensive	lonely
fortunate	carefree	cautious
loved	sensitive	strong
excited	sympathetic	resentful

10. Put some foods with varying textures in a bag and have the children identify the textures that they feel, such as waxy, hard, bumpy, sticky, prickly, seedy, or moist. Also, they can try to identify the foods. Now take these same foods, adding additional ones if desired, and have the children taste them and describe the "eating" textures (the inside texture). Are they the same as or different from the "feeling" textures (the outside texture)?

 UNIT IDEAS ON TEXTURE

ART

- Melted crayon pictures
- Mud pies
- Collage items of different textures: a variety of textures to be pasted, as well as a variety of background textures
- Seed collages: seeds of different textures

- Fabric collages: fabrics of different textures
- Crayon rubbings on paper with textured objects underneath
- Collage of items found on a texture walk
- Cotton swabs used for painting on different grains of sandpaper
- Finger painting with sawdust, sand, or other media added

VISITORS

- Person who is blind
- Carpenter
- Butcher
- Skin diver
- Sculptor
- Cake decorator
- Person from fabric store
- Grocer
- Baker
- Upholsterer

FOOD

- Hamburgers: comparison of textures before and after cooking
- Candied apples
- Gelatin: quick-setting with ice cubes, to see changes as the mixture thickens
- Sponge cake
- Angel food cake
- Soups
- Root beer floats
- Cream puffs or popovers
- Apples: apple cider, applesauce, chopped in salad, or apple strudel
- Potatoes prepared in various ways (raw, mashed, hash browns, fried, or baked)

MUSIC

- Creative movements that depict textures: interpreting butter melting; an ice cube freezing and then melting; a person walking on sand or rocks, walking barefoot, walking or skating on slippery, or cold ice
- Texture band with such items as sandpaper blocks, different textured sticks; washboards, vegetable graters, pots and pans, corrugated cardboard, and sticks or spoons used for striking
- Shakers or containers partially filled with media of various textures: sand, water, macaroni, sawdust, and so on

FIELD TRIPS

- Sawmill
- Furniture store
- Dairy
- Zoo
- Farm
- Bakery
- Lumberyard
- Park
- Fabric store
- Greenhouse
- Upholstery shop
- Carpet store
- "Texture" walk
- Hat store
- Gravel pit

SCIENCE

- Two ice cubes with rock salt rubbed or pressed between them: change in texture of ice cubes
- Chemical garden (see Chapter 9 for recipe)
- Any experiment or experience that involves a texture change; for example, a powder mix before and after liquid has been added
- Making Styrofoam: two chemicals, purchased where Styrofoam or boats are made, mixed together to create an immediate reaction that results in Styrofoam
- Freezing of various substances
- Clay or playdough mixed by children
- Melting of butter, ice, and other substances
- Observation of mold growing during the aging and spoiling process of a substance such as bread

LANGUAGE AND LITERACY

- Make texture booklets by having the children describe textures and write down their own words.
- Encourage the children to dictate and/or write similes for textures such as "as soft as . . ." or "as sticky as . . ."

Sound (Hearing)

APPROACH TO TEACHING. Auditory discrimination is the ability to differentiate sounds, including likenesses and differences in tone, rhythm, volume, or the source of sound. Hearing is one of the 5 senses, and when we teach children to listen carefully, we are teaching auditory discrimination.

Children learn much about their world by listening. Infants, unable to respond to many stimuli, do obviously respond to sounds around them, both familiar and unfamiliar. Perhaps children can be helped to sharpen their awareness of sound when a teacher's own awareness of sound is refined. Considering individual differences also, it must be remembered that people do not respond to sounds in the same way. Even though some adults have lost their sensitivity to pitch (which describes whether a sound is a low, middle, or high tone), young children are extremely sensitive to pitch; in fact, a very high sound can actually cause pain.

New emphasis on hearing and sound can be made by assisting children to learn by listening. For example, when children are taken across a street, they are told: "Stop and look. Do you see any cars coming?" They might also be told: "Stop and listen. Do you hear any cars coming?" A brainstorming session could be the children's responses to the question "What have you heard today?" or "What sounds do you hear right now?" In addition to this exercise, sounds could be selected and then described without using the sound word itself. Riddles could be made in which a child describes and gives clues to a sound, while the other children guess what sound is being described. Older children should be able to write these clues as riddles. For example, "This is a loud, piercing, sharp, continuous sound. It varies regularly from high to low and back. What sound is it?" (siren).

The skill of auditory discrimination is best developed through daily experiences perceiving and interpreting various sounds. Motivating questions should often be asked, such as "What might that sound be?" or "What else has the same sound?" or "How would you describe that sound?" Creative thinking and stimulating brainstorming emerge from explorations with similes and metaphors relating to sounds. For example, the children could describe sounds that are "as soft as _____," "as loud as_____," or "as shrill as _____." Adults have trite phrases such as "as quiet as a mouse," but children will come up with new ideas such as "as quiet as cutting thread," "as quiet as a snowflake hitting my nose," or "as quiet as my mother kissing me goodnight."

As teachers begin providing experiences with sounds, it is wise to start with the familiar before going on to the unfamiliar. Many adults find it difficult to identify specific sounds on the basis of hearing alone. They often use their sense of sight, along with listening, even for identifying familiar sounds. Less familiar sounds are much more difficult to recognize, not only for adults but especially for the less experienced child.

Another skill is auditory memory, or the ability to remember and recall sounds. Often achievement tests for children as young as 4 or 5 years test for auditory memory. A good way to teach younger children this skill is to clap rhythm patterns and have the children clap the exact rhythms back to you. Older children can repeat concept sequences in the exact order; these can be objects, names, colors, numbers, or any variety of items.

Concepts and Ideas for Teaching

1. There are different categories of sounds. For example:
   a. Cleaning
   b. Holidays or other special days
   c. Home
   d. Country and farm
   e. Musical
   f. Machines or automobiles
   g. Animals
   h. Nature and weather: water, wind, thunder, leaves, fire, and rain
   i. Cooking
   j. Human
      1. External: hopping, eating, chewing, scratching, and snapping fingers
      2. Internal: stomach growling, swallowing, hiccupping, and burping

2. Sounds have different qualities and thus can be described in different ways, for example:

   light   noisy
   heavy   pleasant
   soft   fearful
   loud   comforting
   happy   silly
   angry   frightening
   sad   exciting

3. We learn from sounds; they give us information and motivate our behavior.
   a. Hungry baby crying
   b. Something boiling over
   c. Time of day: the clock chiming; children outside playing, indicating that school is over and it is late afternoon
   d. School dismissal: school bell
   e. Someone at the door or waiting outside: doorbell, knock, honking horn
   f. People outside: walking sounds, vocal sounds, laughing
   g. Activity of parent: pounding nails, washing windows, preparing dinner, running sewing machine
   h. Feelings of animals or people: whining, growling, laughing, or crying
   i. Emotional quality of such things as movies, homes, music, television

4. The same sounds can influence or affect people differently.
   a. Alarm clock: pleasant if it rings on the morning of a long-awaited vacation, but unpleasant on a morning when you want to stay in bed
   b. Telephone: unpleasant in the middle of the night, but pleasant when a call is expected from someone special

5. We can hear things we do not see.
   a. Wind
   b. Jet breaking the sound barrier
   c. Stomach growling
   d. Cat purring
   e. Furnace clicking on
   f. Voices in another room

6. Some things are so soft that they cannot be heard.
   a. Snowflakes falling
   b. Feathers falling
   c. Eyes blinking
   d. Worms crawling
   e. Butterflies flying
   f. Foods baking

7. Some sounds are alike.
   a. Thunder and fireworks
   b. Dog barking and seal barking
   c. Telephone and alarm clock
   d. Hair dryer and vacuum cleaner

8. The same items sometimes make different sounds: child, musical instrument, dog, and cars

9. Sound travels both long and short distances.
   a. Through systems of communication such as the telephone, telegraph, radio, television, and satellite
   b. By walkie-talkie: on tightly stretched wire or string
   c. Through a tabletop: a child with an ear placed on the table can easily hear sounds made on the underside at the opposite end of the table.
   d. Through vibrations: a rather abstract concept for young children, but can be introduced by feeling a tuning fork, striking a tuning fork and then putting it in water, or feeling musical instruments that have definite vibrating qualities.

Activities and Experiences

1. Tape-record sounds and have the children determine what the sounds are. The sounds selected should be familiar ones and should be heard long enough on the tape so that the children can hear them adequately. Some sounds should be made twice: for example, a squeaky door. The following are kinds of sounds that can be used with this activity:
   a. Liquid boiling
   b. Food frying
   c. Batter being stirred

d. Carrot being peeled

e. Doorbell ringing

f. Oven timer buzzing

g. Water running

h. Toilet flushing

i. Car starting, windshield wipers working, seat belts being fastened, or gears being shifted

j. Traffic moving

k. Dog barking or other familiar animal sounds

l. Telephone ringing

There are commercial recordings or tapes of these and other sounds; check your library's audio department. (*Note:* modify this activity by having the teacher make sounds behind a screen, and children guess the sound.)

2. Have the children listen to a particular sound and then suggest several adjectives or descriptive words for the sound.

3. Set out pairs of containers, such as empty film containers, that the children cannot see through. Put equal amounts of media in pairs so that when children shake matching pairs, they hear the same sounds. Media or items might include wheat, rice, beans, sugar, paper clips, beads, sand, or seeds. With older children, more pairs can be included.

4. Allow the children to feel and/or see things that vibrate, such as a rubber band stretched between two nails and plucked or a radio, timer, music box, or simple machine that vibrates as it runs. Ask the children what they feel and hear.

5. Assign the children to cooperative learning groups, and give each group a small, wrapped, jewelry-sized box. Each box could contain a small, rubber ball; a flat object such as a coin, paper clip, or washer; a marble; and a nail, screw, or similar item. Have each group try to discover what the four items are in the box by listening carefully as they shake and tap the box at their ears. Each box could have the same items, or they could each have different items. After they have guessed and explored, have the children open the box and see what is in it. If just the lids of the boxes are wrapped in wrapping paper, the boxes can be tied and used again without having to be rewrapped each time.

6. Have the children compare loud and soft sounds. Ask, "Can the same sound be either loud or soft? How about a whistle or pounding with a hammer—can they be either loud or soft?" Tap softly on a wooden table and describe the sound. Then have the children put one ear to the table and cover their other ear. Now tap the table again. Ask, "Was the sound loud with the ear close to the table?"

7. Obtain a set of six or eight bottles of the same size and shape. Fill them with water to various levels. Have the children strike each bottle with a spoon and compare the sounds; order the bottles from lowest to highest sounds; and blow across the tops of the bottles to compare the sounds (if the tops are narrow).

8. Have the children strike various lengths of conduit pipe or the various-sized strikers on a child's xylophone and compare the sounds.

9. Have the children brainstorm and/or describe their favorite or happiest sounds and their most frightening or unpleasant sounds. Write their responses on a chart or collect them in an illustrated booklet.

10. Tape-record each child's voice. Let the children listen to the recordings and discuss the differences.

11. Make a simple telephone system using two tin cans or paper cups and string, wire, or thread. Punch two small holes in the bottom of each can (cup) and fasten the ends of the wire (string) to the can. Stretch the system out and have a child at each end of the wire hold the can. The system functions best when the wire is tight; it should not be allowed to touch anything between the cans. The wire can be several yards long. As a child talks into the can, the sound waves travel from that can along the wire to the other can, where the sound is reproduced.

UNIT IDEAS ON SOUND AND PITCH

VISITORS

- Person to play musical instrument: one instrument making many sounds; many instruments making the same sound
- Ensemble from portion of band or orchestra
- Custodian to bring in materials, equipment, and supplies that make various sounds
- Vocalist
- Baby: comparison of baby's sounds with the sounds that the children in the classroom make; listening to sounds made by the baby's equipment and toys
- Parent to bring in materials or equipment relating to job, hobby, or home activities: electric shaver, power tools, hammer and nails, and so on; pitch of parent's voice compared to that of children's own voices also noted
- Tap dancer
- Garbage collector with truck
- Pet store owner or anyone with animals that make sounds
- Plumber
- Mechanic

- Native American dancer
- Piano tuner

FIELD TRIPS

- Farm
- School where music room, band, or orchestra could be visited
- Pet shop
- Zoo
- Service station or automobile repair garage
- Outside walk to listen to sounds of nature in the everyday environment
- Bird refuge
- Factory: machine sounds
- Office
- Music store
- Sawmill
- Fire station
- Construction or building site
- Barbershop
- Cafeteria: cooking sounds

SCIENCE

- String and cans to make walkie-talkie
- Dry-cell circuit: hooked up to make a buzzing sound or ring a bell
- Lengths and widths of strings on musical instruments (and bottles of water at various levels): variation of the pitch of the sound made when they are plucked or struck
- Experiments with a tuning fork
- Experiences with sounds traveling or vibrating
- Activities with elastics

FOOD

- Popcorn
- Rice Crispy squares
- Grilled or broiled hamburgers or other foods
- Boiled vegetables or other foods
- Chopped foods
- Shredded foods such as cabbage for making coleslaw
- Homemade root beer

ART

- Decorated sound shakers
- Other instruments made and decorated: tambourines, hummers, or drums

MUSIC

- Making any kind of musical instrument for musical band or orchestra
- Shakers made by groups of children, with each group using a different medium; for a music activity using the shakers, the first verse of a song to be accompanied by one group whose shakers have a particular sound, and the chorus accompanied by another group whose shakers have another sound; alternatively, various parts of a record accompanied by individual groups

LITERACY

- At Halloween, write or dictate and illustrate a booklet titled "Spooky Sounds."
- Develop a chart or booklet, with or without illustrations, titled "Sounds We Like—Sounds We Don't Like." Have each child do a page for "Sounds We Like" and a page for "Sounds We Don't Like." The pages can be illustrated and then described with a written or dictated sentence.

TEACHING ABOUT ANIMALS

Animals make excellent visitors to the classroom, where children observe, investigate, learn about, and care for them. It is important for children to develop concern for animals and where they live—just as they should for living things. As children study and learn more, they will be less likely to fear the animals or want to kill them. Children must be able to investigate and explore, without our own concerns that they should not touch or get dirty.

NAEYC (2008) suggests that early childhood classrooms should develop a pet or animal policy of appropriate safety and sanitation procedures. The Centers for Disease Control and Prevention (CDC; n.d.) recommends the following procedures to prevent young children from getting sick while handling animals:

Children should always be supervised.

Wash hands with soap and water after handling.

Children under age 5 should not handle baby chicks, ducklings, amphibians, or reptiles.

The following are general safety precautions around animals:

Do not touch or pet a strange or unfamiliar animal.

Do not bother an animal while it is eating or sleeping.

Do not reach inside a fence or pen to pet an animal.

Do not tease or chase an animal (adapted from Jalongo, 2006, p. 32-G).

Categories of animals appropriate for indoor interest centers include pets, some farm animals, fish, birds,

Dogs are often brought into the classroom when studies focus on pets.

and insects. Some traditional favorites are tadpoles and frogs, turtles, gerbils, hamsters, guinea pigs, goldfish, caterpillars and butterflies, chicks that hatch, rabbits, and hermit crabs. Children also enjoy ant farms, bug cages, and bird feeders. Individually made bird feeders can be taken home, where they further extend children's interest and understanding through continued observation and feeding of the birds.

The world of animals is a big world indeed, and many units of study can develop from this single category. There are numerous forms of animal life, ranging in size from animals so small that they cannot be seen without the aid of a microscope to those that are much larger than humans. Many of the concepts, projects, and units developed may result from the children's inquiries about particular animals or categories of animals or because the children have brought pets or other animals into the classroom. Children will especially enjoy doing a project study on a pet that is their own.

A well-planned animal unit or project should include, if possible, a field trip to visit the animals being studied, a visitor who will bring animals into the classroom, or animals that can stay in the classroom for study and observation. Remember the importance of the firsthand sensory experience. It is difficult to imagine a unit on eggs and chickens without including a visit to a poultry farm; having eggs incubated and hatched right in the classroom; or having chicks, hens, or roosters in the classroom for study and firsthand observation. Even when there are actual animals for classroom observation, misconceptions may occur.

Lyn had been watching the incubator as the chickens hatched from eggs. When only one more egg remained to hatch, Lyn inquired, "But when is the mother going to come out?"

After the experience of having a live angora sheep on the playground, the children discussed it and compared it to pictures of sheep with which they were more familiar. However, one child told his mother as she was picking him up from school that day, "We had a real live buffalo come to our class today."

After several days' experiences with guinea pigs, one child commented, "Baby pigs are guinea pigs." Another child stated, "Baby pigs are skinny pigs."

As animal units, projects, and experiences are planned, do not be afraid to develop units around the most common animals. For example, many new concepts can be taught and many ideas reinforced and clarified through units on dogs, fish, or cows. Many children are familiar with these animals and may even have some for pets; however, new concepts can be built on those already understood, and broader meanings can be obtained. Children can also be introduced to generally less familiar animals, such as tadpoles, guinea pigs, and lizards.

Categorization games help children to distinguish animals from other groups, such as toys, foods, furniture, people, and plants. Even more specifically, animal picture cards can be sorted into categories, such as insects, farm animals, circus animals, pets, animals that live in water, birds, and animals that live underground; many additional categories could be developed as well. A set of animal pictures or flash cards can be used for naming the animals. Pictures can be found in such places as magazines, stickers purchased from stationery stores, or discarded workbooks.

The following is a list of suggested animal unit themes. It is not meant to be inclusive, because the ideas and themes are almost endless, limited only by the teacher's own creative thinking and planning. Also, a unit need not necessarily emerge from each theme; it is possible to use one of the suggested themes for a science experience. For example, a teacher might not wish to do a whole unit on the life cycle of tadpole to frog, but it would provide an excellent experience for the science center or as a single science activity.

Note: The general theme is in boldface, and the subthemes listed may be included in the general unit of study or may stand alone as a project or unit of study.

Farm animals: cows, pigs, rabbits, horses, ducks, chickens, sheep, goats, and turkeys

Zoo animals: elephants, monkeys, lions, tigers, seals, penguins, and bears

Jungle animals

Circus animals

Desert animals

Ocean animals: fish, shellfish, and mammals (whales and dolphins)

Pets: birds, dogs, cats, hamsters, guinea pigs, gerbils, fish, and turtles

Insects, caterpillars: bees, ants, butterflies, and flies

Worms

Birds (perhaps specific birds common to the locale)

Tadpoles and frogs (life cycle)

Animal babies

Animal homes

Hibernation

Animals that live in trees

Animals that live underground

Animals that lived long ago

Concepts and Ideas for Teaching

1. Animals have various physical characteristics.
   a. Various body parts that often serve specific functions
      Wings: how many? Some birds have wings but do not fly.
         Legs: how many?
         Claws
         Shell
         Eyes
         Tail and fins
         Mouth
         Feet (study footprints)
         Nose
         Arms
         Beak
         Antennae
         Lungs
         Gills
         Backbone (or no backbone)
         Other
   b. Various body coverings that have characteristic textures and serve different purposes.
      fur   shell
      skin   hair
      feathers   scales
2. Animals have adapted different ways of locomotion: walking, swimming, flying, and crawling.
3. Animals live in various places or environments and in various kinds of homes.
   a. Trees
   b. Desert
   c. Jungle
   d. Farm
   e. Zoo
   f. On the land
   g. Underneath the ground
   h. Near garbage
   i. In cold climates
   j. In water but not on land
   k. In water and also on land
   l. Change in habitat corresponding to change in season

4. Animals eat various kinds of things.
   a. Plants
   b. Nuts
   c. Other animals
   d. Garbage
   e. Wood
5. Animals reproduce and care for their young in various ways.
   a. Give birth to live young
   b. Lay eggs: with hard shells or without shells
   c. Abandon young after giving birth
   d. Feed milk to young (mammals)
   e. Keep young nearby to nurture and care for
   f. Usually have multiple offspring
   g. Usually have single offspring
   h. Provide the food for the offspring
6. Animal babies have different characteristics in relation to their parents. Animals go through life cycles while changing and growing.
   a. May or may not look like the parent
   b. Sometimes have identifying names
   c. May eat different things or the same things as the parent
   d. May or may not move in the same way as the parent
   e. May or may not sound the same as the parent
   f. Change as they grow
7. Animals may make characteristic sounds; the sounds may have a particular purpose.
8. Some animals are extinct, and we learn about them from fossils.
   a. Dinosaurs: the largest land animals that ever lived on the earth
   b. Mammoths
   c. Saber-toothed tigers
9. Some animals are make-believe, such as dragons.
10. Many animals are useful to humans.
    a. Animals that provide food for humans: cows, chickens, pigs, turkeys, deer, and fish
    b. Animals that provide clothing or apparel for humans: sheep; animals that provide furs, silkworms; animals that provide leather for making shoes, purses, and wallets
    c. Animals that are friends or pets to humans
    d. Animals that eat other animals that are harmful or a nuisance to humans: snakes eating mice, cats eating mice, and birds eating insects such as grasshoppers
    e. Animals that eat plants that are harmful or a nuisance to humans: livestock eating mustard weed, which is harmful to humans
    f. Animals that provide humans with entertainment and recreation
       (1) Animals that are hunted for sporting purposes, as well as meat: deer, elk, fish, rabbits, pheasants, ducks, and geese
       (2) Zoo and circus animals, which are always enjoyable to observe

g. Animals that work for humans
  (1) In some parts of the world, animals provide transportation; horses, donkeys, camels, and dogs
  (2) Dogs that help to herd sheep and cattle
  (3) Dogs that are trained as seeing-eye guide dogs for people who are blind
  (4) Dogs that are used in detective work or serve as guards
  (5) Cattle, mules, and horses, which do farm work
11. Many animals are harmful to humans.
  a. Animals that are dangerous if they are threatened by humans
  b. Animals whose bites are poisonous: coral snake and black widow spiders
  c. Animals whose bites may cause disease, such as rabies or malaria
12. Many animals are a nuisance to humans. Some animals eat plants or animals that are important to humans (insects such as weevils eat wheat and other grains); coyotes eat sheep and chickens; bears eat sheep.
13. Some animals may be useful, while also being either harmful or a nuisance to humans. Range cattle are useful, but because of trampling and overgrazing, the possibility of erosion increases.
14. Animals adapt in various ways to seasonal changes.
  a. Animals that hibernate: fish, frogs, bears, and snakes
  b. Animals that migrate: birds, such as geese
  c. Animals that acquire a heavier fur or covering: cows, horses, sheep, and dogs
15. Animals respond to temperature in various ways.
  a. Dogs and other animals that pant to cool themselves
  b. Pigs, which shunt their blood away from the skin surface in cold weather, but are more susceptible to death in hot weather
  c. Bees, which cluster together in masses to keep warm in cold weather

Activities and Experiences

1. Take field trips to places where animals are found or bring animals to the classroom. When animals are in the classroom, children need to be told exactly what they can and cannot do with them and, if the animals can be handled, how to do that kindly, gently, and properly. The safety of both the children and the animals should be considered. Teachers should check their program or school policies to see whether there are any restrictions or regulations that need to be observed. When the animals are in the classroom, the children should have the opportunity to feed them and care for their needs. In this way, the children learn that all animals need food, but that they do not all eat the same kinds of foods. The children also learn that all animals need water and air.

   A favorite observation activity with animals is observing the life cycles of particular animals such as the frog (tadpole to frog), monarch butterfly (caterpillar to chrysalis to butterfly), or chicken (egg to chick). Whenever possible, return animals to their natural environment.

2. Make a bug cage. Obtain two large lids (at least 3 inches in diameter) of exactly the same size or use two small cake pans. Obtain a piece of heavy, stiff screen about 8 to 10 inches in length and wide enough to fit inside the circumference of the lids or pans plus several inches for overlap. Roll the screen into a cylinder to fit inside the lids or pans exactly, and then, with string or yarn, "sew" around the overlap to hold the screen securely in the roll that will fit inside the lids or pans. Now mix a small amount of plaster of Paris and pour it into one of the lids or pans. Then immediately put one end of the roll of screen into that lid or pan. Hold it until the plaster of Paris dries. A twig or stick may be stuck into the plaster of Paris before it sets so that there will be something for the bugs to crawl on. When bugs are caught in the cage, simply put the other lid or pan on the top of the roll.

3. Collect pictures of many kinds of animals and glue them to cards. They can be sorted into such categories as farm or zoo animals, animals that fly or that do not fly, animals that provide food for humans, and so on. Pass these cards out to the children. Give a characteristic of animals and have the children raise their card (or cards) of animals that have that characteristic. For example, say "Hold up your animal(s) if it eats other animals" or "Hold up your animal(s) if it lives in the jungle."

4. Make animal scrapbooks. Collect as much information or as many pictures as possible for each animal in the scrapbook. The scrapbook could relate to a particular group of animals, such as pets, or it could be for animals in general. Encourage literacy by writing something about each animal.

5. Present animal riddles. Either the teacher or the children can give the clues for a particular animal. The children guess what animal answers the riddle. These can be written in an animal riddle book, with additional riddles added during the year.

6. Use animal stick puppets for dramatizations, for demonstrating animal sounds and other characteristics, or for categorizing by characteristics.

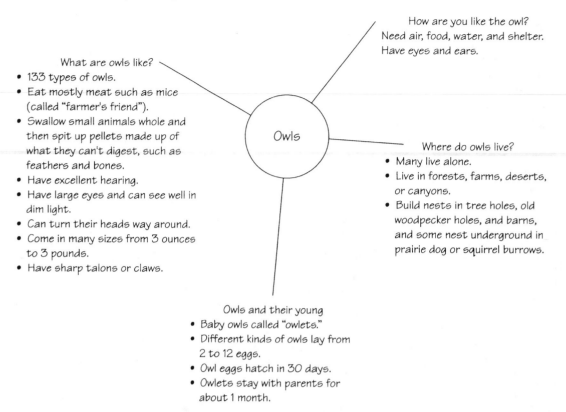

What are owls like?
- 133 types of owls.
- Eat mostly meat such as mice (called "farmer's friend").
- Swallow small animals whole and then spit up pellets made up of what they can't digest, such as feathers and bones.
- Have excellent hearing.
- Have large eyes and can see well in dim light.
- Can turn their heads way around.
- Come in many sizes from 3 ounces to 3 pounds.
- Have sharp talons or claws.

How are you like the owl?
Need air, food, water, and shelter.
Have eyes and ears.

Where do owls live?
- Many live alone.
- Live in forests, farms, deserts, or canyons.
- Build nests in tree holes, old woodpecker holes, and barns, and some nest underground in prairie dog or squirrel burrows.

Owls and their young
- Baby owls called "owlets."
- Different kinds of owls lay from 2 to 12 eggs.
- Owl eggs hatch in 30 days.
- Owlets stay with parents for about 1 month.

FIGURE 11.1   Sample Web: What Has Been Learned About Owls

7. Make plaster molds of animal footprints by mixing plaster of Paris (it sets up quickly, so mix it just as you are preparing to make the mold) and putting a cardboard rim around the footprint. (The cardboard rim could be the rim of a small box such as a jewelry box. Cut out several sizes beforehand.) Place the rim around the footprint and pour plaster into the impression. When dry, remove the plaster and return it to the classroom to classify and label it. Put a picture and the name of the animal next to the footprint cast.

8. Make written or dictated observations of animals that the children see or visit. For example, after visiting a zoo or farm, each child could dictate or write about one animal that he or she has carefully observed. The children could illustrate their observations and these could be put together into a class booklet. First- and second-grade children could add research to their observation report. If the animal is in the classroom, a language experience chart could be recorded on observations made of the animal each day.

9. Following an experience with an animal, have the children help to make a web to review what has been learned. For an example, see Figure 11.1.

10. Compare one animal to another or one group of animals to another group of animals, or animals to people.
    a. Similarities
    b. Differences

Unit Ideas and Project Plans on Animals

Many different unit, project, and lesson plans could be done on animals or concepts relating to animals; the following serve only as examples, and they should spark your imagination and creative planning for other units and lesson plans relating to animals, such as those on hibernation, baby animals, or animal homes.

The following are unit and lesson plans on some animal themes. Again, be aware that they can be either general (such as zoo or farm animals) or specific (such as cows, bees, frogs, or animal babies) and that they make great projects for children to plan.

 UNIT IDEAS ON FARM ANIMALS

ART

- Farm mobiles
- Farm animal collages
- Salt or oil-based clay farm animals
- Finger paint, with media such as oats or wheat: food for farm animals
- Farm animal sack puppets

FIELD TRIPS

- Farm

- Grocery store, to look for products from farm animals
- Butcher shop

VISITORS

- Farmer
- Someone to bring in a pet that is a farm animal
- Storyteller to tell a farm animal story
- Grocer to bring in farm animal products
- Parent to cook a farm animal product

FOOD

- Eggs prepared any way
- Ice cream, milkshakes, or cheese
- Bacon and tomato sandwiches
- Hamburgers or hamburger used in any way
- Chicken prepared in any way
- Turkey prepared in any way
- Jerky or salami pizza
- Various preparations of pork, lamb, or fish

SCIENCE

- Animal corner with live farm animals, eggs incubating, or baby farm animals
- What farm animals eat
- Physical characteristics of some farm animals
- Farm animal babies: what they look like, what they are called, how they are cared for, what they eat
- What happens to farm animals in summer and in winter

MUSIC

- Creative movements dealing with farm animals
- Paper cups decorated and used as rhythm accompaniment to songs about animals walking or running
- Music and movement involving fairy tales with farm animals. For example: "The Three Billy Goats Gruff," "The Three Little Pigs," and "The Little Red Hen," etc.

LANGUAGE AND LITERACY

- Poetry and stories relating to farm animals
- Tape of farm animal sounds; identification of the animals by the children
- Puppets or felt figures of farm animals made by the children; stories dramatized about farm animals; stories made up using animal figures
- Dramatized nursery rhymes, poems, and fairy tales relating to farm animals

- Open-ended stories, with children telling the endings
- Display of pictures of farm animals (Say "I went to the farm and saw a _____"; let the child select a picture and talk about that animal.)
- Slides of farm animals, with discussion about them
- Writing or telling and illustrating stories about favorite farm animals

UNIT IDEAS ON BEES

ART

- Bee mobiles: bees and beehive painted or colored; holes punched in hive, and bees hung all around it with string
- Bees made with Styrofoam base and materials such as pipe cleaners
- Bees made and decorated, using toilet-paper roll as base

FIELD TRIPS

- Bee farm
- Honey distributor
- Flower garden where bees are collecting nectar to make honey
- Library

VISITORS

- Parent or grandparent to make something using honey: honey candy or honey butter
- Beekeeper: description of job, telling how the hive is smoked to obtain honey; demonstration of a beekeeping outfit or uniform, including veil, gloves, and clips around trousers to prevent bees from getting inside pants; equipment used, including smoker machine, bee brush, knife for opening hives, and beehive frames
- Someone to show honeycomb

FOOD

- Honey butter
- Honey candy or cookies
- Muffins with honey butter (see recipe)
- Honey bread (see recipe)

Recipe for Muffins and Honey Butter

2 cups baking mix	1 cup milk
$\frac{1}{4}$ cup sugar	$\frac{1}{4}$ cup oil
1 egg	

Mix baking mix and sugar. Add beaten egg to milk and oil; then add this liquid to the dry ingredients. Stir until moistened; the batter will be lumpy. Fill greased muffin tins two-thirds full. Bake at 400°F for about 20 minutes. Serve with a mixture of butter and honey.

Recipe for Honey Bread

$1\frac{1}{2}$ cups honey	$1\frac{1}{2}$ tsp salt
$1\frac{1}{2}$ cups milk	$\frac{1}{3}$ cup oil
$\frac{3}{4}$ cup sugar	2 eggs
$3\frac{3}{4}$ cups flour	2 tsp vanilla
$1\frac{1}{2}$ tsp soda	

Bring honey, milk, and sugar to a boil and cool the mixture. Mix dry ingredients together; add oil, eggs, and vanilla. Add cooled liquid mixture and beat for 2 minutes. Put in greased loaf pans. Bake at 325°F for about 1 hour.

SCIENCE

- Science corner or table with pictures of bees, beehives, and beekeepers doing their jobs; display of objects such as honeycomb, equipment beekeeper uses, bee eggs, bees, and bee products
- Science discussions, experiments, and observations focusing on the following topics: members of the bee family (queen, workers, and drones and their various functions within the hive); making of honey; characteristics of bees; honeycomb (six-sided wall cells in the hive that bees use for storing food and as a place for hatching young bees); collecting nectar from flowers to make honey; bees' role in pollinating flowers and trees (use pictures and any visual material available)
- Discussion of first-aid treatment for bee stings; discussion of why bees sting people and animals

MUSIC

- Creative movements and dramatics relating to bees: hatching from eggs, flying, moving about in the hive, and searching for nectar in flowers
  - Songs and records relating to bees

LANGUAGE AND LITERACY

- Stories and poems relating to bees
- Making bee puppets or flannel-board figures, with the children telling stories or dramatizing them
- Slides of bees, with discussion and storytelling
- Films and filmstrips relating to bees
- Tape of bee sounds; discussion
- Story writing about bees

UNIT IDEAS ON BIRDS

ART

- Finger painting, with birdseed added
- Feather painting
- Feather collages
- Decoration of eggs (made from plastic colored eggs)
- Bird collages or bird stickers from stationery store
- Birdseed collages
- Decorate birdseed shakers with birdseed and/or other materials
- Use of the outline or form of birds on large sheets of butcher paper; children paint and/or make collages with them
- Bird puppets

FOOD

- Any food activities using poultry products: chicken, turkey, or eggs

FIELD TRIPS

- Pet store
- Bird refuge
- Walk to observe birds and look for birds' nests
- Museum or university ornithology department to observe stuffed birds
- Poultry farm
- Aviary
- Home where pet birds may be observed

VISITORS

- Pet store owner
- Ornithologist
- Bird watcher
- Child or other member of family who can bring a pet bird
- Storyteller to tell stories about birds
- Parent to cook a poultry product
- Person who knows birdcalls; demonstration
- Someone who owns a talking bird such as a parrot

SCIENCE

- Science discussions, experiments, and observations focusing on the following topics: kinds of birds, sizes of birds, characteristics of birds (such as having feathers and having been hatched from eggs), colors of birds, birds that migrate, birds common to the locale, and bird food

- Study of bird eggs: sizes, colors, and so on
- Study of bird's nests: sizes, materials used in construction, and matching of specific birds with their characteristic nests
- Bird feeders; a simple one is a pinecone, with flour and water mixed into a thick paste and stuffed into the pinecone, which is then rolled in birdseed and hung in a tree with a piece of string
- Slides of birds; discussion
- Tape recording of bird sounds from the library or made by the teacher

MUSIC

- Musical games about birds
- Songs about birds
- Creative dramatics relating to birds: hatching from the egg, drying feathers, swimming, flying, and hunting for worms
- Records lending themselves to dramatization of bird characteristics and actions

LANGUAGE AND LITERACY

- Pictures of birds; discussion and storytelling
- Stories and poetry about birds
- Puppets or flannel-board figures, with children dramatizing or telling stories
- Display of pictures of birds with a discussion beginning "I saw a bird that . . .," with individual children selecting a picture and telling about this bird by finishing the statement. These accounts could be written and collected into a book.
- Dramatization of stories, poems, and songs relating to birds

 UNIT IDEAS ON FISH

ART

- Fish made from a small brown-paper sack stuffed with newspaper, tied with string on the open end so that it resembles a fishtail, then painted or decorated
- Fish drawn by each child and put on an overhead or opaque projector for enlarging (older children can trace their own) and then painted or decorated (makes a creative bulletin board)

- Fish made and decorated and then put behind blue cellophane paper to create the illusion of a fishpond or aquarium
- Seafood collage made by cutting types of fish that we eat and fish products from newspaper grocery advertisements

VISITORS

- Parent to cook fish by any method
- Parent to bring in fishing gear and demonstrate its use, perhaps cooking fish as well
- Fish and game officer
- Person from a hatchery, cannery, or restaurant
- Grocer to bring in several varieties of fish, perhaps allowing the children to taste some
- Someone to bring in slides of fishing trips
- Someone to bring in pet fish

MUSIC

- Creative dramatics or movements representing fishing or moving like fish
- Shakers made from tuna fish or shrimp cans; can be decorated with seashells

FIELD TRIPS

- Fish hatchery
- Fish cannery
- Sporting goods store or department store to see fishing gear and supplies, such as salmon eggs and fishing flies
- Pet store with several varieties of fish
- Fish market, to see various cuts of fish and to notice fish odors
- Restaurant that serves fish
- Grocery store

FOOD

- Fish burgers
- Baked, fried, or broiled fish
- Tuna casserole
- Fish patties: salmon or tuna
- Fish salads: tuna or shrimp
- Sandwiches
- Fish and chips
- Chowder

SCIENCE

- Kinds of fish and where they live
- Parts of fish: scales, fins, gills, and so on

- What fish eat
- How fish breathe
- Hibernation of some fish
- Spawning habits of some fish
- Aquarium placed in classroom
- Tasting and comparing of various kinds of fish
- Fish placed in a trough or large container for observation and touching
- Characteristics of a specific kind of fish, such as salmon

LANGUAGE AND LITERACY

- Slides (or PowerPoint), pictures, stories, poetry, songs, films relating to fish
- Teacher-made puppets or flannel-board fish characters for children to dramatize or tell stories about
- Stories about fish: tell or illustrate
- Books about fish

 ## UNIT IDEAS ON PETS

For this unit it is suggested that one particular pet be chosen for each day's focus, with concepts relating to that pet brought into the discussion. The children should be able to handle the pets, feed them, and care for them. Baby pets will also add interest for the children.

ART

- Decoration of rocks to resemble a desired pet, using felt scraps, hobby-store eyes, beans, fabric scraps, and other media
- Sock pets: child's sock decorated with felt scraps, yarn, and other fabrics
- Sack-puppet pets: paper lunch sacks decorated to make pet puppets
- Pet collages: pictures of pets cut from magazines or animal pet stickers purchased from stationery stores
- Salt dough or salt clay pets
- Collages using dry foods for pets, such as birdseed

FIELD TRIPS

- Pet store
- Home where pets can be observed
- Zoo
- Animal hospital

VISITORS

- Pet store owner
- Family member of student to share family pet

- Storyteller to tell pet stories
- Veterinarian
- Zookeeper

FOOD

- Sandwiches cut with pet-animal cookie cutters
- Green salad, with discussion of pets that enjoy vegetables: sesame seeds sprinkled on salad, followed by discussion of which pets enjoy eating seeds
- Bread dough shaped into a favorite pet

SCIENCE

- Science discussion, experiments, and observations focusing on the following topics: kinds of pets; sizes of pets; characteristics such as footprints, colors, sounds, diet, and sleeping habits
- Care and needs of particular pets
- Pet babies: appearance, care required, and diet

MUSIC

- Songs about pets
- Creative dramatics relating to pets: how they move, what they do during the day, how they respond to friends, and how they respond to enemies

LANGUAGE AND LITERACY

- Slides (or PowerPoint) of pets; discussion
- Pets or pictures of current or former pets brought by the children; sharing and discussion
- Puppet or flannel-board figures; dramatization or storytelling by the children; discussion of particular pets by the children
- Tape recording of pet sounds, with the children naming the pet and discussing the sounds that it makes and why
- Stories and poetry about pets
- Game in which individual children select a particular pet and then describe it so that other children can guess which pet has been described
- Game in which a child leaves the room, class members select a particular pet, and then the child returns and tries to discover which pet was selected by asking yes or no questions
- Children illustrating a favorite pet and then dictating or writing something about this pet; children's stories made into a class booklet

 ## PROJECT PLAN ON DINOSAURS

For a project plan on dinosaurs, see Figure 11.2.

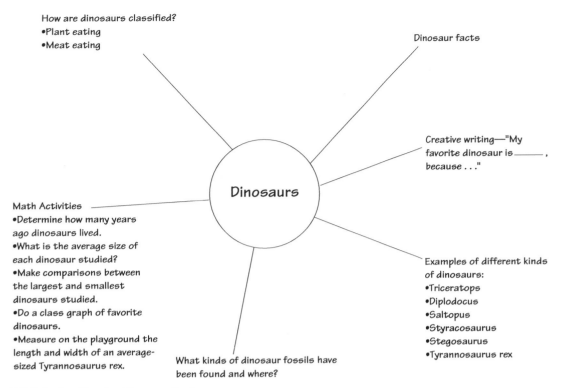

How are dinosaurs classified?
•Plant eating
•Meat eating

Dinosaur facts

Creative writing—"My
favorite dinosaur is ———,
because . . ."

Dinosaurs

Math Activities
•Determine how many years
ago dinosaurs lived.
•What is the average size of
each dinosaur studied?
•Make comparisons between
the largest and smallest
dinosaurs studied.
•Do a class graph of favorite
dinosaurs.
•Measure on the playground the
length and width of an average-
sized Tyrannosaurus rex.

Examples of different kinds
of dinosaurs:
•Triceratops
•Diplodocus
•Saltopus
•Styracosaurus
•Stegosaurus
•Tyrannosaurus rex

What kinds of dinosaur fossils have
been found and where?

FIGURE 11.2 Child's Project Plan for Dinosaur Study

TEACHING ABOUT PLANTS

To select units of study relating to plants, the teacher should use the appropriate seasons and climates and select for study the plants that are most common to the children's surroundings and locality. Where possible, give the children actual experiences with plants. Take advantage of the learning opportunities that are provided in gardening experiences. Concepts in math (counting, measuring, charting, observing, predicting, sorting, comparing, classifying, sequencing, and spatial relationships); language and literacy (plant and animal names, books, recipes); and science (growth from seed to plant; effects of food, water, sun; birds, insects, and animals) are all embedded in gardening (Starbuck & Olthof, 2008). A nature-based curriculum also supports social, health-related, and academic learning and development (Ozer, 2007). Exploring nature helps children to develop skills that will be useful in later learning and academic success (Benson & Miller, 2008).

Plants could be approached as a general theme or unit. However, specific areas such as seeds, vegetables, fruits, trees, wheat, or flowers also provide appropriate units of study. Categorization games help children to distinguish plants from other groups, such as animals, people, or toys. Even more specifically, plant picture cards could be sorted into categories, such as vegetables, fruits, flowers, and trees. The cards could also be used as flash cards for naming the specific plants. Pictures of plants can be found in magazines, stickers

Plant the seed, then check every day to see if it has sprouted.

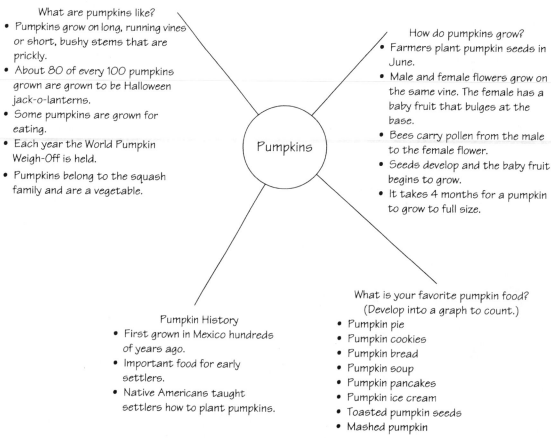

What are pumpkins like?
- Pumpkins grow on long, running vines or short, bushy stems that are prickly.
- About 80 of every 100 pumpkins grown are grown to be Halloween jack-o-lanterns.
- Some pumpkins are grown for eating.
- Each year the World Pumpkin Weigh-Off is held.
- Pumpkins belong to the squash family and are a vegetable.

Pumpkins

How do pumpkins grow?
- Farmers plant pumpkin seeds in June.
- Male and female flowers grow on the same vine. The female has a baby fruit that bulges at the base.
- Bees carry pollen from the male to the female flower.
- Seeds develop and the baby fruit begins to grow.
- It takes 4 months for a pumpkin to grow to full size.

Pumpkin History
- First grown in Mexico hundreds of years ago.
- Important food for early settlers.
- Native Americans taught settlers how to plant pumpkins.

What is your favorite pumpkin food?
(Develop into a graph to count.)
- Pumpkin pie
- Pumpkin cookies
- Pumpkin bread
- Pumpkin soup
- Pumpkin pancakes
- Pumpkin ice cream
- Toasted pumpkin seeds
- Mashed pumpkin

FIGURE 11.3   Sample Web: What We Learned About Pumpkins

purchased from stationery stores, discarded workbooks, or seed packets.

The following is a list of suggested plant unit themes. It is not meant to be inclusive; ideas and themes are limited only by the teacher's own creative thinking and planning. Furthermore, a unit need not necessarily result from each idea or theme; for example, a suggested theme could be used for a science experience supporting any unrelated unit of study.

plants	fruits (also specific)
seeds	vegetables (also specific)
nuts	plants as food for humans
wheat	plants that grow in water
trees	flowers
wood	berries

After a plant unit such as pumpkins is presented, the children can help complete a web such as the one illustrated in Figure 11.3.

Concepts and Ideas for Teaching

1. Most plants need air, light, water, and food in order to grow.
2. We eat different parts of plants.
   a. Roots (turnips, carrots, radishes, parsnips, and onions)
   b. Leaves (cabbage, lettuce, spinach, chard, beet greens, and herbs)
   c. Stems or stalks (asparagus, celery, and broccoli)
   d. Skins (tomatoes, apples, and carrots)
   e. Seeds (nuts, peas, beans, and potatoes)
3. Plants vary in color, size, texture, shape, and weight.
4. Plants may change in appearance as they progress through various stages of growth and as they are affected by temperature, weather, and season.
5. Some plants can grow only in particular seasons and climates.
6. Plants have various characteristics: roots, stems or stalks, flowers, leaves, seeds, and skins.
7. There are many kinds of plants: trees, flowering plants, foliage plants, vegetables, grains, vines, mosses, fruits, molds, and other fungi.
8. Plants have many uses.
   a. Some plants provide food for humans (vegetables, fruits, and grains).
   b. Trees provide products such as wood, paper, gum, drugs, paint, waxes, and dyes.
   c. Some plants provide clothing (cotton and linen).

d. Many plants provide beauty (trees, house-plants, and flowers).

e. Some plants provide shade, shelter, and protection for humans and animals (trees and large plants such as shrubs and bushes).

f. Some plants provide homes for animals (trees, shrubs, and foliage).

g. Many plants are food for animals.

9. Some plants are poisonous or harmful to humans.

10. Some plants are a nuisance to humans (for example, weeds).

11. Some plants grow on land and some grow in water; some grow in light and some grow in shade.

12. Most plants grow from seed, although there are variations. Some plants grow from bulbs, some grow in particular circumstances without seeds (moss and mold), some grow from cuttings (geraniums), and some grow from suckers or runners.

13. Seeds differ in color, shape, size, and texture.

14. We eat some types of seeds.

Activities and Experiences

1. Observe and discuss characteristic parts of different plants: apple tree, geranium, broccoli, and wheat.

2. Have a tasting experience in which the children taste different parts of plants. Ask the children to name and give examples of edible parts of plants. (Refer to teaching concept 2 for ideas.)

3. Observe the growing cycle of several different plants from their beginning to maturity.

   a. Observe the day-by-day stages of a growing seed such as a lima bean seed. Line the inside of a straight-sided jar with a paper towel or blotting paper. Keep water or a soaked sponge in the bottom so that the towel remains wet. Each day put a soaked lima bean seed between the jar and the wet paper. Do this each day for about 5 days so that the changes on each of the 5 days can be observed. Compare differences. Record observations in writing and in drawings or photographs, and put them together in a book to read and reread about the experience. When the seeds are well sprouted, plant them in soil and continue to watch their growth until they bear beans.

   b. Observe the growth of an orange tree from its beginning as a seedling. Record observations in pictures and writing.

   c. Observe the growth of a flower. Record observations in pictures and writing.

   d. Observe the growth of bread mold. Record observations in pictures and writing.

   e. Observe the growth of grass seed by having each child plant some in an eggshell filled with potting soil.

4. Have the class adopt a tree in the neighborhood or schoolyard and observe the tree's changes throughout the year. The class could measure the tree's diameter, examine its bark, observe the leaves during the different seasons, and keep a yearlong book or record describing its growth and changes. Photographs of the tree could be taken at different times during the year and then individually mounted for use as a sequencing material or in a book.

5. Observe how plants absorb water and food. Put a fresh stalk of celery under water; trim the end off and cut it up the center while the stalk is still under water. Cut it almost the entire length of the stem but not quite all the way. Fill two glasses with water and put food coloring of different colors in each (red and blue work well). Put half of the celery in one glass of colored water and the other half in the other glass. Within hours, the veins going up the stem of the celery and the leaves on the top of the stalk will assume the color of the water in the glasses. You can also put a white carnation or Queen Anne's lace (a common wildflower) in the colored water, and the petals will change color.

6. To enable the children to see what happens when a plant does not receive one of the necessary ingredients for growth, perform the following experiment: Obtain 5 similar plants, such as bean plants or flowers. Give one plant all the necessary ingredients except air; another, everything except light (put it in a dark room or closet); another, everything except water; another, everything except soil (food). Provide all the necessary ingredients to the fifth plant. Observe how long each plant grows and lives. Record observations.

7. Put different plants or parts of plants in a paper bag. Have a child describe one of the items, and ask the other children to guess the name or part of the plant from the description given.

8. Compare the sizes of plants, such as a radish plant and a tree or one kind of bean plant and another.

9. Put plant pictures on cards and have the children sort the plants into categories, which might include the following:

   a. Plants that we eat or do not eat

   b. Fruits; vegetables; trees; foliage; flowers

   c. Plants that grow above the ground or below the ground or in water

10. Study and observe plants that do not grow from seeds: plants that grow from bulbs and plants that grow in particular media, such as moss and mold. Allow the children to look at the plants through a magnifying glass. Do forced-bulb planting indoors.

11. To teach the children that stems grow upward and roots grow downward, obtain a clear glass or

Children gain an appreciation for plants as they learn to take care of them.

plastic jar and secure a piece of fine gauze over the top with an elastic band or a string. On top of the gauze, sprinkle seeds such as wheat kernels and then fill the container with water. Make sure that on the first few days the container is filled to the top and that the seeds remain wet enough to sprout. Be sure to put the container in a dish or pie plate, because the gauze absorbs the water. Within a few days the seeds will sprout, with the roots growing downward (because of gravity; this is called *geotropism*) and the stems growing upward (towards the light; this is called *phototropism*).

UNIT IDEAS ON SEEDS

For unit ideas on seeds, see Chapter 4.

UNIT IDEAS ON FRUITS OR VEGETABLES

For unit ideas on fruits or vegetables, see Chapter 6.

UNIT IDEAS ON PLANTS (GENERAL)

ART

- Plant collages: seeds, dried flowers, leaves, sticks, or other parts, in plaster of Paris, playdough, or other medium
- Screen painting with parts of plants
- Painting with flowers, leaves, or grains instead of brushes
- Seeds added to finger paint
- Melted crayon and parts of plants (seeds, leaves, and flowers) between waxed-paper sheets
- Flowers made out of nut cups, egg cartons, or cupcake holders; attached to a pipe cleaner, put in clay base, and arranged in paper-cup vase
- Flowers and leaves cut from wallpaper or fabric to glue on a paper or cardboard base
- Shakers decorated with plant parts

FIELD TRIPS

- Home garden
- Nature walk, with emphasis on looking for plants
- Greenhouse
- Plant nursery
- Flower shop
- Houseplants in home
- Botany department at a college or high school

VISITORS

- Florist
- Person owning houseplants
- Member of one child's family to show seeds that they will plant in a home garden and to discuss the care of plants at home
- Person to build a terrarium
- Person to bring in a pet or animal that eats plants

FOOD

- Any food experience using plants, such as fruits, vegetables, seeds, or nuts

SCIENCE

- Growth cycle of plants
- Needs of plants: air, sun, water, and food
- Uses of plants
- Harmful plants
- Nuisance plants
- Types of plants
- Places where plants grow
- Parts of plants
- Growth of mold; study it under a microscope and discuss which objects grow mold
- Sweet potato supported with toothpicks in a jar of water; observation of growth
- Pineapple planted by twisting the top off a fresh pineapple and then planting it in wet sand
- Carrot tops grown by cutting them $\frac{1}{4}$ to $\frac{1}{2}$ inch down and then putting them in water

MUSIC

- Songs about plants and seeds
- Seed shakers made and used as rhythm instruments; seedpods and gourds used as rhythm instruments
- Creative movements and dramatics relating to growth of plant from seed to mature plant; plants wilting because of lack of water and then being revived; plants following the sun, moving in the wind; seeds traveling and sprouting
- Dramatization of care of plants
- Dramatization of musical story: growth of plant

LANGUAGE AND LITERACY

- Stories about plants
- Poetry
- Slides (or PowerPoint) of plants; discussion
- Different kinds of plants brought by children from their homes; discussion
- Game in which individual children select a particular plant and describe it to the other children; guessing which plant is being described
- Children's own stories based on experiences in planting, growing, and caring for plants or gardens
- Take pictures of various garden plants, such as carrots or peas, and then have the children dictate or write a story about each; assemble the stories into a booklet.

UNIT IDEAS ON TREES

The children should understand that trees are a kind of plant and that trees grow from small seeds. The products of trees, as well as other uses, should be among the concepts studied during this unit. The children should also be exposed to the wide variety of trees. The activities selected will be determined by the goals and objectives desired for the particular unit. A unit on trees would be appropriate around Arbor Day. Children could each do a project on a kind of tree of their choosing.

ART

- Tree product collages using paper and wood products
- Pinecone mice
- Wood collages using wood shavings, sawdust, and wood scraps
- Sawdust painting
- Paper collages

Some houses are made out of wood from trees. Some houses are easier to get out of than others!

- Tree trunk drawn or pasted on paper, with children using sponge painting or handprints from finger paint to paint the leaves
- Nutshell animals
- Four-season paintings or drawings of trees
- Shakers
- Texture smears with leaf rubbings, wood products, or other parts of trees such as twigs
- Leaf collages
- Pinecone printing

FIELD TRIPS

- Nature walk to observe trees
- National or state forest
- Lumberyard
- Carpenter shop
- Home under construction
- Sawmill
- Hobby shop or woodworking shop
- Store where wooden things (furniture, for example) are sold
- Christmas tree farm
- Grocery store to observe edible tree products such as nuts and fruits
- Tree nurseries
- Visit to tree(s) in which the children can see animal homes, such as birds' nests
- Visit to a site where trees are being planted
- High school or university industrial arts shop
- Museum to see wood sculptures
- Activity: Divide the children into pairs. One child in the pair is blindfolded and taken to a tree. The child can hug the tree, feel it, and explore it. The child returns to the starting position, removes the blindfold, and then finds the tree that was explored.

FOOD (SEE ALSO CHAPTER 6)

- Fruit salads, desserts, or juices made from fruits of trees
- Foods that have nuts as an ingredient, such as cakes, cookies, candy (exercise special caution and consider possible food allergies)
- Dried fruits

VISITORS

- Forest ranger or urban forester
- Forest firefighter

- City firefighter
- Carpenter
- Wood carver
- Logger
- Owner of a tree nursery
- Grocery store employee

SCIENCE

- Examination of circles in tree trunks to determine age of tree
- Discussion of tree products
- Tree planted and cared for
- Discussion and study of tree parts
- Observation of how wood burns
- Tasting of foods that are products of trees: fruits and pine gum
- Observation of process of making a tree product such as paper
- Observation of selected tree over a period of time, preferably a year (keep a record in writing and with pictures)

MUSIC

- Creative movements relating to trees growing, moving in the wind, heavily laden with snow, leaves falling
- Use wooden rhythm sticks or wooden blocks as rhythm instruments
- Musical Chairs in which pictures of different kinds of trees or tree products are placed on the front of the chairs: Play music and have the children do locomotor rhythms. When the music stops, give directions such as, for example, "All pine trees stand and hop to this music" or "All weeping willow trees stand and skate to this music." A variation of this is to tape the pictures of the trees or tree products securely to the floor. Have each child stand on one when the music stops and then proceed with the game as suggested.
- Wooden drums
- Shakers with seeds from trees
- Instruments made from wood
- Drumsticks

LANGUAGE AND LITERACY

- Stories about trees written by the children or other authors
- Poetry

- Pictures of trees, and children brainstorming words that come to their minds as they see each tree
- Slides (or PowerPoints) of trees; discussion of characteristics, seasons, and feelings relating to each tree
- Cinquain poetry for trees
- Prepare a book, with each child doing one page. On this page, the child draws a picture of a favorite tree and dictates to the teacher or writes why he or she likes this tree.
- Have children finish the sentence "The best thing about a tree is . . ." or "I like trees because . . ." The children could write or dictate their answers and then illustrate them. These pages could be put together into a book to be enjoyed over and over again.

RELATED ACTIVITIES

- Rope swing in a tree
- Hammering
- Sawing
- Container with wood chips, sawdust, toothpicks, wooden spoons, bark, or leaves

 UNIT IDEAS ON WHEAT AND FLOUR

ART

- Finger painting with flour paste
- Finger painting with wheat kernels added
- Shakers: cans filled with wheat kernels, then decorated with tissue paper, kernels of wheat, or parts of the wheat shaft, and glued with flour paste
- Collages: wheat, parts of the shaft, wheat cereals
- Clay made from flour
- Papier-mâché
- Painting with wheat shaft
- Vase or pencil container made by molding clay around a 6-ounce can and sticking small bits of wheat shaft, kernels of wheat, or other collage items into the soft clay

FIELD TRIPS

- Bakery
- Flour mill
- Wheat field
- Granary, wheat silo, or grain bin

- Home to see how wheat is stored
- Home or bakery to see wheat grinder and observe how it grinds wheat into flour
- Cereal company

FOOD (SEE BREAD UNIT IDEAS IN CHAPTER 6)

- Cooked wheat cereal, whole or cracked
- Sprouted wheat salad
- Chewing of wheat into gum
- Any food activity utilizing flour: cakes, cookies, breads, muffins, biscuits, or pancakes
- Dry wheat cereals eaten as cereals or used in recipes

SCIENCE

- Sprouting of wheat
- Grinding of wheat (blender may be used)
- Observation of growing plant
- Wheat in stages of the growing process
- Equipment farmer uses to plant, harvest, and store wheat
- Kinds of wheat
- Separating of wheat from chaff (shaft rubbed between hands; chaff blown off)

MUSIC

- Shakers used in shaker band or rhythm activity
- Musical dramatization of the story "The Little Red Hen"
- Wheat shafts used to play drums

VISITORS

- Farmer showing kinds of wheat
- Baker
- Parent making bread
- Person grinding wheat with stone
- Botanist showing how wheat grows
- Nutritionist

LANGUAGE AND LITERACY

- Story such as "The Little Red Hen"
- Poems
- Create own stories, for example, "How We Use Wheat"

Note: A lesson plan on wheat and flour can be found in Appendix A.

Summary

This chapter has dealt with the subjects of animals, plants, and sensory-related concepts. Although smell (olfactory) and taste (gustatory) perceptions involve separate senses, they are closely related and influence each other. Texture is the way that the touch of an object can be described. It is important that children be able not only to identify items by feel, but also to use appropriate descriptive words. As children have experiences in listening, they also develop the skill of auditory discrimination. The ability to distinguish sound and pitch is an important aspect of reading readiness. Even very young infants respond to smell, taste, touch, and sound. Experiences with familiar smells, tastes, textures, sights, and sounds should be presented before unfamiliar ones, allowing children opportunities to solidify concepts and continue building new understandings on already established foundations.

Teaching units about animals provide numerous possibilities for explorations and experiences regarding various animal-related concepts. Young children generally have a natural curiosity about animals and their characteristics. Learning about animals provides opportunities for studying size, shape, number, color, texture, classification and sorting, weight, smell, sound, and food. The physical characteristics, habitats, uses, and habits of animals are also rich possibilities for learning. By studying animals, children are able to lessen or overcome fears while gaining insight into and understanding of the proper care of animals. Most of all, children can appreciate animals and sense humans' dependence on them.

Plants are a natural, living part of the children's environment both inside and outside the classroom. Regardless of the locality, climate, and season, there are numerous possibilities for plant studies and experiences. Related concepts such as size, number, color, texture, categorization, shape, characteristics, needs, and uses of various plants can be explored.

When children study animals and plants, they can learn to not disturb trees, bushes, rocks, logs, and streams, which are homes to creatures that live in the outdoors. Whenever possible, animals and plants should remain in, or returned to, their natural environments.

Student Learning Activities

1. Visit with a preschool, kindergarten, or first- or second-grade teacher. Find out whether projects, units, or activities relating to animals and plants are included in the teacher's programs. (Note the units or experiences included in the curriculum.) Ask the teacher to relate to you the children's (and the teacher's) feelings about animal and plant units and experiences in the classroom. Does the teacher ever have live animals in the classroom? Discuss with the teacher any other ideas and questions relating to animals and plants as a part of the curriculum. Following your interview, describe what you learned and your reactions.

2. Visit a classroom where there is a live animal, or bring a live animal into class. What are the children's reactions? Ask the children questions about the animal. Do you see any reinforcement relating to the animal, such as pictures, books, or other materials?

3. Study the unit plans on animals and plants included in this chapter. Then prepare a unit plan, project, or web on an animal, category of animals, topic relating to animals, or plant. From this plan, prepare a 5-day activity plan. Balance your days with a variety of activities that are not theme related.

4. Plan and implement with a group of children at least one of the activities on animals, one on plants, and one on sensory concepts suggested in this chapter or added by you. Evaluate your experience. The group of children may be a classroom group or a small group of relatives or neighborhood children between the ages of 3 and 8 years.

5. Prepare a demonstration or experience for young children to show that texture changes.

Suggested Resources

See additional science resources at the end of Chapters 6, 9, and 10. Space limits the list provided here to only a few of the possible suggestions in this category. Four excellent resources include (a) *Science and Children*, a journal of the National Science Teachers Association that provides in each issue a column on the care of a specific living organism; (b) National Geographic Society, 17th and M Streets, NW, Washington, DC 20036; (c) National Audubon Society, Rt. 4, Box 171, Sharon, CT 06069; and (d) National Wildlife Federation, 1400 16th Street, NW, Washington, DC 20036.

Basile, C., & White, C (2000). Respecting living things: Environmental literacy for young children. *Early Childhood Education Journal 28*(1), 57–61.

Beck, A. G. R., & Beck, A. M. (2000). Kids and critters in class together. *Phi Delta Kappan 82*(4), 313–315.

Jackson, D. (2002). *The bug scientists.* Boston: Houghton Mifflin.

Jalongo, M. R. (Ed.). (2004). *The world's children and their companion animals: Developmental and educational significance of the child/pet bond.* Olney, MD: Association for Childhood Education International.

Melson, G. F. (2001). *Why the wild things are.* Cambridge, MA: Harvard University Press.

National Arbor Day Foundation. (2007). *Learning with nature idea book: Creating nurturing outdoor spaces for children.* Lincoln, NE: Author.

National Gardening Association. (1988). *Grow lab: A complete guide to gardening in the classroom*. South Burlington, VT: Author.

National Geographic. (2000). *National geographic animal encyclopedia*. Washington, DC: Author.

National Geographic. (2002). *Honeybees*. Washington, DC: Author.

Poderscek, A. L., Paul, E. S., & Serpell, J. A. (Eds.) (2000). *Companion animals and us: Exploring the relationships between people and pets*. Cambridge, UK: Cambridge University Press.

Starbuck, S., Olthof, M., & Midden, K. (2002). *Hollylocks and honeybees: Garden projects for young children*. St. Paul, MN: Redleaf.

Worth, K., & Grollman, S. (2003). *Worms, shadows, and whirlpools: Science in the early childhood classroom*. Portsmouth, NH: Heineman; Washington, DC: NAEYC.

Yoon, S. (2001). *Children's preconceptions of human-animal relationships: Dispositions toward a humane consciousness and implications for curriculum and instruction*. (ERIC Document Reproduction Service No. ED 456 039.)

Online Resources

www.nationalgeographic.com/siteindex/animals.html   This site offers the opportunity to explore animals through the lens of National Geographic Society.

http://members.tripod.com/%7EPatricia_F/mathscience.html   Site includes activities and ideas for the biological sciences.

www.teach-nology.com/teachers/early_education/subject_matter/science   Lessons and links to activities in science are provided.

www.eduplace.com/rdg/gen_act/barn/zoo.html   This site includes an activity to explore the relationship between people and animals.

www.sciencemadesimple.com   Science experiments on plants and plant growth offered on this site.

www.pbskids.org/sid   Sid the Science Kid. An educational television program, based on the idea that young children are naturally curious, and can engage in true scientific exploration. It is a collaboration among KCET/Los Angeles, PBS, and the Jim Henson Company.

www.nap.edu/catalog.php?record_id-4962.   National Research Council (1996). This site discusses the National Science Education Standards: Observe, interact, learn, change. Washington, DC: National Academies Press.

www.education-world.com   Lessons and ideas are offered on a variety of topics including science ideas on plants and animals. Spend time searching this site.

chapter 12

Problem Solving
and Mathematics

"High-quality teaching in mathematics is about challenge and joy, not imposition and pressure. Good early childhood mathematics is broader and deeper than mere practice in counting and adding" (Clements, 2001, p. 270). The early years are the time for every child to develop a solid foundation of mathematics understanding and knowledge, the ability to solve problems, and positive beliefs about mathematics. Teachers in early childhood should look at mathematics growth and learning as they do literacy development, because mathematical concepts develop by being exercised and stimulated (Geist, 2001). Therefore, the notion of emergent mathematics, like literacy, begins to develop from the day children are born and they begin to notice patterns, communications, and other things in their environment; later, as toddlers, they being to classify, order, and compare various objects (Geist, 2009). Developing understanding of mathematics is best achieved when children are expected to reason, problem solve, and communicate their ideas and thoughts to others (Wood, 2001). The best context, according to a joint position statement of NAEYC and NCTM, is a rich environment that allows children to explore math concepts in their play. The joint position statement says, "Play does not guarantee mathematical development, but it offers rich possibilities" (NAEYC & NCTM, 2002, p. 11). However, it should be emphasized that play alone is not enough. Children need the support of adults to help them think, understand, and recognize mathematical ideas (Seo, 2003).

A working definition of mathematics that will serve as an educational focus throughout this chapter is this: the science of mathematical understanding achieved through learning to solve problems. Bredekamp and Rosegrant (1992) suggest a repeated learning cycle during early childhood that includes four phases: awareness (recognition of objects, events, and people that develops from the child's experiences); exploration (observing, exploring, discovering, and constructing meaning); inquiry (refine understanding and make connections through examining, investigating, comparing, and generalizing); and utilization (apply and use learning in new situations). The learning cycle reminds teachers of the importance of developmentally appropriate practice.

> Research suggests three principles that guide mathematics instruction: "1. Learning substantial math is critical for primary grade children. 2. All children have the potential to learn challenging and interesting math. 3. Understanding children's mathematical development helps teachers be knowledgeable and effective in teaching math." (Sarama & Clements, 2009)

The National Council of Teachers of Mathematics (NCTM, 2000, p. 16) suggests six principles for school mathematics: equity, curriculum, teaching, learning, assessment, and technology. These principles are issues or features that need to be considered for high-quality math education.

Early childhood classrooms should be communities of inquiry, problem posing, and problem solving, where children perceive that in math lessons they are expected to offer their thoughts about questions posed and to find resolution to these problems. Young children should sense the application of

PRINCIPLES OF SCHOOL MATHEMATICS

- *Equity.* Excellence in mathematics education requires equity—high expectations and strong support for all students.
- *Curriculum.* A curriculum is more than a collection of activities: It must be coherent, focused on important mathematics, and well articulated across the grades.
- *Teaching.* Effective mathematics teaching requires understanding what students know and need to learn and then challenging and supporting them to learn it well.
- *Learning.* Students must learn mathematics with understanding, actively building new knowledge from experience and prior knowledge.

- *Assessment.* Assessment should support the learning of important mathematics and furnish useful information to both teachers and students.
- *Technology.* Technology is essential in teaching and learning mathematics; it influences the mathematics that is taught and enhances students' learning.

Source: Reprinted with permission from *Principles and Standards for School Mathematics,* p. 11, copyright 2000 by the National Council of Teachers of Mathematics. All rights reserved.

mathematical ideas in everyday life. At this level, mathematics learning should be "active, rich in natural and mathematical language, and filled with thought-provoking opportunities" (National Council of Teacher of Mathematics [NCTM], 2000, p. 77). Early childhood teachers should develop a positive attitude toward math, remembering that mathematics learning builds on curiosity and enthusiasm (NCTM, 2000). Rather than teach math concepts with worksheets and rote memorizing, teachers can provide everyday activities and games, and questions can encourage mathematical exploring and understanding (Cutler, Gilkerson, Parrott, & Bowne, 2003; Geist, 2001). There is a plethora of superb children's literature that relates to mathematical learning by incorporating the plot of the story or focusing on a particular math concept (Cutler et al., 2003). Linking literacy and numeracy skills benefits children in many ways, including using the context of a story to discuss and reason about various mathematical ideas

(Whitin & Whitin, 2005). Because early impressions are often lasting impressions, children need to sense the satisfaction of developing math and number skills as they participate and think about their world (Clements, 2001). "Math is a natural part of the everyday world because children are constantly monitoring their position in space, count, gathering data, and comparing" (Eisenhauer & Feikes, 2009, p. 22).

In problem solving and mathematics, teachers traditionally "have been more concerned with getting the 'right' answer than with 'how' children arrived at an answer" (T. L. Anderson, 1996, p. 35). Problem solving emphasizes the process rather than the final product or correct answer (Charlesworth, 2005). Classroom focus should be on thinking, analyzing, understanding, and reasoning, not just facts. It is too easy for children to be overwhelmed with facts but starving for understanding and meaning. Memorizing facts is not the same as understanding the processes.

Children learn mathematical combinations and relationships during play activities.

Problem solving should begin with natural and informal problems such as:

- How many children are in our class today? How many boys? How many girls? How many people?
- Be sure you take enough crackers so that everyone at your table gets four.
- Do you want a big helping of mashed potatoes or a small helping?
- Do more children like chocolate or strawberry ice cream? How do you know? What would it look like in a graph?

Engaging problems and mathematical conversations should be a part of every day, naturally integrated into all parts of the day. Problem solving is related to all areas of learning and involves four basic steps (Diffily & Morrison, 1996):

1. Identify the problem.
2. Brainstorm possible solutions.
3. Choose one solution and try it out.
4. Evaluate what happens.

Problem solving and mathematical thinking are invited when teachers ask thought-provoking and open-ended questions that lead to thinking and discussion (Frakes & Kline, 2000). For example, after making a graph, instead of asking a pointed or specific question, the teacher may ask a more open-ended question, such as "What do you see on the graph?" (Frakes & Kline, 2000). We should teach children to identify, classify, infer, observe, compute, measure, predict, solve problems, think through possibilities, and understand the process.

The use of mathematical thinking is preferred to planned, sequenced mathematics activities in discovering concepts and solving problems in everyday life (Clements, 2001; Clements, Swaminathan, Hannibal, & Sarama, 1999; Greenberg, 1993; Mills, Whitin, & O'Keefe, 1993). A simple problem-solving experience might evolve naturally at snack or lunchtime. If there are not enough forks for everyone, there are more solutions than just having an adult retrieve additional forks. Allowing children to determine various solutions may take more time, but it will increase their problem-solving skills. Children's possible solutions might include using plastic forks, borrowing from another classroom, eating with spoons for a change, taking turns eating, or washing some used forks.

Remember: Experiencing the process of problem solving is more valuable than arriving at a solution! Emphasize the thinking, rather than a specific answer. And look for the thinking that students demonstrate, not just the skills (Frakes & Kline, 2000). Solving problems leads to new ways of thinking and prepares children for future higher-level thinking.

> "Problem solving is the process that underlies all instruction in mathematics" (Charlesworth, 2005, p. 40).

Teaching mathematics is most often done through thoughtful questioning, clarifying, or rich mathematical conversing. In addition, the use of materials such as books and manipulatives supports mathematics learning in the early years. However, mathematical concepts can also be taught in units, lessons, and projects. For example, units, lessons, or projects could be planned on shapes, calculators, recognizing numbers, or measurement notions. Units should be developmentally appropriate and match the interests and needs of the children. Research informs us that young children are capable of complex and sophisticated learning. All children, including those from low-income and minority populations, are interested in and capable of grappling with "big" ideas in mathematics (Clements, 2001).

PROBLEM SOLVING AND MATHEMATICS COMPETENCIES IN THE EARLY CHILDHOOD CURRICULUM

Guidelines for Incorporating Problem Solving and Mathematics into Early Childhood Curriculum

Teachers should avoid gender bias regarding math and must nurture confidence in and enthusiasm for math, problem solving, and reasoning activities in *all* children. If the concepts are geared to their particular level of interest and ability and if the emotional inhibitions that promote a feeling of inferiority are removed, all children are capable of mathematical reasoning and problem solving (Piaget, 1974). Teachers can use specific strategies to improve the performance of girls in problem solving (Casey, 2001). For example, use concrete manipulatives to calculate solutions, and use modeling and counting strategies to clarify problems.

Teachers should recognize that opportunities for teaching math abound in children's daily experiences as they encounter concepts relating to time, distance, measuring, weight, number recognition, and other math notions. During the early childhood years, many understandings of math concepts grow out of experiences with objects, food, play materials, nature, the outdoors, time, and space; in effect, everyday experiences. Teachers should use children's unique experiences as springboards for learning math. Math concepts are often acquired in a spontaneous, natural way because children are normally curious about and interested in them (NCTM, 2000).

However, many math concepts require substantial experience and development time before they can be incorporated into the child's thinking. For example, young children often misunderstand time concepts such as today, tomorrow, and yesterday, and comments such as "I don't want my bath today, I want to have it yesterday" or "I already did that, I did it tomorrow" are very common among young children.

Math in early childhood should be concrete and manipulative. Young children develop abstract reasoning through numerous experiences with manipulative and concrete objects. Teachers should be cautioned against the use of workbook pages and dittos when teaching math in early childhood. "Where children are required to sit down, quiet down, and write it down, excitement about math may never have a chance to emerge" (Stone, 1987, p. 16). Many math understandings grow naturally from experience (NCTM, 2000). Children need to learn the intrinsic rewards of problem solving. Objects and manipulative toys and materials must be an integral part of early childhood math programs. It is difficult, for example, for young children to understand money concepts without opportunities to actually use money. However, although teaching and learning should begin concretely, research warns that concrete manipulatives do not guarantee meaningful learning; manipulatives do not transmit the meaning of a mathematical notion (Clements & McMillen, 1996). "Math manipulatives are just objects until children use them to *think* about mathematical ideas" (Seo, 2003, p. 30). Ideas become meaningful through good mental activity, be it objects, materials, visuals, or an excellent computer program, and students build these ideas from working with and thinking about their actions on such materials (Clements & McMillen, 1996).

Math should be taught and integrated into all curriculum areas, although math learning centers can be set up and specific times allotted in the curriculum for math activities. Math is often a bridge to related fields of the curriculum (Charlesworth, 2005) and should be integrated. Problem-solving skills are related to all areas of learning, not just to math and science. For example, while on field trips, children spontaneously learn concepts relating to money, time, numbers, and other aspects of math; in food experiences, children are exposed to measuring, number concepts, fractions, and other math and problem-solving skills. These skills or concepts include matching (quantities, numbers, shapes, forms, sizes, etc.); making patterns; classifying, ordering, or seriating in order on the basis of size, number, ordinal position, or weight; and making comparisons. Recognizing and using patterns is a valuable problem-solving tool, as is classifying, which helps develop analytical and logical thinking and abstract concepts. Classification relies on the recognition of likenesses and differences.

Children's literature can provide a springboard for teaching math concepts and thereby integrate math

with reading and language arts (Thatcher, 2001; Thiessen, Matthias & Smith, 1998). A wide assortment of picture books and children's literature teaches math concepts and helps young children understand how math is used in the real world (Welchman-Tischler, 1992; Whitin & Wilde, 1992).

Begin with simple concepts and then move to the more abstract. Once a child has had experiences with beginning number concepts (that is, recognizing numbers, counting, understanding the meaning of numbers, and even some simple addition concepts), begin to teach more abstract math concepts, such as time, money, and space. Preschool children have difficulty with math concepts of these kinds because they are in the stage (preoperational) in which their understanding depends on how something appears to them. Consider Piaget's example of conservation: Five buttons, pennies, crackers, or other objects of uniform size are placed close together in one row; in a second row, five like items are spread apart. When children are asked whether both rows contain the same number of items, most preschool children will indicate that the row that is spread apart or is longer has more because it *appears* to have more. After 5 or 6 years of age, most children are able to focus on actual numbers and can separate length from number. Math notions should always be built on prior understanding and children's informal knowledge.

Children learn best when allowed appropriate freedom to explore through their senses of touch, sight, sound, taste, and smell. Therefore, a good early childhood education environment for developing math and other problem-solving concepts should include literature and storytelling; blocks and construction; art; science; water and sand; music; language; food and nutrition; interactions with peers and adults; and other activities suitable for young children.

Recommendations to Guide Early Childhood Classroom Practice

1. Take advantage of children's natural curiosity and inclination.
2. Build on children's prior knowledge and experiences, their culture, and their individual dispositions and interests.
3. Base mathematics curriculum and teaching on developmentally appropriate principles.
4. Support process skills such as problem solving and reasoning in mathematical teaching.
5. Create a mathematical curriculum that is sequential with ideas building on one another.
6. Teach mathematical ideas deeply rather than broadly. Children need repetition and sustained interaction to develop mathematical meaning and understanding.

(continued)

7. Integrate mathematics throughout the curriculum.
8. Use play as the context for teaching mathematics, incorporating manipulatives, materials, and teacher scaffolding.
9. Incorporate a wide variety of strategies and experiences for children's active engagement with mathematical concepts.
10. Assess continually children's mathematical knowledge, skills, and dispositions.

Source: Adapted from Early Childhood Mathematics: Promoting Good Beginnings (Joint Position Statement), by NAEYC and NCTM, 2002, Washington, DC: NAEYC and Reston, VA: NCTM. Reprinted with permission from the National Association for the Education of Young Children. All current NAEYC position statements are available online at www.naeyc.org/positionstatements.

USE OF COMPUTERS IN MATHEMATICS AND PROBLEM SOLVING

Computers are a great asset in learning math skills and enhancing problem-solving competence. Young children can increase such skills as counting, number recognition, one-to-one correspondence, and understanding the relationship between quantity and symbol through the use of computer exploration. Many counting and math computer games are available for young children, and the thinking processes involved in using the computer often utilize mathematical reasoning, problem solving, or even manipulations (Clements, 2001; Clements & McMillen, 1996). Computer manipulatives increase attention and motivation, as well as facilitate precise explanations; they often go beyond what can be done simply using physical manipulatives (Clements & McMillen, 1996). Websites such as http://standards.nctm.org provide electronic examples that give children practice in the standards and expectations outlined by the National Council of Teachers of Mathematics. It has been suggested that using interactive, web-based, computer-generated images of objects that children can manipulate on the computer screen supports mathematics understanding and the use of developmentally appropriate technology (Rosen & Hoffman, 2009). There are many excellent examples of software that are developmentally appropriate and give children experiences in mathematical notions and problem solving.

The National Council of Teachers of Mathematics suggests that technology is one of six principles of high-quality mathematics education. According to the NCTM, "Technology is essential in teaching and learning mathematics; it influences the mathematics that is taught and enhances students' learning" (NCTM, 2000, p. 16). Specifically in the early years, NCTM (2000) suggests that work with calculators provides an opportunity to explore the concepts of number and pattern and to focus on the problem-solving processes. Computers provide feedback and connections between various representations. Computers are especially valuable for students with physical limitations and also for those who prefer technology learning (Clements & Heely, 1999).

TEACHING MATHEMATICS

Mathematics and problem solving involve more than learning about numbers and how to add, subtract, multiply, and divide them. The National Council for Teachers of Mathematics (NCTM, 2000, pp. 78–136) suggests 10 curriculum standards for Pre-K through second grade. These standards provide a guide for early childhood curriculum planning.* Five of them address mathematics *content standards:*

- Number and operations
- Algebra
- Geometry
- Measurement
- Data analysis and probability

The other five are *process standards:*

- Problem solving
- Reasoning and proof
- Communication
- Connections
- Representation

The NCTM standards give a detailed overview of math content and processes for prekindergarten through second grade. The focus in early childhood is on understanding numbers and the number systems and understanding operations, specifically addition ("putting together") and subtraction ("taking apart") (Kline, 2000). Implementing the NCTM standards requires teachers to alter their teaching role from transmitter of information and knowledge to the more constructivist approach of facilitator: "one who engages the class in mathematical investigations, orchestrates class discourse, and creates a learning environment that is mathematically empowering" (Herrera & Owens, 2001, p. 90).

Children become aware of numbers early in life, because daily experiences involve various uses of numbers. Soon after children begin to speak, they use words relating to numbers. But understanding the meanings of these number words comes later, as the child matures, experiences, and develops.

*Reprinted with permission from *Principles and Standards for School Mathematics,* copyright 2000 by the National Council of Teachers of Mathematics. All rights reserved.

Young children are very interested in exploring and experimenting with numbers; math should be concrete and manipulative (Charlesworth, 2005). Intuitively, they like to count and rehearse the sequence of number names. Many experiences with self-correcting manipulatives should be provided throughout the early childhood years. Teachers should take advantage of opportunities that frequently arise in a child's play: pegboards, snap beads, abacus, clay, nesting cups, cooking, taking turns, sharing, climbing stairs, fingerplays, snack time, music, and so on. Before children study mathematics formally, they have had many experiences with math in their play (Eisenhauer & Feikes, 2009). Children can best learn numerical combinations and relationships in the context of their play experiences, rather than with worksheets and skill and drill time (Clements, 2001; Kline, 1999). After children learn to associate a quantity with a number (idea), adults can begin to write down number symbols, or numerals, so that the children can associate the quantity with the numeral.

The classroom and activities of young children abound with opportunities for using numbers that include counting and simple number reasoning concepts; but many of the understandings that children have of numbers are incomplete or even misunderstood or confused. For example, children may enjoy counting, but the cognitive understanding of one-to-one correspondence comes some time later, developmentally, than rote counting ability. Children's understanding of numbers develops as they match, compare, sort, combine, separate, group, question, and order.

Various number concepts, including classification, comparison, ordering, sorting, ordinal and cardinal number, one-to-one correspondence, rational counting, number recognition, and conservation, can be explored through children's books and literature. However, to be successful in teaching math concepts, the teacher must know the level of understanding of individual children and teach to their needs (NCTM, 2000).

Mathematical and number concepts can be taught in a unit theme or in individual or group activities, but must also be an integral part of the entire curriculum or preschool day. Mathematical understanding can be interwoven with literacy learning combined with drama to personalize the story and the math and to relate the literature to real-world activities, as well as to apply and extend the new concept (Harris, 1999).

Children can be given engaging problems to solve in cooperative learning groups. Cooperative learning helps children to share, refine, and include all children in elaborating on information. It is important that adults use math terms correctly in their vocabulary, while listening for any misconceptions that children may have in their striving for understanding.

IDEA: In preschool each group could be given a set of beads or buttons and a set of numeral cards. Each group counts its objects and finds the numeral representing that quantity. For first or second grades, once a day in a cooperative group the children could have a story problem to solve relating to the math concept that they are learning. For example, if they are working on beginning addition, give a problem such as "There are three goldfish in the aquarium, and a class member brings in two more fish. How many fish are there in the tank all together?"

Birthdays and ages are always items of importance to children. They become measures of time, abilities, and achievements. Frequently, the importance of the child's age is apparent in responses to seemingly unrelated stimuli. A 3-year-old may not be satisfied with 1 cookie or with 4 cookies—just 3. Since that age of 3 years is so important, the child can usually count to 3 and desires things in that amount.

Often in children's speech we hear references to ages and birthdays.

"I already did this—when I was only 3."

A soldier was visiting the classroom and explaining to the children about independence and being free. Richard, intently listening, suddenly retorted, "I am not free, I am 4!"

"Yesterday I was 3, today I am 4—and tomorrow I will be 5!"

"My sister is 14 and I am 4, so we are the same age."

The children were being divided into groups for an art activity, the groups being named "1s," "2s," "3s," and so on. The teacher said, "Destry, you are a '2,'" to which he indignantly responded, "I am not 2, I am 5."

A 3-year-old was involved in a discussion with her 4-year-old brother. He had told her that she could not go to preschool because she was not yet 4. She said, "Someday I'll be 5," to which he replied, "Then I'll be 6." She said, "Someday I'll be 10"; he said, "And I'll be 11." They continued on and finally she said, "Well, someday I'll be 100," and he confidently said, "And then I'll be 101!"

To a young child, age and size are directly associated, since the child assumes that the larger and bigger a person is, the older that person is. Children also directly associate age and authority: The more authority a person has, the older that person is. Only after gaining more experience and understanding does the child realize that a large 5-year-old child is younger than a small 8-year-old child or that a 40-year-old parent is older than a 30-year-old firefighter. References to height and weight are often heard as children continue to experiment with their new vocabulary. "I ate 2 pounds of bacon for breakfast; now I weigh 37 pounds." "I weigh 65 feet."

The children were being measured and weighed, and these amounts were being recorded on a chart. Melissa observed the other children for a short time and then declared, "Pound me next."

Numbers are also familiar to children because they appear in telephone numbers, addresses, speedometers, speed limit signs, mileage distance signs, page numbers, clocks, calendars, and thermometers.

Using stickers is one way to practice recognizing the correct number of objects that match a numeral.

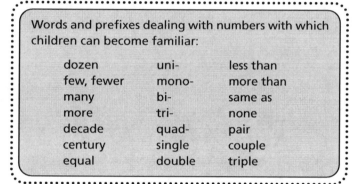

Words and prefixes dealing with numbers with which children can become familiar:

dozen	uni-	less than
few, fewer	mono-	more than
many	bi-	same as
more	tri-	none
decade	quad-	pair
century	single	couple
equal	double	triple

TEACHING NUMBER CONCEPTS

In the process of learning to understand numbers, some basic concepts are developed. Number and operations include concepts of counting, comparing and ordering, grouping, addition, and subtraction (Clements, 2004). As children work on these understandings, they need the example and encouragement provided by the teacher so that misconceptions can be corrected. These concepts are not self-contained, and they may overlap. A child will develop many number concepts during the early child-

NUMBER AND OPERATIONS STANDARDS: PRE-K THROUGH GRADE 2 EXPECTATIONS

Understand numbers, ways of representing numbers, relationships among numbers, and number systems. In pre-kindergarten through grade 2 all students should:

- Count with understanding and recognize "how many" in sets of objects
- Use multiple models to develop initial understandings of place value and the base-10 number system
- Develop understanding of the relative position and magnitude of whole numbers and of ordinal and cardinal numbers and their connection
- Develop a sense of whole numbers and represent and use them in flexible ways, including relating, composing, and decomposing numbers
- Connect number words and numerals to the quantities that they represent, using various physical models and representations
- Understand and represent commonly used fractions such as $\frac{1}{4}$, $\frac{1}{3}$, and $\frac{1}{2}$

Understand meanings of operations and how they relate to one another. In pre-kindergarten through grade 2 all students should understand:

- Various meanings of addition and subtraction of whole numbers and the relationship between the two operations
- The effects of adding and subtracting whole numbers
- Situations that entail multiplication and division, such as equal groupings of objects and sharing equally.

Compute fluently and make reasonable estimates. In pre-kindergarten through grade 2 all students should:

- Develop and use strategies for whole-number computations, with a focus on addition and subtraction
- Develop fluency with basic number combinations for addition and subtraction
- Use a variety of methods and tools to compute, including objects, mental computation, estimation, paper and pencil, and calculators

hood years. Some of the first concepts—becoming aware of the sound and sequence of numbers or **counting** and **one-to-one correspondence**—provide a basis for the acquisition of other number skills. The child then moves from counting to understanding what these numbers mean, and that "2" means 2 objects or things.

Becoming Aware of the Sound and Sequence of Numbers (Counting) and Developing One-to-One Correspondence

Number knowledge develops early in life (Clements, 2004). Children frequently hear counting, as steps are climbed, objects are stacked, foods are distributed, finger and toe games are played, familiar nursery rhymes and songs are enjoyed, and during many other activities. This repetition reinforces the child's ability to begin memorization of the sequence and sounds of numbers even before the meanings of these numbers are understood. The recitation of numbers in the counting sequence has little meaning to very young children; in fact, they probably perceive it as just sound in a particular sequence. Songs, fingerplays, nursery rhymes, and stories utilizing the fingers as counting objects should be heard often. Because the correct number sequence is 1, 2, 3, 4, 5 . . ., these songs and fingerplays should utilize this particular ordering, rather than . . . 5, 4, 3, 2, 1. Learning correct counting is difficult enough for children to grasp; as their understanding increases, they are able to reason about the reverse counting sequences. It is not uncommon in this stage to hear children count 1, 2, 3, 4, 5, 6, 13, 11, 14, 5, 6. . . .

To rote count, verbalizing the number sequence is one thing; but to count items correctly, one number per item, is more difficult. This requires skill in one-to-one correspondence. Often when a young child is given a series of items to count, the child may count two numbers for one item or one number for two items. Thus, children need to be given much time to learn to count; once this concept is mastered, the skill of one-to-one correspondence can be acquired. One way to foster the development of this skill is to have children record what they are counting, using symbols such as rocks, coins, beads, or punched holes in a card to represent numbers of items. They could count cars in a parking lot, children in the group, birds that fly overhead, or many other objects in their environment. Other daily opportunities for fostering one-to-one correspondence include table setting or passing papers or other supplies to class members. There are many children's counting books that can be read and objects counted to give further practice.

Understanding the Meaning of Specific Numbers

As this memorization takes on meaning, the one-to-one correspondence necessary for actual counting is understood; the child learns that "3" means 3 objects or items. Even though a child may not yet be able to recognize the numeral, as objects are counted the child can correctly ascribe a number to them and understand what that number means. To understand the meaning of numbers, the child must be able to associate quantities with symbols. Puzzle matches, in which the numeral is on one side of the block or card and items representing that quantity are on the other side, provide good practice and can be geared to the developmental needs of the child. For example, a child just learning this concept may be given only matches 1 through 4, whereas another child may be ready for 1 through 10.

Zero, or the empty set, is also a rather difficult concept for children to grasp. Zero is less than 1; but when the numeral 1 precedes zero (10), then the numeral has 10 times the value of the 1.

> Eric, who had a 6-month-old brother, was asked, "How old is your new baby brother?" After thoughtful consideration, he answered, "Zero."

Recognizing Numeral Symbols

Children memorize the sequence of numbers, and this sequence broadens into one-to-one correspondence between object and number. Now the task of recognizing the symbol representing the number (the *numeral*) must be mastered. Suppose that you were told to learn the symbols shown in Figure 12.1, which represent the numbers 1 to 5. This makes the child's position easier to understand. Now, if these numerals are written into mathematical problems, the task becomes even more difficult (see Figure 12.2). Through repeated experiences and opportunities, children learn to recognize the numeral symbols and say the names. The old adage that a single experience is not enough to build a reliable concept certainly applies in learning to recognize numerals. It is an exciting accomplishment for children and demonstrates much work and study on their part.

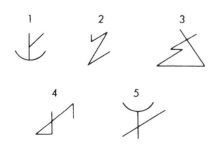

FIGURE 12.1 Example of Symbol-Learning Task

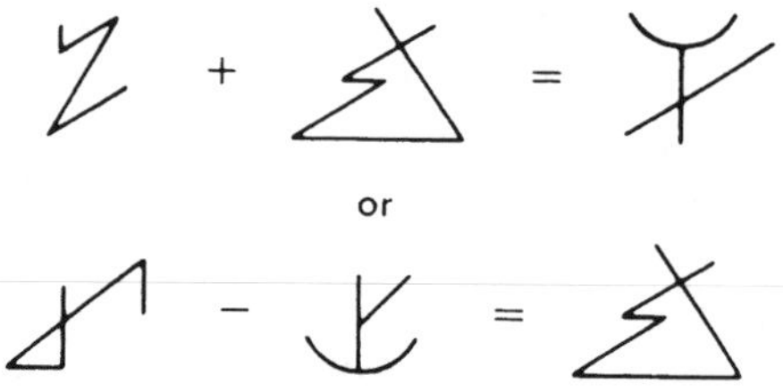

FIGURE 12.2   Sample Symbols in Problem Form

Charlesworth (2005, p. 218) suggests there are 6 number symbol skills young children acquire:

1. Recognizing and saying the name of each numeral
2. Placing the numerals in order
3. Associating numerals with sets: "1" goes with one thing, "2" goes with two things
4. Recognizing that each numeral in sequential order stands for one more than the numeral that comes before it
5. Matching each numeral to a set of the size that the numeral stands for and to do the opposite to make sets that match the specific numerals
6. Ability to write the numerals

Many manipulative toys and materials can be used effectively in teaching numeral recognition. There are also many excellent commercial toys focusing on numerals that can be used in the early childhood classroom. Many of these can be created by the early childhood teacher with a minimum of expense. Once numeral symbol skills are mastered, not only are the numerals correctly ordered and sequenced, but the child is able to place them so that they are positioned correctly. The numerals are not backward, sideways, or upside down; and the numerals 6 and 9 are distinguished.

IDEA: Make separate cards for each numeral, with the numeral cut from sandpaper (they are effective because they encourage tactile learning; the child feels the shape of each numeral as it is being learned). Numerals can be cut from felt to be used at a flannel board, made from wood to give 3-dimensional shape, or cut from index cards or other heavy paper. To make a self-correcting number lotto, numerals can be cut and put on oak tag or poster board; then matching numerals that are exactly the same can be cut and put between clear plastic sheets so that each numeral for matching is separate. As the children match the numerals in plastic to the ones on the board, the plastic allows them to see through and correct themselves if the numerals have been matched backward or upside down.

Comparing and Conserving Numbers

In mathematical comparisons, children learn to make comparisons such as those that relate to size and measurement and to quantity, such as *more than, less than,* and *as many as.* Comparing collections in terms of more than or less than is a way to begin to examine and compare (Clements, 2004). Before children begin adding and subtracting, they should have many experiences comparing sets in terms of *more than, less than,* and *as many as.*

Conservation. Conservation means that if two sets are compared and found to be equal, when they are rearranged so they do not look the same, the child can still determine that the two sets are equal. For example, if 2 rows of buttons, 5 in each row, are arranged in such a way that each button on one row corresponds with a button on the other row, it may be obvious to the child that they are the same or equal. If they are arranged so that the second row is more or less widely spaced than the first row, this concept will not be as obvious. However, the child who can conserve numbers will still recognize that the sets are equal. Number conservation experiences can also be planned with rows of unequal items, making them look either the same or different.

Conservation relates to judging the amount; as with the number, the child recognizes that the arrangement of items does not change the number. Conservation of volume is more challenging, because the child must recognize and understand that changing the shape of something does not change the volume. To understand conservation of weight, the child must recognize that changing the shape or size of something does not change its weight, as long as nothing has been added or subtracted in the transformation.

Ordinal Numbers

As children develop concepts of ordinal numbers (1st, 2nd, 3rd, etc.), they are also able to order items using ordinal numbers and to match ordinal numbers to cardinal numbers (1, 2, 3, etc.). When teaching numerals, it is helpful if other concepts (such as size and color) are kept constant. For instance, it is easier for the child to concentrate on learning the numeral itself if all the numerals are the same size and color. If the numerals are of various colors, the child might think that the red numeral is a 4 and the blue numeral is a 5, rather than learning that the 4 is a 4 and the 5 is a 5, regardless of color. Varying the color, however, adds an element of difficulty to be introduced later to increase the challenge and the children's motivation. Once children understand the meaning of numbers and recognize numerals, they can associate the numeral with the number in the set. For example, the child can now match a set of four peanuts to the numeral or symbol 4. Once children master these basic mathematical number concepts, they are ready for more advanced number skills and usually show signs of wanting to write the numerals.

Adding Sets

As children develop skill in this aspect of mathematics, they are able to determine the number of items in a set when two or more sets are combined. Begin by having the child identify numerals that are one more than a particular number. Use real objects for early experiences. The child can then visualize that two buttons in one box and three buttons in another equal the same as 5 buttons in a box. Many games focus on addition.

> **IDEA:** Frakes and Kline (2000) suggested a game or activity titled Total of 6. Numeral cards from 0 to 6 are put face up in three rows with four cards in each row. Additional cards are put face down in a pile. As players take their turns, they look for combinations of number cards to total 6. When a player finds a combination equaling 6, he or she places these cards together and then adds new cards to the rows. This activity could be adapted for combinations of 5, 7, and so on.

Subtracting Sets

As children develop skill in this aspect of mathematics, they are able to determine the number of items in the set resulting when one set is taken away from another set. Again, begin by having the child identify numerals that are one less than a particular number. Initially, working with manipulatives helps children to "see" what is happening in this kind of operation. As development and understanding progress, story problems can be used to help children to apply this operation to real-life situations.

Concepts and Ideas for Teaching Numbers

1. The words *number* and *numeral* have different meanings. **Number** is the idea, or what is being thought. **Numeral** is the name or symbol of this idea, or what is being written. The numeral, then, represents the number.
2. The correct numeral sequence is 1, 2, 3, 4, 5, ... Therefore, it is important that songs, fingerplays, nursery rhymes, poems, and games utilize this sequence.
3. A group of objects such as buttons, beans, or chips is called a *set*. An *empty set* is 0 (zero).
4. Numbers are used in many ways.

Activities and Experiences for Teaching Numbers

1. Select two pages from a calendar. Leave the numerals on one intact and separate the numerals of the other. The single numerals are then matched to those on the whole page.
2. Cut playing cards in half (make the cutting lines different on the separate cards, so that only the two correct halves will fit together). Then the cards are matched together as puzzles. A variety of number puzzles can be made matching the numeral or symbol to objects and the written name of the numeral to either objects or the numeral symbol. These can be constructed and geared to the developmental levels of the children.
3. Draw a line with numerals in the proper sequence on the floor. Tell the child to stand on a numeral and "move ahead 4 numerals—now move back 2. What numeral are you standing on?" (This exercise also develops basic math understandings of addition and subtraction.)
4. Make a set of cards from pictures on seed packets. These cards can be grouped by flowers and vegetables; classified by kinds of flowers, by vegetables, or by colors; or used to present even more advanced concepts, such as vegetables that grow above the ground as opposed to those that grow beneath the ground.
5. Use a calendar. Children enjoy either marking off each day or adding the days to the calendar.
6. Use a calculator. Children enjoy seeing the numeral appear in response to the button that they have pushed. Older children can do simple addition and subtraction.
7. Make a classroom directory with each child's name, address, and telephone number. Put this list by the toy telephone so that the children can practice dialing numbers.
8. Use the flannel board with felt numerals and felt shapes such as stars, trees, flowers, apples, and others. Challenge the children to organize these shapes into sets representing each numeral. For example, for the numeral 1, one star; for the numeral 2, two apples; and so on.
9. Make a series of cards (at least 5 by 8 inches) with a tree cut from felt glued on the cards. Cut apples from red felt. Children can put apples on the trees and then order them in sequence or make comparisons between trees, such as *more than, less than,* or *the same as.* They can also match the number of apples on a given tree to the numeral.
10. Do a variety of fingerplays, songs, poems, and stories that focus on rote counting.
11. Adapt pages from worksheets and workbooks to make learning games for number concepts. For example, make a matching game from a sheet on money or time on which the children are expected

to write in the time or the amount of money. Write the times or money amounts on cards for the children to match to the clock faces or sets of money on the worksheet.

12. Place pairs of items (shoes, socks, earrings, dice, mittens, cymbals) in a bag and then have the children remove them and match them. Trace right and left hands on various wallpaper patterns (matching patterns for left and right), then cut them out, mix them up, and have the children match them (J. I. Stone, 1987).

13. Mark a numeral (2, 3, 4, 5, . . . 10) on a card. Have the children use paper clips, staples, hole punches, paper reinforcements, clothespins, or other objects to create sets: five staples on a "5" card, eight holes punched on an "8" card, and so on (J. I. Stone, 1987).

14. Prior to an outdoor walk, give paper sacks to pairs of children and assign specific sets to collect: two pinecones, six leaves, eight rocks, and so on (J. I. Stone, 1987).

15. Have the children play a game using a board such as the one shown in Figure 12.3. Each of two to four players has a marker such as a button. The object is to move from square 1 to square 12 and back to 1 again. There are 3 dice, and each player gets a chance to roll. The child must roll a numeral 1 before being able to move to square 1. Each player can add numbers together to try to get the needed numeral. For example, if the child rolls a 1, a 4, and a 2 and is on square 3, the child can move to squares 4, 5 (4 + 1), and 6 (4 + 2).

16. Play a game called "What's My Rule?" in which the children give you a number and you give it back to them, applying your rule. They try to guess the rule, but they do not shout it out. If they think that they know the rule, another child gives them a number and they apply the rule. For example, the rule could be to add or subtract a particular amount, or it could be to always add 10 to the number. You will need to make up rules according to developmental levels. Once the children understand the game, they can divide into cooperative learning groups and take turns thinking up a rule and applying it to numbers given to them by members of their group.

17. Divide the children into cooperative learning groups. Give each group a handout of developmentally appropriate math problems for which they will need to identify the pattern and determine the rule in order to select the number that comes next. For example:
    a. 1, 3, 5, 7. What is my rule?
       What comes next?
    b. 15, 12, 9. What is my rule?
       What comes next?
    c. 10, 20, 30. What is my rule?
       What comes next?

FIGURE 12.3 Board Game

18. Cover 10 soup cans with solid-color contact paper. Using small adhesive circles from an office supply store, put one on the "1" can, two on the "2" can, and so on. Children can put the same number of Popsicle sticks or straws in each can, as there are circles on the can.

19. Number Rainbow is a good game for children to play in cooperative pairs while they develop skill in adding and subtracting. Each child has a card with a rainbow with numerals 2 through 12. The pairs take turns throwing two dice. If a player throws a 4 and a 3, a 7 (4 + 3) or a 1 (4 − 3) on the rainbow can be covered with an object such as a button. As the children take turns, if they throw the dice on a pair of numerals for which they have already covered the answers to the addition and subtraction problems, then they lose that turn. The player who first covers all the numerals on the rainbow wins.

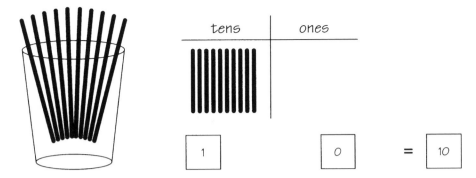

FIGURE 12.4 Sample Number Card Showing the Place Value of 10

20. This activity is for children in first or second grade as they begin to study place value (numbers above 10). To make this concept concrete, they need to see it and work with it manipulatively. Use the soup cans created for activity 19. Show the children that the 10 can, or 10 sticks, is equal to one number 10. Write the numeral on a number card as shown in Figure 12.4. Now do this with a higher number such as 14. Put 10 sticks in the "tens" can and 4 in the "ones" can so the children can learn that 10 + 4 = 1 ten and 4 ones = 14. You can do this same activity with blocks and numeral cards (see Figure 12.5). As children become developmentally ready, you can increase your tens' place value to 2, 3, and so on.

21. Give each child a number line to learn the number sequence from 1 to 10. Then, for addition and subtraction, have the children use buttons or poker chips on the number line as manipulables to compute problems such as "Find 4 more than 1" or "Find 3 less than 5."

22. Make the points of a triangle with empty circles, and place another circle on each of the sides. Ask the children to figure out how to make each row of three circles total 9 (or any number) (Charlesworth, 2005). This is called a "magic triangle" (see Figure 12.6).

23. Take advantage of math experiences arising from the background, experiences, and knowledge of the individual children. In one class, the children illustrated and wrote math equations because of one child's response to his experience of losing some of his teeth. The child drew a picture of his smile and left spaces where he had lost teeth. He counted and drew all the rest of his teeth. Then he made a math problem on his paper to show how many teeth he had left. The whole class then wanted to illustrate their smiles and figure out how many teeth they had (Mills et al., 1993).

24. Play Target Addition with the class. Choose a target number such as 10, 20, 25, or whatever seems appropriate. There are two to four players with a board similar to the one shown in Figure 12.7. Players can work with one board (which would necessitate picking a smaller target number), or each player can have an individual game board. The object of the game is to pick two numbers, add them together, and cover those two numbers with beans or buttons. The next player must start with what the last player's numbers added up to so that each player adds numbers on to the last player's. For example, the first player might select 1 + 1 = 2; the second player, 2 + 1 = 3; the third player, 3 + 2 = 5; the fourth player, 5 + 5 = 10, the fifth player, 10 + 5 = 15, and so on. Once you pass 5, players are only able to cover one of the board numerals since they only go to 5. The first player to reach the exact target number wins (Stenmark, Thompson, Cossey, & Hill, 1986).

25. Using dice, children can either add or subtract the numbers shown on two dice. Dice can also be used to find the different ways that a certain number

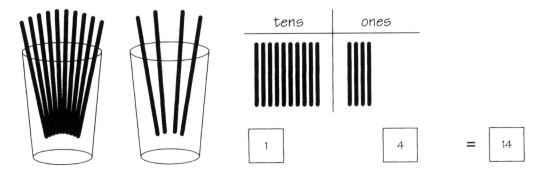

FIGURE 12.5 Sample Number Card Showing the Place Value of 14

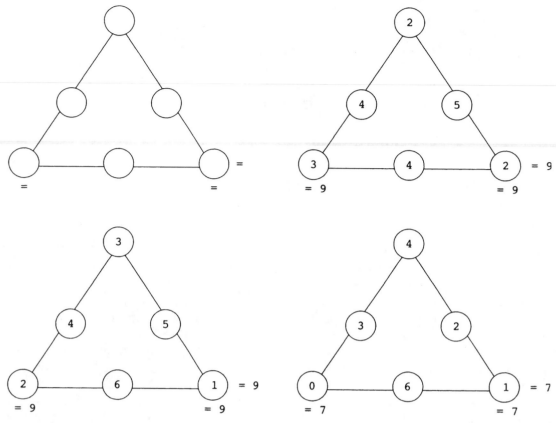

FIGURE 12.6 Magic Triangle

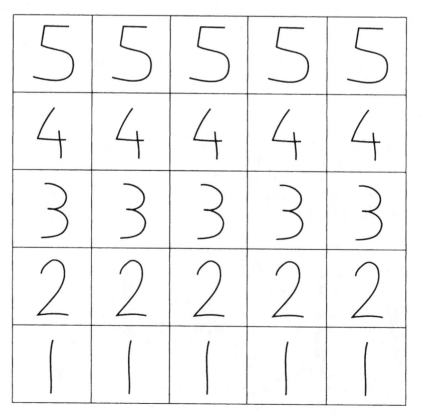

FIGURE 12.7 Target Addition Game Board

ALGEBRA STANDARDS: PRE-K THROUGH GRADE 2 EXPECTATIONS

Understand patterns, relations, and functions. In pre-kindergarten through grade 2 all students should:

- Sort, classify, and order objects by size, number, and other properties
- Recognize, describe, and extend patterns such as sequences of sounds and shapes or simple numeric patterns, and translate from one representation to another
- Analyze how both repeating and growing patterns are generated

Represent and analyze mathematical situations and structures using algebraic symbols. In pre-kindergarten through grade 2 all students should:

- Illustrate general principles and properties of operations, such as commutativity, using specific numbers
- Use concrete, pictorial, and verbal representations to develop an understanding of invented and conventional symbolic notations

Use mathematical models to represent and understand quantitative relationships. In pre-kindergarten through grade 2 all students should:

- Model situations that involve the addition and subtraction of whole numbers, using objects, pictures, and symbols
Analyze change in various contexts. In pre-kindergarten through grade 2 all students should:
- Describe qualitative change, such as a student's growing taller
- Describe quantitative change, such as a student's growing two inches in one year

Source: Reprinted with permission from *Principles and Standards for School Mathematics* (p. 90), by the National Council of Teachers of Mathematics. All rights reserved.

can be made: 5 and 1, 4 and 2, or 3 and 3 can make 6. *Variation:* Face cards can be used to work with the same concepts.

Note: Some stores carry dice with numbers higher than 6.

26. Fair Share: This activity teaches beginning concepts of division and also encourages sharing. In cooperative groups, give each group a container of cereal, crackers, or pretzels. Challenge the children to find a way to divide the treats to ensure that everyone gets an equal amount. Have one person in the group record how many of the treats each member of the group got and whether there

were any left over. This activity can be repeated using nonedible items such as buttons, pennies, paper clips, or other items (*Learning,* 1994).

ALGEBRA CONCEPTS

"Algebra in the early years establishes the necessary groundwork for ongoing and future mathematics learning" (Taylor-Cox, 2003). The generalizations and learning to think algebraically provide a foundation for more challenging mathematical concepts. Algebra includes understanding patterns and being able to sort and classify objects with different criteria or properties.

Algebra includes understanding patterns and being able to sort and classify objects.

Patterns

Children see evidence of patterns in their daily living. For example, they follow a pattern of preparing for school each morning or getting ready for bed each night. **Patterns** are series of repeats. Children learn that patterns can be detected by listening, such as a clapping pattern or the pattern of a ticking clock. They can perform a motor pattern such as three jumps followed by two hops. Many dance steps are simply repeating patterns. Visually children can see patterns such as in quilts or in a series of blocks in a particular pattern based on color and/or shape. Patterns can be seen in science activities such as the various patterns in snowflakes, or the patterns in leaves or flowers. During early childhood children should be able to recognize and extend patterns visually, by auditory means, and in motor responses.

Initial visual patterns with materials can focus on common attributes such as shape, size, and color. However, children can also recognize "growing" patterns where visuals such as blocks increase or decrease by a consistent amount (Taylor-Cox, 2003). Cubes of equal size built into side-by-side towers represent this notion well with each tower one more block. Children's representations of this concept with materials or visual pictures can serve as an assessment of their understanding.

Classification

Classification is a beginning math concept that can be taught in many ways, in different areas of the room, and in various curriculum areas. To classify means to sort or group by some common characteristic, such as size, shape, number, color, or other category. The objects being sorted are not as important as the child's own selection of object relationships. The younger the children, the fewer the sorting groups should be. Older children will determine more ways to categorize. For example, young children would sort buttons by color, and older children would sort by size, shape, number of holes, and so on (Micklo, 1997). Examples of classifying are workers by things that go with their jobs; fruits, vegetables, or flowers by kind or other characteristics; kinds of transportation; and animals by kind, category, size, or color.

Ordering

Whereas classification refers to separating objects, **ordering** (or **seriation** according to Piaget) involves placing objects from first to last. As children experiment with objects, they will compare, sort, and group, but will not actually develop a logical system of ordering or seriating until they are 7 or 8 years of age (Micklo, 1997). The early years should have numerous experiences with comparing tallest to shortest, darkest to lightest, thinnest to thickest, heaviest to lightest, and so on. Even though only two objects are being compared, this is ordering at its beginning. Again, remember that the ideas of tallest–shortest, heaviest–lightest, and other descriptions may be difficult to comprehend because an item may be taller than some objects and shorter than others. Words ending in "er" tend to make it easier to comprehend relationships than those ending in "est."

Ordering Numerals and Sets

Once numerals are recognized, the skill that often follows is the ability to order the numerals in sequence. As the children observe a collection of numerals, they are able to select first the 1, then the 2, the 3, 4, 5, 6, and so on, in correct order.

In addition, they develop the skill of putting sets of objects in order, from those with the fewest number of objects to those with the greatest number of objects. The children should also be able to make comparisons such as *more than, less than,* and *as many as.*

Size

Although color and form are more functional than size in children's perceptions, size distinctions are still an integral part of early learning. Size is one of the functions by which children classify or order objects or other properties. Children learn to classify size through many experiences involving actual objects and construct new knowledge based on previous observations and manipulations (Clements & Battista, 1990; Kamii & Lewis, 1990; Micklo, 1995). Children realize how much they have grown as they compare their size with that of young infants. They see themselves as big. Activities with size can help them to learn to make comparisons and understand size. These activities must be developmentally appropriate for children, with both age and individual differences being considered (Copple & Bredekamp, 2009).

Teaching size involves making comparisons between the sizes of two or more objects. One way to make these comparisons is arranging items in a specific order according to a specific rule, such as size. When children order with regard to size, they arrange items from smallest to largest.

Size is relative or comparative; in other words, the size of a particular object may be larger or smaller, depending on the size of the object to which it is compared or seen in relationship. An exciting brainstorming session can emerge when children are asked, "What is the largest object in the room?" Then they could be asked what would make that object smaller by comparison, then even smaller. The questions could continue until the final answer might be the universe. Because size is relative, it is better to use relative size words: *larger* rather than *large, smaller* rather than *small, bigger* rather than *big,* and so on. With the addition of the suffix *-er,* these words become comparative.

In teaching size and seriation, teachers should give children daily experiences in making size comparisons and in seriating objects. Motivating questions and statements should often be used, such as "Which is the smallest fish in our aquarium?" or "Put the cars in order from smallest to largest as you put them away today." Not only is it important to ask such questions as "Which is larger?" but a follow-up question of "How can you tell?" helps children to further solve problems and determine correct attributes (Kilmer & Hofman, 1995, pp. 43–63).

Many opportunities for becoming familiar with size vocabulary should be provided. The more a child has repeated exposure to words and their meanings, the sooner they become possessions and an active part of the vocabulary.

Examples of Words Relating to Size Aspects

larger/smaller	deeper/shallower
bigger/littler	taller/shorter
wider/narrower	gigantic/tiny
longer/shorter	fatter/thinner

Children often relate size to themselves or their own bodies. The distance an object is from a child affects how the child judges the object's size, and children have difficulty making comparisons and judgments as the distance between themselves and an object increases or decreases. Objects larger than themselves are "big," and objects smaller than themselves are "little." Concepts of age are tied to physical characteristics of size. To a child, the larger people are, the older they are. Children become aware of size early, because they are constantly reminded that they are "too big to . . ." and "too little to . . .," as well as being told that "when you are bigger you will be able to . . ." Thus, children begin to feel that with size and age everything becomes possible, but in the meantime they have to wait because they are too young—and too small.

Many children, especially those who are shorter or smaller than their peers, equate their size with their character, which strongly influences their self-concept. These children not only feel shorter or smaller physically, but also emotionally small, inadequate, and unimportant. Teachers have a responsibility and obligation to all children to focus size remarks on objects rather than children. For example, instead of saying, "You are too small to reach the light switch," it might be better to say, "That light switch is too high—let me help you." Children should be frequently reminded that they *can* do many things because of their size. All too often, they are constantly reminded of things that they *cannot* do

because they are either not old enough or not big enough. It is no wonder that some children are discontented with their size, age, and particular stage of life.

> More than 50 years ago, Davis and Havighurst (1947, p. 28) explained the child's desire to grow up, and their description is still appropriate today:
>
> Age is the ladder by which the young child hopes to climb to his Arcadia . . . . Very early he discovers that other children, whether in his family or his nursery school, measure his prestige by his age. On the ladder of age each step will lead him to higher privileges at home and at school, to sweeter triumphs over more and more "small fry," and to more dazzling signs of prestige . . . . Everything good, he is told by his parents, comes with age. More than anything else, therefore, the child yearns to become bigger and older . . . . To the young child . . . age seems to be the key which unlocks all the forbidden doors of life. It is the magic gift of adults, which brings power and social acceptance. It lifts the barriers to the most inviting and mysterious roads, opening toward freedom and adventure . . . . As long as he is young he must be the underdog, he must yield, he must obey. It is not easy for a child to be always inferior, simply because he is inferior in size.

Because children initially make comparisons of size, it is important to focus on only one aspect or attribute. Micklo (1995, p. 25) refers to "attribute materials" as those items that can be sorted in various ways, such as size, color, shape, or thickness. For example, if sizes of coins or buttons are being compared (larger versus smaller), do not add the comparison of thicker versus thinner. It is also wise to keep other concepts constant, such as color and shape, because changes in these attributes may confuse the child. A piece of equipment such as the familiar stacking cone often fails to focus on size, because the child memorizes the color sequence and knows that the top ring goes on the top because it is orange, not because it is the smallest. This stacking cone actually has at least four attributes for children to learn: small, round, red, and thin, or whatever adjectives are appropriate for the object. Depending on the desired concept focus, concentrate on only one attribute and gradually add the others as children expand their reservoirs of understanding. Take care to avoid this confusion when selecting pieces of commercial or handmade equipment. However, for some pieces of equipment relating to size, variation in color is appropriate. Color can serve as an aid in these kinds of toys, rather than as a distraction. An example is a set of different-sized dowels in which each specific size dowel is a different color.

Concepts and Ideas for Teaching Size

1. The child is bigger than some things and smaller than others. This fact often determines what the child can and cannot do.
2. Size may stay the same, even though it appears to change.
   a. A child growing out of a coat thinks that the coat has changed in size.
   b. Size changes in terms of perspective; the farther away one goes from an object, the smaller it looks.
   c. An airplane in the sky appears smaller and then disappears.
   d. Use of magnifying glass, microscope, binoculars, telescope, or spotting scope demonstrates how size may appear to change.
3. We feel different sizes even though our physical size does not change.
   a. When do we feel big?
   b. When do we feel small?
4. Things do not always look the same when size changes.
   a. Distortion mirrors
   b. Items viewed under a magnifying glass
   c. An inflated balloon compared to a deflated one
5. The same items come in various sizes.
   a. People
   b. Trees
   c. Flowers
   d. Automobiles
   e. Buttons
   f. Macaroni
   g. Cans
   h. Houses
   i. Marbles
   j. Balls
6. Size can change.
   a. Physical growth and aging: This can be seen in the size of a seed in the growing process (fruits, vegetables, plants, etc.); in aging fruits or vegetables as they shrivel up; in a baby compared to an adult.
   b. Cooking: Some foods, such as rice, macaroni, and bakery products, become larger during cooking; others, such as meats, become smaller, or shrink.
   c. Subtracting: As air is taken out of a balloon, it becomes smaller; as wood is sawed, the pieces become smaller.
   d. Adding: Changes can be seen in adding air in an inner tube or water to a dry sponge.
   e. Chemical changes: Combining ingredients such as vinegar and soda changes their size; combining the ingredients that make Styrofoam causes a chemical reaction in

which the material foams up and becomes much larger in size.
   f. Cutting: Changes can be seen in the sizes of materials and items.
   g. Temperature: Freezing water expands.
   h. Bending or folding
   i. Instruments: Microscopes, magnifying glasses, and binoculars all change the apparent sizes of items.

Activities and Experiences to Teach Size

1. Have the children order Styrofoam balls from smallest to largest or match duplicate sizes.
2. Put rods or dowels in matched pairs into containers; the child relies on the sense of touch to match two that are the same size.
3. Use materials such as buttons, gummed stars, lids, beads, feathers, and nails as sensory media, as collage material, or order with regard to size. Also, have the children make size comparisons between two or more of the objects.
4. Have the children order cans or boxes from smallest to largest by placing them inside one another.
5. Have the children order or match washers, plastic rings, or other materials in graduated sizes.
6. Cut geometric shapes in seriated sizes out of wood, felt, or cardboard. Cut two of each size for matching pairs; use one of each size for ordering size.
7. Put lima bean seeds or similar seeds on a glass slab on a damp piece of cotton each day. After several days, the changes in size are evident. The seeds can also be put in a glass between a paper towel and the outside of the glass; keep them moist by means of a continually dampened sponge in the center of the glass.
8. Give the children clay or playdough and have them roll balls of various sizes; then order these balls according to size.
9. Observe pieces of fine art (in books, calendars, postcards, galleries, etc.) and have the children compare lines, shapes, and spaces in terms of sizes and seriations.
10. Fill a shopping bag with pairs of objects that are similar except for size. Empty the bag and have the children match and sort pairs of one big and one little object.
11. Supply greeting cards and envelopes or boxes and lids that are all mixed together. Have the children match the cards to the correctly sized envelopes or lids to the appropriate boxes.
12. Cut and compare various lengths of paper tubes (from toilet paper, paper towels, gift wrapping paper) for size matching.

13. Divide children into cooperative groups and give each group an orange. Using a string, measure the circumference of the orange. Each group determines how long its string is in inches or centimeters. On the chalkboard or chart paper, each group graphs its results. Comparisons are made. Each group then takes its string and finds at least three objects in the room that are the same measurement as the string or the same size as the circumference of the orange (adapted from Misifi, 1993). *Variation:* Adapt as an activity for estimating the circumference of, for example, a watermelon.

14. Place a hula hoop on the floor and have children put the smaller of item pairs inside the circle and the larger items outside the circle (Micklo, 1995).

15. Set a vegetable or fruit, such as a carrot, on the table. Every few days, compare its size with the size of a fresh carrot that has the same length and diameter as the original carrot. Continue this for an extended period of time.

Situations and Structures

Mathematical situations and structures is one of the algebra standards suggested for early childhood mastery by NCTM (2000). To build a foundation for working with algebraic properties such as commutativity, associativity, and equivalent forms, early experiences with equality should be provided. There are a variety of kinds of balance scales for children to work with in developing concepts of equality. (See Chapter 9 or the index for additional experiences with balance.) Algebraic thinking can also be part of everyday activities as children learn to divide materials, toys, art supplies, objects such as napkins, or foods (Taylor-Cox, 2003).

Quantitative Relationships

Young children need to experience concrete models and situations that involve additions and subtractions. For example, there may be 5 children in a group and each child needs 3 crayons for an activity. The teacher may ask how many total crayons are needed and then visually show the five sets of three crayons, determining that the group will need 15 crayons. Pictures, objects, or symbols can be used to model and represent quantitative relationships.

Change

Change, according to the NCTM standards (NCTM, 2000), can be qualitative or quantitative. When relative mathematical labels such as *smaller, heavier,* or *lighter* are used they are showing change over time and represent qualitative change. Experiences with people, animals, or insects give children opportunities to observe and think about both kinds of changes—qualitative and quantitative.

IDEA: Following Halloween, one class sat a carved pumpkin outside on a shelf. They observed and wrote about the changes they saw in the pumpkin over time. These were qualitative changes. The class also weighed and measured the height of the pumpkin the first day they put the pumpkin on the shelf. Each day following they recorded the measurements to observe these changes over time. These were quantitative changes.

GEOMETRY

Geometry includes understanding spatial relationships and studying the characteristics of shapes, both two-dimensional and three-dimensional.

Spatial Relationships

The concept of **spatial relationships** at the early childhood level primarily involves using and understanding prepositional words. Spatial concepts answer *where* questions, *which way* questions, and *distance* questions. In other words, position, direction, and distance ideas are taught through vocabulary and actual experiences. Vocabulary words involving spatial relationships include *over, under, through, around, between, behind, next to, on, off, beside, in front of, outside, inside,* and *in the middle.* Remember to consider the developmental level and ages of the children when selecting activities involving spatial relationships. Becoming familiar with simple maps and using such spatial phrases as "next to" or "near to" provides experience in spatial relationships.

Shape

As early as 3 weeks of age, children begin to distinguish patterns of shape and form. Color is an important aid for identifying shape, but it is also possible that the form or shape of almost any object, for instance, a chair or a table, is more significant than its color. Clements (2004) suggests that to teach shape effectively children need (a) varied examples; (b) discussions relating to shapes and their characteristics; (c) a wider variety of classifications of shapes such as semicircles, quadrilaterals, trapezoids, and hexagons; and (d) opportunity to engage in interesting tasks and activities with shapes.

During early childhood, children learn that shapes are used to understand and recognize objects in our world (Clements, 2004). By the age of 5 or 6 years, children can differentiate geometric shapes: squares, triangles, and circles. Concepts and understandings are formed from observation and manipulation of models and diagrams, rather than by mere definition (Fuys & Liebov, 1997).

GEOMETRY STANDARDS: PRE-K THROUGH GRADE 2 EXPECTATIONS

Analyze characteristics and properties of two- and three-dimensional geometric shapes and develop mathematical arguments about geometric relationships. In pre-kindergarten through grade 2 all students should:

- Recognize, name, build, draw, compare, and sort 2- and 3-dimensional shapes
- Describe attributes and parts of 2- and 3-dimensional shapes
- Investigate and predict the results of putting together and taking apart 2- and 3-dimensional shapes

Specify locations and describe spatial relationships using coordinate geometry and other representational systems. In pre-kindergarten through grade 2 all students should:

- Describe, name, and interpret relative positions in space and apply ideas about relative position
- Describe, name, and interpret direction and distance in navigating space and apply ideas about direction and distance
- Find and name locations with simple relationships such as "near to" and in coordinate systems such as maps

Apply transformations and use symmetry to analyze mathematical situations. In pre-kindergarten through grade 2 all students should:

- Recognize and apply slides, flips, and turns
- Recognize and create shapes that have symmetry

Use visualization, spatial reasoning, and geometric modeling to solve problems. In pre-kindergarten through grade 2 all students should:

- Create mental images of geometric shapes using spatial memory and spatial visualization
- Recognize and represent shapes from different perspectives
- Relate ideas in geometry to ideas in number and measurement
- Recognize geometric shapes and structures in the environment and specify their location

Source: Reprinted with permission from *Principles and Standards for School Mathematics* (p. 96), by the National Council of Teachers of Mathematics. All rights reserved.

Shape and form are important concepts to teach for a number of reasons. "Shape knowledge underlies algebra, geometry, and other domains of higher mathematics" (Diffily & Morrison, 1996, p. 28). Children are interested in the shapes of things: objects in their environments, the shape of their bodies, the shapes that they can make with their bodies, and geometric shapes. They also learn early that most things have a shape and that the shape of something helps to determine what it is or how it is different from other objects in the same category. One of the most important reasons for teaching the perceptual awareness of shapes and noticing fine differences in shapes is that a child's emergent literacy depends in part on visual perception of shape and form. Wide exposure to shapes and forms in the environment can also be enhanced through fine art, which involves more than geometric shapes and combines both regular and irregular shapes.

If a child has been taught to notice differences and to look for differences in the shapes and forms of things, he or she will be more able to read and master other academic skills. For example, in math a child must recognize the differences between the numerals 9 and 6 and learn the correct forms of other numerals in order to recognize them and comprehend their meanings. Work and study on shape and form transfer to other areas and assist the child in progressing in academic understanding.

Objects are identified by shape or form, and the recognition of various forms depends on previous visual experiences with the objects. The shapes illustrated in Figure 12.8 symbolize a concept or organized thought, even though verbal labels have not been ascribed to them. When the shape is observed, it is recognized and identified as having a particular meaning.

Although most things have a shape, it must be remembered that liquids and gases assume the shapes of their boundaries or containers. In teaching shape and form, it is also important to include shapes in addition to the common geometric shapes of a circle, triangle, rectangle, and square. Because shapes aid in or are sources of identification, limiting instruction to the basic shapes excludes from the learning environment the important aspects of recognition of shapes in general. Before uncommon shapes are taught, more familiar ones must be assimilated and understood. Recognition of unfamiliar shapes depends on previous shape identi-

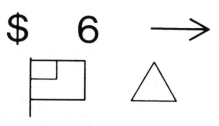

FIGURE 12.8 Examples of Shapes that Symbolize Concepts

fication and recognition. Based on an understanding of simple shapes, the child is able to build more complex structures and schema.

The children were on a field trip observing shapes, and the teacher inquired about the shape of the window in the back of the bus. (The window was rectangular, with rounded corners.) After thinking for a moment, Eric replied, "It isn't a rectangle, because it doesn't have any sharps!" As with the teaching of any idea, various shapes must be found in numerous ways in the child's environment, with many opportunities for manipulation and problem solving.

Words defining shapes should be used often, and words that are usually relied on, such as *that, there,* and *it,* must be accompanied by more detail. Everyday language should include such statements as "That is a square box," rather than "That is square"; "The clock is round," rather than "This is round"; and "Put the book on the square table," rather than "Put it over there." From such sentences, both the object and its characteristic shape become separate and unique ideas. Later more dimensions such as size, texture, and number may be added.

When unfamiliar shapes are introduced, a review of already familiar shapes should precede the introduction. Children need many experiences with shapes and with making comparisons between shapes before focusing on naming shapes. Then the children's thinking can be stimulated with such statements as "How is this new shape the same as . . .?" or "How is this new shape not the same as (or different from) . . .?"

Comparisons provide reinforcement and review of shapes already learned. Too often we begin with naming shapes. This is also true of letters: Children need experiences and opportunities to observe and compare before learning the names of the letters.

Before attaching specific names to shapes, ask such questions as "Who has a shape like this one?" However, do not leave the problem solving there. Follow with, "How do you know?" or "How is it alike?" (Micklo, 1995, p. 25). Identifying similarities and differences is a critical skill that prefaces being able to master reading, writing, spelling, and mathematics. Learning how to solve problems is more important than the solution itself!

To learn about shapes, children need to play with them through games, toys, art activities, fingerplays, songs, poems, and stories. Developmentally appropriate literature, materials, experiences, games, and toys, selected carefully and deliberately, stimulate and increase a child's ability to perceive shapes and forms in the environment (Copple & Bredekamp, 2009). Children's literature is very important in enhancing the learning of prenumber concepts in the early years. The more abstract concepts to grasp, such as time, size, and shape need to be clarified in books, conversation, and activities (Sutherland, 1997).

Concepts and Ideas for Teaching Shape

1. Most things have a shape, and we tell what they are by their shape.
2. Some objects are geometric shapes: circle, square, triangle, and rectangle. (Add the oval, diamond, pentagon, octagon, hexagon, rhombus, ellipse, and other names of specific geometric shapes for older children.) Three-dimensional geometric shapes include the sphere, cone, and cylinder.
3. The same items or objects may be found in different shapes.
   a. Flowers
   b. Hats
   c. People
   d. Dogs
   e. Automobiles
   f. Shoes
   g. Houses
   h. Pasta
4. The same shapes may be found in different objects.
   a. Circle found in a clock, marble, orange, basketball, coin, or plate
   b. Square found in a book, fabric pattern, checkerboard, or block
   c. Triangle found in a tent, house, bridge, musical instrument, or highway sign
5. The same shapes may be found in different sizes.
   a. Suitcases
   b. Crayons
   c. Shoes
   d. Apples
   e. Picture frames
   f. Cans
   g. Balls
   h. Pizza
   i. Fish
6. Shape can be modified.
   a. Growth and aging: Shape of a seed is compared to that of a plant; a fresh fruit or vegetable to an old, shriveled one; a baby to an adult.
   b. Movement: Various shapes achieved by moving different parts of the body or by changing elastic or rope boundaries.
   c. Pressure is applied to a tomato, egg, drying mud, wet cement, rough wood, or inflated balloon alters the original shape.
   d. Temperature changes (heating and freezing): Shapes changed by turning solids into liquids, as well as some liquids into solids.

e. Cutting, crumbling, crushing, bending, folding not only change the original shape, but also may create identifiable new shapes.
f. Natural changes in nature can be seen in wind, water, and so on.
g. Pouring: Liquids take the shape of the containers into which they are poured.
7. One shape, by adding different dimensions, becomes another shape; for example, combining a triangle and a circle results in a face with a hat or an ice-cream cone.

As a shape is named, the children rush to swat the matching shape.

Activities and Experiences for Teaching Shape

1. Shape identification: Circulate containers of objects to be identified by shape; the child feels the shape within the container and then reports the item felt.
2. Silhouette identification: Display outlines of various shapes (simple shapes, such as an umbrella, shoe, chair, or fish, and more complex shapes, such as different shapes of shoes, animals, and flowers, depending on the age level) for the children to identify.
3. Shape collage: Paste variously shaped pieces of paper on a background. Then distribute to the children matching shapes that have been cut smaller than the background shape. As they match the shape, they paste it on the background.
4. Sensory exploration: Put objects of various shapes (of the same category or a different category) in a trough or similar container so that the children can feel and see the various shapes. For instance, objects with circle shapes could include a ball, marble, coin, magnifying glass, and others.
5. Same shape collection: Place a large shape (for example, a circle) on the table or bulletin board. Then invite the children and their families to find photographs, pictures, or objects that are the same shape as the example (for example, a button, ball, coin, mirror, or plate).
6. Pegboard shapes: Supply the children with geoboards or pegboards and pegs and elastic. By stretching the elastic around various patterns of pegs, the children can form shapes. To make a geoboard, sand and finish a board 8-by-8-by-1-inch. Pound small finish nails at equal intervals using five rows of 5 nails each and leaving about $\frac{1}{2}$-inch space between the board and the head of the nail. (Because older children can draw shapes on paper, provide them with pencils and paper on which dots have been placed or drawn. Then they may draw shapes by connecting the dots.)
7. Shape classification: Cut various shapes (geometric and/or objects) in different colors and sizes from felt. The children classify or sort the items according to shape (for example, all the squares together, all the rabbits together).
8. Copying shapes: The 2-, 3-, and young 4-year-olds may have difficulty in copying even such shapes as circles and squares. Most 5-year-olds can begin to copy some shapes. Making a perfect copy will be difficult and challenging, yet enjoyable, for many. By the time children are 6 to 8 years of age, they can copy many-sided geometric shapes and unusual shapes. One way to encourage copying shapes is to draw a particular shape on a series of evenly spaced dots and then, next to this, provide a similar series of dots on which the children can copy the shape.
9. Supply magazines for the children to go through and find objects with obvious geometric shapes. The children can cut out these pictures and make a shape book with a page or pages for each shape.
10. Make individual puzzles from cereal boxes by cutting out the entire front panel from the rest of the box. Then, leaving the four side borders of this panel intact, cut out shapes (triangle, square, circle, etc.) from the center area. Store these puzzle pieces in sealable plastic bags (J. I. Stone, 1987).
11. Prior to cooking pasta for a food activity, mix uncooked pasta of various shapes (shell, elbow, twist) in a bowl. Then have the children sort these

MEASUREMENT STANDARDS:
PRE-K THROUGH GRADE 2 EXPECTATIONS

Understand measurable attributes of objects and the units, systems, and processes of measurement. In pre-kindergarten through grade 2 all students should:

- Recognize the attributes of length, volume, weight, area, and time
- Compare and order objects according to these attributes
- Understand how to measure using nonstandard and standard units
- Select an appropriate unit and tool for the attribute being measured

Apply appropriate techniques, tools, and formulas to determine measurements. In pre-kindergarten through grade 2 all students should:

- Measure with multiple copies of units of the same size, such as paper clips laid end to end
- Use repetition of a single unit to measure something larger than the unit, for instance, measuring the length of a room with a single meterstick
- Use tools to measure
- Develop common referents for measures to make comparisons and estimates

Source: Reprinted with permission from Principles and Standards for School Mathematics *(p. 102), by the National Council of Teachers of Mathematics. All rights reserved.*

into separate bowls. Later, cook the pasta and have the children identify and compare the shapes of the cooked pasta. Various shapes of Styrofoam packing pieces can also be used for shape and form sorting and identification (J. I. Stone, 1987).

12. Assign the children to cooperative learning groups and give each group a sheet with various geometric shapes drawn on it. The children cut out their shapes and glue them on one picture that they work on as a group.

13. Discuss the general characteristics of quadrilaterals (4-sided shapes) and triangles by counting the sides of various figures to select the category to which they belong (Clements & Sarama, 2000).

TEACHING UNITS OF MEASURE

The concept of measurement has real-world applications as children very early realize how often we utilize various measures (Clements, 2004). NCTM (2000, p. 102) expectations for young children for measurement include recognizing the features of length, volume, weight, and time. The concept of measurement develops through five stages including playing and imitating, making comparisons, using arbitrary units of measure, seeing the need for standard units of measurement, and using standard units of measurement (Charlesworth, 2005).

We use measurements whenever we want to know "How far?" or "How much?" We use units of measure to determine length, quantity, temperature, weight, and time. We use various tools and instruments to help measure. Young children easily confuse different standards or units of measurement. For example, a mother was trying to get 4-year-old Kyle to sleep when he said, "Do you know how much I love you, mother?" When she responded with "How much?" he hopped out of

bed, pointed to a numeral on a nearby clock, and said, "This much, 87 pounds!" Another 4-year-old child was weighing herself on the bath scales; reading the numeral 40, she said, "I weigh 40 inches!" It takes time and experience for young children to use units and standards of measurement correctly. We must also point out that early childhood teachers should be familiar with metric units of measurement and vocabulary and understand how to convert standard units to metric units.

Fractions are also a part of measurement. Children during the early childhood years can begin to understand fractional terms such as *one-half* and *one-fourth* and to recognize that these terms indicate a part of a whole. An effective and natural way to introduce fractions to children is through many experiences with recipes. Still another possibility is to divide the class into halves, thirds, fourths, and various other parts of the whole.

> **IDEA:** Fractions can be taught by making a whole circle in one color; making a circle the same size in another color and cutting it in half; making the same size circle in a third color and cutting it in thirds; and making a circle the same size in still another color and cutting it in fourths. Depending on the developmental level of the children, a circle for sixths and one for eighths might be added.

> **IDEA:** Another idea is to put the children in cooperative groups and give each group the same amount of clay. One group is to divide their clay in half, another group in thirds, and another in fourths, extending as far as developmentally appropriate.

Time, another unit of measure, is discussed in this chapter. For more specific information on teaching measurement of temperature and weight, see Chapters 9 and 10 or the index.

Linear Measure

Learning **linear measurement** means understanding that length is measured in terms of inches, feet, and yards and understanding and using tools for linear measurement (for example, ruler, tape measure, or yardstick). Teachers should supply tools for linear measurement in the woodworking area, and it is helpful to add a ruler when using pencils and paper. A tape measure can be included in the dramatic play area for measuring height.

Volume Measurement

The concept of **volume measurement** includes understanding that volumes of materials or quantities of liquids are measured in terms of teaspoon, cup, pint, quart, liter, and gallon and having experiences using containers that equal these amounts. Even more challenging is learning the number of cups in a pint, quart, and so on; the number of pints in a quart; and the number of quarts in a gallon. In addition to sensory media in the trough, add cups and jars for measuring, comparing, and problem solving.

Concepts and Ideas for Teaching Measurement

1. Units of measurement involve assigning a quantitative number to something in order to compare it on some attribute.
2. Measurement attributes include such things as volume, weight, length, and temperature.
3. We use different items or instruments for measuring: clocks, rulers, measuring tapes, scales, measuring cups and spoons, calendars, and thermometers.
4. We measure in standard units of measure such as pints, quarts, feet, pounds, etc. These standards units allow comparisons to be made.

Activities and Experiences for Teaching Measurement

1. Whale on a Playground (adapted from *Learning,* 1994): This activity helps children to apply measurement concepts as well as understand the size of a whale. Research the sizes of several different kinds of whales. Working in groups for each kind of whale, have the group members use chalk and tape measures to mark on the pavement the length of the different whales and measure them in yards or feet. Then they can use a long piece of string to form the outline of the whale. Inside the classroom they can make comparisons of the sizes of the whales and determine the difference between the largest and smallest one.

2. Each child picks an object such as a box, piece of paper, pencil, or crayon that will be his or her unit of measure. Using the object, each child should "measure" several things, such as a desk, a door, or a table, and then record the answers. For example, the desk might be "9 pencils in length" and "7 pencils in width."

3. Using cups, pints, 2-liter bottles, and other containers, have children count the number of cups of water, sand, or other media that it takes to fill a pint, quart, or 2-liter bottle. How many pints will it take to fill a quart? How many quarts to fill a gallon?

4. Measure each child's height using cash register tape, yarn, or string.

5. One-Half: To teach the concept of *one-half* (or any other fraction concept), demonstrate one-half of an apple, cup of sugar, glass of water, licorice stick, and other examples that you choose. Then divide the children into pairs and give each a small candy bar. Let each pair determine how to cut the bar in half to be shared, but the person who cuts takes his or her piece of candy after the one who did not cut.

Measurement of Time

Time is a temporal relationship; and because it cannot be seen, felt, heard, or touched, time is an abstract concept. The notions of *past, present,* and *future* are complicated for young children. **Temporal relationships** refer to the quantitative measurements of time: minutes, hours, days, weeks, months, years, today, yesterday, tomorrow, morning, noon, night. As children begin to understand the concept of time, they usually refer to it in terms of events, such as holidays, birthdays, when a baby is born, attending kindergarten, and so on (VanScoy & Fairchild, 1993).

Children begin to sense the importance and value of time early in their lives, but "have little concept of conventional time, nor will they be ready for instruction in time until well over 7 or 8 years of age" (Seefeldt, 1997).

Every day children hear references to time as they cook, listen to stories, and hear comments regarding time. However, understanding the meanings of these references is a relatively difficult process. To understand quantitative time, children must realize that time flows at a uniform speed that can be divided into equal intervals (VanScoy & Fairchild, 1993). It is important to remember that counting is the basis of time concepts.

Many of the phrases that children hear do not refer to given lengths of time or points in time, and it may be an awesome task for them to grasp the actual meanings. Some of these phrases are "time to go to bed," "time for a bath," "time to eat lunch," "hurry up," "we don't have time to," "not now," "maybe later," "just a minute," "just a second," and "in the olden days."

"Time to have a bath" may be at 6:30 one evening and 8:00 another evening. "Just a minute" could be 50 seconds, 3 hours, or possibly never. To a 5-year-old, "in the olden days" might be only 4 years ago, or it could be a long time ago. This phrase has different meanings for a 30-year-old and an 80-year-old. Thus, it is easy to see why the concept of time is challenging both to teach and to learn.

How long is a minute? Specifically, it is 60 seconds, or one-sixtieth of an hour. Generally, however, the length of time varies in relation to experience. The way a person feels may make this minute feel either long or short. If you are anticipating an important long-distance telephone call, the minute seems much longer than if you are engrossed in an exciting novel—then the minute becomes much shorter. This phenomenon also presents difficulty as children try to grasp time understandings. Also, we often use the word *minute* without meaning the precise time interval of a minute. Young children are just beginning to understand time concepts, and they are often confused. They may know "today" but are still confused that "tomorrow," when it comes, is also "today." Such words as "later" or "after awhile" may mean very little to them. While taking every opportunity to introduce the words and ideas of time, the teacher must also keep in mind that "in a little while" may seem like an eternity to a frightened child waiting for her mother to return.

As children get older, their concept of time also undergoes changes. To a young child, 18 is old; to an 18-year-old, it is young. To a first-grade child anticipating a summer out of school, the summer may seem a long time. But to a 20-year-old college student who is weary of studying, the summer may be much too short. Generally, however, the older a person becomes, the faster the time passes. Because of these varying concepts of time, a preschool child might ask, "Were you alive with the cowboys and Native Americans?" or "Did you know Abraham Lincoln?"

Children invent vocabulary words that are appropriate for their understanding of time; for example, they may say "tomaurieay," "yesternight," or "tosmorning." It is difficult to put words in their proper context when "*to*morrow" does not refer to the same day as "*to*day" or

Timers help children develop concepts of numbers and time. They also remind children when it is their turn.

"*to*night." If today is Wednesday, does "next Saturday" refer to the approaching Saturday or the Saturday following? A visit to the circus may be three sleeps, rather than three nights, away. Teachers can direct children's attention to time and recognize that time words may need to be defined and intentionally taught such as "Yesterday is the day before this day."

Vocabulary Words Relating to Time

yesterday	second	short time
today	minute	long time
tomorrow	hour	never
last night	week	forever
morning	month	past
afternoon	year	present
evening	decade	future
noon	century	new
midnight	B.C.	old
day	A.D.	now
night	early(-ier)	then
spring	late(r)	next
summer	soon(er)	next time
autumn	A.M.	before
winter	P.M.	after

As children work with the calendar in the classroom, they begin to understand the names of the days of the week, the months, and the concepts that there are 7 days in a week, 28 to 31 days in a month, and 12 months in a year. Calendars promote various number concepts: There are 365 days in a year; these 365 days are grouped into 12 months; many months have the same number of days, but some do not; months are divided into weeks, and each week has 7 days; the days of the week have names; calendars tell of special days coming. Calendars should not be overused in early childhood, but only as appropriate. It is not necessary to spend time every day going over calendar concepts, but more meaningful to use the calendar to anticipate and record special events.

Through conversations and experiences, children also develop concepts relating to reading the time on the clock and understanding hours, minutes, and seconds. It is usually around first grade that children begin to use clocks and watches to tell time. Understanding time is much more than being able to "tell time." Often elements other than the clock readings tell of the general time: darkness, overhead sun, snow, jack-o'-lanterns, children playing during recess in the schoolyard, a rooster crowing, and other events and circumstances indicate the possible seasons, hours, and holidays. Children learn that a specific ordering system exists among units of time.

Concepts and Ideas for Teaching Time

1. Time is measured progressively in seconds, minutes, hours, days, weeks, months, years, decades, and centuries.
   a. 60 seconds in a minute
   b. 60 minutes in an hour
   c. 24 hours in a day
   d. 7 days in a week
   e. About 4 weeks in a month
   f. About 52 weeks in a year
   g. 12 months in a year
   h. 10 years in a decade
   i. 100 years in a century
2. The clock has an hour hand and a minute hand (short hand shows the hour, long hand shows the minute), and they move clockwise on the clock.
3. Both the clock and the calendar are measurements of time.
   a. Clock: seconds, minutes, and hours
   b. Calendar: days, weeks, months, and years
4. Even though time is specific, it is flexible; there are 24 hours in 1 day, but a person can structure what will be done within these 24 hours.
5. Time regulates what children do.
   a. School around 9:00 A.M. on weekdays
   b. Church on Sunday for some children
   c. Bedtime around 8:00 P.M.
6. Time influences the food that we eat.
   a. Breakfast food generally different from dinner food
   b. Snacks during favorite television programs
   c. Plentiful and inexpensive vegetables in season
   d. Shortage of fruit supply during spring frosts
7. Time influences recreation.
   a. Basketball in winter, baseball in spring, football in fall
   b. No skiing if the season is sunny and warm
   c. No picnics when the weather is cold or rainy
   d. Outdoor movie theaters are often closed during winter
8. Time influences the clothing that we wear.
   a. Different clothing styles compared to those of 20 years ago
   b. Warmer clothing in cold seasons
   c. Cooler clothing in warm seasons
   d. Bedtime clothes different from daytime clothes
   e. Different clothing at home and at work
   f. Warmer clothing in late evenings and early mornings; cooler clothing in afternoons
9. Time is an element of measurement in holidays, birthdays, and other events.
   a. Operation on child 3 weeks ago
   b. Child's lost tooth on the night of a favorite movie
   c. Christmas always on December 25
   d. Child's birthday on same date each year
   e. New baby expected the first part of October
   f. Visit from a child's grandmother on April 4
10. Time is an element of measurement in seasons, weather, lightness and darkness, and speed.
   a. Four seasons: spring, summer, fall, winter, which always begin on the same dates and follow the same sequence
   b. Car traveling 45 miles per hour (45 miles traveled in an hour)
   c. Distance of lightning indicated by lapse of time between observing lightning and hearing thunder
   d. Warnings of approaching storms usually given in lengths of time
   e. Inches of precipitation said to accumulate in a specific period of time
   f. Rotation of Earth in 24-hour period, resulting in lightness and darkness: contrary to the usual childhood ideas that the sun makes the day light and the moon makes the night dark, and that the sun and moon come up and go down

Activities and Experiences for Teaching Time

1. Make a year's calendar and include dates of importance to the children: their birthdays, closing date of school, holidays, and special events. Refer often to the past, present, and future and how these time perspectives change from day to day.

2. Make a clock with movable hour and minute hands. Have it show appropriate times at the beginning and end of the school day, lunch, snack, outside play, and so on. Match digital times to a traditional clock's time, or vice versa.

3. Measure a 60-second length of time at two different times, one while the children are sitting with nothing to do and one while they are listening to a good story. Discuss the differences that they felt and why.

4. Make a sundial. On a large cardboard circle, attach a perpendicular straw or narrow stick. Leave it in the sun so that the straw will cast a shadow on the circle for 12 hours. Every hour on the hour, mark the position of the shadow of the straw. At the end of 12 hours there will be 12 appropriate marks, but these markings will not be equal distances apart. Then, at the mark indicating when school begins, place a picture or a drawing representing that time. Lunch, school ending, and other events of the day may be designated by drawings or pictures at the appropriate marks. As the day progresses, the children observe the nearness of an event by the shadow of the straw cast on the dial. (This sundial will be accurate for only a few days; then another one must be constructed.)

5. From a calendar, take 2 month pages. Leave one page as is and cut the day numerals apart on the other page. Then have the children use the cut numerals to match the numerals on the page that has been left intact.

6. Measure the time of different egg timers.

7. Do language experience stories titled "Times I Like" and "Times I Do Not Like."

8. A favorite calendar activity is to use 31 sheets of paper, about by 4 inches, representing each day of the month. Number them from 1 to 31 and put them up in correct order, representing a calendar. As each day arrives, a different child can write and draw a picture for that day. For example, on May 2, when Daniel announces that his dog had puppies in the middle of the night, he is invited to draw a picture on the paper with the 2. Either the child or the teacher, depending on the child's level of writing skill, then writes a related sentence on the paper. When the month is finished, the ordered pages are attached to a name-of-the-month cover sheet. The resulting book will be read over and over again. If saved for an entire year, the sheets can be put together into a class yearbook.

9. Read a story that has a definite time sequence such as *Caps for Sale* (Slobodkina, 1987); then go back through the story and label the sequences in terms of the time of day.

10. Using a kitchen timer, have the children first guess how many things can be done in a certain length of time, such as "In one minute, how many times can you bounce a ball?" "In one minute, how many times can you hop on one foot?" Then set the timer to one minute and actually count these out.

11. Take a picture of the children under the same tree at various times during the year to see the changes that result in both the tree and the children. Explain how the passage of time changes things.

12. After the children are able to read hour and half-hour times, teach them how to count by 5 and tell time to the nearest multiple of 5. Teach them to read both traditional hand and digital time.

Teaching Money Concepts

Because of the importance of money in people's lives, children are made aware of its value long before they understand the value meanings. Most young children's concepts of money relate to the understanding that we earn it by working and use it to pay for things that we purchase. Because it is easy for misconceptions to occur, provide many experiences that allow children to work with various amounts of money. When a child has the opportunity to use money, it becomes meaningful. Many games and types of play involve play money, and certainly play money has value as the child learns about payments, cash exchanges, and other concepts. But it is also important that the child experience the use of real money so that the various sizes, amounts, and markings become familiar. Because the child associates size with value, both the nickel and the penny seem to be worth more than the dime. Children are often able to identify different coins, even though they do not know the value of the coins. The vocabulary attests to the child's understandings or misunderstandings. "I need two-seventy pennies." "It costs sixty-eleven monies." George asked his mother for a tricycle. She answered that they did not have any money to buy a tricycle. Being accustomed to seeing the store clerk return change, George answered, "Well, let's go to the grocery store for some money."

It is important for children to experience shopping for food, toys, and clothing. Children will learn that not all items cost the same amount of money, that different items may have the same cost, and that the same item may have various costs. They often see change being returned to the buyer, but they need to learn that the buyer paid for the item before change was made. Perhaps an item costing 79 cents was paid for with a dollar. The change of 21 cents would be returned to the buyer as two dimes and one penny. It is difficult for children to understand that one piece of money ($1.00) is of more worth than three pieces of money (21 cents), because 3 is greater than 1.

The use of checks and credit cards further hinders a child's understanding of the value of money. Often, if a parent responds to a child's request for money with the comment "We don't have enough money," the child will reply, "Then write a check."

Concepts and Ideas for Teaching Money

1. Money is used to purchase things.
2. Coins and dollars are U.S. money, and coins have different names and different values.
3. The sizes of the coins do not correspond with their value.
4. Some coins relate to some bills, for example, a dollar coin is the same value as a dollar bill.

Activities and Experiences for Teaching Money

1. Cut a pig from heavy paper and make a square hole near the top of it. Cut a circle about the size of the pig's body and fasten this circle underneath the pig with a paper fastener. Glue various quantities of money on the circle where they will show through the hole. Turn the wheel so that the different quantities show through the square hole. Write each of the represented quantities on a small card so that the children can match the two. Include a small box or bag of change so that the same amount of money can be shown in ways other than that represented on the wheel or through the hole. For example, if a dime is shown through the hole, the child should find the 10-cent card and also combinations equaling 10 cents (10 pennies, 2 nickels, or 1 nickel and 5 pennies).

2. Newspapers can be used to cut out advertisements on different items for making comparisons. For example, the children could cut out items and their prices and order them from least to most expensive. The children may need assistance in separating items by price per pound and price per individual item.

3. Money Math (ACEI, 1995/1996): As players take turns rolling a die, they get as many pennies as they roll. As soon as the players get 5 pennies, they exchange them for a nickel, 10 pennies for a dime, and so on, depending on the desired difficulty.

DATA ANALYSIS AND PROBABLITY

Data analysis can focus on sorting objects and counting and comparing the groups that are formed. Comparisons can be based on which group has the most or the least. Materials and toys can be easily sorted by various attributes such as color, shape, size, and so forth. As children are involved in various lessons they can graph ideas and data they collect and see the representation of their analysis. Preferences can be represented in numerical representations or pictures in a bar graph. In a lesson on the *w* phoneme the children in one kindergarten were participating in a variety of activities with a watermelon. One of the lessons was predicting the circumference of the watermelon prior to measuring it. Each child made a prediction and the predictions were put on a graph. Following the predictions,

---

DATA ANALYSIS AND PROBABILITY: PRE-K THROUGH GRADE 2 EXPECTATIONS

Formulate questions that can be addressed with data and collect, organize, and display relevant data to answer them. In pre-kindergarten through grade 2 all students should:

- Pose questions and gather data about themselves and their surroundings
- Sort and classify objects according to their attributes and organize data about the objects
- Represent data using concrete objects, pictures, and graphs

Select and use appropriate statistical methods to analyze data. In pre-kindergarten through grade 2 all students should:

- Describe parts of the data and the set of data as a whole to determine what the data show

Develop and evaluate inferences and predictions that are based on data. In pre-kindergarten through grade 2 all students should:

- Discuss events related to students' experiences as likely or unlikely

Understand and apply basic concepts of probability.

Data analysis can focus on sorting objects, then counting and comparing the formed groups.

a tape measure was used to measure the circumference of the watermelon and then an analysis was made with the graph to see how many predictions were under the correct circumference and how many were over.

Whitin and Whitin (2003) described how data analysis was used in a kindergarten classroom where the children did pictographs. From their experience they drew some implications, including that graphing experience should be tied to contexts in the classroom and that various forms of representation can be used for the same data.

In a first-grade classroom the children were involved in a unit on nutrition relating to healthy food choices. They were asked to remember what they had for breakfast the next morning, write it down, and bring their "data" to class. The next day the data were graphed and then an analysis was made in terms of healthy food choices. Following are other activities for data analysis:

- Ask your class, "How many class members have brothers? How many brothers? How many class members have sisters? How many sisters? How many have no brothers or sisters?" Now make a graph of the results. Make other simple graphs for color of hair or eyes, ages, number in family, favorite colors, favorite foods, kinds of pets,

favorite books, number of books read, weather for a month, number of letters in name, number of buttons on clothing, and a comparison of the number of seeds found in a variety of fruits.

- Create a graph of the class members' birthday months. Across the top of the graph, write the months of the year; then, to make the graph, have the children draw pictures of their faces and sign their names. How many birthdays in each month? Which month has the fewest? The most? What does this graph tell us?

Opportunities abound in the early childhood classroom for gathering data and then organizing, classifying, and analyzing the data with a chart or graph. Teachers must be intentional in finding ways to clearly teach data analysis.

TEACHING PROCESS STANDARDS

The following are the five *process standards* suggested by the National Council of Teachers of Mathematics (NCTM) (2000, pp. 116–136).

Problem Solving

Students should:

- Build new mathematical knowledge through problem solving
- Solve problems that arise in mathematics and in other contexts
- Apply and adapt a variety of appropriate strategies to solve problems
- Monitor and reflect on the process of mathematical problem solving

Reasoning and Proof

Students should:

- Recognize reasoning and proof as fundamental aspects of mathematics
- Make and investigate mathematical conjectures
- Develop and evaluate mathematical arguments and proofs
- Select and use various types of reasoning and methods of proof

Communication

Students should:

- Organize and consolidate their mathematical thinking through communication
- Communicate their mathematical thinking coherently and clearly to peers, teachers, and others

(continued)

- Analyze and evaluate the mathematical thinking and strategies of others
- Use the language of mathematics to express mathematical ideas precisely

Connections

Students should:

- Recognize and use connections among mathematical ideas
- Understand how mathematical ideas interconnect and build on one another to produce a coherent whole
- Recognize and apply mathematics in contexts outside mathematics

Representation

Students should:

- Create and use representations to organize, record, and communicate mathematical ideas
- Select, apply, and translate among mathematical representations to solve problems
- Use representations to model and interpret physical, social, and mathematical phenomena

Source: Reprinted with permission from *Principles and Standards for School Mathematics* (pp. 116–136), by the National Council of Teachers of Mathematics. All rights reserved.

UNIT IDEAS ON NUMBERS, MEASUREMENT, AND MONEY

FIELD TRIPS

- Store: weight of items, cost of items, number of objects in each item (12 eggs in one dozen), money exchanges
- Bank
- Telephone company and telephone numbers
- Ride that includes seeing the speedometer, mileage signs, speed-limit signs, and house numbers
- Weather station and thermometer
- Bakery: numbers of ingredients and baking time
- Carpenter shop
- A place where the children ride an elevator

ART

- Numeral collage: children supplied with cut numerals, glue, and paper; numerals pasted randomly or matched to predrawn numerals on background paper

- Block printing, with the raised numerals glued on blocks: numerals glued backward to be correct when printed; blocks dipped into liquid paint, then pressed onto paper or other background material

VISITORS

- Store clerk, with items showing weight and cost
- Bank teller
- Telephone operator
- Police officer: importance of speed limit and mileage signs
- Weather forecaster with thermometer
- Chef, baker, or parent to prepare a food item requiring numbers in amounts and measurements
- Carpenter with measuring tape, yardstick, and ruler

FOOD

- Food experiences requiring recipes with specified amounts and numbers of ingredients
- Food experiences requiring baking and cooking time
- Numeral cookies: numeral shapes cut from rolled cookie dough

MUSIC

- Musical footsteps: footsteps with numerals put in a circle on the floor; children skip, hop, and jump around the circle until the music stops; children name the numerals that they are standing on
- Clapping rhythms: record with definite beat, clapping varieties of rhythms ("This time we will clap three times, then pause one time, then clap three times again.")
- Clapping rhythms of nursery rhymes and familiar songs; clapping the numbers of dots placed on a chalkboard

SCIENCE

- Experiences with scales and balances using numbers for measurements
- Activities with yardsticks, rulers, measuring tapes
- Activities with liquid measurements
- Experiences with a thermometer

LANGUAGE AND LITERACY

- Make number booklets with pictures from magazines or workbooks, photos, or the children's own drawings. Have the children write or dictate a sentence or two for each page.

UNIT IDEAS ON TIME

SCIENCE

- Chemical garden: observation of changes
- Seeds planted: observation of growth over a specific length of time; comparison with original seed size
- Potato left on a table for a period of time: observation of changes
- Sundial

MUSIC

- Musical chairs: music played for varying lengths of time
- Creative movements: being in a hurry, going slowly; pretending to be the hour, minute, or second hand of a clock; dramatizing a day from awakening through going to bed
- Rhythm sticks played along with a metronome, with variation of the beats per minute

FIELD TRIPS

- Clock sales and repair shop
- Science center with fossils
- Historical museum
- Bakery: time the baking time of breads, rolls, and other bakery goods
- Weather station
- Any business that uses a time clock for employees to punch in and out of work

ART

- Individual sundials made and decorated
- Clock face made by each child: paper plate and all numerals needed; numerals pasted on the plate in order or matched to a numeral previously drawn by the teacher

FOOD

- Any food activity requiring a specific cooking time: cookies, cakes, candies, casseroles, puddings, breads, and pies
- Medium- or hard-cooked eggs, depending on the cooking time

VISITORS

- Grandparent, teenager, or baby
- Person from museum of history: objects from the past

- Person with a fossil
- Baker: explanation of the time element in baking
- Person who sells or repairs clocks
- Weather forecaster

UNIT IDEAS ON SHAPE

FIELD TRIPS

- Bakery
- Shape walk
- Furniture store
- Shoe store
- Hat store
- Bus ride
- Construction site
- Art gallery

ART

- Sponge printing (geometric or other shapes)
- Shape collage
- Easel paper cut in various shapes
- Box sculpture: see unit plan on size and seriation
- Tracing around objects similar in shape
- Clay molding
- Different-shaped buttons in a collage
- Shakers of various shapes
- Marshmallow sculpture
- Circle or other shape drawings: draw several circles on a sheet of paper and have the children make something different with each one.
- Various cutout shapes put into patterns or used to make figures

MUSIC

- Twister with shapes, using music
- Playing instruments of varied shapes
- Comparison of sounds from instruments of various shapes
- Musical shapes: pass shapes around; identify or describe them when the music stops
- Different ways we can shape our own bodies
- Ways of moving around shapes or a particular shape

FOOD

- Variously shaped crackers with juice
- Shaped sandwiches

- Napkins folded in shapes
- Cakes baked or decorated in different shapes
- Rolled, shaped cookies
- Gelatin in molds
- Popcorn balls "sculpted" into various shapes
- Bread, molded and then baked
- Hotcakes cooked in various shapes
- Various shapes of pasta, uncooked and cooked

VISITORS

- Carpenter
- Glassblower
- Person from hat store
- Person from shoe store
- Highway flag signaler or police officer
- Artist
- Flower arranger
- Family (comparison of body shapes)
- Parent to make cookie or bread shapes
- Pizza expert
- Wood carver

SCIENCE

- Shape changed by cutting, crumbling, and so on
- Shape changed by adding yeast
- Demonstration of erosion
- Water and air: take the shape of containers
- Balloon experiments
- Observation of snake after feeding time
- Crushing, then releasing of plastic
- Identification of objects from cut silhouettes
- Matching of shapes by feeling
- Bubble blowing ($\frac{1}{2}$-cup liquid dishwashing detergent and $\frac{1}{4}$-cup sugar, or 8 ounces liquid detergent and 1 ounce glycerin; either recipe can be diluted with a small amount of water, if necessary)

LITERACY

- Make a booklet composed of pictures of various shapes. Add sentences created by the children (written by the children or teacher, depending on the children's writing ability). Even the booklet pages can be cut into shapes; either each page is different, or all pages within the booklet match.

UNIT IDEAS ON SIZE

FIELD TRIPS

- Sports store: observe balls of various sizes.
- Clothing store: clothing too large and too small for children; clothing to fit parent(s)
- Grocery store: different items of the same size; the same items in various sizes
- Cycle shop: cycles of different sizes
- Carpenter shop: drill bits, pieces of wood, nails, and screws in various sizes
- Tire store: tires and inner tubes of various sizes
- Bakery: observe process of bread baking.
- Greenhouse: many kinds of plants in different stages (sizes) of growth
- Shoe store
- Art gallery

VISITORS

- Mother and baby
- Grocer with canned goods of various sizes
- Baker to make doughnuts
- Service station attendant to fix an inner tube
- Teenager to inflate tires on bicycle
- Sports store clerk: seriation of balls (golf, baseball, softball, volleyball, basketball)
- Scientist with microscope or magnifying glass
- Carpenter with saw and boards
- Two grandfathers of different sizes
- Clothing store clerk with some clothes too small, some just right, and some too large for the children

SCIENCE

- Planting seeds: compare growing seeds and plants with the size of the original seeds
- Mixing vinegar and soda together
- Two similar sponges: allow one to become saturated with water and then compare the sizes of the two sponges.
- Freezing of water: draw a line on a clear bottle, fill to the line with colored water, let freeze, observe level of ice, and then let thaw and observe as the liquid returns to the original mark.
- Planting young tree: caring for it and watching its growth over an extended period of time
- Lighting a candle: observe the change in size (start with 2 candles, so that the lighted candle can be compared to the unlighted one)

FOOD

- Bread: mix and bake, cool, eat
- Raised doughnuts
- Hamburgers
- Marshmallow squares: butter and marshmallows change size as they melt
- Popcorn
- Cookies
- Ice cream: size changes in ice, salt, and amount of ice-cream mixture
- Whipped cream or egg whites
- Egg soufflé
- Rice, spaghetti, or macaroni dish
- Snapping spaghetti into various lengths prior to cooking
- Cake
- Hotcakes cooked in various sizes

ART

- Collage with paper circles of various sizes, either of the same color or of different colors
- Button collage: buttons of many sizes pasted on Styrofoam trays
- Various lengths of straws, cut and strung
- Papier-mâché applied to an inflated balloon and allowed to dry; the balloon then popped and the resulting ball decorated

- Box sculpture: boxes of various sizes pasted together, allowed to dry, and then decorated
- Clay modeling of balls or ropes
- Smallest to largest pictures: draw pictures of objects, ordering them from smallest to largest; or pictures of animals, comparing smaller animals to larger animals.

MUSIC

- Creative movements: of a child or seed growing, bread or cake baking, ice cube or icicle melting, balloon being inflated and popped, sponge absorbing water, vinegar and soda being mixed
- Music shakers: of varying sizes or of the same size, containing unlike sizes of materials (sand, berries, rocks, wheat, or rice)
- Small musical instrument (such as a harmonica) compared to larger musical instrument (such as an accordion)
- Similar musical instruments of varying sizes (violin, cello, or bass violin)

LITERACY

- Write stories titled "As Big as . . .," "As Small as . . .," "As Tall As . . .," or use other size words as similes.

Summary

As we have discussed problem solving and its relationship to all aspects of the early childhood education curriculum, we have stressed that the critical thinking required to reach a solution to a problem is much more valuable than the solution itself. This does not minimize the importance of learning facts, but it does maximize the lifelong rewards of being able to assess problems and evaluate possible solutions. Problem solving is a particularly necessary ingredient when working with mathematics and numbers.

Even though children become aware of numbers early in life through daily experiences, the actual understanding of number words depends on experiences, maturation, and intellectual development. Generally, number concepts are best acquired through incidental, active learning, rather than from formalized structured lessons or worksheets. Carefully planned and prepared lessons assist children in assimilating concepts relating to numbers. For children in preschool and the early primary grades, math studies are most effective when the activities and experiences include concrete objects that relate to the concepts being taught and are individually and age appropriate (Charlesworth, 2005). Copley (2010, p. 12) addresses three components of teaching mathematics to young children: "(1) curriculum—what mathematics content and processes should be taught; (2) instruction—how children should be taught that curriculum; and (3) assessment—finding out what children know and can do and what more they need to learn." These three ingredients of teaching are critical to all areas of early childhood curriculum, and we have addressed all three in the early chapters of this text as well as this chapter.

Math activities should be enjoyable and challenging, worked on gradually, and repeated often. Although often informal and integrated into the entire curriculum, math learning is not "unplanned or unsystematic" (Clements, 2001, p. 273). As children gain experience and knowledge in measuring, counting, ordering, telling time, matching, comparing, estimating, and so on, their ability to recognize and ascribe appropriate ideas with number concepts increases.

Concepts relating to time and telling time are abstract, but they develop in early childhood as a result of daily experiences with time words and concepts and clocks. Children learn that time exists in units and, as they understand specific units, they extend their mathematical thinking and reasoning.

Shape and size were two mathematical concepts also presented in this chapter. Even in their first few months of life, children are able to distinguish shapes. While they are relatively young, they also demonstrate interest in the various shapes in their environment. Familiar and common shapes should be discussed and taught before more unfamiliar and uncommon shapes are introduced. Not only are objects identified by shape, but the recognition and perception of shapes are also basic ingredients in reading readiness. Children should have numerous experiences with the shapes in their environment. They should be encouraged to notice the differences and similarities among various shapes.

Size and ordering manipulatives or other things involves both making comparisons between two or more objects of different sizes and arranging items from smallest to largest. Size is relative; the size of an object depends on the size of another object with which it is being compared. In teaching size and seriation, provide children with many opportunities for practicing size comparisons, seriating objects, and hearing related vocabulary words.

Student Learning Activities

1. Discuss why you agree or disagree with the authors' premise that the critical thinking required to reach a solution to a problem is more valuable than the solution itself.

2. Visit a preschool, kindergarten, or first- or second-grade classroom. From the equipment and materials in the environment, list the opportunities that you see for teaching concepts relating to numbers, shape, and size. For example, you may see unit blocks of various sizes that could be compared on the basis of size or even ordered according to size.

3. With a group of children, implement at least one of the activities and experiences related to number, shape, or size concepts in this chapter. The children may be a classroom group or simply a small group of relatives or neighborhood children. Evaluate your experience.

4. Observe and talk with a preschool child, listening for comments and understandings related to numbers. Ask such questions as "How old are you?" "What is your favorite number?" "How far can you count?" and "Where do you see numbers?" Now make a comparison. Then observe and talk with a child between ages 5 and 6 and ask some of the same questions. You will want to ask additional questions, such as "Show me how you can add some items. Here are three pencils. What will you have if you add three more pencils?" You may wish to relate problems to money, time, weight, measurement, and other concepts. Challenge the child with number questions and problems. Now compare the differences in the two children that you observed, keeping in mind the differences in their ages.

5. Visit a classroom and observe an activity or lesson for teaching numbers, shape, or size. Evaluate the activity. Was it appropriate for the age of the children? Was the emphasis on thinking and understanding the mathematical process(s)? Would you have made any changes in the lesson or activity? Was it effective? Did the teacher use materials? Was a workbook sheet used and, if so, was it effective?

6. Prepare a 5-day activity plan, unit plan, or lesson plan on shape, size, or number. You could select a concept relating to one of the number concepts.

Suggested Resources

Hurst, C. O. (1997). *Picturing math: Using picture books in the math curriculum* (pre-kindergarten through second grade). DeSoto, TX: McGraw-Hill Learning Materials.

Kessler, C. (2007). *Picturing math: Hands-on activities to connect math with picture books.* Waco, TX: Prufrock Press.

Krasa, N., & Schunkwiler, S. (2009). *Number sense and number nonsense: Understanding the challenges of learning math.* Baltimore, MD: Brookes.

Roberts, P. L. (1990). *Counting books are more than numbers.* Hamden, CT: Shoe String Press.

Zaslavsky, C. (2001). *Number sense and nonsense: Building math creativity and confidence through number play.* Chicago: Chicago Review Press.

CHILDREN'S BOOK CITED

Slobodkina, E. (1987). *Caps for sale.* New York: Harper Trophy.

Online Resources

www.naeyc.org/resources/position_statements?psmath.htm This site covers early childhood mathematics: Promoting good beginnings—A joint position statement of NAEYC and NCTM.

www.nctm.org National Council of Teachers of Mathematics site includes information about the principles and standards addressed in this chapter. It also includes links to mathematics resources.

www.ed.gov/pubs/EarlyMath (1999). This is a government publication that provides early math activities for 2- to 5-year-old children.

www2.ed.gov/pubs/parents/math/title.html   (1999). Helping your child learn math. This is a government publication that provides support for parents in working with math with young children.

www2.ed.gov/parents/academic/help/math/math.pdf.   (2005). Helping your child learn math. This is an updated PDF file or booklet for parents to use as they support young children with math concepts and activities.

www.math.rice.edu/~lanius/counting   A fun and colorful set of counting activities.

www.math.com   Math resources for both parents and teachers are available at this site.

www.goenc.com   Eisenhower National Clearinghouse includes links to a variety of sites.

www.mathforum.org   This math forum has links to many resources and sites.

www.learner.org/teacherslab/math/patterns/index.html   The focus of this is on the importance of patterns and how to teach them. You may also want to visit the site www.learner.org/ and check the Teacher Resources for many ideas for math grades K–2.

www.terc.edu/ourwork/elementarymath.html   This site offers ways to improve math education.

www.gse.buffalo.edu/org/conference   This site includes a list of website sources for mathematics standards for early childhood.

www.ncsmonline.org   A professional association to provide leadership in math education.

http://members.tripod.com/~Patricia_F/mathscience.html   This website has great math activities with easy-to-follow directions.

part 4

Aesthetic and Creative Development

The next two chapters address the aesthetic development of young children, especially in the areas of creativity in music and art. To educate the whole child, the arts must be part of the curriculum (Pica, 2009b)! The Educate America Act places dance, drama, music, and the visual arts at the very center of the curriculum (C. M. Thompson, 1995). The United States Department of Education (2004) proposes that the arts are essential to the education of our children, and should be included in the core curriculum of our classrooms.

Aesthetic awareness involves the ability to discern and be sensitive to things in the environment and to human creations. **Aesthetic development** encompasses the young child's individual taste, love of beauty, and criteria for judging beauty. Whether creativity is defined in terms of art, thinking, writing, or any other activity, certain words and ideas come to mind. **Creativity** appears to involve intuition, elaboration, fluency, flexibility, originality, evaluation, and divergent thinking. Most researchers believe that all human beings possess the capacity or potential for creativity. Teachers need to believe that all children possess creativity. When children express thoughts, feelings, or actions in original, self-initiated, or inventive ways, they are being creative.

During a unit on fish, the children were participating in an art activity in which they were making a collage of fish cutouts. One child put a group of them together, and the teacher, thinking this would be a great time for discussing the meaning of the term *school of fish,* asked the child if she knew what a group of fish is called. The child confidently responded, "Of course, it is a bouquet of fish!"

Remember, *all* children are creative. Creative children often manifest a determination to express their creativity. They display characteristics such as the following:

- Have the ability to perceive unusual and broad relationships
- Have a different time–space perspective
- Have a sense of humor
- Enjoy inquiring and asking questions, as well as solving problems
- Show great ingenuity and imagination
- Offer many ideas and a variety of valid alternatives in problem solving
- Enjoy taking risks and participating in adventure
- Are often persistent in reaching a goal
- Enjoy firsthand investigative activities that provide the opportunity to probe, explore, discover, and create
- Use elaborate language and often express themselves in unique ways

Participating in creative activities perpetuates creativity. "Imagination opens new worlds, discloses new vistas, and makes life enjoyable" (Mulcahey, 2009, p. 109). The joy of discovery is its own reward and provides the incentive for continuing exploration and discovery.

Too often our schools are not designed to promote or encourage creative thinking or creative art. Too often, children are expected to limit their individuality to achieve a set mold or pattern. **Convergent thinking,** arriving at the same "right" answer, is often the type of conformity encouraged and rewarded. This type of thinking is uncreative, less time consuming, easy to evaluate, and, in some areas, essential to education. However, a balanced view makes room for **divergent thinking,** too.

Any activity can become educationally meaningful when we stimulate imagination, which is the realm of possibilities and the source of all creativeness. Imagination can and should be a part of all mental functions. We should design our schools to encourage children to think, for all children can think both competently and creatively. Yet society and schools seem to discourage divergence, and pressures on children often cause them to surrender their natural creativity. All children engage in creative thinking, but they will not continue to do so if their ideas are discouraged and they are told that there is only one correct way to do something (Pica, 2009a). Teachers frequently cover too much material too quickly. They do not ask enough questions or give children adequate time to think and respond verbally, with questions, in speaking or writing, or in art expression. Our schools often expose children to the constant fear of evaluation.

Children can be taught in a way that their creative thinking abilities become useful in attaining educational competencies. These creative skills and abilities are very different from those measured by intelligence and scholastic aptitude tests, but they are important to both mental health and vocational success. It is imperative that teachers strive to foster creativity during the early childhood years, because it is the child's creativity that kindles a new idea, that motivates the child to accept a challenging task or assignment, or that fosters the spirit of independence. Creativity offers the child the chance to change things that are or have been to things that might be or may yet be discovered.

Children grow, work, and learn better when there are periodic times set aside for self-expression. Creativity is not just for thinking, art, and music—it is an integral part of all areas in the curriculum. Arts education contributes to and improves such areas as critical thinking and problem solving (Edwards, 2009). Children are able to naturally practice math concepts, patterns, and symbolic thinking skills while participating in music and movement activities. Many music activities involving keeping time and rhythm help establish a sense of one-to-one correspondence, which is a basic math skill (Armistead, 2007). These activities also support the development of language and literacy, physical, cognitive, and socio-emotional skills (Parlakian & Lerner, 2010).

It has been suggested that three key ingredients are necessary for creativity to flourish in any classroom and in any part of the curriculum: (a) appropriate teacher attitude, (b) appropriate classroom atmosphere, and (c) appropriate activities and materials (M. K. Smith, 1996).

The ability to create new ideas and solve problems is one of the most important competencies for children to develop. Music and creative arts provide numerous opportunities for solving problems with creative thinking. Specific conditions that facilitate the development of creativity in the classroom include the following:

- Giving responsibility and independence
- Valuing the expression of feelings and individual divergence
- Emphasizing self-initiated exploring, observing, and questioning
- Creating a feeling of freedom and openness, and encouraging spontaneous expression
- Developing an accepting atmosphere
- Providing a wealth of stimulation from a rich and varied environment
- Asking provocative, thoughtful questions
- Valuing originality
- Providing many opportunities for achievement
- Providing differentiated, meaningful interaction

Experiences and activities in the creative arts reduce stress, enhance development, facilitate learning, and balance children's often-hurried lives (Elkind, 2007a). The arts provide children opportunities for creative thinking as well as creative production. Children enjoy experimenting with words, paints and other materials, and music; they find it rewarding to dream and to create something of their own, something unique and original. Music and creative arts can give children opportunities for a creative outlet to use divergent, as opposed to convergent, thinking. Teachers must be careful not to teach these art areas in rigid, structured ways, thereby stifling children's creative potential. Teachers' techniques, approaches, and activities need to be open ended, giving children the opportunity to use their creative imagination. "It is an early childhood teacher's challenge to create a musically stimulating classroom environment and enjoyment with music materials and activities" (Kim & Robinson, 2010, p. 46).

chapter 13
Music and Movement

There are many benefits of music and movement. No special training in music is necessary.

"The benefits of music and motion are numerous, and no special training is needed to have fun with music" (Foley, 2006, p. 176). Music and movement provide an outlet for young children to express themselves, respond to rhythm, enhance oral language, investigate space, and increase sensory acuity (L. C. Edwards, 2009). Recent neuropsychology research suggests that music and movement integrate the functions of both hemispheres of the brain and contribute to the language, social/emotional, cognitive, and physical development of young children (Dodge, Colker, & Heroman, 2003; Neelly, 2001). Engaging the brain through movement is central to learning (Jensen, 2004). Although music promotes learning, it "is usually ignored as a talent for the select few or indulged as fun-time diversion. Musical illiteracy is all too often accepted as the norm" (Kenney, 1997, p. 104). Too often teachers in early childhood education appear unprepared to use music, and programs lack musical direction (Scott-Kassner, 1999). But, according to Gardner (1999b) music is one of the basic intelligences possessed by all humans and, as such, is an aspect of human potential. There is a musical impulse in young children, and their potential and aptitude for music are nurtured by the musical environment provided them during infancy and early childhood. Music activities require neither specific skills nor competence, and all children are able to participate at varying levels of involvement from listening, to singing, to active movement (Humpal & Wolf, 2003).

Reasons for Including Music in Early Childhood Programs

- Music can foster appreciation of various cultures, as well as one's own heritage. It is a part of every culture's uniqueness (Lazdauskas, 1996). Children enjoy learning songs and dances from various cultures and nations.
- Through music, children experience pleasure, joy, creative expression, and other emotional responses.
- Music is one of the acceptable avenues for release and expression of feelings, moods, and emotions. Music can reduce stress (Davies, 2000) and facilitate the development of desirable feelings and moods and the dissolving of undesirable feelings and moods.
- Music can quiet or calm children, create listening moods, or soothe hurt and troubled feelings.
- Music has therapeutic value and, as a result, can also enhance the child's feelings of self-worth. Songs can include the child's name, or children can write words, phrases, or verses of songs. Children should be permitted to interpret music in their own style and to make up new words, new melodies, and new movements.
- Children's listening skill, attention span, auditory discrimination, and memory develop through music. Listening to songs that tell a story (ballads) or give directions to follow provides an excellent opportunity for careful concentration and attention.
- Language and concepts can be developed through music as children sing using correct language form. New songs often introduce new words, concepts, and cognitive skills. Music can wake up the brain and increase the child's productivity (Davies, 2000).
- Research supports the notion of the physical and psychological advantages of music on the body and mind (Davies, 2000; Neely, 2001).
- The rhythm and rhyme of music make it easier to remember factual information. Putting concepts and ideas to music often commits them to memory, because music aids recall (Davies, 2000).

activities. They can name a locomotor skill or other activity and dramatize it while singing about it. Reading and singing are closely connected. Reading lyrics while singing helps to develop reading and language skills. Additionally, it has long been recognized that music is a valuable memorization tool. Children are able to learn and remember information taught through singing songs—the 50 states, telephone numbers, addresses, mathematical facts, spelling. These teaching songs are actually types of storytelling and story songs (Ringgenberg, 2003).

Music skills such as rhythm, meter, pitch, and tone are introduced to young children through music. Music enhances a sense of belonging to and functioning within a group (Neely, 2001). Most of all, children enjoy music; the intricate tunes and melodies; the words, which often tell a story or capture their sense of humor; and the rhythms, which often create spontaneous body movements such as swaying, toe tapping, or hand clapping. When responding to music and movement, the whole child is involved with voice, body, and emotions: listening, singing, moving to the beat, playing instruments, and imitating simple movements of objects or concepts (Edwards, Bayless, & Ramsey, 2008). "Physical movement tasks demand full engagement of mind and body" (Armistead, 2007, p. 90).

Shore and Strasser (2006, pp. 66–67) provide suggestions for helping children expand their thinking:

- Use notes and rhythm to teach phone numbers and addresses.
- Clap rhythm of children's names.
- Clap out simple songs.
- Use counting songs.
- Make rhythm instruments.
- Have children provide sound effects for a story.
- Sing simple rounds.
- Create story songs to familiar melodies.
- Include music in science and social studies lessons.
- Have children teach others their songs.
- Increase our own knowledge and abilities in music.
- Do not let personal feelings of embarrassment about our own music abilities interfere with the music and movement opportunities we should provide in our classroom.

"Music helps young children synthesize experiences, transition into new activities, calm down during naptime, share cultural traditions, and build self-esteem and a sense of community" (Shore & Strasser, 2006, p. 62). "Learning music and words together, often accompanied by hand and body motions, is a wonderful way to wire brain connections for children's learning" (Honig, 2005, p. 30). Songs can teach about children's clothing or attributes. Children can sing about their

Through fingerplays, action songs, music games, writing words for songs, composing melodies, and other music-related activities, children are able to utilize creative thinking in problem solving. Musical experiences are bridges to children's overall growth (Neely, 2001).

MUSIC GOALS

". . . music should not be taught just for its ability to enhance other subjects . . . it should be taught for its own worth" (Greata, 2006, p. 74). Remember that in all areas of the aesthetic aspects of the early childhood curriculum, the emphasis must be on the child, not the teacher; the enjoyment, not the skill; the process, not the product. Because music should be an integral part of the early childhood curriculum, its main objective for this age group is the child's enjoyment of music. "A child-centered curriculum is based on the assumption that the learner is more important than that which is being learned. The child is more important than the music; music has the power, however, to make the child's life more important" (Andress, 1995, p. 100). "Giving children time and space in which to grow socially, emotionally, and cognitively may rely upon their daily participation in music making, which, in turn, may set the foundation for healthy development throughout the life span" (Zur & Johnson-Green, 2008, p. 299).

> ### Benefits of the Music Programs in Early Childhood Education
>
> - Success, joy, and pleasure through participation
> - Opportunities to experience music through a variety of relevant activities, materials, instruments, and movements
> - Acquaintance with a variety of types of music
> - Provision for listening activities to foster music understanding
> - Awareness of contrasts in music, such as fast and slow, high and low, loud and soft
> - Responsiveness to simple rhythms through locomotor movements, body movements such as clapping, or the use of rhythm instruments
> - Opportunity to sing a variety of songs
> - Ability to express the mood or feelings of a musical selection through body movements, and opportunity to express emotion through music

Kim and Robinson (2010) suggest four steps to becoming familiar with early music standards:

- Read the music standards.
- Learn the music related to the standards.
- Implement the music standards.
- Check to make sure the music standards are satisfied.

The teacher should individualize these goals for the particular group and also for the individual children within the group. Too often teachers plan from an activ-

ity approach; they think of a "fun" activity instead of a developmentally appropriate music activity. Music activities must be developmentally appropriate if they are to be effectively incorporated into all curriculum areas. While working, if all the students do not want to listen to music or a particular type of music, those who do wish to listen can use headphones (Davies, 2000). The teacher should know each child's functioning level with regard to musical skills and interests. A good music program should incorporate the goals of music in singing, rhythm experiences, movement, listening and through active involvement. The Music Educators National Conference (MENC, 1994a) advocates that music in the curriculum be consistent with appropriate practice. According to Kenney (1997, pp. 106–107), that means it demonstrates the following principles:

- Age appropriateness, individual appropriateness, and context must be taken into account when planning music learning environments.
- Play is a primary vehicle for musical growth.
- Every student should have access to a balanced, comprehensive, and sequential program of study in music.

> ### The Teacher's Role in Music Education
>
> - Show an interest in the spontaneous beginnings of music that the child creates.
> - Make time available for music and not just listening to music; active involvement is best (D. B. Fox, 2000). The power and benefit of music are in "doing" the music (Guilmartin, 2000).
> - Be confident in your own musicianship.
> - Plan for every day, but also use music spontaneously to support other parts of the curriculum, to create variety, and to provide transitions to activities.
> - Provide adequate space for musical activities, particularly during creative movements and expressions.
> - Allow for freedom of expression, as well as some freedom regarding participation. Young children should be free to become involved in music and to express their own feelings, moods, and interpretations.
> - Avoid criticism and demands for perfection in performance skills.
> - Create an appropriate music learning environment by planning activities that will encourage music participation and expression, as well as providing materials and experiences that will stimulate creative thinking and action.
> - When possible, take children to see various musical performances.

NATIONAL STANDARDS FOR MUSIC EDUCATION K–4

Content Standard	Sample Activities
1. Singing, alone and with others, a varied repertoire of music.	Singing a variety of folk songs, lullabies, familiar tunes—during centers, circle time, transitions, indoor/outdoor play.
2. Performing on instruments, alone and with others, a varied repertoire of music.	Playing instruments, making rhythm instruments, playing various rhythms and beats.
3. Improvising melodies, variations, and accompaniments.	Making various changes in rhythm, words, melodies to familiar tunes.
4. Composing and arranging music with specified guidelines.	Using chants, repeated sounds, and other sounds when expanding familiar songs.
5. Reading and notating music.	Recognizing the typical lines and notes patterns of music on a page, compared to words only on text pages.
6. Listening to, analyzing, and describing music.	Responding to music by moving fast or slow, softly or loudly, swaying, dramatizing, marching, walking, running, skipping.
7. Evaluating music and music performances.	Attending musical performances. Visiting high school band and music departments. Visitors to class playing a variety of selections.
8. Understanding relationships between music, the other arts, and disciplines outside the arts.	Using expandable songs to teach address and phone numbers, math concepts. Songs that help teach social skills, character education. Creating songs relating to various science objects or concepts.
9. Understanding music in relation to history and culture.	Incorporating visitors who have roles in music: band leader, drummer, pianist, singer. Learning songs typical to specific cultures. Observe and learn dances from various cultures. Sing traditional folksongs from history.

Source: From National Standards for Arts Education. Copyright © 1994 by MENC: The National Association for Music Education. Used with permission. Further information relating to the National Standards is available at the MENC website *National Standards* (http://www.menc.org/resources/view/national-standards-for-music-education)

Because young children are highly motivated by praise, the teacher should further motivate musical competencies by praising individuals. Comments such as "Jimmy has found a different way to use the rhythm sticks" or "Lori has learned that you can even jump sideways" provide individual motivation.

> According to Kenney (1997, p. 108), as adapted from the MENC (1994a), "The music curriculum should be conceived not as a collection of activities but rather as a well-planned sequence of learning experiences leading to clearly defined skills and knowledge."

The experiences should be challenging, but reflect the joy and personal satisfaction that are inherent in music. The purpose of studying music should be to enable children to enhance the quality of their lives by participating fully in their musical culture.

Teacher-initiated activities include teaching songs and musical games, planning music activities that support and relate to curriculum areas, planning musical dramatizations, using rhythm activities and rhythm instruments, and encouraging creative body movements. Because play is the primary vehicle for music experiences in early childhood, the teacher should also take advantage of child-initiated, child-directed activities

(MENC, 1994a). The children may begin singing or chanting during play. They may sing familiar songs, make up their own tunes, or use new words to familiar melodies. A child may begin spontaneously to hum or move rhythmically; the teacher should take advantage of the opportunity to praise the effort and encourage the child to continue. Musical experiences, then, should be both structured and open-ended.

Teachers should create opportunities for increasing their own musical competencies. Even when we are not confident in our musical talents, reaching to increase our abilities is certainly an expression of creativity. Teachers should develop enthusiasm for the music program, since their own feelings will be *caught* by the children, rather than *taught* to them. Children do not necessarily respond to our abilities in music—they respond to us, as teachers, to our willingness, enthusiasm, enjoyment, spontaneity, and interest (Edwards, 2009; Neely, 2002). Positive music attitudes are the key. With a teacher's positive attitude, all children will enjoy participating in various singing and other music activities. Teachers who enjoy music and sing with enthusiasm, regardless of ability or training, are the ones who receive the greatest response and involvement from children. Music is a universal language; we do not have to understand the terminology or musical mechanics to enjoy it. It is most effectively approached in early childhood as an experience to be lived, rather than a subject to be taught.

Five suggestions (Gharavi, 1993) for expanding music and singing in the curriculum are:

1. Singing at a comfortable pitch for young voices
2. Expanding our own musical repertoire
3. Becoming familiar with quality music available for young children
4. Providing opportunities for quiet listening
5. Providing a variety of musical styles, especially ethnic music

SONGS AND SINGING

Think about favorite songs from your own childhood. Why do you think you have remembered them all your life? Do you remember how and when you learned them, and from whom? What kinds of feelings stir or awaken as you recall these songs? The young children in your classrooms should have the opportunity of building the same kinds of memories. Listening to music and singing songs from children's home cultures create continuity between home and school, and help children feel more comfortable in the school setting (Parlakian & Lerner, 2010). Moore (2002) reminds us that because of music in various media forms in this country, we do not sing as much as we used to. Passively we listen to and watch performers, rather than making our own music. "There are more and more trained singers, but they are trained to perform music, not to connect with the community" (p. 84). Developmentally appropriate musical activities in the early childhood classroom allow just that—opportunities for children to connect with the community as together they share songs, rhymes, chants, singing, lullabies, and other musical activities (Humpal & Wolf, 2003).

Honig (1995) proposes that songs soothe, express love, promote cooperation and learning daily routines, help to smooth transitions, ease separation, build trust and self-esteem, encourage enjoyment for poetry and imagery, stretch memorization skills, develop humor, build motor skills, and increase group cohesiveness. "Singing is an intimate expression of who we are and what we feel" (Neelly, 2002, p. 83). Even as infants, children benefit from musical exposure. Learning songs and singing are probably the most common musical experiences in the early childhood years. The key to the child's total musical growth is cheerful singing. Teachers should build a repertoire of songs, and it is imperative that they use caution and wisdom when selecting songs to teach to young children to insure the songs are developmentally appropriate. Children should have daily experiences with singing.

Toddlers imitate singing and often tag on to the end of a phrase or song. They move to the music and enjoy very simple songs. As 5-year-olds learn songs, they "first learn the words, followed by rhythm, then melodic contour, and finally intervals" (Kenney, 1997, p. 112). Music preferences are formed by the age of 5, but can be changed as a result of music in the environment and by the caregiver's love for various kinds of music.

Guidelines for Teaching Songs in Early Childhood

1. Competition has no place in teaching children to sing; for example, when children compete to sing the loudest their voices become distorted and the melodies suffer. Comparisons between children should not be made.
2. Practice and learn the song before trying to teach it (Dodge et al., 2003) and then sing the song to the children several times while they listen. Listening to good singing is a significant factor in children's vocal development (Haines & Gerber, 1999). Do not teach a song by repeating the words separately from the music. You might play a recording of the song for the children to hear; then they can join in and sing with the recording and the teacher. When selecting records or tapes, make sure that the voices are in tune and the instrumentation is uncomplicated.
3. Some songs should be taught in sections: phrases, sentences, or short verses at one time. This is particularly true of longer songs that are more difficult to learn. Then these sections can all be put together. However, when the children are first introduced to the song, they should hear it in its entirety so that they experience it as a whole unit.
4. Use a variety of approaches and teaching techniques (discussed throughout this chapter) in teaching songs and singing familiar songs. Do not always teach songs in the same way. Use pictures, hand and finger actions, and simple props that will involve the children to assist them in remembering the words (Dodge et al., 2002; Edwards et al., 2008).
5. Do not force children to sing. Often a child does not sing at school, but sings all the songs at home. Some children take time to feel comfortable singing with the group, and pressure to sing does not make them more willing to participate. However, involve the reluctant singer whenever possible. The more involved

the children become in a song, the more comfortable they feel in participating.

6. Eye-to-eye singing, like eye-to-eye teaching, is most effective. The mood and feeling of the song, along with the teacher's enjoyment of singing, will be caught through the expressions that you convey to the children.

7. Sing songs to the children in a lower range (A or B below middle C to G or A above).

8. Make sure that children understand the meanings of new words in the song, as well as the meaning of the song. However, make certain that the content of the song is on the level of the children's understanding and interest.

9. You may want to discuss the feeling, mood, repetition of melodies or words, tempo, or rhythm of the song.

10. As you teach songs, enunciate clearly and distinctly.

11. If there is a part of a song that is particularly difficult for the children to learn, isolate this part and sing it to the children while they listen. Also, sing this part of the song much more slowly until the children have learned it. Other suggestions include having them clap the rhythm or use their hands to show how the melody moves.

12. To motivate children to listen to a song, ask questions about the song that prompt them to listen.

13. Use instruments often to accompany the children's singing, but *teach* the songs without accompaniment. Even if you are not skilled in music reading, there are still many instruments that can be learned or played easily (autoharp, baritone or tenor ukulele, guitar, rhythm sticks, or other rhythm instruments).

14. Children enjoy songs with simple and clear melodies, although they are also eager to learn longer and more intricate tunes. When selecting songs for young children, remember that those with repetition of melody and words are generally both easy and enjoyable to learn (Dodge et al., 2002).

15. When teaching new songs, hum and sing the song spontaneously to the children as they work and play; they may also hum along.

16. Songs with half-steps in the melody line, unusually large intervals between tones, or a broad range should be avoided because they are often too difficult for very young children to learn.

17. Whenever simple actions, motions, or dramatizations are appropriate, incorporate them into the singing time.

18. Sing confidently, and do not apologize for your singing.

19. When involved in a singing time, you may invite the children to sing along; usually you need only begin to sing and they will join in. Beware of asking, "Do you want to sing this song?" unless you are prepared to accept a negative answer.

20. Sing songs about familiar things or feelings.

21. Make a tape recording or CD of favorite classroom songs, and add new favorites to it. Encourage parents or children to take it home for listening and singing along.

Variety in Singing

Routine approaches or techniques in any curriculum area tend to become boring to children. Thus, we need to focus on ways to add variety to singing songs.

Ways to Add Variety in Singing

1. Use visual aids (such as overhead transparencies, movie boxes, charts, posters, or chalk talk) to help teach a song. The children will also enjoy assisting with the visual aids. Puppets (finger, sack, stick, or commercial) add friendly interest. Stories that tell the content of the song can be used. As you tell stories about animals, places, or things, sing songs about them also.

2. Make up guessing games to utilize variety in songs. Say, "I'm thinking of a song that tells me to put my finger in different places" ("Put Your Finger in the Air"). Or start the singing time with a question that will arouse interest and gain attention (see item 12).

3. Put the names of songs on the backs of objects or pictures pinned to a chart or bulletin board, or put the names of songs in a sack or box. The children select the object from the chart or the paper from the box to determine the songs to be sung. Also, many songs that utilize action words such as skipping, painting, and so on, can be depicted in pictures.

4. Have children sing songs, or parts of songs, as a solo, duet, or trio.

5. Where accompanying chants are appropriate, have some of the children chant and others sing the song. For example, in the familiar folk song "I've Been Working on the Railroad," some of the children chant "choo, choo, choo, choo." In the familiar folk song "Little White Duck," have some of the children accompany

with "quack, quack, quack." In "Hush, Little Baby," have the accompaniment of "hush, hush."

6. Use sounds or instruments as accompaniment. Some of the children accompany while others sing.

7. Sing a song and pause while the children sing the end of the line, the next phrase, or the end of the sentence; the children fill in the words.

8. Write the words of a song on the chalkboard or a chart. Erase or cover words or phrases as the children are learning the song.

9. Have children pantomime a song for the rest of the group. Follow up with singing the song.

10. Have the children add new words to a familiar song in order to make or weave nonsense into them. For example, when singing "London Bridge," change "Build it up with iron bars" to "Build it up with bacon and eggs" or "Build it up with cats and dogs." In the song "Mary Had a Little Lamb," ask what silly thing Mary might have instead of a lamb (a centipede, for example).

11. Use pitch-level conducting in teaching a song. In other words, use your arm and hand to show the changes in pitch level.

12. Before you sing or play a new song, create a listening experience by asking the children the following kinds of questions:
    a. Who? ("Listen to this song and tell me *who* it is about.")
    b. Where? ("Listen to this song and tell me *where* the animal is going.")
    c. What? ("Listen to this song that I am going to sing for you and tell me *what* new word you hear" or "*What* words rhyme?" or "*What* parts of the melody or tune are alike?" or "*What* words are repeated?")
    d. How? ("Listen to this song ['Michael Finnegan,' a familiar folk song] and tell me *how* Michael Finnegan's whiskers got in again.")
    e. Why? ("*Why* did Jack and Jill go up the hill?")

13. Incorporate a variety of other teaching methods, such as role playing or dramatizing a song.

14. Hum the song or parts of it.

15. Sing a song from a record or a tape by a children's recording artist such as Ella Jenkins, Joe Wayman, Raffi, Miss Jackie, Hap Palmer, Steve Millang, Pete Seeger or Greg Scelsa. Discover your favorites at educational toy stores or at your library, where they can be checked out. Include them in your classroom for easy sing-alongs.

16. Teachers can use song picture books such as *The Lady with the Alligator Purse* (Westcott, 1990), *I Know an Old Lady* (Karas, 1995), *Six Little Ducks* (Conover, 1976), *The Itsy Bitsy Spider* (Trapani, 1993b), *I'm a Little Teapot* (Trapani, 1993a), and *Five Little Monkeys Jumping on the Bed* (Christelow, 1989) to link songs to literacy. The song can be sung, the book read, and then a variety of activities in other curriculum areas planned to extend the learning (Barclay & Walwer, 1992). Song picture books facilitate literacy growth in young children and contribute to aesthetic development in music, art, literature, and creative writing (Jalongo & Ribblett, 1997). Barclay (2010) suggests three steps to assist teachers in using song picture books to support early language and literacy development: Learn the song, link the song to print, then extend the song.

17. See Figure 13.1 for a web for one of the song picture books called *The Wheels on the Bus* (a variety of authors and illustrators have done this song in picture book form). For complete references for the titles given here, see the Suggested Resources at the end of the chapter.

Specific Kinds of Songs

Literally, thousands of excellent songs can be selected for teaching young children. Some of the categories of songs from which teachers should surely make some selections are discussed here. There are songs to teach almost every one of the concepts discussed in this book. A teacher who desires a song about a specific concept for which a song cannot be found should write new words about the concept to a familiar tune or make up both the words and melody for a new song. The following categories of songs are valuable in teaching young children.

EXPANDABLE SONGS. Expandable songs offer opportunities for children to help to create the songs, thus creating feelings of pride, confidence and accomplishment (Ringgenberg, 2003). Because songs are language, they can be used to study parts of speech as one particular part of the song is "expanded" or changed each time it is sung. For example, change the nouns in a song, or change the verbs or "doing" parts of a song. For instance, the familiar folk song "If You're Happy and You Know It" becomes an expandable song as children add their own phrases: "If you're happy and you know it (blink your eyes)." Another way of changing this song is to change the word *happy* to different moods or emotions, such as "If you're mad and you know it, take a walk."

FIGURE 13.1 Web for *The Wheels on the Bus*

Suggestions for Songs that Contain Expandable Phrases and Words

"Mary Wore a Red Dress"
"Look Around the Room"
"I See a Boy"
"Sing with Me"
"My Little Soul's Gonna Shine"
"Over in the Meadow"
"Bumble Bee"
"The Wheels on the Bus"
"Come On and Join into the Game"
"Put Your Finger in the Air"
"Rig-a-Jig Jig"
"Johnny Works"
"Blue, Blue"

I Went to Visit a Friend

(To the tune of "Oats, Peas, Beans, and Barley Grow")
  Underlined words and phrases are those that can be changed by the children.

I went to visit a friend one day,
She only lived across the way.
She said she couldn't come out to play,
Because it was her <u>cleaning day</u>.
This is the way <u>she cleans</u> away,
This is the way <u>she cleans</u> away,
This is the way <u>she cleans</u> away,
Because it was her <u>cleaning day</u>.

To the tune of "Mary Had a Little Lamb," sing the following:
Pass a napkin to your friend, to your friend, to your friend.
Pass a napkin to your friend. Now take one yourself.

or

It's time for us to go outside, go outside, go outside.
It's time for us to go outside, for soon we're going home.

or

Jimmy has some jingle bells, jingle bells, jingle bells.
Jimmy has some jingle bells, that he plays for us.

or

Martha brought a pair of skates, pair of skates, pair of skates.
Martha brought a pair of skates to our sharing time.

or

Eric has a shape that's blue, shape that's blue, shape that's blue.
Eric has a shape that's blue. What shape and color can you find?

or

Now it is cleanup time, cleanup time, cleanup time.
Now it is cleanup time, I will need your help.

To the tune of "Lazy Mary" (also "Here We Go 'Round the Mulberry Bush'"), sing the following:

What is the color of the shoes, of the shoes, of the shoes?
What is the color of the shoes you're wearing on your feet?

or

Stand up if you are wearing red, wearing red, wearing red.
Stand up if you are wearing red, and show us what to do.

or

This is the way I nod my head, nod my head, nod my head.

This is the way I nod my head; you can join me too.

or

We are getting ready, ready, ready.
We are getting ready, to go outside and play.

or

Jimmy and Susie, you can go out, you can go out, you can go out.
Jimmy and Susie, you can go out; Bobby, you can go too.

or

We are working stirring the batter, stirring the batter, stirring the batter.
We are working stirring the batter, soon our cake will be done.

Many of the songs that you already know and sing are expandable. They provide a valuable exercise in creative thinking and problem solving as children create their own words and phrases.

NURSERY RHYMES. Preschool and kindergarten children delight in singing nursery rhyme songs. The simple melodies and short verses (most of them four-line songs) make them very appropriate for young children. The familiar, simple, catchy tunes also make them easily adapted to new words. These suggestions should only serve to stimulate your own imagination. Think of additional possibilities for other nursery rhymes. Some favorite nursery rhymes follow:

"Twinkle, Twinkle, Little Star"
"Old MacDonald"
"Sing a Song of Sixpence"
"Hickory, Dickory, Dock"
"Baa, Baa, Black Sheep"
"Jack and Jill"
"Peter, Peter, Pumpkin Eater"
"The Muffin Man"
"Three Blind Mice"

OLD TRADITIONAL AND FOLK SONGS. Children's musical heritage surely must include many of the songs that have been sung by children for centuries. A majority of children's songs are traditional or folk songs from around the world. Folk and traditional songs are an important part of our heritage and provide generational ties and appreciation.

Some Favorite Traditional and Folk Songs

"This Old Man"
"Pop Goes the Weasel"
"Eensy-Weensy Spider"
"Where Is Thumbkin?"
"Rig-a-Jig Jig"
"If You're Happy"
"Little Peter Rabbit"
"My Pigeon House"
"I'm a Little Teapot"
"Yankee Doodle"
"B-I-N-G-O"
"Six Little Ducks"
"Michael Finnegan"
"The Noble Duke of York"
"The Bear Went Over the Mountain"

LULLABIES. The main purpose of lullabies is to help young children relax, settle down, go to sleep. It does not matter in what language the lullabies are sung, the soothing, gentle, repetitive melodies all have the same calming results. Often, these lullabies produce the same feelings in the person singing them (Honig, 2005)! Have preschool and kindergarten children pretend that they have a baby that they are trying to get to sleep. They may rock it in their arms or pretend to rock it in a cradle. The following lullabies are suggested:

"Hush, Little Baby"
"Brahms' Lullaby"
"Rock-a-Bye Baby"
"All Through the Night"
"Kum Ba Yah" (African folk song)

BALLADS OR STORY SONGS. These traditional songs have been handed down from generation to generation and enjoyed by many. Children love them because of the stories that they tell. After a ballad was sung to a group of children, Rachel immediately said, "Oh, sing me that story again!" The following will be enjoyed by the children time and time again:

"Hush, Little Baby"
"I've Been Working on the Railroad"
"Frog Went a-Courting"
"I Know an Old Lady Who Swallowed a Fly"

Haines and Gerber (1999) suggest an approach that they call "add-a-song": Children role play or dramatize favorite fairy tales or nursery rhymes, then add a song with simple words and possibly a tune that is familiar such as a nursery rhyme, and repeat them when certain actions occur or recur in the story line. This approach combines music, listening, and storytelling and adds a new dimension to storytelling.

ROUNDS. Even preschool children enjoy singing simple rounds, and they like to hear different words sung at the same time. However, when using rounds in early childhood, it is important to have an adult leader for each group. For younger children, usually two groups are adequate, even though some songs have more parts to them. One of the simplest ways to sing a round with the very young is to combine two songs with different tunes: Have one group sing one song while the other group sings another song. Examples of such combinations include "Three Blind Mice" with "Row, Row, Row Your Boat" and "Are You Sleeping?" or "The Farmer in the Dell" with "Skip to My Lou." You can also have the children sing rounds by combining two or more songs that have the same melodies:

"Twinkle, Twinkle, Little Star" with "Baa, Baa, Black Sheep" or "The ABC Song"
"The Farmer in the Dell" with "A-Hunting We Will Go" or "I Put My Right Foot In"
"Frère Jacques" with "Are You Sleeping?" or "Where Is Thumbkin?"
"The Mulberry Bush" with "Lazy Mary" or "The Wheels on the Bus"
"The Bear Went Over the Mountain" with "My Thumbs Are Starting to Wiggle"

When teaching rounds sung in the traditional way, make sure that the children know the song well before trying it as a round and remember to have a leader for each group. Some rounds that can be sung in parts and are simple enough for children in the early childhood years include the following:

"Frère Jacques" or "Are You Sleeping?"
"Row, Row, Row Your Boat"
"Sweetly Sings the Donkey"
"Kookaburra"

WRITING AND CREATING SONGS. New words can be written to familiar old tunes or melodies. Children also enjoy learning new words to the familiar melodies of television commercials. Children and teachers can also enjoy writing new words to new tunes. It is amazing how easy it is to create original words and a simple, original melody to go with them. Just be sure to record or write the words and melody, because they are often difficult to remember until they become familiar. Choose a topic, and then begin brainstorming short phrases about that topic. A small group of children could work cooperatively on an appropriate melody for these short phrases. The entire group could work on the words and then in small groups, each group being responsible for one or two lines; then the melody could be developed and finally recorded.

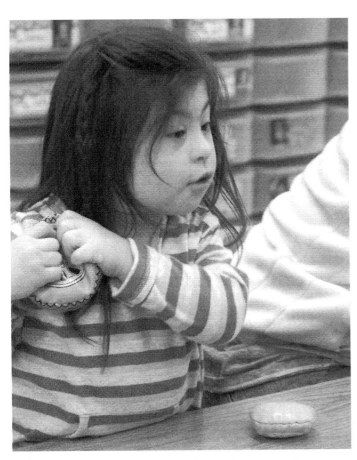

"Passing the Bean Bag" increases ability to follow directions and interact with a group in an enjoyable music activity.

A simple way of creating songs is to work with **scale songs.** The melody is the scale, beginning at middle C or lower and then climbing to upper C (or to the note on which you began). Then go back down the scale. For each scale song, you will need a sentence or phrase with eight syllables to go up the scale, and then a sentence or phrase with eight syllables to go down the scale. For example, the following words could be sung up and down the scale:

Mr. Jones, the carpenter, came.

He showed us how to build a frame.

Musical Games

Young children enjoy the involvement that comes with musical games. Some are simple enough that the children need only follow along and do as the words tell them. However, others need careful instruction, and it may be wise to role-play or go through these games before combining music and game. Also, the musical background can be provided in a number of ways. For familiar songs, the children can sing as the game is played. Sometimes a piano or other musical instrument is available for accompaniment. Many of these musical games are also on CDs.

RHYTHM ACTIVITIES

In many ways, each musical experience that a child has will be a rhythm experience, because children begin to feel the rhythm pattern of music very early. Even infants begin to sense the beat, or rhythm, of musical selections. By age 3, children will repeat musical patterns, and by 5, they are able to demonstrate a steady beat. However, it is common to find a young child who has difficulty in sensing the rhythm pattern of music, or a child might have a keen sense of rhythm and still not be able to carry a tune. These children should not be singled out and embarrassed, which will take away their enjoyment of the music. Children's first experiences in finding or experimenting with rhythm patterns will probably be with clapping or other spontaneous body movements and then playing the beat on an object (with a spoon on a pan or hand on a drum).

Initially, some children may simply enjoy the experience of hand clapping or playing the instrument and may not be aware of the rhythm. The teacher's role in these early rhythmic experiences should be to encourage sound and rhythm exploration and participation, not to mandate repetition. During rhythm experiences, the teacher can pat the beat on the child's knees. Being able to keep time to music develops gradually, and there is much individual variation among children.

Early exposures to rhythm should involve simple and definite sounds, with even or steady rhythm patterns. A good beginning to rhythm activities is the exploration of sounds in the environment, not necessarily actual musical sounds. For example, encourage the children to listen for sounds that have definite beat patterns, such as a clock ticking, a water faucet dripping, or a jackhammer drilling. Then encourage them to listen to the sounds twice and try to reproduce them by clapping hands or tapping feet. Another possibility is to listen to the sound of different rhythmic vocal sounds. Select a particular vowel or consonant sound and sing it to a familiar melody. Other vocal sounds that can be set to rhythm patterns include buzzing, laughing (ha-ha-ha or ho-ho-ho), hissing, and chanting. Games can be made out of this kind of rhythm experience. In one game, the children sit in a circle, and as a beanbag or ball is thrown to a child, that child creates a vocal rhythm pattern and then tosses the beanbag or ball to another child. The second child must repeat the same rhythm pattern. Then the beanbag or ball is tossed to others, and they must come up with new patterns.

Chants can also be used for early rhythm exploration. Four- or five-word sentences can be made into chants and different rhythm patterns clapped or beaten out as the children repeat the sentences. For example, the sentence "You can't catch me!" can have a variety of patterns. Emphasis may be put on the first, second, third, or fourth words (*You* can't catch me; You *can't* catch me; You can't *catch* me; You can't catch *me*). Chants can be altered in other ways: they can be soft or loud, fast or slow, steady or wavering. Chants adapted from rhymes, stories, or fingerplays can be developed for children's actions, including jump-rope chants. If young children are not familiar with the chants, invite a person into the classroom to teach some of them to the children. After they listen, they can play the rhythm patterns of these chants on rhythm instruments or use "body instruments" such as hand clapping.

Children can pretend to do some of the following activities and develop a rhythm pattern by clapping or beating the rhythm pattern of each sound: chair rocking, clock ticking, washing machine agitator turning, water dripping, knocking on a door, hammering a nail, sawing a log or piece of wood, sweeping the floor, or shining a window.

Many excellent tapes and CDs can give children experience in rhythm exploration. Some can be used for basic introduction to rhythm, and others are used for more advanced explorations (see the Suggested Resources at the end of this chapter).

---

clicking tongue   gasping
blinking eyes   sh-h-h-h (gentle, or explosive
                              and loud)

In addition, the children could take just one part of the body, such as the hands, elbows, or feet, and discover ways of using that body part to beat rhythm. For example, the hands could be used to clap, tap on the floor, or tap some part of the body such as the chest or back. The tapping could also alternate from head to floor or from shoulder to knees.

Rhythm Instruments

Give children frequent experiences using rhythm instruments. Many early childhood teachers do not like to use them because the children become difficult to control when the instruments are brought out for use. If these instruments are seldom used, the children may become too excited about them. Lack of variation in presentation and direction also encourages lack of control. When introducing an instrument, make sure to use its proper name and give the children ample opportunity to become familiar with it. Freedom to explore instruments should be provided in various ways, not always in a rhythm band marching around in a circle and following a leader. The teacher might even allow exploration during free play.

Children's first experience with rhythm will probably be with clapping hands or spontaneous body movements.

Body Instruments

Clapping is probably the most commonly used body rhythm instrument, and we have cited it often. However, other body instruments can be used in rhythm activities:

whistling	speaking
humming	thigh slapping (patting)
hissing	head tapping, head nodding
snapping fingers	stamping feet

Instruments can be purchased, collected, or made by the teacher or children. They can be as easy as collecting dried gourds or seed pods. Usually, school budgets determine the kinds and amounts of rhythm instruments purchased. With handmade instruments, it is usually possible to have greater numbers of the same kinds. The following is a discussion of many rhythm instruments that can be obtained in a variety of ways.

BELLS.   Bells and jingles can be made simply by lacing bells on a cord and tying the ends of the cord together. Another method is to sew bells onto a mitten or glue them across the top of a wide elastic band. You can also drill holes in bottle caps, string them on a cord, and then tie the ends of the cord together.

CLAPPERS.   The effect of castanets can be obtained by selecting a stiff piece of cardboard approximately the size of a matchbook (an empty matchbook could be used). Fold the cardboard piece in the middle, just as a matchbook is folded. Tape or glue a bottle cap on each inside end, but do not put the tape over the outside of the caps. The clapper is held between the thumb and the index and middle fingers and then is secured in this position with a rubber band. As the fingers and thumb are brought together, the bottle caps should strike each other, making the sound of castanets (see Figure 13.2).

CORRUGATED CARDBOARD WASHBOARD.   Pieces of heavy corrugated cardboard (or lighter pieces pasted on heavy cardboard or wood) are strummed with a spoon, dowel, or nail for a washboard sound effect.

CYMBALS.   Kettle lids or other lids with knobs attached can serve as cymbals. (Small pieces of wood screwed onto the lid will also serve as knobs.)

DRUMS.   Use coffee cans, or obtain large metal cans from the cafeteria. On the open end, stretch inner-tube rubber, chamois, Naugahyde, or similar material as tightly as possible and secure it with wire or cord. When making a drum, the tighter the ends, the sharper the sound. Wiring is recommended over lacing, because

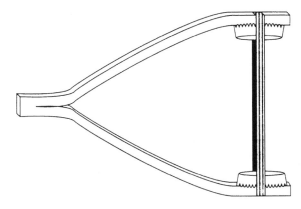

FIGURE 13.2 Clapper

lacing does not seem to be tight enough and the lacing holes may tear easily. A drumstick can be made out of a dowel or stick. Secure a piece of fabric-covered foam rubber to one end. Decorate the drum by dipping magazine scraps and pieces of tissue paper into liquid starch and then placing them on the sides of the can.

Drums can also be made out of oatmeal or hat boxes, nail kegs, or large barrels; or two different-sized cans may be tied together to make bongo drums. Drumsticks can be improvised from a dowel, spoon, eraser end of a new pencil, wire brush, rubber spatula, drawer-pull nailed to a dowel, or dowel inserted in a Styrofoam ball.

GONGS.   The sound of a gong can be obtained by setting a steel or brass hubcap on a block of wood to strike it or by drilling a hole in the hubcap and attaching a wire or rope as a handle. The sound will differ according to where the gong is struck and what is used to strike it. Possible strikers include a dowel, stick, spoon, or nail.

HUMMERS.   Obtain cardboard tubes from the inside of paper rolls (waxed paper, paper towels, toilet paper, etc.). On one end of the tube, punch a hole, using a paper punch and punching down as far as possible. Cover that same end of the tube with either waxed paper or aluminum foil (about a 3-inch square is adequate for each hummer). Secure this covering with a rubber band, but make sure that the punched hole is not covered. The tube can be decorated in any desired way. The children put their mouths up to the open ends of the tubes to blow and hum at the same time.

JINGLE CLOGS.   These instruments can be made by flattening bottle caps and then making a hole in the middle of each bottle cap with a nail. (This hole should be larger than the nail used to attach the tops to the dowel so that the tops can jingle.) Loosely nail the bottle caps to the ends of a 4- to 6-inch dowel. Bells may be used in place of bottle caps. Decorate them. Small wooden wheels, buttons, or metal washers could be used in place of bottle caps. Also, a nail could be pounded in one end of a piece of wood, bells joined loosely on a string, and the string tied to the nail (see Figure 13.3).

HOLLOW CLAPPERS.   Two same-sized paper cups are provided for each child. They may be decorated. Play them by bringing together either of the two ends or alternating them—the larger ends together, then the smaller ends together. When using a coconut, cut it in half, hollow out the meat, and then strike the cut ends of the halves together.

PLUCKED INSTRUMENTS.   Drill a hole through the bottom of an old washtub. Fasten a screw eye or a large bolt through the hole. Secure a heavy wire to the bolt; attach the other end of the wire to the top of a broomstick or long dowel. Secure the lower end of the stick or

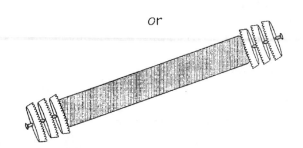

FIGURE 13.3   Jingle Clogs

FIGURE 13.5   Shakers

dowel in the bottom of the washtub by drilling a hole in the tub. Play it by plucking the wire; obtain pitch variations by tightening the wire by pulling on the broomstick. Make a rubber-band banjo by obtaining a sturdy open box and stretching a few rubber bands of different sizes, spaced widely, around it. Place the box on a wooden table for more resonant tones.

RHYTHM STICKS.   Cut dowels of any width into lengths of 8 to 12 inches. Cut them all the same length and make enough to provide the children with two each. These sticks can be struck together or tapped on an aluminum pie plate, a steel bowl, or the floor. One stick could be serrated so that a different sound would be made by rubbing the smooth stick over the serrated one (see Figure 13.4).

SHAKERS.   Dried seed pods or gourds often make the sound of maracas or shakers. Empty containers such as gourds, metal cans, or film containers; small boxes or cartons such as gelatin boxes, cottage cheese cartons, or half-pint milk cartons; paper plates stapled together; baby food jars; plastic bottles; or empty bandage boxes can be partially filled with sand, rice, dry beans, maca-

roni, pebbles, shells, paper clips, or similar items. Use small amounts of these items. The shakers can be decorated (see Figure 13.5).

TAMBOURINES.   Tambourines can be made using either two lightweight paper plates with the rims attached together or one heavy paper plate. Attach bells or bottle caps to the edges. Aluminum pie plates also work well.

CHIMES.   A chime can be made by obtaining a 3- to 5-inch length of metal pipe and a piece of heavy string 10 to 15 inches long. Run the string through the pipe and tie the ends of the string together. The children hold the string and strike the suspended pipe with a nail or other metal implement. Nails also make good instruments, producing the sounds of chime bands or triangles. Purchase one nail 5 inches in length or longer for each child in the class (a variety of lengths or the same length may be used). In addition, purchase a striker nail approximately 4 inches in length for each child. To the head of the longer nail, tie a string to be used as a handle for the nail. A horseshoe suspended by a string, with a nail for a striker, can also be used (see Figure 13.6).

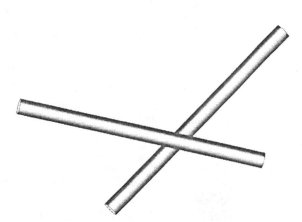

FIGURE 13.4   Rhythm Sticks

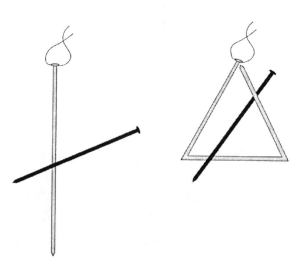

FIGURE 13.6   Chimes

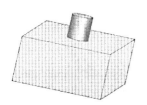
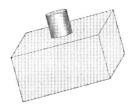

FIGURE 13.7   Wooden Blocks

TUNED GLASSES OR BOTTLES.   Fill glasses, soda bottles, or other glass bottles with water to different levels. If the water levels are properly varied, the tones achieved will represent a scale. Tap the bottles lightly with a spoon to produce the sound. (Cover these bottles so the measured water will not evaporate as readily.)

TUNING FORK.   A tuning fork, which can be obtained commercially, will vibrate and produce a certain tone, depending on the size of the fork.

WOODEN BLOCKS.   Wooden blocks are made of hardwood and provided in pairs. They can be cut into any shape, including geometric shapes, and sanded. Handles of spools, knobs, or wooden pieces can be bolted or screwed on. For variations, materials such as corrugated cardboard, sandpaper, or foam rubber could be thumb tacked on or attached to create different sounds (see Figure 13.7).

XYLOPHONE.   Obtain electrical conduit pipe from a hardware store. It should be cut into the following lengths, but the cutting must be exact. Therefore, it is best to use a power saw. (If the hardware store has a power saw, have the pipes cut there.)

middle C	$12\frac{1}{2}$ in.	G	10 in.
D	$11\frac{3}{4}$ in.	A	$9\frac{1}{2}$ in.
E	11 in.	B^{b}	$9\frac{3}{8}$ in.
F	$10\frac{3}{4}$ in.	B	9 in.
F$^{\#}$	$10\frac{1}{2}$ in.	C	$8\frac{3}{4}$ in.

Make a wooden xylophone using balsa wood $1\frac{1}{2}$ inches wide in the following lengths:

middle C	9 in.	G	7 in.
D	$8\frac{1}{2}$ in.	A	$6\frac{1}{2}$ in.
E	8 in.	B^{b}	6 in.
F	$7\frac{5}{8}$ in.	B	$5\frac{1}{2}$ in.
F$^{\#}$	$7\frac{9}{8}$ in.	C	5 in.

Other Rhythm Instruments

1. Hair-comb harmonicas or kazoos (waxed paper over the edge of a comb)
2. Pots and pans
3. Pages of a book ("strummed")
4. Wooden rungs of chair
5. Vegetable grater

Specific Activities with Rhythm

There are many delightful ways of using rhythm activities in the classroom. The teacher should incorporate rhythm activities into the music curriculum, as well as into other parts of the curriculum.

Rhythm Activities

1. Have the children use body instruments or rhythm instruments to beat the rhythm of nursery rhymes, poems, names, colors, places, or songs. Alternatively, rhythm patterns can be suggested by using marks on the chalkboard or felt pieces on the flannel board. The following patterns could be put on the chalkboard and the children asked to clap them:

    // //
    /// ///
    /// // /// //

    More difficult patterns can be given as children's experience increases. Tell the children that you are clapping the name of a child, and have them stand if they think their name is being clapped. For example, the pattern for Allison McKean would be /// //. You could combine names such as Brandon and Marilyn as // / ///. As the children grow in experience, substitute note patterns for the marks or felt pieces. For example, Mary Lou Smith might be (♫♩); Phillip White might be (♫♩). The children will learn that the pause indicates the separation between words. Also, make guessing games by using the rhythm patterns of songs, familiar poems, nursery rhymes, animals, and other categories.

2. Give each child one rhythm stick or dowel. On the verse of the song, use locomotor movements to move around or over the dowel. On the chorus, the dowel is picked up and the rhythm tapped out on the floor. For example, on the first verse of the song "Rig-a-Jig Jig," the children find some way of walking around or over the dowel (backward, sideways, forward, or other), and on the chorus the children pick up the dowel and tap the rhythm. On the second verse, the children might hop as they sing, instead of walking; thus they must find a way of hopping around or over the dowel. Songs can either be sung by the children or played on tapes or CDs. Directions could be given to find a way to go *around* the dowel on the first verse and *over* the dowel on the second verse. On the third verse, encourage the

children to find a different way of moving, but always on the chorus they pick up the dowel and tap out the rhythm.

3. Have the children pretend to be conductors, inventing their own arm and hand movements. They could use a dowel for a baton.

4. As the children are given an instrument, they can be encouraged to find two different ways of playing it or holding it.

5. As an accompaniment to the children's singing of or a recording of "Horsey, Horsey," provide each child with a pair of paper cups. As they play or beat the rhythm of the song, first striking the tops and then the bottoms of the paper cups together, the sound will resemble the "clip-clop" of horses' hooves.

6. Accompaniments for stories, songs, poems, and nursery rhymes can be devised. For example, drums of three different sizes could be used to tell the story of "The Three Bears." The larger, deeper-sounding drum would be the papa bear; the middle-sized drum, the mama bear; and the smallest drum, the baby bear. As an alternative, on a 4-line song, one instrument (such as a triangle) could play the first line, wooden tone blocks could play the second line, the maracas could play the third line, and all could join in for the last line. For a nursery rhyme such as "Hickory, Dickory, Dock," some of the children could pretend to be the pendulum on a grandfather clock and "tick-tock" back and forth to the rhythm of the rhyme or song. On the first line, tapping instruments (such as wooden blocks or triangles) could

"tick-tock"; on the second line, when the mouse runs up the clock, the xylophone could be played up the scale; on the third line, when the clock strikes one, the cymbal or gong could strike; also on the third line, when the mouse runs down, the xylophone could play down the scale; and on the last line, the tapping instruments could again "tick-tock."

CREATIVE OR EXPRESSIVE MOVEMENTS

"Creative movement is an art form whose medium is the human body in motion" (Dow, 2010, p. 30). Through dancing and creative movements, children are able to respond to music, express ideas, and convey feelings (Dodge et al., 2002; Edwards et al., 2008). This creates an atmosphere that supports individuality, divergent thinking, and positive feelings in all areas of the curriculum. Movement activities build a classroom environment of trust that encourages everyone to interact, think, and learn within and without the walls of the classroom (Vagovic, 2008).

To add movement to your curriculum, you need just willingness and imagination. To the young child, music and movement are often one and the same. Movement to music gives children another way to explore music. Whenever possible, involve some kind of finger, hand, or body movement or rhythm with songs.

Dow (2010) suggests the benefits of creative movement include:

- Access for all children
- Accommodating children with special needs

NATIONAL STANDARDS FOR DANCE EDUCATION K–4

Content Standard	Sample Activities
1. Identifying and demonstrating movement elements and skills in performing dance.	Responding by walking, running, sliding, hopping; moving in various directions.
2. Understanding the choreographic principles, processes, and structures	Responding creatively with individual movements, ideas, and feelings.
3. Understanding dance as a way to celebrate and communicate meaning.	Discuss the ways dance is different from sports, talking, and sleeping.
4. Applying and demonstrating critical and creative thinking skills in dance.	Watch two separate dances, then compare how they are the same and how they are different.
5. Demonstrating and understanding dance in various cultures and historical periods.	Observe and learn dances from various cultures or historical periods.
6. Making connections between dance and healthful living.	Learning that dance and movement help us to *stay* healthy, and that we enjoy them more when we *are* healthy.
7. Making connections between dance and other disciplines.	Learning dance steps and movements involves counting. Specific dance instructions help us learn such concepts as shape, size, and color.

Source: Reprinted by permission of the National Dance Association (of the American Alliance for Health, Physical Education Recreation & Dance). The complete *National Standards for Dance Education and Opportunity-to-Learn Standards in Dance Education* (1996) may be purchased from: National Dance Association, 1900 Association Drive, Reston, VA 20191-1599; nda@aahperd.org or phone 1-800-231-7193.

Note: *The Sample Activities are the authors' ideas.*

Music, in its many forms and variations, is a universal language and should be part of the daily curriculum.

- Curriculum enrichment
- Physical development
- Movement as an antidote to obesity
- Social and emotional development
- Creativity
- Brain development

Movement and dance are children's play and they naturally respond to music by moving (Edwards et al., 2008). Even adults often nod heads, tap feet, and move bodies to the rhythm and sounds of music. Teachers need not try to "teach" children creative movements, but rather help them to discover and release the creative movements that already exist. Creative movement to music enhances children's physical health and development, balance and coordination, rhythm and beat, ability to predict what happens next, self-esteem, and body awareness. "Movement to music provides children with opportunities to occupy their own kinesphere, to express the qualities of the music, to respond to rhythm and melody, and to interact musically with other children" (Neely, 2001, p. 37).

Creative movements require limitations and rules that must be explained carefully to the children. When and if they break a rule, they need to be reminded that if they choose to participate they must abide by the rules; if they cannot abide by the rules, they must be watchers. One basic rule of any movement experience is that children must move in their own space and not touch others. This rule helps children to become responsible for their own behavior. Another basic rule is to stop when the signal is given (music stops, hands clap, whistle blows). You may need additional rules, depending on your space, materials, and the children that you are working with.

Guidelines for Effective Creative Movements

1. Children need as much space as possible; therefore, if a game room, gymnasium, or similar space is available, use it. If you must stay in the classroom, move furniture aside to give adequate space. If you are planning the experience for outside, provide some limitations as to space.

2. Children's inhibitions can be avoided more easily if the teacher is not inhibited and is an active participant. Do not press a child to join the group; sometimes shy children need to observe several times before joining. This is one of the values of having movement activities during free play. Inhibitions may begin with too much adult interference or with negative comments from either children or adults. Build confidence and give individual praise, especially to children who show some signs of hesitation.

3. Do not set up yourself or any child as a model to be copied by others. Respect individual differences and abilities. Do not make comparisons among children. In creative movements, the idea is to develop individuality of expression.

4. Do not use music as the only stimulus for creative movements. Sometimes no music at all is appropriate. Perhaps a story or poem will give a suggestion for creative movements, and sound effects made by the children could serve as the background for these movements.

5. As children become involved in movement explorations, try to redirect, challenge, and stimulate their discoveries by suggestions such as "Do what you are doing now in a slower way," or "Try moving in a different direction or at a different level," or "Try the same thing you were doing, but make it smoother or lighter." Verbalize or describe to the child what she or he is doing.

6. Avoid trite phrases such as "light as a feather." Instead, use phrases such as "Move as if you were a feather," "as if snow were hitting your nose," or "as if you were a butterfly landing on a flower." Children will make their own suggestions.

Movement Interpretations

Movement explorations, creative movement, and dance experiences can be used to interpret nearly every experience, thing, or phenomenon. Dance movements blend three basic qualities: time, space, and force. **Time** refers to tempo (fast, slow) and rhythm (from music or dance). **Space** refers to the movement area: personal—own exclusive area, or general—everywhere else. **Force** refers to pushing, pulling, balancing, heaviness, or lightness involved in the dancing and movements (Edwards, 2009). Dance and movement can be integrated throughout the early childhood curriculum. (See the music sections in the unit ideas in various chapters.) For example, children can use their bodies to form the shape of alphabet letters as they are learning them.

Suggested Movement Interpretations

This list can be easily expanded.

1. Life cycle of the butterfly
   a. Caterpillar crawling
   b. Caterpillar eating milkweed
   c. Caterpillar hanging very still from a branch or twig
   d. Chrysalis hanging very still
   e. Butterfly emerging from the chrysalis
   f. Butterfly drying its wings
   g. Butterfly flying
2. Piece of cellophane or lightweight plastic
   a. Plastic crumpled in the teacher's hands without children seeing; children encouraged to guess what it might be, interpreting their guesses through movement
   b. Teacher's hands opened, with children watching plastic move, and then interpreting what they see through movement
3. Shaving cream
4. Airplane sequence
   a. Starting motor
   b. Taking off
   c. Flying
   d. Coming in
   e. Landing safely
5. Popcorn
   a. Butter melting
   b. Popping
6. Water
   a. Dripping
   b. Flooding
   c. Flowing in a fountain
   d. Freezing
   e. Melting
   f. Spilling
   g. Sprinkler

---

7. Laundry
   a. Inside a washing machine
   b. Inside a dryer
   c. Being scrubbed on a washboard
   d. Being pinned to a clothesline
   e. Drying in a breeze
8. Fishing
   a. Casting out
   b. Reeling in
   c. Pretending to be a fish
   d. Fly fishing
   e. Pretending to have a hooked line
   f. Frying and eating fish

These suggestions offer opportunities for sequences and a number of interpretations relating to a single idea. Also, many items, activities, and experiences allow for a single possible interpretation, such as "Move like a pair of scissors," "Show me how you would move if you were a needle on a sewing machine," or "Show me how your dog moves when you have just come home after being gone for a while and the dog is glad to see you." As teachers train themselves to become aware of movement opportunities, they will be amazed at the daily experiences that lend themselves to these kinds of activities. Movement ideas work well for transitions.

Although materials are not necessary for movement interpretations, they can add variety and stimulate more movement exploration.

Suggested Materials for Movement Exploration

1. Plastic or cellophane (with a rule that the plastic cannot be put up to the face)
2. Scarves, drapery materials, or pieces of lightweight fabric
3. Ribbons, pieces of string or yarn, strips of crepe or tissue paper
4. Hoops
   a. Placed on floor to determine space
   b. Children do movements inside the hoop or around the outside
   c. Used with a partner
   d. Children moving in and out of a hoop in different ways
5. Balloons
   a. Children throwing and catching them with music
   b. Children following movements
   c. Balloon let go and deflated, and then movements followed

6. Balls
   a. Many different kinds
   b. Different parts of body moved to represent a bouncing ball
   c. Comparison of movements of different kinds of balls (e.g., Ping-Pong, foam)
7. Ropes
8. Batons
9. Boxes
10. Rubber or elastic bands
11. Feathers
12. Crumpled paper
13. Tubes (from waxed paper or paper towel rolls, decorated as desired)
    a. Story told, with children allowed to respond, imitate, and move with tubes
    b. Many different kinds of objects created for interpretations: oar, ski pole, telescope, fishing pole
14. Parachute
    a. Children encouraged to move around the parachute, using locomotor movements or any kind of movement patterns
    b. Parachute moved up and then down, with children and adults gathered around; then movements interpreted without the parachute
    c. Ball placed on top of the parachute, with each person trying to prevent it from going out or off the parachute at a particular spot

Musical Dramatizations

Musical dramatizations also tie in closely with creative movements. Many stories have possibilities for excellent dramatization, or parts of stories can be dramatized as the children interpret some situation, action, or incident. Songs also have possibilities for musical dramatization, because they allow opportunities for children to interpret through body movements. Many music books for early childhood provide musical dramatizations and tell stories interspersed with music. Children also enjoy dramatizing poetry and nursery rhymes and often wish to repeat the same activity over and over again.

MUSICAL INSTRUMENTS

Whenever possible, children should be exposed to musical instruments. We have mentioned the use of rhythm instruments because children will enjoy playing them. However, if other musical instruments can be played by the children, their use is encouraged. A tuba was placed in one preschool classroom to be explored and tried out during free play. Although many of the children had difficulty getting enough wind into the tuba to produce sound, they enjoyed having an adult blow into it while they pushed the buttons to alter the sounds. Other kinds of instruments can be explored by the children, and including visitors in this objective broadens the many possibilities.

Teachers who possess skills playing a specific instrument can enrich children's experiences by using those skills often in the classroom. There are many instruments that a teacher can learn to play with relative ease: the ukulele, guitar, autoharp, resonator bells, song bells, recorder, or Orff instruments. In one preschool classroom, a grandfather who played the fiddle entertained the children with his music for 45 minutes. Another group of children were entertained when a visitor played a saw. Take the children on field trips to places having instruments and musicians: music stores, junior high school band period, high school orchestra period, a concert or concert rehearsal. A group of Head Start children visited a nearby high school during the orchestra period and listened to the orchestra practice for a performance. Then they were invited to wander among the musicians, who encouraged the children to touch and explore. The children could begin to classify or sort instruments into groups such as stringed, percussion, wood, and metal instruments, or even to organize them by size.

Pictures of individual musical instruments can also be displayed around the room. Young children can become familiar with musical symbols and notes through matching or lotto games. It is not intended that music theory be taught in early childhood, but rather that children be encouraged to become acquainted with related symbols and vocabulary. Music and stationery stores often carry stickers, posters, and other items with pictures of musical symbols or instruments, or they can be ordered online.

LISTENING AND DEVELOPMENT OF APPRECIATION FOR MUSIC

If music is made an important part of the curriculum, children should develop an appreciation for music and its many assets and should learn to listen carefully. In addition to the planned musical activities, it is hoped that teachers will see the value of music used spontaneously throughout the day and in different areas of the curriculum. Often, all that is needed is to provide a setting and materials and an encouraging comment. It is also hoped that throughout the day music will provide a background for play and activities; Music often has a calming influence on young children. However, music should often be really listened to, without distractions. Children should listen to others, to themselves, to live music, and to recorded music (including marches, polkas, and

Children should be exposed to a variety of musical instruments. Field trips and visitors can enrich music appreciation and exploration.

waltzes). They should eventually learn to listen to various elements of the music. Classical music can be included in various ways throughout the day. Children can be exposed to the masterpieces in all types of music performances directly through observation and listening experiences. (If you do not have them in your classroom or library, they can often be borrowed from the public library.) These masterpieces can provide a musical background for free play, art activities, science activities, or other desired projects. Children can listen to and learn to appreciate the music and dance of different cultures, which provides a link among people. All these associations with good music assist children in developing appreciation for music and movement.

> Music, a universal language, is a most important element of the early classroom curriculum.

Summary

Music should be developmentally appropriate and meet the needs of individual children. According to Gardner (1999b), music is one of the human intelligences, and recent research indicates that *all* people possess some degree of musical competence.

Performance should not be the focus in early childhood music; early experiences with music should be varied and should consist of both listening and active participation. Teachers also need to be active participants, whether they are skilled musicians or music novices.

Music can be the springboard for units and projects for study, or it can be integrated into every part of the curriculum. Music allows and encourages enjoyment, attentive listening, moving to the beat, pleasure, creative expression, emotional balance, positive self-concept, music appreciation, and development of musical-related skills (rhythm, meter, pitch, melody, tone).

The most important emphasis on music, however, should be enjoyment.

As teachers' own musical competencies and abilities increase, they become much more capable of providing the kinds of activities that result in the development of children's own musical competencies and abilities.

Although songs and singing are the most common experiences, there are many others: musical games, rhythm activities, fundamental locomotor movements, musical instruments, and the development of musical appreciation. Music engages children and fosters developmental growth in other areas such as socialization, emotional satisfaction, cognitive growth in language and math, and opportunity for physical activity and movement. It is an integral part of the early childhood curriculum and should be experienced by each child every day.

Student Learning Activities

1. Examine why music is an important part of the early childhood curriculum. How do you plan to implement it as a part of your curriculum? How could you improve your music skills? Are there particular areas that you could work on?

2. Begin a music file of songs that you plan to use in your curriculum. Include folk songs and rhymes for a variety of ages and from a variety of cultures.

3. Using at least one of the suggestions for providing variety in singing given in this chapter, teach a song to a group of children between 3 and 8 years of age.

4. Visit a preschool, kindergarten, or first-grade classroom and observe how music is included in the curriculum. Are music tools and instruments a part of the learning environment? Are appropriate tapes and/or CDs available and used? Does the teacher sing to and with the children? Did you see any musical games, rhythm activities, or creative movements being used with the children? Were rhythm instruments available? Were they teacher made or commercial?

5. Add to the list of suggested movement interpretations or creative movements given in this chapter. With a group of children, use one of the suggestions and evaluate your experience.

6. What songs do you remember from your childhood? How did you learn them? From whom? What feelings are stirred when you think about them? What does this tell us about the importance of music in the lives of young children?

Suggested Resources

TEACHER DEVELOPMENT, CHILDREN'S BOOKS, EARLY CHILDHOOD MUSIC, AND SONGBOOKS

Many excellent early childhood songbooks are no longer in print. However, they are often available and have good selections of songs. Consult libraries, bookstores, schools, the Internet, and other sources for out-of-print books and for those currently on the market.

CHILDREN'S BOOKS CITED

Christelow, E. (1989). *Five little monkeys jumping on the bed.* New York: Houghton Mifflin.

Conover, C. (1976). *Six little ducks.* New York: Crowell.

Karas, G. B. (1995). *I know an old lady.* New York: Scholastic.

Trapani, I. (1993a). *I'm a little teapot.* Boston: Whispering Coyote.

Trapani, I. (1993b). *The itsy bitsy spider.* Boston: Whispering Coyote.

Westcott, N. B. (1990). *The lady with the alligator purse.* New York: Little, Brown.

Online Resources

www.pbs.org/teachersource/arts_lit/k2-music.html   This site offers a variety of early childhood music lessons and activities from PBS matched to standards.

www.ecmma.org   This is the official site of a professional association for early childhood supporting music and movement.

www.theideabox.com/ib.php?web=ideasbytype&type=Music/Song   The Idea Box section provides lyrics to many early childhood songs.

www.nyphilkids.org/main.phtml   The New York Philharmonic kids site offers many great adventures in music for children including exploring instruments and instructions for making instruments.

www.nncc.org/Series/good.time.music.html   National Network for Child Care resource offered called "Good Times with Music and Rhythm" from Colorado State University Cooperative Extension.

www.nncc.org/Curriculum/cc21_music.movement.html   National Network for Child Care resource is offered here, called "Music and Movement Activities."

chapter 14
Creativity, Art, and Dramatic Activities

"Creativity is the ability to invent or make something new, using one's own skills without the specific use of patterns or models" (Mitchell, 2004, p. 46). This creativity develops as children daily participate in activities involving music, movement, dramatic play, and the visual arts (Mitchell, 2004). "Creative expression develops creative thinking" (de la Roche, 1996, p. 82). If presented properly, art offers great potential for developing the child's creativity, imagination, thinking, and emotions. "Play and the creative arts are the child's natural medium for self-expression; they allow trained adults to determine the nature and causes of behavior; they allow children to express thoughts and concerns for which they may not have words; and they allow for the cathartic release of feelings and frustrations" (Frost, 2005, p. 5).

Developmentally appropriate art for children is personal, spontaneous, inventive, imaginative, unique, therapeutic, and fun (Diffily & Morrison, 1996). "Art prompts students to empathize—to feel the experiences of others—and, perhaps most important, to understand themselves" (Zwirn & Graham, 2005, p. 273).

> Matthew, a preschool child, ran to the teacher excitedly one morning and announced: "Come over to the easel. I just painted a red bird with yellow eyes, and it looks like it is *really* flying!" As the teacher went to the easel, she beheld a red bird with yellow eyes that did indeed look as if it were really flying. The freeness of Matthew's painting created an impression of movement—a red bird with yellow eyes, in flight!

The main goal in creative art should be to communicate an idea, not to please the teacher. Children need art for art's sake, as well as for their understanding of their world; it also contributes to their intellectual development. Creative art activities enhance children's development in such areas as perception, cognition, fine motor skills, language, social interaction, problem solving, and mathematics (A. S. Epstein, 2001). Additionally, when original ideas with art are encouraged, children's motivation, confidence, and self-esteem are reinforced (de la Roche, 1996).

Because of the emphasis on testing in education, there seems to be little room or motivation to include the creative arts in the classroom curriculum (Zwirn & Graham, 2005). However, "In this era of performance standards and skill-based/outcome-based education, it is more important than ever for educators and families to articulate the values and support the creativity of play and exploration as ways to meet the standards—and to go beyond them" (Drew & Rankin, 2004, p. 44).

Art materials should be readily accessible to young children and carefully introduced to them. Markers, paste, playdough, crayons, and paints should be in a place where children have ready access to them, along with paper, cardboard, fabrics, and other supplies. Not only is it important to provide appropriate art materials and the opportunities to freely explore them, but we must also provide support and direction in skills and techniques for appropriate use of the materials. As children draw, they learn about

Creativity develops as children participate in music, movement, dramatic play, and the visual arts.

such art qualities and properties as color, line, shape or form, space, design, mass or volume, pattern, and texture; they also practice visual problem-solving skills.

As the young artist smears, brushes, dabs, and swirls paint or glue, we must remember that the efforts and process are more important than the product. Even though we often are unable to recognize and identify objects or symbolism in a child's particular drawing or painting, the progressive steps and understandings are valuable. Much of young children's art is personal, experimental, and not intended to look like something. As young children make attempts at representation of objects, remember in art there is no right or wrong (Edwards, 2009). The fact that children *do* draw, paint, and glue is far more important than *what* or *why* they do (Edwards, 2009). Appropriate comments, sincerely and carefully expressed, provide encouragement and support to young children in their art endeavors and explorations.

Art pieces do not always need to be discussed. Our responses to children regarding their artwork must be genuine and directly related to the product. This will increase the child's self-esteem, interest in painting, and possible incentive to continue personal expression

through art (Engel, 1996). Rinker (2000) reminds us that it is inappropriate to ask children in advance what they are going to create, to quiz them on the colors, to identify what it looks like, or to focus on neatness. Children should not be expected to "name" their drawings or explain why they drew what they did. However, they should be encouraged to put their names on their projects—because that is what artists do (Rinker, 2000). "Tell me about your picture" is an open-ended comment that encourages positive interaction with the child. Engel (1996) suggests six questions to consider that help us to look more carefully at a young child's art (p. 78):

1. What is it made of?
2. What does the observer see (lines, angles, colors, etc.)?
3. What does it represent?
4. How is it organized?
5. What is it about (humor, sadness, or experimentation)?
6. Where does the idea come from (a story, an outing, or imagination)?

ART AND CREATIVITY GOALS

"Thinking in art is the traditional approach to early childhood art: planning and doing art activities. Thinking about art, on the other hand, is art appreciation: reflecting on artists, artwork, and their meaning in our lives" (A. S. Epstein, 2001, p. 38). As with all areas of the curriculum, art needs to have purpose and meaning. Too often in early childhood education, art is added to the curriculum for fun and creativity only. For each art experience planned, teachers should reflect on the purpose and intent of the activity. How will the activity affect the students' learning and achievement? The National Art Education Association outlined the national standards for arts education, which are organized around content and achievement. Following are the content standards with some ideas of sample early childhood activities.

Value of Children's Artwork

Children's artwork has many benefits, and art is an important area of the curriculum. When art is integrated with other subjects in the curriculum, it encourages creative ways of understanding, thinking, and representing knowledge. However, the art curriculum and environment need to be assessed to determine if they are developmentally appropriate for young children. Developmentally appropriate art for young children enhances all areas of the curriculum; it provides children with opportunity to explore more deeply the content studied with a variety of art media. Inappropriate practice approaches art with little time, attention, or meaning.

THE NATIONAL VISUAL ARTS STANDARDS

Content Standard	Sample Activities
1. Understanding and applying media, techniques, and processes.	Using various paints (watercolors, markers, crayons, tempera) and glue, in different ways (fingers, brushes, sponges), and on varied surfaces (table top, smooth or textured paper, fabric, plastic, carpet swatches).
2. Using knowledge of structures and functions.	Learning that ideas can be conveyed by using a variety of paint media and surfaces.
3. Choosing and evaluating a range of subject matter, symbols, and ideas.	Studying different types of artwork and identifying subjects and ideas portrayed. Using art media to communicate meaning.
4. Understanding the visual arts in relation to history and cultures.	Observing artworks depicting past histories and how they compare with our world today. Observing and discussing artworks typical to specific cultures.
5. Reflecting upon and assessing the characteristics and merits of their work and the work of others.	Helping children understand and accept that there are individual differences and preferences among various artists, including their peers.
6. Making connections between visual arts and other disciplines.	Using visual arts to deepen understanding of other content and disciplines studied. Illustrating stories, poems, music they read or heard.

Source: Reprinted with permission from The National Art Education Association, © 1994. See www.arteducators.org.

Young children "exhibit a sense of joy and excitement as they make and share their artwork with others. Creation is at the heart of this instruction. Students learn to work with various tools, processes, and media" (National Art Education Association, 1994, p. 15).

Creative experiences require careful preparation on the part of the teacher, appropriate supervision during the experience, and may require cleanup afterwards. The early childhood teacher's role in art is to provide experiences with a variety of media and to encourage participation and the development of artistic potential through exploration. In addition, an atmosphere of trust, and genuine acceptance for children and their work is needed to facilitate children's artistic efforts and development. Unfortunately, sometimes art activities are limited because teachers have doubts regarding their value or concern with preparation and cleaning up after an art project.

Benefits of Art Experiences for Young Children

1. Art offers opportunities for self-expression and individualism. For some children, art media experiences may be one of the few means of self-expression. Young children's art expresses their thinking *and* feelings. There are children who do not communicate feelings well through verbal language, music, physical activities, writing, or other areas; however, they are able to express themselves through art media. For every child, art materials should offer the opportunity for self-expression, for celebrating individual uniqueness.

2. Art activities and experiences can deepen children's comprehension of the world, their perception of it or the way they view it, and can enrich their lives and understanding (A. S. Epstein, 2001).

3. Art experiences are satisfying to most children. They enjoy creating, working with the raw materials, the processes involved in the art activity, and the product achieved through creative art endeavors.

4. Art activities are therapeutic. Whatever the kind of art project, it offers a catharsis for the child's feelings and emotions that may not be expressed in any other kind of activity. Art activities provide a time to relax from the structure and sometimes the rigidity of the school day. They can be the means by which many children free themselves of pent-up tension and frustration and create feelings of pleasure and joy.

5. Art activities offer training, skill, and development in eye–hand coordination. Children learn to use scissors, manipulate and handle glue and paste, and work with a paintbrush and other tools, all of which promote eye–hand coordination. Most art activities require small-muscle skill and, as the child practices, this skill is improved.

6. As children mature and advance through the stages of art, they devote more thinking, planning, and organizing to their projects. Thus, the

way that they interpret ideas, solve problems, and think through concepts can be reflected in their artwork. Much can be learned about a child's feelings and knowledge through artwork.

7. Art activities provide opportunities for language and communication skills as children listen to directions, talk to one another as they work, and describe their efforts and products as they finish.

8. Science skills and concepts are often demonstrated before their eyes as they work with and combine various media. For example, finger painting provides (literally) hands-on experience in combining colors or making shades of colors. Substances such as glitter, sand, or spices added to art media such as paints add texture and smell to artwork.

Children find great satisfaction in sensory exploration with the various media provided in art activities. Their satisfaction in the process and their pride in the product can make valuable contributions to boosting their self-esteem.

FOSTERING CREATIVITY THROUGH THE ARTS

Teachers play a key role in helping children to develop their creative abilities.

Guidelines for Using Art to Foster Creative Expression

- Avoid patterns, ditto outlines or blacklines, and coloring books. Provide stimulus to generate ideas and then plain drawing paper.
- Through art, help the children to develop positive views of themselves. Let them know that you have faith in their efforts.
- Do not force or pressure children into telling you what their artwork is; it may not be anything at all, but rather an exploration of the media. Comment on designs, shapes, and colors and invite them to tell you about their picture. If they describe their artwork, an adult or older child may wish to write their descriptive words (exactly as they are said) on the picture, but gain permission to do so.
- Give affirmation and praise of the children's work. Let them know that you value uniqueness, diversity, and difference.
- Display children's artwork at their eye level, not the adult's. Avoid displaying any of the children's artwork unless they can all be displayed.

- Show children how to use materials and media provided, but then remove the example and allow them to explore, experience, try out, and manipulate media. Do not do the children's artwork for them, do not edit their work, and do not provide specific models for them to follow.
- Expose children to quality artwork through visits to art shows, bookstores, and museums.
- Avoid evaluating and grading artwork; look on it as a personal expression.

Because we consider the process to be more important than the product, Edwards (2009) challenges us to: put away patterns and coloring books; accept and encourage individual differences; include free art periods; positively acknowledge children's work; and recognize their creativity. The use of patterns or dittos is defended by some who say that children enjoy them. "But many children also love sweets, violent superheroes, and staying up all night. Everything children like is not always what is best for them" (Dodge et al., 2003, p. 347). Children enjoy experiencing freedom and risk taking with art materials and media, and in appropriate practice they are encouraged to create their own drawings based on their own ideas (Dighe, Calomiris, & Van Zutphen, 1998). In developmentally inappropriate practice, children are given examples and models to follow and told what to do with materials. We do children a disservice when we require them to work with prefabricated, uniform pictures. Only when art activities are unstructured and utilize raw materials does the child have an opportunity for creative expression. But teachers can and should teach skills and model and support techniques that encourage artistic growth and teach graphic representation (Dighe et al., 1998). "Must all snowflakes and shamrocks and turkeys be the same shape?. . . . Is regularity and sameness what we want from preschool, kindergarten and first-grade children?" (de la Roche, 1996, p. 82).

Structured art experiences do not recognize the value of art as both a process and a product in the curriculum. The *process* of making art allows children a creative activity in which they learn to manipulate and use art materials. The *product* provides a means of expression and communication that can be shared with others. If approached in the right way, every art project offers possibilities for encouraging creativity.

Children sometimes say, "I can't do it. Will you draw it for me?" Encourage them to draw on their own by such approaches as helping them think about the object they want to draw—size, color, body parts, shapes, their favorite part about the object, and other related ideas (Healy, 2001). When children become dependent on the lines or patterns of others, they begin to think that they cannot perform on their own. For example, when a pattern of a horse is given to them to color, they will notice the sophistication of the drawing and how much it really does look like a horse. When they next try to make a horse, the pattern comes to mind, and since they might not be able to duplicate it, they say, "I can't draw a horse." Perhaps not long before they colored the horse, they had happily and confidently sketched a picture of a horse. To many adults it may not have looked exactly like a horse, but they enjoyed the freedom of using their self-expression in creating their horse. This freedom, this creative expression, becomes lost for many children when they become dependent on the outlines of adult artists. Children may enjoy coloring books because they are not required to think for themselves. They become dependent on someone else's art, impression, or outline and in so doing become less confident in their own expression. The outlines of others so closely resemble the actual objects that children no longer consider their own efforts correct or worthwhile. When children think their end product must look like some else's product, they lose confidence in their work and efforts, and lack a sense of their own creative self-expression (Edwards, 2009). Art is an activity that is a personal expression of one's own ideas or reactions. "The children care more, learn more, and enjoy an activity more when they produce their own creations—not copies of ours" (Diffily & Morrison, 1996, p. 38).

Through art, help the children to develop positive views of themselves. Let them know that you have faith in their efforts. Tell them often, "You can." Praise their unique efforts. Help the children to know that what they create is their own and that they should strive to please themselves—not you, not other children, and not other adults. When a child has a positive view of self, he or she can risk taking chances. A positive view of self allows the individual to be creative.

Avoid evaluating children's artwork. Teachers are conditioned to evaluate, but children should be free in the art area to express themselves without fear of being evaluated. The teacher's role is to provide the appropriate attitude, time, materials, and encouragement for children and then allow them the dignity of doing their own work (M. K. Smith, 1996). Do not grade art; rather, collect a sampling of their artwork for their portfolio. Encourage parents to display children's artwork in a professional manner—framed, mounted in appealing and attractive positions (Dodge, Colker, & Heroman, 2003).

Shane had painted his first finger painting, but he was unable to take it home because it had not dried adequately. It was difficult for him to leave the painting at school, and he made sure that he knew where it would be waiting for him the next day. His first words after arriving at school the following day were, "Do I get to take my picture home today?"

Young children are proud of their work; teachers and parents should also be proud of the work. Help parents to acknowledge their children's creative efforts, to recognize that the product, the artwork itself, is not as important as the process used in the art project. This appreciation can be fostered by educating parents regarding the stages of artistic development through which children progress. Children universally progress through the same series of stages in their early art development, but individual children go through these stages at individual rates and have unique results (Kellogg, 1967). Scribbling is a valuable stage of artistic development. Scribbling begins at age 2 or earlier, extending up to the age of 4 or 5, at which time the child begins to draw symbolically (Kellogg, 1967). Kellogg (1970) has described at least 20 basic scribbles used by children, such as vertical, horizontal, and diagonal lines and other lines and patterns.

Expose children to quality artwork through visits to art shows, bookstores, and museums (Diffily & Morrison, 1996). Visit galleries; borrow reproductions of paintings by famous artists from your public library and display them in your room. Comment on the art or illustrations in picture books. Young children can begin to develop artistic taste and appreciation during their impressionable years.

> **IDEA:** Using postcard-sized reproductions of artwork available from museum gift shops, have the children match or pair those that are identical. The cards can also be grouped into such categories as subject, color, artist, size, or others. If the children know how to read, they can learn the names of artists and the titles of paintings.

PREPARING AND ORGANIZING ART ACTIVITIES

When planning creative curriculum activities, Mitchell (2004) suggests we consider using the "MOST" strategy—M (materials are appropriate), O (objectives are embedded), S (space is adequate), T (time is sufficient). Art activities require careful planning and preparation on the part of the teacher. Very often, the success of a project rests on its preparation, not on the project itself. Sometimes, creative art projects with children may seem like failures—but they actually can result in additional creative solutions and expanded learning opportunities (Bisgaier, Samaras, with Russo, 2004). The following guidelines are useful.

> ### Guidelines for Planning and Preparing Art Activities
>
> 1. Establish rules with the children concerning the care and use of art materials. They need to know that supplies and materials cannot be

wasted. They cannot damage school property or other children's property with art supplies. Young children must be taught that art supplies are not for eating.

2. Have all the materials and supplies needed for the project set up and organized.

3. Try out art activities ahead of time so that you know how to use the materials and can assist the children in learning how to use them. A student teacher was planning an art activity using plaster of Paris. She had not worked with it before and was not familiar with its properties. In making preparations for the day's activity, she carefully mixed the plaster of Paris before class began. Two hours later, the children were prepared for their art activity, but the plaster of Paris had already set! For each activity planned, the teacher should know what kinds of materials are needed, what thickness of paint is desired for a particular activity, how long the string should be for string painting, or whether glue or paste works better with a button collage.

4. Cleanup should be organized and made as easy as possible. For many art activities, tabletops can be covered with butcher paper or old newspapers for rapid change and cleanup. Containers of soapy water can be provided for glue brushes or paintbrushes as soon as children are finished with them. Aprons or old short-sleeved shirts should be worn by the children to protect their clothing. A sponge, soapy water, and other necessary cleanup materials should be available for the children to use; they can be encouraged to clean up when they are finished.

5. The children should have adequate working space during the activity. If no large space is available, perhaps the activity can be done in smaller groups during free play. Or the children could be divided into groups; while one group is participating in the activity, the other children are involved in other projects.

6. Art activities need plenty of time—time for setting up, time for exploring and creating with the raw materials provided, and time for proper cleanup. Too often art experiences become rushed, taking the enjoyment and even some of the creativity out of the projects.

7. If paintings need to dry, plan ahead of time for a drying place. Also, provide a place for finished products.

MATERIALS FOR ART ACTIVITIES

When children use open-ended materials (i.e., paint, clay, writing and drawing tools) that have no predetermined expectations, they are able to explore, create, make choices, and freely express themselves (Drew & Rankin, 2004). Materials for art activities should be handled carefully and should not be wasted. Children need ample supplies. Thus, if costly supplies are desired, use them less frequently, but when they are used, supply an adequate amount. Be on the lookout for discarded items that may be collected and stored in clean containers in an art-supply storage area. Empty plastic containers, aluminum containers and plates, aerosol lids, and so on are useful for many art projects. Some of the supplies may belong to an individual child, whereas other materials are shared by several children.

Many of the materials discussed in the following sections can be combined with other media. For example, instead of using finger paint alone, add sand, confetti, or glitter. Combine crayon drawings with finger painting for an interesting effect. First make crayon drawings and then finger paint over them. Or use cut-up tissue paper with paint at the easel. Let the child first paint a picture or explore with the paints and brush and then place pieces of tissue paper on the paint before it dries.

Surfaces

Children can create art on butcher paper (cut into individual pieces or left longer for murals), construction paper, paper bags, paper towels, newspaper, sandpaper, newsprint, cardboard, and scraps of wood. Styrofoam meat or pastry trays, paper plates, wallpaper, wrapping paper, printshop end rolls (often available from newspaper printers), boxes (any kind or size), cans, and ice-cream cartons can also be used.

Variety increases interest. Vary the surface of the child's artwork; the novelty makes the activity and the product exciting for the child. Art activities can be done on various sizes of paper, from very small bits to large pieces. Murals may be displayed either outside or inside the building. The individual child's portion may be cut out for taking home, or the mural may be done as a class project, with none of it taken home. Use simple geometric shapes and unusual shapes and designs of paper, as well as shapes and designs cut into the paper.

Finger Painting

Using fingers and hands in a paint medium is called **finger painting**. Some children are hesitant to become involved in this kind of activity and are concerned about being messy. Provide encouragement for these children, but do not force them to become involved. Heather was not willing to join in the first three times the class finger painted. However, the fourth time the activity was provided, she painted with one finger; the next time, she became completely involved with all her fingers. Finger painting must be well organized and supervised, and children should wear aprons. The painting

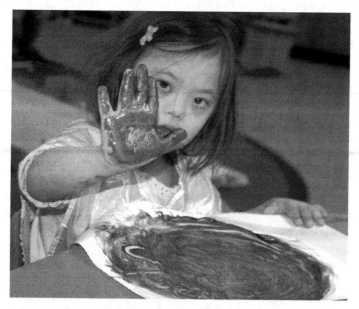

Children seem to respond to creative art activities with an intrinsic desire to express themselves.

can be done on many of the previously mentioned surfaces. Some kinds of paper should be either taped down or dampened on the underside so that they will adhere to the table. The entire table can be covered with butcher paper on which the children can finger paint. Or, children will enjoy finger painting directly on the tabletop and then will not worry about sliding, slipping, or tearing the paper. If the child wants a product to save, you can print a reverse simply by blotting the design onto paper. Children may sit or stand while painting, depending on the freedom of movement desired. The following are possibilities for finger paint mixtures:

1. Soap flakes: water added and the mixture beaten to the desired consistency
2. Cream: shaving cream or other cosmetic creams; food coloring or dry, powdered paint added for color
3. Liquid starch: dry, powdered paint added for color

Foot Painting. Using any of the media mentioned under Finger Painting, have the children paint with their feet instead of with their fingers and hands. After the children remove their shoes and socks, put the desired kind of paper on the floor, which you previously covered with newspapers. The paper should be taped down at least on the corners. One successful method is to put two rows of children's chairs parallel and facing one another. Then put one long strip of large-sized butcher paper between the two rows of chairs. Put a spoonful of finger paint in front of each chair. While painting, the children should stay seated in their chairs so that they do not slip. When they are finished, a plastic tub of water and a bar of soap can be brought to their chairs so that their feet can be washed. This activity can also be done outside in warm weather, with a hose handy to wash their feet.

Painting and Printing

Although liquid paints may be purchased from commercial supply houses, mixing paint from powder is more economical and provides many opportunities for child involvement. Vary the color and the consistency of the paints. Sometimes provide only one color; at other times, provide two or more colors. Combine some of the colors to obtain more unusual colors. Try adding small amounts of dark colors to darken the colors, or add white to make pastel colors.

The consistency of the paint will often be determined by the project. Straw painting requires fairly thin paint, whereas other paintings require thicker consistencies. Various media can be added to change the consistency of the paint. A frequently added medium is soap or detergent, which makes the paint go farther, makes cleanup easier, and makes the paint adhere to waxy surfaces (such as milk cartons). Other added media include sand, sawdust, and confetti, which vary in both consistency and texture. One teacher added strong spices to the paint during a unit on smells.

Paints are used differently for painting and printing projects. In **painting,** the tool (brush) is used to rub or brush the paint on the surface. In **printing,** the tool is dipped into the paint and then applied to the paper with no movement to leave the imprint of the tool shape. In this case, a sponge or paper towel saturated with paint may work better than a container of paint. Often printing turns out to be painting, but interest and involvement are of much more value than the end product.

- *Brush Painting.* Probably the most frequently used type of painting is brush painting. Although it is often done at the easel, it can be done in different areas and on a variety of surfaces. Vary the size of the brush and the consistency of the paint.
- *Sponge Painting.* Cut sponges into small pieces; clip each piece inside a clothespin for a handle, or tie it to a tongue depressor or stick. Sponges can be used for both painting and printing.
- *Feather Painting.* Use several feathers clipped inside a clothespin, a feather duster, or a single feather of any size or kind dipped into paint and used like a brush. If single feathers are used, they may be attached to the picture, resulting in both a painting and a collage of feathers.
- *Cotton Swab Painting.* Dip the cotton swabs into the paint and use them as brushes, pens, or sponges.
- *Vegetable and Fruit Printing.* Pour the paint over a sponge or absorbent paper placed in a small dish or container. Press the fruit or vegetable into the paint and then onto a surface. Oranges,

lemons, apples, grapefruits, onions, potatoes, green peppers, celery, pieces of corn on the cob, corncobs, and others work well. When potatoes are used, designs may be cut into the potatoes, or the potatoes may be cut around the design. (This is a good use of vegetables and fruits that grocery stores would otherwise discard.)

- ***Button Printing.*** Using epoxy glue, glue buttons onto small wooden dowels, and then use the buttons for printing. Vary the sizes, shapes, and designs of the buttons.

- ***Spool Painting.*** Attach empty thread spools to a handle made from an old coat hanger or other wire. Make small nicks on the ends of the spools to create variation in the design.

- ***Yarn-on-a-Metal-Can Painting.*** Glue yarn or string with strong glue to a small metal can. Brush paint over the yarn, and then roll the can over a surface.

- ***Fabric Printing.*** Wrap small pieces ($2\frac{1}{2}$ to 3 inches square) of burlap, nylon netting, or other textured fabrics over a sponge that has been attached to a clothespin or secured to a dowel with a piece of string or elastic. Then dip the fabric into paint and print on a surface.

- ***Pinecone Printing.*** Roll whole pinecones or pieces in paint, and then roll them over a surface. The large ones with flat bottoms can be dipped into paint to make an impression of the bottom on a surface.

- ***String–Block Printing.*** Glue string, yarn, rickrack, lace, or similar materials onto small wooden blocks or scraps of wood. Dip the blocks into the paint (or brush the paint on), and print the design onto a surface.

- ***Blot Painting.*** Fold the paper or other material in half; drop small amounts of paint with either a spoon or an eyedropper on one inside half. Then fold the paper over, blot the halves together, and open up the paper.

- ***String Painting.*** Attach one end of a piece of string or yarn, 8 to 10 inches in length, to a clothespin. Dip the string into the paint. Then place the string in a design on one inside half of a piece of paper or other material. Fold the paper over the string. One hand presses on the paper and string, and the other hand pulls the string out in different directions to make a design. If desired, dip the string into paint of a different color and repeat the same procedure.

- ***Straw Painting.*** Drop paint onto a surface with an eyedropper or spoon. Then blow the paint in different directions with a short straw.

- ***Gadget Printing.*** Gadgets (washable only) found around the house are dipped into paint and then onto a surface to make the design. Gadgets such as forks, potato mashers, jar ring tops, and rubber doorstoppers make interesting choices.

Collages

When collages are made, some materials or combinations of materials are glued onto a surface. Many different kinds of materials and scrap items can be used for collages. Children can tear or cut their collage materials out of paper. "As children create collages with cut and torn papers, photographs, fabrics, natural objects, and other materials, they are practicing an art technique used by many fine artists" (Prudhoe, 2003, p. 10).

GLUES. A variety of substances can be used for glue or paste. For gluing paper of any kind, an inexpensive paste may be used, such as *library* or *school paste*. It can be thinned, if desired, by whipping or beating with a rotary beater. Do not add water. It can also be used directly out of the jar. For heavier items, such as scraps of fabric or macaroni, *white glue* is suggested. Homemade *flour paste* can be used as glue, along with homemade *cornstarch paste* (flour or cornstarch mixed with a small amount of water). *Wheat paste* can be purchased inexpensively. *Plaster of Paris* can be purchased economically in bulk and mixed to a thick consistency. A small amount can be put on a base and then various collage items pressed into it. Tissue paper, cut-up scraps of magazines, or similar light media can be glued to any kind of surface with *liquid starch*. Dip the pieces into the starch and then press them onto such surfaces as plastic aerosol caps (two of the same size could be glued together, with some objects placed inside, to make a musical shaker); empty baby food jars (to make banks, vases, pencil holders, etc.); or half-pint milk cartons (to make musical shakers). Although a little more difficult to use, *rubber cement* is another possibility. The kinds of glues and pastes mentioned can be put as a blob on waxed paper, aluminum foil, a metal lid, or a paper towel (easily cleaned up) and applied with the finger or a brush; or the collage items can be dipped into the paste or glue and then onto the surface.

SUGGESTED MEDIA. When children make a collage, they arrange a medium or combination of media in desired ways on a surface. Their designs are often intricate and unusual. Collage media can be found anywhere, including in the garbage can, and practically everywhere indoors and outdoors. Paper can be torn or cut for collage work; three-dimensional objects also offer good possibilities. Collages can become part of class murals in various sizes and shapes. Be sure that the glue is strong enough to hold the medium or media chosen. The following list of suggested media is only a beginning; use your own imagination, along with the materials and discarded items on hand in your environment. You can use combinations of items, one item, a variety of one item such as buttons, or even a category of items such as beans, seeds, sewing items, or wood.

Suggested Media for Collages

rubber bands	seeds
all kinds of paper	sawdust
keys	Styrofoam
wallpaper	wrappers from candy bars
sequins	wood chips
tissue paper	toothpicks
any kind of tape	labels from cans
crepe paper	small rocks and/or gravel
gummed stars, reinforcements	dried flowers and weeds
labels	leaves
newspaper	lace
magazine scraps	hardware items
cotton balls	yarn scraps
straws	carpet scraps
confetti	linoleum scraps
old jewelry	beans
feathers	canceled stamps
spices	colored salt or sand
bottle caps	eggshells, including dyed
string	brads
craft items	fabric scraps

Sculpturing

When children sculpt, they pile on, build high, pat, roll, flatten, poke, and squeeze, depending on the materials provided.

CLAY SCULPTURE. The most frequently used sculpture medium is clay. It should always be available in every early childhood classroom. Clay must be neither too sticky nor too dry. It should be pliable and workable. Children should be exposed to different kinds.

1. *Playdough*
   2 cups boiling water
   Food coloring (about 4 to 6 drops)
   3 T. oil
   $2\frac{1}{2}$ cups flour
   $\frac{1}{2}$ cup salt
   1 T. alum

Mix the food coloring with the water, and then add the oil. Add the liquid ingredients to the dry ingredients and knead them together well. Form the material into balls and refrigerate in an airtight container. This playdough must be kept covered and refrigerated when not in use. It will not dry out like other salt–flour doughs. The texture and consistency are excellent.

2. *Salt–Flour Clay or Dough*
   3 cups flour
   $\frac{3}{4}$ cup salt
   $\frac{1}{2}$ tsp oil
   Water to achieve the right consistency

   Mix together the dry ingredients with dry powdered paint for coloring, or add food coloring to the water. Gradually, add the water and oil, and continue kneading and mixing until the clay is the desired consistency. This clay can be mixed and stored in an airtight container for a long period of time. It can be used to make beads: Roll it into small balls and poke holes through each bead with a nail, then let dry. The clay can also be used for making handprints, or it can be molded around a can, with collage items pressed into it for decoration. The clay can be left out to air-dry or can be baked until hard.

3. *Oil-based modeling clay* is very pliable and workable. It can be purchased from school stores or art-supply stores. It can be used over and over. Store it in plastic bags so that it retains moisture.

4. *Pottery clay* is a moist clay used by potters. It can be purchased from art-supply stores or from a college art department. It should be stored in plastic bags so that it remains moist and workable.

5. *Bread dough* can be molded like clay, baked in the oven like ordinary bread, and then eaten.

WOOD SCULPTURE. Small scraps of wood (obtained from a mill or construction site) are combined with other items and glued or nailed to a wood base. Paint the dried sculpture.

BOX SCULPTURE. An assortment of boxes of different sizes and shapes is glued together. A cereal box makes an excellent base, and then smaller boxes may be used to complete the sculpture. The sculpture can be painted; if powdered detergent is added to the paint, it will adhere to a wax-coated box.

STYROFOAM SCULPTURE. A structure can be built with a Styrofoam base and scraps and pieces of Styrofoam attached with toothpicks.

Miscellaneous Art Activities

NECKLACES. Children enjoy making things that they can wear. Both boys and girls delight in constructing necklaces. Make sure to put a piece of tape on one end of the string or tie a small object to it to hold the objects on. The end being used for stringing should be stiff; dip the yarn or string in wax, glue, or nail polish, or wrap tape around the end. Combinations of the following are suggestions for stringing media.

1. ***Colored macaroni.*** Use smaller-sized macaroni, because it will go farther and the child can spend more time stringing it. If large macaroni is used, the necklace will hold only 6 to 10 pieces. To color macaroni or similar media, put rubbing alcohol and food coloring in a jar. The darker and more intense the desired color, the more food coloring should be added. Put the macaroni in the jar and shake it for a few minutes. Then spoon it out onto paper towels to dry. (Use macaroni or pasta that is too old to eat.)
2. ***Paper.*** Use small pieces of paper cut into shapes or designs with holes punched in the middle. Flower shapes are easily made this way.
3. ***Horse chestnuts or small blocks of wood.*** Drill holes through each for stringing.
4. ***Plastic straws.*** Cut into varying lengths for stringing.

HATS. Various kinds of hats can be made for use in parades, games, musical activities, and so on.

1. ***Paper plate hats.*** Paper plate hats work best if a smaller paper plate is stapled to the back of a larger plate so that they are back to back. The smaller paper plate may have a hole punched on each side, with ribbons or strings attached to make the ties. The smaller plate then fits around the child's head and is not decorated. The larger paper plate will appear to sit on top of the head and can be decorated with collage paper flowers, cotton balls, flowers, or other objects.
2. ***Crowns.*** Cut a crown pattern for each child out of heavy paper such as poster paper. The paper can be decorated by painting, collaging, or printing. Add such items as gummed stars, glitter, aluminum foil, or old jewelry stones. Staple bands of the heavy paper to the crown, and then staple these two ends together to fit the child's head.
3. ***Newspaper hats.*** Fold newspapers into various hat shapes and then decorate them.
4. ***Spring hats or bands.*** Make a band of paper about $1\frac{1}{2}$ inches wide and long enough to extend about three-quarters of the way around the child's head; attach string or ties to the ends. Paper flowers can be cut out and glued on. Flowers can also be made by forming 1-inch squares of crepe paper over the eraser end of a pencil to make a flower formation, which is then glued to the headband. Bows can be made by twisting rectangular-shaped crepe paper in the middle and then gluing the bows to the band. Another spring band can be made by cutting out the inside portion of a paper plate, decorating the rim, and attaching ties.
5. ***Wigs.*** A brown paper bag may be used to make a wig. Cut a face hole in one side of the bag, and then cut the rest of the bag into strips. Roll each strip on a pencil, crayon, or pen to curl it.

COTTON-BALL PAINTING. Dip cotton swabs or balls into dry, powdered paint and smear them on paper. Pastel colors or shades work best. When the picture is finished, spray it with lacquer hair spray so that the paint does not rub off.

MELTED CRAYON PICTURES. Using a vegetable grater or a small plastic pencil sharpener, make crayon shavings using old crayons. Do not use many of the darker colors. Mix the shavings together and put them in small containers for each child. Sprinkle a few shavings onto half of the inside of a folded paper. Waxed paper works especially well because the finished picture is transparent and the two sides of the paper are sealed together. After the crayon shavings have been sprinkled onto one side of the paper, the other side is folded on top of the shavings. The picture is then placed between several layers of newspaper and ironed with a hot iron. The heat will melt the crayon shavings together. If waxed paper is used, the two portions will melt together. Small collage items may also be added with the shavings. For example, at Christmas time, cut holiday objects and shapes from tissue paper and add them, with glitter, to the shavings. Things from nature and the outdoors could be collected and added with the shavings. For example, one group of children made place mats in the fall by adding small seeds, dry weeds, and other outdoor fall treasures to the crayon shavings.

SALT OR SAND PAINTING. Although termed *painting*, this process is actually a collage activity. Spread glue onto a surface, and then sprinkle sand or salt that has been put in saltshakers or other containers onto the wet glue. Then shake off the excess salt or sand. (Color the salt or sand by adding a few drops of food coloring or powdered paint.)

PAPER PLATE CRAFTS. Some suggestions for using paper plates have already been presented. Three paper plates of varying sizes can be stapled together and then decorated to make snow figures. They can also be decorated to make turtles or masks. Eyeholes can be cut out, with big, floppy bunny ears and a bunny nose and mouth added, to make a bunny mask.

EGG CARTON CRAFTS. Egg cartons can be used to make insects, ants, caterpillars, or other animals. They can be painted and then items glued on to make faces. Pipe cleaners can be used for legs and feelers.

COFFEE FILTER BUTTERFLIES AND FLOWERS. Dip the filters in water colored with food coloring. After they dry, pull them together across the diameter of the circle and attach with a clothespin. Glue a head on and attach pipe cleaner feelers for a butterfly, or attach a pipe cleaner stem for a flower.

MILK CARTON CRAFTS. Milk cartons can be decorated and used to make the sections of a train or to make other vehicles such as boats or wagons. They can also be decorated as planting boxes or as baskets.

ICE CREAM TUB CRAFTS. These containers can be made into wastebaskets, flowerpots, drums, curler boxes, helmets, hats, or storage containers by collaging, painting, or finger painting them.

PAPER CUP OR ALUMINUM CAN CRAFTS. Paper cups or aluminum cans can be decorated with desired media and used for pencil holders, planting containers, flowerpots, clay gardens, or musical instruments.

ROCK CRAFTS. Rocks can be painted and decorated as animals, pets, or other objects. They can also be glued together for sculpturing.

CAMERAS. Provide each child with a box that has holes punched in the longest sides so as to create a lens hole through which the child can see. The boxes can be decorated with collage items or using marking pens. Put a picture of the child inside the box, along with cutout magazine pictures of other people. Decorate the pretend cameras. When dry, put a rubber band around the box. As the children peer through the punched holes, they pretend to take pictures by snapping the rubber band. Then they can take out the picture inside that has already been "developed."

SOAP BUBBLES. Make blowers out of old coat hangers bent to the desired size, or use the plastic holders that link six-packs of sodas. Mix one of the following two recipes and give each child a small portion in an aerosol lid or similar small container. Let them blow bubbles outside; it prevents a sticky film from collecting on the floor.

Recipe 1

$\frac{1}{2}$ cup liquid dishwashing detergent

$\frac{1}{4}$ cup sugar

A little water to dilute solution, if necessary

Recipe 2

8 oz liquid detergent (quality brand)

1 oz glycerin

CRAYON AND FELT-TIP PEN ART. These art tools are easy to obtain and offer great creative opportunities for children when used on a variety of surfaces. Use water-based markers, rather than permanent markers, because

the permanent markers may contain toxic solvents and can stain clothing.

CHALK ART. Chalk can be used dry and then sprayed with lacquer hair spray to prevent it from rubbing off. Wet a paper with water, buttermilk, or liquid starch, and then use the chalk. Using these dampening methods makes the paintings much more brilliant, and the chalk sticks better to the paper. Chalk can also be dipped into sugar water (a few tablespoons of sugar mixed with half a cup of water), buttermilk, or water for the same results.

BOX CRAFTS. Large boxes can be painted, sculpted, collaged, or decorated for play. A train could be made from a number of boxes, with ice-cream tubs being used on the front box to make the engine.

DRAMATIC PLAY

"Dramatic play is the most highly developed form of symbolic play, in which the child begins the incredible process of using objects as symbols for objects and events in the real world" (S. J. Stone, 1995, p. 47). Dramatic play is one of the great joys of childhood, helping children to develop interpersonal skills of conflict resolution and cooperation and improve their problem-solving and language abilities. There are many types of dramatic play activities, and each offers opportunities for all children to talk and listen, thus developing the language arts. These activities promote socialization and release of feelings and attitudes. Dramatic play encourages creativity and offers the opportunity for children to play out their own personal culture and world. The importance of dramatic play in the early years should not be underestimated (S. J. Stone, 1995).

The following strategies can be used to help incorporate dramatic play in the classroom curriculum:

1. Provide children with opportunities to create and explore in dramatic play centers.
2. Use drama in both large- and small-group situations in all curriculum areas.
3. Provide children with opportunities to act out stories they have heard.
4. Use drama to help to resolve conflicts, express emotions, and teach/extend social skills (Howell & Corbey-Scullen, 1997).

Free Dramatic Play

Teachers support dramatic play by recognizing its importance in developing language and literacy skills, and planning opportunities for its inclusion in the everyday early childhood classroom (Hatcher & Petty, 2004). During the early childhood years, children naturally

Cash registers not only support dramatic play, but also enhance practice of mathematical skills.

engage in much dramatic play, acting out various play themes and character portrayals. Dramatic play activities, often referred to as **free dramatic play,** or, more informally, "Let's pretend," are set up during individual play for children who choose to participate. An area of the room is set up with appropriate props, changed often to suggest various kinds of dramatic play. The children need not be told what to do, because the materials will suggest possibilities to them. To pretend, children draw on their own experiences and imaginations; this is all they need. Dramatic play is especially enjoyed by 3- to 8-year-olds because they like pretending. It is easy for a child to become a police officer, farmer, mother, father, beautician, or whatever role the materials inspire. Teachers must encourage diversity of roles and watch for stereotyped comments and behaviors.

Large, hollow blocks provide a great chance for dramatic play in which children add props to expand their imaginative play. The children choose whether the play is housekeeping, farming, aviation, fishing, boating, or something else. When the accessories are unstructured, even more imagination and creativity can be tapped. For example, fabrics can be furnished for dressing up; small-unit blocks for small accessories; paper, tape, and crayons for signs.

Suggested Props for Dramatic Play Areas

1. *Housekeeping:* Any housekeeping and domestic tools and equipment, such as brooms, mops, stove, table, refrigerator, dress-up clothes for boys and girls (child sized), hats, purses, shoes, gloves, ties, and eyeglass frames; in addition, towels, washtub, and dolls (of both genders and diverse ethnic and racial backgrounds), along with dishes, cooking utensils, equipment, and pretend foods

2. *Barbershop and beauty shop:* Actual materials and cosmetics, such as rollers, combs, brushes, hair dryer, mirror, fingernail polish, nail file, cotton balls, old makeup, perfume, lotions, shaving cream, play razor, and aftershave lotion, together with soap and water, as well as cleansing cream, if possible

3. *Camping:* Sleeping bags, small tent, backpacks, canteens, mess kits, compass, hiking boots, rope, flashlight, food, as well as rocks and campfire logs

4. *Picnic:* Tablecloth, napkins, picnic basket, jug for drinks, sandwiches, cookies, rocks and wood to represent fire, and other equipment

5. *Carpenter shop:* Hammers, saws, other tools, nails with large heads, scrap lumber, sandpaper, and woodworking bench

6. *Plumbing:* Pipes of all lengths, widths, and shapes; monkey wrenches, plungers, hose and nozzles, and box for tools

7. *Restaurant:* Small tables set up with matching tablecloths; old menus obtained from restaurants; placemats, napkins, place settings, and any other restaurant supplies obtained from local places that might be willing to give you these materials; an area where food is prepared, with both pretend and real foods available to serve customers

8. *Grocery store:* Foods, empty cartons and empty metal cans with labels; large-unit blocks or small tables, with aisles and shelves set up for display of grocery items; cash register, real money (small change), cart or carriage, and bags and/or boxes

9. *Hospital:* White shirts, stethoscope, adhesive bandages, elastic bandages, cotton balls, cots, pillows and sheets, scales, tongue depressors, flashlight, syringes, masks, rubber gloves, crutches, pill bottles for medicine, and unused supplies donated from a doctor's office (sterilized or disposed of after use)

10. *School:* Desks, chalk, chalkboard, erasers, paper, pencils, crayons, books, flannel board and flannel figures, and any other school supplies

11. ***Office:*** Typewriter, paper, pen, pencils, telephone, briefcase, and any other office supplies available
12. ***Post office:*** Envelopes (both new and used), rubber stamp and ink pad (perhaps discarded from a post office), scales, used stamps, mail-bag (old newspaper bag or large purse with shoulder strap), mailboxes (small and large shoe boxes), and mail sorting box (box with cardboard sections in it)
13. ***Bakery:*** Bowls, rolling pins, playdough or clay, cookie cutters, muffin tins, cookie sheets, baker's hat, and aprons
14. ***Service station:*** Air pumps, boxes, ropes, hoses for pump, tools such as wrench and screwdriver, oil can, cash register, sponges, and paper towels

Additional possibilities for dramatic play areas include a shoe store (complete with shoeshine area), dentist's office, television station, dress shop, men's clothing store, airport, space station, gardening center, farm, circus, fashion show, greenhouse, and pet store. Even a few materials will promote dramatic play. Another idea is to have a couple of suitcases ready to pack for trips. Line up chairs for an airplane, boat, automobile, bus, train, or whatever means of travel has been chosen. Children, calling on their own experience or reading, will decide where they are going.

In many early childhood classrooms, the only dramatic play area set up is a housekeeping area. Over time, the children tire of it and do not use it as often. Regularly rotating the props in dramatic play areas will spark interest and enthusiasm in the children.

Creative Dramatics

Creative dramatics is more sophisticated than free dramatic play. Davis and Behm say, "Creative dramatics is an improvisational, non-exhibitional, process-centered form of drama in which participants are guided by a leader to imagine, enact, and reflect on nursery rhymes, folktales, and other stories" (quoted by Cline & Ingerson, 1996, p. 4). It is planned by the teacher, but acted and played out by the children. **Creative dramatics** has more form and structure than free dramatic play. Creative dramatics is creativity, whole language, cooperative learning, and problem solving combined (Cline & Ingerson, 1996). A great benefit of creative dramatics is the full participation and involvement of all the children. Children's social play, role-playing, and dramatizing are the avenues through which they learn about themselves, others, and their world (Edwards, 2009). "Preparing for and engaging in sociodramatic play provides a nonthreatening, child-centered environment where children teach, learn, and experience real-life roles. It provides a meaningful context in which children use their developing skills for authentic purposes" (Cooper & Dever, 2001, p. 62).

Types of Creative Dramatics in Early Childhood

- *Pantomime:* students act out situations within their own self-space using only actions and gestures as a means of expression
- *Story Dramas:* acting out whole stories or parts of stories
- *Role-Playing:* various events, people, stories, and situations, are acted out, usually spontaneously. By acting out roles, students are able to think, feel, and act as other persons. This activity is effective for resolving conflicts, practicing appropriate behavior, and creating empathy.
- *Choral Reading and Choral Speaking:* the oral interpretation of literature. **Choral speaking** refers to experiences in which students recite passages from memory. In **choral reading** the students read text, such as poetry or stories.
- *Reader's Theater:* minimal theater in support of literature and reading. Usually, there is no full memorization and scripts are held during the performance. It is rather informal without full costume and no full stage sets.

Dramatizations can be stimulated and motivated in many ways. They must be geared to the ages of the children, and younger children will need more coaching and help from the teacher. Even though these children enjoy dramatizations, they do not often have the know-how to carry them out without guidance and assistance. The teacher may need to participate or simply give much prompting and assistance. Older children require fewer suggestions, possibly only a story plot or idea.

IDEA: One kindergarten group was dramatizing "The Three Billy Goats Gruff." The teacher first told the story and then parts were assigned. The children who did not have parts were the audience. A plank was set up between two chairs to represent the bridge, the troll wore an old coat and hat, and the three billy goats wore simple paper-sack masks. As the teacher helped the children with this dramatization, she used such motivating questions as "What happened next?" "What did the first billy goat do then?" and "What did the troll say?" If the children taking the parts could not remember, they were coached by the audience. They enjoyed participating, and it was not important that each "actor" have the part memorized or even remember it. What was important was that the children were involved in making the story come to life for them.

THE NATIONAL STANDARDS FOR THEATRE EDUCATION

Content Standard	Sample Activities
1. Script writing by planning and recording improvisations based on personal experience, imagination, literature, and history.	Planning the dramatization of familiar stories or fairy tales, including determining necessary props and characters.
2. Acting by assuming roles and interacting in improvisations.	Pretending to be the characters in stories or fairy tales as they are dramatized.
3. Designing by visualizing and arranging environments for classroom dramatizations.	Deciding where the dramatization will take place (outside, inside), how much space will be needed, where the props will be placed, what dress-up clothes will be gathered.
4. Directing by planning classroom dramatizations.	Determining how the dramatization will take place, where the narrator will be, who and where the audience will be.
5. Researching by finding information to support classroom dramatizations.	Learning about the various aspects of the story: What were the people like, and what did they do? What happened, and where?
6. Comparing and connecting art forms by describing theatre, dramatic media (such as film, television, and electronic media), and other art forms.	Discussing the differences and similarities between live action and television/video/DVD. Choosing songs, dances, artwork to be included.
7. Analyzing and explaining personal preferences and constructing meanings from classroom dramatizations and from theatre, film, television, and electronic media productions.	Learning about and accepting individual differences in preferences and themes of stories to dramatize and characters to portray.
8. Understanding context by recognizing the role of theatre, film, television, and electronic media in daily life.	Discussing the value of television/video/DVD in our lives, and what kinds of concepts and ideas we are able to observe. Learning about various cultures and their characteristics.

Source: The National Standards for Theatre Education. Copyright © 1994 by the American Alliance for Theatre & Education. Used by permission. The complete National Standards for Theatre Education (K-4) and additional materials relating to the Standards are available at www.aate.com.

Skills That Children Acquire Using Creative Dramatics

1. Problem solving
2. Literacy (reading, writing, speaking, listening)
3. Analyzing
4. Planning
5. Self-confidence
6. Courage
7. Creativity
8. Empathy
9. Communication
10. Social interaction

7. Dramatizations centered on an object or series of objects: an object or objects put in a bag, with the children making up stories about the object(s)
8. Pretend activities: pretending to be seeds growing or sprouting, a worm crawling along a branch, or the like (especially enjoyed by younger children)
9. Plays
10. Role playing: specific role or character for an individual child or a story role-played by the entire group to promote understanding of feelings and actions
11. Puppet shows

Suggestions to Prompt Creative Dramatizations

1. Stories: read in class or in a reading group
2. Poems
3. Musical stories
4. Situations: a friend unwilling to share a toy with you, what to do if a friend gets hurt, being lost
5. Field trips: to the farm, to the zoo, or elsewhere
6. Events: a birthday party, a hike, a hunting expedition; trips to outer space, to Mexico, or any other place

Choral readings can easily be organized and "cast" using either poems or simple stories. For younger children, simple poems, rhymes, or fingerplays can be used. For second- and third-grade children, longer poems or short stories can be scripted for choral readings. A choral reading can be as simple as girls and boys alternating lines or stanzas. Another way to script choral readings is to divide the class into smaller groups with each group assigned particular lines or passages. Once children have introductory experiences with choral reading, scripts can be introduced that are more complicated. For example, a poem or story can be divided into parts for girls and boys, group parts, and solo parts. Third-grade children enjoy scripting or casting choral

Two or more telephones in the dramatic play area encourage development and expression of social, emotional, communication, and creative skills.

readings either as a class experience or as a smaller group. Poetry or stories prepared as choral readings and presented at parent or community programs are inclusive, build fluency, and give all children an opportunity to perform.

Puppets

"Using puppets is a safe, creative way for children at varied developmental levels to express feelings, act out roles, create play scenarios, and reenact stories" (Esch & Long, 2002, p. 90). In the dramatic play area, children expand their knowledge and abilities in literacy, mathematics, science, social studies, the arts, perception, cognition, and technology (Dodge et al., 2003). Use of puppets is a kind of dramatic play, and it offers many opportunities for both speaking and listening. Because young children are fascinated by puppets, they make effective attention getters. They can be used in unstructured situations such as individual play; but sometimes children become aggressive when using them, particularly if animal puppets are being used, so limits and guidelines must be established. Puppets can be used to capture attention in a discussion, tell a story or poem, teach a song, or give children directions. Puppet skits can be used to help children to develop problem-solving skills such as sensitivity to problems or alternative-solution

thinking. Younger children use puppets in less formal and structured ways.

Puppets can be made in numerous ways. The puppets that children make should be simple in design and easy to use, such as those made from paper sacks, sticks, felt, socks, vegetables, paper plates, cardboard cylinders, or gloves.

Examples of Using Puppets

1. Storytelling
2. Play acting
3. Puppet show
4. Singing songs: puppets used by one or more children when singing songs; often helps shy children to sing or speak out more
5. Children in stories: participation by children in parts of stories
6. Stimulation of a dialogue or conversation between two or more children
7. Television shows: television set made out of a large box such as a store or refrigerator box; puppets used for quiz shows, talk shows, movies, or even commercials

Summary

Many values emerge from children's creative art activities. A great deal of freedom lies within the bounds of limits, rules, and responsibilities. Individualism flourishes, self-expression flows, and there is satisfaction in both the process and the product. Art activities also have sensory qualities, often involving several of the senses at one time. All professionals who work with young children should support and encourage these young ones in art education assuring that their creative expression is not usurped or controlled (Edwards,

2009). As teachers foster creativity in art during the early childhood years, children's abilities to kindle new ideas, accept challenging tasks, and discover horizons not yet imagined are expanded. Ideas for better ways of doing things exist in the human mind, not in computers or other machines. The sooner the mind is encouraged and invited to create, the more able it will be to expand its capabilities and the more time it will have to reach its potential. What is most important in art expression is "to ensure that each child grows and develops, learns to think and express his feelings and ideas, and creates new and original responses within an environment that is supportive, validating, and inclusive" (de la Roche, 1996, p. 83).

Dramatic activities have also been included in this chapter. Their value has been clearly defined, and they can be embraced for their cognitive, emotional, and social benefits.

Student Learning Activities

1. Visit an early childhood classroom when children are participating in an art activity. Evaluate how effectively creativity was fostered. Notice individual children and their various stages of art. Was the activity well planned and set up, implemented, and cleaned up?
2. Make a list of the art supplies and equipment that you would want to have in your classroom.
3. Begin an art portfolio of children's art activities by completing a sample of at least two art activities suggested for each section in this chapter. For example, do at least two finger paintings, two paintings, two printings, two collages, and so on. Label them and describe the materials needed on the back. Add to the collection each time a new art activity is done.
4. Observe a classroom where a dramatic play area is set up. Describe the area, the play that occurred during your observation, and the benefits for the children from this kind of play.
5. Plan, implement, and evaluate at least one creative dramatics activity with a group of children aged 3 to 8 years.

Suggested Resources

CREATIVE ART REFERENCES

Amabile, T. M. (2001). Beyond talent: John Irving and the passionate craft of creativity. *American Psychologist 56*(3), 12–16.

Chenfeld, M. B. (2002). *Creative experiences for young children* (3rd ed.). Portsmouth, NH: Heinemann.

Cherry, C., & Nielsen, D. M. (2001). *Creative movement for the developing child: An early childhood handbook for non-musicians* (3rd ed.). Torrance, CA: Fearon Teacher Aids.

Crawford, L. (2004). *Lively learning: Using the arts to teach the K–8 curriculum*. Greenfield, MA: Responsive Classroom, Northeast Foundation for Children.

Isenberg, J. P., & Jalongo, M. R. (2006). *Creative thinking and arts-based learning* (4th ed.). Upper Saddle River, NJ: Merrill/Prentice Hall.

Jalongo, M. R. (2003). The child's right to creative thought and expression. *Childhood Education 79*, 218–228.

Koster, J. B. (1997). *Growing artists: Teaching art to young children*. Albany, NY: Delmar.

Mayesky, M. (2003). *How to foster creativity in all children*. Albany, NY: Delmar.

Nyman, A. L. (2002). Cultural content, identity, and program development: Approaches to art education for elementary teachers. In Y. Gaudelius & P. Spiers (Eds.), *Contemporary issues in art education* (pp. 61–69). Upper Saddle River, NJ: Prentice Hall.

Schirrmacher, R. (2002). *Art and creative development for young children*. Albany, NY: Delmar Thomson Learning.

Wigg, P. R., Hasselschwert, J., & Wankelman, W. F. (1997). *A handbook of arts & crafts*. Madison, WI: Brown & Benchmark.

Winer, K. (2003). Learning about art. No. 4 of the *Learning at Home* series. Watson, ACT, Australia: Early Childhood Australia.

Wyrick, M. (2002). Art for issues sake: A framework for the selection of art content for the elementary classroom. In Y. Gaudelius & P. Spiers (Eds.), *Contemporary issues in art education* (pp. 212–225). Upper Saddle River, NJ: Prentice Hall.

Online Resources

http://members.tripod.com/~Patricia_F/art.html   This site contains a variety of early childhood art activities.

www.nncc.org/Curriculum/art_recip.html   A National Network for Child Care resource is offered called "Favorite Recipes for Art Materials" that includes recipes for bubbles, fingerpaint, clay, and other media.

www.kidsart.org.uk   A site for children of all ages to share their art.

www.naturalchild.com/gallery   A site for children around the globe to submit their art and for other children to view children's art.

www.teachnet.com/lesson/art/index.html   This site provides a variety of art lessons.

appendix A
Lesson Plans

The following concepts or themes are included in this appendix as examples of lesson plans:

Seeds

Emotions

Water

Wheat and flour

Community helpers

Fruit

Light (shadows)

Texture

Sound

Numbers

Honeybees

Fish

Trees

UNIT PLAN ON SEEDS (FIVE DAYS)

UNIT OBJECTIVES

Students will:

- Describe concepts associated with seeds, specifically the following:
  1. Seeds come from the fruits of plants.
  2. Seeds are different from one another in color, shape, size, and texture.
  3. Seeds need water to grow. (Warmth, food, and air could also be included.)
  4. We eat some seeds.
  5. Plants grow from seeds.

- Demonstrate basic understanding of some positional words through concrete, repeated experiences with such words and their meanings.

DAY 1

Whole-Group Activity

SCIENCE—HOW SEEDS GROW

Objective: Students will identify how seeds grow over time. Students will recognize words relating to plants and use these in conversation.

- On this day, and on each of the four following days, put a presoaked lima bean seed between glass and a moist paper towel. (By the end of the unit, the children will be able to see the first five daily stages of growth of the seeds.) Ask the children what seeds need to survive and grow and help them to discover (if not the first day, during subsequent experiences) seeds' need for water, light, air, and soil.

Teach language labels such as *root, sprout,* and *stem* with a drawing of a plant and a real plant, pointing out each part of the plant.

Small-Group Activity

FIELD TRIP—SEED WALK

Objective: Students will observe and collect seeds in their natural environment and discuss differences in the variety of seeds they collect.

- In small groups, the children will walk around the area observing plants, trees, and weeds that are shedding seeds at this time of year. Give a sack to each child for gathering seeds. Ask them to look for differences in seeds, such as texture, shape, size, and color, and clues to how they might travel.

INDIVIDUAL ACTIVITIES

- Bubble blowing
- Seeds in sensory area

DAY 2

Whole-Group Activities

MUSIC—RHYTHM EXPERIENCES USING SEEDPODS

Objective: Students will examine a catalpa seedpod (or other gourd or pod) and observe the seeds inside. They will recognize that because the pod is dried out, the pod can be used as a rhythm instrument or shaker.

Students will sense the rhythm of the songs selected.

- The children will use seedpods to accompany the rhythm of familiar songs and a record with a definite beat. Break open one seedpod and let the children raise questions and observe the seeds inside the pod.

SCIENCE—SEEDS THAT TRAVEL

Objective: Students will learn a variety of ways seeds travel.

- Raise the question of how a seed goes from one child's house to another child's house. Use a toy town to focus on a demonstration. Then discuss how seeds travel in various ways: burrs cling to animals and people, some seeds fly through the air, some seeds roll.

Small-Group Activity

ART—SEED SHAKERS

- Provide juice cans or half-pint milk cartons in the art center. The children put some seeds inside and glue seeds on the outside. They can secure the lids with tape. Encourage questions and comparisons between seeds.

Individual Activities

ART

- Easel, with seed-shaped paper and green paint

SCIENCE

- Observe the growth of the lima bean seed planted yesterday and plant another today.

DAY 3

Whole-Group Activity

VISITOR—MUSICIAN

Objective: Students will identify a variety of natural musical shakers and use them in shaking the rhythm of a song.

- The visitor will play various musical instruments for the children. Then show the children how different kinds of seeds can be used to provide music (seed pod shakers, dried gourds, seeds sealed in containers).

Small-Group Activity

ART—SEED COLLAGES

Objective: The students will identify the great variety of seeds and use them in creating a collage.

- The children will make seed collages from the seeds that they collected on the field trip the first day. They will make plaster of Paris, put the plaster on a paper plate, and then put the seeds in the soft plaster to harden. (If you do not wish to use plaster of Paris, seeds can be glued on the paper plate or stuck into potter's clay.) Encourage questions and observations of various seeds.

Individual Activities

SCIENCE

Objective: Children will compare and contrast seeds and determine that we eat some seeds.

- Observe the growth of the lima beans planted the two previous days and plant another today.
- Display foods with seeds for children to explore, such as watermelon, cantaloupe, tomato, orange, lemon, cucumber, apple, peach, cherry, plum, or others that are in season. Provide plastic, serrated-edged knives and encourage the children to cut the fruits and observe the seeds. Are the seeds edible? Compare sizes, shapes, colors, numbers, textures, and other similarities and differences. Ask the children which of the foods have seeds that we can eat.

ART—PAPERWEIGHT OF POTTER'S CLAY WITH SEEDS PRESSED IN

Objective: The children will creatively use a variety of seeds, comparing and contrasting them, to create a useful object.

- Provide the children with aprons, potter's clay, and a variety of seeds. They will roll the clay into balls, flatten one side, and then push seeds into the clay.

DAY 4

Whole-Group Activity

SCIENCE—WE EAT SOME SEEDS

Objective: Students will name seeds that we eat.

- Show the children examples of seeds that we eat, such as peanuts, peas, corn, beans, nuts, squash seeds, cucumber seeds, and potatoes. Show the difference between vegetable seeds that we plant and those that are edible in the vegetable (such as bean or pea seeds). Make comparisons. Show the children examples of some seeds that are not edible only because they have not been cooked (chili beans, lima beans, etc.).

Small-Group Activities

FOOD—CHILI

Objective: Students will make chili and then taste a seed that we eat.

- The beans will already be soaked and ready for cooking. In small groups, have the children watch and help grind the onion. Then the children will brown the hamburger and onion and add seasonings and tomatoes. These ingredients will be added to one or two large pots and allowed to cook. The children can individually stir and watch the chili as it cooks. Point out that the beans are actually seeds that are eaten once they have been cooked.

- In small groups, serve chili for the children to eat. While the children are eating, reinforce concepts relating to beans being seeds, how the chili was prepared and mixed, and its nutritional value to our health. Provide opportunity for the children to raise questions and explore concepts that they suggest.

Individual Activities

SCIENCE

- Observe the growth of the lima bean seeds and plant another one.

SENSORY AREA

- Peanuts and edible nuts, with nutcrackers
Caution: Be aware of children with peanut allergies.

SHAPE TRACING AND CUTTING

Objective: Children will practice small muscle skills as they recognize and create various shapes.

- Provide various shapes, such as toys and cookie cutters, for the children to trace, and provide scissors for them to cut out the shapes.

DAY 5

Whole-Group Activity

PHOTOGRAPHS ON BULLETIN BOARD

Objective: Children will sense an identity as they see their own picture on the bulletin board.

Children will recognize and use a variety of positional words such as *under, over, beside,* and *between.*

- Put pictures of the children on the bulletin board, providing an opportunity to use positional words. Each day, rearrange each child's picture so that the pictures vary in position: beside, under, over, or between circles of a particular color. It will now be easy to divide the children into groups. For example, say, "All those who are beside a blue circle go with (teacher's name) group." Review the positional words by having all the children in particular positions stand, hop around the circle, change places, or perform some other movement.

Small-Group Activity

ART—FINGER PAINTING WITH SEEDS ADDED

Objective: Using a creative and sensory medium, such as finger paint or whipped soap flakes, children will create pictures and feel and describe the difference in the texture when seeds are added.

- In small groups, have the children finger paint with a mixture to which seeds have been added. When the paint dries, the seeds will stick to the paper.

Individual Activities

SCIENCE

- Observe the growth of the lima bean seeds and plant another one.

SORTING AND CLASSIFYING SEEDS

Objective: Children will use different criteria to classify seeds.

- Use muffin tins to sort seeds by various characteristics, such as the way they travel, color, size, kind, and whether they are edible or inedible.

LESSON PLAN ON EMOTIONS (FOUR DAYS)

OBJECTIVES

The students will:

- Recognize emotions and the expression of them.
- Recognize the kinds of things that stimulate emotions and how to work with them.

Note: Many of the whole- and small-group activities in this lesson plan work well as cooperative learning projects, especially those that address happy and unhappy emotions, curiosity, fear, anger, and so on.

DAY 1

Whole-Group Activity

INTRODUCTION TO UNIT ON FEELINGS AND/OR EMOTIONS

- Place felt cutout faces representing various moods or emotions on the flannel board and discuss them with the children. Afterward, tell the children a story about feelings and discuss it with them.

Small-Group Activity

ART—CONSTRUCTION PAPER COLLAGES

- Provide school paste, a sheet of white construction paper, and many cutout shapes of colored construction paper for each child. Divide the children into small groups after the introduction to the unit. The cutout shapes (similar to the felt ones used in the introduction) can be put together to represent faces with different moods. The children may wish to make faces, or they may want to paste the shapes in any collage design.

Individual Activities

- Large trough with wheat
- Paint at the double easel

DAY 2

Whole-Group Activities

DISCUSSION AND STORY ON HAPPY EMOTIONS— LOVE, JOY, AND EXCITEMENT

- Show the children a picture of a child with a happy expression and ask them such questions as: "How do you think this child feels? What could have caused the feeling? Have you ever felt happy, excited, joyful? What told you that this child was happy?" Share a story about love between a parent and children, and then follow it with a discussion on love. Emphasize that loving others or being loved by others makes us happy.

VISITOR—CLOWN

- Have a visitor come dressed in a clown costume. While the children are gathered as a group, the visitor puts on the greasepaint and makes up a clown face. The clown discusses the concept that dressing up as a clown makes people happy.

DISCUSSION AND STORY ON UNHAPPY EMOTIONS— SADNESS, LONELINESS

- Tell an open-ended story to the children and, with a partner or in cooperative groups, encourage them to supply possible endings. Show the children a picture of a crying child, and use the same kinds of questions listed in the preceding discussion. Tell a story to the children that will elicit how it feels to be rejected.

Individual Activity

- Large trough with snow or ice

DAY 3

Whole-Group Activities

DISCUSSION AND INTRODUCTION TO THE EMOTION OF CURIOSITY

- Use an unfamiliar book, a pair of magnets, and a picture of children observing and playing with a frog to stimulate interest in the emotion of curiosity. Since the word *curiosity* will probably be new to the children, describe what it is: wondering about, investigating, and exploring something. Use questions to stimulate thought and discussion.

DISCUSSION AND OPEN-ENDED STORY ABOUT ANGER, FRUSTRATION, AND JEALOUSY

- Tell an open-ended story about a girl who is angry. The children will discover that the girl is angry; have them describe what made her feel that way. Show several pictures of angry children and discuss what might have made the children angry and what can be done to solve the problem. Also, introduce *frustration* to the children as a new word, and have them talk about things that frustrate them and how they may become angry about them. Show the children a picture of a new baby and discuss jealousy. (These pictures could be distributed among cooperative groups so that more children would have an opportunity to participate and share ideas.)

MUSIC—CREATIVE MOVEMENTS WITH PLASTIC

- Play music of various moods. Give the children a scarf or piece of colored plastic, allow them to move about the area, and encourage them to interpret the music and how it makes them feel. Ask them whether the music makes them feel afraid, curious, happy, excited, or sad. Accept any answer or response.

Small-Group Activity

MAKING UP STORIES FOR PICTURES

- After the discussion on anger, divide the children into small groups for cooperative learning. Send the groups to various areas of the room, where they will be given several pictures of children depicting specific emotions. In the groups, have the children make up stories for their pictures. If they want the stories written down, make lined paper available.

Individual Activities

- Magnets on science table

DAY 4

Whole-Group Activity

SCIENCE—DISCUSSION ON FEAR

- Have the children discuss some of the situations that stimulate fear: going to the doctor or dentist, getting shots, taking medicine, going on an elevator, hearing loud noises, being near animals, being in the dark, or parents leaving. Discuss how to overcome these fears, mainly by having more experiences with the things feared. Afterward, discuss and display some things that the children should be cautious with: fire, matches, poisons, broken glass, medicines, and so on.

Small-Group Activity

FOOD—POPCORN WITH CHEESE

- See recipe in appendix B.

INDIVIDUAL ACTIVITIES

- String painting
- Trough with manipulative toys

LESSON PLAN ON WATER (THREE DAYS)

OBJECTIVES

The students will:

- Recognize that humans have many uses for water: to dissolve some things, to drink, to cleanse some of the foods we eat, to swim, to wash our own bodies, to wash automobiles, to cool our bodies on a hot day, to put out fires, to cook, and as an ingredient in many substances.
- Name five of the preceding uses of water by humans.
- Identify the three forms of water.

DAY 1

Whole-Group Activity

INTRODUCTION TO UNIT

Tell a story about a child who went swimming. The story leads into a discussion about some other uses humans have for water. Put pictures illustrating some of these uses on a flannel board as they are discussed.

MUSIC—RHYTHM STICKS

Give each child a pair of rhythm sticks and have the children tap the rhythm as an appropriate record is playing that imitates the falling of rain and then the sound of thunder.

Small-Group Activity

FIELD TRIP TO A GYMNASIUM

When the children first arrive, give them the opportunity to take a drink from the water fountain. At the gymnasium, lead the children on a tour and give them an explanation of the swimming pool, shower room, and steam room. Take special precautions to ensure the safety of the children. Soon after returning, hold a discussion on the field trip.

DAY 2

Whole-Group Activity

DISCUSSION

Review some of the uses of water discovered yesterday and discuss how we use water in our homes: for cooking, for drinking, for bathing, for watering yards, and so forth. Do role plays of some of the activities involving the use of water.

Small-Group Activity

FOOD—VEGETABLE SOUP

Form cooperative learning groups for making homemade vegetable soup. Provide each group with a large bowl, scrub brush, paper towels, peeler, cutting board, and small knife. The children in each group will take turns doing the various steps. First, they will wash and scrub the vegetables in a large dishpan. Then, under close supervision, they will peel and slice the vegetables. One child will take the group's sliced vegetables to a large pan placed on a hotplate in the classroom. When all the groups are finished, add several quarts of hot water to the vegetables. Caution the children that the pan will soon be hot. Allow the soup to simmer for several hours to be eaten the next day.

Individual Activities

- Watercolor painting with primary colors at the double easel
- Water in the trough with sponges and other materials

DAY 3

Whole-Group Activity

SCIENCE EXPERIMENT

Show ice cubes and ask the children if they know what they are. Using a hot plate with a pan of boiling water, put the ice cubes in a pie plate and put this above the boiling water on the hot plate. Observe what happens as the heat from the boiling water changes the ice cubes to liquid. When the ice has changed to liquid, with the pie plate still on the boiling pan of water, put another pie plate over the water. As it heats watch it change to steam and then collect onto the second pie plate. Explain that they have observed three forms of water: solid (ice), liquid (water), and gas (steam).

Small-Group Activity

FOOD ACTIVITY AND DISCUSSION

Eat soup made the day before and review the concepts learned about water: the uses of water and the three forms of water.

Individual Activities

- Books and stories about water
- Water and ice cubes in the trough

LESSON PLAN ON WHEAT AND FLOUR (ONE DAY)

OBJECTIVES

The students will:

- Describe the following basic concepts of wheat:

  What wheat is

  What it looks like. Wheat has three basic forms: seed, greens (sprouts), and mature shaft.

  How it tastes, feels, smells

  How it grows; where it grows

  Different forms: Flour is ground wheat.

  Uses as food: whole wheat, cracked wheat, sprouted wheat, as well as flour (a basic element in many products)

- Recognize what *growing* is by watching wheat sprout.

Whole-Group Activities

DISCUSSION

Show kernels of wheat to the children and ask if they know what wheat is or from where it comes. Explain that these are wheat seeds taken from a mature shaft, and the shaft was grown on a farm and comes from a seed (the kernel). When the wheat is mature, it is harvested, and the kernels are removed from the wheat shaft and then ground into flour. If a wheat grinder is available, demonstrate how the wheat is ground into flour. Ask the children what the flour is used for. Explain that flour is a plant product that is vital to our diet. We use it in tortillas, breads, and many other foods that we eat every day.

DEMONSTRATION OF FORMS OF WHEAT

Gather the children at the rug covered with a large tarpaulin. Have containers of whole-kernel wheat, sprouted wheat (greens), and mature-shaft wheat. Explain to the children the relationship among the three forms. To reinforce this concept, separate the wheat from the chaff of the mature wheat so that they can see that it is a whole kernel of wheat and begin to grasp the cycle. Give each child the opportunity to explore a shaft of wheat and extract the kernels onto the tarp. Put some kernels of wheat on a piece of gauze and put this over a jar of water. Keep the gauze moist and over a period of days observe the kernels sprout.

RHYTHM AND CREATIVE MOVEMENT ACTIVITY

Gather the children at the rug and have them participate in several well-known fingerplays and songs. Have them play the game The Farmer in the Dell, and then introduce them to the following new song by singing it several times to the melody of "I'm a Little Teapot":

> *I'm a little wheat stock, short and stout.*
> *Here is my kernel, and here is my sprout.*
> *When I get all grown up, then I'll shout—*
> *Just pick me, farmer, and shake me out.*

Small-Group Activities

ART—PAINTING WITH WHEAT SHAFT

Divide the children into groups by color squares, and ask each child to go to the table that has the appropriate color of paint. Provide the children with white paper on which their names have been printed and a bundle of three wheat shafts tied together to serve as a paintbrush. Put the paint on the paper in drops with a spoon (it should have a rather thick consistency), and have the children paint with the wheat. They may create whatever design they wish.

FOOD—COOKED WHOLE-WHEAT CEREAL

Cook the cereal beforehand. Divide the children into small groups by means of their names placed on small disposable bowls. Give each group containers of milk and brown sugar. Serve the cereal from the pan in which it was cooked. Give each child a very small amount, along with a spoon, and encourage them to try it. Serve juice also.

Individual Activities

- Trough filled with whole kernels of wheat

LESSON PLAN ON COMMUNITY HELPERS (FOUR DAYS)

OBJECTIVES

The students will:

- Demonstrate involvement in the functions of a community so that they gain a realistic understanding of community helpers.
- Show awareness of how community helpers aid us and the necessity for the skills that they possess.
- Describe ways of assisting the community helpers.
- Identify a variety of tools and equipment used by community helpers.
- Appreciate various occupations and respect workers for the jobs they do.

Note: Activities in this unit plan are listed in order of schedule.

DAY 1—FARM DAY (FOOD SOURCES)

Small-Group Activity

FOOD—MAKING BREAD

As the children come in, greet them and give each one a name tag in the shape of stalks of grain, a loaf of bread, a sack of flour, or a grocery store. Set up four centers in the room, and instruct the children to go to any one of them and see what the teacher is doing. At the tables are small amounts of bread dough, one for each child. The teachers instruct the children to knead and fold it. Give the children adequate time to work the dough until all the children have arrived; then show them how to shape the dough into a small loaf and place it in their own individual small bread pans. Each group will take its bread to a warm place to rise and then go over to the rug and sit down. The bread will rise and bake while the children listen to the record containing farm animal sounds.

Whole-Group Activity

FARM DISCUSSION

Begin singing the song "Old MacDonald Had a Farm" as the children begin coming over to the rug, and encourage them to join in. When everyone gets to the rug, tell a story about a vegetable and then lead into a discussion of farms. Talk about what is grown on farms and why they are important. Emphasize that wheat is grown on the farm and is later made into bread.

TRANSITION

Tell the children to look at their name tags. In the classroom, there is a table with some stalks of grain on it, a table with a flour sack on it, a table with a loaf of bread on it, and a table with a miniature grocery store on it. Tell the children to go to the table that corresponds to their name tag.

Small-Group Activity

ART—PUPPETS

Spread out on the table materials with which the children can make sack puppets of farm animals, including pigs, cows, chickens, and horses. They can have their choice, and creativity is the key. The basic patterns are there for them to cut out and use; what they do is up to them. Also make available construction paper, blunt-end scissors, and glue. As the children finish, they will assist in cleaning up.

Individual Activities

- Stage on which to play with puppets
- Table with seeds, grains, feathers, and eggshells for making a collage
- Cups, dirt, and seeds that can be worked and planted
- Playhouse

Whole-Group Activity

FARM RECORDING

Put on a record of farm animal sounds while children clean up and come to the rug. Then read stories and sing songs about cows. Talk about how the cream in the milk turns into butter, and show the children how it is done by bringing out a churn. Let them all take a turn at churning for a little while. When everyone has had a chance and the butter is all churned, add some salt for flavor. Then all the children will be able to eat their small loaf of bread with some of the churned butter on it and have a small glass of milk. After finishing, they will go outside to play until it is time to go home.

DAY 2—OUR HEALTH HELPERS

When the children arrive, give them name tags that are like little Red Cross badges. Ask them to hang up their coats and explore the different areas in the room.

Individual Activities

- Area with collections of books about community helpers
- Housekeeping area with hospital arrangement (bandages, small pillows, adhesive bandages, empty spray cans, gauze, syringes, and tape)
- Art area, constructing nurses' or doctors' hats from available materials
- Dentist's office, complete with magazines, reception desk, phone, office chair, teeth models, white coats, cloth to go over patients, and tongue depressors

Whole-Group Activity

DISCUSSION ON CHECKING AND MAINTAINING HEALTH

Use a large freezer box that has been previously decorated to look like an ambulance. Make a siren noise and have the children hook onto the teacher's back like a train. Go around the room for everyone, and then go to the rug. After watching a filmstrip about health helpers and safety, have a discussion about the ambulance, doctors, nurses, and dentists. Stress the point that they are available to help us, not to harm or hurt us. Pull out a satchel and begin taking items out of it. The items should include a microscope, slides, and instructions for use; measuring tape; elastic bandage; reflex hammer; tongue depressor; stethoscope; sphygmomanometer; balloons; thermometer; and a dental hygiene kit. Discuss what each item is and how it is used. Also explain how to make microscope slides. As soon as everyone knows what the items are and how to use them, send an equal number of students to each of the four different areas for the science experiences.

Small-Group Activities

SCIENCE EXPERIENCES

Each group will spend about 10 minutes in each interest center, and the signal to change will be a siren.

1. Set up microscopes with certain prepared slides, and provide materials for the children to make their own slides showing such items as salt, pond water, sugar, and others. They will be able to see the slides under the microscopes.
2. Place a long piece of butcher paper along one wall. Set up a scale to weigh each child, and mark the child's height by a line on the butcher paper. On that line, write the child's name, height, and weight. These measurements are not mandatory, and children who are reluctant and do not want to participate should be allowed this choice. During this process, the others can occupy themselves with wrapping each other up in elastic bandages, checking each other's reflexes, and looking at each other's tonsils using the tongue depressors.
3. Provide several stethoscopes so that the children can hear each other's heartbeats. Set up a sphygmomanometer to take blood pressure. Have the children blow up balloons so that they can see what their lungs do, and provide thermometers so that they can take their own temperatures. (Properly sterilize thermometers or provide disposable plastic sheaths or covers.)
4. By the sinks, provide a toothbrushing kit for each child, and set up mirrors. Have the children brush once and then chew the little red tablets to see where they have brushed their teeth inadequately; then have them brush again. Show them how to brush their teeth properly.

ART—MOBILES OR AMBULANCES

In a large group, discuss the doctor, dentist, and first-aid kit. Make sure the children understand that both males and females can be doctors and dentists. Then divide into smaller groups. At the tables, the children will have materials before them for one of two activities: (a) making mobiles of teeth out of string, paper, cardboard, crayons, sticks, tape, pictures of teeth and mouths, glue, and marking pens; or (b) making ambulances out of matchboxes and white paper by adding details such as wheels with black construction paper, doors, a red beacon light, stripes, headlights, and so on. (Ambulances could also be made out of rectangular-shaped pieces of Styrofoam, with red gumdrops for the sirens and black circles for wheels.)

DAY 3—THE MAIL CARRIER

The children's name tags today will be in the shapes of business envelopes, letter envelopes, packages, or stamps. As the children come in, direct them to tables where there is cookie dough. They may all help to drop the dough on cookie sheets and bake them in the oven while waiting for everyone to arrive.

Whole-Group Activity

INTRODUCTION TO THE MAIL CARRIER

Have everyone gather on the rug. Read a story about the mail carrier, and talk about the forthcoming field trip to the post office and some of the things to observe. Explain that both males and females can be mail carriers and postal workers. Assign the children to cars and adults according to their name tags. Before going, they will first go over to tables where there are certain materials.

Small-Group Activity

WRAPPING COOKIES AND FIELD TRIP TO THE POST OFFICE

At the tables, each child finds a small box, some brown wrapping paper, and some string. Give the children two of the cookies to put in their boxes and wrap like presents. Then put the children's names on their boxes. When they are finished, have each group get into a car for the field trip. When they are all out of the room, put the packages in a big bag to be used later, after returning.

After returning from the post office, go to the rug and discuss the day and the mail carrier. Then have another teacher bring out the bag and pass out the packages of cookies and juice to each child; the cookies are eaten with the juice.

DAY 4—THE FIREFIGHTER

This morning welcome the children and encourage them to explore freely the different areas of the room.

Individual Activities

- Trough filled with wood and twigs
- Housekeeping
- Easel for painting
- A tape playing a story about a firefighter
- Blocks for constructing a fire station; ladders and trucks, along with striped overalls, bell, fire hats, and long hose

Whole-Group Activity

VISITOR—FIREFIGHTER

When the sound of the siren begins, gather all the children in the center of the room and ask them what they think it is. Then go to see that it is a firefighter who has come to visit and has brought the truck. The firefighter will tell the children all about the truck, show them all its parts, and then come in to talk to them. The firefighter will discuss safety measures and how to prevent forest fires, house fires, and accidents. Emphasis will be placed on the fact that, although some fire is good for heat and cooking, it is harmful when it gets out of hand. Emphasize that firefighters can be women or men. When the visitor has gone, make a long fire engine "train" and drop off "firefighters" at the different tables.

Small-Group Activity

FOOD—FONDUE

At the tables are fondue pots over small Sterno fires. Each child will prepare several kinds of fondue and have juice.

Whole-Group Activity

DRAMATIZATION

Have the children, in three groups, pretend that they are on fire and must find a way to extinguish the fire. The firefighter comes to the rescue and saves the people. The firefighter demonstrates the ways to put out clothing fires. This should include these three main ways: (a) put a blanket around you, (b) lie down on the rug and roll, or (c) lie on the ground and roll. Emphasize the phrase "Stop, drop, and roll." Stress walking, rather than running. Talk about how water is important in putting out fires. Then tell the children the story of Smokey Bear.*

After the firefighter is finished, the three groups will be ready for the art activity.

Small-Group Activity—Working Cooperatively

ART—MAKING SMOKEY BEAR

Place art supplies at the tables for the children to construct a Smokey Bear on a piece of contact board. Materials available will include fuzzy fur for the body, which will be cut in the proper shape, and construction paper, string, yarn, and glue for the features. Have each group work together on one Smokey Bear. After the children finish, have them go over to the rug, where someone will be reading stories until all groups have finished the art project.

 LESSON PLAN ON FRUIT (TWO DAYS)

OBJECTIVES

The students will:

- Label a variety of fruits, both familiar and unfamiliar.
- Recognize that fruit comes in many different sizes, shapes, colors, textures, and tastes.
- Recall that fruit has seeds and match the fruit with its seed.
- Explain that fruits can be eaten: how they can be eaten, which parts of the fruit we eat, and which parts we throw away.
- Review that fruit must be preserved to avoid spoilage.

*Teacher's Forest Fire Prevention and Conservation Kit. Forest Service. U.S. Department of Agriculture and your state Forestry Department. See www.smokeybear.com for more information.

DAY 1

Whole-Group Activities

INTRODUCTION AND LABELING

Have an apple, orange, and banana at the rug. Talk about each one with the children. Determine whether the children can identify fruit as a category. Discuss each fruit with the children: what it is, what part we eat, what part we throw away, whether it is soft or crunchy to eat, where it is seen on the bulletin board, where it grows, how many seeds it has, and whether it tastes like anything else. (The bulletin board will display several familiar fruits in several different forms: on the tree, in a bottle or can, peeled, cut, sectioned, and so on.)

VISITOR—DEMONSTRATION OF MAKING FRUIT JUICES

Have the children gather at the rug and watch as the visitor makes a variety of juices. (The visitor's demonstration should precede the children's own juice-making experience.)

Small-Group Activities

FOOD—MAKING FRUIT JUICE

Divide the children into four cooperative learning groups. Have enough grapefruits, juicers, knives, strainers, and cups for one group; enough oranges and equipment for another; enough limes and equipment for another; and enough lemons and equipment for the fourth group. Each group makes its own kind of juice, adding sugar if necessary. Then they go to the rug to taste the various juices and talk about the experience.

MUSIC—MUSICAL CHAIRS

Divide the children and teachers into two groups to create more room for each group. Place fruit shapes in a circle around each group, one for each person. The fruit shapes that are being used should be presented first to the children; use only familiar fruits at this stage. Play music, and when the music stops, all sit down. Ask the children what fruits they are sitting on.

Individual Activities

- Red sand in trough, together with funnels, utensils, and bottles
- Science bench with dried fruit, jar of moldy fruit, jar of good fruit

MATCHING FRUIT LOTTO

Set out lotto games and dominoes made with various fruit pictures from seed packets or catalogs.

DAY 2

Small-Group Activities

FIELD TRIP—FRUIT STAND OR STORE

Divide the children into groups, and assign to cars and an adult. First, check with the store or stand and notify the owner before you go. Tell the children that they may each choose one piece of fruit to buy and that the fruit that they choose will go into a fruit salad that they will help to prepare. At the stand, have one supervisor for every few children to watch them for safety reasons and to supervise what they choose for the salad. Let each group buy its fruit separately so that the children will have more individual involvement in the buying process. Each supervisor should tell the children something about the fruits that they see at the stand.

FRUIT STAND CENTER

Set up an actual fruit stand with fruit on it for the rest of the unit during free play. Make shopping bags and money available to create a more realistic situation.

LESSON PLAN ON LIGHT (SHADOWS) (FOUR DAYS)

OBJECTIVES

Students will:

- Describe the concept of shadows and their origin.
- Recognize types of shadows, and then generalize the knowledge that a shadow's size and darkness are changeable, according to the light source and the distance from the object.
- Identify the shapes of objects by their shadows.
- Create interest in and appreciation for poetry.
- Increase body awareness through creative movement, body shadow pictures, and rhythm activities.

Note: Because of the nature of this unit plan, one corner of the room will be darkened to be the "shadow corner," where many of the individual activities throughout the unit will be performed. The plans may have to be altered or changed if the weather is not sunny.

DAY 1

Whole-Group Activity

INTRODUCTION TO UNIT ON LIGHT AND SHADOWS

As an introduction to this unit, give a slide presentation. The slides will consist of many pictures of shadows in our everyday lives and what causes shadows. A tape may accompany the presentation. Questions that may concern the young child will be answered during this presentation. Such topics as the causes of shadows, the shapes of shadows, the light source, and the size of shadows will be illustrated during this short presentation. Afterward, read a poem about shadows.

Small-Group Activities

SCIENCE—SHADOWS

After dividing the children into cooperative learning groups, tell them to go outside. Each group will have a dowel or stick to place in the ground; then they will measure its shadow. Later in the morning, each group will go back to its own stick and again measure the shadow. Place a marker at the locations of both shadows to allow the children to see how shadows change as the day progresses.

ART—PAPER HATS

Have the children, in groups, make pointed paper hats, which will be used for the "shadow parade" on day 2. They can decorate the hats with paint, crepe paper streamers, scraps of paper, and other materials.

Individual Activities

- *Tracing Shadows Outside.* Provide butcher paper and trace each child's complete body shadow while the child stands still and watches. Encourage the child to find a unique position or stance. Emphasize the body parts and help to increase the child's body awareness during this experience. Cut out the bodies so that the children can paint them on day 2. Each picture must be carefully labeled.
- *Object Printing.* Have the children make printings with various types of objects using a variety of colors of paint.
- *Lotto Shape Games.* Develop a set of black shadow shapes as a lotto game for matching and discrimination purposes. This game can be used at any time, but it will be especially effective during this unit or a shape unit.
- *Bubble Blowing.* Place the trough in the shadow corner. Mix 1 cup of granulated soap in 1 quart of warm water. Small open-ended cans and straws should be available for each child. It is interesting for the children to observe the bubbles that they blow and see whether the shadows are cast on the wall when the light in the shadow corner is switched on.

DAY 2

Whole-Group Activity

MUSIC—SHADOW PARADE

Have the children participate in a "shadow parade" with musical instruments. They wear the hats that they

made on day 1 and carry a flag, baton, or rhythm instrument. Beat a rhythm on a drum, and encourage the children to beat out the rhythm as they march around the playground and especially to watch their shadows during the parade.

Small-Group Activity

FOOD—FRUIT SALAD (COOPERATIVE LEARNING)

Ask the children to guess the shapes of certain fruits from their shadows. Place the fruits behind a sheet, with a light shining from behind. Each fruit will be guessed separately. Show the following fruits (easily identified): grapes, pineapple, watermelon, cantaloupe, bananas, and apple. They will be combined to make a fruit salad in each group. Each child will have a chance to cut some fruit into pieces and then each group's salad will be shared among the group. Because sharp knives will be used, carefully supervise this activity, and thoroughly caution the children about the dangers of sharp instruments.

Individual Activities

- *Painting the Shadows Outside.* Hang the traced shadows on the fence on the playground to be painted. Offer several colors of paint. Leave the pictures on the fence to dry.
- *Shadow Puzzles.* Cut the silhouettes of certain objects into puzzles, which the children will have the opportunity to put together and use, along with the other manipulative toys.
- *Puppets and Overhead Projector.* Set up an overhead projector in the shadow corner. Here the children can have creative play with the puppets and their shadows on the wall. Music may be played to stimulate creative movement.
- *Science.* On the science table, place several shoeboxes with balls of clay, a small flashlight, and a pencil. The pencil is supported in the shoebox by the clay. The flashlight is then used at various angles and distances from the box to produce different types of shadows. Help the children to observe the various angles of shadows that can be produced, making the pencil shadows both long and short.

DAY 3

Whole-Group Activities

VISITOR—PERSON TO DEMONSTRATE SHADOW PLAYS

Ask a visitor to show a variety of finger shadow plays on a screen or wall in the classroom. In these plays, use simple shapes that children can quickly learn to imitate, such as those of a rabbit, duck, elephant, or dog. A light shining on the wall helps to produce the dark shadows. Encourage group involvement and have the children practice some of these shadow plays while the visitor is there to assist.

DISCUSSION—SHADOWS AT NIGHT

Encourage discussion of the kinds of shadows that the children see at night in their bedrooms. Talk about how quiet, dark, and dim the shadows are. Help the children to talk about their fears, but minimize this aspect of the darkness. Discuss how shadows are not always what they seem to be. Emphasize the positive.

Small-Group Activity

SHADOW TAG

Divide the children into small groups and have them go outside. There each group will play Shadow Tag. In this game, one person is "It" and tries to step on another child's shadow. When he or she does step on another child's shadow, that child then becomes "It." Several children can be "It" at once. Be sensitive to each child and careful not to let anyone feel that he or she is not a part of the game. Another variation to this game is Shadow Touch Shadow, in which the children try to let their shadows touch hands, feet, and so on.

Individual Activities

- *Trace Silhouettes.* Trace the children's profiles on black paper as silhouettes (with a sheet and light). Later, cut the silhouettes out and mount them on pieces of white paper. Provide a learning experience on day 4 with the silhouettes, and then let the children take their own silhouettes home.
- *Shape Collage.* Cut all kinds of shapes out of black paper, and have the children paste collages on white paper. Provide scissors if the children want to cut.
- *Shadow Plays.* Place the screen in the shadow corner so that the children can experiment with the shadow plays that they have been taught. Other media and shapes may also be provided to increase experimentation with the light and shadows.

DAY 4

Whole-Group Activities

PREPARE A SHADOW PLAY

The shadow play will be performed completely behind a sheet, so that the children will see only shadows of what is happening. The shadows might

be activities such as jumping rope, directing music, using a fly swatter, or a variety of motions. When the play is over, talk about what happened and remove the sheet so that the children can actually see the actions taking place.

MUSIC—CREATIVE DRAMATICS

Give each child a piece of plastic to move creatively with the music. Place a light behind the children to cast shadows on the wall. Encourage discussion about the shadows and why the plastic shadows are so much lighter than the children's shadows.

Small-Group Activity

SILHOUETTE GAME

Divide the children and their silhouettes made the previous day into small groups, and have each child try to guess his or her own silhouette.

Individual Activities

- *Shape Game.* Cut shapes of familiar objects out of black Pellon®, and have the children match pictures of them to the actual objects.
- *Trough.* Set a trough full of sand in the shadow corner. Put figures of animals and people in it to promote play. The children can observe the shadows cast from the animals and other objects.

 LESSON PLAN ON TEXTURE (FIVE DAYS)

OBJECTIVES

Students will:

- Describe textures that are common to their environment and attach descriptive language labels to textures.
- Differentiate and identify various textures.
- Identify basic concepts related to textures.

DAY 1

Whole-Group Activity

INTRODUCTION TO THE CONCEPT OF TEXTURE

To lay a foundation for the study of textures, introduce the word *texture* to the children, along with the meaning of the word. Items having various textures will be available for the children to feel, see, and hear. Adjectives such as *rough, hard, soft, smooth, bumpy,* and *velvety* will be applied to the texture feelings.

Small-Group Cooperative Activity

MAKING CLAY

The children prepare clay in three small groups. Each group has 4 cups of flour and 1 cup of salt, as well as water and some coloring. Because all the clay is approximately the same color, it can be put into one plastic container to ripen.

Individual Activities

- Autoharp
- *Material and Yarn Sewing.* Make available various pieces of textured material, along with threaded needles, for sewing and stitching.
- *Trough with Water in Various Forms.* Put containers of ice, snow (if available), and water in the trough, along with various measuring and pouring utensils.
- *Art—Crayons at the Easel.* Provide crayons to be used for drawing and sketching at the easel. Along with the regular easel paper, provide background papers of various textures. One side of the easel has textured material underneath the easel paper; the other side has textured wallpaper and other materials.

DAY 2

Small-Group Activity

FOOD—GELATIN

Have four groups of children make gelatin, each group making a different flavor. The gelatin will be set with ice cubes and then put into the refrigerator until firm. Later in the day, allow the children to eat the gelatin in a large group at the table.

Whole-Group Activity

MUSIC WITH TEXTURE SOUNDS

Demonstrate musical "instruments," such as sand blocks, corrugated cardboard, and washboards that have various textures and that make sounds of various textures. Then let the children use the instruments to accompany familiar songs. Then the children go to the large table to eat the gelatin that they have made.

Individual Activities

- Small trough containing sawdust and wooden cars
- Double easel with sponges and brushes
- **Texture Collage on Styrofoam Meat or Pastry Trays.** Make materials and items having various textures available for pasting on the meat or pastry trays, which also provide an example of an unusual texture. Put paste into individual containers, and set out a jar of warm water for soaking the used brushes.

DAY 3

Whole-Group Activity

FIELD TRIP—LUMBERYARD

As the children arrive, attach an identification badge to each child's coat. Explain the reason for the visit to the lumberyard. Then divide the children into smaller groups according to their badges. At the lumberyard the children will feel and see the various textures of wood, glass, and other products. They will also be able to see ways in which texture may be changed.

Small-Group Activity

STORIES ABOUT THE FIELD TRIP

After the field trip, have the children return to the same groups that they had at the lumberyard. While the groups discuss the field trip, have a teacher or aide write down what the children say. Then read the "story" back to the children while they are still in the groups.

Individual Activities

- Small trough containing bark, with wooden and rubber cars and trucks

DAY 4

Whole-Group Activity

SCIENCE—CHANGING TEXTURE

Demonstrate changes in texture by adding water to dry dirt or sand, by adding water to a very dry sponge, or by adding a smooth coat of paint to a rough surface. Have the children perform an experiment of their own as they make root beer floats.

Small-Group Activity

FOOD—ROOT BEER FLOATS

Divide the children into smaller groups to make and eat root beer floats. Put ice cream into the cups first, and then add the root beer.

Individual Activity

- Small trough with wooden blocks, hammers, and nails

DAY 5

Whole-Group Activity

VISITOR

Have a person who has various materials and items of similar and different textures visit the classroom. Explain the uses of the items and review appropriate texture labels.

Small-Group Activity

TEXTURE BOOKS

Give each child a sheet of poster paper and a sample cut from fabric. Each child in each group will have a different textured fabric. Have the children discuss the texture and how it feels and then paste it on the paper. Their ideas will be written on their own sheets as they suggest them. If children are able to write, they should write their own ideas. Then combine these sheets to form a book for the children to read.

Individual Activities

- Small trough with dolls and sponges
- Xylophone

LESSON PLAN ON SOUND (FIVE DAYS)

OBJECTIVES

Students will:

- Discriminate among sounds and categorize them.
- Recognize the loudness–quietness and highness–lowness that can be characteristic of most sounds.
- Explain the emotional qualities of sound (happy, sad, fearful, light, comforting sounds).
- Identify and classify sound further by the object or objects that created it, such as human, animal, farm, and city sounds.
- Detect that sounds can communicate (for example, the sound of a siren can mean an accident or a fire; a car pulling into the driveway at the end of the day can mean that Mom or Dad is home).

DAY 1

Whole-Group Activity

DISCUSSION OF LOUDNESS, QUIETNESS, HIGHNESS, AND LOWNESS OF SOUNDS

At the rug, sing songs (with fingerplays) loudly, then quietly, and then in normal voices. Then play several tape-recorded sounds. These sounds will be high or low, and

in some cases the same object will create both sounds. Imitate the sounds and discuss which are liked or not liked and how they make one feel when they are heard.

Small-Group Activities

SOUND HUNT FOR TREASURE

This activity takes place outdoors if the weather permits, and each group has a different route to follow. This game is comparable to a treasure hunt. Each new clue is found only when the children answer questions on whether certain objects make high, low, loud, or quiet sounds. Show the children that some objects can produce all these sound qualities. The treasure could be hidden inside a large chest or buried in the sandbox, depending on what the treasure is.

ART—STARCH AND TISSUE SCULPTURED DRUMS

Give the children an opportunity to create a collage on the sides of drums made from large empty cans obtained from cafeterias, with a piece of inner tube stretched over the open end and secured with wire. The drums will be used the following day during a story. Explain this plan to the children while they are making their collages. Tissue paper dipped in starch is the collage medium.

Individual Activity

- ***Feathers, Hammers, and Water-Filled Pop Bottles.*** Place the feathers in the trough, place the hammers on stumps with nails, and line up the pop bottles on a table. Vary the water level in the bottles so that a person blowing on the openings will be able to produce both high and low sounds. The hammers, when used to pound nails, provide a loud sound, and the feathers provide an almost noiseless quality, bordering on a soft sound, which is discussed along with the emotional qualities of sounds.

DAY 2

Whole-Group Activity

FLANNEL-BOARD STORY

Tell the story outside. Pass out the drums made the previous day before telling the story. Have the children help to tell the story by playing the drums when given certain signals.

Small-Group Activity

"SOUND" WALK ON THE PLAYGROUND AND IN THE CLASSROOM

Have two groups of children begin outside and two inside. With eyes closed and ears close to objects so that sounds can be heard, the children strike or listen to various objects, such as a drum, an autoharp, a seashell, or a music box.

DAY 3
Whole-Group Activity
VISITORS—HUMAN SOUNDS

Ask a small group of high school drama students to perform a segment of the children's theater version of "Hansel and Gretel."

Small-Group Activity
ANIMAL SOUNDS

Bring four animals (or figures of animals) to the class and place them around the room. For this activity, each group of children has an animal at its table. The children discuss the sounds that the animal makes and then use clay to sculpt either an animal or an object representing an animal sound.

Individual Activity
- *Recording the Children's Voices.* Provide two or more tape recorders in various areas of the room, such as in the block or manipulative area. Have teachers in these areas record the voices of the children there and then play the tape back to them. Emphasize the idea that children make human sounds and that these sounds are meaningful.

DAY 4
Whole-Group Activity
MUSIC—RHYTHM BAND

Provide each child with an instrument, and use several different instruments. Have the children accompany a musical selection on a record or their singing.

Small-Group Activities
SCIENCE—GUESSING OBJECTS BY THE SOUND THAT THEY MAKE

Assign the children to cooperative learning groups. Give each group a wrapped, jewelry-sized box containing three or four objects such as a coin, marble, bell, and screw or nail. Have them listen carefully and then brainstorm possibilities for what is inside. After they have guessed, have them open the container to see what is inside.

ART—STRING PAINTING

Have small groups of children gather at the tables. The children dip strings into liquid paint and then put them

between the two halves of a folded paper. With one hand, they press the two sides together; with the other hand, they pull the string out. Make sure they leave an end of the string protruding so that it can be grasped for pulling out.

Individual Activity
- *Matching Sounds.* Use small boxes or film cans and put duplicates of different objects inside pairs of containers. For example, in each of two cans, put six paper clips; in two others, put five buttons; in two others, put one tablespoon of rice. Ask the children to shake the cans or boxes and listen to identify which pairs match.

DAY 5
Whole-Group Activities
SIRENS

As the children brown meat for sloppy joes, turn on a recording of a siren. From the sound heard, have the children try to determine what it could have been. Have some pictures to show possibilities. A review of the week may be given at this time.

FOOD—MAKING SLOPPY JOES

Have the children gather at the rug as you combine the ingredients. Use a hot plate or electric fry pan. (The hamburger will have been browned by the children in their small groups.) Call attention to the cooking sounds.

Small-Group Activities
FOOD—SETTING THE TABLE AND BROWNING THE HAMBURGER

Have the children set the tables while listening to the sounds of setting the table. After establishing the idea that the sounds made while setting the table are dish sounds, introduce the final concept for the week by asking, "What do we think of when we hear the sounds of dishes being set on the table?" Because these sounds usually mean food, begin browning the hamburger to be made into sloppy joes.

FOOD—EATING LUNCH

Go inside and dish up the sloppy joes. Have the children eat them with carrots and juice, observing the sounds that the different foods make as they chew.

LESSON PLAN ON NUMBERS (FIVE DAYS)

OBJECTIVES

Students will:

- Recognize that numbers are used in the environment.
- Recall the sound and sequence of counting numbers.
- Identify the correct position of numerals.
- Match the numeral or symbol of the number with its meaning (that is, the numeral 7 will be matched to 7 dots).
- Order numerals from 1 to 10 or beyond if they are ready.

DAY 1

Whole-Group Activities

INTRODUCTION TO THE UNIT ON NUMBERS

Have the children gather on the rug, and place a sack in front of them containing various items that use numbers. Ask the children to guess what is in it. It will contain some of the following items: clock, recipe, book, newspaper advertisement, measuring cup, and toy.

FLANNEL-BOARD STORY

While the children are gathered on the rug, tell a flannel-board story. One relating to number concepts would be especially appropriate.

Small-Group Activity

NUMERAL COLLAGES

Divide the children into small groups, and give each child an ice cream tub, a dish of liquid starch, and various numerals cut from lightweight paper, such as gift wrap. The children will paste the numerals on their cartons, using the starch as glue.

Individual Activities

- Paint at the single easel
- Put soapy water in the trough
- Number manipulatives

DAY 2

Small-Group Activities

MATCHING NUMERALS

Direct the children to small groups as they arrive. Give each child one calendar page with the numerals intact. Also give each child a set of numerals cut out of a page. Direct the children to match the cut-up numerals to the sheet of numerals. If they have difficulty, select the numerals 1 to 3 and then point to these same numerals on the calendar, asking the child to match them. It is the responsibility of the teacher in each group to simplify the task as needed for individual children. They will stay in these small groups until all the children arrive and have an opportunity to participate in the matching activity. Give books to each teacher in case the children arriving first tire of the matching activity.

FIELD TRIP—GROCERY STORE

Have the children gather at the rug after their matching activity, and explain the field trip to them. Explain and discuss the use of numbers in the grocery store. Encourage the children to look at prices on food items, weights on food items, and the use of numbers at the checkout stand in determining the total grocery bill. Also encourage them to weigh some produce items. Divide them into four groups. Give each group some money with which to purchase one large package of pudding, which will be used in a food activity later in the unit.

Whole-Group Activities

DISCUSSION ON COUNTING AND POSITION AND ORDERING OF THE NUMERALS 1 TO 10

Have the children gather on the rug, and count the number of boys, girls, and teachers separately and then all together to give practice in rote counting. After some counting songs have been sung, place poster paper with the numbers 1 to 10 outlined at the top where all the children can see it. Hold up individual numerals in correct order and match them to the corresponding outlined numerals on the poster paper. Emphasize the correct order and orientation of the numerals as they are pasted on the paper. Point out that numerals have to go a certain way, or else they will be upside down or backward.

ART—GADGET PRINTING

Place gadgets that make a circular imprint on a large table, along with black and yellow paint and white paper.

DAY 3

Whole-Group Activity

VISITOR—PARENT, GUARDIAN, OR GRANDPARENT OF ONE OF THE CLASS MEMBERS

The visitor will be invited into the classroom to measure and cut wood for a simple birdhouse. He will focus particularly on the use of numbers in measuring and the importance of measuring accurately so that the pieces of wood will fit together properly. He will point out the numbers on his tape measure. During this activity the children will be gathered around a sawhorse, with a dropcloth and plenty of room for the visitor to work. If weather permits, the activity could take place outdoors. The birdhouse, when completed, will be put in the art center for the children to paint as they wish. When completed, it will be installed in a tree on the playground.

Small-Group Activities

FOOD—MAKING PUDDING

After the visitor's presentation, while the children are still in a whole group, introduce and explain the food experience. Tell the children that the numerals on the package indicate the price and the weight. Then tell them how they will make the pudding that will be eaten the next day. Place particular emphasis on the use of numerals in measuring and timing the cooking of the pudding. Then divide the children into four small groups. Two of the groups will go outside while the other two groups stay in and make their pudding. One of the two groups that stays inside will use the hot plate in the room for cooking, while the other uses the stove in the kitchen. Then the groups will change places, and the ones that were outside will make their pudding. Pour the pudding into small bowls labeled with each child's name, cover, and refrigerate until they eat it the next day.

DISCUSSION AND STRUCTURED COLLAGES: MATCHING NUMERALS AND DETERMINING THE MEANING OF NUMERALS 1 TO 10

Using the poster paper with the numerals 1 to 10 printed across the top (used the day before), have the children review the orientation, counting, and sequence of numerals 1 to 10. Then explain the meaning of these numerals. Under each numeral, paste the number of squares representing that numeral. Then divide the children into smaller groups and give one piece of construction paper to each child. On one side, the numerals 1 to 5 will be outlined; on the other side, 6 to 10. Give each child numerals to match and paste, providing guidance and help where needed. Then give the children squares to paste below each numeral to represent the meaning of this numeral. Dots will be placed on the construction paper to aid the children in this task; they can match the square to the dot. For example, one dot will be placed below the numeral 1 for its matching square. This activity must be individualized to meet the developmental needs of each child. It is not expected that all children will be able to complete the activity as described.

Individual Activities

- Bubble blowing
- Trough containing number toys
- Number manipulatives

DAY 4

Small-Group Activities

EATING PUDDING

In the same groups as the previous day, allow the children to eat their bowls of pudding. During the interaction, review and reinforce concepts relating to numbers.

READING STORIES; MANIPULATIVE PLAY WITH NUMBER TOYS

Read various number stories to the children. Then give each group several number of toys for play and exploration.

Individual Activities

- ***Measuring in the Trough.*** Allow the children to play at the trough, filled with bits of paper such as confetti or hole punches, along with funnels, cups, spoons, and other measuring and pouring devices.

- ***Locomotor Rhythms Using Numerals.*** Designate one area of the room for this activity, and tell the children that those wishing to participate may do so. Tape pieces of paper, each with one numeral on it, to the floor (use only numerals 1 to 10). Give each participating child a small card with a numeral or with dots representing one of the numerals on it. Put on a recording, and have all the children do locomotor movements appropriate to the rhythm of the music (hopping, skipping, jumping, leaping, and so forth). When the music stops, the children are to stand on the numeral that either matches the numeral or represents the number of dots on their card. Cards can be exchanged and the activity repeated many times.

DAY 5

Whole-Group Activities

CLAPPING RHYTHMS

Have the children first clap the rhythm of some familiar nursery rhymes. Then clap some simple rhythm patterns, such as / //, /// /, or ////. The children will listen to the patterns and then clap them. Then place some black dots on the flannel board in different rhythmic patterns, one pattern at a time, and have the children clap them.

SCIENCE—ADDITION AND BALANCE RELATED TO NUMBER CONCEPTS

Have the children gather on the rug, and by means of a balance stick (see chapter 9), explain the concept of balance as equal weight on two sides. First, focus on placing a disk on, for example, the numeral 5 on one side, and make it balance with a disk on the numeral 5 on the other side. Then, show another way to make it balance by putting, on the second side, a disk on 3 and a disk on 2. Use real objects to illustrate that 3 and 2 are the same as 5. Then, with five beans, show ways of grouping to make 5, that is, combinations of 4 and 1 and 3 and 2. Divide the children into four smaller groups, and give each child 10 beans. The teacher in each group asks such questions as "Show me six beans." "Now show me another way of showing six, such as three and three."

Daily Activity

During the unit, put out a number-concept table so that children can go there during free play and participate in games and activities or play with pieces of equipment related to number concepts.

Individual Activities

- Painting with brushes and water outside
- Dramatization of nursery rhymes
- Number manipulatives

LESSON PLAN ON HONEYBEES (ONE DAY)

OBJECTIVES

Students will:

- Describe the honeybee and its characteristics: habitat, body parts, food, reproduction, locomotion.
- Recognize how the honeybee helps humans.
- Recall some uses of honey.
- Overcome fears of bees.
- Know that bees and flowers are necessary to each other for survival.

Whole-Group Activity

INTRODUCTION TO HONEYBEES

Tell the children that bees are the only insects that provide any important part of our food. Include questions such as "What is the food that they provide for us?" "What body parts do bees have? Do they have a head and legs?" "Where do honeybees live?" Have

flannel-board cutouts showing body parts of bees: head, thorax, abdomen, legs, wings, and antennae. Point out fuzz, pollen, and baskets, and talk about the nectar or honey sack. Show pictures of honeybee farms beehives; compare the differences. Ask what bees eat. Emphasize that bees are constantly seeking flowers because they use the pollen for protein and the nectar for carbohydrates. They convert the nectar to honey inside the hive.

Small-Group Activities

FOOD—SAMPLING BREAD AND HONEY

Following the discussion on honeybees and honey, each child will be given a piece of bread, some butter, and honey to eat. Teachers will reinforce that the honey has come from bees. They will also brainstorm and teach how we use honey (that is, on bread or rolls, as honey butter, or in recipes such as in whole wheat bread).

ART—MAKING BEEHIVES

Provide the children with yellow and brown flour clay, as well as a piece of Styrofoam in the shape of a beehive. Encourage the children to roll their clay into a "snake" and then mold it around the Styrofoam, layering the yellow and brown clay. When the children are finished, each child will be given a purchased bee (purchased by the teacher from a hobby store) to place anywhere on the beehive. Compare the texture of the clay to that of the Styrofoam.

FIELD TRIP—LIBRARY

Divide the children into groups by pinning different-colored bees on them. Parents will drive the children to the library. The children will listen to stories about honeybees read by the librarian.

Individual Activities

- Easel with brown and yellow paint
- Bees in aquarium

LESSON PLAN ON FISH (FOUR DAYS)

OBJECTIVES

Students will:

- Recognize different kinds of fish and their uses.
- Name the body parts of fish such as fins, tail, scales, and gills.
- Identify several uses for fish (food, pets, recreation).

- Recognize that although there are certain elements that all fish have in common (backbone, mouth, gills, swimming), there are many kinds of fish. Fish differ in size, color, shape, habit, taste, and use, as well as kind.

DAY 1

Whole-Group Activity

INTRODUCTION TO UNIT

Introduce the topic of the unit, as well as some of the basic concepts, such as what fish look like, where fish live, and how fish are cared for and used. Ask questions concerning what to observe on the field trip, such as "Do all fish look alike?" "Are all fish the same size and color?" "What odor does a fish have?"

Small-Group Activities

FIELD TRIP—FISH HATCHERY

Divide the children into groups with badges shaped like fish that are the same except for the fins. The fins will distinguish the groups. Teachers help the children to label this part of the fish and discuss the number or shape of fins to enable the children to find their own groups. Drive to the hatchery and tour the grounds. A guide should be available to show the children the fish equipment and to answer questions. Point out the various things to be observed: smell, size, and variations of fish.

EXPERIENCE CHART

Gather the children into groups to make experience charts. Title the piece. Let the children contribute the observations that they would like to remember about the trip. Write these observations on a piece of butcher paper as the children watch.

Individual Activities

- Aquarium with goldfish
- Paper and crayons at easel

DAY 2

Whole-Group Activity

STORY ABOUT A FISH

Read the story *Fish Is Fish* (L. Lionni, New York: Pantheon, 1970) at the rug, with special emphasis given to the fish characteristics that are common in the pictures. Point out and label these characteristics.

Small-Group Activities

SCIENCE—AIR IN WATER

Divide the children into small groups to discuss why the fish in the story had to live in the water. Let the children express their knowledge of fish. Bring in the concept of gills, and reinforce any correct concepts that the children discuss. Then perform the following science experiment: Before the children arrive, clear glasses will have been filled with water, one for each group. As the children finish discussing gills, underwater breathing, and living on land and in water, fill other glasses with fresh water, one for each group. Show the group the glass that was previously filled with water. The air in the water will have formed bubbles on the side of the glass. Explain that just as people can breathe air, fish have special equipment, gills, to get the air out of the water.

ART—PAPER BAG FISH

Provide the children with a paper bag taped into a fish shape, string for the tail, newspapers with which to stuff the fish, and paint to decorate it. Show the children how to stuff the fish with paper, and tie each bag to make the tail, with the child assisting. The children can then paint their fish. The fish will be set somewhere to dry until day 3, when collage items (eyes, gills, fins) will be added. Names will be taped to the fish.

Individual Activity

- Fish in the trough

DAY 3

Whole-Group Activities

ART—COLLAGE

As the children enter at the beginning of the day, direct them to the art activity of gluing collage items to their fish (made yesterday). The children can decorate their fish as they wish. Use this opportunity to reinforce knowledge of the parts of the fish.

MUSIC—RHYTHM

Gather the children at the rug for a rhythm activity. Pass out instruments so that the children can accompany songs, fingerplays, and records. Explore various beats.

Individual Activities

- Watercolors and salt at easel
- Water and objects in a container

DAY 4

Whole-Group Activity

DISCUSSION AND REVIEW—FILM ABOUT FISH

At the rug, involve the children in a discussion of what they have learned about fish: physical characteristics, where fish live, how they breathe, the uses of fish. Then present the concept that all fish are not alike. The class will discuss how the fish that they have seen have various characteristics (color, size, location, uses). Show a film that presents many unusual as well as common fish. Allow for discussion and comments.

VISITOR, WITH TASTING EXPERIENCES

Ask the visitor to demonstrate how fish is cooked, including the preparation required before cooking and the method of cooking. While the fish is being cooked, have the visitor show the children fishing equipment and tell them about fishing as a sport. Then divide the children into groups for a tasting experience. At the tables, set up prepared samples of fish, which have been carefully deboned. Use two or three different kinds of fish, including one prepared in class. Encourage the children to try each of the samples and compare the tastes.

Small-Group Activity

DRAMATIZATION OF POEMS, SONGS, OR RHYMES

Gather half of the children inside, and send the other half outside. Give the inside group a nursery rhyme, poem, or song to act out or perform as they wish. When they have practiced, have the other group come in and practice. Then each group will dramatize their selection for the other group, who will try to guess what is being dramatized.

Individual Activities

- Trough with balance scales and corn
- Pictures of various kinds of fish on display
- Fish specimens and aquatic insects

LESSON PLAN ON TREES (FIVE DAYS)

OBJECTIVES

Students will:

- Recognize the different parts of a tree (roots, trunk, branches, leaves).
- Develop an awareness of the nature around them.

- Recall the many types, uses, values, and products of trees (shade, ornamentation, fruit, nuts, lumber, homes).
- Define vocabulary terms relating to trees.

DAY 1

Whole-Group Activities

INTRODUCTION TO UNIT

Gather the children together at the rug. Sing a few songs about trees. Then tell the children about the different parts of the tree and show them pictures of many different kinds of trees. Read the book *A Tree Is Nice* (J. M. Udry, New York: Harper & Row, 1956).

DISCUSSION OF NATURE WALK

Gather the children at the rug to discuss the nature walk. Then guide them in a discussion on the uses of trees (shade, ornamental, building homes, fuel for fires). Use pictures as illustrations.

Small-Group Activities

ART—LEAF COLLAGES

Assign the children to small groups at separate tables. Give each group a piece of construction paper and some glue. Make many different shapes and kinds of leaves available for the children to use. The children will glue them on the paper in any desired way.

NATURE WALK

Divide the children into groups of three or four, with a leader for each group. The groups will walk through the area, looking at the many different trees. The leaders will obtain feedback from the children and help to clear up any misconceptions that they might have. This is also a good time to reinforce knowledge of the parts of the tree.

DAY 2

Whole-Group Activities

Visitor—Forest Ranger

Invite a ranger to talk to the children about forests and the trees in them. The discussion should include some of the problems involving trees, such as fires, diseases, winterkill, and insects that destroy the wood, as well as some of the uses of our national forests.

MUSIC AND CREATIVE MOVEMENT

Gather the children at the rug; after a brief introduction, put on a recording. Have the children use their shakers to keep time with the music, and encourage them to move like a tree on a hot summer day, in the wind, in the rain, when thirsty, and so on.

Small-Group Activity

ART—SHAKERS

At the tables, give each child two paper plates with holes punched all around the outside, as well as yarn, snips of colored paper, and liquid starch to use as paste. The children put seeds from a honey locust or other tree inside the two plates and then lace them up with yarn. They can decorate them with the paper snips. They will use these shakers for the music activity.

Individual Activity

TROUGH WITH WOODEN ITEMS

Possible items include wood chips, sawdust, toothpicks, wooden spoons, bark, and wooden boxes.

DAY 3

Whole-Group Activities

MOVIE EXPLAINING LOGGING

Show a movie as soon as all the children have arrived. It should be a short movie, so that the children will not lose interest.

FIELD TRIP—SAWMILL

In groups of three or four, the children ride with parents and teachers to the sawmill. Here, they see how the trees are cut into usable sizes and observe treatments used to cure the wood. The children see how many wood products are made (rough-cut lumber, planed lumber, sawdust, pressed plywood).

Small-Group Activity

ART—SAWDUST PICTURES

Give each child a piece of paper and some glue. Make sawdust available at each table in several different colors, to be used as desired.

DAY 4

Whole-Group Activity

DISCUSSION OF THINGS THAT GROW ON TREES

Discuss with the children the many types of trees and the different things that grow on them. Use pictures of the trees and items or the actual items if available. Read the book *Apple Tree! Apple Tree!* (M. Blocksma, Chicago: Children's Press, 1983).

Small-Group Activities

FOOD—NUTS

Divide the children into groups with name tags shaped like different kinds of nuts. Give them the opportunity to crack many different kinds of nuts and see how they taste. Save the shells.

ART—NUTSHELL ANIMALS

Have the children take the nutshells and sort out some that they would like to use. Make available paint, pieces of paper, glue, and small pieces of yarn. These materials will be used for making animals out of the shells.

DAY 5

Whole-Group Activities

MUSIC

Set out such things as wood blocks and log drums for the children to make music. They can also use these items with a record for variety.

SCIENCE

Set out many different preparations of apples so that the children will be able to see the results of some of the processes that can alter the form of food. Some of the items shown can include raw apples, canned applesauce, dried apples, and apple juice. The children will be able to see how the dried apple soaks up water and swells to a larger size.

VISITOR

Invite a person with an apple press to come in and show the children how apple juice, or cider, is made. The children will then drink the juice.

Small-Group Activity

ART—TOOTHPICK SCULPTURE

Give each of the children toothpicks, some fast-drying glue, and a cardboard base on which to put the sculpture. The children put toothpicks into the glue and stick them together.

Recipes for Food Experiences

Recipes are grouped under the headings Fruit–Vegetable; Grain; Milk, Yogurt, and Cheese; and Protein to assist in planning a variety of selections from each group using the MyPyramid (USDA, 2005) described in Chapter 6. Recommended daily servings are also included. Some recipes include foods from more than one group, and some include foods from all the groups. The "Quick and Easy" ideas at the beginning of each section, along with many of the recipes, have been taken from a publication on food and nutrition by the U.S. Department of Agriculture that provides a variety of healthy recipes for children at the following site: http:kidshealth.org/kids/recipes/index.html. This publication is not copyrighted and contains public information. We appreciate it as a source for nutritious food recipes for children.

In presenting recipes, our goals are fourfold: (a) emphasize ingredients that provide nutrients, (b) be practical in the selection of foods, (c) plan activities that are developmentally appropriate, and (d) allow children to learn by preparing foods from scratch.

A modest number of recipes that are rich in fat, cholesterol, sugar, or salt have been included; these should be used sparingly. Also, meat and eggs should be adequately cooked, and children should not be allowed to taste preparations containing raw eggs.

FRUIT–VEGETABLE GROUP (RECOMMENDED DAILY SERVINGS: VEGETABLES, 3; FRUIT, 2)

Quick and Easy

- Finger fruits such as grapes, apple sections, pear sections, and so on
- Dried fruits such as apricots, raisins, prunes, bananas, pineapple, or dried fruit leathers
- Mini kabobs of bite-sized fruit chunks strung on a toothpick

- Banana chunks dipped in orange juice; shaken in a bag with chopped peanuts; speared with toothpicks
- Juice cubes made by freezing fruit juice in an ice cube tray; other fruit drinks chilled with the cubes
- Grapefruit half, sprinkled with brown sugar and broiled
- Tomato half, sprinkled with bread crumbs and Parmesan or grated cheese, and broiled
- Tomato sections, cucumber slices, and cauliflowerets marinated in French dressing
- Raw vegetable sticks or pieces (radishes, celery, cauliflower, zucchini, green pepper, carrots, cucumbers, parsnips); try cutting them in various shapes
- Mini kabobs of bite-sized vegetable chunks strung on a toothpick
- Celery stuffed with cottage cheese, cheese spread, or peanut butter; raisins added for "ants on a log"
- Sliced zucchini, cauliflowerets, broccoli, and alfalfa sprouts with greens such as lettuce
- Cooked baby lima beans, sliced mushrooms, and green onions, seasoned with oregano; serve with dressing as desired

Banana Smoothie

The children mash pieces of banana on waxed paper. Add this to vanilla ice cream and milk. Stir together.

Orange Frost

6-oz can frozen orange juice concentrate

1 cup milk

1 cup water

$\frac{1}{4}$ cup sugar

$\frac{1}{2}$ tsp vanilla

10 ice cubes

Place all ingredients in a blender. Cover and blend until smooth. Serve immediately.

Fruit Dip

10-oz pkg frozen strawberries

8-oz pkg cream cheese

$\frac{1}{2}$ tsp lemon juice

Thaw and drain strawberries. Combine all ingredients in a blender and blend until smooth. Use as a dip for bite-sized fruit pieces.

Fruit-Nut Snack

$6\frac{1}{2}$-oz can Spanish peanuts, salted

1 cup raisins

4 oz chopped dates

(Other fruits and nuts such as dried banana slices, sunflower seeds, coconut, or other raw nuts can be added for variety or taste. Carob pieces can also be added if desired.)
Mix all ingredients.

Frozen Fruit Pops

1 cup frozen or fresh unsweetened fruit (strawberries, peaches, raspberries, blueberries, kiwis, mixed fruit)

1 cup plain low-fat yogurt

5 Tbsp honey

Put fruit in blender. Cover and blend for 45 seconds at medium speed until smooth. Pour into 1-quart measuring cup, add yogurt and honey, and mix well. Pour mixture into $3\frac{1}{2}$-oz paper or plastic cups (about seven) and put a wooden stick in the center of each cup. Freeze for 1 to 2 hours until firm. Remove cup from frozen pop and serve.

Apple Crisp

$3\frac{1}{2}$ cups sliced apples

1 Tbsp lemon juice

2 Tbsp water

$\frac{1}{2}$ cup flour (may use whole wheat)

$\frac{1}{2}$ cup quick-cooking oats

$\frac{3}{8}$ cup brown sugar

$\frac{3}{8}$ tsp salt

$\frac{1}{4}$ cup melted butter

1 tsp cinnamon

Combine apples, lemon juice, and water. Place in baking dish. Mix together remaining ingredients and sprinkle on apple mixture. Bake at 375°F for 35 to 40 minutes.

Applesauce

6 apples

4 Tbsp honey or brown sugar

Wash, core, and slice apples. Put in saucepan with a little water. Add honey and sugar and cook slowly until tender. Strain or force through sieve or food mill or puree in blender (if apples were peeled).

Pumpkin Drop Cookies

$\frac{1}{3}$ cup shortening

$\frac{3}{4}$ cup sugar

1 egg

1 cup canned pumpkin

$2\frac{1}{4}$ cups flour (part whole wheat)

4 tsp baking powder

1 tsp cinnamon

$\frac{1}{4}$ tsp ginger

$\frac{1}{4}$ tsp nutmeg

$\frac{1}{2}$ tsp salt

$\frac{1}{2}$ tsp vanilla

Cream sugar and shortening; add egg, blend well, and add pumpkin. Add dry ingredients, sifted together, and flavoring. One cupful of raisins and $\frac{1}{2}$ cup chopped nuts could be folded in. Drop by spoonfuls on greased cookie sheet. Bake at 350°F for 15 minutes. (Makes about 3 dozen cookies.)

Raggedy Ann Salad

Fresh or canned peach halves

Celery sticks

Shredded cheese

Nuts and raisins

Use a peach half for the body, celery for legs, and cheese for hair. Make the face with raisins and nuts. Place on a lettuce leaf.

Breakfast on a Stick

Bananas

Yogurt

Dry cereal or granola

Craft sticks

Peel bananas, cut into halves or thirds, depending on size of banana. Insert craft stick about $\frac{1}{2}$ way into banana section. Dip in yogurt and roll in dry cereal or granola.

Stew

Vegetables

Liquid

Browned stew meat, if desired

Have each child bring a vegetable. Prepare vegetables and add liquid. If desired, add browned stew meat. Simmer for at least an hour and a half. (Add a cleaned rock or stone for Stone Soup.)

Vegetable Dip

$\frac{1}{4}$ cup chives or onion tops

$\frac{1}{4}$ cup parsley

$\frac{1}{6}$ pkg (3 oz) fresh spinach (not frozen)

$\frac{1}{4}$ tsp salt

$\frac{1}{4}$ tsp ground pepper

1 cup mayonnaise

Place chives, parsley, and spinach in blender with a small amount of mayonnaise. After blending, add remaining ingredients and run blender again. (Half-and-half cream can be used to make the dip thinner.) Dip zucchini slices, cucumber, carrots, celery, and other vegetables into the dip.

Tempura Vegetables (single portion)

Batter:

1 Tbsp water

2 tsp beaten egg

2 Tbsp flour

Combine to make batter. Put carrot strips, green pepper, raw green beans, or other vegetables on a skewer and dip into batter. Cook in hot oil and serve with soy sauce.

Coleslaw

4 cups shredded or finely chopped cabbage

Pinch of salt

1 cup plain yogurt or salad dressing

Mix together. (May add diced apples, raisins, pineapple, marshmallows, etc.)

Salads with Vegetable and Fruit Combinations

To grated carrots, add any or all of the following:

Crushed or tidbit canned pineapple, drained

Raisins

Diced banana

Coconut

Salad dressing or plain yogurt to moisten

To chopped or shredded cabbage, add any or all of the following:

Diced celery

Diced apple

Chopped peanuts

Raisins

GRAIN GROUP (RECOMMENDED DAILY SERVINGS, 6)

Quick and Easy

- Raisin bread, toasted and spread with peanut butter
- Sandwiches using a variety of breads: raisin, cracked wheat, pumpernickel, rye, and black

- Date–nut roll or brown bread spread with cream cheese
- English muffins, served open faced for sandwiches such as hot roast beef or turkey, chicken salad
- Individual pizzas: English muffin halves topped with cheese slices, tomato sauce, and oregano and then broiled
- Waffles topped with yogurt and fruit
- Wheat or rye crackers topped with seasoned cottage cheese, cheese, meat spread, or peanut butter

Bread or Bread Sticks

1 cup milk

3 Tbsp shortening

1 Tbsp salt

1 cup cold water

2 yeast cakes

1 cup warm water

3 Tbsp sugar

8 cups flour (or 4 cups white and 4 cups whole wheat)

Scald milk, shortening, and salt; dissolve. Then add cold water. Soak yeast cakes in warm water and sugar in large bowl. Next, add 2 cups flour to yeast mixture and mix well. Add the milk, shortening, salt, and water mixture; add 6 cups flour. Mix well, pour out, and knead for 5 minutes on floured board. Place mixture back in bowl and let rise until double in bulk, about 90 minutes. Turn out on floured surface and knead for 5 minutes. Make two loaves, let rise in lightly greased pans until doubled in bulk, about 45 to 90 minutes, or let children shape into individual rolls or sculptures. Bake for 20 to 30 minutes at 425°F.

Navaho Fry Bread (Pahnelaquiz)

2 cups flour

$\frac{1}{2}$ cup dry milk

1 Tbsp baking powder

$\frac{3}{4}$ tsp salt

2 Tbsp shortening

$\frac{3}{4}$ cup lukewarm water

Mix flour, milk, baking powder, and salt together and then cut in shortening. Mix in water (more if necessary) and knead until smooth and elastic. Let stand at least 30 minutes or refrigerate overnight. Cut into pieces and deep fry in small amount of hot oil.

Fry Bread (single portion)

2 Tbsp flour

$\frac{1}{4}$ tsp baking powder

Pinch of salt

2 tsp water

Mix and then shape into thin pancake shape. Deep fry and drain on paper towel.

Hole-in-One

Bread slices

Eggs

Cut circle center out of bread slice. Heat a non-stick pan or pan coated with cooking spray. Place bread in pan and add cracked egg. Cook until bottom side is toasted and egg is partially cooked, turn bread and egg over to finish cooking.

Grits

$\frac{1}{3}$ cup grits

$6\frac{2}{3}$ cups boiling water

$1\frac{1}{2}$ tsp salt

3 Tbsp butter

Pour grits into boiling water, add salt, and stir until it thickens (2 to 3 minutes). Cover and cook over low heat 25 minutes; stir twice during that time. Dot with butter and serve.

Hoecakes (single portion)

2 Tbsp cornmeal

Pinch of salt

1 Tbsp boiling water

Mix, form into pancake, and cook on greased griddle. Serve with syrup or molasses.

Popcorn with Cheese

$\frac{1}{3}$ cup popcorn kernels, popped

2 Tbsp melted butter or margarine

$\frac{1}{2}$ cup Parmesan cheese

$\frac{1}{2}$ tsp salt, if desired

Place popped corn in a shallow baking pan. Drizzle with melted fat; mix. Sprinkle with cheese and salt, if desired; mix. Heat for 8 to 10 minutes in oven, stirring frequently.

Scones

2 cups unsifted flour

$\frac{1}{4}$ cup sugar

2 tsp baking powder

$\frac{1}{2}$ tsp baking soda

$\frac{1}{2}$ tsp salt

$\frac{1}{4}$ cup butter or margarine

2 eggs

$\frac{1}{3}$ cup sour milk (or combine 1 tsp vinegar or lemon juice with enough sweet milk to make $\frac{1}{3}$ cup)

Grease a baking sheet. Mix dry ingredients thoroughly. Mix in fat only until mixture is crumbly, using a pastry blender, two table knives, or a fork. Beat eggs; add milk. Stir into dry ingredients, mixing just until moistened. Divide dough in half. Place on baking sheet and shape each half of the dough into a 7-inch circle about inch thick. Cut each circle of dough into six wedges. Prick with a fork. Bake at 375°F for 12 minutes or until lightly browned.

Bran Cereal or Whole Wheat Muffins

1 cup whole bran cereal

$1\frac{1}{2}$ to 1 cup milk

1 egg, beaten

$\frac{1}{4}$ cup oil

$\frac{1}{4}$ cup honey, molasses, or brown sugar

$1\frac{1}{4}$ cups unsifted whole wheat flour

2 tsp baking powder

$\frac{1}{4}$ tsp baking soda

$\frac{1}{2}$ tsp salt

Grease muffin tins. Stir bran cereal and milk together in a bowl. Let stand for a minute or two, then add egg, oil, and honey. Beat well. Stir remaining ingredients together until well mixed. Add to liquid mixture and stir only until moistened. Put into muffin tins, filling only about two-thirds full. Bake at 400°F for about 20 to 25 minutes or until lightly browned. (*Option:* Eliminate bran cereal and increase whole wheat flour to 2 cups. If bran is eliminated, mix milk with other liquids.)

Red Beans and Rice

$\frac{1}{2}$ cup chopped onion

$\frac{1}{2}$ cup chopped celery

1 clove garlic

2 Tbsp butter or margarine

16-oz can kidney beans

2 cups cooked rice

1 Tbsp chopped parsley

$\frac{1}{2}$ tsp salt

$\frac{1}{8}$ tsp pepper

Cook onion, celery, and garlic in fat until tender; remove garlic. Add remaining ingredients. Simmer together for 5 minutes to blend flavors.

Whole Wheat Drop Cookies

2 cups brown sugar, packed

1 cup shortening

2 eggs, beaten

2 tsp baking soda, dissolved in 2 Tbsp water

$\frac{1}{2}$ tsp baking powder

$\frac{1}{2}$ tsp salt

$2\frac{1}{2}$ cups whole-wheat flour

1 cup chopped dates or raisins

$\frac{1}{2}$ cup nuts (optional)

Cream shortening and sugar. Mix remaining ingredients and add to creamed mixture; mix to a soft dough. Drop about 2 inches apart on baking sheet. Bake for 8 to 10 minutes at 375°F.

Individual Carrot Cakes

$\frac{1}{3}$ cup grated carrot

3 Tbsp yellow cake mix

$\frac{1}{4}$ tsp cinnamon

Pinch nutmeg

6 raisins

2 Tbsp beaten egg

Mix all ingredients together. Bake in muffin tin at 375°F for 10 to 15 minutes. Frost if desired.

RECIPES USING REFRIGERATOR BISCUITS

Pigs in a Blanket

Small sausages or hot dogs

Refrigerator biscuits

Fold refrigerator biscuits around sausages. Place in pan and bake at 450°F for 8 to 10 minutes. Cool slightly and serve with mustard or catsup, if desired.

Doughnuts or Scones

Refrigerator biscuits

Cooking oil (approximately $\frac{1}{4}$ in. deep in skillet)

Sugar, cinnamon–sugar mixture, or glaze

Poke small hole in biscuit with finger or thimble. Fry in heated oil for about 2 minutes or until done, turning once. Drain on paper towels. Roll in sugar or cinnamon–sugar mixture, or glaze. (For scones, eliminate hole in center.)

Bread Sticks

Refrigerator biscuits

Butter

Seeds, such as sesame seeds

Roll each biscuit into a long cylinder. Roll in butter and then, if desired, in any kind of seed, such as sesame seeds. Bake according to package directions. Serve in a basket with any kind of preserves or honey, or just butter.

Individual Pizzas

Refrigerator biscuits

1 lb ground beef

2 cups tomato sauce

$\frac{1}{4}$ cup finely chopped onion, if desired

Finely chopped small garlic bud, if desired

Grated cheese

On lightly greased cookie sheet, flatten biscuits and press up rim on edge. Fill with mixture of tomato sauce, browned hamburger, onion, and garlic. Top with grated cheese. (Other ingredients that may be used include sliced wieners, pepperoni, Parmesan cheese, oregano, parsley flakes, onion, garlic, basil, pepper.) Bake at 425°F for 10 minutes.

MILK, YOGURT, AND CHEESE GROUP (RECOMMENDED DAILY SERVINGS, 2)

Quick and Easy

- Milkshakes with mashed fresh berries or bananas
- Parfait of cottage cheese, yogurt, or ice milk combined with fruit, sprinkled with chopped nuts, wheat germ, or crisp cereal
- Fruit-flavored yogurt
- Custard
- Ice-milk sundae topped with fresh, canned, or frozen fruits
- Cheese cubes plain, or speared with pretzel sticks, or alternated with mandarin orange sections on a toothpick
- Assorted cheeses with crackers or fresh fruits
- Dips for vegetables sticks (for fewer calories and more nutrition, substitute cottage cheese or plain yogurt for sour cream and mayonnaise in preparing dips)

Butter

$\frac{1}{2}$ pint whipping cream

Dash of salt

Yellow coloring, if desired

Warm cream to room temperature. Shake in bottle until butter and milk separate. Pour milk off and continue to separate the milk from the butter. Salt to taste. Add yellow food coloring, if desired.

Chili con Queso Dip

16-oz box pasteurized processed cheese spread, cut in cubes

$\frac{3}{4}$ cup canned tomatoes, chopped

1 Tbsp finely chopped chili peppers

Place cheese cubes in the top of a double boiler over boiling water. Stir constantly until cheese is melted. Stir in tomatoes and peppers until well blended and creamy. Serve hot with tortilla or corn chips.

Eggnog

3 eggs, slightly beaten

$\frac{1}{2}$ cup sugar

$\frac{1}{4}$ tsp salt

3 cups milk

1 cup half-and-half

$\frac{1}{2}$ tsp vanilla

$1\frac{1}{2}$ tsp imitation rum flavoring

Nutmeg as desired

Mix beaten eggs with sugar and salt in the top of a double boiler. Add milk and half-and-half. Cook over boiling water, stirring constantly, just until mixture coats spoon, about 10 to 15 minutes. Cool. Add vanilla and rum flavorings.

Chill. Immediately before serving, strain eggnog. Beat with rotary beater until frothy. Pour into chilled cups. Sprinkle each serving with nutmeg, as desired.

Banana Smoothie (single serving)

Mash $\frac{1}{2}$ banana, mix with $\frac{1}{2}$ cup ice milk, and $\frac{1}{4}$ cup milk

Banana–Orange Shake

4 ripe bananas, sliced

$\frac{1}{3}$ cup orange juice

6 Tbsp honey

Salt

$\frac{1}{4}$ tsp vanilla

4 cups reconstituted nonfat dry milk (To make 4 cups reconstituted nonfat dry milk mix $3\frac{3}{4}$ cups water with $\frac{3}{4}$ cups nonfat dry milk. Or, you may use 4 cups milk instead.)

Put in blender and beat until smooth.

Strawberry–Yogurt Pops

2 10-oz pkg frozen strawberries, thawed (conserve liquid)

1 Tbsp unflavored gelatin

16 oz plain yogurt

3-oz paper cups

Wooden sticks

Drain strawberries. Place drained liquid in a saucepan and sprinkle with gelatin. Cook over low heat, stirring constantly, until gelatin dissolves. Mix strawberries, yogurt, and gelatin mixture in a blender until smooth. Place cups on a tray or in a baking pan. Fill with blended mixture and cover cups with a sheet of aluminum foil. Insert a stick in each pop by making a slit in the foil over the center of the cup. Freeze pops until firm. Run warm water on outside of cup to loosen each pop from the cup.

PROTEIN GROUP (MEAT, POULTRY, EGGS, NUTS, FISH, BEAN) RECOMMENDED DAILY SERVINGS, 2)

Quick and Easy

- Nuts, sesame seeds, or toasted sunflower seeds
- Sandwich spread of peanut butter combined with raisins or chopped dates
- Peanut butter and honey spread on an English muffin, sprinkled with chopped walnuts and heated under broiler
- Grilled open-faced peanut butter and mashed banana sandwich
- Tomatoes stuffed with egg salad
- Melon wedges topped with thinly sliced ham

Toasted Sunflower Seeds

1 cup sunflower seeds

1 tsp oil, if desired

$\frac{1}{4}$ tsp salt, if desired

Mix sunflower seeds with oil only if salt is used. Spread plain or oiled seeds on baking sheet. Bake at 325°F for about 8 minutes or until lightly browned. (Watch carefully, these seeds brown quickly.) Sprinkle oiled seeds with salt while hot.

Quick-Cook Chili

1 lb ground beef

$\frac{1}{2}$ cup chopped onion

16-oz can pinto beans

1 can condensed tomato soup

2 to 3 tsp chili powder

Heat beef and onion in a skillet until beef is browned and onion is tender. Drain off excess fat. Stir in remaining ingredients, cover. Simmer for 30 minutes, stirring occasionally.

Chao Fan

1 Tbsp oil

4 eggs, well beaten

2 green onions, chopped

$\frac{1}{2}$ cup ham, diced

4 oz frozen peas, thawed

2 cups rice, cooked and cooled

Soy sauce (optional)

Scramble eggs in oil and add green onion. Add chopped ham and cooked peas. Serve over cooked rice. Add soy sauce, if desired. (Adapted from Kositsky, 1977, p. 30).

Wontons

Wonton skins

Hamburger

Soy sauce

Bean sprouts

Green onion

Combine raw hamburger, a little soy sauce, some cut-up bean sprouts, and a little minced green onion. Put a teaspoon of the mixture into the center of the wonton skin and fold in half to make a triangle. Dampen the edges so they stick together. Simmer in chicken soup, or deep-fat fry until meat is cooked (5–10 minutes). (Adapted from Kositsky, 1977, p. 30).

Chicken–Fruit Salad

3 cups cooked chicken, cut in chunky pieces

$\frac{3}{4}$ cup chopped celery

$\frac{3}{4}$ cup grape halves, seeded

20-oz can pineapple chunks in natural juice, drained

11-oz can mandarin oranges, drained

$\frac{1}{4}$ cup chopped pecans

$\frac{1}{4}$ cup salad dressing or plain yogurt

$\frac{1}{8}$ tsp salt

Lettuce leaves

Toss chicken, celery, grapes, pineapple, oranges, and 3 Tbsp of the pecans together lightly. Gently mix salad dressing or yogurt and salt with chicken mixture. Chill. Serve on lettuce leaves. Garnish with remaining pecans.

Mexicale Hot Dog (single portion)

1 flour tortilla

1 slice cheese

1 hot dog

Salsa (optional)

Lay flour tortilla out. Put slice of cheese on tortilla, spread with salsa, put hot dog on top, and roll up. Microwave for 1 minute.

Open-Faced Submarine Sandwiches

6 English muffin halves, toasted

1 Tbsp butter or margarine

6 slices meat

1 cup chopped lettuce

$\frac{1}{2}$ small onion, thinly sliced and separated into rings

1 medium tomato, thinly sliced

$\frac{1}{2}$ tsp basil leaves

6 slices pasteurized process American cheese

Spread toasted muffin halves with butter or margarine. Layer meat slices, lettuce, onion, and tomato slices on muffins. Sprinkle with basil. Top each sandwich with cheese slice. Broil until cheese is melted and lightly browned, about 5 minutes.

Refried Beans

1 lb pinto beans, dried

1 qt water

Salt to taste

Dash of cumin

$\frac{1}{4}$ cup lard or bacon fat (optional)

Sort and wash pinto beans. Cover with water generously; let stand overnight. Next day, pour off liquid. Put in large pot and add twice as much water as there are beans. Stir in salt and cumin. Quickly bring to a boil. Lower heat. Simmer for 2 to 3 hours (until tender). Drain; mash beans. Heat lard or fat. Add very hot lard to beans. Stir and simmer until fat is absorbed. Use as is or refry. To refry, fry mashed beans in hot lard or fat until completely dry.

Peanut Butter

$1\frac{1}{2}$ Tbsp oil

1 cup peanuts

Salt

Put the oil in a blender and gradually add the peanuts, blending well; sprinkle in a little salt.

Peanut Butter Balls

15 oz graham crackers

2 Tbsp corn syrup

2 Tbsp milk

$\frac{1}{2}$ cup peanut butter

4 Tbsp butter or margarine

2 tsp vanilla

Crush crackers with a rolling pin or in a blender. Cream butter and add syrup, milk, vanilla, and peanut butter. Add 1 cup of the graham cracker crumbs and set the remainder aside. Mix the ingredients thoroughly; then roll into 1-inch balls. Roll the balls in the remaining cracker crumbs and serve.

Baked Kidney Beans

3 cups kidney beans, dried

2 large onions, sliced

2 cups canned tomatoes

3 Tbsp chopped green pepper

1 Tbsp salt

2 Tbsp brown sugar

3 Tbsp vegetable oil

Cover beans generously with water and soak overnight. Parboil with onions in the morning and then turn into bean pot. Add the rest of the ingredients and bake for 5 to 6 hours.

Mexican Loaf

1-lb can kidney beans

$\frac{1}{2}$ lb cheddar cheese

1 finely chopped onion

1 Tbsp butter

1 cup bread crumbs

2 eggs

Seasonings

Green pepper rings

Tomato sauce

Drain liquid from beans. Grind beans with cheese. Saute onion in butter. Combine beans, cheese, $\frac{3}{4}$ cup bread crumbs, onion, eggs, and seasonings. Put in buttered baking dish, cover with the rest of the bread crumbs, and bake in 350°F oven for 30 to 40 minutes. Garnish with green pepper rings and serve hot with heated tomato sauce.

FATS AND SWEETS GROUP (RECOMMENDED DAILY SERVINGS, SMALL AMOUNT) MISCELLANEOUS GROUP

Pudding Squares

5 envelopes unflavored gelatin

1 small pkg vanilla or butterscotch instant pudding

$1\frac{1}{2}$ cups boiling water

$\frac{1}{2}$ cups cold milk

In large bowl, combine unflavored gelatin and pudding mix. Add boiling water and beat with wire whisk or rotary beater until well blended; stir in milk. Pour into 8- or 9-inch square pan and chill until firm. Cut into squares to serve.

Gelatin Squares (sometimes called Finger Gelatin)

2 large pkg flavored gelatin

3 cups water

$\frac{1}{2}$ cup sugar

3 envelopes unflavored gelatin

$2\frac{1}{2}$ cups cold water

Boil the first three ingredients together and add the unflavored gelatin that has been dissolved in the cold water. Pour all ingredients into a 9- by 13-inch pan. Let set for about 2 hours. Cut into bite-sized pieces and eat with fingers, or cut with cookie cutters into desired shapes.

REFERENCES

Media and Software Resources

Davidson & Associates
P.O. Box 2961
Torrance, CA 90509
(800–545-7677)
www.education.com

Davidson Films
668 Marsh Street
San Luis Obispo, CA 93401–3951
(888–437-4200)
www.davidsonfilms.com

Films for the Humanities & Sciences
P.O. Box 2053
Princeton, NJ 08543–2053
(800–257-5126)
www.films.com

Insight Media
2162 Broadway
New York, NY 10024–0621
(800–233-9910)
www.insight-media.com

National Geographic
Educational Services
1145 17th Street, NW
Washington, DC 20036–4688
(800–368-2728)
www.nationalgeographic.com

Riverdeep Interactive Learning
P.O. Box 97021
Redmond, WA 98073–0721
(800–362-2890)
www.riverdeep.net

Sunburst
101 Castleton Street
P.O. Box 100
Pleasantville, NY 10570
(800–321-7511)
www.sunburst.com

The Video Journal of Education
8686 South 1300 East
Sandy, UT 84094
(878–350-6500)
www.schoolimprovement.net

Adams, M. J. (1990). *Beginning to read: Thinking and learning about print.* Champaign, IL: University of Illinois Press—Center for the Study of Reading.

Albert Shanker Institute. (2009). *Preschool curriculum: What's in it for children and teachers?* Washington, DC: Author. Retrieved July 9, 2010, from http://www.ashankerinst.org

Allington, R. L., & McGill-Franzen, A. (1995). Flunking: Throwing good money after bad. In R. L. Allington & S. A. Walmsley (Eds.), *No quick fix* (pp. 45–60). New York: Teachers College Press.

American Academy of Pediatrics (AAP). (2003). Prevention of pediatric overweight and obesity. *Pediatrics, 112,* 424–430.

American Academy of Pediatrics, American Public Health Association, & National Resource Center for Health and Safety in Child Care (APA, APHA, & NRCHSCC). (2002). *Caring for our children: National health and safety performance standards: Guidelines for out-of-home child care programs* (2nd ed.). Elk Grove Village, IL: Authors.

American Association for Health Education. (2006). Cited from pre-publication document of National Health Education Standards, PreK–12. Retrieved from http://www.aahperd.org/aahe/pdf_files/standards.pdf

American Heart Association. (2010). *Heart disease and stroke statistics–2010 update.* Dallas, TX: Author. Retrieved from www.americanheart.org/downloadable/heart/126566515297ODS-3241%20HeartStrokeUpdate-2010.pdf

Anderson, S. J. (2002). He's watching! The importance of the onlooker stage of play. *Young Children, 57*(6), 58.

Anderson, T. L. (1996). "They're trying to tell me something": A teacher's reflection on primary children's construction of mathematical knowledge. *Young Children, 51*(4), 34–42.

Andrade, H. (2008). Self-assessment through rubrics. *Educational Leadership, 65*(4), 60–63.

Andress, B. (1995). Transforming curriculum in music. In S. Bredekamp & T. Rosegrant (Eds.), *Reaching potentials: Transforming early childhood curriculum and assessment,* (Vol. 2, pp. 99–108). Washington, DC: National Association for the Education of Young Children.

Armbruster, B. B., Lehr, F., & Osborn, J. (2001). *Put reading first: The research building blocks for teaching children to read.* Washington, DC: Center for the Improvement of Early Reading Achievement.

Armistead, M. E. (2007). Kaleidoscope: How a creative arts enrichment program prepares children for kindergarten. *Young Children, 62*(6), 86–93.

Armstrong, T. (2009). *Multiple intelligences in the classroom* (3rd ed.). Alexandria, VA: Association for Supervision and Curriculum Development.

Arndt, J. S., & McGuire-Schwartz, M. E. (2008). Early childhood school success: Recognizing families as integral partners. *Childhood Education, 84*(5), 281–285.

Arnqvist, A. (2000). Linguistic games as a way to introduce reading and writing in preschool groups. *Childhood Education, 76*(6), 365–367.

Association for Childhood Education International (1995c). President's message: Reconsidering developmentally appropriate practices. *Childhood Education, 71*(4), 224-A, 224-D.

Association for Childhood Education International (1995/1996). Money math. *Childhood Education, 72*(2), 96-I.

Association for Childhood Education International (1996b). Issues of diversity in teacher education. *Childhood Education, 72*(3), 160-L, 160-O.

Association for Childhood Education International (1996c). Reduce, reuse, recycle. *Childhood Education, 72*(5), 288-G.

Auxter, D., Pyfer, J., & Huettig, C. (2009). *Principles and methods of adapted physical education and recreation* (11th ed.). St. Louis: McGraw-Hill.

Bagdi, A., & Vacca, J. L. (2005). Supporting early childhood socio-emotional well being: The building blocks for early learning and school success. *Early Childhood Education Journal, 33,* 145–150.

Baker, A. M., & Manfredi/Petitt, L. A. (2004). *Relationships, the heart of quality care: Creating community among adults in early care settings.* Washington, DC: National Association for the Education of Young Children.

Bakley, S. (1997). Love a little more, accept a little more. *Young Children, 52*(2), 21.

Bales, D., Wallinga, C., & Coleman, M. (2006). Health and safety in the early childhood classroom: Guidelines for curriculum development. *Childhood Education, 82*(3), 132–138.

Balke, E. (1997). Play and the arts: The importance of the "unimportant." *Childhood Education, 73*(6), 355–360.

Ball, R. A. H. (2006). Supporting and involving families in meaningful ways. *Young Children, 61*(1), 10–11.

Banks, J. A. (1993). Multicultural education: Development, dimensions, and challenges. *Phi Delta Kappan, 75*(1), 21–27.

Barclay, K., Benelli, C., & Curtis, A. (1995). Literacy begins at birth: What caregivers can learn from parents of children who read early. *Young Children, 50*(4), 24–28.

Barclay, K., & Walwer, L. (1992). Linking lyrics and literacy through song picture books. *Young Children, 47*(4), 76–85.

Barclay, K. H. (2010). Using song picture books to support early literacy development. *Childhood Education, 86*(3), 138–145.

Batsche, G. M., Elliott, J., Graden, J., Grimes, J., Kovaleski, J. F., Prasse, D., et al. (2005). *Response to intervention: Policy considerations and implementation.* Alexandria, VA: National Association of State Directors of Special Education.

Bauer, K. L., Sheerer, M. A., & Dettore, E., Jr. (1997). Creative strategies in Ernie's early childhood classroom. *Young Children, 52*(6), 47–52.

Bear, D. R., Invernizzi, M., Templeton, S., & Johnston, F. (2008). *Words their way: Word study for phonics, vocabulary, and spelling instruction* (4th ed.). Upper Saddle River, NJ: Merrill/Prentice Hall.

Beck, I. L. (2006). *Making sense of phonics: The hows and whys.* New York: Guilford Press.

Beck, I. L., & McKeown, M. G. (2006). *Improving comprehension with questioning the author: A fresh and expanded view of a powerful approach.* New York: Scholastic.

Bennet-Armistead, V. S., Duke, N., & Moses, A. M. (2006). *Literacy and the youngest learner: Best practices for Educators of Children from Birth to 5.* New York: Scholastic.

Bennett, L. (1995). Wide world of breads in children's literature. *Young Children, 50*(5), 64–68.

Bennett, T. (2007). Mapping family resources and support. In D. Koralek (ed.), *Spotlight on young children and families.* Washington, DC: National Association for the Education of Young Children.

Bennett, W. J. (Ed.) (1993). *The book of virtues.* New York: Simon & Schuster.

Benson, J., & Miller, J. L. (2008). Experiences in nature: A pathway to standards. *Young Children, 63*(4), 22–28.

Bewick, C. J., & Kostelnik, M. (2004). Educating early childhood teachers about computers. *Young Children, 59*(3), 26–29.

Biggar, H., & Pizzolongo, P. J. (2004). School readiness: More than ABCs. *Young Children, 59*(3), 64–66.

Birchmayer, J. Kennedy, A., & Stonehouse, A. (2008). *From lullabies to literature: Stories in the lives of infants and toddlers.* Washington, DC: National Association for the Education of Young Children and Pademelon Press: Castle Hill, NSW, Australia.

Bisgaier, C. S., Samaras, T., with Russo, M. J. (2004). Young children try, try again: Using wood, glue, and words to enhance learning. *Young Children, 59*(4), 22–29.

Blake, S. (2009). Engage, investigate, and report: Enhancing the curriculum with scientific inquiry. *Young Children, 94*(6), 49–53.

Bloom, B. S. (Ed.). (1956). *Taxonomy of educational objectives: The classification of educational goals: Handbook I, cognitive domain.* New York, Toronto: Longmans, Green.

Bloom, B., Englehart, M., Hill, W., Furst, E., & Krathwohl, D. (1956). *Taxonomy of educational objectives. The classification of educational goals. Handbook I: Cognitive domain.* New York: Longman Green.

Bodrova, E., & Leong, D. J. (2003). Chopsticks and counting chips: Do play and foundational skills need to compete for the teacher's attention in an early childhood classroom? *Young Children, 58*(3), 10–17.

Bodrova, E., & Leong, D. J. (2008). Developing self-regulation in kindergarten: Can we keep all the crickets in the basket? *Young Children, 63*(2), 56–58.

Bodrova, E., Leong, D. J., & Paynter, D. E. (1999). Literacy standards for preschool learners. *Educational Leadership, 57*(2), 42–46.

Bond, T. F. (2001). Giving them free rein: Connection in student-led book groups. *Reading Teacher, 54*(6), 574–584.

Booth, D., & Barton, B. (2000). *Story works: How teachers can use shared stories in the new curriculum.* Portland, ME: Stenhouse.

Bosse, S., Jacobs, G., & Anderson, T. L. (2009). Science in the air. *Young Children, 64*(6), 10–15.

Bosworth, K. (1995). Caring for others and being cared for. *Phi Delta Kappan, 76*(9), 686–693.

Bothmer, S. (2003). *Creating the peaceable classroom: Techniques to calm, uplift, and focus teachers and students.* Tucson, AZ: Zephyr Press.

Bouhebent, E.A. (2008). Providing the best for families: Developing appropriate home visitation services. *Young Children, 63*(2), 82–87.

Bowman, B., Donovan, M. S., & Burns, M. S. (Eds.). (2002). *Eager to learn: Educating our preschoolers.* Washington, DC: National Academy Press.

Bowman, B., & Moore, E. K. (Eds.). (2006). *School readiness and social-emotional development: Perspectives on cultural diversity.* Washington, DC: National Black Child Development Institute, Inc.

Brabham, E. G., & Villaume, S. K. (2001). Building walls of words. *The Reading Teacher, 54*(7), 700–702.

Bradley, D. H., & Pottle, P. R. (2001). Supporting emergent writers through on-the-spot conferencing and publishing. *Young Children, 56*(3), 20–27.

Bradley, J., & Kibera, P. (2006). Closing the gap: Culture and promotion of inclusion in child care. *Young Children, 61*(1), 34–40.

Brandt, R. S. (2000). *Education in a new era.* Alexandria, VA: Association for Supervision and Curriculum Development (ASCD).

Bredekamp, S. (2010). Learning and cognitive development. In V. Washington & J. Jenkins-Scott (Eds.), *Children of 2020: Creating a better tomorrow* (pp. 48–53). Washington, DC: Council for Professional Recognition; and Washington, DC: National Association for the Education of Young Children.

Bredekamp., S., & Rosegrant, T. (Eds.). (1992). *Reaching potentials: Appropriate curriculum and assessment for young children* (Vol. 1). Washington, DC: National Association for the Education of Young Children.

Bredekamp, S., & Shepard, L. (1989). How best to protect children from inappropriate school expectations, practices, and policies. *Young Children, 44*(3), 14–24.

Brenneman, K. (2009). Preschoolers as scientific explorers. *Young Children 94*(6), 54–60.

Breslin, D. (2005). Children's capacity to develop resiliency: How to nurture it. *Young Children, 60*(1), 47–52.

Brewer, J., & Kieff, J. (1996/1997). Fostering mutual respect for play at home and school. *Childhood Education, 73*(2), 92–96.

Briody, J., & McGarry, K. (2005). Using social stories to ease children's transitions. *Young Children, 60*(5), 38–42.

Brodmann, A. (1993). *The gift.* New York: Simon & Schuster.

Bromley, K. D. (1996). *Webbing with literature: Creating story maps with children's books.* Boston: Allyn & Bacon.

Bronson, M. B. (2004). Choosing play materials for primary school children (ages 6–8). In *Spotlight on young children and play* (pp. 22–23). Washington, DC: National Association for the Education of Young Children.

Brown, W. (2008). Young children assess their learning: The power of the Quick Check strategy. *Young Children, 63*(6), 14–20.

Buchanan, B. L., & Rios, J. M. (2004). Teaching science to kindergartners: How can teachers implement science standards? *Young Children, 59* (3), 82–87.

Buchoff, R. (1995). Jump rope rhymes. .. in the classroom? *Childhood Education, 71*(3), 149–151.

Buehl, D. (2009). *Classroom strategies for interactive learning* (3rd ed.). Newark, DE: International Reading Association.

Bulach, C. R. (2002). Implementing a character education program and assessing its impact on student behavior. *The Clearing House, 76*(2), 79–83.

Burke, A. (2010). *Reading to learn.* Portland, ME: Stenhouse.

Burningham, L. M., & Dever, M. T. (2005). An interactive model for fostering family literacy. *Young Children, 60*(5), 87–94.

Burns, M. S., Griffin, P., & Snow, C. E. (1999). *Starting out right: A guide to promoting children's reading success.* Washington, DC: National Academy Press.

Byrnes, D. A., & Kiger, G. (2005). *Common bonds: Anti-bias teaching in a diverse society* (3rd ed.). Olney, MD: Association for Childhood Education International.

Calkins, L. M. (1994). *The art of teaching writing.* Portsmouth, NH: Heinemann.

Campbell, R. (2001). *Read-alouds with young children.* Newark, DE: International Reading Association.

Carlson, F. M. (2006). *Essential touch: Meeting the needs of young children.* Washington, DC: National Association for the Education of Young Children.

Carson, R. (1956). *A sense of wonder.* New York: Harper & Row.

Carter, P. (2008). Smile on your brother: Teaching siblings together. *Young Children, 63*(5), 18–23.

Cartwright, S. (2004). Teachers on teaching: Young citizens in the making. *Young Children, 59*(5), 108–109.

Casey, M. B. (2001). Spatial–mechanical reasoning skills versus mathematics: Self-confidence as mediators of gender differences in mathematics. *Journal for Research in Mathematics Education, 32*(1), 28–58.

Casey, M. B., & Lippman, M. (1991). Learning to plan through play. *Young Children, 46*(4), 52–58.

Cassidy, D. J., Mims, S., Rucker, L., & Boone, S. (2003). Emergent curriculum and kindergarten readiness. *Childhood Education, 79*(4), 194–199.

Centers for Disease Control and Prevention (CDC). (2002). Prevalence of overweight among children and adolescents. Retrieved November 7, 2006, from http://www.cdc.gov/nchs/

Centers for Disease Control and Prevention (CDC). (n.d.) *Infants and young children: Animal safety tips.* Retrieved from http://www.cdc.gov/healthypets/child.htm

Chalufour, I., & Worth, K. (2007). Science in kindergarten. In D. F. Gullo (Ed.), *K Today: Teaching and learning in the kindergarten year* (pp. 95–106). Washington, DC: National Association for the Education of Young Children.

Chapman, M. L. (1996). The development of phonemic awareness in young children: Some insights from a case study of a first-grade writer. *Young Children, 51*(2), 31–37.

Chard, S. C. (1992). *The project approach: A practical guide for teachers.* Edmonton: University of Alberta Printing Services.

Chard, S. C. (1998). *The project approach: Making the curriculum come alive.* NY: Scholastic.

Charlesworth, R. (2005). *Experiences in math for young children* (5th ed.). Belmont, CA: Wadsworth.

Charlton, B. C. (2005). *Informal assessment strategies: Asking questions, observing students, and planning lessons that promote successful interaction with text.* Portland, ME: Stenhouse.

Charney, R. S. (2002). *Teaching children to care: Classroom management for ethical and academic growth K–8.* Portland, ME: Stenhouse.

Checkley, K. (1997). The first seven. . . and the eighth: A conversation with Howard Gardner. *Educational Leadership, 55*(1), 8–13.

Chenfeld, M. B. (1991). Wanna play? *Young Children, 46*(6), 4–6.

Chenfeld, M. B. (1995). Do spiderwebs ever wake you up? *Young Children, 50*(5), 70–71.

Chenfeld, M. B. (1997). Telling time. *Phi Delta Kappan, 78*(6), 475.

Children's Defense Fund. (2005). *State of America's children.* Washington, DC: Author.

Cianciolo, S., Trueblood-Noll, R., & Allingham, P. (2004). Health consultation in early childhood settings. *Young Children, 59*(2), 56–61.

Clements, D. H. (2001). Mathematics in the preschool. *Teaching Children Mathematics, 7*(5), 270–276.

Clements, D. H. (2004). Major themes and recommendations. In D. H. Clements & J. Sarama (Eds.), *Engaging young children in mathematics: Standards for early childhood mathematics education,* (pp. 7–72). Mahwah, NJ: Lawrence Erlbaum.

Clements, D. H., & Battista, M. T. (1990). Constructivist learning and teaching. *Arithmetic Teacher, 38*(1), 34–35.

Clements, D. H., & Healy, J. M. (1999). Computers and young children. *Scholastic Early Childhood Today, 13*(2), 44–47.

Clements, D. H., & McMillen, S. (1996). Rethinking "concrete" manipulatives. *Teaching Children Mathematics, 2*(5), 270–279.

Clements, D. H., & Sarama, J. (2000). Young children's ideas about geometric shapes. *Teaching Children Mathematics, 6*(8), 482–488.

Clements, D. H., & Swaminathan, S. (1995). Technology and school change—New lamps for old? *Childhood Education, 71*(5), 275–278.

Clements, D. H., Swaminathan, S., Hannibal, M. A. Z., & Sarama, J. (1999). Young children's concepts of shape. *Journal for Research in Mathematics Education, 30*(2), 192–212.

Cline, D. B., & Ingerson. D. (1996). The mystery of Humpty's fall: Primary-school children as playmakers. *Young Children, 51*(6), 4–10.

Cohen, L. E. (2009). Exploring cultural heritage in a kindergarten classroom. *Young Children, 64*(3), 72–77.

Cole, R. (2004). *Children and fire.* Rochester Fire-Related Youth Project progress report (3). Unpublished.

Cole, R. E., Crandall, R., & Kourofsky, C. E. (2004). We can teach young children fire safety. *Young Children, 59*(2), 14–18.

Colker, L. J. (2002). Teaching and learning about science. *Young Children, 57*(5), 10–11.

Colker, L. J. (2005). *The cooking book: Fostering young children's learning and delight.* Washington, DC: National Association for the Education of Young Children.

Collins, N. L. D., & Shaeffer, M. B. (1997). Look, listen, and learn to read. *Young Children, 52*(5), 65–68.

Collinson, V. (1995). Making the most of portfolios. *Learning, 24*(1), 43–46.

Conezio, K., & French, L. (2002). Science in the preschool classroom: Capitalizing on children's fascination with the everyday world to foster language and literacy development. *Young Children, 57*(5), 12–18.

Conlon, A. (1992). Giving Mrs. Jones a hand: Making group story time more pleasurable and meaningful for young children. *Young Children, 47*(3), 14–18.

Cook-Cottone, C. (2009). Eating disorders in childhood: Prevention and treatment supports. *Childhood Education 85*(5), 300–305.

Cooper, J. D., Kiger, N. D., & Au, K. H. (2009). *Literacy: Helping children construct meaning* (7th ed.). Boston: Houghton Mifflin.

Cooper, J. L., & Dever, M. T. (2001). Sociodramatic play as a vehicle for curriculum integration in first grade. *Young Children, 56*(3), 58–63.

Copple, C., (Ed.) (2003). *A world of difference: Reading on teaching young children in a diverse society.* Washington, DC: NAEYC.

Copple, C., & S. Bredekamp. (2006). *Basics of developmentally appropriate practice: An introduction for teachers of children 3 to 6.* Washington, DC: NAEYC.

Copple, C., & Bredekamp, S. (2009). *Developmentally appropriate practice in early childhood program serving children from birth through age 8* (3rd ed.). Washington, DC: National Association for the Education of Young Children.

Copley, J.V. (2010). *The young child and mathematics* (2nd ed.). Washington, DC: National Association for the Education of Young Children; and Reston, VA: National Council of Teachers of Mathematics.

Council of Chief State School Officers. (1987). Interstate new teacher assessment and support consortium (INTASC). Retrieved from http://www.ccsso.org

Council of Chief State School Officers. (1992). *Model standards for beginning teacher licensing, assessment, and development: A resource for state dialogue.* Washington, DC: Author. Retrieved from http://www.ccsso.org/content/pdfs/corestrd.pdf

Council of Chief State School Officers (CCSSO). (2005). The Individuals with Disabilities Education Act. Retrieved November 7, 2006, from http://www.ccsso.org/federal_programs/IDEA/index.cfm.

Council of Chief State School Officers (CCSSO) and the National Governors Association (NGA). (June 2010). Common core state standards for English language arts and literacy in history/ social studies, science, and technical subjects. Retrieved http://www.corestandards.org

Cowan, I. W., & Ciprani, S. (2009). Of water troughs and the sun: Developing inquiry through analogy. *Young Children* 64(6), 62–67.

Crawford, E. O., Heaton, E .T., Heslop, K., & Kixmiller, K. (2009). Science learning at home involving families. *Young Children, 94*(6), 39–41.

Crim, C., Desjean-Perrotta, B., & Moseley, C. (2008). Partnerships gone wild: Preparing teachers of young children to teach about the natural world. *Childhood Education, 85*(1), 6–12.

Crosser, S. (1992). Managing the early childhood classroom. *Young Children, 47*(2), 23–29.

Cullinan, B., Galda, L., & Sipe, L. (2010). *Literature and the child* (7th ed.). Florence, KY: Cengage Learning/Wadsworth.

Cunningham, P. (2005). "If they don't read much, how they ever gonna get good?" *The Reading Teacher, 59*(1), 88–90.

Cunningham, P. (2009). *Phonics they use: Words for reading and writing* (5th ed.). Boston: Allyn & Bacon.

Curran, L. (1991). *Cooperative learning lessons for little ones: Literature-based language arts and social skills.* San Juan Capistrano, CA: Resources for Teachers.

Curtis, D., & Carter, M. (2005). Rethinking early childhood environments to enhance learning. *Young Children, 60*(3), 34–38.

Cutler, K. M., Gilkerson, D., Parrott, S., & Bowne, M. T. (2003). Developing math games based on children's literature. *Young Children, 58*(1), 22–27.

Dabkowski, D. M. (2004). Encouraging active parent participation in IEP team meetings. *Teaching Exceptional Children, 36*(3), 34–39.

Daniel, J. (2009). Intentionally thoughtful family engagement in early childhood education. *Young Children, 64*(5), 10–14.

Daniels, H. (1994). *Literature circles: Voice and choice in the student-centered classroom.* York, ME: Stenhouse.

Daniels, H. (2002). *Literature circles: Voice and choice in book clubs and reading groups.* Portland, ME: Stenhouse.

Darling-Hammond, L. (1997). Quality teaching: The critical key to learning. *Principal, 77*(1), 5–11.

Diversity and Equity Interest Forum, Derman-Sparks, L., Amihault, C., Simpson, C., & Duke, L. N. (2009). Children – socioeconomic class and equity. *Young Children, 64*(3), 50–53.

Davies, M. A. (2000). Learning. . . The beat goes on. *Childhood Education, 76*(3), 148–153.

Davis, A., & Havighurst, R. J. (1947). *Father of the man.* Boston: Houghton Mifflin.

DeBord, K., Hestenes, L. L., Moore, R. C., Cosco, N., & McGinnis, J. R. (2002). Paying attention to the outdoor environment is as important as preparing the indoor environment. *Young Children, 57*(3), 32–35.

de la Roche, E. (1996). Snowflakes: Developing meaningful art experiences for young children. *Young Children, 51*(2), 82–83.

Derman-Sparks, L., & ABC Task Force. (1989). *Anti-bias curriculum: Tools for empowering young children.* Washington, DC: NAEYC.

Derman-Sparks, L., & Edwards, J.O. (2010). *Anti-bias education for young children and ourselves.* Washington, DC: NAEYC.

Derman-Sparks, L., & Ramsey, P. G. (2005). What if all the children in my class are white? Anti-bias/multicultural education with white children. *Young Children, 60*(6), 20–24, 26–27.

DeVault, L. (2003). The tide is high, but we can hold on. One kindergarten teacher's thoughts on the rising tide of academic expectations. *Young Children, 58*(6), 90–92.

Dever, M. T., & Hobbs, D. E. (1998). The learning spiral: Taking the lead from how young children learn. *Childhood Education, 75*(1), 7–11.

Diffily, D. (1996). The project approach: A museum exhibit created by kindergartners. *Young Children, 51*(2), 72–75.

Diffily, D. (2003). Creating a videotape about hurricanes: Experiences in project-based learning. *Young Children, 58*(4), 76–81.

Diffily, D., & Morrison, K. (Eds.) (1996). *Family-friendly communication for early childhood programs.* Washington, DC: NAEYC.

Diffily, D., & Sassman, C. (2002). *Project-based learning with young children.* Portsmouth, NH: Heinemann.

Dighe, J., Calomiris, Z., & Van Zutphen, C. (1998). Nurturing the language of art in children. *Young Children, 53*(1), 4–9.

Dillingham, B. (2005). Performance literacy. *The Reading Teacher, 59*(1), 72–75.

DiNatale, L. (2002). Developing high-quality family involvement programs in early childhood settings. *Young Children, 57*(5), 90–95.

Dockett, S., & Perry, B. (2007). *Transitions to school: Perceptions, expectations, experiences.* Sydney, Australia: University of New South Wales Press.

Dockett, S., & Perry, B. (2008). Starting school: A community endeavor. *Childhood Education, 84*(5), 274–280.

Dodge, D. T., Colker, L. J., & Heroman, C. (2003). *The creative curriculum for preschool* (4th ed.). Washington, DC: Teaching Strategies.

Dodge, D. T., Heroman, C., Charles, J., & Maiorca, J. (2004). Beyond outcomes: How ongoing assessment supports children's learning and leads to meaningful curriculum. *Young Children, 59*(1), 20–28.

Dole, J. A. (2004). The changing role of the reading specialist in school reform. *The Reading Teacher, 57*(5), 462–471.

Dow, C. B. (2010). Young children and movement: The power of creative dance. *Young Children, 65*(2), 30–35.

Dow, R. S., & Baer, G. T. (2006). *Self-paced phonics: A text for educators* (4th ed.). Upper Saddle River, NJ: Merrill/Prentice-Hall.

Drew, W. F., & Rankin, B. (2004). Promoting creativity for life using open-ended materials. *Young Children, 59*(4), 38–45.

Duffelmeyer, F. A. (2002). Alphabet activities on the internet. *The Reading Teacher, 55*(7), 631–635.

Duke, N. (2000). 3.6 minutes per day: The scarcity of information texts in first grade. *Reading Research Quarterly, 35*, 202–224.

Duke, N. (2003). Reading to learn from the very beginning: Information books in early childhood. *Young Children, 58*(2), 14–20.

Duke, N. K., & Bennett-Armistead, V. S. (2003). *Reading and writing informational text in the primary grades: Research-based practices.* New York: Scholastic.

Dunston, P. J. (1992). A critique of graphic organizer research. *Reading Research and Instruction, 31*(2), 57–65.

Duyff, R. (2002). *American Dietetic Association complete food and nutrition guide* (2nd ed.). Hoboken, NJ: John Wiley.

Dymock, S. (2005). Teaching expository text structure awareness. *The Reading Teacher, 59*(2), 177–182.

Dyson, A. H. (1990). Symbol makers, symbol weavers: How children link play, pictures, and print. *Young Children, 45*(2), 50–57.

Edmiaston, R., Dolezal, V., Doolittle, S., Erickson, C., & Merritt, S. (2000). Developing Individualized Education Programs for children in inclusive settings: A developmentally appropriate framework. *Young Children, 55*(4), 36–41.

Edmunds, K. M., & Bauserman, K. L. (2006). What teachers can learn about reading motivation through conversations with children. *The Reading Teacher, 59*(5), 414–424.

Edwards, L., Bayless, K. M., & Ramsey, M. E. (2008). *Music and movement: A way of life for the young child.* Upper Saddle River, NJ: Merrill/ Prentice Hall.

Edwards, L. C. (2009). *The creative arts: A process approach for teachers and children* (5th ed.). Upper Saddle River, NJ: Merrill/Prentice Hall.

Eisenhauer, M. J., & Feikes, D. (2009). Dolls, blocks, and puzzles: Playing with mathematical understandings. *Young Children, 64*(3), 18–24.

Eldridge, D. (2001). Parent involvement: It's worth the effort. *Young Children, 56*(4), 65–69.

Elias, M. (1996). Teens do better when dads are more involved. *USA Today,* 22 August, D-1.

Elkind, D. (1986). Formal education and early childhood education: An essential difference. *Phi Delta Kappan, 67*(9), 631–636.

Elkind, D. (1987). *Miseducation: Preschoolers at risk.* New York: Knopf.

Elkind, D. (1996). Early childhood education: What should we expect? *Principal, 75*(5), 11–13.

Elkind, D. (2003). Thanks for the memory: The lasting value of true play. *Young Children, 58*(3), 46–51.

Elkind, D. (2005). Early childhood amnesia: Reaffirming children's need for developmentally appropriate programs. *Young Children, 60*(4), 38–40.

Elkind, D. (2007a). *The hurried child: Growing up too fast too soon.* Cambridge, MA: Perseus Books.

Elkind, D. (2007b). *The power of play: Learning what comes naturally.* Philadelphia, PA: Perseus Books.

Elswood, R. (1999). Really including diversity in early childhood classrooms. *Young Children, 54*(4), 62–66.

Engel, B. S. (1996). Learning to look: Appreciating child art. *Young Children, 51*(3), 74–79.

Epstein, A. S. (2001). Thinking about art: Encouraging art appreciation in early childhood settings. *Young Children, 56*(3), 38–43.

Epstein, A. S. (2007). *The intentional teacher: Choosing the best strategies for young children's learning.* Washington, DC: NAEYC.

Epstein, A. S. (2009). *Me, you, us: Social-emotional learning in preschool.* Ypsilanti, Michigan: High Scope Press; and Washington, DC: NAEYC.

Epstein, J. L. (2000). *School and family partnerships: Preparing educators and improving schools.* Boulder, CO: Westview.

Esch, G., & Long, E. (2002). The fabulously fun finger puppet workshop. *Young Children, 57*(1), 90–91.

Espinosa, L. (2010). *Getting it right: For young children from diverse backgrounds.* Upper Saddle River, NJ: Prentice Hall; and Washington, DC: National Association for the Education of Young Children.

Fadiman, C. (1984). *The world treasury of children's literature, Book One.* Boston: Little, Brown.

Feeney, S., & Moravcik, E. (2005). Children's literature: A window to understanding self and others. *Young Children, 60*(5), 20–28.

Felon, A. (2005). Collaborative steps paving the way to kindergarten for young children with disabilities. *Young Children, 60*(2), 32–37.

Ferguson, C. (2001). Discovering, supporting, and promoting young children's passions and interests: One teacher reflects. *Young Children, 56*(4), 6–11.

Fields, M. V., & DeGayner, B. (2000). Read my story. *Childhood Education, 76*(3), 130–135.

Fields, M. V., Groth, L., & Spangler, K. L. (2007). *Let's begin reading right: A developmental approach to emergent literacy* (6th ed.). Upper Saddle River, NJ: Merrill/Prentice Hall.

Filler, J., & Xu, Y. (2006/2007). Including children with disabilities in early childhood education programs: Individualizing developmentally appropriate practices. *Childhood Education, 83*(2), 92–98.

Fisher, D., Flood, J., Lapp, D., & Frey, N. (2004). Interactive read-alouds: Is there a common set of implementation practices? *The Reading Teacher, 58*(1), 8–17.

Flippo, R. F. (2005). *Personal reading: How to match children to books.* Portsmouth, NH: Heinemann.

Foley, M. B. (2006). "The music, movement, and learning connection": a review. (A review of Hap Palmer's article in *Young Children,* September 2001.) *Childhood Education, 82*(3), 175–176.

Fountas, I. C., & Pinnell, G. S. (2005). *Leveled books, K–8: Matching texts to readers for effective teaching.* Portsmount, NH: Heinemann.

Fountas, I. C., & Pinnell, G. S. (2006). *Teaching for comprehending and fluency: Thinking, talking, and writing about reading, K-8.* Portsmouth, NH: Heinemann.

Fountas, I. C., & Pinnell, G. S. (2009). *When readers struggle: Teaching that works.* Portsmouth, NH: Heinemann.

Fountas, I. C., & Pinnell, G. S. (2010). *The continuum of literacy learning, PreK-2* (2nd ed.), Portsmouth, NH: Heinemann.

Fox, B. J., & Hull, M. A. (2009). *Phonics for the teacher of reading* (10th ed). Upper Saddle River, NJ: Merrill/Prentice Hall.

Fox, D. B. (2000). Music and the baby's brain early experiences: *Music Educators Journal, 87*(2), 23–27.

Fox, L., & Lentini, R. H. (2006). "You got it!" Teaching social and emotional skills. *Young Children, 61*(6), 36–42.

Frakes, C., & Kline, K. (2000). Teaching young mathematicians: The challenges and rewards. *Teaching Children Mathematics, 6*(6), 376–381.

French, K., & Cain, H. M. (2006). Including a young child with Spina Bifida. *Young Children, 61*(3), 78–84.

Fromberg, D. P. (1999). A review of research on play. In C. Seefeldt (Ed.), *The early childhood curriculum: Current findings in theory and practice* (3rd ed., pp. 27–53). New York: Teachers College Press.

Fromberg, D. P. (2001). *Play and meaning in early childhood education.* Boston: Allyn & Bacon.

Frost, J. L. (2005). Lessons from disasters: Play, work, and the creative arts. *Childhood Education, 82*(1), 2–8.

Frost, J., Wortham, S., & Reifel, S. (2007). *Play and child development* (3rd ed.). Upper Saddle River, NJ: Merrill/Prentice Hall.

Fulmore, J. S., Geiger, B. F., Werner, K. A., Talbott, L. L., & Jones, D. C. (2009). Sun protection education for healthy children. *Childhood Education, 85*(5), 293–299.

Fuys, D. J., & Liebov, A. K. (1997). Concept learning in geometry. *Teaching Children, Mathematics, 3*(5), 248–251.

Gadsden, V., & Ray, A. (2002). Engaging fathers: Issues and considerations for early childhood educators. *Young Children, 57*(6), 32–42.

Gallagher, K. C. (2005). Brain research and early childhood development: A primer for developmentally appropriate practice. *Young Children, 60*(4), 12–18, 20.

Gallagher, K. C., & Mayer, K. (2008). Enhancing development and learning through teacher-child relationships. *Young Children, 63*(6), 80–87.

Gallahue, D. I. (1996). *Developmental physical education for today's children* (3rd ed.). Madison, WI: Brown & Benchmark.

Gallahue, D. L. (1995). Transforming physical education curriculum. In S. Bredekamp & T. Rosegrant (Eds.), *Reaching potentials: Transforming early childhood curriculum and assessment* (Vol. 2, pp. 125–144). Washington, DC: National Association for the Education of Young Children.

Gardner, H. (1999a). *Intelligence reframed: Multiple intelligences for the 21st century.* New York: Basic Books.

Gardner, H. (1999b). *The disciplined mind: What all students should understand.* New York: Simon & Schuster.

Gargiulo, R. M. (2006). *Special education in contemporary society: An introduction to exceptionality.* Belmont, CA: Thomson Wadsworth.

Garman, C. G., Garman, F. J., & Brown, W. K. (2009). *Teaching young children effective listening skills* (3rd ed.). York, PA: William Gladen Press.

Gately, S. E., (2004). Developing concept of word. *Teaching Exceptional Children, 36*(6), 16–22.

Gatewood, T. E., & Conrad, S. H. (1997). Is your school's technology up-to-date? A practical guide to assessing technology in elementary schools. *Childhood Education, 73*(4), 249–251.

Geist, E. (2001). Children are born mathematicians: Promoting the construction of early mathematical concepts in children under 5. *Young Children, 56*(4), 12–19.

Geist, E. (2009). Infants and toddlers exploring mathematics. *Young Children, 64*(3), 39–41.

Geist, E., & Baum, A. C. (2005). "Yeah, but's" that keep teachers from embracing an active curriculum: Overcoming the resistance. *Young Children, 60*(4), 28–36.

Gennarelli, C. (2004). Communicating with families: Children lead the way. *Young Children, 59*(1), 98–99.

Gentry, J. R. (2006). *Breaking the code: The new science of beginning reading and writing.* Portsmouth, NH: Heinemann.

Gerard, M. (2004). What's a parent to do?: Phonics and other stuff. *Childhood Education, 80*(3), 159–160.

Gharavi, G. J. (1993). Music skills for preschool teachers: Needs and solutions. *Arts Education Policy Review, 94*(3), 27–30.

Gillespie, C. W., & Chick, A. (2001). Fussbusters: Using peers to mediate conflict resolution in a Head Start classroom. *Childhood Education, 77*(4), 192–195.

Gillespie, L.G. (2006). Cultivating good relationships with families can make hard times easier. *Young Children 61*(5), 53–55.

Gillies, R. M. (2007). *Cooperative learning: Integrating theory and practice.* Thousand Oaks, CA: Sage Publications.

Glasser, W. (1997). A new look at school failure and school success. *Phi Delta Kappan, 78*(8), 597–602.

Goldberg, M. F. (1997). An interview with Dr. James P. Comer. *Phi Delta Kappan, 78*(7), 557–559.

Goldberg, M. F. (2001). An interview with Linda Darling-Hammond: Balanced optimism. *Phi Delta Kappan, 82*(9), 687–689.

Gonzalez-Mena, J. (2008). *Diversity in early care and education: Honoring differences*. (5th ed.). Washington, DC: NAEYC; and New York, NY: McGraw-Hill.

Gonzalez-Mena, J., & Eyer, D. W. (2004). *Infants, toddlers, and caregivers: A curriculum of respectful, responsive care and education*. New York: McGraw-Hill.

Greata, J. (2006). *An introduction to music in early childhood education*. Clifton Park, NY: Delmar Learning.

Greenberg, P. (1993). Ideas that work with young children. How and why to teach all aspects of preschool and kindergarten math naturally, democratically, and effectively (For teachers who do not believe in educational excellence, and who find math boring to the max), Part I. *Young Children, 48*(4), 75–84.

Greenberg, P. (2001). The irreducible needs of children: An interview with T. Berry Brazelton, M.D. and Stanley I. Greenspan, M.D. *Young Children, 56*(2), 6–14.

Grisham-Brown, J. (2000). Transdisciplinary activity-based assessment for young children with multiple disabilities. *Young Exceptional Children, 3*(2), 3–10.

Gronlund, G. (2001). Rigorous academics in preschool and kindergarten? Yes! Let me tell you how. *Young Children, 56*(2), 42–43.

Gronlund, G. (2006). *Make early learning standards come alive: Connecting your practice and curriculum to state guidelines*. St. Paul MN: Readleaf Press and Washington, DC: NAEYC.

Guilmartin, K. (2000). Early childhood music education in the new millennium. *American Music Teacher, 49*(6), 40–41.

Gullo, D. F. (1992). *Developmentally appropriate teaching in early childhood*. Washington, DC: NEA.

Gullo, D. F. (Ed.). (2006). *K Today: Teaching and learning in the kindergarten year*. Washington, DC: NAEYC.

Guthrie, L. F., & Richardson, S. (1995). Turned on to language arts: Computer literacy in the primary grades. *Educational Leadership, 53*(2), 14–17.

Guthrie, J. T., & Wigfield, A. (2000). Engagement and motivation in reading. In M. L. Kamil, P. B. Mosenthal, P. D. Pearson, & R. Barr (Eds.), *Handbook of reading research* (Vol. 3, pp. 403–422). Mahwah, NJ: Erlbaum.

Hachey, A. C., & Butler, D. L. (2009). Seeds in the window, soil in the sensory table: Science education through gardening and nature-based play. *Young Children, 64*(6), 42–48.

Hahn, M. L. (2002). *Reconsidering read-aloud*. Portland, ME: Stenhouse.

Haines, J. E., & Gerber, L. L. (1999). *Leading young children to music: A resource book for teachers* (6th ed.). Upper Saddle River, NJ: Merrill/Prentice Hall.

Halgunseth, L. (2009). Family engagement, diverse families, and early childhood education programs: An integrated review of the literature. *Young Children, 64*(5), 56–58.

Hammeter, M. L., Ostrosky, M. M. Artman, K. M., & Kinder, K. A. (2008). Moving right along. . . Planning transitions to prevent challenging behavior. *Young Children, 63*(3), 18–25.

Harris, J. (1999). Interweaving language and mathematics literacy through a story. *Teaching Children Mathematics, 5*(9), 520–524.

Harris, M. E. (2009). Implementing portfolio assessment. *Young Children, 64*(3), 82–85.

Hart, B., & Risley, T. (1995). *Meaningful differences in the everyday experiences of young American children*. Baltimore: Brookes.

Hart. B., & Risley, T. (2003, spring). The early catastrophe: The 30 million word gap by age 3. *American Educator, 27*(1), 4–9.

Hart, C. H., Burts, D. C., & Charlesworth, R. (1997). Integrated developmentally appropriate curriculum: From theory and research to practice. In C. H. Hart, D. C. Burts, & R. Charlesworth (Eds.), *Integrated curriculum and developmentally appropriate practice: Birth to age eight* (pp. 1–27). Albany, NY: SUNY Press.

Hartman, J. A., & Eckerty, C. (1995). Projects in the early years. *Childhood Education, 71*(3), 141–148.

Harvey, S., & Goudvis, A. (2007). *Strategies that work: Teaching comprehension to enhance understanding* (2nd ed). Portland, ME: Stenhouse.

Hatcher, B., & Petty, K. (2004). Seeing is believing: Visible thought in dramatic play. *Young Children, 59*(6), 79–82.

Haugland, S. (1992). The effect of computer software on preschool children's developmental gains. *Journal of Computing in Children's Education, 31*(1), 15–30.

Haugland, S. (1995). Classroom activities provide important support to children's computer experiences. *Early Childhood Education Journal, 23*(2), 99–100.

Hawkins Centers of Learning (2009). Resources for science education activities. *Young* Children *64*(6), 23. Available at http://www.hawkinscenters.org/resources

Healy, L. I. (2001). Applying theory to practice: Using developmentally appropriate strategies to help children draw. *Young Children, 56*(3), 28–30.

Hefflin, B. R., & Barksdale-Ladd, M. A. (2001). African American children's literature that helps students find themselves: Selection guidelines for grades K–3. *Reading Teacher, 54*(8), 810–819.

Heimes, Maegan. (2009). Teachers on teaching: Building positive relationships. *Young Children, 64*(1), 94–95.

Helm, J. H. (2008). Got Standards? Don't give up on engaged learning. *Young Children, 63*(4), 14–20.

Helm, J. H., & Beneke, S. (2003). *The power of projects: Meeting contemporary challenges in early childhood classrooms—strategies and solutions*. New York: Teachers College Press.

Helm, J. H., Beneke, S., & Steinheimer, K. (1997). Documenting children's learning. *Childhood Education, 73*(4), 200–205.

Helm, J. H., Beneke, S., & Steinheimer, K. (2007). *Windows on learning: Documenting young children's work* (2nd ed.) New York: Teachers College Press.

Helman, L. A., & Burns, M. K. (2008). What does oral language have to do with it? Helping young English-language learners acquire a sight word vocabulary. *The Reading Teacher, 62*(1), 14–19.

Herbert, E. A., & Schultz, L. (1996). The power of portfolios. *Educational Leadership, 53*(7), 70–71.

Hernandez, L.A. (2010). Hopes, dreams, intentions. In V. Washington & J. Jenkins-Scott (Eds.), *Children of 2020: Creating a better tomorrow* (pp. 19–23). Washington, DC: Council for Professional Recognition; and Washington, DC: NAEYC.

Herrera, T. A., & Owens, D. T. (2001). The "new new math"?: Two reform movements in mathematics education. *Theory into Practice, 40*(2), 84–92.

Heuwinkel, M. K. (1996). New ways of learning = new ways of teaching. *Childhood Education, 73*(1), 27–31.

Hillman, C. B. (1995). *Before the school bell rings.* Bloomington, IN: Phi Delta Kappa Educational Foundation.

Hobbs, D. E., Dever, M. T., & Tadlock, M. (1995). A curriculum planning tool: The learning spiral. *Transcendence: The Journal on Emerging Adolescent Education, 23*(2), 28–33.

Holland, M. (2004). "That food makes me sick!" Managing food allergies and intolerances in early childhood settings. *Young Children, 59*(2), 42–46.

Honig, A. S. (1995). Singing with infants and toddlers. *Young Children, 50*(5), 72–78.

Honig, A. S. (2005). The language of lullabies. *Young Children, 60*(5), 30–36.

Honig, A. S. (2007). Play: Ten power boosts for children's early learning. *Young Children, 62*(5), 72–78.

Howell, J., & Corbey-Scullen, L. (1997). Out of the housekeeping corner and onto the stage—Extending dramatic play. *Young Children, 52*(6), 82–88.

Hudson, R. F., Lane, H. B., & Pullen, P. C. (2005). Reading fluency assessment and instruction: What, why, and how? *The Reading Teacher, 58*(8), 702–714.

Huettig, C. I., Sanborn, C. F., Dimarco, N., Popejoy, A., & Rich, S. (2004). The O generation: Our youngest children are at risk for obesity. *Young Children, 59*(2), 50–55.

Humpal, M. C., & Wolf, J. (2003). Music in the inclusive environment. *Young Children, 58*(2), 103–107.

Hurst, D. S. (1994). Teaching technology to teachers. *Educational Leadership, 51*(7), 74–76.

Hyson, M. (2008). *Enthusiastic and engaged learners: Approaches to learning in the early childhood classroom.* New York, NY: Teachers College Press; and Washington, DC: NAEYC.

Individuals with Disabilities Education Act (IDEA) Amendments of 1997. (1997). P.L. 105–17, 105th Congress, 1st Session, 13 May 1997. (20 U.S.C. 1400 et seq., 111 STAT, 37).

International Reading Association (IRA). (2000). *Make a difference means making it different: Honoring children's rights to excellent reading instruction* (Position statement of the IRA). Newark, DE: Author.

International Reading Association (IRA). (2005). *Literacy development in the preschool years: A position statement of the International Reading Association (IRA),* adopted 2005. Newark, DE: Author.

International Reading Association (IRA), & National Association for the Education of Young Children (NAEYC). (1998). Learning to read and write: Developmentally appropriate practices for young children. *Reading Teacher, 52*(2), 193–216. Also in *Young Children, 53*(4), 30–46. (Also available from http://www.naeyc.org/about/positions.asp.)

International Society for Technology in Education (ISTE). (2007). *National educational technology standards for students* (2nd ed.). Eugene, OR: Author.

Isenberg, J. P., & Jalongo, M. R. (2009). *Creative thinking and arts-based learning: Preschool through 4th grade* (5th ed.). Upper Saddle River, NJ: Merrill/Prentice Hall.

Jacobs, G., & Crowley, K. (2010). *Reaching standards and beyond kindergarten: Nurturing children's sense of wonder and joy in learning.* Thousand Oaks, CA: Corwin.

Jacobs, G. M., Power, M. P., & Loh, W. I. (2002). *Teacher's sourcebook for cooperative learning: Practical techniques, basic principles, and frequently asked questions.* Thousand Oaks, CA: Corwin Press.

Jalongo, M. J. (2004). *Young children and picture books* (2nd ed.) Washington, DC: National Association for the Education of Young Children.

Jalongo, M. R. (1995). Promoting active listening in the classroom. *Childhood Education, 72*(1), 13–18.

Jalongo, M. R. (2006). Children and dogs. *Childhood Education, 83*(1), 32-G.

Jalongo, M. R., & Ribblett, D. M. (1997). Using song picture books to support emergent literacy. *Childhood Education, 74*(1), 15–22.

Jegatheesan, B., & Meaden, H. (2006). Pets in the classroom: Promoting and enhancing social-emotional wellness of young children. In E. M. Horn, & E. Jones (Eds.), *Supporting social emotional development in young children* (pp. 77–88). Missoula, MT: Division for Early Childhood.

Jenkins, S. (2009). How to maintain school reading success: Five recommendations from a struggling male reader. *The Reading Teacher, 63*(2), 159–162.

Jensen, E. (2000). Moving with the brain in mind. *Educational Leadership, 58*(3), 24–27.

Jensen, E. P. (2004). *Brain-compatible strategies.* (2nd ed.). Thousand Oakes, CA: Corwin.

Johnson, D. W., & Johnson, R. T. (1999). *Learning together and alone: Cooperative, competitive and individualistic learning* (5th ed.). Boston: Allyn & Bacon.

Johnston, P. H., & Rogers, R. (2002). Early literacy development: The case for "informed assessment." In S. B. Neuman & D. K. Dickinson (Eds.), *Handbook of early literacy research* (pp. 377–389). New York: Guilford Press.

Jolliffe, W. (2007). *Cooperative learning in the classroom: Putting it into practice.* Thousand Oaks, CA: Sage Publications.

Jones, E. (1997). Play is my job. *Principal, 76*(5), 18–19.

Jones, E., & Cooper, R. M. (2006). *Playing to get smart.* New York: Teachers College Press.

Jones, E., Evans, K., & Rencken, K. (2001). *The lively kindergarten: Emergent curriculum in action.* Washington, DC: NAEYC.

Jones, J. (2004). Framing the assessment discussion. *Young Children, 59*(1), 14–18.

Jones, N. P. (2005). Big jobs: Planning for competence. *Young Children, 60*(2), 86–93.

Jones, N. P. (2008). 2, 4, or 6? Grouping children to promote social and emotional development. *Young Children, 63*(3), 34–39.

Jones, R. B. (2004). Playing with your child. *Childhood Education, 80*(5), 272.

Kagan, S., & Kagan, M. (2009). *Kagan cooperative learning.* San Clemente, CA: Kagan Publishing.

Kalmar, K. (2008). Let's give children something to talk about! Oral language and preschool literacy. *Young children, 63*(1), 88–92.

Kamii, C. (Ed.) (1990). *Achievement testing in early childhood education: The games grown-ups play.* Washington, DC: National Association for the Education of Young Children.

Kamii, C., Clark, F. B., & Dominick, A. (1994). The six national goals: A road to disappointment. *Phi Delta Kappan, 75*(9), 672–677.

Kamii, C., & Lewis, B. A. (1990). Constructivism and first-grade arithmetic. *Arithmetic Teacher, 38*(1), 36–37.

Kamii, C., & Manning, M. M. (2002). Phonemic awareness and beginning reading and writing. *Journal of Research in Childhood Education, 17*(1), 38–46.

Karnes, M. B., & Johnson, L. J. (1989). Training for staff, parents and volunteers working with children, especially those with disabilities and from low-income homes. *Young Children, 44*(3), 49–56.

Kato, T., & Van Meeteren, B. D. (1008). Physical science in constructivist early child classrooms. *Childhood Education 84*(4), 234–236.

Katz, L. G. (1990). Impressions of Reggio Emilia preschools. *Young Children, 45*(6), 11–12.

Katz, L. G. (1994). Perspectives on the quality of early childhood programs. *Phi Delta Kappan, 76*(3), 200–205.

Katz, L. G. (1995). *Talks with teachers of young children: A collection.* Norwood, NJ: Ablex.

Katz, L. G., & Chard, S. (1997). Documentation: The Reggio Emilia approach. *Principal, 76*(5), 16–19.

Katz, L. G., & Chard, S. C. (2000). *Engaging children's minds: The project approach* (2nd ed.). Stamford, CT: Ablex.

Kellogg, R. (1967). Understanding children's art. *Psychology Today, 1*(1), 16–25.

Kellogg, R. (1970). *Analyzing children's art.* Palo Alto, CA: Mayfield.

Kelman, A. (1990). Choices for children. *Young Children, 45*(3), 42–45.

Kemple, K. M., & Johnson, C. A. (2002). From inside out: Nurturing aesthetic response to nature in the primary grades. *Childhood Education, 78*(4), 210–218.

Kenney, S. H. (1997). Music in the developmentally appropriate integrated curriculum. In C. H. Hart, D. C. Burts, & R. Charlesworth (Eds.), *Integrated curriculum and developmentally appropriate practice: Birth to age eight* (pp. 103–144). Albany, NY: SUNY Press.

Kersey, K. C., & Malley, C. R. (2005). Helping children develop resiliency: Providing supportive relationships. *Young Children, 60*(1), 53–58.

Kersey, K. C., & Masterson, M. L. (2009). Teachers connecting with families – in the best interest of children. *Young Children, 64*(5), 34–38.

Keyser, J. (2006). *From parents to partners: Building a family-centered early childhood program.* St. Paul, MN: Red Leaf Press; and Washington, DC: NAEYC.

Kilmer, S. J., & Hofman, H. (1995). Transforming science curriculum. In S. Bredekamp & T. Rosegrant (Eds.), *Reaching potentials: Transforming early childhood curriculum and assessment* (Vol. 2, pp. 43–63). Washington, DC: NAEYC.

Kim, A. K., & Yeary, J. (2008). Making long-term separation easier for children and families. *Young Children, 63*(5), 32–36.

Kim, J., & Robinson, H. M. (2010). Four steps for becoming familiar with early music standards. *Young Children, 65*(2), 42–48.

Kirmani, M. H. (2007). Empowering culturally and linguistically diverse children and families. *Young Children, 62*(6), 94–98.

Kline, K. (1999). Helping at home. *Teaching Children Mathematics, 5*(8), 456–460.

Kline, K. (2000). Early childhood teachers discuss the standards. *Teaching Children Mathematics, 6*(9), 568–571.

Kline, L. W. (1995). A baker's dozen: Effective instructional strategies. In R. D. Cole (Ed.), *Educating everybody's children: Diverse teaching strategies for diverse learners* (pp. 21–43). Alexandria, VA: Association for Supervision and Curriculum Development.

Kohl, H. (2009). *The Herb Kohl reader: Awakening the heart of teaching.* New York: The New Press.

Kohn, A. (1993). Choices for children: Why and how to let students decide. *Phi Delta Kappan, 75*(1), 8–19.

Kohn, A. (1997). How not to teach value: A rational look at character education. *Phi Delta Kappan, 78*(6), 429–437.

Koralek, D. (Ed.). (2007). *Spotlight on young children and families.* Washington, DC: National Association for the Education of Young Children.

Korte, K. M., Fielden, L. J., & Agnew, J. C. (2005). To run, stomp, or study: Hissing cockroaches in the classroom. *Young Children, 60*(12), 12–19.

Kositsky, V. (1977). What in the world is cooking in class today? Multiethnic recipes for young children. *Young Children, 33*(1), 23–31.

Krathwohl, D. R. (2002, p. 215). A revision of Bloom's taxonomy: An overview. *Theory Into Practice, 41*(4), 212–218.

Kristo, J. V., & Bamford, R. A. (2005). *Nonfiction in focus.* New York: Scholastic.

Kuhn, M. (2004/2005). Helping students become accurate, expressive readers: Fluency instruction for small groups. *The Reading Teacher, 58*(4), 338–344.

Kupetz, B. N., & M. M. Twiest. (2000). Nature, literature, and young children: A natural combination. *Young Children, 55*(1), 59–63.

Lally, J. R. (1995). The impact of child care policies and practices on infant/toddler identity formation. *Young Children, 51*(1), 58–67.

Laminack, L. L., & Wadsworth, R. M. (2006). *Learning under the influence of language and literature: Making the most of read-alouds across the day.* Portsmouth, NH: Heinemann.

Larkin, B. R. (2001). "Can we act it out?" *Reading Teacher, 54*(5), 478–481.

Lazdauskas, H. (1996). Music makes the school go 'round. *Young Children, 51*(5), 22–23.

Learning (1994). Math. *Learning, 23*(1), 58–68.

Lewin-Benham, A. (2006). One teacher, 20 preschoolers, and a goldfish: Environmental awareness, emergent curriculum, and documentation. *Young Children, 61*(2), 28–34.

Lewis, B. A. (2005). *What do you stand for? A kid's guide to building character.* Minneapolis, MN: Free Spirit.

Lidz, C. S. (2003). *Early childhood assessment.* Hoboken, NJ: John Wiley.

Louie, B. Y. (2006). Guiding principles for teaching multicultural literature. *The Reading Teacher, 59*(5), 438–448.

Louv, R. (2005). *Last child in the woods.* Chapel Hill, NC: Algonquin Books.

Lubeck, S. (1994). The politics of developmentally appropriate practice: Exploring issues of culture, class, and curriculum. In B. L. Mallory & R. S. New (Eds.), *Diversity and DAP: Challenge for early childhood education* (pp. 17–43). New York: Teachers College Press.

Lucht, L. B. (2006). *The wonder of word study: Lessons and activities to help create independent readers, writers, & spellers.* Portsmouth, NH: Heinemann.

Lundgren, D., & Morrison, J. W. (2003). Involving Spanish-speaking families in early education programs. *Young Children, 58*(3), 88–95.

Machado, J. M. (2010). *Early childhood experiences in language arts* (9th ed.) Belmont, CA: Wadsworth.

Maple, T. L. (2005). Beyond community helpers: The project approach in the early childhood social studies curriculum. *Childhood Education, 81*(3), 133–138.

Marcon, R. A. (2003). Growing children: The physical side of development. *Young Children, 58*(1), 80–87.

Marotz, L. R., Cross, M. Z., & Rush, J. M. (2005). *Health, safety and nutrition for the young child* (6th ed.). Clifton Park, NY: Thomson Delmar Learning.

Marshall, H. (2003). Research in review. Opportunity deferred or opportunity taken? An updated look at delaying kindergarten entry. *Young Children, 58*(5), 84–93.

Matt, M. M. (2008). Plant part snacks – A way to family involvement, science learning, and nutrition. *Young Children, 63*(6), 98–99.

Maxwell, K. L., & Clifford, R. M. (2004). School readiness assessment. *Young Children, 59*(1), 42–46.

Mazzoni, S. A., Gambrell, L. B., & Korkeamaki, R. L. (1999). A cross-cultural perspective of early literacy motivation. *Reading Psychology, 20,* 237–253.

McAfee, O., & Leong, D. (1994). *Assessing and guiding young children's development and learning.* Boston: Allyn & Bacon.

McAfee, O., Leong, D. J., & Bodrova, E. (2004). Gathering information about children. In *Basics of assessment: A primer for early childhood educators* (pp. 35–50). Washington, DC: NAEYC.

McDermott, D. R. (2003/2004). Building better human connections: Parenting/caring education for children and teens in school. *Childhood Education, 80*(2), 71–75.

McElveen, S. A., & Dierking, C. C. (2000/2001). Children's books as models to teach writing skills. *Reading Teacher, 54*(4), 363–364.

McGee, L. M., & Richgels, D. J. (2007). *Literacy's beginnings: Supporting young readers and writers* (5th ed.). Boston: Allyn & Bacon.

McKean, B. (2000/2001). Speak the speech, I pray you! Preparing to read aloud dramatically. *Reading Teacher, 54*(4), 358–359.

McLaughlin, M. (2010). *Guided comprehension in the primary grades* (2nd ed.). Newark, DE: International Reading Association.

McWayne, C., Hampton, V., Fantuzzo, J., Cohen, H. L., & Sekino, Y. (2004). A multivariate examination of parent involvement and the social and academic competencies of urban kindergarten children. *Psychology in the schools, 41*(3), 363–377.

Meisels, S. (1993). Remaking classroom assessment with the work sampling system. *Young Children, 48*(5), 34–40.

Melchior, A. (2000). Service learning at your service. *Education Digest, 66*(2), 26–32.

Mercurio, M. L., & McNamee, A. (2006). Healing words, healing hearts: Using children's literature to cope with the loss of a pet. *Childhood Education, 82*(3), 153–160.

Mere, C. (2005). *More than guided reading: Finding the right instructional mix, K–3.* Portland, ME: Stenhouse.

Merkley, D. M., & Jefferies, D. (2000/2001). Guidelines for implementing a graphic organizer. *Reading Teacher, 54*(4), 350–357.

Mesmer, H. A. E., & Griffith, P. L. (2005/2006). Everybody's selling it—But just what is explicit, systematic phonics instruction? *The Reading Teacher, 59*(4), 366–376.

Micklo, S. J. (1995). Developing young children's classification and logical thinking skills. *Childhood Education, 72*(1), 24–28.

Micklo, S. J. (1997). Math portfolios in the primary grades. *Childhood Education, 73*(4), 194–199.

Miles, L. R. (2009). The general store: Reflections on children at play. *Young Children, 64*(4), 36–41.

Miller, D. (2002). *Reading with meaning: Teaching comprehension in the primary grades.* Portland, ME: Stenhouse.

Miller, H. M. (2001). Teaching and learning about cultural diversity: A dose of empathy. *Reading Teacher, 54*(6), 380–381.

Miller, J. (1990). Three-year-olds in their reading corner. *Young Children, 46*(1), 51–54.

Mills, H., & Clyde, J. A. (1991). Children's success as readers and writers: It's the teacher's beliefs that make the difference. *Young Children, 46*(2), 54–59.

Mills, H., Whitin, D. J., & O'Keefe, T. (1993). Teaching math concepts in a K–1 class doesn't have to be like pulling teeth—But maybe it should be! *Young Children, 48*(2), 17–20.

Mills, K. A. (2009). Floating on a seat of talk: Reading comprehension through speaking and listening. *The Reading Teacher, 63*(4), 325–329.

Mindes, G. (2005). Social studies in today's early childhood curricula. *Young Children, 60*(5), 12–18.

Misifi, F. L. (1993) A sense of science. *Science and Children, 30*(4), 28–29.

Mitchell, L. C. (2004). Making the MOST of creativity in activities for young children with disabilities. *Young Children, 59*(4), 46–49.

Moomaw, S., & Jones, G. W. (2005/2006). Native curriculum in early childhood classrooms. *Childhood Education, 82*(2), 89–94.

Moore, T. (2002). If you teach children, you can sing! *Young Children, 57*(4), 84–85.

Moriarty, R. F. (2002). Entries from a staff developer's journal. . . Helping teachers develop as facilitators of three- to five-year-olds' science inquiry. *Young Children, 57*(5), 20–24.

Morrow, L. M. (2002). *The literacy center: Contexts for reading and writing* (2nd ed.). Portland, ME: Stenhouse.

Morrow, L. M. (2008). *Literacy development in the early years: Helping children read and write* (6th ed.). Boston: Allyn & Bacon.

Morrow, L. M. (2004). Developmentally appropriate practice in early literacy instruction. *The Reading Teacher, 58*(1), 88–89.

Morrow, L. M., & Gambrell, L. B. (2002). Literature-based instruction in the early years. In S. B. Neuman and D. K. Dickinson (Eds.), *Handbook of early literacy research* (pp. 348–360). New York: Guilford Press.

Morrow, L. M., Freitag, E., & Gambrell, L. B. (2009). *Using children's literature in preschool to develop comprehension: Understanding and enjoying books* (2nd ed.). Newark, DE: IRA.

Morrow, L. M., & Smith, J. K. (1990). Introduction. In L. M. Morrow & J. K. Smith (Eds.), *Assessment for instruction in early literacy* (pp. 1–6). Upper Saddle River, NJ: Prentice Hall.

Moutray, C. L., & Snell, C. A. (2003). Three teachers' quest: Providing daily writing activities for kindergartners. *Young Children, 58*(2), 24–28.

Mulcahey, C. (2009). Providing rich art activities for young children. *Young Children 64*(4), 107–112.

Murray, C. D. (2000). Learning about children's social and emotional needs at snack time—Nourishing the body, mind, and spirit of each child. *Young Children, 55*(2), 43–52.

Music Educators National Conference (MENC). (1994a). *The school music program: A new vision.* Reston, VA: Author.

Music Educators National Conference (MENC). (1994b). *National Standards for music education K–4.* Retrieved from www.menc.org

Myers, J. W., & Myers, B. K. (2005). Challenges, conflict, and core condition: Working together with young children and their families. *ACEI Focus on Pre-K & K, 17*(4), 1–6.

Narvaez, A., Feldman, J., & Theriot, C. (2006). Virtual pre-k: Connecting home, school, and community. *Young Children 61*(1), 52–53.

Nation, K., & Snowling, M. J. (2004). Beyond phonological skills: Broader language skills contribute to the development of reading. *Journal of Research in Reading, 27*(4), 342–356.

National Art Education Association (NAEA). (1994). *The national visual arts standards.* Reston, VA: NAEA.

National Association for the Education of Young Children (NAEYC). (1993). Position statement: Violence in the lives of children. Retrieved from http://www.naeyc.org/about/positions/PSVIOL98.asp

National Association for the Education of Young Children (NAEYC). (1995). *Responding to linguistic and cultural diversity: Recommendations for effective early childhood education.* Washington, DC: Author. Brochure. Available online at http://www.naeyc.org.

National Association for the Education of Young Children (NAEYC). (1996a). *Guidelines for preparation of early childhood professionals.* Washington, DC: Author.

National Association for the Education of Young Children (NAEYC). (1996b). Position statement: Responding to linguistic and culture diversity: Recommendations for effective early childhood education. *Young Children, 51*(2), 4–12.

National Association for the Education of Young Children (NAEYC). (1996c). Position statement: Technology and young children—Ages three through eight. *Young Children, 51*(6), 11–16.

National Association for the Education of Young Children (NAEYC). (1998a). Section II of Ideals and principles about our ethical responsibilities of families. *Young Children, 53*(1), 65.

National Association for the Education of Young Children (NAEYC). (1998b). The value of school recess and outdoor play. Retrieved from http://www.naeyc.org/ece

National Association for the Education of Young Children (NAEYC). (2004). Final draft: Early childhood program standards and accreditation performance criteria. Available online at www.naeyc.org/accreditation/

National Association for the Education of Young Children (NAEYC). (2007). *NAEYC early childhood program standards.* Retrieved from http://www.naeyc.org/accreditation/criteria/program_standards.html

National Association for the Education of Young Children (NAEYC). (2008). Collage. 10X. Choosing a classroom pet. *Teaching Young Children, 1*(2), 5.

National Association for the Education of Young Children (NAEYC). (2008). NAEYC early childhood program standards and accreditation criteria: The mark of quality in early childhood education (Rev. ed.). Washington, DC: Author. Available online at http://www.naeyc.org/academy/primary/standardsintro

National Association for the Education of Young Children (NAEYC). (2009a). Position statement on developmentally appropriate practice in early childhood programs serving children from birth through age 8. In C. Copple & S. Bredekamp (Eds.), *Developmentally appropriate practice in early childhood programs.* Washington, DC: Author.

National Association for the Education of Young Children (NAEYC). (2009b). Position statement: NAEYC standards for early childhood professional preparation programs. Washington DC: Author. Available online at http://www.naeyc.org/positionstatements.

National Association for the Education of Young Children (NAEYC) & National Association of Early Childhood Specialists in State Departments of Education (NAECS/SDE) (1991). Guidelines for appropriate curriculum content and assessment in programs serving children ages 3 through 8 (joint position statement). *Young Children, 46*(3), 21–38.

National Association for the Education of Young Children (NAEYC) & National Association of Early Childhood Specialists in State Departments of Education (NAECS/SDE). (2003). Early childhood curriculum, assessment, and program evaluation: Building an effective, accountable system in programs for children birth through age 8. (Position statement.) Retrieved from http://www.naeyc.org

National Association for the Education of Young Children (NAEYC) & National Council of Teachers of Mathematics (NCTM). (2002). Early childhood mathematics: Promoting good beginnings. (Joint position statement.) Washington, DC: NAEYC and Reston, VA: NCTM. Retrieved from http://www.naeyc.org

National Association for Music Education (NAME). (1994). *National Standards.* Reston, VA: Author.

National Association for Sport and Physical Education (NASPE). (1995). *Moving into the future: National standards for P.E.—A guide to content and assessment.* St. Louis, MO: Mosby.

National Association for Sport and Physical Education (NASPE). (1995). *Looking at physical education from a developmental perspective: A guide to teaching* (position statement). Reston, VA: Author. Retrieved from http://www.aahperd.org/naspe/pdf_files/pos_papers/Developmental_Perspective.pdf

National Association for Sport and Physical Education (NASPE). (n.d.). *What constitutes a quality physical education program?* Reston, VA: Author. Retrieved from http://www.aahperd.org/naspe/template.cfm?template = qualityPEPrograms.html

National Association for Sport and Physical Education (NASPE). (2000). Appropriate practices in movement programs for young children ages 3–5. NASPE Position Statement. Reston, VA: Council on Physical Education for Children.

National Association for Sport and Physical Education (NASPE) (2001). *Physical education is critical to a complete education* (position statement). Reston, VA: Author. Retrieved from http://www.aahperd.org/naspe/pdf_files/pos_papers/pe_critical.pdf

National Association for Sport and Physical Education (NASPE). (2004). *Moving into the future: National standards for physical education* (2nd ed.). Reston, VA: Author.

National Association of Early Childhood Specialists in State Departments of Education (NAECS/SDE). (2002). Recess and the importance of play: A position statement on young children and recess. Retrieved from http://www.naecs-sde.org

National Association of Elementary School Principals (NAESP). (1990). *Standards for quality programs for young children: Early childhood education and the elementary school principal.* Alexandria, VA: Author.

National Coalition for Parent Involvement in Education. (2006). What's happening. A new wave of evidence: The impact of school, family, and community connections on student achievement. Available online at http://www.ncpie.org

National Council of Teachers of Mathematics. (1989). *Curriculum and evaluation standards for school mathematics.* Reston, VA: Author.

National Council of Teachers of Mathematics (NCTM). (2000). *Principles and standards for school mathematics.* Reston, VA: Author.

National Center for Improving Science Education. (1990). *Getting started in science: A blueprint of elementary school science education.* Colorado Springs, CO: Author.

National Dance Association (of the American Alliance for Health, Physical education, Recreation & Dance). (1994). National standards for dance education K-4. Retrieved from http://www.aahperd.org/nda/

National Governors Association. (2002). NGA Task Force on school readiness: A discussion framework. Retrieved from http://www.nga.org/cda/files/1102SchoolReadiness.pdf

National Institute of Child Health and Human Development. (2000). *Report of the National Reading Panel. Teaching children to read: An evidence-based assessment of the scientific research literature on reading and its implications for reading instruction* (NIH Publication No. 00–4769). Washington, DC: U.S. Government Printing Office.

National Parent Teacher Association. (2008). National standards for family-school partnerships. Retrieved from http://www.pta.org/documents/National_Standards.pdf

National Reading Panel. (2000). *Report of the National Reading Panel: Teaching children to read* (NIH Publication No. 00–4769). Washington, DC: National Institute of Child Health and Human Development.

National Research Council. (1996). *National science education standards*. Washington, DC: National Academy Press.

National Research Council. (1996). National Science Education Standards: Observe, interact, change, learn. Retrieved from http://www.nap.edu/catalogue.php?record_id = 4962

National Science Teachers Association (2009). NSTA position statement: Parent involvement in science education.Retrieved from http://www.nsta.org

Neelly, L. P. (2001). Developmentally appropriate music practice: Children learn what they live. *Young Children, 56*(3), 32–37.

Neelly, L. P. (2002). Practical ways to improve singing in early childhood classrooms. *Young Children, 57*(4), 80–83.

Nel, E. M. (2000). Academics, literacy, and young children. *Childhood Education, 76*(3), 136–141.

Nelson, B. G. (2002). *The importance of men teachers: And reasons why there are so few.* Minneapolis, MN: MenTech.

Nelson, B. G., Carlson, F. M., & West, R., Sr. (2006). Men in early childhood: An update. *Young Children, 61*(5), 34–36.

Nemeth, K. (2009). Meeting the home language mandate: Practical strategies for all classrooms. *Young Children, 64*(2), 36–42.

Neuman, S. B. (2004). The effect of print-rich classroom environments on early literacy growth. *The Reading Teacher, 58*(1), 89–91.

Neuman, S. B., & Celano, D. (2001). Books aloud: A campaign to "put books in children's hands." *The Reading Teacher, 54*(6), 550–557.

Neuman, S. B., Copple, C., & Bredekamp, S. (2000). *Learning to read and write: Developmentally appropriate practices for young children.* Washington, DC: NAEYC.

Neuman, S. B., & Dwyer, J. (2009). Missing in action: Vocabulary instruction in pre-k. *The Reading Teacher, 62*(5), 384–392.

Neuman, S. B., & Roskos, K. (2005). Whatever happened to developmentally appropriate practice in early literacy? *Young Children, 60*(4), 22–26.

Neuman, S. B., Roskos, K., Wright, T. S., & Lenhart, L. (2007). *Nurturing knowledge: Building a foundation for school success by linking early literacy to math, science, art, and social studies.* New York: Scholastic.

New, R. S. (1999). An integrated early childhood curriculum: Moving from the *what* and the *how* to the *why.* In C. Seefeldt (Ed.), *The early childhood curriculum: Current findings in theory and practice* (3rd ed., pp. 265–287). New York: Teachers College Press.

New, R. S., & Mallory, B. L. (1994). Introduction: The ethics of inclusion. In B. L. Mallory & R. S. New (Eds.), *Diversity and developmentally appropriate practices: Challenges for early childhood education.* (pp. 1–13). New York: Teachers College Press.

Newberger, J. J. (1997). New brain development research—A wonderful window of opportunity to build public support for early childhood education. *Young Children, 52*(4), 4–9.

Nissen, H., & Hawkins, C. J. (2010). Promoting emotional competence in the preschool classroom. *Childhood Education, 86*(4), 255–259.

Novick, R. (1999/2000). Supporting early literacy development: Doing things with words in the real world. *Childhood Education, 76*(2), 70–75.

Oczkus, L. D. (2003). *Reciprocal teaching at work: Strategies for improving reading comprehension.* Newark, DE: International Reading Association.

Ogle, D. M. (1986). K–W–L: A teaching model that develops active reading of expository text. *Reading Teacher, 39,* 564–570.

Ogle, D. & Correa-Kovtun, A. (2010). Supporting English-language learners and struggling readers in content literacy with the "partner reading and content, too" routine. *The Reading Teacher, 63*(7), 532–542.

Ogu, U., & Schmidt, S. R. (2009). Investigating rocks and sand: Addressing multiple learning styles through an inquiry-based approach. *Young Children, 64*(2), 12–18.

Ozer, E. J. (2007). The effects of school gardens on students and schools. Conceptualization and considerations for maximizing healthy development. *Health Education, 34*(6), 846–863.

Palmer, S., & Bayley, R. (2005). *Early literacy fundamentals: A balanced approach to language, listening, and literacy skills, ages 3 to 6.* Portland, ME: Stenhouse.

Parlakian, R., & Rovaris, J. M. (2009). Celebrating fathers as a resource in early child care settings. *Young Children, 64*(5), 64–65.

Parlakian, R., & Lerner, C. (2010). Beyond twinkle, twinkle: Using music with infants and toddlers. *Young Children, 65*(2), 14–19.

Patrick, H., Mantzicopoulos, P., & Samarapungavan, A. (2009). Reading, writing, and conducting inquiry about science in kindergarten. *Young Children, 94*(6), 32–38.

Pattnaik, J. (2004/2005). On behalf of their animal friends: Involving children in animal advocacy. *Childhood Education, 81*(2), 95–100.

Patton, M. M., & Kokoski, T. M. (1996). How good is your early childhood science, mathematics, and technology program? Strategies for extending your curriculum. *Young Children, 51*(5), 38–44.

Pentimonti, J. M., Zucker, T. A., Justice, L. M., & Kaderavek, J. N. (2010). Informational text use in preschool classroom read-alouds. *The Reading Teacher, 63*(8), 656–665.

Perkins, D., & Blythe, T. (1994). Putting understanding up front. *Educational Leadership, 51*(5), 4–7.

Perrone, V. (1994). How to engage students in learning. *Educational Leadership, 51*(5), 11–13.

Perry, J. P. (2003). Making sense of outdoor pretend play. *Young Children, 58*(3), 26–30.

Petty, K. (2009). Using guided participation to support young children's social development. *Young Children, 64*(4), 80–85.

Piaget, J. (1952). *The origins of intelligence in children.* New York: International Universities Press.

Piaget, J. (1970a). Piaget's theory (G. Gellerier & J. Langer, trans.). In P. H. Mussen (Ed.), *Carmichael's manual of child psychology,* Vol. 1 (3rd ed., pp. 703–732). New York: Wiley.

Piaget, J. (1970b). *Science of education and psychology of the child*. New York: Viking.

Piaget, J. (1973). *The child and reality*. New York: Viking.

Piaget, J. (1974). *To understand is to invent*. New York: Viking.

Pica, R. (2006). Physical fitness and early childhood curriculum. *Young Children, 61*(3), 12–19.

Pica, R. (2009a). Can movement promote creativity? *Young Children, 64*(4), 60–61.

Pica, R. (2009b). Make a little music. *Young Children, 64*(6), 74–75.

Pierson, C. A., & Beck, S. S. (1993). Performance assessment: The realities that will influence the rewards. *Childhood Education, 70*(1), 29–98.

Pikulski, J. J., & Chard, D. J. (2005). Fluency: Bridge between decoding and reading comprehension. *The Reading Teacher, 58*(6), 510–519.

Pincus, A. R. H. (2005). What's a teacher to do? Navigating the worksheet curriculum. *The Reading Teacher, 59*(1), 75–80.

Pinnell, G. S., & Fountas, I. (1998). *Word matters: Teaching phonics and spelling in the reading/writing classroom*. Portsmouth, NH: Heinemann.

Pinnell, G. S., & Scharer, P. L. (2003). *Teaching for comprehension in reading: Grades K–2*. NY: Scholastic.

Poest, C. A., Williams, J. R., Witt, D. D., & Atwood, M. E. (1990). Challenge me to move: Large muscle development in young children. *Young Children, 45*(5), 4–10.

Pohan, C. A. (2003). Creating caring and democratic communities in our classrooms and schools. *Childhood Education, 79*(6), 369–373.

Popham, W. J. (2009). Assessment literacy for teachers: Faddish or fundamental? *Theory Into Practice, 48*(1), 4–11.

Porth, D. (2002). The Portland report 2002: A report on the juvenile firesetting issue in Portland, Oregon. Retrieved from http://sosfires.com/new.html

Powell, D. R. (1998). Reweaving parents into the fabric of early childhood programs. *Young Children, 53*(5), 60–67.

Prudhoe, C. M. (2003). Picture books and the art of collage. *Childhood Education, 80*(1), 6–11.

Putnam, J. W., & Slavin, R. W. (Ed.). (1993). *Cooperative learning and strategies for inclusion: Celebrating diversity in the classroom*. Baltimore, MD: Paul H. Brookes.

Rafferty, C. D. (1999). Literacy in the information age. *Educational Leadership, 57*(2), 22–25.

Raikes, H. H., & Edwards, C. P. (2009). Staying in step: Supporting relationships with families. *Young Children, 64*(5), 50–55.

Raines, S. C. (1997). Developmental appropriateness: Curriculum revisited and challenged. In J. P. Isenberg & M. R. Jalongo (Eds.), *Major trends and issues in early childhood education: Challenges, controversies, and insights* (pp. 75–89). New York: Teachers College Press.

Raines, S. C., & Isbell, R. (1988). Talking about wordless books in your classroom. *Young Children, 43*(6), 24–25.

Ramsey, P. G. (1995). Growing up with the contradictions of race and class. *Young Children, 50*(6), 18–22.

Ramsey, P. G. (2004). *Teaching and learning in a diverse world: Multicultural education for young children* (3rd ed.). New York: Teachers College Press.

Raphael, T. E., & Au, K. H. (2001). *Super QAR for testwise students: Teacher resource guide, Guide 6*. Chicago: McGraw-Hill/Wright.

Raphael, T. E., Highfield, K., & Au, K. H. (2006). *QAR now: A powerful and practical framework that develops comprehension and higher-level thinking in all students*. New York: Scholastic.

Rasinski, T. V. (2000). Speed does matter. *The Reading Teacher, 54*(2), 146–150.

Rasinski, T. V. (2008). *From phonics to fluency: Effective teaching of decoding and reading fluency in elementary school* (2nd ed.). Boston: Allyn & Bacon.

Rasinski, T. V. (2010). *The fluent reader: Oral reading strategies for building word recognition, fluency, and comprehension* (2nd ed.). New York: Scholastic.

Rasinski, T. V., Rupley, W. H., & Nichols, W. D. (2008). Two essential ingredients: Phonics and fluency getting to know each other. *The Reading Teacher, 62*(3), 257–260.

Ray, J.A., Pewitt-Kinder, J., & George, S. (2009). Partnering with families of children with special needs. *Young Children, 64*(5), 16–22.

Ray, J. A., & Shelton, D. (2004). E-pals: Connecting with families through technology. *Young Children, 59*(3), 30–32.

Renaissance Partnership for Improving Teacher Quality. (n.d.). Renaissance teacher work samples (RTWS). Retrieved from http://www.uni.edu/itq

Reutzel, D. R. (1997). Integrating literacy learning for young children: A balanced literacy perspective. In C. H. Hart, D. C. Burts, & R. Charlesworth (Eds.), *Integrated curriculum and developmentally appropriate practice: Birth to age eight* (pp. 225–254). Albany, NY: SUNY Press.

Reutzel, D. R., & Cooter, R. B. (1992). *Teaching children to read: From basals to books* (2nd ed.). Upper Saddle River, NJ: Merrill/Prentice Hall.

Reutzel, D. R., & Cooter, R. B. (2009). *The essentials of teaching children to read: The teacher makes the difference* (2nd ed.). Boston, MA: Allyn & Bacon.

Riel, M. (1994). Educational change in a technology-rich environment. *Journal on Computing in Education, 26*(4), 452–474.

Riley, D., SanJuan, R. R., Klinkner, J., & Ramminger, A. (2008). *Social and emotional development: Connecting science and practice in early childhood settings*. Washington, DC: National Association for the Education of Young Children; and St. Paul, MN: Redleaf Press.

Ringgenberg, S. (2003). Music as a teaching tool: Creating story songs. *Young Children, 58*(5), 76–79.

Rinker, L. (2000). Active learning through art. *Child Care Information Exchange, 135*, 72–75.

Rivkin, M. S. (1995). *The great outdoors: Restoring children's right to play outside*. Washington, DC: National Association for the Education of Young Children.

Roberts, L. C., & Hill, H. T. (2003). Come and listen to a story about a girl named Res: Using children's literature to debunk gender stereotypes. *Young Children, 58*(2), 39–42.

Robinson, E. H., & Curry, M. J. R. (2005/2006). Promoting altruism in the classroom. *Childhood Education, 82*(2), 68–73.

Rosen, D., & Hoffman, J. (2009). Integrating concrete and virtual manipulatives in early childhood mathematics. *Young Children, 64*(3), 26–33.

Roskos, K. A., Christie, J. F., & Richgels, D. J. (2003). The essentials of early literacy instruction. *Young Children, 58*(2), 52–59.

Roskos, K. A., Tabors, P. O., & Lenhart, L. A. (2009). *Oral language and early literacy in preschool: Talking, reading, and writing* (2nd ed.). Newark, DE: IRA.

Ross, M. E. (2000). Science their way. *Young Children, 55*(2), 6–13.

Rousseau, J. J. (1911). *Emile* (trans. B. Foxley). London: J. M. Dent. (Original work published in 1762.)

Rule, A. C. (2001). Alphabetizing with environmental print. *Reading Teacher, 54*(6), 558–562.

Rump, M. L. (2002). Involving fathers of young children with special needs. *Young Children, 57*(6), 18–20.

Russell-Fox, J. (1997). Together is better: Specific tips on how to include children with various types of disabilities. *Young Children, 52*(4), 81–83.

Sanders, K. (2002). Men don't care? *Young Children, 57*(6), 44–48.

Sandstrom, S. (1999). Dear Simba is dead forever. *Young Children, 54*(6), 14–15.

Sarama, J., & Clements, D.H. (2009). Teaching math in the primary grades: The learning trajectories approach. *Young Children, 64*(2), 63–65.

Savage, J. F. (2007). *Sound it out! Phonics in a comprehensive reading program* (3rd ed.). New York: McGraw-Hill.

Scherer, M. (1996). On our changing family values: A conversation with David Elkind. *Educational Leadership, 53*(7), 4–9.

Schickedanz, J. A. (2008). *Increasing the power of instruction: Integration of language, literacy, and math across the preschool day*. Washington, DC: National Association for the Education of Young Children.

Schickedanz, J. A., & Casbergue, R. M. (2004). *Writing in preschool: Learning to orchestrate meaning and marks*. Newark, DE: International Reading Association.

Schwartz, R. M., & Raphael, T. E. (1985). Concept of definition: A key to improving students' vocabulary. *Reading Teacher, 39*, 198–203.

Scott-Kassner, C. (1999). Developing teachers for early childhood programs. *Music Educators Journal 86*(1), 19–25.

Seefeldt, C. (1997). Social studies in the developmentally appropriate curriculum. In C. H. Hart, D. C. Burts, & R. Charlesworth (Eds.), *Integrated curriculum and developmentally appropriate practice: Birth to age eight* (pp. 171–199). Albany, NY: SUNY.

Seefeldt, C. (Ed.). (1999a). *The early childhood curriculum: Current findings in theory and practice* (3rd ed.). New York: Teachers College Press.

Seitz, H. (2008). The power of documentation in the early childhood classroom. *Young Children, 63*(2), 88–93.

Seo, K-H. (2003). What children's play tells us about teaching mathematics. *Young Children, 58*(1), 28–33.

Seplocha, H. (2004). Partnerships for learning: Conferencing with families. *Young Children, 59*(5), 97–99.

Shaffer, L. F., Hall, E., & Lynch, M. (2009). Toddlers' scientific explorations: Encounters with insects. *Young Children, 64*(6), 18–23.

Shepard, L. A. (1994). The challenges of assessing young children appropriately. *Phi Delta Kappan, 76*(3), 206–212.

Shepard, L. A. (2001). The role of classroom assessment in teaching and learning. In V. Richardson (Ed.), *Handbook of research on teaching* (4th ed., pp. 1066–1101). Washington, DC: American Educational Research Association.

Shepardson, D. P. (2002). Bugs, butterflies, and spiders: Children's understanding about insects. *International Journal of Science Education, 24*(6), 627–643.

Sherman, J. L. (1979). Storytelling with young children. *Young Children, 34*(1), 20–27.

Shidler, L. (2009). Setting an example in the classroom: Teaching children what we want them to learn. *Young Children, 64*(5), 88–91.

Shore, R., & Strasser, J. (2006). Music for their minds. *Young Children, 61*(2), 62–67.

Sid the Science Kid. (2009). An educational television program, a collaboration among KCET/Los Angeles, PBS, and the Jim Henson Company. Available online at http://www.pbskids.org/sid

Sidelnick, M. A., & Svoboda, M. L. (2000). The bridge between drawing and writing: Hannah's story. *Reading Teacher, 54*(2), 174–184.

Smith, A. F. (2000). Reflective portfolios. *Childhood Education, 76*(4), 204–208.

Smith, C. A. (2004). *Raising courageous kids: Eight steps to practical heroism*. South Bend, IN: Sorin. Retrieved from http://www.raisingcourageouskids.com

Smith, C. A. (2005). First steps to mighty hearts: The origins of courage. *Young Children, 60*(1), 80–87.

Smith, L. (1995). Guess what: Fathers matter, too. *Kansas City Star*, 26 March, H-2, H-4.

Smith, M. K. (1996). Fostering creativity in the early childhood classroom. *Early Childhood Education Journal, 24*(2), 77–82.

Snow, C. E., Burns, M. S., & Griffin, P. (Eds.) (1998). *Preventing reading difficulties in young children*. Washington, DC: National Academy Press.

Soalt, J. (2005). Bringing together fictional and informational texts to improve comprehension. *The Reading Teacher, 58*(7), 680–683.

Souto-Manning, M. (2010). Family-involvement: Challenges to consider, strengths to build on. *Young Children, 65*(2), 82–88.

Spangler, S. (2009). Beyond the fizz: Getting children excited about doing real science. *Young Children, 64*(4), 62–64.

Spring, J. H. (2004). *American education* (12th ed.). Columbus, OH: McGraw-Hill.

Stahl, S. A. (2001). Teaching phonics and phonological awareness. In S. B. Neuman & D. K. Dickinson (Eds.), *Handbook of early literacy research: Vol 1* (pp. 333–347). New York: Guilford.

Staley, L., & Portman, P. A. (2000). Red Rover, Red Rover, it's time to move over. *Young Children, 55*(1), 67–72.

Starbuck, S., & Olthof, M. R. (2008). Involving families and community through gardening. *Young Children, 63*(5), 74–79.

Stead, T. (2005). *Reality checks: Teaching reading comprehension with nonfiction, K–5.* Portland, ME: Stenhouse.

Stegelin, D. A. (2005). Making the case for play policy: Research-based reasons to support play-based environments. *Young Children, 60*(2), 76–85.

Stenmark, J. K., Thompson, V., Cossey, R. & Hill, M. (1986). *Family math.* Berkeley: Regents of the University of California.

Stiggins, R. (2005). From formative assessment to assessment FOR learning: A path to success in standards-based schools. *Phi Delta Kappan, 85*(4), 325–328.

Stiggins, R., & Duke, D. (2008). Effective instructional leadership requires assessment leadership. *Phi Delta Kappan, 90*(4), 285–291.

Stiggins, R., & DuFour, R. (2009). Maximizing the power of formative assessments. *Phi Delta Kappan, 90*(9), 640–644.

Stone, J. I. (1987). Early childhood math: Make it manipulative! *Young Children, 42*(6), 16–23.

Stone, S. J. (1995). Wanted: Advocates for play in primary grades. *Young Children, 50*(6), 45–54.

Stone, S. J. (1995/1996). Integrating play into the curriculum. *Childhood Education, 72*(2), 104–107.

Stone, S. J., & Glascott, K. (1997/1998). The affective side of science instruction. *Childhood Education, 74*(2), 102–104.

Strecker, S. K., Roser, N. L., & Martinez, M. G. (1998). Understanding oral reading fluency. In T. Shanahan & F. V. Rodriquez-Brown (Eds.), *47th Yearbook of the National Reading Conference* (pp. 295–310). Chicago: National Reading Conference.

Strickland, D. S. (2004). Working with families as partners in early literacy. *The Reading Teacher, 58*(1), 86–88.

Strickland, D. S., & Schickedanz, J. A. (2009). *Learning about print in preschool: Working with letters, words, and beginning links with phonemic awareness* (2nd ed.). Newark, DE: International Reading Association.

Strickland, D. S., & Shanahan, T. (2004). Laying the groundwork for literacy. *Educational Leadership, 61*(2), 74–77.

Sutherland, Z., (1997). *Children and books* (9th ed.). Boston: Allyn & Bacon.

Sutterby, J. A., & Thornton, C. D. (2005). It doesn't just happen! Essential contributions from playgrounds. *Young Children, 60*(3), 26–33.

Swick, K. J., & Freeman, N. K. (2004). Nurturing peaceful children to create a caring world: The role of families and communities. *Childhood Education, 81*(1), 2–8.

Swim, T. J., & Freeman, R. (2004). Time to reflect: Using food in early childhood classrooms. *Young Children, 59*(6), 18–22.

Tarr, P. (2004). Consider the walls. *Young Children, 59*(3), 88–91.

Taylor, B. M., & Heibert, E. H. (1994). Early literacy interventions: Aims and issues. In E. H. Hiebert and B. M. Taylor (Eds.), *Getting reading right from the start* (pp. 3–12). Boston: Allyn & Bacon.

Taylor-Cox, J. (2003). Algebra in the early years? *Young Children, 58*(1), 14–21.

Teale, W. H. (1990). The promise and challenge of informal assessment in early literacy. In L. M. Morrow & J. K. Smith (Eds.), *Assessment for instruction in early literacy* (pp. 45–61). Upper Saddle River, NJ: Prentice Hall.

Ten Boom, C. (1971). *The hiding place.* New York: Bantam.

Tener, N. (1995/1996). Information is not knowledge. *Childhood Education, 72*(2), 100.

Thatcher, D. H. (2001). Reading in the math class: Selecting and using picture books for math investigation. *Young Children, 56*(4), 20–26.

Thiessen, D., Matthias, M., & Smith, J. (Eds.). (1998). *The wonderful world of mathematics: A critically annotated list of children's books in mathematics* (2nd ed.). Reston, VA: National Council of Teachers of Mathematics.

Thompson, C. M. (1995). Transforming curriculum in the visual arts. In S. Bredekamp & T. Rosegrant (Eds.), *Reaching potentials: Transforming early childhood curriculum and assessment* (Vol. 2, pp. 81–98). Washington, DC: NAEYC.

Thompson, J. (2004). Strategies to increase parent involvement that really work! *CEC Today, 11*(2), 8.

Thompson, S. (2004). Choosing and using accommodations on assessments. *CEC Today, 10*(6), 12, 18.

Torbert, M. (2005). Using active group games to develop basic life skills. *Young Children, 60*(4), 72–78.

Torbert, M., & Schneider, L. B. (1992). *Follow me too: A handbook of movement activities for three-to five-year-olds.* Washington, DC: NAEYC.

Torp, L., & Sage, S. (1998). *Problems as possibilities: Problem-based learning for K–12 education.* Alexandria, VA: Association for Supervision and Curriculum Development (ASCD).

Torquati, J., & Barber, J. L. (2005). Dancing with trees: Infants and toddlers in the garden. *Young Children, 60*(3), 40–46.

Trelease, J. (2006). *The read-aloud handbook* (6th ed.). New York: Viking.

Tsao, L. (2002). How much do we know about the importance of play in child development? *Childhood Education, 78*(4), 230–233.

Turbiville, V. P., Umbarger, G. T., & Guthrie, A. C. (2000). Father's involvement in programs for young children. *Young Children, 55*(4), 74–79.

Turner, S. B. (2000). Caretaking of children's souls: Teaching the deep song. *Young Children, 55*(1), 31–33.

Ulmen, M. C. (2005). Hey! Somebody read to me! Ten easy ways to include reading every day. *Young Children, 60*(6), 96–97.

U.S. Department of Agriculture. (2005). MyPyramid.gov. Retrieved from http://www.mypyramid.gov

U.S. Department of Education. (1997). Fathers' involvement in their children's schools (online). Retrieved from http://www.ed.gov/NCES/pubs98/fathers

U.S. Department of Education. (2004). Teacher update: The importance of arts education. Retrieved from http://www.ed.gov/teachers/how/tools/initiative/updates/040826.html

U.S. Department of Education. National Center for Education Statistics. (2006). Internet access in public schools and classrooms: 1994–2005 (NCES 2007–020). Washington, DC: Author. Retrieved from http://www.nces.ed.gov

Vagovic, J. C., (2008). Transformers: Movement experiences for early childhood classrooms. *Young Children, 63*(3), 26–32.

Vance, E., & Weaver, P. J. (2002). *Class meetings: Young children solving problems together.* Washington, DC: NAEYC.

Van Hoorn, J., Nourot, P. M., Scales, B., & Alward, K. R. (2007). *Play at the center of the curriculum* (4th ed.). Upper Saddle River, NJ: Merrill/Prentice Hall.

VanScoy, I. J. (1995). Trading the three R's for the four E's: Transforming curriculum. *Childhood Education, 72*(1), 19–23.

VanScoy, I. J., & Fairchild, S. H. (1993). It's about time! *Young Children, 48*(2), 21–24.

Volk, D., & Long, S. (2005). Challenging myths of the deficit perspective: Honoring children's literacy resources. *Young Children, 60*(6), 12–19.

Vukelich, C., & Christie, J. (2009). *Building a foundation for preschool literacy: Effective instruction for children's reading and writing development* (2nd ed.). Newark, DE: International Reading Association.

Vygotsky, L. S. (1962). *Thought and language* (trans. E. Hanfmann & G. Vakar). Cambridge, MA: MIT Press.

Vygotsky, L. S. (1978). *Mind in society: The development of psychological processes.* Cambridge, MA: Harvard University Press.

Wardle, F. (1990). Endorsing children's differences: Meeting the needs of adopted minority children. *Young Children, 45*(5), 44–46.

Washington, V., & Andrews, J. D. (Eds.). (2010). *Children of 2020: Creating a better tomorrow.* Washington, DC: Council for Professional Recognition; and Washington, DC: NAEYC.

Wasik, B. A. (2001a). Phonemic awareness and young children. *Childhood Education, 77* (3), 128–133.

Wasik, B. A. (2001b). Teaching the alphabet to young children. *Young Children, 56*(1), 34–39.

Watson, A., & McCathren, R. (2009). Including children with special needs: Are you and your early childhood program ready? *Young Children, 64*(2), 20–26.

Welchman-Tischler, R. (1992). *How to use children's literature to teach mathematics.* Reston, VA: National Council of Teachers of Mathematics.

Wheatley, K. F. (2003). Promoting the use of content standards: Recommendations for teacher educators. *Young Children, 58*(2), 96–101.

Whitin, D. J., & Wilde, S. (1992). *Read any good math lately? Children's books for mathematical learning, K–6.* Portsmouth, NH: Heinemann.

Whitin, P., & Whitin, D. J. (2003). Developing mathematical understanding along the yellow brick road. *Young Children, 58*(1), 36–40.

Whitin, P., & Whitin, D. J. (2005). Pairing books for children's mathematical learning. *Young Children, 60*(2), 42–48.

Wien, C. A. (2008). Emergent curriculum. In C. A. Wien (Ed.), *Emergent curriculum in the primary classroom: Interpreting the Reggio Emilia approach in schools* (pp. 5–16). New York: Teachers College Press and Washington, DC: NAEYC.

Wien, C. A., Coates, A., Keating, B. L., & Bigelow, B. C. (2005). Designing the environment to build connection to place. *Young Children, 60*(3), 16–24.

Wiencek, B. J. (2001). Teaching ideas: The daily news. *Reading Teacher, 54* (7), 658–659.

Williams, J. A. (2001). Classroom conversations: Opportunities to learn for ESL students in mainstream classrooms. *Reading Teacher, 54*(8), 750–757.

Williams, K. C. (1997). "What do you wonder?" Involving children in curriculum planning. *Young Children, 52*(6), 78–81.

Williams, K. C., & Cooney, M. H. (2006). Young children and social justice. *Young Children, 61*(2), 75–82.

Wilson, L. J. (1997). Technology in the classroom. *Childhood Education, 73*(4), 249–251.

Winter, S. M. (1997). "SMART" planning for inclusion. *Childhood Education, 73*(4), 212–218.

Winter, S. M. (2009). Childhood obesity in the testing era: What teachers and schools can do. *Childhood Education, 85*(5), 283–288.

Winters, J., Ring, T., & Burriss, K. (2010). Cultivating math and science in a school garden. *Childhood Education, 86*(4), 248-G to 248-J.

Wolery, M., & Wilbers, J. S. (Eds.). (1994). *Including children with special needs in early childhood programs.* Washington, DC: NAEYC.

Wolf, A. D. (2000). How to nurture the spirit in nonsectarian environments. *Young Children, 55*(1), 34–36.

Wolk, S. (1994). Project-based learning: Pursuits with a purpose. *Educational Leadership, 52*(3), 42–43.

Wolter, D. L. (1992). Whole group story reading? *Young Children, 48*(1), 72–75.

Wood, F. S. (2008). Grief: Helping young children cope. *Young Children, 63*(5), 28015031.

Wood, T. (2001). Teaching differently: Creating opportunities for learning mathematics. *Theory into Practice, 40*(2), 110–117.

Woodward, M. M., & Talbert-Johnson, C. (2009). Reading intervention models: Challenges of classroom support and separated instruction. *The Reading Teacher, 63*(3), 190–200.

Worth, K., & Grollman, S. (2003). *Worms, shadows, and whirlpools: Science in the early childhood classroom.* Portsmouth, NH: Heinemann and Washington, DC: NAEYC.

Wortham, S. C. (1997). Assessing and reporting young children's progress: A review of the issues. In J. P. Isenberg & M. R. Jalongo (Eds.), *Major trends and issues in early childhood education: Challenges, controversies, and insights* (pp. 104–122). New York: Teachers College Press.

Woyke, P. O. (2004). Hopping frogs and trail walks: Connecting young children ansd nature. *Young Children, 59*(1), 82–85.

Xu, S. H., & Rutledge, A. L. (2003). Chicken starts with ch! Kindergartners learn through environmental print. *Young Children, 58*(2), 44–51.

Yopp, H. K. (1995). A test for assessing phonemic awareness in young children. *Reading Teacher, 49*(1), 20–29.

Yopp, R. H., & Yopp, H. K. (2000). Sharing information text with young children. *The Reading Teacher, 53*(5), 410–423.

Yopp, R. H., & Yopp, H. K. (2004). Preview-predict-confirm: Thinking about the language and content of informational text. *The Reading Teacher, 58*(1), 79–83.

Yopp, R. H., & Yopp, H. K. (2006). Informational texts as read-alouds at school and home. *Journal of literacy Research, 38*(1), 37–51.

Yopp, H. K., & Yopp, R. H. (2009). Phonological awareness is child's play! *Young Children on the Web.* Retrieved from http://www.naeyc.org/files/yc/file/200910/BTJPhonologicalAwareness/pdf

Youngquist, J., & Martinez-Griego, B. (2009). Learning in English, learning in Spanish: A Head Start program changes its approach. *Young Children, 64*(4), 92–99.

Zan, B., & Geiken, P. (2010). Ramps and pathways: Developmentally appropriate, intellectually rigorous, and fun physical science. *Young Children, 65*(1), 12–17.

Zeece, P. D. (1995). Laughing all the way: Humor in children's books. *Early Childhood Education Journal, 23*(2), 93–97.

Ziemer, M. (1987). Science and the early childhood curriculum: One thing leads to another. *Young Children, 42*(6), 44–51.

Zur, S. S., & Johnson-Green, E. (2008). Time to transition: The connection between musical free play and school readiness. *Childhood Education, 84*(5), 295–300.

Zwirn, S. G., & Graham, M. (2005). Crossing borders: The arts engage academics and inspire children. *Childhood Education, 81*(5), 267–273.

Zygouris-Coe, V., Wiggins, M. B., & Smith, L. H. (2004/2005). Engaging students with text: The 3–2–1 strategy. *The Reading Teacher, 58*(4), 381–384.

NAME INDEX

A

AAHE. *see* American Association for Health Education (AAHE)

ABC Task Force, 28, 120

ACEI. *see* Association for Childhood Education International (ACEI)

Adams, M. J., 164, 182, 183, 184, 187, 192, 193, 194, 195

Agnew, J. C., 263

AHA. *see* American Heart Association (AHA)

Ahlberg, A., 177, 188–189

Ahlberg, J., 177, 188–189

Albert Shanker Institute, 169, 172

Allingham, P., 131

Allington, R. L., 52

Alward, K. R., 18

American Academy of Pediatrics (APA), 125, 132

American Association for Health Education (AAHE), 131

American Heart Association (AHA), 19

American Public Health Association (APHA), 132

Amihault, C., 96

Anderson, T. L., 213, 214, 264, 295

Andrade, H., 55

Andress, B., 335

Andrews, J. D., 8, 29, 93, 94

APA. *see* American Academy of Pediatrics (APA)

APHA. *see* American Public Health Association (APHA)

Armbruster, B. B., 195

Armistead, M. E., 330, 334

Armstrong, T., 83

Arndt, J. S., 32, 39

Arnqvist, A., 165

Artman, K. M., 82

Association for Childhood Education International (ACEI), 97, 239

Atwood, M. E., 28

Au, K. H., 193, 199, 201

Auxter, D., 18

B

Baer, G. T., 196

Bagdi, A., 155

Baker, A. M., 7, 8, 32

Bakley, S., 7, 154

Bales, D., 124, 133

Balke, E., 21

Ball, R. A. H., 32

Bamford, R. A., 184

Banks, J. A., 93

Banks, L. R., 93, 187

Barber, J. L., 239, 264

Barclay, K. H., 78, 339

Barksdale-Ladd, M. A., 184

Barton, B., 174

Batsche, G. M., 201

Battista, M. T., 308

Bauer, K. L., 88

Baum, A. C., 13

Bauserman, K. L., 182, 193

Bayless, K. M., 334, 337, 348, 349

Bayley, R., 172

Bear, D. R., 182, 196

Beck, I. L., 195, 199

Beck, S. S., 55

Beneke, S., 51, 54, 62, 76

Benelli, C., 78

Bennet-Armistead, V. S., 182

Bennett, L., 138

Bennett, T., 39

Bennett, W. J., 154

Bennett-Armistead, V. S., 182, 184, 199

Benson, J., 285

Bewick, C. J., 87

Bigelow, B. C., 23

Biggar, H., 6

Birchmayer, J., 174, 175

Bisgaier, C. S., 264, 358

Blake, S., 220

Bloom, B. S., 67

Blythe, T., 76

Bodrova, E., 18, 19, 30, 53, 146, 180, 182, 193

Bond, T. F., 188

Boone, S., 6

Booth, D., 174

Bosse, S., 213, 214, 264

Bosworth, K., 14

Bothmer, S., 153

Bouhebent, E.A., 45

Bowman, B., 5, 6, 155

Bowne, M. T., 295

Brabham, E. G., 200

Bradley, D. H., 204

Bradley, J., 204

Brandt, R. S., 88

Breathed, B., 185

Bredekamp, S., 14, 16, 18, 29, 32, 38, 49, 50, 51, 64, 66, 70, 88, 94, 101, 109, 133, 135, 185, 198, 294, 308, 313

Brenneman, K., 213, 214, 237

Breslin, D., 154

Brewer, J., 20

Briody, J., 110

Brodmann, A., 185

Bromley, K. D., 201

Bronson, M. B., 215

Brown, W., 55, 56

Brown, W. K., 171

Buchanan, B. L., 217

Buchoff, R., 178

Buehl, D., 68

Bulach, C. R., 155

SUBJECT INDEX

A

Visitors (*Continued*)
on fire, 226
fish, 283
on food, 139, 142, 143, 145
and lesson plans/projects on seeds, 78
musical, 351
on myself, 159
numbers/money/measurement, 322
people, 119
pets, 284
plants, 288
rain, 259
shape, 324
size, 324
on smell, 267–268
on sound, 275–276
on summer/sun, 258
taste, 269–270
time, 323
trees, 290
on water, 246
on weight/balance, 234
wheat/flour, 291
on wind, 259
Visual impairments, 104–105
Vocabulary
color, 224
development of, 166, 168, 170, 196–197
in mathematics, 300
shape, 313
size, 309
of smell, 265
spatial relationships, 311
of taste, 268
of textures, 270
time, 317
weight, 230
Vocalizations, 166
Volume measurement, 316
Volunteers
parents as, 35, 46
Vygotsky, Lev, 4

W

Water
activities, 245–246
characteristics of, 245
consumption of, 245
cycle, 245
on earth, 245
experiences, 245–246
forms of, 245
lesson plans on, 375–376
pollution, 239
teaching about, 244–246
unit ideas on, 246–247
uses of, 245
Weather
activities, 256–257
experiences, 256–257
rain, 253–254
snow, 253
sun, 255–256

teaching about, 247–249, 252–259
wind, 254–255
Webbing, 78, 120–121
Webs
pumpkins, 286
storybook, 177
for *The Wheels on the Bus,* 340
Weight
and balance, 229–234
comparisons of, 231–232
concepts about, 230–231
daily experiences with, 230
defined, 229
gravity and, 229
unit ideas on, 234
Whale on a Playground (activity), 316
What's My Rule, game, 304
Wheat/flour
lesson plans on, 376–377
unit ideas on, 291
Whole child, development of, 5–6
Whole-group activity, 70
Wind, 254–255
unit ideas on, 258–259
Winter, 249–250
Wooden blocks, rhythm instruments, 347
Wood sculpture, 362
Word banks, 197, 200
Word logs, 197
Word maps, 197, 201
Words, 193. *See also* Vocabulary
defined, 192
Word walls, 196–197, 200
Worksheets, 195
Writer's workshop, 203
Writing, 202–209
aloud, 187
book, 188
early, 181
effective experiences, 204
experimental, 181
guided, 187–188
handwriting, 202–203
independent, 181, 188–189
journals, 203–204
process, components of, 203
productive, 181
reading and, 190–191
shared, 188
strategies to support, 204–209
transitional, 181
Writing center, computer as, 206
Written communication, 40–41

X
Xylophone, rhythm instruments, 347

Y
Yarn-on-a-metal-can Painting, 361

Z
Zero, concept of, 301